# Dictionary of the Modern Politics of South-East Asia

# Dictionary of the Modern Politics of South-East Asia

## Third Edition

*Michael Leifer*

**London and New York**

First published in 1995
by Routledge
11 New Fetter Lane, London EC4P 4EE

Simultaneously published in the USA and Canada
by Routledge
29 West 35th Street, New York, NY 10001

Second edition 1996

This edition first published 2001

*Routledge is an imprint of the Taylor & Francis Group*

Typeset in Palatino by Keystroke, Jacaranda Lodge, Wolverhampton
Printed and bound in Great Britain by
St Edmundsbury Press, Bury St Edmunds, Suffolk

*British Library Cataloguing in Publication Data*
A catalogue record for this book is available from the British Library

*Library of Congress Cataloging in Publication Data*
A catalog record for this book is available from the Library of Congress

ISBN 0–415–23875–7 (hardback)
ISBN 0–415–23876–5 (paperback)

# Contents

x  **Contents**

# Introduction

Since the end of the Pacific War in August 1945, South-East Asia has evolved from a category of convenience employed by a military command for dispossessing Japan of its wartime gains into a distinct region within which geographic and institutional bounds coincide, with the notable exception of East Timor. The separate regional identity of South-East Asia has been registered primarily through the institutional evolution of the Association of South-East Asian Nations (ASEAN), which, from an inauspicious beginning by five states in August 1967, has expanded to incorporate ten members by the end of the twentieth century. ASEAN has enjoyed mixed fortunes, however. In its enlarged form, it has failed to sustain the culture of close consultation and the self-confidence that distinguished its collective practice prior to the end of the Cold War and the advent of an acute economic adversity that afflicted the region with devastating effect towards the end of the 1990s.

South-East Asia comprises ten states (excepting the prospective new state of East Timor) situated to the east of the Indian sub-continent, to the south of the People's Republic of China and to the north of Australia with combined populations of just over 500 million. The region divides into mainland and island zones and displays a variety of cultural and religious legacies, which are a product of historical waves of migration. South-East Asia's human diversities are contained within territorial bounds inherited in the main from colonial rule so that society and polity are not necessarily congruent. And yet, despite an incipient separatism within the states of the region, secession has been the exception rather than the rule, so far. The circumstances surrounding the independence of Singapore from Malaysia in August 1965 do not fit the conventional separatist model. The former Portuguese colony of East Timor, annexed by Indonesia in 1975 but whose inhabitants voted overwhelmingly for independence in August 1999, was never within the bounds of the Dutch East Indies. Those bounds served as the rationale for the territorial definition of the

Republic of Indonesia proclaimed in August 1945. The colonial territorial legacy has been challenged in Indonesia's case, however, where political alienation in the Province of Aceh in northern Sumatra has been stimulated by the precedent of a referendum in East Timor. A corresponding alienation has been registered in Irian Jaya, the western half of the island of New Guinea. Irredentism has also been a general feature of the region but where successful it has been realized as a delayed process of decolonization; in the case of Irian Jaya, which was transferred from Dutch to Indonesian rule in 1963, and in Vietnam, which was united under Communist rule in 1975.

Within South-East Asia, there is no standard model of political system. Authoritarian governments prevail, however, despite a regional trend towards market-driven economics which has given rise to social changes of democratizing political consequence. At issue is the extent to which a process of economic recovery around the turn of the new millennium will accelerate that democratization. Parliamentary systems with prime ministers as heads of government exist in Cambodia, Malaysia, Singapore and Thailand but with very mixed expressions of democratic practice. The Philippines and Indonesia apply executive presidential systems but again very different in their models of democratic practice. Since 1998, Indonesia has emerged from authoritarian rule to a quasi-democracy but without totally eliminating the political role of its military establishment. Military-based administration is exercised blatantly in Burma (officially Myanmar since 1989), while Brunei provides the sole example of a governing monarchy. Vietnam and Laos continue to be subject to the monopoly rule of their respective communist parties.

Despite its political diversity, South-East Asia is not beset by a central conflict of the kind that continues to trouble neighbouring South Asia. There is great irony in the fact that during the early phase of the Cold War, the region was often described as the Balkans of the Orient in an analogy with the turbulent and foreboding condition of south-eastern Europe before the outbreak of the First World War. At the end of the Pacific War, nationalism and communism, often opposite sides of the same political coin, contended with a weakened colonialism. The process of regional decolonization became drawn into global conflict, especially in Indochina that was to be afflicted by three successive wars over four and a half decades. By the onset of the 1990s, and with the end of the Cold War, the challenge of revolutionary communism had petered out, while governments in Vietnam and Laos had acknowledged the failings of Socialist economic dogma in the interest of market-driven development. Moreover, the international settlement of the Cambodian conflict in October 1991 marked a historic disjunction between global and regional issues leaving South-East Asia in a condition of relatively good regional order.

At the turn of the century, South-East Asia is not free of bilateral tensions, while contention over sovereign jurisdiction within the South China Sea puts four of ASEAN's ten governments at odds with one another. By contrast with the recent experience of south-eastern Europe, however, its relative condition suggests a zone of peace, which has been the idealized goal of ASEAN's governments since 1971. Such a picture is both valid and misleading. It is valid because of the absence of war, despite the domestic and international impact of acute economic adversity towards the end of the century. It is also misleading because of the possible return of the volatile contagion inherent in economic globalization with its devastating impact on currency, stock and property values with attendant social dislocation and consequences for political order and inter-state relations. In addition, the post-Cold War regional environment is notable for the shadow cast by a military modernizing China with irredentist claims at the maritime heart of South-East Asia.

ASEAN has attempted to cope with an uncertain environment marked by the disintegration of the Soviet Union and residual uncertainty about the staying power of the United States as well as a rising China by expanding its strategic horizons beyond its regional bounds. Its success in 1993 in promoting the ASEAN Regional Forum

(ARF), a multilateral security dialogue with the participation of all major Asia-Pacific powers, as well as the Asia–Europe Meeting (ASEM) in 1996, has had only limited benefit, while the Association is no closer to approximating to its ideal declaratory role of prime manager of regional order based on an adherence to common norms of inter-state conduct. Indeed, the so-called 'ASEAN Way' has been exposed as a piece of diplomatic rhetoric.

This dictionary of the politics and international relations of primarily post-Pacific War South-East Asia attempts to encapsulate the changing nature and experience of the region through individual entries arranged in alphabetical order. Information, analysis and commentary are provided about significant episodes and treaties, indigenous concepts and political parties and movements, and regional organizations. Biographical data are included on principal political figures, past and present, without any claim to being exhaustive. In an opening section, short essays deal generally with each of the ten states of the region, while the embryonic state of East Timor is dealt with in the body of the text. A guide to further reading, both general for the region and particular to individual states, has been included to aid further enquiry.

This volume is the third edition of a work that appeared first in 1995. Apart from filling in gaps brought to the attention of the author by diligent reviewers and readers, this edition incorporates significant political events and changes that were precipitated by the impact of regional economic adversity in the late 1990s. In preparing its different versions, I have enjoyed assistance at Routledge from Mark Barragry, Alex Clark, Christine Firth, Colville Wemyss, Victoria Smith, Fiona Cairns, Dominic Shryane and Sarah Eden as well as encouragement from John Ashworth, when Director of the London School of Economics and Political Science, as well as the loving support of my wife, Frances. Helpful advice on content has come from Kathleen Kazer, Duncan McCargo, Derwin Pereira, James Putzel, Paul Reddicliffe, Sabam Siagian and Michael Vatikiotis.

Michael Leifer
London, September 2000

# Brunei, Sultanate of

The Sultanate of Brunei or *Brunei Darussalam* (Abode of Peace), which is located along the northern coast of Borneo, is the sole ruling monarchy in South-East Asia. Its head of state and government, Sultan **Hassanal Bolkiah** has been on the throne since October 1967. In August 1998, he installed his eldest son, Al-Muhtadee Billah, as Crown Prince. In the fifteenth and sixteenth centuries, Brunei exercised suzerainty over much of Borneo (giving its name to the island) and into the south of the Philippines archipelago. Its territorial extent was whittled down considerably over the centuries, while its separate identity was only preserved through British colonial intervention, albeit with further loss of territory. Brunei became a protected state in 1888 and only acquired internal self-government in 1959, with internal security powers transferred in 1971 when Britain gave up an automatic defence guarantee for a consultative defence arrangement. It became fully sovereign in January 1984 when Britain transferred its residual responsibility for foreign affairs. Brunei then comprised two territorial enclaves of some 5,765 square kilometres accessible from one another only by water and surrounded on the landward side by the Malaysian state of Sarawak. Its population is estimated at around 300,000, of whom some 230,000 are Malay-Muslim who dominate the political and bureaucratic life of the sultanate. Ethnic-Chinese, most of whom lack citizenship, number around 50,000. Non-Malay indigenous people add up to about 10,000, while the balance is made up of expatriates, including skilled professionals from the West and construction and factory workers from other parts of South-East Asia. The official religion is **Islam**, while the state is represented as a Malay Islamic Monarchy (*Melayu Islam Beraja*) in the interest of sustaining political conservatism. The sultan, by combing religious and royal roles, seeks to contain radical Islam, which is viewed as a threat to the established political order.

Modern Brunei is bound up with the discovery and exploitation of oil and natural gas. Onshore production of oil began in 1929 with the active involvement of the Shell Company, which in time became the joint venture Brunei Shell in which the government of the sultanate owns a 50 per cent share. Offshore oil production began in 1963 and corresponding natural gas production in 1973 with the involvement of Mitsubishi with the subsequent engagement of Elf Petroleum. A consortium comprising Fletcher Challenge Energy of New Zealand, Unocol Borneo Utara and the government of Brunei is involved in the biggest offshore drilling programme for a decade. Six operational offshore oil and gas fields account for virtually the whole of the sultanate's great wealth, either directly or indirectly through overseas investments funded from oil and gas revenues. National reserves have never been disclosed, nor has the great personal wealth of the Sultan and other members of the royal family. At one time, national reserves were estimated at over US$100 billion but are believed to have been run down dramatically as a result of the collapse with losses estimated at US$15 billion of the country's largest private company, Amedeo Development Corporation, headed by the Sultan's youngest brother, Prince Jefri. In March 2000, he was the subject of a civil law suit brought by the Brunei government for misappropriating funds from the Brunei Investment Agency (BIA), which he also used to head. The government sought to recover B$25.8 billion but the matter was settled out of court in May 2000 with an agreement that all assets acquired with funds derived from the BIA and under the control of Prince Jefri and his family be returned to the agency.

Brunei's economic tribulations came to a head during the peak of economic crisis within South-East Asia compounded in its case by the relatively low world oil price. By the turn of the century that price had recovered significantly to Brunei's advantage. In the past, the huge resources at the disposal of the state, which gave it (at US$25,000) one of the highest average per capita incomes in the world, enabled the introduction of a unique system of social welfare. Free education and health care as well as guaranteed pensions and housing have been provided on a generous basis but have been under review because of changing economic circumstances. Economic planning has concentrated on developing alternative forms of employment to the energy industry and government service in the interest of political stability but with very limited success. In July 2000, radical economic reforms were announced in an attempt to broaden the revenue base before oil and gas reserves run out in twenty-five years.

The government of Brunei is literally a family business with the sultan as prime minister as well as holding the portfolios of finance and defence. One brother, Prince **Mohamed Bolkiah**, has been foreign minister since January 1984, while Prince Jefri was finance minister until his dismissal in 1998. During British protection, the current Sultan's father, the late Sir Omar Ali Saifuddin, was persuaded to introduce a measure of democracy. Elections in September 1962 gave a majority of elective seats to the radical **People's Party** (*Partai Ra'ayat*) with links to the Indonesia of President **Sukarno**. In December 1962, after the Sultan had refused to convene the Legislative Council, the People's Party led by **A. M. Azahari**, launched a revolt, which was put down through British military intervention from Singapore. Brunei has been ruled by decree ever since without any reversion to electoral politics and with all political parties effectively proscribed. Moreover, in order to hold off British pressure for democratization, Sultan Sir Omar Ali Saifuddin abdicated in favour of his son Hassanal Bolkiah in October 1967 shortly before he was due to graduate from the British Military Academy at Sandhurst. Sir Omar remained a powerful and decisive influence behind the throne until his death in 1986. Following his father's death, Sultan Hassanal Bolkiah sought to throw off the playboy image depicted in western media and to demonstrate a seriousness of political purpose in the absence of political change. Despite the neo-conservatism associated with the sultan, expressed in a ban on the public consumption of alchohol in

January 1991, social delinquency has grown among a young unemployed sector. The vulnerability of monarchical rule is well understood in royal circles, especially to a military coup arising from social discontent. For that reason, the armed forces, on whom some 10 per cent of the national budget is spent, are well paid and provided for in modern equipment. The officer corps is also monitored and personal interests balanced in a way that ensures loyalty. Since the revolt was crushed in 1962, a battalion of British Gurkha Rifles had been deployed in the sultanate on rotation from their brigade headquarters in Hong Kong under a secret exchange of letters, ostensibly in a training role. In addition, the sultanate recruits an additional battalion of retired Gurkhas directly from Nepal. These forces serve as a deterrent against any challenge by rebellious elements.

In September 1984, shortly after independence, Sultan Hassanal Bolkiah addressed the General Assembly of the United Nations maintaining: 'We wish to be left alone and free from foreign intervention'. Brunei had been reluctant to assume full independence from Britain because of an acute sense of vulnerability arising from experience of hostile relations with both Indonesia and Malaysia. At one stage, Brunei had contemplated joining the Federation of Malaysia on its inception in 1963 but decided against political union. The **Brunei Revolt** had served as Indonesia's pretext for its campaign of **Confrontation**, while, during the mid-1970s, Malaysia had sought to destabilize the sultanate in part to consolidate its control in northern Borneo. It was only in the late 1970s that the evident cohesion of **ASEAN** (Association of South-East Asian Nations), to which Indonesia and Malaysia were strongly committed, encouraged Brunei to assume full independence and place its security in membership of ASEAN; which was openly pledged to uphold the sanctity of national sovereignty. Even then, independence was accomplished through a treaty of friendship with Britain in 1979 which contained a unique five-year grace period before the transfer of full sovereign status in January 1984. On independence, Brunei joined the Commonwealth and the Organization of the Islamic Conference as well as the United Nations and

ASEAN. It also participated in **APEC** from its advent in 1989 and the **ASEAN Regional Forum** (ARF) and the **Asia–Europe Meeting** (ASEM) from their respective inceptions in 1993 and 1996. Diplomatic relations have been gradually expanded beyond Britain, the United States, ASEAN and other major powers to the Islamic world and the People's Republic of China. Tensions still obtain with Malaysia, with whom Brunei is in dispute in its **Limbang Claim**: the district of Limbang was incorporated into Sarawak in 1890 after Britain's protectorate had been established. In addition, there are differences with Malaysia over maritime jurisdiction in Brunei Bay and also with China and Vietnam over corresponding jurisdiction within that part of the sea-space within the **Spratly Islands** which falls within Brunei's continental shelf. Among its neighbours, Brunei has enjoyed a special relationship with Singapore with which a common vulnerability over size and location has been shared. Singapore bases an infantry battalion in the Temburong enclave, while military exercises are conducted with Australian forces. Relations have improved significantly with Indonesia, which has assumed a protective regional role, while an underlying coolness remains in the relationship with Malaysia. A residual relationship has been maintained with Britain, which still plays an important role in training and servicing the Royal Brunei Armed Forces. An agreement to deploy the Gurkhas beyond 1998 was concluded between the Sultan and Britain's prime minister in London in December 1994, when they also signed a memorandum on defence sales. In addition, limited military links have been established with the United States.

see also: APEC; ARF; ASEAN; ASEM; Azahari, A. M.; Bolkiah, Hassanal; Bolkiah, Mohamed; Brunei Revolt 1962; Confrontation; Islam; Limbang Claim; *Melayu Islam Beraja*; People's Party; Spratly Islands.

# Burma/Myanmar

Burma is the second largest country in South-East Asia with an area of 676,000 square kilometres. It is situated to the east of India and Bangladesh, to the south-west of the People's Republic of China and to the west of Laos and Thailand. Its coastline extends from Bangladesh to Thailand and fronts the Bay of Bengal. The country has a population of over 50 million, the vast majority of whom are devotees of Theravada **Buddhism**. A host of ethnic minorities, long disaffected from the central government, inhabit a horseshoe-like zone around the northern periphery of the state. Burma's primarily agricultural economy has not advanced beyond its condition under colonialism. Indeed, for some forty years, it has regressed economically in the charge of a military junta for whom power has become an end in itself reflected in defence expenditure consuming a third of the annual budget. In reconstituted form since 1988, that junta attempted to open the county to foreign investment and trade, in particular from the early 1990s but with only superficial success. The initial momentum of foreign investment has been reversed, partly as a consequence of external sanctions driven by a deplorable human rights record and evidence that the regime is engaged in narcotics production and trafficking. By the end of the decade, a World Bank study exposed the full depths of the country's economic malaise, including rising inflation and poverty as well as a high level of child malnutrition, which was attributed to incompetent management by the military regime. Its recommendation that major political and human rights were required before economic development could proceed fell on deaf ears in Rangoon.

Burma has been ruled continuously by a military regime since March 1962 when the armed forces, led by General **Ne Win**, seized power. In September 1998, in response to a popular challenge put down with great violence and bloodletting, Ne Win having abdicated formal responsibility in the previous July, the military government transformed itself into the **State Law and Order Restoration Council** (SLORC).

In November 1997, SLORC was replaced by the **State Peace and Development Council** (SPDC). The change in nomenclature and in implied orientation did not change the substance of military despotism. Political opposition has been ruthlessly repressed, including the use of torture, while a continuing practice of forced labour led to Burma's being censured within the International Labour Organization in June 2000. On 18 June 1989, the name of the state was changed from the Socialist Republic of Burma to *Myanmar Naingngan*, which is a direct transliteration in English meaning Union of Peoples. The English spelling of the capital Rangoon was changed to Yangon. Under a draft constitution approved in April 1994 by a national convention but not yet in force, Burma will become known as the Republic of the Union of Myanmar.

Burma was colonized by Britain from the early nineteenth century and was accorded a limited form of self-government only in the late 1930s, when it was separated from the administration of India against a background of nationalist challenge. It was occupied by the Japanese during the Pacific War with the support of Burmese nationalists, who in 1943 were accorded a nominal independence. When it became apparent that the Japanese were going to lose the war, the Burma National Army rebelled against its military mentors in support of the Allied cause. Burma attained full independence in January 1948 after the British Labour Party administration had revised its gradualist timetable in the light of the demonstrable support enjoyed by the **Anti-Fascist People's Freedom League**, the militant nationalist movement led by **Aung San**. Initially self-styled as the Union of Burma, its governments have struggled to overcome the centrifugal political pull of its ethnically diverse population. Geography has combined with ethnicity to obstruct the reach of central power. The majority of Burmans adhere to Theravada Buddhism, as do some of the ethnic minorities, who also observe **Islam** and Christianity.

Burma began independence as a parliamentary democracy in inauspicious circumstances.

Nationalist leader Aung San had come to an agreement in January 1947 with the British government for the transfer of sovereignty a year later but in July 1947 he was assassinated together with six cabinet colleagues in a plot mounted by a political rival. Independence went ahead on 4 January 1948 with **U Nu** as prime minister. From independence, Burma was subject to violent internal upheaval as the government in Rangoon was confronted with insurrection by two Communist and a number of ethnic-minority insurgencies challenging both the identity and the constitutional arrangements of the new state. The ethnic minorities (including the Arakanese, **Chin, Kachin, Shan** and **Karen**) were distributed in concentrations around the northern perimeter of the country from east to south-west and tensions between them and the Burman majority had been inflamed during the Pacific War. These mixed challenges were contained by the early 1950s, in part because of the inability of the opponents of the central government to unite among themselves and also because of the success of the Burmese army in putting them down.

Because of its roots in the nationalist movement against both the British and the Japanese, the army led by General Ne Win displayed a sense of political entitlement which came to affect the future of the country. Violent challenge to the state and its integrity was succeeded by ferocious factional fighting within the ruling political party. It was to repair this situation that in July 1958, the prime minister, U Nu, invited General Ne Win to form a caretaker government and to prepare the country for fresh elections. Power was returned to civilian government in March 1960. With the electoral success of his faction of the Anti-Fascist People's Freedom League, U Nu resumed office as prime minister. In March 1962, however, Ne Win mounted a coup in response to concessions by the government to the insurgent ethnic minorities and set up a Revolutionary Council to run the country.

Under military rule, the country became committed to an ersatz ideology called the **Burmese Way to Socialism**, which was a potted version of Marxist and Buddhist formulae. The declared purpose of the undertaking was Burma's development on an autonomous basis. In July 1962 the Revolutionary Council established the **Burma Socialist Programme Party** (BSPP) with the mission to realize the Burmese Way to Socialism. All other parties were abolished, while the BSPP served as the political arm of the army. In 1974 a new constitution was promulgated, the BSPP was opened up to a mass membership and the name of the state was changed to the Socialist Republic of Burma, with Ne Win in the office of president. Ne Win stepped down in November 1981 but remained in control as chairman of the BSPP. These changes in political form did nothing to arrest a relentless economic decline as the dogma, bureaucracy and corruption of the so-called Burmese Way to Socialism, combined with a policy of international isolation, affected the availability and distribution of basic goods in a country rich with natural resources and once regarded as the rice-bowl of South-East Asia. In addition, the cost of containing the disparate insurgencies served to bring the country closer to economic collapse. For a decade and a half, this continuing decline did not lead to any political reaction beyond the ready control of the military. However, acute economic crisis was signalled in 1987, when the government in Rangoon applied to the United Nations for Burma to be accorded the status of 'least developed country' in order to secure grants in aid.

Burma erupted in political turmoil when the government adopted desperate measures to cope with a deteriorating economy. Demonetization of larger currency notes in circulation in September 1987 provoked student unrest which exploded in demonstrations and violence in March 1988. This challenge was matched by ruthless military repression, which came to a head in August and September. In the interim, Ne Win resigned as chairman of the BSPP in July but failed to stem popular protest which responded to the inspiring leadership provided by **Aung San Suu Kyi**, the daughter of national hero Aung San, who had returned to Burma coincidentally to nurse her ailing mother. On 18 September 1988 the army chief of staff, General Saw Maung, assumed power on behalf of the military in an incumbency coup marking the culmination of an awesome bloodletting. All state organs were abolished by the new junta, which styled itself the State Law and Order Restoration Council (SLORC). The country was placed under martial law but SLORC promised that multi-party elections would be held for a constituent assembly. In the mean time, all references to the Burmese Way to Socialism disappeared from public pronouncements, while the junta sought foreign exchange to buy arms by according foreign entrepreneurs logging and fishing rights.

Political parties were allowed to register during 1989. Although more than two hundred emerged, only a handful of any significance were formed, above all, the **National League for Democracy** (NLD) led by Aung San Suu Kyi. She was placed under house arrest in July 1989 just prior to the anniversary of the period of bloodletting in 1988. Nonetheless, the National League for Democracy won an overwhelming electoral victory at the polls in May 1990 over the **National Unity Party**, which was the political reincarnation of the BSPP. The constituent assembly in the form of a National Convention was not convened until 1993, however, while the position of the National League for Democracy was undermined through contrived expulsions, including that of Aung San Suu Kyi, who was kept in incarceration. SLORC's attempt to discredit her nationally and internationally was thwarted when she was awarded the Nobel Peace Prize in October 1991. However, despite almost universal condemnation of its appalling human rights record, the ruling junta has held on to power, with Ne Win apparently influential in the background despite his ailing condition.

General Saw Maung stepped down as head of SLORC in April 1992, believed to be suffering from mental disorder, to be succeeded by General **Than Shwe**, who also assumed the office of prime minister. However, Ne Win's close confidant and head of intelligence as well as SLORC's first secretary, General **Khin Nyunt**, has been regarded as the more powerful figure and his proxy. He inspired the inauguration of the constituent assembly or National Convention in Rangoon in January 1993 suitably purged of dissident political elements. It took over a year of intermittent meetings before the armed forces were able to have their own way over a draft constitution promulgated in Jan-

uary 1994 but without the National Convention completing its work. At issue had been the insistence of the armed forces that the constitution make provision for their leading political role in a corresponding way to the amended terms of Indonesia's constitution. The draft constitution stipulated that the country's executive president, his or her parents, spouse and children must not be citizens or entitled to the rights or privileges of another state and must also have lived in Burma continuously for at least twenty years prior to election. This provision would disqualify Aung San Suu Kyi, whose late husband was a British citizen, who returned to Burma only in 1988. She was released unexpectedly from detention in July 1995 but without any other political concessions by SLORC. A boycott of the National Convention in November 1995 by the NLD had no political impact.

An ability to reinforce power at the centre has been matched with an increasing assertion of state power against dissident ethnic minorities. The revolt of northern Wa tribesmen against ethnic-Chinese dominance of the Communist Party in the late 1980s enabled the Rangoon government to exercise greater control over the flow of opium and military supplies to rebel minorities. Such control has been facilitated by effective cooperation with the government in Beijing, which has been a major source of arms transfers but in return for access to intelligence facilities in the Andaman Sea. In October 1993 a cease-fire was concluded with the Kachin Independence Army, regarded as the most significant of the insurgent groupings fighting against the government, which was formalized in February 1994. This accord meant that the armed forces could concentrate their efforts against the Karen and the Shan rebels to great military effect. By 1996, the government in Rangoon had effectively turned the tide of battle against the country's ethnic insurgencies, although armed resistance has been sustained by the Karen minority.

In foreign relations, Burma had been an early advocate of non-alignment, being represented at the historic **Asian-African Conference** in Bandung in 1955 and at the founding conference of the Non-Aligned Movement in Belgrade in 1961. Indeed, a passionate anti-colonialism had prevented membership of the Commonwealth in advance of the arrangement made to accommodate India, which as an independent republic could not pledge loyalty to the British Crown. The military regime which assumed power in 1962 maintained the same commitment to non-alignment which complemented the aims of the Burmese Way to Socialism. The commitment did not prevent the development of a close association with northern neighbour China. That relationship was never allowed to become unduly deferential, however. During the period of the Cultural Revolution, Burma displayed a testy independence in response to evident intimidation. In September 1979 at the summit meeting in Havana, Burma withdrew from the Non-Aligned Movement on the ground that it had ceased to be neutral enough under Cuba's chairmanship, which claimed a special relationship for the Soviet Union. However, international reaction to SLORC's violation of human rights, especially against its Muslim minority, caused the government in Rangoon to revise its view by the time of the Non-Aligned Summit in Jakarta in September 1992. Repressive action in 1992 against the Muslim **Rohingyas** minority in Arakan Province bordering Bangladesh drew condemnation from Islamic states, which Burma sought to counter by securing readmission to the Non-Aligned Movement. Moreover, Burma has been able to attract China's support as both an arms supplier and a patron of a kind, willing to help contain international criticism of its brutal repressive regime in return for extensive economic opportunities. China is also developing communication facilities which will enable direct physical access from its borders to the Indian Ocean while an extensive Chinese business/migrant presence has been established in upper Burma. The government of Thailand has been the most active among **ASEAN** (Association of South-East Asian Nations) states in practising the association's policy of constructive engagement viewed as more appropriate than one of shunning the Rangoon regime. In consequence, a Burmese delegation was invited by the Thai government to attend as guests at the annual meeting of ASEAN's foreign ministers held in Bangkok in July 1994. Equivalent status was accorded in July

1995 in Brunei when Burma's foreign minister signed ASEAN's Treaty of Amity and Cooperation and at the Bangkok Summit in December 1995, attended by Prime Minister Than Shwe. Singapore has been even more forthcoming with a visit to Rangoon by its prime minister, **Goh Chok Tong**, in March 1994. His appearance in the Burmese capital marked only the second visit by a head of government since SLORC assumed power. The prime minister of Laos had visited the country in 1992. Despite the release of Aung San Suu Kyi, western countries including the United States have continued to treat Burma as a political outcast. Burma joined the **ASEAN Regional Forum** (ARF) in August 1996 and ASEAN in July 1997 but without its government making any substantive concessions to Aung San Suu Kyi and her followers, who have been marginalized politically. Burma's integration within ASEAN has given rise to difficulties between the Association and some of its dialogue partners. For example, the European Union has denied visas to senior members of the military junta and refused to engage in multilateral meetings until a compromise agreement with the EU in August 2000.

The military government in Burma rules without consent but retains its position because of a caste-like sense of identity and loyalty among the officer corps and a system of patronage which ensures that commands to rank-and-file troops to fire on unarmed demonstrators are obeyed without dissent. One key to the political future of the country is the mortality of General Ne Win, who despite his advancing years and ailing physical condition remains the ultimate authority, like an oriental Stalin. Political change can only follow his death but will not be guaranteed by it.

*see also:* Anti-Fascist People's Freedom League; ASEAN; ASEAN Regional Forum; Aung San; Aung San Suu Kyi; Bangkok Summit 1995; Buddhism; Burma Socialist Programme Party; Burmese Way to Socialism; Chin; Kachin; Karen; Khin Nyunt; Khun Sa; National League for Democracy; National Unity Party; Ne Win; Nu, U; Rohingyas; Shan; State Law and Order Restoration Council; State Peace and Development Council; Than Shwe; Treaty of Amity and Cooperation 1976.

# Cambodia, Kingdom of

Cambodia is situated in the central-south of the Indochina peninsula and is 181,000 square kilometres in size. Its population numbers around 11 million and adheres in the main to the Theravada branch of **Buddhism**, which overlays an historically prior Hindu culture that still plays an important part in informing political traditions. A location to the west of Vietnam and to the east of Thailand has been an important factor in a turbulent and painful political experience since effective independence from French rule in 1954. Cambodia's location drew it into the **Vietnam War** at the end of which, in April 1975, the country descended into barbarism under the murderous rule of a local communist movement, the **Khmer Rouge**. That rule was overturned through an invasion by Vietnam in December 1978, which established a client government that endured changing form in the face of international ostracism to participate in a fragile coalition government with UN endorsement in October 1993. That coalition was displaced through a violent coup in July 1997 to leave government exclusively in the hands of **Hun Sen**, who had defected from the Khmer Rouge in the late 1970s and who had been prime minister under the Vietnamese-sponsored regime. His stable, albeit authoritarian, rule was confirmed by internationally-endorsed elections in July 1998.

Cambodia had become a protectorate of France in the mid-nineteenth century, which had the inadvertent consequence of preserving a separate identity from rapacious neighbours, especially the Vietnamese. The French restored Cambodia's historical monuments from the glorious Angkor period, which served to generate a sense of ethnic and cultural pride but hardly brought the country into the modern world. The French ruled Cambodia through the legitimizing vehicle of the royal family, preserving the institution of monarchy in the process. In 1941 they returned the title of king to the senior branch of the royal family in favour of **Norodom Sihanouk**, then in his late

teens. It was assumed that he would be a pliant instrument of colonial rule, then subject to the authority of the government in Vichy. It was a gross miscalculation which had failed to take account of his innate ability to exploit the aura of monarchy among a predominantly peasant population which regarded him as semi-divine.

Cambodian politics after the end of the Pacific War was marked by factional struggles, which King Norodom Sihanouk overcame to personal advantage. The origins of those contemporary factions may be traced to the modest opening of the political system by the French on the restoration of their rule following the brief wartime interregnum inspired by the Japanese. In simple terms, these factions represented royalist, republican and revolutionary interests, with the latter enjoying support initially from the insurgent Vietnamese Communists. King Norodom Sihanouk exploited the aura of monarchy and French failure to restore colonial authority to outmanoeuvre his republican and revolutionary opponents. Through political theatre, he was able to claim the credit for France conceding independence in November 1953. After that independence had acquired international recognition with the **Geneva Agreements on Indochina** in July 1954, he went on to divest himself of the form of monarchy while retaining its substance. In order to enjoy full political freedom, he abdicated the throne in favour of his father Norodom Suramarit, reverting to the title of prince. He ruled the Kingdom of Cambodia as a populist but ruthless leader in part through the vehicle of *Sangkum Reastre Niyum* (Popular Socialist Community), a mass movement subject to his manipulation. Prince Sihanouk became head of state after the death of his father in April 1960 but was removed from power by a military coup in March 1970.

Prince Sihanouk's commitment to neutrality in foreign policy had served to keep Cambodia out of the Vietnam War until Communist use of his country's territory provided a pretext for his republican opponents to oust him when he was visiting the Soviet Union. Cambodia then experienced five years of civil war, becoming the **Khmer Republic** under the leadership of Marshal **Lon Nol**, who proved to be incompetent and corrupt. Prince Sihanouk went into exile in Beijing where he established a united front in opposition to the new regime in Phnom Penh. He was joined in this front by a revolutionary faction led by a close-knit group of Cambodian intellectuals who had developed a salvationist ideology as students in France in the late 1940s and early 1950s, when the local Communist Party espoused Stalinist dogma. The Khmer Rouge, as Prince Sihanouk had labelled them in a differentiation from the right-wing Khmer *Bleu*, were only a limited insurgency by the late 1960s. The overthrow of Prince Sihanouk changed matters, however, because of the threat which the coup appeared to pose to the revolutionary interests of Vietnam's Communists. They then invaded Cambodia to destroy Lon Nol's army and extracted the administration of the eastern part of the country from the government in Phnom Penh, within which they assisted the Khmer Rouge to become a formidable military force. Aided by association with Prince Sihanouk, the Khmer Rouge fought their way to power by mid-April 1975 just two weeks before the fall of Saigon.

The Khmer Rouge under the leadership of the notorious **Pol Pot** subjected the people of Cambodia to a terrible ordeal in the name of revolutionary idealism between April 1975 and the end of 1978. They sought the total transformation of Cambodian society by murdering its political and religious elite and by driving the inhabitants of the towns into the countryside, where they engaged in a primitive and punishing agriculture. The failure of this crude collectivization by the newly named state of **Democratic Kampuchea** generated paranoid intra-party purges as treachery was deemed to be its cause, especially on behalf of the Vietnamese depicted as historical enemies and not ideological soul-mates. Military interventions into southern Vietnam in the late 1970s together with a tacit alliance with China caused the government in Hanoi to respond with *force majeure*. The Vietnamese invaded Cambodia on 25 December 1978 (as the Kampuchean National

United Front for National Salvation) and by early January 1979 had established a new government of their own fabrication in ostensible charge of the **People's Republic of Kampuchea**. Prince Sihanouk, who had returned to Cambodia to experience house arrest, was able to leave the country on a Chinese aircraft and to go on from Beijing to the United Nations in New York to condemn both his jailors and the Vietnamese occupiers.

The Vietnamese invasion revealed the full extent of the horrors inflicted on the Cambodian people with an estimate of at least 1 million dead through execution, overwork, malnutrition and disease. Nonetheless, the new government in Phnom Penh failed to receive full international recognition. Vietnam's invasion of Cambodia had taken place with the support of the Soviet Union and therefore was treated as a dimension of both Sino-Soviet and US-Soviet antagonisms. With the backing of a group of states in coalition which wished to reverse Vietnam's occupation, Cambodia was returned to civil war. The remnant of the Khmer Rouge army was given sanctuary in Thailand, where it was restored through Chinese military aid. Non-Communist factions, representing royalist and republican interests, emerged under freebooting leaderships but in June 1982 a coalition of all anti-Vietnamese factions was set up under the auspices of **ASEAN** (Association of South-East Asian Nations) which had assumed diplomatic responsibility for challenging Vietnam. That so-called **Coalition Government of Democratic Kampuchea** (CGDK), which served to register the international legitimacy of the Khmer Rouge, held together while Vietnam's circumstances changed adversely. Economic failure and the loss of Soviet countervailing power obliged it to withdraw its main force units in September 1989 and to leave the government in Phnom Penh to its own devices.

After a protracted diplomacy, an **International Conference on Cambodia** in Paris concluded an accord in October 1991 whereby the United Nations would assume responsibility for implementing a peace plan tied to general elections in 1993. The United Nations became involved when it had been demonstrated that the warring Cambodian factions were unwilling to come to terms. They did agree on establishing a **Supreme National Council** under Prince Sihanouk's chairmanship as a formal repository of sovereignty which would delegate powers to **UNTAC** (United Nations Transitional Authority in Cambodia) with a supervisory role in administration and responsibilities for peacekeeping and conducting elections. That ambitious undertaking geared to establishing a neutral political environment which would permit popular choice to determine the country's future ran into early difficulty. The Khmer Rouge refused to cooperate with UNTAC in disarming and demobilizing their forces and in permitting access to its zones of control for registration of voters and actively harassed UN personnel. Their initial expectations of the collapse of the government in Phnom Penh had proved mistaken so they refused to participate in an electoral process seen as stacked against them. They charged that UNTAC had failed to verify the withdrawal of Vietnamese forces and called for the replacement of the Phnom Penh administration by the Supreme National Council. They were prepared to participate in elections only if they would serve to advance their prospect of resuming power. The government in Phnom Penh engaged in lesser acts of violence in attempts to intimidate the faction nominally led by Prince **Norodom Ranariddh**, Prince Sihanouk's eldest son, which had attracted popular support. Those contending factions with force at their disposal were bent on abusing the rules of the electoral game in their own interest.

By early 1993, the Paris agreement appeared to be in serious jeopardy. The Khmer Rouge had called for a boycott of the elections, which they seemed determined to disrupt through acts of violence. Nonetheless, UNTAC went ahead with the elections as scheduled during 23–8 May, which were conducted surprisingly without serious disruption, despite intimidation of opponents by the **Cambodian People's Party** (CPP). Some 4.6 million voters had been registered, of whom nearly 90 per cent cast their ballots in a poll which the United Nations Security Council judged to have been free and fair. **FUNCINPEC** (National United Front for an Independent, Neutral, Peaceful and Cooperative Cambodia) led by Prince Norodom Ranariddh won a narrow plurality with 58 seats

in the Constituent Assembly of 120 members. The incumbent government's Cambodian People's Party secured 51, while the **Buddhist Liberal Democratic Party** obtained 10 seats.

The CPP contested the outcome, threatening territorial secession in eastern provinces; UNTAC stood firm but conceded a provisional coalition government, while the Constituent Assembly set about drafting a new constitution. That constitution, which reinstated the monarchy, was promulgated by Norodom Sihanouk on 24 September 1993. He was then enthroned nearly four decades after he had abdicated the throne. A new government was not announced until the end of October because of factional divisions within the CPP over how to cope with its political failure. Prince Ranariddh and the former prime minister, **Hun Sen**, became First and Second prime ministers respectively in a fragile coalition sustained from a common fear of the Khmer Rouge and of a loss of external assistance. Control of the armed forces and the police remained with the CPP, whose dominant position in the rural administration had not been challenged, despite the greater electoral success of FUNCINPEC.

The last UN peacekeepers left the country towards the end of 1993 with Cambodia displaying a measure of political stability beyond all expectations. That stability was illusory because of tensions within and between the component parties of the ruling coalition pointed up by an abortive coup in July 1994. The practice of coalition government pivoted initially on a working relationship between prime ministers Prince Norodom Ranariddh and Hun Sen at the expense of the short-lived senior political position of FUNCINPEC attained through its electoral performance. Effective administrative and military power remained with the Cambodian People's Party, with the security forces at times a greater threat to law and order than even the Khmer Rouge, which had become a marginal factor in national politics. Corruption became endemic and attempts to curb it met with opposition from the political centre because of a need to reward and sustain key constituencies of support. For example, Finance Minister Sam Rainsy was dismissed in October 1994 because of his persistence in seeking to eliminate corruption. He continued his campaign out of office and was stripped of his membership of FUNCINPEC before being expelled from the National Assembly in June 1995 without debate or vote. More draconian measures, inspired by Hun Sen, were taken against Foreign Minister Prince Norodom Sirivudh, who was imprisoned on a trumped-up charge of attempted assassination after being removed from office. Other human rights abuses and draconian press laws, on top of the murder and intimidation of journalists, pointed to the distance that Cambodia had travelled within only a few years since UNTAC had conducted free and fair elections in May 1993. By 1997, the working relationship between Norodom Ranariddh and Hun Sen had broken down with both sides competing to solicit defections from the Khmer Rouge. That issue served as a pretext for Hun Sen to seize power through a violent coup in Phnom Penh in July 1997, while Norodom Ranariddh was out of the country. That coup effectively ended coalition government to the advantage of the Cambodian People's Party, although its form was maintained with Foreign Minister Ung Huot assuming the office of First Prime Minister in place of Norodom Ranariddh. In the event, Prince Ranariddh and other FUNCINPEC exiles were prevailed upon to return to Cambodia to participate in elections in July 1998, which were supervised up to a point by international monitors. Those elections were won unsurprisingly by the Cambodian People's Party after which Hun Sen assumed the exclusive office of prime minister with Norodom Ranariddh relegated to chair the National Assembly. An ageing and ailing Norodom Sihanouk played a role in brokering an agreement whereby a new coalition government was formed in November 1998 but without any effective sharing of power, which had become concentrated in the ruthless hands of Hun Sen.

Ironically, the Khmer Rouge were unable to benefit from the degeneration of Cambodian politics after the advent of the coalition government in October 1993. The outcome of the UN-supervised elections in the previous May was a political defeat for them with defections ensuing. Initially, they controlled swathes of territory around Cambodia's periphery and about 10 per cent of its population. The coalition government in Phnom Penh mounted military actions against their positions in the west of the country in early 1994 without a conclusive outcome. Talks on national reconciliation in June 1994 failed; the Khmer Rouge were outlawed by the National Assembly in July. The Khmer Rouge responded by proclaiming a provisional government with **Khieu Samphan** as prime minister, while still acknowledging Norodom Sihanouk as king. Their military and political fortunes dwindled, however. A major blow to their credibility was the defection in August 1996 of **Ieng Sary**, a one-time deputy prime minister of Democratic Kampuchea and brother-in-law of Pol Pot. The final act to the tragic saga of the Khmer Rouge involved characteristic self-destruction. In June 1997, Pol Pot ordered the murder of his former defence minister, **Son Sen**, and members of his family, in an attempt to prevent a deal with the Phnom Penh government. He was then detained and sentenced to life imprisonment by a 'people's court' in July. He died in April 1998 in a remote jungle base, apparently of a heart attack. The final surrender of Khmer Rouge forces took place in December 1998 ending any prospect of a return to a murderous rule, whose legacy casts a continuing shadow over Cambodia.

After October 1993, despite persisting tensions with immediate neighbours Thailand and Vietnam, Cambodia sought regional integration through engagement with ASEAN. On signing the Association's **Treaty of Amity and Cooperation** in 1995, it became an observer at annual meetings of foreign ministers and also joined the **ASEAN Regional Forum** (ARF). Cambodia was expected to join ASEAN towards the end of July 1997, together with Burma and Laos, at a meeting of foreign ministers commemorating the thirtieth anniversary of its formation. The violent coup in Phnom Penh earlier in the month caused political embarrassment to ASEAN whose governments decided to postpone Cambodia's entry. Membership was attained only in April 1999 after fresh elections and a new government in Cambodia. Although Cambodia has been confirmed in its membership of ASEAN, its government has participated in an alignment of Indochinese states reminiscent of a pattern of relations during the 1980s when the country was subject to Vietnam's tutelage. In October 1999, Prime Minister Hun Sen took part in a meeting in Vientiane with counterparts from Laos and Vietnam at which they stressed the need to further strengthen their traditional solidarity.

see also: ASEAN; ASEAN Regional Forum; Bangkok Summit 1995; Buddhism; Buddhist Liberal Democratic Party; Cambodian People's Party; Democratic Kampuchea; Democratic Kampuchea, Coalition Government of; Domino Theory; FUNCINPEC; Geneva Agreements on Indochina 1954; Hun Sen; Ieng Sary; Indochina Wars; International Conference on Cambodia, Paris 1991; Kampuchea, People's Republic of; Khieu Sampan; Khmer Republic; Khmer Rouge; Missing in Action; Nol, Lon; Pol Pot; Ranariddh, Norodom; *Sangkum Reastre Niyum*; Sihanouk, Norodom; Son Sen; Supreme National Council; Treaty of Amity and Cooperation 1976; United Nations: Cambodia 1991–3; UNTAC; Vietnam War.

# Indonesia, Republic of

The Republic of Indonesia is the largest and most populous country in South-East Asia. It comprises a distended archipelago of some 13,000 islands that extend from south of the Indian sub-continent to north of Australia; the most sizeable and important of which are Sumatra, Java (on which is located the capital Jakarta), the major portion of Kalimantan (Borneo), Sulawesi (Celebes) and **Irian Jaya** (West New Guinea). They comprise a land area of almost 2 million square kilometres. Its population of around 210 million is the fourth largest after China, India and the United States. Some 90 per cent of its citizens profess an adherence to **Islam** and constitute statistically the largest Muslim community in the world. The degree of religious observance varies, however, and orthodox Islamic practice is diluted and combined regionally with underlying Hindu–Buddhist and animist traditions. Islam has been denied a prerogative place in political life through a state philosophy, *Pancasila*, which was enunciated before independence by the country's first president, **Sukarno**. *Pancasila* enjoins all Indonesians to believe in a single deity but permits them to worship any god of their choice. This philosophy was introduced initially in the interests of religious and cultural tolerance but was then exploited to serve the cause of political demobilization during the authoritarian rule of the country's second president, and former general, **Suharto**. An Islamic revival encouraged from the late 1980s for political advantage found expression in sectarian conflict between Muslims and the country's Christian minority from the late 1990s attendant on an acute economic adversity, which paved the way for the resignation of President Suharto in May 1998. A transitional rule under his constitutional successor, Vice-President **Habibie** enabled a return to democratic practice, which was followed by the election in October 1999 of **Abdurrahman Wahid** as Indonesia's fourth president. Although Indonesia is a unitary republic, a law came into effect in January 2001 that gave provincial administrations greater autonomy in education, health, land rights and transport policies as well as investment approvals.

Indonesia is a unitary republic without historical antecedent within its contemporary territorial bounds, which were established by a waxing Dutch colonial rule from the end of the sixteenth century. Independence was proclaimed by Sukarno and Vice-President **Hatta** on 17 August 1945 shortly after a cruel Japanese occupation from March 1942. Full international status was attained only on 27 December 1949 after a bitter national revolutionary struggle against the returning colonial Dutch, who refused to transfer the western half of the island of New Guinea. Their abortive attempt to undermine the integrity of the revolutionary republic through exploiting the cultural diversity of the archipelago left an abiding apprehension of foreign intervention among the country's political elite. Indonesian independence began with the practice of parliamentary democracy which was marked by fragile coalition governments and regional rebellion. In July 1959 President Sukarno set aside the parliamentary constitution with military support and imposed a **Guided Democracy** by restoring the revolutionary constitution which provided for an executive presidency. This political system was distinguished by intense competition between Sukarno, the armed forces and the large Communist Party of Indonesia. A conventional non-alignment in foreign policy was set aside in favour of membership of radical **New Emerging Forces** ranged against so-called **Old Established Forces** in company with the People's Republic of China. Sukarno embarked on a policy of coercive diplomacy (self-styled as **Confrontation**) which was successful in recovering the western half of New Guinea from Dutch control in 1963. Confrontation was employed again in an abortive attempt to thwart and then to dismantle the Federation of Malaysia. Indonesia left the United Nations in January 1965 in pique at its failure when Malaysia was elected to a non-permanent seat on the Security Council.

In October 1965 an abortive coup (*see* **Gestapu**) attributed to the Communist Party paved the way to a fundamental change in Indonesia's political system and priorities. The circumstances of the coup discredited Sukarno and enabled the armed forces led by Major-General Suharto with Muslim support to take violent measures against the Communists and their alleged supporters. On 11 March 1966 Sukarno was obliged to transfer executive authority (*Supersemar*) to Suharto, promoted to lt-general, who became acting president in the following year. Confirmed as president in March 1968, Suharto held office continuously with military support for over three decades. He secured re-election for a seventh successive term in March 1998 but was obliged to give up office within two months against a background of social and political unrest generated by economic collapse. For the most part, however, his authoritarian rule had provided a stable background for notable economic development, which rested initially on the exploitation of natural resources, especially oil and natural gas. Foreign direct investment enabled that process of development to extend to manufacturing for export generating high levels of growth. However, with accelerated development came a culture of corruption to the advantage, in particular, of Suharto's close family and business circle. The attendant structural weaknesses in the economy were exposed with the onset of devastating economic crises from the late 1990s.

Under President Suharto's proclaimed **New Order**, political participation was strictly controlled, while the media were subject to draconian controls. Parliamentary elections were resumed in 1971 but political parties were compelled to merge into two groupings entitled to canvass popular support only every five years. The government revived an association of functional groups, *Golkar*, to serve as its electoral vehicle. *Golkar* secured approximately two-thirds of the votes cast in parliamentary elections between 1971 and 1997 but lost support dramatically after the political downfall of Suharto. Members of Parliament and political nominees, including representatives of the armed forces, made up the constitutionally supreme **People's Consultative Assembly**, which re-elected Suharto to a seventh consecutive five-year term of office in March 1998. Suharto had previously assumed the title of 'father of development' in a demonstration of his claim to legitimacy. By that juncture, however, Indonesia was deep in economic crisis. Suharto appeared determined to soldier on to the end of his term and had secured the appointment of Dr B. J. Habibie as vice-president on the assumption that he would be a politically unwelcome successor. In the event, a reluctance to meet the economic priorities of the International Monetary Fund served to accelerate the process of economic crisis, which gave rise to serious social and political unrest in Jakarta, in particular, including anti-Chinese violence. The catalyst in generating political change was a student-led activism, which was met by force from the security services killing four students at Trisakti University in Jakarta. It was in this turbulent context that Suharto found himself unable to reconstitute his cabinet and without the support of the armed forces leadership decided to resign on 21 May 1998. The end of his personalized quasi-monarchical rule left a political vacuum distinguished by the absence of viable national economic and legal institutions.

He was succeeded by Vice-President Habibie who restored the practice of democracy but attempted to use it to secure a fresh term of office. With the restoration of democracy, there was an explosion in the number of political parties. Forty-eight of them contested parliamentary elections in June 1999. The most successful was the **Indonesian Democratic Party (Struggle)** (PDI-P), which secured approximately 154 of 462 elective seats. It was led by **Megawati Sukarnoputri**, the daughter of the republic's first president. The PDI was one of three legal parties during Suharto's rule but PDI-P was its prevailing faction. A much diminished and divided *Golkar* came second with 120 seats. In third place with 58 seats, in alliance with smaller parties, was the Islamic **United Development Party** (PPP), another legal party from the Suharto era. Fifth with 51 seats was the **National Awakening Party**, which was new in form but represented the interests of the moderate-Islamic *Nahdatul Ulama* and its leader Abdurrahman Wahid, which had once been a constituent part of the PPP. The ostensibly constitutionalist but modernist-Islamic **National Mandate Party** with 35 seats came last among the more successful participants. With the exception of the Islamic Crescent Star Party with 14 seats, 13 other parties secured 6 seats or less each.

The parliamentary elections placed Megawati as front runner for president. President Habibie faced resistance from a progressive wing within *Golkar* and was tainted politically by his close association with the Suharto regime. His political prospects were damaged irretrievably by a scandal at Bank Bali over funds siphoned off to fund *Golkar*'s and his election campaign as well as by his handling of the problem of **East Timor**. In the event, Habibie withdrew from the presidential contest. The way was not automatically left open for Megawati, however. She did not command a working majority either in the Parliament or in the People's Consultative Assembly (MPR), the electoral college that elected the president and the vice-president. Moreover, an Islamic-based coalition had coalesced against her organized by Amien Rais of the National Mandate Party, who became the speaker of the MPR. In the event, Abdurrahman Wahid was elected president on 20 October 1999 defeating Megawati by 373 votes to 313. She was then elected vice-president on the following day in an act of political reconciliation. President Addurrahman Wahid appointed a coalition government, including Professor **Juwono Sudarsono**, the first civilian minister of defence for some four decades. An early political confrontation occurred with General Wiranto, the former armed forces commander and minister of defence, who occupied the office of coordinating minister for political and security affairs. President Wahid suspended him from office in February 2000, from which he formally resigned in May, in a demonstration of supremacy of civilian authority. A subsequent cabinet reshuffle to the advantage of his political party suggested a reversion of Indonesian politics to the financially-driven factionalism of the 1950s as well as a neglect of national economic

priorities reflected in the progressive weakening of the currency. President Wahid has adopted a populist style, marred by a willingness to tolerate the youth wing of his party acting as street gangs against his political critics. From before the onset of his presidency, Indonesia was wreaked with sectarian conflict between Muslims and Christians on the Moluccan Island chain with around 4,000 fatalities as well as on Sulawesi and the island of Lombok. Separatist challenge in **Aceh** in northern Sumatra was mitigated with a cease-fire signed in May 2000, but it has rumbled on without imminent threat in Irian Jaya. The early promise of President Wahid's tenure gave way after six months to disillusionment at home and abroad as a result of his erratic and even inconsequential style of leadership, which neglected economic priorities. In August 2000, he sought to reassert his authority through reconstituting his cabinet at the cost of alienating the majority parties in the parliament as well as his vice-president. However, he failed to impose any effective control over the armed forces.

Indonesia returned to the United Nations in September 1966 and reinstated a declaratory policy of Non-Alignment, while forging close economic and political links with the United States and Japan as well as suspending diplomatic ties with China. General Suharto presided over the end of Confrontation of Malaysia and played a decisive role in cementing regional reconciliation through promoting the formation of **ASEAN** (Association of South-East Asian Nations) in August 1967. Within Indonesia, ASEAN was conceived as a vehicle for managing regional order to the exclusion of the major powers. Accordingly, its foreign minister, **Adam Malik**, opposed a Malaysian proposal to neutralize South-East Asia and pressed successfully in November 1971 for the ASEAN states to commit themselves to establishing the region as a **ZOPFAN** (Zone of Peace, Freedom and Neutrality), albeit without operational expression. Indonesia's central place within ASEAN was registered in June 1976 when its secretariat was located in Jakarta. After Vietnam's invasion of Cambodia in December 1978, Indonesia experienced frustration in its regional policy because ASEAN's opposition to its military occupation facilitated Sino-Soviet involvement in the conflict in contradiction to the Zone of Peace formula. However, its foreign ministers were able to play leading roles in the diplomacy of the Cambodian conflict. **Ali Alatas** served as co-chair of the international conference in Paris in October 1991 which resolved the conflict, although it was the permanent members of the United Nations Security Council which were instrumental in fashioning the final settlement. In August 1990, after the end of the Cold War, Indonesia restored diplomatic relations with China, which removed an impediment to a long-sought goal of assuming the chair of the Non-Aligned Movement, whose summit was held in Jakarta in September 1992. Indonesia also hosted an **APEC** summit in Bogor in November 1994. Despite recurrent tensions with the United States over human rights, Indonesia has maintained an informal strategic relationship and has permitted US naval vessels access to the port of Surabaya for repair and supply. That relationship was augmented indirectly in December 1995 through an unprecedented security agreement with Australia that then fell victim to acrimony over East Timor in September 1999.

Indonesia had seized the eastern half of the island in December 1975 in an act of strategic denial to prevent the Portuguese possession from becoming subject to a left-wing government. Its integration into the republic in July 1976 was never endorsed by the United Nations. Under President Suharto's rule, Indonesia maintained its hold over the territory through ruthless repression. In January 1999, President Habibie unexpectedly offered the inhabitants of East Timor the choice between autonomy with Indonesia and full independence. A referendum in August 1999 under UN auspices produced an overwhelming vote in favour of independence but so-called pro-integrationist militia inspired and armed by the armed forces engaged in a scorched-earth policy in an abortive attempt to hold on to the territory. Indonesia's condition of economic adversity and international pressure obliged President Habibie to tolerate the intervention of a United Nations-sanctioned international force led by Australia to restore order and to transfer responsibility for the territory to the world body in October 1999. The initial act of annexation in 1975 had marked a continuity in strategic perspective from December 1957 when an **Archipelago Declaration** was proclaimed. That declaration asserted the same right of jurisdiction over waters surrounding and intersecting the islands of Indonesia as over its land space. Indonesia's archipelagic status, with prerogative rights, was recognized in the Convention concluded at the Third United Nations Conference on the Law of the Sea in 1982, which came into force in 1994. At issue is the ability of Indonesia's navy to command that archipelago with only fifteen patrol vessels at its disposal.

see also: *Abangan*; ABRI; Alatas, Ali; APEC; Archipelago Declaration 1957; ASEAN; Confrontation; Crocodile Hole; *Dwi Fungsi*; *Gestapu*; *Golkar*; Guided Democracy; Habibie, Dr B. J.; Hatta, Mohammad; Indonesian Democratic Party-Struggle; Irian Jaya; Islam; Malik, Adam; Megawati Sukarnoputri; *Nahdatul Ulama*; National Awakening Party; National Mandate Party; New Emerging Forces; New Order; Old Established Forces; *Pancasila*; People's Consultative Assembly; *Santri*; Sudarsono, Juwono; Suharto; Sukarno; *Supersemar*; Timor, East; United Development Party; Wahid, Abdurrahman; ZOPFAN.

# Laos, People's Democratic Republic of

The People's Democratic Republic of Laos was established on 2 December 1975 in succession to the Kingdom of Laos. The political change was effected by the ruling **Lao People's Revolutionary Party**, which had been created in the 1950s as a virtual branch of the Communist Party of Vietnam. The party had assumed power progressively during 1975 as a direct consequence of Communist victories in Cambodia and Vietnam in April that year. It has ruled Laos continuously with close reference to the changing priorities of its senior fraternal partner in Hanoi.

Laos is an elongated landlocked state of around 240,000 square kilometres situated in the mainland of South-East Asia. The country is bounded to the north by the People's Republic of China, to the east by Vietnam, to the south by Cambodia, to the west by Thailand and minimally to the north-east by Burma/Myanmar. Its topography is very mixed with a great contrast between the fertile valley of the River Mekong to the west and the forested mountainous uplands in the east. A population of some 5 million is distinguished by an ethnic diversity, in particular between the lowland Lao with linguistic and cultural affiliations to Thailand, and the upland hill tribes who have kinship links across the eastern border in the upland area of Vietnam. The contemporary configuration of the state owes much to colonial intervention in the late nineteenth century, with a French protectorate established initially over the Kingdom of Luang Prabang in 1893. The imposition and expansion of French colonial domain prevented the absorption of the several local principalities between expanding Thai and Vietnamese states. An occupied France was obliged to give up territory west of the Mekong to Thailand in May 1941. Japan inspired the independence of Laos in April 1945 but the protectorate was reinstated at the end of August 1945 after Japan's surrender to the Allied powers.

The restoration of French rule and the establishment of the Kingdom of Laos was resisted by a nationalist revolutionary movement which received direction and military support from a patron movement in Vietnam. From the end of the Pacific War, the country was caught up in a wider struggle for Indochina whose prime locus was in Vietnam (*see* **Indochina Wars**). Civil conflict within the Lao elite over ideology and external patronage attracted intervention from the United States and Thailand as well as from China, the Soviet Union and Vietnam and was contained only temporarily by the settlement reached in the **Geneva Agreements on Indochina** in July 1954 which confirmed national independence. After a revival of conflict, a further settlement exclusively for Laos was reached in the **Geneva Agreements on Laos** in July 1962 and the country was ostensibly neutralized under a coalition government comprised of warring political factions. Neutralization failed and the country continued to be a hostage to the fortunes of competing sides in the **Vietnam War**. On 21 February 1973, just weeks after the **Paris Peace Agreements** for Vietnam, hostilities in Laos were ended by the **Vientiane Agreement on the Restoration of Peace and Reconciliation in Laos**. Another coalition government was established in which the balance of advantage shifted inexorably to the Communist side until their complete seizure of power in December 1975, when King Savang Vatthana abdicated.

Laos began its socialist era with a commitment to the same doctrinal priorities that inspired the ruling party in Hanoi. Indeed, Laos has moved in both domestic and international policy in parallel with that of its eastern neighbour, which has served as mentor and patron for a decade and a half. In July 1977 a **Treaty of Friendship and Cooperation** between Laos and Vietnam affirmed a special relationship in a context of deteriorating Sino-Vietnamese relations which overcame any Laotian desire at the time for greater political autonomy. Laos shared Vietnam's experience of miscalculating the pitfalls of an accelerated collectivization of agriculture and nationalization of industry and commerce and suffered economic distress as a consequence. That distress was aggravated from the onset of the Cambodian conflict in which Laos sided with Vietnam to its cost. Parallel with Vietnam, Laos was obliged from the onset of the 1980s to sacrifice ideology and to embark tentatively on market-based economic reforms while striving to maintain single party rule. Those reforms were pursued vigorously from the mid-1980s concurrently with the ending of the Cold War and Vietnam's loss of Soviet patronage, which had the attendant effect of weakening but not dissolving the special relationship enshrined by treaty. Laos made corresponding adjustments in foreign policy by improving fractured ties with China and Thailand which have become important economic partners. In July 1992 in Manila, Laos acceded to **ASEAN's Treaty of Amity and Cooperation** thereby securing observer status at annual meetings of ASEAN's foreign ministers. In July 1993 in Singapore, Phoune Sipaseuth, the foreign minister of Laos, took part in the inaugural dinner meeting of the **ASEAN Regional Forum**. Laos became a member of ASEAN in July 1997. However, in October 1999, a meeting in Vientiane of the heads of government of Cambodia, Laos and Vietnam indicated a reversion to a political alignment in opposition to ASEAN that had been forged during the height of the Cambodian conflict.

Laos has long ceased to be a battleground in Indochina but has been troubled by a limited revival of insurgency on the part of the *Hmong* minority that were recruited by the American CIA to fight on the anti-communist side in the spill-over from the Vietnam War. Laos continues to be governed by an administration drawn from the Lao People's Revolutionary Party, which is the sole legal political organization and in which the military exercise a leading role. Since November 1992, the party has been headed by General **Khamtay Siphandon** following the death of the founding leader, **Kaysone Phomvihan. Nouhak Phoumsavan** assumed the office of state president, which Kaysone had also held but was replaced in February 1998 by Khamtay who gave up office as prime minister, while remaining party leader. General Sisavath Keobounphanh took over as prime minister. The ease with which political succession was accomplished indicated an underlying party control.

Only one out of ninety-nine members of the National Assembly elected in December 1997 was not from the ruling party. Despite that control, Laos is a weak state with few resources in which substance agriculture is the primary occupation. Annual average per capita income is around US$250. Apart from limited exports of hydro-electric power, timber and coffee, Laos has been dependent on tourism, including gambling, economic aid and investment for foreign exchange. It was badly hit by the economic crisis that afflicted South-East Asia at the end of the 1990s, primarily as a result of Thailand's acute difficulties leading to collapse of its currency, the *kip*. In August 1999, its finance minister and the governor of its central bank were dismissed on grounds of mismanaging the country's fiscal and banking policy in terms that suggested an involvement in corruption. Laos faces major problems in creating an adequate infrastructure to overcome physical and human resources barriers to development. Despite the limited economic opportunities that Laos provides, its ruling party, like that in Vietnam, has been cautious in opening up the country to foreign influences that might pose a threat to its conservative political system. In that respect, the bridge across the River Mekong linking the country with Thailand, that was built with Australian aid and opened in April 1994, has not been a major stimulus to economic advance. From early 2000, Vientiane experienced indiscriminate bombings, while Vietnamese military assistance was provided to counter a revival of *Hmong* rebellion in moutainous Xiang Khouang Province.

*see also:* APEC; ASEAN; ASEAN Regional Forum; Domino Theory; Geneva Agreements on Indochina 1954; Geneva Agreements on Laos 1962; Indochina wars; Kaysone Phomvihan; Khamtay Siphandon; Lao People's Revolutionary Party; Nouhak Phoumsavan; Paris Peace Agreements 1973; *Pathet Lao*; Treaty of Amity and Cooperation 1976; Treaty of Friendship and Cooperation 1977; Vientiane Agreement on the Restoration of Peace and Reconciliation in Laos 1973; Vietnam War.

# Malaysia, Federation of

The Federation of Malaysia was established on 16 September 1963 from former British colonial possessions in South-East Asia around the core of the Federation of Malaya. It contains a population of some 22 million within a land area of around 330,000 square kilometres. Comprising the Malay Peninsula and much of northern Borneo, Malaysia shares common land and maritime boundaries with Thailand, Brunei and Indonesia and maritime boundaries with Singapore, the Philippines and Vietnam, some of which are contested. The federal enterprise was designed primarily to protect the political dominance of the indigenous Muslim community of the Malay peninsula from the economically based challenge of ethnic-Chinese of migrant origin (*see* **Overseas Chinese**). It was intended also to facilitate a smooth process of decolonization.

Malay-Muslim political dominance in the federation is symbolized in a constitutional monarchy whose incumbent is drawn, on a rotating five-year basis, from the sultans or rulers of the states of the Malay peninsula (*see* **Yang di-Pertuan Agong**). It has more practical expression in the commanding role of **UMNO** (United Malays National Organization), the distribution of parliamentary seats and cabinet posts. As that political dominance has become more entrenched under the leadership of the prime minister, Dr **Mahathir Mohamad** since 1981, intra-Malay contention has become more evident. Successful economic development with diversification into export-led growth in manufactures in addition to plantation agriculture and extractive industry, including oil and natural gas, has provided a strong material base for political stability in a plural society. Such stability has been enforced also by authoritarian government which has curbed the role of independent institutions in providing those political checks and balances associated with parliamentary democracy. That authoritarianism became more pronounced in the wake of economic crisis at the end of the 1990s during which Dr Mahathir met a political challenge by removing his deputy **Anwar Ibrahim**. Malay reaction to his arrest, trial and imprisonment on charges of corruption and sexual misconduct provided an opportunity for *Parti Islam Se-Malaysia* (PAS), the main Malay opposition party, to make considerable gains at UMNO's expense in elections in November 1999. But Dr Mahathir was re-elected as president of UMNO without a contest in May 2000.

Malaysia superseded the Federation of Malaya, which had been independent since 31 August 1957. The ambit of the government of Malaya, based in Kuala Lumpur, was extended to the self-governing island of Singapore and two British colonial possessions in northern Borneo – Sarawak and Sabah – located several hundred miles away across the **South China Sea**. The British-protected Sultanate of Brunei, also in northern Borneo, had contemplated membership but in the event did not join. Singapore's membership was short-lived. The island constituent was expelled from the federation on 9 August 1965.

Malaysia was established in a climate of controversy because of objections, from President **Sukarno**'s Indonesia in particular, at the extension of Kuala Lumpur's political domain across the South China Sea to a common border in Borneo. That dispute was resolved after Sukarno's downfall in 1966 and Indonesia and Malaysia had become founder members of **ASEAN** in 1967. The initiative for extending Malaya into Malaysia came from the prime minister, **Tunku Abdul Rahman**, who viewed the federal undertaking as a way of securing the dominant political position of the Malay community represented by the United Malays National Organization which he led. That initiative, first made public in May 1961, had been inspired by apprehension at the prospect of the self-governing island of Singapore, joined to the Malay peninsula by a causeway, becoming fully independent. Its predominantly Chinese population and the growing influence of the

Communist Party of Malaya made Singapore a potential source of political infection. The Malayan government's wish to neutralize Singapore through political encapsulation was tempered by a fear of the consequences of the demographic change for the Malay community. It was to avoid such an outcome that the two Borneo states were included in Malaysia on the facile assumption that their non-Chinese indigenous people, akin to Malays, would help to maintain the right kind of racial and political balance.

The peninsular Malaya model of politics – based on intercommunal coalition government led by its Muslim component – was extended to northern Borneo. The attempt to sustain this Alliance Party model in a very different racial context provoked recurrent federal–state tensions which have persisted. When Singapore's ruling People's Action Party (PAP) entered peninsular Malaysia elections in 1964 to challenge the Chinese partner of UMNO in the federal coalition cabinet, it laid the ground for expulsion from Malaysia in August 1965. The challenge was construed as masking an ulterior intent to displace UMNO from its leading political role. The sequel took the form of intercommunal violence (the **May 13 Racial Riots**) in Kuala Lumpur in 1969 in the wake of general elections. UMNO had lost support from its communal constituency, while non-Malay opposition parties publicly trumpeted their success at the expense of its non-Malay coalition partners. A state of emergency was imposed and government placed in the hands of a National Operations Council. When it was lifted, the rules of politics had been revised in the Malay interest. To that end, a **New Economic Policy** was introduced to ensure that a constitutionally founded dominance would be underpinned by corporate economic ownership. Prime minister Tunku Abdul Rahman, associated with appeasing Chinese interests, was obliged to resign. He was succeeded in September 1970 by his deputy, **Tun Abdul Razak**, who was identified with Malay rural development. From that juncture, Malay political dominance has never been challenged. The significance of non-Malay voting support for the wider ruling intercommunal *Barisan Nasional* (National Front), which replaced the

Alliance, has paradoxically increased rather than diminished. The reason is that the centrality of intercommunal contention in politics has been succeeded up to a point by intra-Malay contention.

A critical factor in modifying the pattern of politics in Malaysia has been the resurgence of **Islam** as a result of international and local causes. The experiment of incorporating the Malay opposition *Parti Islam Se-Malaysia* (PAS) into the ruling coalition from the early 1970s failed by the end of the decade. More successful was the cooption of non-Malay parties, including those from the northern Borneo states. When Dr Mahathir became Malaysia's fourth prime minister in July 1981, he decided to reinforce UMNO's Islamic identity in order to overcome its political vulnerability because of its close cooperation with non-Malay parties. That policy was expressed more in form than in substance. It proved effective, however, for example, through his cooption of Anwar Ibrahim, a one-time radical Islamic youth leader, who rose rapidly through ministerial ranks to become deputy prime minister by the end of 1993.

Dr Mahathir found himself troubled far more by challenge based on personal ambition from among his cabinet colleagues than from racial tension or Islamic resurgence. Major internal discord was signalled from February 1986, when the deputy prime minister, **Musa Hitam**, resigned from the government complaining of Dr Mahathir's managerial style. In April 1987 **Tengku Razaleigh Hamzah**, minister for trade and industry, who had been demoted from finance, launched an abortive challenge to Dr Mahathir for the presidency of UMNO at the party's triennial elections. He did so in tandem with Musa Hitam, who failed to retain the office of deputy president. The contest exposed deep factional divisions within UMNO. Those divisions became institutionalized after a challenge in the courts to the credentials of a number of UMNO branches led to the party being declared an unlawful society. After a confrontation between Dr Mahathir and senior members of the judiciary, during which its head was removed from office, UMNO was reconstituted as a new party with the power to screen applications for admission. In May 1988 Tengku Razaleigh registered *Semangat '46* as a new party. Its meaning (Spirit of 1946) was intended to convey direct lineal descent from UMNO, which had been established in that year. The sustained challenge to Dr Mahathir was then mitigated by Musa Hitam's announcement in January 1989 that he was rejoining UMNO; this was possibly prompted by the heart attack suffered by the prime minister, whose health was restored through bypass surgery.

Any doubts about Dr Mahathir's mastery of Malaysian politics were laid to rest in October 1990 when he led UMNO to a third successive electoral victory since assuming office. *Semangat '46* had entered into an electoral pact with PAS within a Muslim Unity Front which gave them an overwhelming victory only in the legislature in Tengku Razaleigh's home state of Kelantan, where his nephew was sultan. The ruling coalition was also unable to displace *Parti Bersatu Sabah* (PBS), the **Sabah United Party**, which had defected from the ruling federal coalition only days before the election. Nonetheless, UMNO secured more than the two-thirds parliamentary majority required to amend the federal constitution at will. At the end of the month, Dr Mahathir was returned unopposed as president of UMNO at its General Assembly. His political dominance was further asserted when an impetuous act by the Sultan of Johor provided the opportunity in 1993 to have the legal immunity of the Malay rulers removed by constitutional amendment and to diminish their political influence. Dr Mahathir's position has been underpinned by the good health of Malaysia's economy as well as by a skilful employment of attendant patronage. Jockeying for political succession, however, became evident in the run-up to UMNO's general elections in November 1993 at which Anwar Ibrahim displaced the deputy prime minister, **Ghafar Baba**, from the office of deputy president in a generational change reflected also in the team which he carried into the three posts of vice-president. Prime minister Mahathir was returned unopposed as president of the dominant party but its activists had indicated their choice of the next prime minister. Dr Mahathir showed no inclination to step aside; instead he indicated a strong determination to lead the ruling coalition to a further electoral victory. He did so in a resounding manner in April 1995 when the *Barisan Nasional* won 162 seats in an expanded federal parliament of 192, but not placing himself beyond political challenge. That victory owed much to a successful economic policy which began to run into difficulties from 1996.

Malaysia was afflicted by regional economic crisis, which came to a head during 1998. In the wake of the downfall of President Suharto in May 1998, Dr Mahathir judged that his deputy prime minister and finance minister, Anwar Ibrahim, was making a bid to replace him. He was dismissed from both offices on 2 September 1998 and expelled from UMNO on the following day. He was arrested later in the month and charged with corruption (abuse of power) and sexual misconduct. On his first appearance in court, Anwar's neck and arms were badly bruised and he had a black eye. He was found guilty on four charges of corruption in April 1999 and of a further count of sodomy in August 2000. One reaction to Anwar's arrest, trial and imprisonment was public disorder in Kuala Lumpur put down with a heavy hand by security forces. Another was the emergence of a new political entity, *Parti Keadilan Nasional* (National Justice Party), promoted by Anwar's wife, Wan Azizah Ismail. A political sequel to the Anwar affair was the outcome of elections in November 1999 in which the *Barisan Nasional* was returned to federal office with a reduced majority of 148 seats in a legislature expanded to 193. UMNO suffered a major reverse, however, to the advantage of *Parti Islam Se-Malaysia* (PAS), which increased its federal representation to twenty-seven seats from seven. PAS had entered into an electoral pact with other Malay opposition parties, including *Parti Keadilan Nasional*, which won five seats, and the non-Malay **Democratic Action Party** within a **Barisan Alternatif** (Alternative Front). PAS also displaced UMNO as the government in the state of Trengannu, while holding onto that in Kelantan and provided the leader of the federal parliamentary opposition for the first time. Dr Mahathir replaced Anwar with **Abdullah Ahmad Badawi** as deputy prime minister in January 1999. He was confirmed, without contest, as deputy president of UMNO in May 2000.

Dr Mahathir has announced that he would not seek another term as prime minister on the grounds of age but has been equivocal about automatic succession on the part of his fourth deputy prime minister.

Malaysia's foreign policy has reflected domestic political change. Its first prime minister, Tunku Abdul Rahman, was an Anglophile who valued the Commonwealth connection and who was obliged to draw on British and Commonwealth support to cope with the threat posed by Indonesia's **Confrontation**. Reconciliation with Indonesia and membership of ASEAN encouraged an extension of international links, especially membership of the Non-Aligned Movement, under the leadership of Tun Abdul Razak. He was identified with a proposal to neutralize South-East Asia and took the initiative in 1974 in establishing diplomatic relations with the People's Republic of China to manage domestic politics. Following Razak's premature death in 1976, **Hussein Onn** succeeded but without imposing any distinctive stamp on foreign policy. He did, however, curtail an adventurist tendency expressed in particular in an attempt to destabilize Brunei.

Foreign policy did not change in great substance when Dr Mahathir became prime minister in 1981 after Hussein Onn had retired because of ill-health. ASEAN remained at the centre of regional calculations but Malaysia became more self-assertive under his leadership. He acquired a reputation as a sharp-tongued spokesman in support of Third World causes and early in his tenure directed his anger on Britain, which was subject to economic discrimination (*see* **Buy British Last Policy**) in retaliation for insensitivity to Malaysia's interests. Membership of the Commonwealth was reconsidered, while international Islamic links were strengthened. Initiatives were taken to promote international cooperation in control of drug trafficking and over Antarctica and South-South relationships. A change of political heart over the utility of the Commonwealth resulted in Malaysia playing host to the meeting of its heads of government in October 1989. In 1994 Dr Mahathir returned to attack the former colonial power over British press allegations of his financial impropriety. He has also been vocal over the alleged hypocrisy

of the west through its failure to safeguard human rights in Bosnia.

Dr Mahathir's personal role in foreign policy has given rise to some tensions in regional relations. For example, he interpreted Singapore's willingness to receive the president of Israel in November 1986 as an insult because of his own identification with the Palestinian cause. Relations with Indonesia have been uneasy partly because of an unwillingness to respect President **Suharto**'s seniority. Such unease was reinforced in the early 1990s, after Dr Mahathir had unilaterally put forward a proposal for the establishment of an **East Asian Economic Caucus** to cope with a global trend towards trade blocs. That proposal has generated tensions with the United States and Australia. Tensions with the United States were generated also during 1998 when Dr Mahathir claimed that an international Jewish conspiracy was behind Malaysia's economic tribulations. Malaysia took a strong stand on incorporating Burma (Myanmar) and the states of Indochina within ASEAN and aligned with Vietnam against other regional partners in supporting Cambodia's early membership, despite the violent coup in Phnom Penh in July 1997. Malaysia has also been prominent within ASEAN in promoting close relations with China. An agreement to boost defence cooperation and to use peaceful means to resolve tensions over disputed maritime jurisdiction in the **South China Sea** was concluded in Beijing in June 1999. That agreement gave rise to suspicions that Malaysia had come to terms with China at the expense of ASEAN partners, with which both China and itself dispute jurisdiction in the **Spratly Islands**. In June and August 1999, Malaysia occupied two unoccupied features in the Spratly group, which provoked a strong protest from the Philippines but only a mild rebuke from China. The key to Dr Mahathir's ability to receive a hearing internationally for his outspoken views has been the underlying success of Malaysia's economy. The economic crisis of the late 1990s had the effect of diminishing his credibility in preaching to the West.

*see also:* Al-Arqam; Alliance Party; Anwar Ibrahim; APEC; ASEAN; Badawi, Abdullah Ahmad; *Barisan Alternatif; Barisan Nasional;* Buy British Last Policy; Confrontation;

Democratic Action Party; East Asian Economic Caucus; Ghafar Baba, Abdul; Hussein Onn; Islam; Mahathir Mohamad, Datuk Sri; May 13 Racial Riots 1969; Musa Hitam, Datuk; New Economic Policy; Overseas Chinese; *Parti Islam Se-Malaysia*; *Parti Keadilan Nasional* (National Justice Party); People's Action Party; Rahman, Tunku Abdul; Razak, Tun Abdul; Razaleigh Hamzah, Tengku; Sabah United Party; *Semangat '46*; South China Sea; Spratly Islands; Suharto; Sukarno; UMNO; Yang di-Pertuan Agong.

# Philippines, Republic of

The Republic of the Philippines was established as an independent state on 4 July 1946 when sovereignty was transferred by the US colonial power. The US model of democracy was replaced by authoritarian rule under President **Ferdinand Marcos** from 1972 until 1986. Constitutional democracy was restored by President **Corazón Aquino**, who was succeeded in office by **Fidel Ramos** after elections in May 1992. From Corazon Aquino onwards, the tenure of presidential office was restricted to a single six-year term. Incumbent Vice-President **Joseph Estrada** was elected president in May 1998.

The Philippines is made up of an archipelago of some 7,000 islands extending for nearly 1,000 miles from north to south, which are located at the eastern periphery of South-East Asia and to the south of the People's Republic of China. Its land area is 300,000 square kilometres. Three principal geographic divisions comprise the main northern island of Luzon, on which is located the capital Manila, the central Visayan islands and the southerly islands of Mindanao and Sulu. The archipelago was given political coherence through Spanish colonial intervention from the late sixteenth century and was named for the crown prince who became Philip II. The Spanish also left a profound religious legacy, with over 90 per cent of the population of some 75 million adhering to the Catholic faith. The Spanish were responsible also for containing Islamic settlement to the extreme south of the archipelago. **Islam** is the religious faith of about 5 per cent of the population, who have a tradition of resistance and rebellion against the government in Manila.

The United States succeeded Spain as the colonial power through military action at the end of the nineteenth century. A commitment to self-government produced a promise of independence in the 1930s which was fulfilled on time despite a cruel and devastating Japanese occupation during the Pacific War. On independence, the Philippines replicated the US constitutional model with an elected presidential system of government constrained in principle by congressional and judicial checks and balances. Two main political organizations, the **Nacionalista Party** and the **Liberal Party**, contended for office and spoils but did not represent fundamental alternatives. In effect, the two parties served as vehicles for advancing and enriching competing provincial-based elite groups whose power rested on a network of local and personal loyalties. Politics involved the alignment and realignment of these fractious elite groups which switched promiscuously from party to party for electoral advantage. That pattern of politics changed in September 1972 when Ferdinand Marcos, elected in November 1965 and re-elected in November 1969, declared martial law in order to overcome the constitutional limitation of two presidential terms. He concentrated power at the centre at the expense of provincial elites with the exception of cronies from his home base of Ilocos Norte. Initially, the inauguration of Marcos's so-called **New Society Movement** appeared to address the country's economic and political ills. Law and order visibly improved, bureaucratic corruption was reduced while land reform measures were begun. In the event, adverse economic factors precipitated by the energy crisis together with a gross abuse of personal power and financial mismanagement led to decline and disillusionment as all political and legal institutions were rendered impotent. Martial law was ended formally in January 1981 but without significant political change. Political decay was accelerated after the assassination in August 1983 of President Marcos's principal opponent, **Benigno Aquino**, at Manila airport on his return from exile in the United States. Political change was precipitated by a snap presidential election in February 1986 in which Marcos was challenged by Corazón Aquino, Benigno Aquino's widow. Against a background of charges of electoral fraud, the defence minister, **Juan Ponce Enrile**, and the deputy chief of staff of the armed forces, Fidel Ramos, led a military mutiny. That mutiny inspired a popular demonstration (**People Power**) in central Manila against Marcos and in favour of Mrs Aquino. With the refusal of the security forces to act against civilians, the United States intervened to persuade Marcos and his notorious wife, **Imelda Marcos**, to leave the country on 25 February for exile in Hawaii.

Corazón Aquino was declared president and set about restoring a legitimate constitutional structure. The previous US model was reinstated in slightly modified form with a bicameral congress but with provision for a single presidential term of six years. The new constitution was approved with an overwhelming vote in favour in a national referendum in February 1987, while candidates endorsed by Mrs Aquino won a decisive majority in congressional elections in May. Mrs Aquino faced a series of major political challenges during her tenure. First, she was confronted by a series of abortive coups by a group of alienated army officers who felt that as they were responsible for the fall of Marcos, the armed forces should be his political beneficiaries. Her chief of staff and then defence minister, Fidel Ramos, remained loyal and mobilized military support for constitutional government, which came also from the United States. Second, she was opposed by the Communist Party of the Philippines, which had made great strides as a result of Marcos's years of misrule. Its leadership, which miscalculated popular support for a return to constitutional government, also felt cheated by Mrs Aquino's political success and sought to sustain a military challenge in the rural areas where poverty was most acute. Finally, she had to contend with rumbling Muslim rebellion in the southern islands which had been precipitated by the declaration of martial law in 1972.

In the event, Mrs Aquino saw out her tenure and was succeeded through the ballot box in May 1992, when Fidel Ramos was elected with only 23.6 per cent of the vote, less than 1 million more than his nearest rival in a contest against five other candidates. Her presidency was not marked by the regeneration of the Philippines, which failed to demonstrate the vigorous economic growth exhibited by its regional partners. She became chief executive with a great opportunity to provide decisive political leadership. However, the very qualities of non-worldliness which made her such a potent opponent of Marcos failed to equip her for the responsibilities of high office, while the prominence of her family in the decision-making process further reduced national confidence. Mrs Aquino restored constitutional government but in so doing enabled a reversion rather than a reform of the political process. Fidel Ramos assumed office in June 1992 without generating the same political expectations and was also not faced with the same challenges to his rule encountered by Mrs Aquino. His political party *Lakas ng Edsa* or Edsa Struggle – recalling the site of the mutiny of February 1986 – was very much a personal following, formed only in 1991 (*see* **EDSA**; *Lakas*-**NUCD**). Nonetheless, he was able to work with the Congress in which he commanded a majority only in the House of Representatives and also demonstrated early success in overcoming military dissidence. He acted to neutralize the persisting Communist challenge through persuading the Congress to legalize the party, while Indonesia's good offices were employed to begin negotiations over regional autonomy with Muslim separatists. An agreement on provincial autonomy in part of Mindanao was reached with the **Moro National Liberation Front** in 1996 but a matching accord could not be realized with the rival and fundamentalist **Moro Islamic Liberation Front**, which continues to resist the assaults of the Philippine army. Under Fidel Ramos, modest economic improvement was demonstrated with continuing support from multilateral agencies but without transforming the poverty-stricken condition of the majority of the population dependent on remittances from family members working overseas. The elite-driven and fractious nature of Philippine politics served to obstruct economic reform, especially over land tenure. Political realignment within Congress occurred in reaction to proposed tax legislation intended to strengthen the resources of central government. President Ramos also attracted strong opposition from his predecessor when it was suspected that he had an interest in amending the constitution to permit him a second term of office. Although the

Philippines was afflicted by regional economic crisis from the middle of 1997, its limited degree of development and restrictions on international borrowing softened its impact compared, say, to Indonesia. Economic difficulty, however, served to influence the presidential campaign in 1998, which was marked by the break-down of the ruling coalition in jockeying for political advantage. Incumbent Vice-President Estrada posed as the populist champion of the poor through the electoral vehicle of the **Struggle of the Nationalist Filipino Masses** formed in June 1997. He secured a landslide victory over Jose de Venecia, the speaker of the lower house and the candidate of the ruling party. Venecia's electoral partner, **Gloria Macapagal-Arroyo**, was elected vice-president.

The promise of President Estrada's victory had soured by the turn of the new millennium as the managerialism of Fidel Ramos was succeeded by a reversion to traditional patron–client politics. In January 2000, Finance Secretary Edgardo Espiritu resigned in a protest against corruption and cronyism. In February 2000, President Estrada dismissed his Justice Secretary, Serafin Cuevas, ostensibly over a decision to pardon a murderer but in reality over decisions against the business interests of close associates. His reputation was tarnished also with allegations of share manipulation by another close associate. Charges of corruption and cronyism and failings of leadership provided the background to President Estrada's reversal of a declared policy of amending the constitution. His proposal for removing provisions barring foreigners from owning land and controlling key industries in the interests of economic development had met with strong opposition on the grounds that it could serve as a precedent for securing a second term of presidential office. The fall in the popularity of President Estrada was compounded by the failure of his hard-line policy against Muslim separatists in the south of the country who reacted with a campaign of kidnapping and violence. A concurrent spate of bombings in Manila, however, occurred without an evident locus of responsibility. In May 2000, President Estrada was obliged to cut short a visit to China and to cancel a visit to Europe in order to be seen to take charge of a crisis of

international significance because of foreign hostages involved.

The presidency of Fidel Ramos marked a major discontinuity in relations with the United States, which withdrew its military presence completely in November 1992. After independence, the former colonial power had been accorded sovereign rights over extensive military base facilities through a treaty in 1947. In 1951 the two countries also entered into a mutual security treaty which constituted an American guarantee in the context of the Cold War. The US military presence became a controversial factor in domestic politics made acute by Washington's support for Marcos's regime until virtually the last possible moment when he was discarded. Nationalist agitation against the US military presence revived during Mrs Aquino's tenure. Negotiations for an agreement to phase out that presence by the end of the decade failed because the nationalist card was employed by members of the Senate with presidential ambitions. The prospect of the end of the US military presence after nearly a century removed any obstacle to the Philippines joining the Non-Aligned Movement in September 1992. The republic had been a founder of **ASEAN** (Association of South-East Asian Nations) in August 1967 but differences with Malaysia over the **Philippines' Claim to Sabah** soured the relationship and enthusiasm for ASEAN. Less than convincing offers to drop the claim were treated sceptically in Kuala Lumpur until Fidel Ramos announced in September 1992 that it would no longer be pursued. An improvement in relations was marked by Fidel Ramos's official visit to Kuala Lumpur in January 1993, the first by a Philippine president since 1968. The claim to Sabah has continued to interpose in the relationship because of the vagaries of Philippine domestic politics. In May 1994 Fidel Ramos appeared to go back on his previous commitment when he announced that the Philippines had not given up its territorial claim. Membership of ASEAN has come to be of increasing importance to the Philippines with a changing relationship with the United States. In December 1987 the ASEAN heads of government persisted in holding a third meeting at their **Manila Summit** in order to demonstrate solidarity with Mrs Aquino, who had nearly been toppled by a coup attempt. The Philippines has long asserted sovereignty over a number of the **Spratly Islands** which lie to its west. In July 1992 at a meeting of its foreign ministers in Manila, ASEAN served as a vehicle for a **Declaration on the South China Sea** calling on claimants to jurisdiction to settle disputes by peaceful means. That declaration did not inhibit China from seizing a reef near the Philippines island of Palawan in February 1995; nor Malaysia from seizing two others in 1999. The military weakness of the Philippines in the face of China's maritime assertiveness prompted a reconsideration of relations with its main treaty partner. In May 1999, the Philippines Senate approved a visiting forces agreement with the United States. In February 2000, the first large-scale joint military exercise was conducted with American forces. The Philippines had embarked on a US$8.7 billion military modernization programme but its implementation has been delayed by a lack of funds.

*see also:* Abu Sayyaf; APEC; Aquino, Benigno; Aquino, Corazón; ASEAN; Contemplacion, Flor; Declaration on the South China Sea; EDSA; Enrile, Juan Ponce; Estrada, Joseph; Islam; Liberal Party; Macapagal-Arroyo, Gloria; Manila Summit 1987; Marcos, Ferdinand; Marcos, Imelda; Moro Islamic Liberation Front; Moro National Liberation Front; Nacionalista Party; New People's Army; New Society Movement; Philippines' Claim to Sabah; Philippines–US Security Treaty 1951; Ramos, Fidel; Struggle of the Nationalist Filipino Masses; Subic Bay Naval Base.

# Singapore, Republic of

The island-state of Singapore, with a land area of just over 600 square kilometres, is located at the southern tip of peninsular Malaysia. It is separated from Malaysia by the Strait of Johor but is joined to the mainland by a causeway carrying road and rail traffic as well as by a road bridge that was opened in 1998. The **Singapore Strait** to the south separates the republic from the Riau Islands of Indonesia. It has a population of around 3.2 million citizens, three-quarters of whom are ethnic Chinese of migrant origin (**Overseas Chinese**). Some 15 per cent are ethnic Malay, many with links across the Strait of Johor from whose sultan the British pro-consul Sir Stamford Raffles acquired the island in 1819.

Singapore has become an exemplar of post-colonial Asian modernization and achievement, especially under the dynamic leadership of **Lee Kuan Yew**, who served as its prime minister from June 1959 until November 1990. The island is a model of urban planning and design, with remarkable accomplishment in public housing and environmental provision as well as in technological achievement. Astounding economic success beyond a traditional role as a regional trading entrepôt has taken place within a stable and authoritarian political system in which a mandatory democracy to the advantage of the ruling **People's Action Party** (PAP) has not provided opportunity for effective opposition. That form of democracy is based on an informal social contract whereby authoritarian government is accepted in return for material advantages. In September 2000, in a token gesture of democratization, the government authorized a public forum, named 'Speaker's Corner', modelled loosely on that in London's Hyde Park.

Singapore had been separated from Britain's local colonial domain after the Pacific War partly because of its strategic importance as a military base. It acquired self-governing status in 1959 concurrent with the electoral success of the PAP, which has been continuously in power ever since. The leadership of that party judged then that Singapore did not have any future as an independent entity and persuaded Malaya's prime minister, **Tunku Abdul Rahman**, to include it within a wider Federation of Malaysia, which was established in September 1963. Singapore's tenure within Malaysia was stormy and brief because of the attempt by the PAP (seen as a Chinese party) to become a part of the federal political establishment. On 9 August 1965 against a background of rising racial tension, Singapore formally separated from Malaysia to become an independent republic. That enforced independence, at a time when Indonesia was still engaged in active **Confrontation** against Malaysia, gave rise to an acute vulnerability which has become part of the political culture of the state. An initial abrasiveness of tone in foreign policy has been succeeded over time by a greater moderation based on national accomplishment and a more assured regional place within **ASEAN** (Association of South-East Asian Nations), but an underlying sense of vulnerability pervades the calculations of the political elite. The deputy prime minister, **Lee Hsien Loong**, elder son of Lee Kuan Yew, expressed the national outlook well in a speech in October 1984 shortly before resigning from the armed forces to enter politics. He pointed out that 'overnight an oasis can become a desert'. That fear has translated itself into a recurrent practice of mobilizing the population, who are told that the world does not owe them a living and that the material advantages which they now enjoy can not be taken for granted. Order and stability have in consequence been given a higher priority than political freedoms justified on the ground that Singapore's prosperity depends much on the confidence reposed in the state by foreign investors whose flow of capital has been responsible for successful economic development based on export-led growth.

Initially, the PAP had faced political challenge from a radical left-wing faction which split off in 1961 in opposition to membership of Malaysia. The *Barisan Sosialis* (Socialist Front) then withdrew from parliamentary politics, leaving the field to the PAP until the early 1980s. In October 1981, however, a by-election was won by **J. B. Jeyaretnam** representing the **Workers Party**, which had been a Communist front in the late 1950s. In general elections in 1984, he retained his seat, while another opposition candidate from the **Singapore Democratic Party** was also successful at the expense of the PAP, which suffered an adverse voting swing of over 12 per cent. Generational change and a resentment of high-handedness by government had led to a growing measure of political alienation to which the PAP responded by harassing opposition, including drumming J. B. Jeyaretnam out of Parliament. That voting trend against the PAP was sustained marginally in elections in September 1988 and again in August 1991, when the PAP was led by the prime minister, **Goh Chok Tong**, who had succeeded Lee Kuan Yew in November 1990. Four seats were lost to opposition members in 1991. Moreover, in elections for a president with reserve powers in August 1993, the incremental voting trend against the PAP continued when an unknown candidate secured more than 40 per cent against Ong Teng Cheong, who had resigned from the office of deputy prime minister in order to stand.

In January 1997, the PAP made an electoral recovery in winning 81 out of 83 parliamentary seats, only 36 of which were contested by opposition candidates, with 65 per cent of the vote. A close call in a bitterly fought five-member group constituency was made more dramatic by a successful libel action against Workers Party candidate, Tang Liang Hong, who subsequently left Singapore. Tension between President Ong Teng Cheong and members of the cabinet over the interpretation of his responsibilities led him to stand down at the end of his term. He was succeeded in August 1999 by S. R. Nathan, a former intelligence chief and diplomat, who was not opposed.

At issue in Singapore is the question of leadership and political change as succeeding generations come of age without direct experience of the difficulties faced by their parents and grandparents both before and after Singapore became independent. Singapore's vulnerability based on size, location, ethnic identity and economic

role has been buffered by success in development and engagement in regional cooperation but has not been erased. The prime minister, Goh Chok Tong, has not really been able to stamp his political imprint on Singapore, living in the shadow of his illustrious predecessor, who has remained in the cabinet with the rank of senior minister. Moreover, Lee's brilliant and dynamic elder son, Lee Hsien Loong, has been seen as a restless political crown prince. In November 1992 it was announced that both he and Ong Teng Cheong were suffering from cancer of the lymphatic system, which cast a pall over the republic. By October 1993 Lee Hsien Loong had appeared to have made sufficient a recovery to resume ministerial responsibilities. In December 1997, he was appointed chairman of the Monetary Authority of Singapore (MAS) and played a central role in directing the island-state's response and marked speedy recovery from regional economic crisis. In August 1999, in his National Day address, Prime Minister Gok Chok Tong indicated that his most likely successor would be Lee Hsien Loong.

Internationally, Singapore has enjoyed an influence out of proportion to its minuscule scale and limited population. That reputation has owed much to a reputation for excellence, exemplified by the performance and standing of its national airline and also to the intellectual calibre of its first prime minister, Lee Kuan Yew, who has remained in the cabinet with the office of senior minister. Independence coincided with tense relationships with its closest neighbours, Malaysia and Indonesia. Those relationships have never been easy, especially with Malaysia with which a structural tension obtains expressed in recurrent open antagonism, most recently coincident with regional economic adversity at the end of the 1990s. Those tensions have been contained up to a point through common membership and interest in ASEAN but Singapore has continually looked beyond the Association, exemplified by its initiative in promoting the **ASEAN Regional Forum** (ARF) and the **Asia–Europe Meeting** (ASEM). Singapore's foreign policy has been directed to preventing the dominance regionally of any state that might be able to challenge its independence. To that end, its leaders have been keen to sustain the regional security engagement of the United States. In 1990, it entered into a memorandum of understanding for America's use of military facilities in the island. And with its withdrawal from the Philippines in 1992, the US naval logistics command headquarters was relocated to Singapore. In November 1998, an additional memorandum of understanding was concluded under which the United States was offered the use of the new Changi naval base for its aircraft carriers. That security relationship has withstood differences over political values, exemplified in the controversy over the caning of an American teenager for vandalism in 1994.

Singapore was an active diplomatic adversary of Vietnam within ASEAN during the Cambodian conflict but with the end of the Cold War and the **International Conference on Cambodia** in Paris in October 1991, its policy towards Indochina was transformed exemplified by its support for Vietnam's membership of ASEAN. However, strong resistance was mounted to Cambodia's early membership after the violent coup in July 1997 in Phnom Penh that displaced the coalition government set up under the Paris agreement. Relations with China have steadily progressed, especially after communism had ceased to generate political concerns and to be closely associated in Asia with the Chinese, who are the majority community in Singapore. Diplomatic relations were established in October 1990 but Singapore's enthusiasm for economic cooperation with China soured somewhat after a joint venture to set up a model township in Suzhou, near Shanghai, foundered because the local authority failed to keep to contractual undertakings. Moreover, Lee Kuan Yew was not inhibited in admonishing China in March 1996 when the government in Beijing attempted to intimidate Taiwan's electorate through live-firing missile exercises. Within its own region of South-East Asia, Singapore is viewed with a mixture of respect and resentment because its remarkable economic accomplishments have been realized by a majority Chinese population who have succeeded in adapting a traditional entrepôt role to the conditions of modern globalization. Its political culture, however, registers an abiding sense of vulnerability, compensated for by an annual defence budget of over US$4 billion and the most technologically advanced armed forces in the region.

see also: APEC; ASEAN; ASEAN Regional Forum (ARF); Asia–Europe Meeting (ASEM); Barisan Sosialis; Confrontation; Goh Chok Tong; Jeyaretnam, J. B.; Lee Hsien Loong; Lee Kuan Yew; Overseas Chinese; People's Action Party; Rahman, Tunku Abdul; Shared Values; Singapore Democratic Party; Singapore Strait; Strait of Johor; Workers Party.

# Thailand, Kingdom of

The Kingdom of Thailand, once known as Siam, is situated in the centre of the mainland of South-East Asia with a land area of some 500,000 square kilometres. It is the only regional state not to have been subject to European colonialism. Thailand is a constitutional monarchy where the reigning King Bhumibol Adulyadej has exercised a unique personal authority which has mitigated and controlled the prerogative political assertiveness of a military establishment.

To Thailand's west and north lie Burma (now Myanmar), Laos is to its north and east, Cambodia is to its east and it shares a southern border with Malaysia. Thailand does not have a direct frontier with the People's Republic of China but is separated from it by only narrow stretches of territory extending from Burma and Laos, which touch to its extreme north. Thailand has a population of some 63 million, primarily composed of ethnic T'ai whose religion is the Theravada branch of **Buddhism**. In addition to tribal minorities, such as the **Hmong** in northern provinces, there is a significant concentration of Muslims (*see* **Islam**) in the southern provinces bordering Malaysia, where irredentist movements have operated. The largest minority is that of ethnic Chinese, who comprise some 10 per cent of the population. A considerable proportion, however, have intermarried into Thai families with a notable degree of cultural assimilation (*see* **Overseas Chinese**).

The origins of the Thai state date from the tenth century, when ethnic T'ai migrated from south-west China towards the central plain then under the control of the Cambodian empire based around Angkor. The current Thai state dates from the eighteenth century when King Rama I sited his capital at Bangkok and founded the Chakri dynasty, which is represented by its ninth incumbent, Bhumibol Adulyadej. From the mid-nineteenth century, modernizing Chakri monarchs opened the country to commercial contact with the west, with the rice trade as the staple basis for economic development. Western

skills were drawn on to develop the machinery of state, which over time had the effect of creating tensions between the monarchy and an emerging military-bureaucratic class. In 1932 the absolute monarchy was overthrown by a military coup to be replaced by a constitutional monarchy. Since then, two principal internal conflicts have dominated the political life of the country. One was within the armed forces, including the police, for the dominant position; this was resolved in 1957 when Marshal **Sarit Thanarat** seized power on behalf of the army. More protracted has been the problem of establishing a political format acceptable to all competing interests, including the armed forces.

The issue of political format has tested the stability of the state on numerous occasions, with recurrent acts of military intervention serving as the vehicle of political change. After the Pacific War, during which Thailand was allied with Japan, constitutional government of a kind alternated with direct military rule. Until the early 1990s, however, constitutionalism was subject to the tolerance of the military, who removed an elected government as recently as February 1991. They sought without success to impose their will again in 1992 against a background of bloodletting on the streets of Bangkok. The ability of the military to impose their will was facilitated during the 1960s and into the 1970s by the **Vietnam War**, to which Thailand was a party, as well as by the active insurgent role up to the end of the 1970s played by the Communist Party of Thailand. Moreover, Vietnam's invasion of Cambodia and the ensuing third phase of the Indochina Wars during the 1980s also served to maintain the political centrality of the armed forces.

The political pre-eminence of the military began to be challenged from the early 1970s as a consequence of successful economic development, which was accompanied by social change foreshadowed by student activism. In addition, King Bhumibol, who had acquired considerable popular respect for his commitment to rural development, employed the aura of monarchy in the interest of democratization. Violent military reaction to student protest in October 1973 led to the removal of the military regime and its succession by a raucous democratic interlude which was brought to an end with decisive military intervention in October 1976 (on the same day as the **Thammasat University Massacre**). The tempestuous politics of the mid-1970s concurrent with the Communist victories in Indochina alarmed the king, who lent his weight to a period of more benign military rule in the 1980s under the leadership of the army commander and prime minister, **Prem Tinsulanond**. Two abortive military coups in 1981 and 1985 failed to arrest the gradual return to constitutionalism concurrent with remarkable economic development by the end of the 1980s.

When the military removed the elected government of **Chatichai Choonhavan** in February 1991, the king distanced himself from the successful junta. Indeed, they found themselves obliged to appoint a civilian caretaker prime minister, **Anand Panyarachun**, until fresh elections were held in March 1992, ostensibly to return the country to civilian rule. Massive vote-buying in the rural areas led to a victory by military-affiliated political parties. The appointment of the former army commander-in-chief, General **Suchinda Krapayoon**, as an unelected prime minister of a military-based coalition, provoked angry demonstrations in Bangkok in May led by the opposition *Palang Dharma* (Moral Force party). When a bloody confrontation ensued, the king intervened and General Suchinda resigned office. Anand Panyarachun was reappointed acting prime minister at the head of a technocratic government. Elections in September 1992 produced a new civilian-based coalition with **Chuan Leekpai**, the leader of the **Democrat Party**, as prime minister. The return to civilian rule marked a notable decline in the prerogative political outlook of the armed forces. Political parties outside of the capital have tended to be fleeting constellations of personal and regional interests bound together in the main by considerations of patronage and not by coherent programmes linked to distinctive constituencies. After the 1991 coup, three new

political parties were created. Five disappeared, while others splintered and regrouped. The frustrations of coalition government were exemplified by the experience of the administration headed by Chuan Leekpai, which was thwarted in attempting to secure democratic amendments to the constitution imposed by the military after 1991. His success in January 1995 in securing constitutional amendments in the interest of greater democratization was followed by the loss of office through elections in July 1995, which were precipitated by the defection of *Palang Dharma*. A new seven-party coalition with the **Chart Thai Party** at its core and **Banharm Silpa-archa** as prime minister was formed without any threat of military intervention. That coalition collapsed and then lost power in elections in November 1996 to be succeeded by a six-party counterpart headed by former army commander, **Chavalit Yong-chaiyut**, the leader of the **New Aspiration Party**. The onset of economic crisis following the dramatic float of the currency in July 1997 precipitated the fall of his government and the emergence of a new political alignment with the Democrat Party at its core. Chuan Leekpai assumed high office for the second time in November 1997 with royal and military support. Initial success in coping with economic adversity gave way to intra-coalition tensions by the turn of the century. Ironically, a new democratic constitution had been promulgated during Chavalit Yongchaiyut's tenure in September 1997. Elections to replace the appointed Senate of soldiers and businessmen were held on 4 March 2000. Seventy-eight of the 200 winning candidates were then rejected by the election commission over allegations of malpractice. By that juncture, the Democrat Party had lost national standing partly through the decision to decorate Field Marshal **Thanom Kittikachorn**, a disgraced former military dictator. At the end March 2000, Sanan Kachornprasart, the interior minister, was obliged to resign his portfolio after the newly-formed National Counter Corruption Commission had charged that he had concealed his assets by fabricating a US$1 million loan. The decline in the political fortunes of the Democrat Party lent significance to the rising electoral challenge of the new

*Thai Rak Thai* Party headed by **Thaksin Shinawatra**.

By contrast with the mercurial quality of most political parties, the monarchy stands as a pillar of stability. However, the role of King Bhumibol as political mediator in the conservative democratic interest will not necessarily be sustained should he be succeeded by his only son. Crown Prince **Maha Vajiralongkorn** does not give the impression of sharing his father's sense of duty and is not as well regarded by the Thai people. For those reasons, the stability of the Thai state remains in some doubt.

Thailand's geographic location and historical experience have moulded a foreign policy outlook of signal consistency over time. Thailand was a beneficiary of Anglo-French imperialist competition whereby the two European states found it politic to have an interposing buffer between their respective realms in Burma and Indochina. Before colonial intervention in mainland South-East Asia, Thailand had experienced armed invasion from Burma as well as competition from Vietnam for influence in the trans-Mekong zone. Suspicion of both close and near neighbours survived the end of colonialism, while during the Pacific War Thailand enjoyed Japanese support in prosecuting irredentist claims against Burma, Laos, Cambodia and Malaya. After the Pacific War, Thailand secured international rehabilitation with US support. Prime international concern came to focus on Indochina, where the restored French colonial position was subject to strong challenge from the Communist Party of Vietnam, perceived as a more fearsome historical enemy. Independent Burma, subject to ethnic minority rebellion, was a lesser priority. Indeed, Thai military support was provided for **Karen** and **Shan** rebels close to the common border.

Fear of a resurgent Communist Vietnam with dominion over Laos and Cambodia was reinforced with the advent of a Communist China in 1949. Concurrently, US containment policy served both the domestic and foreign policy interests of the postwar Thai military regime through diplomatic, material and security support. Thai troops participated in the Korean War under the United Nations flag and its government signed the US-inspired **Manila Pact**, the South-East Asia Collective Defence Treaty, in September 1954. In February 1955 Thailand contributed further to this attempt to shore up the non-Communist position in the region by providing the headquarters of **SEATO** (South-East Asia Treaty Organization) which served as an institutional base for the Manila Pact until dismantled in 1977.

Thailand maintained its assertive anti-Communist policy until the fall of Indochina in 1975, sending troops to Vietnam and permitting US aircraft to bomb the north of the country from Thai airfields. In addition to the American connection, Thailand promoted the cause of regional cooperation; initially with Malaya/Malaysia and the Philippines within **ASA** (Association of South-East Asia), and then more vigorously within **ASEAN** (Association of South-East Asian Nations), with the addition of Indonesia and Singapore and later of Brunei. With the Communist victories in Indochina that followed US military disengagement, confidence waned in the United States as a security partner. Diplomatic relations were established with the People's Republic of China and with the successor governments in Indochina. A traditional geopolitical perspective persisted, however. Advantage was taken of growing antagonism between China and Vietnam and also between Vietnam and Cambodia to uphold a physical buffer in Indochina and to eliminate external patronage for an insurgent Communist Party. When Vietnam invaded Cambodia in December 1978, Thailand drew on the support of its ASEAN partners to mobilize international opinion in its strategic interest. In addition, territorial asylum was given to military resistance groups engaged in insurgency in Cambodia. Particular support was provided for the ousted notorious **Khmer Rouge**, who were supplied with equipment from China. Pressure on Vietnam was applied with effect during the 1980s, culminating in a political settlement of the Cambodian conflict at the **International Conference on Cambodia** in Paris in October 1991, facilitated by the end of the Cold War. Thailand progressively repaired its relations with Vietnam and endorsed the outcome of elections in Cambodia conducted in May 1993 under United Nations auspices (*see* **UNTAC**) but its military establishment sustained its links with the Khmer Rouge for reasons of financial advantage and also of geopolitical insurance lest the government in Phnom Penh come under Vietnamese influence. These links disintegrated with the Khmer Rouge, while correct rather than close ties have been maintained with the government in Phnom Penh.

With the end of the Cold War and the Cambodian conflict, the civilian government of Thailand engaged more vigorously in regional multilateral dialogue with ASEAN at its core. It reconciled with Vietnam and welcomed it into the Association. It also sought to modify, albeit without success, the Association's rule of non-interference in the domestic affairs of regional partners where its domestic circumstances spill over its borders with an adverse effect. In that respect, frustration has been experienced in trying to promote a working relationship with the military regime in Rangoon through a policy of so-called constructive engagement intended partly to counter its close ties with China.

Geography and history have combined also to sustain a traditional strategic perspective towards the trans-Mekong of Indochina required as a buffer if it cannot be dominated. Defence co-operation has been sustained with the United States and with Singapore, in particular, among ASEAN states.

*see also:* Anand Panyarachun; ASA; ASEAN; Banharn Silpa-archa; Buddhism; Bhumibol Adulyadej; Chavalit Yongchaiyut; Chart Thai Party; Chatichai Choonhavan; Chuan Leekpai; Democrat Party; *Hmong*; Indochina Wars; International Conference on Cambodia, Paris 1991; Islam; Karen; Khmer Rouge; Manila Pact 1954; New Aspiration Party; Overseas Chinese; *Palang Dharma*; Prem Tinsulanond; Sarit Thanarat; SEATO; Shan; Suchinda Krapayoon; *Thai Rak Thai Party*; Thaksin Shinawatra; Thanom Kittikachorn; Thammasat University Massacre 1976; UNTAC; Vajiralongkorn, Maha; Vietnam War.

# Vietnam, Socialist Republic of

The Socialist Republic of Vietnam was established on 2 July 1976 through the formal unification of the country, which had been effectively joined through *force majeure* at the end of April 1975. The title of the reunified state registered its political identity subject to the monopoly power of the Communist Party, which had been formed in 1930 as the Communist Party of Indochina when the country was under French colonial rule. That party in a changing nomenclature had led the nationalist movement in an armed struggle for independence from the end of the Pacific War. A Democratic Republic of Vietnam had been proclaimed in Hanoi by the Communist leader, **Ho Chi Minh**, on 2 September 1945 following the **August Revolution** but was displaced by the restoration of French rule. The French were obliged to abdicate their position after July 1954 when an international conference, leading to the **Geneva Agreements on Indochina**, endorsed a cease-fire agreement with a temporary division of the country along the line of the 17th parallel of latitude. That division hardened into a political boundary which endured for over twenty years. The Democratic Republic of Vietnam succeeded to power north of the line of division, while a US-backed State (subsequently Republic) of Vietnam assumed the administration to its south. The challenge of Communist insurgency in the south of the country in the early 1960s led to progressive military intervention by the United States, including the aerial bombardment of the north. The failure of the United States to impose a political solution by military means and growing domestic opposition to the loss of blood and treasure led to the **Paris Peace Agreements** in January 1973. US military withdrawal followed soon after and a military offensive launched by the northern army in March 1975 paved the way to final military victory with the investment of Saigon on 30 April 1975.

Vietnam is located in the mainland of South-East Asia and comprises an elongated territory of nearly 330,000 square kilometres which resembles a pole with baskets at either end. It shares its northern border with the People's Republic of China and its western borders with Laos and Cambodia. To its east and south, Vietnam is bounded by the **South China Sea** whose islands have been the subject of contested jurisdiction, especially with China. The Vietnamese people, who number some 80 million, are in the main ethnically homogeneous. There are hill tribe minorities and a sizeable Cambodian community in the south as well as an ethnic Chinese community of migrant origins.

An autonomous Vietnamese polity located in southern China and northern Vietnam dates from the third century and the basis of Vietnamese statehood came to be centred on the Red River delta. Vietnamese history has comprised a dual process. On the one hand, struggle against and resistance to Chinese hegemony, while assuming its cultural and religious traditions, has served to define national identity. Concurrently, a movement southwards through pioneer settlement took place at the expense of weaker kingdoms. That movement, which gave rise to two competing economic centres in the Red River and Mekong River deltas, provided Vietnam with a precarious unity, which after consolidation in the early nineteenth century was overtaken by French colonial rule which expanded to the whole of Indochina. The French facilitated Vietnamese territorial expansion, while the military struggle from the end of the Pacific War reinforced a geopolitical prerogative on the part of the Communist Party expressed in the concept of a special relationship with Laos and Cambodia. A reunited Vietnam sought to assert that relationship with Cambodia in the context of a revival of antagonism with China from the mid-1970s. An invasion of Cambodia provoked by cross-border military incursions by the **Khmer Rouge** government in Phnom Penh was followed by a punitive intervention by Chinese forces into northern Vietnam. Vietnam was then confronted by an alignment of China, the United States, Japan and **ASEAN** (Association of South-East Asian Nations) which through a division of labour in isolating it diplomatically and imposing sanctions was able to impose breaking strain on its government and society. When it became apparent that countervailing support from the Soviet Union was likely to be withdrawn, Vietnam adjusted by changing its domestic and international policies in a radical way.

On unification in 1976, Vietnam had embarked dogmatically on the creation of a socialist state but within a short time was embroiled in conflict over Cambodia. The economic condition of the country became parlous and the position of the ruling Communist Party was placed in some jeopardy. In December 1986, at its sixth national congress, a policy of **Doi Moi** (economic renovation) was adopted which took the form of a commitment to market-driven economics. A liberal investment law soon followed as well as a more accommodating attitude over Cambodia, with a settlement reached through United Nations involvement in October 1991. Relations were restored with China and developed with the states of ASEAN, while the United States phased out a longstanding trade and investment embargo which was finally withdrawn in February 1994. Continuing progress in accounting for Americans missing in action during the **Vietnam War** (MIA) produced an agreement in May 1994 to set up liaison offices in respective capital cities. Diplomatic relations were established in August 1995 and an American ambassador, who was a former prisoner of war in Vietnam, took up residence in May 1996. Although the memories of war continue to cast a shadow over the relationship, William Cohen, America's Defence Secretary, visited Hanoi in March 2000 where he stated that the US had resolved to move forward with Vietnam 'in a manner that serves our mutual interests in regional stability, security and stability'. For its part, however, Vietnam had been reluctant to press ahead with the relationship exemplified by the delay in signing a trade agreement with the United States that embodies the free-market prescriptions of the International Monetary Fund. An underlying concern about the loss of central government control has been an impediment to economic progress. Vietnam made

signal economic advances during the 1990s, exemplified in success in controlling inflation and in moving from a rice-deficit country to the world's third largest exporter of rice within a period of five years. Foreign investment was attracted from Taiwan, Hong Kong and Japan. By the turn of the century, however, the momentum of economic reform had been retarded as a consequence of bureaucratic impediments and corruption but, above all, by the failure of the ruling Communist Party to embrace the spirit of *Doi Moi*. Its narrow interpretation of the maxim that development will follow 'a market-based, but socialism-driven structure of economic development' suggested a loss of nerve on the part of a leadership fearful of social and political change represented euphemistically as 'peaceful evolution'. A Cold War rhetoric prevails in the claim by party leader, **Le Kha Phieu**, in February 2000 that the battle with the West was still on with the economy as the arena. In consequence, foreign investors have been voting with their feet and economic growth has failed to keep pace with a rising population and unemployment. In July 2000, however, the trade agreement with the US was concluded shortly after Vietnam had relaxed regulations on private enterprise and foreign investment.

Vietnam's commitment to economic reform stands in contradiction to the ruling party's determination not to permit any fundamental change to the political system. The Communist Party refuses to allow the formation of any other political organization and has exercised tight repressive control over Buddhist and Christian associations. Fear of the political chaos which has been the fate of eastern Europe in the wake of the end of communism has been a critical factor in the judgement of the party leadership. The circumstances of the assumption of Communist rule and its nature has meant that there is no alternative locus of political activity other than the armed forces, which have been integrated with the party in classical manner. Moreover, the Communist Party has maintained a remarkable measure of internal cohesion despite factional differences. For example, the death of Ho Chi Minh in 1969 did not give rise to a visible power struggle. Moreover, the party has never experienced Soviet-style purges, nor has it had to cope with the kind of popular protest confronted by its Chinese counterpart in June 1989.

Vietnam may have given up its revolutionary identity as an outpost of socialism, which was proclaimed with unification in 1976, but it has yet to adjust politically to a post-war world driven by the forces of globalization. It has adjusted, of necessity, to an adverse strategic environment. In armed struggle against France and the United States, it attracted Chinese and Soviet support. That from the former was always problematic, exemplified by Beijing's toleration of the division of Vietnam in 1954. Sino-Vietnamese tensions became open after Sino-US rapprochement in the early 1970s and culminated in a limited punitive invasion in February 1979 in retaliation for Vietnam's invasion and occupation of Cambodia. The Soviet Union sustained Vietnam during the conflict over Cambodia during the first half of the 1980s but became an unreliable partner even before the end of the Cold War. The disintegration of the Soviet Union in December 1991 was a profound political shock to the leadership of a party whose greatest luminary had served part of his political apprenticeship in Moscow. Vietnam was obliged to cope unaided with the transformation in its strategic circumstances by appeasing China over Cambodia, from which it withdrew its forces from 1989. After the **International Conference on Cambodia** in Paris in 1991, a process of Sino-Vietnamese rapprochement was set in train with a meeting of party and state leaders in Beijing in November 1991. A working relationship has been based in part in a common interest in upholding the hegemony of respective communist parties. Vietnam was able to accede to ASEAN's **Treaty of Amity and Cooperation** in July 1992, which gave it observer status at the annual meetings of the Association's foreign ministers. In July 1993, at a meeting in Singapore, Vietnam became a founding member of the **ASEAN Regional Forum** (ARF), the Asia-Pacific-wide multilateral security dialogue that began its working life in Bangkok in July 1994. It was admitted to ASEAN as the first communist member in July 1995. It was a founding member of the **Asia–Europe Meeting** (ASEM) in March 1996 and was admitted to **APEC** in November 1998. Vietnam's degree of success in integration within ASEAN was demonstrated in December 1998 when the sixth summit meeting of the Association convened in Hanoi. Despite its developing regional ties, Vietnam faces an intimidating China with which it is in contention over islands and maritime space in the **South China Sea**. Progress has been made, however, in demarcating their common land border. Vietnam is also in contention over some of the **Spratly Islands** with ASEAN partners, Malaysia and the Philippines. Despite this unresolved problem, Vietnam conducts its international relationships with the prime object of developing ties that will reduce its vulnerability to pressure from a resurgent China. In that respect, an historical experience predating French colonial rule and the rise of communism has served to inform contemporary Vietnamese international outlook. An example of more recent historical continuity, possibly in reaction to democratization within ASEAN, has been Vietnam's participation from October 1999 in exclusive trilateral meetings of Indochinese states, which were a feature of the polarization of South-East Asia over Cambodia during the 1980s.

see also: APEC; ASEAN; ASEAN Regional Forum; Asia–Europe Meeting; August Revolution 1945; *Doi Moi*; Domino Theory; Geneva Agreements on Indochina 1954; Ho Chi Minh; Indochina wars; International Conference on Cambodia, Paris 1991; Khmer Rouge; Le Kha Phieu; Missing in Action (MIA); Paris Peace Agreements 1973; South China Sea; Spratly Islands; Treaty of Amity and Cooperation 1976; Vietnam War.

# A

## *Abangan* (Indonesia)

*Abangan* is the term applied to rural Javanese who acknowledge an adherence to **Islam** but order their lives according to precepts and practices drawn from animist and Hindu–Buddhist values. The distinguishing feature of *Abangan* culture is its syncretic quality expressed partly in a refusal to define identity with exclusive reference to Islam by contrast with the alternative *Santri* tradition. That refusal assumed political significance prior to the proclamation of Indonesia's independence in August 1945 when an attempt was made to impose a constitutional obligation on all professing Muslims to observe *Sharia* (Islamic) law. That Islamic initiative was frustrated by Indonesia's first president, **Sukarno**, who insisted on religious pluralism expressed through the pre-eminent of five principles, *Pancasila*, which he enunciated and which became the philosophical bases of the post-colonial Republic. *Pancasila* served to protect *Abangan* cultural identity and was entrenched in the constitution during the rule of President **Suharto**. The distinction between *Abangan* and *Santri* became blurred from around the seventh decade of the twentieth century with rapid economic development and urbanization, which has provided a social context within which a burgeoning Islam has become increasingly assertive.

see also: Islam; *Pancasila*; *Santri*; Suharto; Sukarno.

## ABIM (Malaysia)

ABIM is an acronym drawn from *Angkatan Belia Islam Malaysia*, which translates as Islamic Youth Movement of Malaysia. It was set up in 1971 on the campus of the University of Malaya as a vehicle of Islamic revivalism (see **Dakwah**). ABIM represented an expression of political as well as religious dissent against a Malay–Muslim-dominated government, which had allegedly compromised the political birthright of the indigenous Malays to the advantage of non-Malays, especially the Chinese. The lead-

ing role in ABIM's formation was played by **Anwar Ibrahim**, then a student of Malay studies, who exercised a truly charismatic influence on his fellow students. In December 1974, he was detained for twenty-two months for leading a demonstration against peasant poverty in the state of Kedah. ABIM was for a time regarded as the youth wing of the principal Malay opposition **Parti Islam Se-Malaysia** (PAS) and some of its members campaigned for PAS in the 1978 elections. It lost national standing as an agent of Islamic resurgence when Anwar Ibrahim joined **UMNO** (United Malays National Organization) shortly before general elections in April 1982. He stood successfully as an UMNO candidate in those elections and then entered the government as a junior minister in the Prime Minister's Department, after which he enjoyed a spectacular political rise, reaching the office of deputy prime minister by the end of 1993. Anwar Ibrahim retained his ABIM intellectual links but the movement had ceased to serve as a vigorous vehicle for Islamic-based challenge to government well before his political downfall in September 1998. Without Anwar's leadership, ABIM concentrated its efforts on Islamic education and assumed a non-partisan role, while its politically-disposed members joined either PAS or UMNO.

see also: Anwar Ibrahim; *Dakwah*; Islam; *Parti Islam Se-Malaysia*; UMNO.

## ABRI (Indonesia)

ABRI is an acronym drawn from *Angkatan Bersenjata Indonesia* which translates as Armed Forces of the Republic of Indonesia. Indonesia's armed forces, which include the army, navy, air force and police, have long enjoyed a central place in the political and business life of the country and served as the power-base for President **Suharto** during his extended rule. As a serving general, he assumed its leadership during a coup attempt in October 1965 and with military support seized political control in March 1966. Within the armed forces, the army has occupied the dominant position. It draws its tradition from Japanese military culture, inculcated during the Pacific War occupation, and from the experience of national revolution against the Dutch. With the political downfall of President Suharto in May 1998, the national standing and morale of the armed forces was diminished as its record of human rights abuses was publicized. An attempt to cleanse its sullied reputation in April 1999 by changing its name to *Tentara Nasional Indonesia* (Indonesia's National Army) failed conspicuously with the revelation of its brutal conduct in **East Timor**.

ABRI's origins may be traced back to 5 October 1945 when President **Sukarno** inaugurated the People's Security Army under the initial command of an Indonesian officer from the former Dutch colonial army. That leadership was soon challenged by Indonesians who had been trained in Japanese paramilitary organizations, such as the *Peta*. By mid-November, leadership had passed to Sudirman, a former *Peta* battalion commander, who distinguished himself in directing guerrilla resistance against the Dutch in the closing stages of the revolutionary war, despite being terminally ill with tuberculosis. The formative moment in the development of the political culture of the armed forces occurred in December 1948 when the Dutch occupied the revolutionary capital of Yogyakarta. The civilian government headed by President Sukarno surrendered, while the army opted to continue resistance by irregular warfare. From this juncture, the military took the view that politics was too serious a matter to be left exclusively in the charge of civilians who had abdicated their responsibility at a time of gravest national peril. Moreover, independence was depicted as having been achieved primarily through armed struggle and not the diplomacy of irresolute politicians. The armed forces represented themselves as the legitimate guardians of the state.

After independence, this prerogative view was confirmed for the leadership of the armed forces by the political instability and economic failings of parliamentary democracy during the 1950s. During this period, the army chief of staff, General **Abdul Haris Nasution**, formulated a theory of the 'Middle Way' to justify a political role for the military. Although the armed forces were instrumental in helping President Sukarno to establish the authoritarian political system of **Guided Democracy** in July 1959, they were neutralized by his manipulative skills. In the wake of an abortive coup in October 1965 (see *Gestapu*), the armed forces reasserted themselves and seized power in March 1966 under the leadership of then Lt-General Suharto (see *Supersemar*). Indonesia reverted to the form of constitutionalism with parliamentary and presidential elections revived from the early 1970s but ABRI's right to a prerogative place in political life on account of its *Dwi Fungsi* (or dual role) was embodied in legislation in 1982. The special place of the armed forces was acknowledged also by allocating them 100 seats in the Parliament of 500 members, justified in addition by a denial of their right to vote.

In April 1995, ABRI's parliamentary representation was reduced to seventy-five seats. This reduction was justified ostensibly with reference to Indonesia's democratic progress. It was interpreted, however, as an indication of a rising tension between the military establishment and President Suharto, which had showed itself first in February 1988 with the premature removal from office of armed forces commander, General **L. B. Murdani**. President Suharto's determination to rule independently of the armed forces as well as his toleration of the extensive business activities of his family caused a progressive alienation. This alienation was aggravated in December 1990 when the president encouraged the formation of an Association of Indonesian Muslim Intellectuals (**ICMI**) in apparent emulation of the practice of the late President Sukarno of mobilizing countervailing political support against the armed forces. Up to his resignation in May 1998, President Suharto dominated the armed forces by controlling the promotion of its most senior officers with ABRI commanders drawn from the ranks of former personal aides. General Wiranto, his last nominee as ABRI commander, endorsed the transfer of executive authority to Vice-President **Habibie**. An initial working relationship gave way to political tension, especially from January 1999 after President Habibie had offered the people of East Timor the choice between autonomy within Indonesia or full independence without reference to the armed forces, which had an emotional stake in the territory because of casualties incurred in counter-insurgency and also because of a guardian role in upholding the integrity of the republic.

The armed forces were obliged to tolerate a further reduction of their parliamentary representation to thirty-eight seats prior to elections in June 1999. They withheld support for President Habibie's bid to retain high office and did not try to obstruct the election of **Abdurrahman Wahid** as president by the **People's Consultative Assembly** in the following October. His appointment of Professor Juwono Sudarsono as the first civilian minister of defence for several decades indicated the president's determination to reduce the political role of the armed forces. Tension became manifest between the president and General Wiranto, appointed coordinating minister for political and security affairs, especially after President Abdurrahman Wahid endorsed the right of a national commission of enquiry into human rights violations in East Timor to hold him and other senior officers accountable. General Wiranto was suspended from cabinet office in February 2000 (resigning formally in May), while armed forces commander Admiral Widodo Adisutjipto informed a parliamentary committee that the military was prepared to give up its thirty-eight legislative seats at the next elections in 2004. By then, the concept of *Dwi Fungsi* had lost credibility and the armed forces had lost the cohesive capability to mount a coup but a significant vestigial influence in politics and business remained. In April 2000, Admiral Widodo announced the armed forces were out of politics and wanted to concentrate on their professional role. However, tension has remained with civil authority reflected in the statement in May 2000 by defence minister Juwono Sudarsono that the armed forces could no longer guarantee the country's security and unity because of excessive cuts in their budget. In August 2000, the People's Consultative Assembly decided that the armed forces would retain a token representation until 2009.

*see also: Dwi Fungsi; Gestapu;* Guided Democracy; Habibie, B. J.; ICMI; Murdani, L. B.; Nasution, Abdul Haris; People's Consultative Assembly; Peta; Sudarsono, Juwono; Suharto; Sukarno; *Supersemar;* Timor, East.

## Abu Sayyaf  (Philippines)

Abu Sayyaf, which means bearer of the sword, is a militant Muslim group which seeks a separate Islamic state in the southern Philippines. It was established in 1991 on the island of Basilan by Abubakar Janjalani after he had returned from a period of religious study in Saudi Arabia and Libya sponsored by the **Moro National Liberation Front** (MNLF). His movement is opposed to any accommodation with the Philippines government over Muslim political autonomy and has declared its intention of driving Christian inhabitants from the southern islands of the republic by acts of force which were undertaken first during 1992. He attracted a constituency of politically discontented and radical younger Muslims, including disaffected members of the MNLF, whose numbers grew from 100 to over 500. Initially engaging in kidnappings, bombings and grenade attacks, the Abu Sayyaf group achieved international notoriety in April 1995 for a daring surprise seaborne raid by some two hundred armed men on the small predominantly Christian town of Ipil on the south-western tip of the island of Mindanao. In the course of the raid, which devastated the commercial district, the town's seven banks were robbed and fifty-three residents were killed. The raiders then fled into the jungle with hostages, many of whom were hacked to death with knives. The Abu Sayyaf group is believed to be stiffened by Filipino Muslims with military experience gained in Afghanistan and to have received financial support from external Islamic sources. It has been linked to the international terrorist network implicated in the bombing of the World Trade Center in New York in 1993 and in a plot to kill the Pope during his visit to the Philippines in January 1995. It has been suggested also that it enjoys a covert relationship with the Moro National Liberation Front which it exploited in protracted negotiations with the Philippines government. In a second raid in April 1995, Abu Sayyaf insurgents attacked the coastal town of Tungawan located about 12 miles south-east of

Ipil. At the end of 1998, Abubakar Janjalani was killed in a gun-battle outside of the provincial capital of Isabela. Since his death and under the leadership of his brother Khaddafi, Abu Sayyaf has degenerated into a quasi-criminal organization engaging in kidnapping and hostage-taking justified by outlandish political demands, such as the release of Ramzi Yousef who was convicted of masterminding the bombing in 1993 of the World Trade Centre in New York. A group of about fifty Filipino hostages were seized from two schools on the island of Basilan in March 2000, two of whom were beheaded. In late April that year, a group of twenty-one foreign and local tourists were seized from the Malaysian-held resort island of **Sipadan** and taken by boat to the Philippine island of Jolo. Recurrent assaults by units of the armed forces failed to dislodge the insurgents from their jungle redoubt only forty minutes' drive from Jolo town. Hostages were released in batches in return for millions of dollars in ransom. In September, following the seizure of a further three hostages from Malaysia, President Estrada ordered a military operation against the Abu Sayyaf movement.

see also: Moro National Liberation Front; Sipadan.

## Aceh Independence Movement
(Indonesia)

The Aceh Independence Movement (*Gerakan Aceh Merdeka*) is a separatist organization, which was set up on 4 December 1976 by Hasan di Tiro, an American-educated expatriate businessman. In his mid-seventies, he has resided in exile in Sweden since 1979. However, his leadership has been contested by another exile-based faction resident in Sweden and Malaysia. Aceh is the northern-most province of Sumatra whose population of over 4 million shares a strong Islamic historical identity going back to a powerful seventeenth-century sultanate from which di Tiro claims descent. It was the last part of the Indonesian archipelago to fall to Dutch colonial rule, which was not effectively consolidated until the early years of the twentieth century. Although an active source of resistance to the return of the Dutch after the Pacific War, on Indonesia's independence Aceh became a seat of the Muslim-inspired rebellion known

as *Darul Islam*, which challenged the unity of the Republic over the next decade, partly in reaction to the new republic merging Aceh into the province of North Sumatra. The source of political alienation, that formed the context to di Tiro's separatist initiative, was Jakarta's failure to honour a promise of provincial autonomy in 1959 and the meagre returns to Aceh from the exploitation of the rich Arun offshore oil and natural gas fields.

The Aceh Independence Movement made only a limited impact until the late 1980s when a government clampdown on marijuana growing by army deserters against a context of economic and religious discontent provoked a surge of local dissent with armed attacks mounted on police posts. Brutal military repression followed with the deployment of special forces. The limited rebellion was sufficiently crushed by mid-1991 that the government political party *Golkar* was able to assert its dominance in the province in parliamentary elections in June 1992. By then, however, several hundred young Acehnese had received military training in Libya. The underlying resentment of rule from Jakarta and demand for independence came to a head again after the political downfall of President **Suharto** in May 1998 and gained momentum after the seeming precedent of a referendum in **East Timor** in August 1999. It was reinforced by the indiscriminate nature of military repression, which had been responsible for the loss of some 5,000 lives from the early 1990s. Moreover, statements by **Abdurrahman Wahid**, before and even after he became president, that he supported a corresponding vote in Aceh aroused strong political expectations within the disaffected province. He subsequently ruled out independence as an option in any referendum partly under pressure from the armed forces (see **ABRI**) leading to a political impasse between the government in Jakarta and the separatists in Aceh. The strength of support for independence within Aceh was demonstrated in November 1999 when over 500,000 protesters converged on the province's capital, Banda Aceh, to demand a referendum. The independence movement, led militarily within Aceh by Abdullah Syafie, claims to have around 1,000 men under arms supplied by sympathizers in Malaysia and Thailand. The prospect of Indonesia's balkanization alarmed the country's regional partners and major Asia-Pacific powers who have lent their support to the government in Jakarta for the continued integrity of the Republic after the independence of East Timor. President Abdurrahman Wahid played on the popular desire for peace within the province by offering a range of concessions, including a much greater share of natural-gas revenues and latitude in applying Islamic law as well as countenancing a human rights trial of soldiers charged with murdering students at an Islamic school in July 1999, who were found guilty in mid-May 2000. On 12 May, after several months of secret negotiations, a cease-fire described as a humanitarian pause was signed in Davos, Switzerland, between a representative of the Indonesian government and of the faction loyal to Hasan di Tiro. However, under pressure from its Parliament, Jakarta refused recognition to the insurgents who also sustained their demand for independence. The ceasefire, renewed in August, failed to end recurrent violence in the province. In September, a prominent Islamic university rector, who was a leading candidate for governor, was assassinated.

*see also:* ABRI; *Darul Islam*; East Timor; *Golkar*; Islam; Suharto; Wahid, Abdurrahman.

## AFTA  (Association of South-East Asian Nations Free Trade Area) 1993– (Brunei/Burma(Myanmar)/Cambodia/Indonesia/Laos/Malaysia/Philippines/Singapore/Thailand/Vietnam)

At the fourth meeting of heads of government of **ASEAN** held in Singapore in January 1992, an agreement was reached on establishing a free trade area with effective tariff reductions ranging from 5 to 0 per cent during a fifteen-year period beginning from 1 January 1993. ASEAN had been established with an ostensible prime commitment to economic cooperation, which had not been realized that far. Political co-operation had taken pride of place, especially during the course of the Cambodian conflict during the 1980s. With its resolution as an international problem and the attendant marginalization of ASEAN as a diplomatic community,

its members became conscious of the need for corporate renewal. This concern coincided with a collective fear of global trading blocs as well as with a contrasting opportunity of being able to benefit from a potential single market, then of over 300 million people.

The notion of a free trade area had been suggested by Thailand in September 1991 and was approved in principle the next month at a meeting of ASEAN's economics ministers in Malaysia. The initiative to establish an AFTA marked an attempt to repair the Association's failure to raise intra-mural trade beyond around 15 per cent. The main mechanism chosen was the Common Effective Preferential Tariff (CEPT) Scheme. In January 1992, fifteen groups of manufactured goods and processed agricultural products were initially identified for inclusion in the scheme of accelerated tariff reductions. A meeting of economics ministers convened in Manila in October that year, which reached agreement on trying to expedite the process of tariff reduction. A new target of five to eight years was set for lowering tariffs to 20 per cent before realizing the goal of a maximum of 5 per cent by the end of the fifteen-year implementation period. At issue for ASEAN at the outset was how to overcome the persisting problem of reconciling the conflicting economic interests of member states reflected in their different tariff levels. By October 1993, at a subsequent meeting of economics ministers, it was evident that the CEPT Scheme had stalled. It was agreed to re-launch it, with all members (with the exception of Brunei) beginning tariff cuts from January 1994. In July 1995, despite reservations on the part of Indonesia and the Philippines, ASEAN's foreign ministers supported the reduction of the time-frame for implementing tariff cuts of from 5 to 0 per cent to eight years. Vietnam, which joined the Association in that month, was granted a dispensation to defer its obligations under AFTA until 2006.

At the ASEAN Summit in Bangkok in December 1995, it was agreed to reduce all intra-mural tariff barriers under the CEPT Scheme by 2003. Despite the impact of regional economic adversity from mid-1997, the ASEAN Summit in Hanoi in December 1998 sanctioned an advance by one year to 2002 for tariff reductions

to between 5 and 0 per cent, with more recent members, including Vietnam and Burma (Myanmar) and Laos which had joined in July 1997, given a dispensation up to 2008. At an informal summit in Manila in November 1999, the target date for the final elimination of all duties was advanced from 2015 to 2010 for Brunei, Indonesia, Malaysia, the Philippines and Thailand, while remaining members, including Cambodia which had joined in April 1999, had their target advanced from 2018 to 2015. In the light of the regional impact of economic adversity at the end of the twentieth century and the disarray within ASEAN over collective measures to cope with it, a general scepticism has obtained about the Association's ability to keep to its declared target dates for tariff reductions. Indeed, at a meeting of trade ministers in Rangoon in May 2000, an extension of two years was granted to Malaysia on the deadline for tariff cuts on cars and selected agricultural products. It has been pointed out that most of the increase in intra-ASEAN trade has been in parts and components for assembly lines in factories set up by multinationals in the region.
*see also:* ASEAN; Bangkok Summit 1995; Hanoi Summit 1998; Singapore Summit 1992.

## *Al-Arqam* (Malaysia)

*Al-Arqam* was an Islamic revivalist organization of some 100,000 members named after a companion of the Prophet Muhammad; known originally as *Darul Arqam*, it translates literally as House of Arqam. It was founded in 1968 by a religious teacher, Ustaaz Ashaari Muhammed, with the object of recreating an Islamic way of life based on personal morality and social responsibility. To that end, a number of village communities were established on a self-sufficient and sexually segregated basis as well as factories which processed *halal* (religiously permitted) foodstuffs. The ultimate purpose of the experiment was to create an Islamic state as a result of creating an Islamic society and was tolerated by government as a counter to *Parti Islam Se-Malaysia*. From 1991 the movement came into conflict with the government for flouting its ban on activities in any of its offices and was subject to severe constraints. It remained active, however, and attracted support from disaffected members of **UMNO** (United Malays National Organization) and discontented youth. In April 1994 a number of Malaysian students and members of *Al-Arqam* were arrested during an Islamic fundamentalist demonstration in Cairo. The sect was banned in Malaysia in August 1994, after prime minister Dr **Mahathir Mohamad** had described it as a threat to national security because of its deviant teaching; in the following month, Ashaari was detained after being deported from exile in Thailand. He was released in October 1994 and appeared on television to renounce his movement's policies. *Al-Arqam* was formally disbanded in November 1994.
*see also:* ASEAN; *Dakwah*; Islam; Mahathir Mohamad, Datuk Sri; *Parti Islam Se-Malaysia*; UMNO.

## Alatas, Ali (Indonesia)

Ali Alatas has been the longest serving foreign minister of Indonesia. He was first appointed to that portfolio in March 1988, which he held continuously through the last decade of the rule of President **Suharto** until May 1998 and then during that of interim-President **Habibie** who lost office in October 1999. He was born in Jakarta on 4 November 1932. A Dutch-language secondary education was followed by enrolment in the Academy for Foreign Service from which he graduated in 1953. After receiving a law degree from the University of Indonesia in 1955, he was posted to Bangkok. Ali Alatas assumed responsibility for information services during Indonesia's **Confrontation** of Malaysia. With the change of political order in Indonesia in 1966, he served in Washington and then during 1972–5 was *chef de cabinet* to foreign minister Adam Malik, in which role he distinguished himself. A short term as his country's permanent representative to the United Nations in Geneva was followed by secondment as secretary to the vice-president when that office was held by Adam Malik between 1978 and 1983. In 1983, he was appointed permanent representative to the United Nations in New York where he served until his elevation to foreign minister.

As foreign minister, Ali Alatas was one of the most articulate exponents of Indonesia's interests in the English language. He played a leading role in the negotiations leading to the formal settlement of the Cambodian conflict and served as co-chair of the **International Conference on Cambodia** in Paris in October 1991, which sanctioned it. He was also instrumental in Indonesia becoming chair of the Non-Aligned Movement in September 1992. His last decade in office was taken up with defending Indonesia's position in **East Timor** but his attempt to secure international support for a policy of provincial autonomy was undermined by President Habibie's unilateral initiative in January 1999 in offering its residents a choice between autonomy and independence. In the event, Ali Alatas did not resign office but negotiated the terms of reference of the referendum held in East Timor in August 1999 with Portugal and the Secretary General of the United Nations.

*see also:* Confrontation; Habibie, B. J.; International Conference on Cambodia, Paris 1991; Malik, Adam; Suharto; Timor, East.

## Alex Boncayao Brigade (Philippines)

The Alex Boncayao Brigade is a breakaway urban assassination unit from the Communist **New People's Army**, named after a labour leader who was killed by security forces in 1983. It was set up in May 1984 at a time when the martial law regime of President **Ferdinand Marcos** had failed to realize its initial promise and had lost its legitimacy as a result of the assassination of opposition leader **Benigno Aquino**. The Brigade became especially active, however, during the late 1980s after the downfall of Marcos and his replacement as president by Corazón Aquino. This fundamental political change led to a significant draining of support from the Communist movement, which sought to compensate by engaging in a campaign of urban terror with armed attacks on government officials, police and US military advisers. The Alex Boncayao Brigade failed to sustain its momentum into the 1990s, partly as a consequence of an ideological split within Communist ranks which generated internecine tensions. One faction was led by **José María Sisón**, in exile in Holland, who had founded the movement, and another by Felimón Lagmán, the leader

of the Manila wing which controlled the Alex Boncayao Brigade. The Brigade's activities revived briefly in early 1994 but its fortunes were dealt a heavy blow in May 1994 when Felimón Lagmán was arrested in the Quezón City district of Manila, probably as a result of an act of betrayal. Acts of assassination were resumed at the end of 1995 under the leadership of Sergio Romero but attracted the suspicion that they served as a cover for criminal interests. In June 1996, the Brigade claimed responsibility for assassinating Rolando Abadilla, an intelligence colonel during the Marcos era. In October 1997, Sergio Romero was arrested in Marilao in Bulacan Province after his car crashed into a lamppost while being pursued by military intelligence agents. The security forces then announced that Romero was an alias for Nilo dela Cruz, who also headed another breakaway faction of the New People's Army known as the Revolutionary Proletarian Army. In March 2000, in a display of continuing hit-and-run tactics, an attack was launched on the offices of the government's department of energy and those of two oil companies in Negros Oriental province.

*see also:* Aquino, Benigno; Aquino, Corazón; Marcos, Ferdinand; New People's Army; Sisón, José María.

## Aliran (Malaysia)

*Aliran* is the shortened form of the Malay term *Persatuan Aliran Kesesdaran Negara* (National Consciousness Society). *Aliran* is a multiracial intellectually based interest group dedicated to social and political reform which was founded on the Malaysian island of Penang in 1977. Its leading figure from the outset has been Dr Chandra Muzaffar, a convert to **Islam** and at one time a lecturer at the university in Penang. *Aliran* has stood out as a focus for political dissent within a society in which civil liberties have been constrained. Its pamphlets and monthly journal have been a recurrent source of irritation to the government, which has come close to banning it on a number of occasions. Its full title conveys the declared goal of raising political consciousness. However, its constituency is limited in the main to only a section of the middle class, which restricts *Aliran*'s political impact; this is probably why it is tolerated by the government, which has been successful in coopting the organization. *Aliran's* political constituency became alienated from government, however, following the dismissal of **Anwar Ibrahim** as deputy prime minister in September 1998 and his subsequent detention, trial and imprisonment. Chandra Muzaffar became deputy leader of the opposition *Parti Keadilan Nasional* (National Justice Party), which secured five federal parliamentary seats in elections in November 1999.

see also: Anwar Ibrahim; Islam; *Parti Keadilan Nasional* (National Justice Party).

## All-Malaya Council of Joint Action (Malaya)

The All-Malaya Council of Joint Action was established initially as the Pan-Malayan Council of Joint Action in December 1946. That body was set up as a united front to challenge the revised constitutional provision for a Federation of Malaya by the Colonial Office in the wake of Britain's withdrawal of the controversial **Malayan Union Proposal**. The core of the council was a group of left-wing non-Malays based in Singapore who had earlier formed the **Malayan Democratic Union** to oppose the Malayan Union Proposal. They had objected to Singapore's separation from mainland Malaya and the limited provision for self-government. They expressed even stronger objections to the new proposal for a Federation of Malaya and entered into association with the radical Malay Nationalist Party and its affiliates who joined with the All-Malaya Council of Joint Action, which became the new name of the organization in August 1947. The council organized a protest strike in October and published a model people's constitution at the end of the year. Their efforts were to no avail, especially given their links with the Communist Party of Malaya (see **Emergency 1948–60**). The Federation of Malaya was inaugurated on 1 February 1948.

see also: Emergency 1948–60; Malayan Democratic Union; Malayan Union Proposal 1946.

## Alliance Party (Malaya/Malaysia)

The Alliance Party is the name adopted by the governing intercommunal coalition which assumed the administration of Malaya on independence in August 1957. The Alliance remained continuously in power after the formation of the wider Federation of Malaysia in September 1963 until superseded in June 1974 by a larger intercommunal arrangement, the *Barisan Nasional* (National Front), based on the same political model and of which it has been the core. The Alliance emerged out of a pact between **UMNO** (United Malays National Organization) led by **Tunku Abdul Rahman** and the Malayan (subsequently **Malaysian**) **Chinese Association** (MCA) to contest elections for the municipality of Kuala Lumpur in 1952 in competition with the multicommunal **Independence of Malaya Party** (IMP). At issue was the appropriate political format for a communally divided society. The British colonial power had made the grant of independence contingent on a working relationship among the Malay, Chinese and Indian communities, ideally within the framework of a single political organization. Indeed, during the **Emergency 1948–60**, they had set up a Communities Liaison Committee on an intercommunal basis. The IMP proved to be an abortive attempt to realize the ideal of a truly multiracial party. The electoral success of the pact between UMNO and the MCA demonstrated the prospect of an alternative arrangement whereby exclusively communal parties through inter-elite bargaining and accommodations about political prerogatives and economic advantage could sustain government on a harmonious basis. When the first federal-wide elections were held in July 1955, the initial pact had evolved into an institutionalized undertaking with the additional participation of the Malayan (subsequently **Malaysian**) **Indian Congress** (MIC). The Alliance went on to win fifty-one out of the fifty-two elective seats, proving itself to be the legitimate representative to negotiate the independence of Malaya from Britain. The Alliance model in which UMNO was the dominant partner was expanded from the early 1970s after elections in May 1969 in which the ruling coalition suffered a major reverse followed by racial violence. Coalition building at state level in northern Borneo, Penang and Perak led on to an arrangement at federal level initially with *Parti Islam Se-Malaysia*, which came into effect in January 1973. *Barisan Nasional* as the successor of the Alliance was registered formally as a political party on 1 June 1974.

*see also: Barisan Nasional*; Emergency 1948–60; Independence of Malaya Party; Malaysian Chinese Association; Malaysian Indian Congress; *Parti Islam Se-Malaysia*; Rahman, Tunku Abdul; UMNO.

## Alwi Shihab  (Indonesia) *see* Shihab, Alwi.

## Anand Panyarachun  (Thailand)

Anand Panyarachun served with distinction as interim prime minister of Thailand on two occasions during 1991–2. He was born in Bangkok on 9 August 1932 and received his secondary and higher education in England, graduating in law from Cambridge University in 1955. He then entered the Thai Ministry of Foreign Affairs, serving in later years as ambassador to the United States and then permanent representative to the United Nations. He returned to Thailand in 1976 with a reputation as a skilful diplomat to become permanent secretary (head) of the Ministry of Foreign Affairs but fell victim to the political purge by the military following a bloody coup in October 1976. During 1977–8, Anand served as ambassador to West Germany, resigning from the foreign service in 1979 to go into private business. In February 1991 a military coup removed the government of **Chatichai Choonhavan**. In March, Anand was persuaded by King **Bhumibol Adulyadej** to accept the post of interim prime minister until fresh elections were held. His mainly technocratic administration took a number of important and successful economic initiatives and enjoyed considerable popular support in great part because of Anand's reputation for ability and integrity. He relinquished office with the elections in March 1992 but was asked by the king to resume it again after political violence in May, which was precipitated by the non-elected, retired general **Suchinda Krapayoon** taking over as prime minister. Anand returned to high office in June

1992 and held it until elections in September produced a coalition government led by **Chuan Leekpai**. During his second and more limited tenure, Anand acted with royal and popular approval to circumscribe the powers and privileges of the military establishment.

*see also:* Bhumibol Adulyadej; Chatichai Choonhavan; Chuan Leekpai; Suchinda Krapayoon.

## Ananda Mahidol, King  (Thailand)

King Ananda Mahidol succeeded to the Thai throne in March 1935 following the abdication and exile of his uncle King Prajadhipok, who had conceded the end of the absolute monarchy in 1932. Born in 1925, he was then 9 years old and at school in Lausanne. Apart from a brief visit to Bangkok in 1938, he remained in Switzerland until after the end of the Pacific War, returning to Thailand in December 1945 with his younger brother **Bhumibol Adulyadej**. At the time, Thailand was adjusting to the end of a discredited collaborationist military rule and the introduction of civilian politics with **Pridi Phanomyong**, who had opposed the Japanese, as prime minister. On the morning of 9 June 1946, however, King Ananda was found shot dead in his bed in the Grand Palace in Bangkok. The initial official explanation was that the death had been an accident; the king and his brother had been known to play with guns. Rumours of regicide in order to create a republic prompted prime minister Pridi to appoint an official commission into the fatality but public unrest was unabated, aggravated by economic problems and corrupt practice. Ultimately, the death of the king served as a pretext for a military coup in November 1947 which restored to power the wartime leader Field Marshal **Phibul Songkram**. With the change of regime, further investigation of the death led to a prolonged trial and then the execution in 1955 of two royal pages and a friend of Pridi, which confirmed public suspicion of a plot. King Ananda was succeeded in June 1946 by his brother Bhumibol; the circumstances of his death have never been satisfactorily explained and have remained a forbidden topic in Thailand.

*see also:* Bhumibol Adulyadej; Phibul Songkram; Pridi Phanomyong.

## Angkatan Belia Islam Malaysia
(Malaysia) *see* ABIM.

## Angkatan Perpaduan Ummah
(Malaysia)

*Angkatan Perpaduan Ummah*, which translates as Muslim Unity Front, is an electoral coalition which was formed by opposition Malay parties in June 1990 in the wake of the split within **UMNO** (United Malays National Organization) that occurred during 1987 when **Tengku Razaleigh Hamzah** unsuccessfully challenged Dr **Mahathir Mohamad** for the leadership. The coalition comprised *Parti Islam Se-Malaysia* (PAS), *Semangat '46, Berjasa* and another minor grouping, *Parti Nasional Muslimin Malaysia*. The Muslim Unity Front contested concurrent federal and state elections in October 1990 but was successful only in the state of Kelantan, where it won all thirty-nine seats in the legislature. It formed the state government but under the effective control of PAS which was repeated after election in April 1995. The Front provided an electoral vehicle of convenience for disparate political interests but by 1996, tensions between the coalition partners reached breaking point over the division of political spoils and PAS's policy of Islamization. *Semangat '46* was formally dissolved in October 1996 and its members were admitted *en bloc* into UMNO, which marked the effective end of the Muslim Unity Front.

*see also:* Berjasa; Mahathir Mohamad, Datuk Sri;
   *Parti Islam Se-Malaysia*; Razaleigh Hamzah,
   Tengku; *Semangat '46*; UMNO.

## Anglo-Malayan/Malaysian Defence Agreement 1957–71
(Malaya/Malaysia/Singapore)

A commitment by Britain to the external defence of Malaya in return for which it was granted the right to maintain military forces 'for the fulfilment of Commonwealth and international obligations' came into effect on 12 October 1957. In April 1959, through an exchange of letters with the government of Malaya, Australia and New Zealand formally associated themselves with those articles in the agreement which provided for the stationing of Commonwealth forces. The terms of the agreement were extended to all the territories of the enlarged Federation

of Malaysia in an undertaking in November 1961, which came into effect with its advent from 16 September 1963. That extension of commitment was successfully tested during Indonesia's **Confrontation** of Malaysia during 1963–6. It was sustained to include Singapore, despite the island's separation from the Federation in August 1965. A meeting in London in April 1971 between representatives of Britain, Australia, New Zealand, Malaysia and Singapore reached an accord on the termination of the agreement on 1 November 1971. It was succeeded by a **Five Power Defence Arrangements** in which the explicit commitment to the external defence of the two South-East Asian states was replaced by a provision for consultation only.

*see also:* Confrontation; Five Power Defence
   Arrangements 1971–.

## Anh, Le Duc (Vietnam) *see* Le Duc Anh.

## Anti-Fascist People's Freedom League (AFPFL) (Burma/Myanmar)

The Anti-Fascist People's Freedom League (AFPFL) was a political organization set up in 1944 by the nationalist leader, **Aung San**. It was intended initially to challenge Japanese occupation in the context of changing military fortunes in the Pacific War but then became the vehicle for nationalist opposition to British plans for postwar Burma. Britain's political accommodation with the AFPFL paved the way for negotiations for independence which were concluded harmoniously in January 1947. In elections in April 1947, the AFPFL won 172 of the non-communal seats and thereby demonstrated its political dominance. It formed the first government after independence in January 1948 with **U Nu** as prime minister, Aung San having been assassinated in July 1947. Over the next decade as the country faced turbulence from ethnic-minority and communist rebellion, the AFPFL proceeded to fragment. In April 1958 it split into two factions, with U Nu leading the majority alignment. It was then that the prime minister turned to General **Ne Win** to request that the army assume a caretaker role, which lasted for two years. U Nu's so-called 'clean'

faction won elections held in February 1960 but the AFPFL government was removed with the military coup in March 1962 which also made the party illegal.
see also: Aung San; Ne Win; Nu, U.

## Anwar Ibrahim (Malaysia)

Anwar Ibrahim became deputy prime minister of Malaysia in December 1993 after having been elected unopposed to the office of deputy president of **UMNO** in the previous November. At the beginning of September 1998, against a context of economic adversity and political differences with prime minister **Mahathir Mohamad**, he was dismissed as deputy prime minister and finance minister and also as deputy president of UMNO. After mounting a campaign for political reform, he was detained later in the month under the Internal Security Act and beaten up in custody by the head of the national police force, which provoked anti-government protests and international criticism. He was then charged with corruption and sexual misconduct and the first phase of his trial began in November. Anwar pleaded not guilty claiming that he was the victim of a political conspiracy, while his cause was taken up by his wife Wan Azizah Ismail who founded the *Parti Keadilan Nasional* (National Justice Party) in his support. In April 1999, Anwar was found guilty of four charges of corruption (abuse of power) and sentenced to six years' imprisonment, which precipitated public disorder in Kuala Lumpur. Later that month, he was charged with a further count of sodomy. The second trial began in June but was suspended in mid-November 1999 shortly before general elections and resumed in January 2000. In April 2000, the anniversary of his conviction and imprisonment was marked by public demonstrations in Kuala Lumpur and also by a severe crack-down against his supporters by the security forces.

Anwar Ibrahim was born on 10 August 1947 in Bukit Mertajam and was educated at the University of Malaya in the late 1960s where he read Malay Studies. He became the charismatic leader of **ABIM**, the Islamic Youth movement, which he founded in 1971 and which posed a radical challenge to the UMNO-dominated government. In 1974, Anwar was detained for leading a protest in support of rice farmers in the state of Kedah. It came as a great surprise, therefore, when he announced that he was joining UMNO to stand as a parliamentary candidate in general elections in April 1982. His Islamic credentials and close association with the prime minister, Dr Mahathir Mohamad, were judged to have been important factors in helping to fend off the electoral challenge of the opposition *Parti Islam Se-Malaysia*. With electoral success, he was appointed a junior minister in the prime minister's office. In September 1982, Anwar was elected a vice-president of UMNO and head of the party's youth wing. He then rose steadily in government, assuming in succession the youth culture and sport, agriculture and education portfolios. During the power struggle within UMNO in 1987 in which Dr Mahathir was challenged by **Tengku Razaleigh Hamzah**, the minister for trade and industry, Anwar remained fiercely loyal to the prime minister, who triumphed over his political adversary. In March 1991, after the resignation of the incumbent **Daim Zainuddin**, he was appointed minister of finance. Although he entered politics from an Islamic base, Anwar Ibrahim advocated religious pluralism in a Malaysian society divided along racial–religious lines. He also repudiated the notion of authoritarian Asian values, espoused by Mahathir Mohamad. Prior to the onset of economic adversity in the late 1990s, Anwar Ibrahim was widely regarded as the prime minister's chosen successor. However, his perceived challenge to Dr Mahathir at a time of economic adversity prompted the prime minister to act to destroy politically his younger protégé in order to try to salvage his own historical reputation. In August 2000, he was found guilty of sodomy and sentenced to nine years imprisonment.
see also: ABIM; Daim Zanuddin; Mahathir Mohamad; *Parti Islam Se-Malaysia; Parti Keadilan Nasional* (National Justice Party); Razaleigh Hamzah, Tengku; UMNO.

## ANZAM (Malaya)

ANZAM is an acronym drawn from Australia, New Zealand and the Malayan area registering

an informal consultative framework (established in May 1948) through which Australia
and New Zealand made contributions to the
defence of British Malaya from 1950. Initial
token deployments of air support were augmented following decisions to commit limited
ground forces in early 1955 prompted by
Communist military success in Indochina in
1954. An Australian battalion landed in Penang
in July 1955 and a New Zealand company in
Singapore in November. These forces were
incorporated within a Commonwealth Strategic
Reserve under British command set up with its
divisional headquarters in Penang in December.
The ANZAM defence framework was subsequently subsumed within the structure of the
**Anglo-Malayan Defence Agreement** concluded
in October 1957 after the independence of the
Federation of Malaya in August 1957.

*see also:* Anglo-Malayan/Malaysian Defence
  Agreement 1957–71.

## APEC  (Asia-Pacific Economic Cooperation) 1989–(Brunei/Indonesia/Malaysia/Philippines/Singapore/Thailand/Vietnam)

APEC is an organization of twenty-one mem-
bers set up in November 1989 as a result of an
Australian initiative with the object of promoting freer multilateral trade and investment
within Asia-Pacific. That initiative was prompted
by concern over lack of progress in the Uruguay
Round of the General Agreement on Tariffs and
Trade (GATT) and the prospect of exclusive
trade blocs developing in North America and
Europe. For that reason, all members of **ASEAN**
(Association of South-East Asian Nations) joined
APEC at the outset but with mixed feelings over
the extent to which the association might have
its separate regional identity diluted as a consequence. Indeed, it was in January 1992, not
long after APEC's formation, that ASEAN's
heads of government decided to establish a free
trade area, known in acronym as **AFTA**, for
members of the association. Although APEC
was represented initially as a loose consultative
body, its members agreed in September 1992
to set up a small permanent secretariat in
Singapore. That sign of institutionalization may
well have prompted Malaysia's prime minister,

Dr **Mahathir Mohamad**, to propose an alternative East Asian Economic Grouping at the end
of the year, subsequently modified to an **East
Asian Economic Caucus** (EAEC).

The character of APEC changed as a result of
an initiative by US President Bill Clinton in July
1993 to hold a meeting of APEC's political leaders following a scheduled ministerial meeting
in Seattle in November. His grandiose scheme
to use APEC as the prime vehicle for creating a
so-called 'New Pacific Community' was greeted
without enthusiasm by ASEAN governments,
while Dr Mahathir took particular offence and
boycotted the meeting. In the event, the summit
passed off without incident but failed to rise
above declaratory commitments on trade liberalization. However, it did mark a qualitative
change in the structure and intended role of
APEC because President **Suharto** agreed to host
a second summit in Indonesia in the following
year which has set an annual pattern. In Bogor
in November 1994, the members of APEC agreed
on a two-step approach to free and open trade
and investment in the region by 2020. Industrialized economies were to achieve that target
by 2010 and developing economies by 2020.
Much of the impetus for an accord on general
principles came from the host government of
President Suharto, which saw the occasion as an
opportunity to demonstrate the international
standing of Indonesia while chair of the Non-
Aligned Movement. Once again, the only openly
discordant note was struck by Malaysia's prime
minister, Dr Mahathir Mohamad, who attended
the meeting but issued reservations to the effect
that his government would commit itself to
trade liberalization on a unilateral basis only
at a pace and capacity commensurate with
Malaysia's level of development. Private reservations about the pace of trade liberalization are
more widely shared within ASEAN because of
concerns about the vulnerability of national
markets to seemingly unfair competition. At
Osaka in November 1995, the Bogor Action
Agenda was reaffirmed but also qualified by
provision for flexibility "in the liberalization
and facilitation process" to take account of the
different levels of development and diverse circumstances in APEC economies. No substantive progress was made at the meeting at Subic

Bay in the Philippines in November 1996, while the meeting in Vancouver in November 1997 was dominated by the Asian economic crisis and revealed the limitations of APEC whose leaders acknowledged the central role of the International Monetary Fund. Plans were made for liberalizing trade in nine sectors but there was an impasse at the meeting in Kuala Lumpur in November 1998 over fast-track liberalization. The meeting in Auckland in September 1999 confined itself to reaffirming the guiding principles of the forum. The meeting in 1997 had admitted Peru, Russia and Vietnam to membership but also imposed a ten-year moratorium on new entries. By the end of the century, in addition to the seven ASEAN states listed above, the members of APEC were Australia, Canada, Chile, China, Hong Kong, Japan, South Korea, Mexico, New Zealand, Papua New Guinea, Peru, Russia, Taiwan and the United States.
*see also:* AFTA; ASEAN; East Asian Economic Caucus; Mahathir Mohamad, Suharto.

## Aquino, Benigno (Philippines)

Benigno (popularly known as Ninoy) Aquino was the most prominent and effective opposition leader during the first decade of President **Ferdinand Marcos**'s authoritarian rule. He was imprisoned on the introduction of martial law in September 1972 and remained in detention until the end of the decade, when he was allowed to travel to the United States for heart surgery. After recovery, he remained in the United States as a rallying point for political dissent. He returned to the Philippines in August 1983, driven by a concern to sustain his political appeal and encouraged by evidence that Marcos was mortally ill. Aquino arrived at Manila airport on 21 August and was taken off the plane by armed members of the Aviation Security Command, one of whom shot him in the head as he was being led down stairs from the exit to the runway and a waiting car (see **Fabian Ver**). His blatant murder served to transform the political condition of the Philippines by arousing great popular anger against President Marcos and his regime. The assassination marked a political turning-point which led directly to the collapse of Marcos's

rule following fraudulent elections in February 1986.

Benigno Aquino was born on 27 November 1932 into an elite landowning family from Tarlac Province, north of Manila. His father had been a member of the prewar Senate and controversially the speaker of the Legislative Assembly set up under the Japanese occupation. Aquino first made his mark as a journalist for the *Manila Times* at the age of 17 when he covered the Korean War. Then after qualifying as a lawyer, he married Corazón Cojuangco, a member of an immensely wealthy Sino-Philippine family (see **Corazón Aquino**). He entered politics in 1955 and secured election as Mayor of Tarlac but was then disqualified for being below the minimum age of 23. Two years later, he successfully contested the office of vice-governor of the province and became governor at the age of 27 when the incumbent joined the national cabinet. Over the next five years, Aquino acquired a national reputation as a capable administrator. In 1967 he stood successfully for the Senate but was obliged to win a court case to hold on to his seat because he had reached the minimum age of 35 only on taking the oath of office after the elections had taken place. In the Senate, Aquino became a vigorous opponent of Marcos, who had been president for two years. He was returned to the Senate for a second term in 1971 and was regarded as the politician most likely to succeed Marcos, who was permitted to serve only two terms under the Philippine Constitution. In September 1972 Marcos declared martial law in an attempt to retain power. Aquino was then arrested and charged with murder and the illegal possession of fire-arms; he was ultimately sentenced to death by a military tribunal. In the event, he was executed in cold blood because his return to the Philippines in 1983 constituted a direct political threat to the decaying Marcos regime. Ironically, that execution served only to accelerate that decay.
*see also:* Aquino, Corazón; Marcos, Ferdinand; Ver, Fabian.

## Aquino, Corazón (Philippines)

Mrs Corazón Aquino was president of the Philippines from February 1986 until June 1992, when she gave up office without seeking re-election. She was born on 25 January 1933 into the extremely wealthy landowning Cojuangco family from Tarlac Province. She entered politics as a result of personal tragedy: her husband Benigno Aquino – whom she married in 1954 and by whom she had four children – had been murdered at Manila airport in August 1983 on his return from exile in the United States. As an aggrieved widow, she became politically active in challenging President **Ferdinand Marcos**, whom she held personally responsible for her husband's fate. When Marcos announced a snap election in late 1985, Corazón Aquino was persuaded to stand against him. That election was fraudulently conducted and provoked a military rebellion. The rebellion was on the point of being crushed when Church leaders mobilized massive popular support in Manila in Mrs Aquino's name (*see* **EDSA**; **Jaime Sin**). This display of so-called '**People Power**' together with US encouragement persuaded Marcos to go into exile. Mrs Aquino succeeded him as the first woman president of the republic.

As a political leader, Mrs Aquino suffered from the defects of her qualities. As the saintly widow of Benigno Aquino, she represented moral virtue. Indeed, the very lack of political experience and taint seemed to qualify her for high office. But in office, moral strength was translated into political weakness and indecisiveness. Mrs Aquino's prime achievement was in restoring constitutional democracy but she was never able to capitalize on her national standing to contain the political contention which followed and which obstructed any attempt to address deep-seated economic and social problems. Buffeted from both right and left, Corazón Aquino sought to lead through conciliation, which exposed her to charges of weakness and encouraged military challenges. The most serious of these took place in December 1989, when she was saved from political overthrow only by US military intervention. By that juncture, the high promise of her assumption of office had gone sour as she became identi-fied with vacillation and drift. Moreover, her personal credibility had been tainted by the financial malpractices of members of her family. She salvaged some of her initial reputation, however, when she kept her word in not seeking a second term of presidential office, through exploiting the letter of the constitution. Moreover, she was able to play an important role in determining the identity of her successor through public support for **Fidel Ramos**, who as chief of staff of the armed forces and then minister of defence had acted loyally to obstruct military coups against her. Out of office, Mrs Aquino has avoided political activity with the important exception of defending her democratic legacy against attempts by Presidents Fidel Ramos and **Joseph Estrada** to change the constitution for possible personal advantage.

*see also:* Aquino, Benigno; EDSA; Estrada, Joseph; Marcos, Ferdinand; People Power; Ramos, Fidel; Sin, Jaime.

## Archipelago Declaration 1957
(Indonesia)

On 13 December 1957 Indonesia's government unilaterally extended the breadth of its territorial waters from 3 to 12 nautical miles. Concurrently, it asserted the right to establish a system of linked straight baselines around the archipelago connecting the outermost points of its outermost islands. This claim to the same quality of jurisdiction over waters surrounding and intersecting the island constituents of the republic as applied to its territory was pressed by Professor **Mochtar Kusumaatmadja** at successive United Nations Conferences on the Law of the Sea from 1958. Indonesia's claim was conceded at the conclusion of the Third Conference in November 1982 and incorporated in the UN Convention on the Law of the Sea in return for rights of maritime passage through the archipelago also incorporated in the convention. In October 1999, in an indication of a renewed interest in protecting Indonesia's archipelagic interests, President Abdurrahman Wahid appointed a minister with special responsibility for maritime exploration, in addition to a minister of communications, to his cabinet.

*see also:* Mochtar Kusumaatmadja.

## ARF (Brunei/Burma(Myanmar)/Cambodia/Indonesia/Laos/Malaysia/Philippines/Singapore/Thailand/Vietnam) *see* ASEAN Regional Forum (ARF) 1994–.

## Arthit, General Kamlang-Ek (Thailand)

General Arthit held the post of commander-in-chief of the Thai army between 1982 and 1986. He was born on 31 August 1925 in Bangkok and was educated at the Chulachomklao Royal Military Academy. He achieved high military office through his role in helping to put down an abortive coup in April 1981. He became commander of the first military region around Bangkok and then army commander from September 1982. In that position, he demonstrated overweening political ambition but limited political acumen and was dismissed by the prime minister, **Prem Tinsulanond**, in May 1986 after strong suspicion that he had inspired the government's defeat in the Parliament. After retiring from the armed forces, Arthit went into politics and in May 1988 assumed the leadership of the Thai People's Party (*Puang Chon Chao Thai*), which included former **Democratic Soldiers**. Arthit stood successfully for Parliament in July 1988 and in August 1990 he was brought into the coalition government of the prime minister, **Chatichai Choonhavan**, as deputy prime minister. He and the prime minister were arrested by the military in February 1991 in the first successful coup mounted since 1977, precipitated in part by the appointment of Arthit to the additional post of deputy defence minister with some control over the budget and promotions. He was released from detention in March 1991 and allowed to travel abroad. In January 1992 Arthit resigned from the Thai People's Party and joined the air force-backed *Sammakkhi Tham*, which had a measure of success in inconclusive elections in March. Arthit was not involved directly in the political turmoil and violence in May 1992 sparked off by the appointment of former army commander-in-chief General **Suchinda Krapayoon** as non-elected prime minister. *Sammakkhi Tham* disintegrated with the collapse of the Suchinda government. He subsequently joined the **Chart Pattana** Party after its establishment in July 1992 and served from December 1994 until July 1995 as a deputy prime minister in the coalition government headed by **Chuan Leekpai**. Then, when Chart Pattana went into opposition, he ceased active political life.

*see also:* Chatichai Chunhavan; Chart Pattana; Chuan Leekpai; Democratic Soldiers; Prem Tinsulanond; Suchinda Krapayoon.

## ASA (Association of South-East Asia) 1961–7 (Malaya/Malaysia/Philippines/Thailand)

The Association of South-East Asia (ASA) was a short-lived experiment in regional co-operation established on 31 July 1961 in Bangkok between the governments of Malaya, the Philippines and Thailand. It was intended to offer an alternative approach to security to that provided by military alliances and especially by the ill-regarded **SEATO** (South-East Asia Treaty Organization). Its underlying rationale was that economic progress provided the foundation for political stability and the best guarantee for political independence. ASA foundered within two years without significant practical achievement, primarily because of a territorial dispute between the Philippines and Malaya over the **Philippines' Claim to Sabah**, a northern Borneo territory. The dispute was aggravated at ASA's expense because of the concurrent challenge of **Confrontation** by Indonesia, supported by the Philippines, to the legitimacy of Malaya's constitutional successor Malaysia. ASA was revived temporarily in March 1966 as Confrontation waned but was superseded in the following year, in a concession to Indonesia, by the new **ASEAN** (Association of South-East Asian Nations). ASEAN adopted the institutional structure and also the approach to security pioneered without success by ASA.

*see also:* ASEAN; Confrontation; Philippines' Claim to Sabah; SEATO.

## ASEAN (Association of South-East Asian Nations) 1967–
(Brunei/Burma(Myanmar)/Cambodia/Indonesia/Malaysia/Laos/Philippines/Singapore/Thailand/Vietnam)

The Association of South-East Asian Nations (ASEAN) was established on 8 August 1967 at a meeting in Bangkok of the foreign ministers of Indonesia, the Philippines, Singapore and Thailand and the deputy prime minister of Malaysia. Brunei joined in January 1984, Vietnam was admitted in July 1995, while Burma and

Laos entered in July 1997 but Cambodia's membership was delayed until April 1999. Although bound by common Cold War concerns, the initial objective of the founding members was to locate regional reconciliation (in the wake of Indonesia's **Confrontation** of Malaysia) within an institutionalized structure of relations. Under the terms of the **Bangkok Declaration 1967**, ASEAN's prime formal purpose was to promote economic and social cooperation but its underlying undeclared goal was political cooperation. That cooperation has expressed itself in an intra-mural practice of conflict avoidance and management and in a role as a diplomatic community on regional issues. The founding Declaration also indicated a prerogative aspiration to manage regional order, which was registered in a declaratory commitment by its foreign ministers in Kuala Lumpur in November 1971 to make South-East Asia a **ZOPFAN** (Zone of Peace, Freedom and Neutrality). That aspiration has not been realized, in important part because of the absence of a shared strategic perspective among members' governments.

A meagre performance in economic cooperation, an aversion to formal defence cooperation and only limited political cooperation made up the sum of ASEAN's record until the success of revolutionary communism in Indochina during 1975. Moreover, the viability of the Association had been tested in the late 1960s by the revival of the **Philippines Claim to Sabah**, a part of Malaysia. Its members responded to political change in Indochina by closing ranks and convening the first meeting of heads of government at the **Bali Summit** in February 1976. A formal commitment to political cooperation was expressed in a **Declaration of ASEAN Concord**, while provision for a norms-based regional order and for dispute settlement was contained in a **Treaty of Amity and Cooperation**. Defence cooperation under ASEAN's aegis was ruled out but sanctioned on a primarily bilateral basis outside of the walls of the Association. A second **Kuala Lumpur Summit** in August 1977 failed to generate an anticipated economic cooperation but attracted the presence of the Prime Ministers of Australia, New Zealand and Japan who began a practice of ASEAN Post-Ministerial Conferences with dialogue partners,

which has become institutionalized. Political cooperation among member governments was effectively displayed in the wake of Vietnam's invasion of Kampuchea (Cambodia) in December 1978. By employing their regional credentials and highlighting the sanctity of national sovereignty, the ASEAN states were able to deny legitimacy to the government conveyed into Phnom Penh by Vietnam's occupying army. During the 1980s, they attracted strong voting support in the General Assembly of the United Nations for an annual resolution calling for its military withdrawal from Cambodia, which took place from September 1989.

With the end of the Cold War and the attendant resolution of the Cambodian conflict as an international problem, ASEAN was faced with a new and uncertain strategic environment distinguished by a change in the pattern of international alignments that had sustained its collective diplomacy against Vietnam. It responded to the challenge by pioneering an historically unique multilateral security dialogue encompassing the Asia-Pacific. At its fourth **Singapore Summit** in January 1992, the heads of government agreed that security dialogue beyond conventional regional bounds could be undertaken through the vehicle of the Post-Ministerial Conference (PMC). A meeting of ASEAN's foreign ministers together with those from the United States, China, Russia and other regional states in Singapore in July 1993 agreed to inaugurate the **ASEAN Regional Forum** (ARF) as a wider vehicle for addressing security issues, which held its first working session in Bangkok in July 1994. ASEAN's successful ARF initiative demonstrated the political standing of the Association in the wake of the Cambodian conflict but it also indicated an abdication from a prerogative attitude to managing regional order based on excluding major powers from a superintending role. The Singapore Summit also saw a commitment to establishing an **AFTA** (ASEAN Free Trade Area) as well as an agreement to hold formal meetings of heads of government every three years.

Although ASEAN's foreign ministers were able to issue a **Declaration on the South China Sea** in Manila in July 1992, which called for peaceful resolution of jurisdictional disputes, the end of the Cold War and the attendant enlargement of the Association generated intra-mural discord as well as problems in external relations. Vietnam's entry in July 1995 was regarded as an historic reconciliation and uncontroversial. At the fifth **Bangkok Summit** in December 1995, a treaty was concluded on creating a **South-East Asia Nuclear Weapon-Free Zone** (SEANWFZ) as a contribution to ZOPFAN. It also took the initiative which led to the establishment of the **Asia–Europe Meeting** (ASEM), which held its first working session in Bangkok in March 1996. However, the entry of Burma (Myanmar) in July 1997 attracted strong criticism from Western states because of its deplorable human rights record with, for example, a disruption of dialogue with the states of the European Union. Additional controversy arose over the membership of Cambodia, which had also been expected to join in July 1997 close to the thirtieth anniversary of ASEAN's foundation. A bloody coup in Phnom Penh to the political advantage of Second Prime Minister **Hun Sen** just days before entry led the foreign ministers to defer Cambodia's membership. That issue proved to be contentious at the sixth **Hanoi Summit** in December 1998 and served to exemplify the greater difficulty in managing consensus within the enlarged Association. In the event, Cambodia was admitted to ASEAN in April 1999. The disarray within the Association has been generated also by the impact of regional economic adversity at the end of the century, which began with the devaluation of the Thai *baht* in July 1997. That impact had profound political consequences within Indonesia, in particular, which left the Association without a natural political leader. Indeed, Indonesia's contribution to ASEAN had been a conspicuous rejection of past hegemonic ambitions and a willingness to defer to the strategic priorities of other members, exemplified in the case of Thailand during the Cambodian conflict, in the interests of regional harmony. ASEAN at the beginning of the twenty-first century is not the same organization as that set up in 1967 with a commitment to regional reconciliation and a shared anti-communist agenda. It remains an institutional going-concern but with enlarge-ment to ten members has lost a collective sense of common purpose exemplified in its institutional paralysis over intervention in **East Timor**.

ASEAN is an intergovernmental body without aspirations to political integration of the kind associated with the European Union. A permanent secretariat was set up in Jakarta in June 1976 with limited service functions. The title of its principal administrative officer was secretary-general of the ASEAN Secretariat *not* of ASEAN, for over a decade and a half until redesignated secretary-general of ASEAN at the Singapore Summit in January 1992. The office of secretary-general rotates among member states. In January 1998, former Philippine foreign affairs undersecretary, Rodolfo Severino, assumed the office for a five-year term. ASEAN's principal organ is an annual meeting of foreign ministers serviced by a prior meeting of senior officials. With the addition of annual informal summits to the triennial formal meetings, the role of heads of government has become more significant. Day-to-day business is in the hands of a Standing Committee located in the capital of the country hosting the next meeting of foreign ministers and presided over by its incumbent and attended also by the heads of ASEAN diplomatic missions.

*see also:* AFTA; ASA; Asia–Europe Meeting; ASEAN Regional Forum; Bali Summit 1976; Bangkok Declaration 1967; Bangkok Summit 1995; Confrontation; Declaration of ASEAN Concord 1976; Declaration on the South China Sea; East Timor; Hanoi Summit 1998; Hun Sen; Kuala Lumpur Summit 1977; Philippines Claim to Sabah; Singapore Summit 1992; Treaty of Amity and Cooperation 1976; South-East Asia Nuclear Weapon-Free Zone (SEANWFZ) 1995; ZOPFAN 1971.

## ASEAN Regional Forum (ARF) 1994–
(Brunei/Burma(Myanmar)/Cambodia/ Indonesia/Laos/Malaysia/Philippines/ Singapore/Thailand/Vietnam)

The ASEAN Regional Forum is an embryonic structure for multilateral security dialogue with the participation of twenty-three states which was established at the initiative of **ASEAN** during the annual meeting of its foreign ministers held in Singapore in July 1993. Its prime function is confidence-building and not conventional defence cooperation. At its **Singapore Summit** in January 1992, ASEAN's heads of government had agreed that security dialogue beyond conventional regional bounds could be undertaken through the vehicle of the Post-Ministerial Conference (PMC). This conference, which convenes immediately after the annual meeting of foreign ministers, then involved seven dialogue partners: Australia, Canada, the European Union, Japan, New Zealand, South Korea and the United States. At Singapore's initiative and with backing from its regional partners, an unprecedented meeting of senior officials from ASEAN states and their dialogue partners was convened on the island in May 1993. It was agreed to invite the foreign ministers of China, Russia, Vietnam, Laos and Papua New Guinea (the latter three as signatories of ASEAN's **Treaty of Amity and Cooperation**) to a special meeting in Singapore in July 1993 concurrent with that of ASEAN's foreign ministers and their dialogue partners. The declared purpose was 'for ASEAN and its dialogue partners to work with other regional states to evolve a predictable and constructive pattern of relationships in Asia-Pacific'. However, the more practical purposes were to encourage the post-Cold War regional security commitment of the United States and the international good citizenship of an irredentist China.

At the inaugural dinner meeting in July, it was decided that the ARF would convene formally in Bangkok in July 1994, to be preceded by a meeting of senior officials. At the first working session, only three hours were allocated for substantive discussion but it was agreed to reconvene the Forum on an annual basis and to endorse the purposes and principles of ASEAN's Treaty of Amity and Cooperation as a code of conduct for regional relations. At the second session in Brunei in August 1995, a 'concept paper' was endorsed in the chairman's statement, which affirmed that the ARF should adopt an evolutionary approach at a pace comfortable to all participants moving in stages from the promotion of confidence-building, development of preventive diplomacy and elaboration of approaches to conflict; the latter a concession to China's objection to conflict resolution. Apart from its annual meetings of senior officials and foreign ministers, the ARF works through inter-sessional meetings, the most important of which is the Inter-Sessional Support Group on Confidence Building which reports to the annual working meeting. At its annual meeting in Kuala Lumpur in July 1997, the ARF agreed to address preventive diplomacy where it overlapped with confidence-building but the outcome has been a cosmetic exercise, so far, while confidence-building measures have not progressed beyond a primitive level. Nonetheless, the ARF has maintained a cordial tone, which has been reflective of an underlying accommodation between the United States and China. The title of the security dialogue is indicative of the diplomatic centrality of ASEAN, which has been concerned to uphold its international standing with the establishment of a structure of relations involving all the major powers. Despite objections from some Western states to ASEAN's claim to be the 'prime driving force' of the ARF as iterated in the concept paper, rivals of the United States such as China, India and Russia have supported ASEAN's diplomatic assertiveness. The annual sessions of the ARF are held in the capital where ASEAN's annual meeting of foreign ministers convenes and is chaired by the appropriate incumbent, while all inter-sessional meetings are co-chaired by an ASEAN member. Apart from ASEAN founding members, Cambodia became a participant in August 1995 and Burma in July 1996. In addition to all ASEAN states listed above, the participants in the ARF comprise: Australia, Canada, China, European Union, India, Japan, Mongolia, New Zealand, Papua New Guinea, Russia, South Korea and the United States. North Korea became a member in July 2000.

see also: ASEAN; Singapore Summit 1992; Treaty of Amity and Cooperation 1976.

## Asia–Europe Meeting (ASEM) 1996–
(Brunei/Indonesia/Malaysia/Philippines/
Singapore/Thailand/Vietnam)

The Asia–Europe Meeting was established at a meeting of heads of government in Bangkok in March 1996 where it was agreed to continue the inter-governmental dialogue on a biannual

basis. A second meeting convened in London in April 1998 and a third in Seoul in October 2000. The initiative came from Singapore's Prime Minister, **Goh Chok Tong**, who was conscious of the lack of a third structure of global dialogue to that between the United States and Europe and the United States and Asia. He was also keen to encourage greater European investment and a greater political interest in the region to counter the influence of China and the United States. He received ready support from **ASEAN** partners, especially Malaysia whose prime minister, Dr **Mahathir Mohamad**, recognized a correspondence between the Asian composition of the dialogue, including China, Japan and South Korea as well as ASEAN states, and his proposal for an **East Asian Economic Caucus**. In that respect, the distinguishing feature of ASEM was the absence of the United States, which had staked a claim to the leadership of **APEC** at a meeting of heads of government on Blake Island in 1993. At its first working session, the buoyancy of the Asian economic situation provided a nexus for dialogue but in London in 1998 economic adversity interposed to weaken it. ASEAN membership has been limited with a line drawn after the admission of Vietnam, partly to avoid controversy over Burma.
see also: APEC; ASEAN; East Asian Economic Caucus; Goh Chok Tong; Mahathir Mohamad.

## Asian–African Conference, Bandung 1955 (Indonesia)

An unprecedented conference of representatives from twenty-nine Asian and African states took place 18–24 April 1955 in the Indonesian city of Bandung. The initiative for calling the meeting rested with Indonesia's prime minister, **Ali Sastroamijoyo**, who raised the idea at a gathering of five Asian prime ministers in Colombo in April 1954 at a time of growing international concern at the prospect of US military intervention in Indochina. A key factor in convening the conference was the opportunity seen by India's prime minister, Jawaharl al Nehru, of using the occasion to welcome the People's Republic of China into the comity of Asian and African states. In the event, Sino-Indian tensions were exposed by the conference but the occasion was significant for being the

first time that post-colonial states had come together to register their own international agenda. Colonialism in all its manifestations was denounced as an evil. The Bandung Conference gave its name to a new spirit of international conciliation in the context of the Cold War and to that extent was a stage in the emergence of the Non-Aligned Movement. The initiative failed to assume institutionalized form. Moreover, the participation of China excluded the Asian-African undertaking from the mainstream of non-alignment, while an attempt to convene a second meeting in Algeria in June 1965 with a greater African participation had to be called off because of the military coup which brought Colonel Boumedienne to power. The so-called Afro-Asian Movement was accordingly discredited, while President **Sukarno** of Indonesia was more interested in convening a conference of the more radical **New Emerging Forces**. Nonetheless, the Bandung Conference enjoys an honoured place in Indonesia's history and in 1985 President **Suharto** convened a thirtieth anniversary meeting as a way of registering his country's restored international standing.
see also: New Emerging Forces; Sastroamijoyo, Ali; Suharto; Sukarno.

## Asri, Datuk Mohamad Muda
(Malaya/Malaysia)

Datuk Mohamad Asri was a prominent figure in *Parti Islam Se-Malaysia* (PAS) and Malayan/Malaysian politics for a quarter of a century. He was born on 10 October 1923 in Kota Bharu, Kelantan, and received only a basic Malay education. He became alternately a schoolteacher and journalist in the Malay medium. After the Pacific War, Datuk Asri became involved in radical Malay politics, inspired by Islamic modernism and the success of revolutionary nationalism in Indonesia. He joined PAS in 1953 and rose rapidly in its organization, playing a major role in its electoral achievement in 1959 in capturing the state government in Kelantan. Datuk Asri was elected to both state and federal seats during successive elections from 1959 to 1974 and became president of PAS and chief minister of Kelantan in 1964. When PAS joined the **Barisan Nasional** (National Front) in January 1973, Asri gave up his state office to become federal minister for lands and special functions. The political association was short-lived, however, and **UMNO** (United Malays National Organization) displaced PAS in Kelantan in elections in March 1978. The subsequent consolidation of UMNO's position following the succession of Dr **Mahathir Mohamad** as its leader and prime minister in 1981 led to tensions within PAS which were aggravated when **Anwar Ibrahim**, head of **ABIM**, the Islamic Youth Movement of Malaysia, entered Parliament in UMNO's interest in April 1982. Datuk Asri was forced from the presidency of PAS in October 1982 by a younger generation of party members disappointed by his lack of political achievement. He subsequentlyfounded *Parti Hisbul Muslimin Malaysia (Hamim)* but failed to make any political impact with it on its own. He joined it to *Angkatan Perpaduan Ummah* (Muslim Unity Front), which included PAS, to contest general elections in October 1990 but without individual success, despite the Front's victory in Kelantan.

see also: ABIM; *Angkatan Perpaduan Ummah*; Anwar Ibrahim; *Barisan Nasional*; Mahathir Mohamad, Datuk Sri; *Parti Islam Se-Malaysia*; UMNO.

## Association of Indonesian Muslim Intellectuals  (Indonesia) *see* ICMI.

## August Revolution 1945  (Vietnam)

The August Revolution describes the seizure of power in Hanoi on 19 August 1945 by armed units of the Communist-led **Viet Minh** in the wake of Japan's surrender four days before. Although short-lived, this seizure of power marked the beginning of a national revolution which was not fully realized until April 1975. Japan's military occupation of Indochina from 1940 did not displace French colonial administration, which remained subject to the nominal authority of the government in Vichy. The reversal of its military fortunes prompted the Japanese to remove French administration by force on 9 March 1945 and to sponsor independence in Indochina, in the case of Vietnam under the leadership of Emperor **Bao Dai**. Japan's surrender to the Allies on 15 August cre-

ated a political vacuum which the Viet Minh filled. On 25 August they secured Bao Dai's abdication and his acceptance of the post of supreme political adviser in a provisional government established on 28 August. The Communist leader **Ho Chi Minh** reached Hanoi on 30 August and proclaimed the independence of the Democratic Republic of Vietnam on 2 September. His statement included extracts from the US declaration of independence in an abortive attempt to attract international recognition, while the French set about trying to restore their colonial position. Viet Minh rule was displaced from 9 September as Chinese troops began occupying Vietnam down to the 16th parallel of latitude under an agreement among the Allies to take the surrender of Japanese forces. On 28 February 1946 a Sino-French treaty provided for the return of French troops. Britain had assumed responsibility for the surrender of Japanese troops south of the 16th parallel. Its local commander, General Gracey, faced with the Viet Minh challenge, armed French prisoners of war and thus enabled it to be contained. French troops returned to the south in October 1945. Negotiations between the Viet Minh and the French broke down at the end of 1946 and armed conflict ensued in two stages until the unification of Vietnam in April 1975.

see also: Bao Dai; Ho Chi Minh; Viet Minh.

## Aung San  (Burma/Myanmar)

Aung San is the acknowledged father of Burmese nationalism whose life was cut short by assassination in July 1947 before independence was obtained from Britain. He was born in 1915 in Magwe district and rose to prominence as a radical nationalist student leader in Rangoon during the 1930s. In 1939 he founded the Communist Party of Burma and the next year left the country by ship with the intention of making contact with the Communist Party of China. He arrived in Japanese-occupied Amoy from where he was sent to Tokyo to enjoy the patronage of the military government. In 1941 Aung San returned secretly to Burma to recruit contemporaries for military training in Japan. Aung San led twenty-eight comrades out of an initial thirty back to Burma with the Japanese army when it invaded the country from Thailand in December 1941. Aung San proceded to establish the Burma Independence Army, which fought alongside the Japanese. Political tensions arose, however, when it became evident to the Burmese nationalists that the independence granted by the Japanese in August 1943 was spurious. Links were then established with the Allies and in March 1945 the reorganized Burma National Army under Aung San declared war against the Japanese, attracting recognition from the Supreme Allied Commander in South-East Asia, Lord Louis Mountbatten (see **South-East Asia Command**). After the end of hostilities, Aung San led the **Anti-Fascist People's Freedom League** (AFPFL) in the political struggle for independence stiffened by a paramilitary force. In this role, he came to enjoy the support of Mountbatten, who used his influential position to urge the British government to make concessions to the young nationalist leader. On 27 January 1947 Aung San signed an agreement in London with the prime minister, Clement Attlee, which promised full independence within a year. Despite acute factional divisions within the Burmese nationalist movement as well as the competing interests of apprehensive ethnic minorities, Aung San appeared to enjoy sufficient confidence to set up a viable Union of Burma with a federal constitution. On the morning of 19 July 1947, however, while the provisional cabinet was in session, a group of armed men burst into the room and sprayed it with machine-gun bullets. Aung San, then only 32, was killed together with six of his ministerial colleagues. He had been murdered on the instructions of a political rival, U Saw, who was subsequently tried, convicted and hanged. Aung San was succeeded by his deputy **U Nu**, who negotiated the eventual independence of Burma on 4 January 1948. Aung San has since been revered as the outstanding figure in the pantheon of Burmese nationalism, a status which has helped his daughter, **Aung San Suu Kyi**, in her persistent political resistance against the ruling military government in Rangoon.

see also: Anti-Fascist People's Freedom League; Aung San Suu Kyi; Nu, U; South-East Asia Command 1943–6.

## Aung San Suu Kyi (Burma/Myanmar)

Aung San Suu Kyi has been the most credible opposition leader to have challenged military rule in Burma since its establishment in 1962. Aung San Suu Kyi is the daughter of the legendary leader and martyr of Burma's independence movement, **Aung San**. He was assassinated in July 1947 when she was only 2 years old, having been born on 19 June 1945. She left Burma at the age of 15 to study abroad and eventually married a British citizen and settled in Oxford. Aung San Suu Kyi returned to Burma in April 1988 to nurse her ailing mother. By then, popular unrest against the military regime established by General **Ne Win** had attained a strong momentum. She quickly assumed a leading role in political challenge, attracting support because of lineage and personal qualities. After a bloody confrontation on the streets in August and September 1988, the military reasserted control but also promised free elections. Aung San Suu Kyi and supporters then formed the **National League for Democracy**, which became the foremost opposition party attracting widespread popular backing. She became its main asset, able to mobilize tens of thousands in rallies against the martial law regime. On 19 July 1989, the anniversary of her father's death, celebrated as Martyr's Day, she cancelled marches and a rally because of the prospect of another bloodletting. The next day, Aung San Suu Kyi was placed under house arrest for 'endangering the state' and thousands of her party members were arrested. She then embarked on a hunger strike which raised the political temperature for a time. When she called off the strike, the military regime was granted a political reprieve because there was no other figure in the country with the courage to face up to the ruthless intimidation of the armed forces. The National League for Democracy achieved an overwhelming victory in elections called by the military regime in May 1990 while Aung San Suu Kyi remained incarcerated. The ruling **State Law and Order Restoration Council** (SLORC) set up in September 1988 refused to accept the outcome of the elections and agreed to release Aung San Suu Kyi only if she gave up her political beliefs and left the country, which she has refused to do. In September 1991 Aung San Suu Kyi was awarded the Nobel Peace Prize for her non-violent struggle for democracy and human rights. She has been allowed limited family visits and in February 1994 was permitted to receive a visit from US Congressman William Richardson. But the effective head of Burma's military junta, Lt-General **Khin Nyunt**, refused to provide an indication of her likely release after describing Aung San Suu Kyi's attitude as negative and counter-productive. Mr Richardson was refused a second visit in May 1995. Therefore it was with some surprise that Aung San Suu Kyi was released from detention on 10 July 1995. No conditions were imposed formally on her release but Aung San Suu Kyi pointed out: 'I have been released, that's all. . . . The situation has not changed in any other ways.' SLORC has not faced a renewed challenge to its rule as a result of her release from house arrest. Moreover, its leaders have refused to engage in political dialogue with her. The negative attitude of the military government did not change when SLORC dissolved itself to re-appear under new nomenclature as the **State Peace and Development Council** (SPDC) in November 1997. Its lack of compassion was displayed in early 1999 when Aung San Suu Kyi's English husband, Michael Aris, terminally ill with cancer, was refused a visa to visit his wife in Rangoon. He died in March 1999. In July 1999, she was denounced in the official press as a traitor who should be driven out of the country. She remains a symbol of the lack of legitimacy of the military regime. In April 2000, in a videotape delivered to the United Nations Human Rights Commission, she maintained that government oppression had worsened greatly on a scale that the world had not yet grasped. In September 2000, she was forcibly detained and returned to house arrest in Rangoon after attempting to leave the capital to visit NLD party workers.

*see also:* Aung San; Khin Nyunt; National League for Democracy; Ne Win; State Law and Order Restoration Council; State Peace and Development Council.

## Azahari, A. M. (Brunei)

A. M. Azahari was the leader of the **People's Party** (*Partai Ra'ayat*) of Brunei, which has been banned in the sultanate since it mounted a revolt in December 1962. He was born on the island of Labuan in 1928 of Arab-Malay parents. During the Japanese occupation, he was sent t o study veterinary science in Indonesia. He participated in the national revolution against the Dutch, returning to Brunei in 1952. He then became involved in a series of unsuccessful business ventures before turning to politics in 1956. He founded the People's Party, which was modelled on a radical Malayan equivalent and attracted considerable support from among Brunei Malays. In April 1962 as a nominated member of the Legislative Council, he failed to secure passage of a motion seeking to restore Brunei's sovereignty over northern Borneo. He then went into exile to Johor Bahru in Malaya where he campaigned against Brunei's membership of the proposed Federation of Malaysia. He was in the Philippines in December 1962 at the time of the **Brunei Revolt** and took refuge in the Indonesian Embassy after its failure. He was not allocated any public role during Indonesia's **Confrontation** of Malaysia. He is believed to have resided in the Indonesian town of Bogor, constrained by the government of Jakarta from engaging in political activity, especially after Brunei became independent and a member of **ASEAN** in January 1984.

*see also:* ASEAN; Brunei Revolt 1962; Confrontation; People's Party.

# B

**Badawi, Abdullah Ahmad** (Malaysia)
Abdullah Ahmad Badawi was appointed deputy prime minister and minister of home affairs in January 1999 in the wake of the dismissal of **Anwar Ibrahim** from high office in the previous September. In those portfolios, he demonstrated consistent loyalty to Prime Minister **Mahathir Mohamad**, against whom he had been aligned politically during the late 1980s. Abdullah Ahmad Badawi was born in Penang on 26 November 1939 and was educated at the University of Malaya. He was first elected to Parliament in 1974 and was appointed a minister in the prime minister's department in 1982. He served subsequently as minister of education and of defence but was dismissed from the cabinet in 1987 because of his identification with a dissident wing within **UMNO** led by former minister of trade and industry, **Tengku Razaleigh Hamzah**. Badawi did not sever his formal affiliation to UMNO and was a successful parliamentary candidate in its interest in October 1990. Moreover, he demonstrated his personal standing within UMNO by securing election to one of the three senior posts of party vice-president but behind his main rival Anwar Ibrahim, who was promoted from education to finance on Badawi's return to the cabinet as foreign minister in March 1991. He was reappointed to that office in May 1995. As deputy prime minister, he has been acknowledged by Dr Mahathir as his likely political successor and commands general support because of his reputation as 'a safe pair of hands', rather than as a dynamic leader. He was elected unopposed to the office of deputy president of UMNO in May 2000, confirming his earlier appointment by UMNO's Supreme Council and the prospect of his succession both to party leadership and to the office of prime minister.
see also: Anwar Ibrahim; Mahathir Mohamad; Razaleigh Hamzah, Tengku; UMNO.

## *BAKORSTANAS* (Indonesia)
*BAKORSTANAS*, which is an acronym drawn from *Badan Koordinasi Bantuan Pemantapan* *Stabilitas Nasional* (Coordinating Body for the Enforcement of National Stability), was established as a so-called non-structural organization on 5 September 1988 by presidential decree. The following day the armed forces commander, General **Try Sutrisno**, was appointed its head. It was made clear, however, that *BAKORSTANAS* was under the direct command of President **Suharto**. State secretary Murdiono declared its primary task to be the coordination of efforts among departments and other government agencies so as to restore, maintain and consolidate national stability. It was apparent, however, that the agency was little more than a political device designed to reduce further the power of the former armed forces commander and then minister of defence, General **L. B. Murdani**, from whom President Suharto had become estranged. Benny Murdani had been relieved of his military command earlier in the year but had retained the office of head of *KOPKAMTIB*, the Operational Command for the Restoration of Security and Order, which had enjoyed extraordinary powers ever since it had been established in 1966. *KOPKAMTIB* was dissolved on 5 September 1988 under a presidential decree on the establishment of *BAKORSTANAS*. The following day General Murdani was discharged as *KOPKAMTIB* commander and General Sutrisno appointed to head the new agency. Its terms of reference were such as to enable President Suharto to give *BAKORSTANAS* a key security role should he deem it appropriate. With his resignation from high office in May 1998, the organization became defunct. It was dissolved by President **Abdurrahman Wahid** in March 2000.
see also: KOPKAMTIB; Murdani, L. B.; Suharto; Sutrisno, Try; Wahid, Abdurrahman.

## Bali Summit (ASEAN) 1976 (Indonesia/ Malaysia/Philippines/ Singapore/ Thailand)
The first meeting of heads of government of **ASEAN** (Association of South-East Asian Nations) took place on the island of Bali in

February 1976. It was significant as a display of solidarity and collective nerve in the close wake of the success of revolutionary communism in Indochina and also because it registered a political role for ASEAN after nearly a decade of unconvincing claims of interest in only economic and social cooperation. That role was defined in a **Declaration of ASEAN Concord 1976** whose objectives and principles were designed to promote political stability within member states and also within South-East Asia. The declaration reaffirmed a commitment to a regional **ZOPFAN** (Zone of Peace, Freedom and Neutrality). In addition, the member governments concluded a **Treaty of Amity and Cooperation** which included machinery for regional dispute settlement and made provision for accession to it by non-members. To that extent, the treaty represented a political opening to the revolutionary states of Indochina and an attempt to interest them in a common code of conduct as a basis for regional order. The initial response was negative and it was only after the end of the Cold War and the formal settlement of the Cambodian conflict that Vietnam and Laos indicated a willingness to adhere to the treaty, which occurred at an ASEAN ministerial meeting in Manila in July 1992. The Bali Summit was significant also for an agreement to establish a secretariat to be based in Jakarta as well as for excluding defence cooperation from within the walls of the Association.

see also: ASEAN; Declaration of ASEAN Concord 1976; Treaty of Amity and Cooperation 1976; ZOPFAN.

## Baling Talks 1955  (Malaya)

A meeting was held in December 1955 in the Malayan town of Baling close to the Thai border at the initiative of **Chin Peng**, the leader of the Communist Party of Malaya, which had mounted an armed insurrection from 1948. He had offered to negotiate with **Tunku Abdul Rahman**, chief minister of Malaya, and **David Marshall**, chief minister of Singapore, both of whom owed their positions to general elections. Tunku Abdul Rahman had declared an amnesty for all insurgents but the talks failed because Chin Peng's demand that the Communist Party

be made legal was rejected. His initiative reflected the international Communist reorientation to peaceful coexistence as well as the slackening momentum of insurgency. The **Emergency**, as it was generally known, continued officially until 1960, even though Malaya became fully independent in 1957 and Singapore self-governing in 1959. The insurgency continued in sporadic form beyond 1960, but the Baling Talks marked a turning-point after which the Communist challenge lost its initial force.

see also: Chin Peng; Emergency 1948–60; Marshall, David; Rahman, Tunku Abdul.

## Ban Me Thuot Offensive 1975  (Vietnam)

A successful attack on the town of Ban Me Thuot in the central highlands of Vietnam was launched on 10 March 1975 by the army of North Vietnam. It precipitated the rout of southern forces and their total defeat by the end of April. On the morning of 11 March, President **Nguyen Van Thieu** made the fateful decision to abandon all of the highlands (except the Ban Me Thuot region) and to hold only the coastal cities in the centre of the country. The outcome was a military catastrophe as the withdrawal generated panic and chaos and the virtual disintegration of the southern army, which its northern adversary exploited by revising the timetable for seizing Saigon and bringing the **Vietnam War** to a speedy conclusion.

see also: Thieu, Nguyen Van; Vietnam War.

## Bandung Conference 1955  see Asian-African Conference, Bandung 1955.

## Bangkok Declaration (ASEAN) 1967  (Indonesia/Malaysia/Philippines/Singapore/Thailand)

The founding document of **ASEAN** (Association of South-East Asian Nations) was promulgated in the Thai capital on 8 August 1967. The Bangkok Declaration's prime formal commitment was to accelerate economic growth, social progress and cultural development in the region. However, a proprietary aspiration in the preamble affirmed 'that the countries of South-East Asia share a primary responsibility for strengthening the economic and social stability of the region and ensuring their peaceful progressive national development, and that they are determined to ensure their stability and security from external interference in any form or manifestation in order to preserve their national identities in accordance with the ideals and aspirations of their peoples'. That proprietary aspiration with security in mind was given formal content in a declaration by ASEAN's foreign ministers in November 1971 to secure the recognition and respect for South-East Asia as a **ZOPFAN**, a Zone of Peace, Freedom and Neutrality. The commitment to a ZOPFAN was reaffirmed in the **Declaration of ASEAN Concord** at its first summit in February 1976 but the goal has never been realized in practical terms.

see also: ASEAN; Bali Summit 1976; Declaration of ASEAN Concord 1976; ZOPFAN.

## Bangkok Summit (ASEAN) 1995
(Brunei/Burma (Myanmar)/Cambodia/ Indonesia/Laos/Malaysia/Philippines/ Singapore/Thailand/Vietnam)
The fifth meeting of **ASEAN**'s heads of government convened in the Thai capital in mid-December 1995. The meeting was notable for the attendance of the Prime Minister of Vietnam as the representative of the first communist member following his country's entry in the previous July. Present also were heads of government of Cambodia and Laos, with observer status, and that of Burma as a guest, making it the first occasion at which all ten South-East Asian governments had been so represented. A corresponding commitment was made to enlarge the Association to include all the states of South-East Asia by the year 2000. An accord was reached on removing all tariff barriers within the ASEAN Free Trade Area (**AFTA**) by 2003 and a treaty was concluded with the object of establishing a **South-East Asia Nuclear Weapon-Free Zone (SEANWFZ)**.
see also: AFTA; ASEAN; SEANWFZ.

## Banharn Silpa-archa (Thailand)
Banharn Silpa-archa was prime minister of Thailand between July 1995 and November 1996. He led the **Chart Thai Party** (Thai National Party) to victory with the largest number of seats in elections in July 1995 and formed a seven-party coalition, which broke up over political spoils in September 1996 and lost office after elections in November 1996. Banharn Silpa-archa was born on 20 July 1932 in Suphanburi in central Thailand of Chinese immigrant parents. He was educated initially at Bangkok Business College and started working life as an office boy. He entered politics as a member of the municipal assembly for Suphanburi in 1974 at the inception of the Chart Thai Party, which was partly based on provincial business networks. Banharn had already established a strong local base through public benefaction from wealth accumulated from his success in the construction industry. He rose quickly to the office of deputy secretary-general of his party and entered the national parliament in its interest in 1976. He held a number of ministerial appointments during the 1980s, including the agriculture, communications and finance portfolios, and enjoyed a reputation as a political fixer and an exponent of 'money politics'. Banharn was the subject of an inconclusive investigation by an anti-corruption committee after his party was removed from government by a military coup in 1991. He sought to demonstrate a seriousness of mind by studying law but, in office, was accused of plagiarizing his master's thesis. He took over the leadership of the Chart Thai Party in May 1994 after the resignation of a caretaker leader who had assumed the position following the defection of former prime minister **Chatichai Choonhavan**. After a significant electoral set-back in November 1996, Banharn took his party into opposition but then negotiated its entry into a coalition government headed by **Chuan Leekpai**, which was formed in Nov-ember 1997. Banharn has remained in parliament but has not held cabinet office since resigning as prime minister. He has remained an influential political fixer and is said to run his party with an iron fist.
see also: Chart Thai Party; Chatichai Choonhavan; Chuan Leekpai.

## Bank Bumiputera Crisis (Malaysia)
In September 1984 Malaysia's minister of finance, **Daim Zainuddin**, announced that Petronas, the national oil company, had assumed financial responsibility for Bank Bumiputera, the country's

largest bank, in a multi-million dollar rescue operation. Bank Bumiputera had been created as a prime vehicle for promoting the **New Economic Policy** launched at the outset of the 1970s in order to redress the balance of material advantage between the indigenous Malays (*Bumiputera*) and the non-Malays of migrant origin. Bank Bumiputera had established a subsidiary company in Hong Kong called Bumiputera Malaysia Finance Ltd. This subsidiary engaged in speculative involvement in the territory's property market between 1979 and 1983 through loans to the Chinese-owned Carrian Group of companies, whose chairman was George Tan. These loans were placed in serious jeopardy with the collapse of the property market and the Carrian Group, which exposed not only Bumiputera Malaysia Finance Ltd but the parent Bank Bumiputera. The consequence was effectively to wipe out its total capital and reserves. The issue became a national scandal because the nature of the speculative involvement, through a Hong Kong Chinese company, had violated the spirit and purpose of the New Economic Policy. It also gave rise to accusations that the abortive undertaking was riddled with personal and political corruption; two deaths in Hong Kong in suspicious circumstances were linked to the episode. Criminal proceedings in Hong Kong continued into the 1990s without giving rise to a satisfactory account of the episode or to an adequate explanation of its Malaysian dimension, involving **UMNO** (United Malays National Organization) and its leadership.

see also: *Bumiputera*; Daim Zainuddin; New Economic Policy; UMNO.

## Bao Dai, Emperor (Vietnam)
Bao Dai was the last emperor of Annam, the central part of Vietnam, which became a French protectorate in 1874. Although never more than a figurehead, he was of political significance from 1940 until 1955 because of his successive collaboration with the Japanese, the **Viet Minh**, the French and finally the anti-communist nationalists who deposed him. His genuine attempts at political reform never bore fruit. Bao Dai was born in Hue, October 1913, the son of the Emperor Khai Din, and ascended the throne in January 1926 on the death of his father. He was denied a political role by the French but in March 1945 proclaimed Vietnam's independence under Japanese auspices. With their surrender to the allies and the **August Revolution**, he was persuaded to abdicate in favour of a provisional government set up by the Communist-led Viet Minh, headed by **Ho Chi Minh**, in which he accepted the nominal role of supreme counsellor. He left Vietnam in March 1946, initially for Hong Kong, with the restoration of French rule. Bao Dai returned to Vietnam encouraged by French assurances. On 8 March 1949, he entered into an exchange of letters (known as the **Elysée Agreement**) with President Vincent Auriol, which restored him as head of state of a nominally independent Vietnam. This attempt to demonstrate a semblance of independence failed to stem the political and military advance of the Viet Minh. In June 1954, following the French defeat at the **Battle of Dien Bien Phu**, he called on the anti-communist exile **Ngo Dinh Diem** to form a government, which he did in the southern half of a Vietnam partitioned by the **Geneva Agreements on Indochina of July 1954**. With US backing, Diem organized a referendum in October 1955, which deposed Bao Dai and established the Republic of Vietnam. He left the country soon after to spend the remainder of his life in exile, mainly in the south of France where he earned a reputation as a playboy. He died in Paris on 31 July 1997.

see also: August Revolution 1945; Diem, Ngo Dinh; Dien Bien Phu, Battle of, 1954; Elysée Agreement 1949; Geneva Agreements on Indochina 1954; Ho Chi Minh; Viet Minh.

## Barisan Alternatif (Malaysia)
The Malay term *Barisan Alternatif* (Alternative Front) is the name of an electoral pact set up in June 1999 to challenge the *Barisan Nasional* in federal and state elections, which were held in the following November. It comprised *Parti Islam Se-Malaysia* (PAS) and the **Democratic Action Party** (DAP), both well-established, the newly-established *Parti Keadilan Nasional* (National Justice Party) and the minor *Parti Ra'ayat Malaysia* (Malaysian People's Party). The significance of the pact was the attempt to appeal across racial bounds in the manner of the *Barisan Nasional*. In the event, only *Parti Islam*

made a major electoral impact by increasing its federal parliamentary strength from 7 to 27 seats as well as gaining control of the Terengganu state legislature. The Democratic Action Party increased its federal representation from 9 to 10, while *Parti Keadilan Nasional* won 5 seats. *Parti Ra'ayat Malaysia* failed to win any seats. Despite this mixed electoral showing and fundamental differences between PAS and the DAP over the issue of Malaysia becoming an Islamic state, the *Barisan Alternatif* held together as an opposition replica of the ruling coalition. When Malaysia's federal Parliament re-assembled in December 1999, the Front named Fadzil Nor, the president of PAS, as leader of the opposition to replace Lim Kit Siang of the DAP who had lost his seat in the elections.

see also: Barisan Nasional; Democratic Action Party (DAP); *Parti Islam* (PAS); *Parti Keadilan Nasional* (National Justice Party).

## Barisan Nasional (Malaysia)

The Malay term *Barisan Nasional* (National Front) is the name of the ruling federal coalition and of all the state governments, with the exception of those in Kelantan and Terengganu in the charge of *Parti Islam Se-Malaysia* (PAS). The coalition is constituted on an inter-communal basis but subject to Malay dominance, which is reflected in the distribution of cabinet portfolios. The *Barisan Nasional* is the direct successor to the **Alliance Party** coalition, which formed the first government of Malaya before independence in August 1957. The Alliance was also an inter-communal coalition: the politically predominant **UMNO** (United Malays National Organization), the Malayan (subsequently **Malaysian**) **Chinese Association** (MCA) and the Malayan (subsequently **Malaysian**) **Indian Congress** (MIC). The rationale of coalition politics is that bargaining and compromise at the elite level serve to ensure the exercise of collective power, the control of patronage and racial peace.

The *Barisan Nasional* employs the same inter-communal governing model but on a far more extensive coalition basis, with fourteen parties contesting general elections under its banner in November 1999. Its origins are to be found in the electoral reverse suffered by UMNO in May 1969, which was followed by inter-communal

violence in the **May 13 Racial Riots**. Prime Minister **Tun Abdul Razak** employed the device of a wider coalition to entrench the position of UMNO and to ensure political stability. In February 1972, the primarily non-Malay *Gerakan Ra'ayat Malaysia* Party, which provided the state government on the island of Penang, was brought within the Alliance federal structure, to be followed in April by a coalition arrangement at the state level in Perak between the Alliance and the Indian-led People's Progressive Party. More significant, however, was the agreement in September 1972 between the ruling Alliance and PAS, the principal Malay opposition party, to establish coalition governments at both state and federal levels. That coalition was constituted formally on 1 January 1973. *Barisan Nasional* was registered as a political party on 1 June 1974 and went on to secure a resounding electoral success in August.

The *Barisan Nasional* survived a major crisis in December 1977 when PAS was expelled after a revolt within the Kelantan state legislature against a chief minister appointed by the federal government. That expulsion was not permitted to undermine the political centrality of the national coalition, which was extended to Malaysian Borneo. Despite reverses in state elections, continuous success at the polls has been demonstrated at the federal level from 1978, the first election after the expulsion of PAS. The *Barisan Nasional* enjoyed its greatest political success in April 1995 when it was returned to office with 162 seats in a federal Parliament of 192. In subsequent elections in November 1999, that number was reduced to 148 seats in a Parliament of 193, while PAS secured control of the state legislature in Terengganu, while holding on to Kelantan which it had recovered in 1990.

see also: Alliance Party; *Gerakan Ra'ayat Malaysia*; Malaysian Chinese Association; Malaysian Indian Congress; May 13 Racial Riots; *Parti Islam Se-Malaysia* (PAS); Razak, Tun Abdul; UMNO.

## Barisan Sosialis (Singapore)

The *Barisan Sosialis* (a Malay term meaning Socialist Front) was a radical left-wing party, which was established in July 1961 as a result of a split within Singapore's ruling **People's**

**Action Party** (PAP). At issue was the prospect of the self-governing island becoming part of a new Federation of Malaysia, comprising also Malaya and British territories in north Borneo, which had been proposed by Malaya's prime minister, **Tunku Abdul Rahman**, in May 1961. That proposal was welcomed by Singapore's prime minister, **Lee Kuan Yew**, and his cabinet colleagues but was denounced as a neo-colonialist plot by a left-wing faction within the PAP. Thirteen parliamentary dissidents crossed the floor of the house to jeopardize the PAP's working majority and to precipitate a major political crisis.

For a short period, the *Barisan Sosialis* gave the impression of being an alternative government in waiting with the capability of thwarting the Malaysia project. However, through political intimidation and the support of conservative opposition parties, the PAP maintained itself in office until after the formation of Malaysia on 16 September 1963. Elections were held in Singapore a week later in which the PAP was returned to office with 37 out of 51, which marked a loss of only 6 seats from its political triumph in May 1959. The *Barisan Sosialis* retained its 13 seats but failed to make a significant political impact, especially after Singapore became independent in August 1965 on its separation from Malaysia. The PAP increased its seats to 49 by the next elections in April 1968 through winning a series of by-elections caused by the resignation of *Barisan Sosialis* members. The party then ceased to function as a credible political entity when it decided to boycott the polls and the PAP won all 58 seats in an enlarged Parliament. From then on, it maintained a vestigial existence; for example, nominating only 4 candidates without success in elections in September 1988. After those elections, its long-standing leader, Dr Lee Siew Choh, took a place in the Parliament as a 'non-constituency MP' with restricted voting rights as one of two defeated candidates with the highest number of votes. However, the *Barisan Sosialis* failed to nominate candidates in subsequent elections in September 1991 and January 1997 and has ceased to be of any political relevance.

see also: Lee Kuan Yew; People's Action Party (PAP); Rahman, Tunku Abdul.

## Barisan Tiga  (Malaysia/Sarawak)

*Barisan Tiga* (Front of Three) is the name for the ruling coalition in the Malaysian state of Sarawak in northern Borneo which is affiliated with the ruling federal **Barisan Nasional** (National Front). Dating from 1976, it comprises **Parti Pesaka Bumiputera Bersatu**, the **Sarawak United People's Party** and the **Sarawak National Party**, which together won forty-nine out of fifty-six seats in elections for the state legislature in September 1991. *Parti Pesaka Bumiputera Bersatu* is the dominant partner in the coalition. In May 1994, the breakaway **Parti Bangsa Dyak Sarawak** was admitted into the ruling coalition. In elections in September 1996, the ruling coalition was returned to office with 57 out of 62 seats in the state legislature.

see also: Barisan Nasional; Parti Bangsa Dyak Sarawak; Parti Pesaka Bumiputera Bersatu; Sarawak National Party; Sarawak United People's Party.

## Bayan  (Philippines)

The *Partido ng Bayan* (People's Party) was set up in the wake of **Corazón Aquino**'s assumption of power in February 1986 in an attempt by the Communist Party of the Philippines to exploit so-called democratic space. The term *bayan* had been used previously for united front purposes. The first major congress was held in August 1986 attended by *Bayan*'s founder, **José María Sisón**, a former chairman of the central committee of the Communist Party, and Bernabé Buscayno, the head of its military wing, the **New People's Army**. Both men had been released from detention in March 1986. At the congress, demands were advanced for the removal of US bases and for controlling multinational corporations. *Bayan* participated in congressional elections held in May 1987 but without success. It failed to make any impact in the face of popular support for candidates endorsed by Mrs Aquino. When José María Sisón went into voluntary exile in the Netherlands, Fidel Agcaoli became chairman. At the subsequent presidential and concurrent congressional elections in May 1992, *Bayan* did not fare any better, despite the failure of Mrs Aquino's administration to overcome the country's economic difficulties. The party ceased to serve any political purpose after her successor,

President **Fidel Ramos**, endorsed congressional legislation which repealed an anti-subversion statute of 1957 under which the Communist Party had been declared illegal. It failed to participate in congressional elections in May 1997.
*see also:* Aquino, Corazón; New People's Army; Ramos, Fidel; Sisón, José María.

## Berjasa (Malaysia)

*Berjasa* is an acronym from *Barisan Jama'ah Islamiah Se Malaysia* (Malaysian Islamic People's Front). This political party was established in the state of Kelantan in late 1977 in the wake of a crisis within the ruling **Barisan Nasional** (National Front) federal coalition which resulted in the expulsion of *Parti Islam Se-Malaysia* (PAS), which commanded a majority in the state legislature. The crisis had been precipitated by a vote of no confidence in Kelantan's chief minister, Datuk Mohamad Nasir, who had been appointed by the late prime minister, **Tun Abdul Razak**, followed by rioting in the state capital, Kota Bahru. PAS was expelled from the *Barisan Nasional* after its parliamentary members, with one exception, voted against a Bill in the federal legislature dissolving the state legislature and imposing emergency rule but were not dismissed from the party.

After the expulsion, Datuk Mohamad Nasir set up *Berjasa* in direct competition to PAS with undoubted encouragement from the federal government. *Berjasa* aligned with *Barisan Nasional*, led by **UMNO** (United Malays National Organization), in elections for the state legislature in March 1978, when emergency rule had been lifted. The result was a victory for the *ad-hoc* coalition which formed a new government. *Berjasa* subsequently joined the *Barisan Nasional* but ceased to play a significant political role, having served its primary purpose in helping to remove PAS from government in Kelantan. Following the split within UMNO in the late 1980s, *Berjasa* became aligned with that wing of the party led by **Tengku Razaleigh Hamzah**, whose home state was Kelantan. In June 1989 *Berjasa* left the *Barisan Nasional* to join the *Angkatan Perpaduan Ummah* (Muslim Unity Front) together with PAS and Tengku Razaleigh's **Semangat '46** as well as another minor Malay party. In general elections for federal and state

legislatures in October 1990, the Muslim Unity Front was successful in Kelantan where it was able to form the state government but individual *Berjasa* party candidates failed to win any seats and it has survived in political form only, without any impact in elections in April 1995. The party became moribund after Tengku Razaleigh announced in May 1996 that he was dissolving *Semangat '46* to return to UMNO.
*see also: Angkatan Perpaduan Ummah; Barisan Nasional; Parti Islam Se-Malaysia*; Razak, Tun Abdul; Razaleigh Hamzah, Tengku; *Semangat '46*; UMNO.

## Berjaya (Malaysia/Sabah)

*Berjaya*, which means 'success' in Malay, is an acronym formed from *Bersatu Rakyat Jelata Sabah* (Sabah People's Union). *Berjaya* was set up in June 1975 in Sabah in Malaysian Borneo by defectors from the ruling **United Sabah National Organization** (USNO) who with evident encouragement from the federal government in Kuala Lumpur sought to challenge the leadership of the state chief minister, **Tun Mustapha Harun**, who was suspected of secessionist ambitions. The new party was led initially by **Datuk Harris Salleh**, a former minister, but on 27 July **Tun Mohammad Fuad** (formerly Donald Stephens before his conversion to **Islam**) announced his resignation as head of state and his adherence to *Berjaya*. The next day, he assumed the leadership of the new party. In elections held in April 1976, *Berjaya* won twenty-eight of the forty-eight seats contested and Tun Mohammad Fuad was sworn in as chief minister at the head of a coalition of Muslim and indigenous factions acceptable to the federal government, which welcomed the victorious party into the ruling **Barisan Nasional**. Tun Mohammad Fuad held office for only fifty-three days, however. On 6 June 1976 he was killed, together with his son and four of his ministers, in a plane crash. He was succeeded as head of the party and state government by his deputy Harris Salleh, who served as chief minister for nearly a decade. During that time the inter-ethnic coalition which had brought *Berjaya* to power began to break up as the government increasingly favoured the interests of the Muslim community as well as appearing subservient to the federal authorities. Of particular significance was the transfer of the island of Labuan to federal jurisdiction in April 1984. Only weeks before state elections in April 1985, a countervailing inter-ethnic opposition coalition was formed called the **Sabah United Party** (*Parti Bersatu Sabah*). This party scored an overwhelming electoral victory which left *Berjaya* devastated politically.

see also: *Barisan Nasional*; Fuad, Tun Mohammad; Harris Mohamad Salleh, Datuk; Mustapha bin Datuk Harun, Tun; Sabah United Party; United Sabah National Organization.

## Bhumibol Adulyadej, King (Thailand)

King Bhumibol Adulyadej is the reigning constitutional monarch of Thailand and the longest-living member of a dynasty, which was founded in 1782 by King Rama I. He has exercised a remarkable political influence by augmenting the traditional aura of the throne through an exemplary personal life. He became king on 9 June 1946 after the still unexplained death of his elder brother, **Ananda Mahidol**, from a gunshot wound. Bhumibol was then 19; he had been born on 5 December 1927 in Boston, Massachusetts, where his father Prince Mahidol was studying medicine. Ananda had ascended to the throne following the abdication of his uncle King Prajadhipok in 1935 in the wake of the coup that abolished the absolute monarchy. Both brothers lived in Switzerland, except for a brief visit to Thailand in 1938, until their return in December 1945. After his accession, King Bhumibol went to live again in Switzerland to return to Bangkok in 1950 for his coronation as Rama IX of the Chakri dynasty. By then, Thailand had reverted to military rule for which the monarchy served as a compliant symbol despite an underlying tension which was a legacy of the coup of 1932.

After Field Marshal **Sarit Thanarat** seized power from Field Marshal **Phibul Songkram** in 1957, a conscious policy was adopted of grooming the young king for a national role by exposing him and other members of the royal family to popular contact through an extensive range of ceremonial and civic duties. He took a special interest in rural development and social welfare and began to speak out on constitutional matters after Sarit's death in 1963 when the successor military government lost its authority. King Bhumibol first demonstrated his political facility and authority in October 1973 in reaction to bloodshed in the streets when university students demonstrated against military rule. He intervened to end the violence and was responsible for the prime minister, **Thanom Kittikachorn**, and deputy prime minister, **Praphas Charusathien**, going into exile, which paved the way for a democratic political interlude. The king endorsed democracy but as a conservative became alarmed at the breakdown in public order coincident with the success of revolutionary communism in Indochina in 1975, which resulted in the Laotian monarchy being overthrown. A right-wing assault on students protesting at the return of exiled prime minister Thanom resulted in the **Thammasat University Massacre** on 6 October 1976; this provided the pretext for a military coup, which installed a nominee of the king as prime minister. The king came down on the side of political conservatism and lost popularity as a consequence. With the return to military rule, Thailand began to experiment with a series of constitutions over which the role of the armed forces was centrally at issue. In this chequered process, the king played a cautious part, being careful not to tarnish the throne by too close an association with political life.

During the 1980s King Bhumibol supported the non-elected administration of General **Prem Tinsulanond** without loss of popular respect because it conducted itself with regard for the virtues of good government. When the elected government of **Chatichai Choonhavan** was overthrown by a military coup in February 1991, he indicated his mild disapproval. In May 1992 popular demonstrations against the unelected retired general **Suchinda Kraprayoon** assuming the office of prime minister were dispersed by the military with great loss of life. After initial hesitation, the king intervened personally to defuse the crisis, which was brought to an end with Suchinda's resignation and fresh elections in September, which produced a democratically elected prime minister, **Chuan Leekpai**. By that intervention, the king restored his political standing and that of the

Thai monarchy. After the election of a government dominated by the **Chart Thai** Party in July 1995, he engaged in unprecedented public criticism of politicians for failing to address Bangkok's traffic and flood problems as well as lecturing on the need for honesty and responsibility in government. In late 1997, during a devastating economic crisis, he let it be known that he was opposed to military intervention and in favour of democratic political change.

King Bhumibol and his consort Queen Sirikit have four children, three daughters and one son, Crown Prince **Maha Vajiralongkorn**, who has one daughter by his official wife. Prince Vajiralongkorn is the heir apparent but he does not command the reverence and respect enjoyed by his father. The king's highly respected second daughter, Princess Sirindhorn, who is not married, was elevated to the status of an heir presumptive on his fiftieth birthday in December 1977. Despite the many accomplishments of his reign and his sustained reputation, King Bhumibol has not been able to assure the future of the Chakri dynasty. He has a history of cardiac problems which required angioplasty treatment on two occasions during 1995. The golden jubilee of his assumption of the throne in June 1996 was a great national occasion. Lavish celebrations continued and merged into those commemorating the king's sixth twelve-year life cycle in his seventy-second year.

see also: Ananda Mahidol; Chart Thai Party; Chatichai Choonhavan; Chuan Leekpai; Phibul Songkram; Praphas Charusathien; Prem Tinsulanond; Sarit Thanarat; Suchinda Krapayoon; Thammasat University Massacre 1976; Thanin Kraivichian; Thanom Kittikachorn; Vajiralongkorn, Maha.

## Boat People (Vietnam)

The term Boat People has been associated exclusively with more than 1.5 million refugees who fled from Vietnam in the wake of the Communist seizure of power in the southern half of the country in April 1975. Initially, the exodus was composed of indigenous Vietnamese linked in some way with the defeated Saigon administration who had reason to fear the retribution of the revolutionary government.

They left in small boats and undertook perilous journeys across the **South China Sea**, braving the elements and pirates to make landfall in particular in Thailand, Malaysia and Indonesia as well as travelling in a north-easterly direction to reach Hong Kong when the prevailing winds blew that way. The composition of the Boat People changed over the years, however. For example, as the Socialist Republic of Vietnam applied economic dogma in agriculture and directed urban dwellers to new economic zones in the countryside in the late 1970s, Boat People came to be driven by a determination to seek a better life, often to join relatives in the United States and Australia. Then in the late 1970s, with a marked deterioration in Sino-Vietnamese relations which was expressed in discrimination against the Chinese community, Vietnamese of ethnic Chinese identity increasingly made up the flow of Boat People coming from both north and south of the country. That flow was aggravated with Vietnam's invasion of Cambodia in December 1978 and the People's Republic of China's retaliatory military intervention in Vietnam in February 1979. During the course of the 1980s, however, the flow of Boat People was sustained by economic circumstances in the main which coincided with a decline in global compassion for their condition. The growing refusal of western governments to accept economic refugees led to a slowing down in the rate of their movement from camps in South-East Asia to final destinations. The issue of economic refugees from Vietnam came to a head during the late 1980s in Hong Kong, whose camps harboured at one stage over 60,000 refugees, some of whom had travelled overland via China. The solution to the problem of the Boat People came about as a function of Vietnam embarking on market-driven economics followed by concessions over the Cambodian conflict. Under the terms of a comprehensive plan of action agreed in 1989, Vietnam accepted the involuntary repatriation of economic refugees from Hong Kong while the United Nations High Commission for Refugees applied increasing pressure on the population of the Hong Kong camps to return. By the early 1990s, only a handful of Boat People continued to arrive in the territory with matching figures for

South-East Asian landfalls. In February 1994 the United Nations High Commission for Refugees announced that Vietnamese people would no longer be automatically eligible for consideration as political refugees, which meant that all those resident in camps could be returned home under international law. By 1995, after the United States had lifted its trade and investment embargo against Vietnam, the number of refugees remaining in camps amounted to around 40,000, half of whom were in Hong Kong. In January 1996, the United Nations High Commission for Refugees announced that it would halt funding for all boat people in first asylum camps by the following July, while Vietnam agreed to speed up repatriation. In the special case of Hong Kong, China urged that all Vietnamese refugees be repatriated before it resumed sovereignty in July 1997, by which time only a remnant were left in one holding camp. In January 1998, the Hong Kong Special Administrative Region abolished the port of first asylum policy, which had applied for the past nineteen years, while the last holding camp was closed in May 2000 with some 1,400 remaining refugees being offered local identity cards.

see also: South China Sea; Vietnam War.

## Bolkiah, Prince Mohamed (Brunei)

Prince Mohamed Bolkiah, a younger brother of the Sultan, has been Brunei's foreign minister ever since it assumed full independence in January 1984. As such, he is the longest-serving foreign minister within **ASEAN** and has been continuously responsible for representing his country within the **ASEAN Regional Forum** (ARF) since its first working session in 1994. Prince Mohamed was born in Bandar Seri Begawan on 27 August 1947 and was educated initially in Malaysia and Brunei. He graduated from Britain's Royal Military Academy at Sandhurst in 1967. In 1985, he was appointed chairman of Brunei's Council of Succession. Prince Mohamed enjoys a reputation for political and religious conservatism. He has become increasingly influential in affairs of state with the resignation of another brother, Prince Jefri, as minister of finance in 1997 and as head of Brunei's Investment Agency in 1998 against

a context of economic mismanagement and personal scandal. Prince Mohamed has extensive business interests and heads the QAF group of companies.

see also: ASEAN; ASEAN Regional Forum (ARF).

## Bolkiah, Sultan Hassanal (Brunei)

Sultan Hassanal Bolkiah is the twenty-ninth absolute ruler of the Sultanate of Brunei. He was born on 15 July 1946 and succeeded his father Sultan Omar Ali Saifuddin in October 1967 when he abdicated the throne in order to thwart British attempts to promote greater democratization. At the time, Hassanal Bolkiah was only a few weeks from graduating from the Royal Military Academy at Sandhurst. He was crowned as head of state in August 1968. For nearly twenty years, however, until the former sultan's death in 1986, he was overshadowed by his domineering father, from whom he became progressively estranged. Brunei assumed full independence in January 1984 following which a cabinet system of government was established with the sultan as prime minister. In that role, Hassanal Bolkiah consolidated his position, assuming also the portfolio of minister of defence after the death of his father. Hassanal Bolkiah has acquired notoriety by becoming known as the richest man in the world, exemplified by his private collection of 153 Rolls-Royce cars. Since the death of his father, however, he has adopted a more serious frame of mind, exhibiting greater interest in the business of government of the oil-rich state. He was obliged to assume the additional portfolio of finance minister in February 1997 following the resignation of his brother, Prince Jefri. In August 1998, against a background of economic adversity and fraternal tensions, the Sultan had his eldest son, Prince Billah, invested as Crown Prince in order to assure the succession. Although the Sultan has been obliged to take a firmer grip on affairs of state, at issue is whether he possesses the ability and the application to maintain intact an absolutist political system whose form (*Melayu Islam Beraja*, meaning Malay Islamic Monarchy) is an anachronism within South-East Asia.

see also: Melayu Islam Beraja.

## Brevié Line  (Cambodia/Vietnam)

The Brevié Line is a delimitation drawn on a map in 1939 to differentiate administrative and police responsibilities over offshore islands between Cochin China (southern Vietnam) and Cambodia, then both subject to French control. Named after Jules Brevié, a governor-general of Indochina, the line extended into the Gulf of Siam from the land border between the two territories without confirming sovereign jurisdiction. The line was recognized as a maritime boundary in 1967 after negotiations between the government of Cambodia and representatives of the Democratic Repulic of (North) Vietnam and the National Liberation Front of South Vietnam. It became a matter of contention after the **Khmer Rouge** assumed power in Cambodia in April 1975. Talks with Vietnam in May 1976 broke down over the proposal by its government to modify the line so as to redefine the configuration of territorial waters to permit easier access to the Vietnamese island of Phu Quoc. The status of the line remains unclear in the wake of the settlement of the Cambodian conflict at the **International Conference on Cambodia** in Paris in October 1991. Although relations between Phnom Penh and Hanoi have been repaired, an underlying historical tension has prevented any conclusive agreement on the definition and demarcation of territorial waters.
see also: International Conference on Cambodia 1991; Khmer Rouge.

## Brunei Revolt 1962  (Brunei)

An abortive uprising was staged in the British-protected Sultanate of Brunei on 8 December 1962 by members of the opposition **People's Party** (*Partai Ra'ayat*) led by **A. M. Azahari**. The People's Party had won an overwhelming majority of elective seats in the first general elections to the Legislative Council in August 1962 on a platform of opposition to Brunei joining the projected Federation of Malaysia. Expressing a local irredentism, Azahari had called for the establishment of a state of North Borneo (to include adjacent Sarawak and Sabah). Frustrated in its attempt to have the Legislative Council convened, the clandestine military wing of the People's Party – the self-styled North Borneo National Army – made an attempt to seize power.

The sultan called on British military support under a treaty of 1959; troops were dispatched from Singapore and put down the revolt within a matter of days. Since then, a state of emergency has been in force in the sultanate. The constitution has remained suspended and the People's Party proscribed. Azahari's absence from Brunei at the time of the uprising suggests an ill-planned exercise, although material support and training is believed to have been provided from Indonesian Borneo. He had enjoyed close political associations with President **Sukarno**'s Indonesia where he found asylum and diplomatic support after the uprising had failed. Domestically, the Brunei Revolt arrested political development in the sultanate. Internationally, it provided the pretext for Indonesia's policy of **Confrontation** of Malaysia with support preferred for the so-called state of North Borneo. The revolt almost certainly was a factor in the decision by Sultan Sir Omar Ali Saifuddin in July 1963 not to take Brunei into Malaysia.
see also: Azahari, A. M.; Confrontation; People's Party.

## Buddhism  (Burma (Myanmar)/ Cambodia/Laos/Thailand/Vietnam)

The Buddhist faith in South-East Asia is identified primarily with countries of the mainland part of the region. It draws its name from the philosopher Gautama Buddha, who lived in the sixth century BC in Nepal. His personal revelation came from an attempt to transcend the constraints of Hinduism based on a continuing cycle of life, death and reincarnation. He claimed to have found the secret to *nirvana* or personal salvation from the suffering of life through renouncing all worldly possessions and desires and by total immersion in meditation, not through worship of any deity. His example lives on in the regime of saffron-robed monks who eat only one meal a day provided by benefactors who fill their bowls at the roadside.

Buddhism came to South-East Asia through two routes and has taken two forms. Mahayana Buddhism (the greater vehicle) is to be found primarily in Vietnam, where it was brought from India via China. Theravada Buddhism (the lesser vehicle) is believed to have penetrated

Burma, Thailand, Laos and Cambodia from India via Sri Lanka (formerly Ceylon). Although Buddhism is a religious philosophy which renounces the material world, its clergy and adherents have been directly involved in political activity. In Burma and Cambodia before the Pacific War, Buddhism served as a vehicle for expressing nationalist sentiment against the colonial powers (see, for example, **Son Ngoc Thanh**). In South Vietnam in 1963, Buddhist agitation against the government of the Catholic **Ngo Dinh Diem** was an important factor in US support being withdrawn and a military coup being mounted during which he was killed. In Thailand, the *Palang Dharma* (Moral Force party) led by retired general **Chamlong Srimuang**, which challenged military rule on the streets of Bangkok in May 1992, has been closely identified with the *Santi Asoke* Buddhist sect. In September 1998, Buddhist monks were in the forefront of a mass protest outside the US embassy in Phnom Penh against prime minister **Hun Sen** whose **Cambodian People's Party** had secured victory in general elections in the previous July. Although Buddhism stresses peace and harmony, the political cultures of countries in mainland South-East Asia have not been informed by its ethics and political violence has been commonplace.

see also: Cambodian People's Party; Chamlong Srimuang; Diem, Ngo Dinh; Hun Sen; *Palang Dharma*; *Santi Asoke*; Son Ngoc Thanh.

## Buddhist Liberal Democratic Party (Cambodia)

The Buddhist Liberal Democratic Party was the direct successor of the **Khmer People's National Liberation Front** (KPNLF) with a middle-class constituency of a republican disposition. The KPNLF was established among refugees along the border with Thailand in October 1979 as an anti-Vietnamese resistance movement by the former prime minister, **Son Sann**. It was a party to the **Coalition Government of Democratic Kampuchea** (CGDK) set up in June 1982. The KPNLF transferred its activities from the border with Thailand after a political settlement was reached at the **International Conference on Cambodia** in Paris in October 1991. In January 1993, when

UNTAC (United Nations Transitional Authority in Cambodia) registered political parties for elections in May, the KPNLF entered as the Buddhist Liberal Democratic Party, hoping to employ its range of symbols for political advantage. In the event, it secured only 10 seats with some 4 per cent of the vote in a constituent assembly of 120 members. With the formation of a coalition government at the end of October 1993, the Buddhist Liberal Democratic Party was allocated minimal representation, with only the information portfolio held by one of its representatives. Its marginal position was weakened further by personal tensions between party president Son Sann and minister for information Ieng Mouly, who succeeded him in party office in July 1995. The party then split, ceasing to be of political significance. Son Sann then formed his own party based on personal following. His 'Son Sann Party' contested general elections in July 1998 without any success. Ieng Mouly led a Buddhist Liberal Party (*sic*) into those elections with an equal lack of success.

see also: Democratic Kampuchea, Coalition Government of; International Conference on Cambodia, Paris 1991; Khmer People's National Liberation Front; Son Sann; United Nations: Cambodia 1991–3; UNTAC.

## Bumiputera  (Malaysia)

*Bumiputera* is a Malay term which translates as sons of the soil or indigenous people. In practice, the term has been applied exclusively to the Malays and not the *orang asli* (aborigines) whose settlement predates them. *Bumiputera* entered the vocabulary of Malaysian politics with a vengeance after racial violence in the **May 13 Racial Riots 1969**. That violence, which followed an electoral rebuff to **UMNO** (United Malays National Organization), was interpreted as a strong indication that the principal Malay party was losing its traditional constituency. To counter this trend, in 1970 the Malay-dominated government introduced a **New Economic Policy** whose objective was to redress the balance of economic advantage in favour of the *Bumiputera* or Malays. Underlying the affirmative action was a Malay anxiety that they would lose their political birthright to the non-Malays of migrant origin, especially the

Chinese, unless control of the economy was radically revised. Communal prerogative in economic affairs was demonstrated from then on by financial and trade portfolios being held exclusively by Malay ministers, by the redistribution of corporate wealth and by the allocation of educational scholarships and access to government-controlled employment. The allocation of shares in publicly listed companies in order to give Malays a greater stake in corporate wealth has been controversial, with recurrent charges of corrupt practice. However, by the 1990s, the *Bumiputera* policy had borne fruit to the extent of having created an increasingly self-confident Malay middle class without the earlier held fear of being politically dispossessed by the non-Malays. The equivalent term in Indonesia is *Pribumi*.

see also: Bank Bumiputera Crisis; May 13 Racial Riots, 1969; New Economic Policy; *Pribumi*; UMNO.

## Burhanuddin Al-Helmy (Malaya/Malaysia)

Dr Burhanuddin Al-Helmy was the leader of *Parti Islam Se-Malaysia* (PAS) from the mid-1950s until the mid-1960s, making his major contribution as a radical nationalist rather than as an Islamic thinker. He was born near Ipoh in Perak in 1911 and received a Malay-Islamic primary and secondary school education before studying homeopathy and philosophy at Aligarh University in India in the late 1920s. He was away from Malaya for some ten years, becoming drawn into anti-colonial activities in India and Palestine. On his return, Dr Burhanuddin became involved in radical Malay politics and was employed as adviser on Malay custom and culture during the Japanese occupation. He was much influenced by the example of Indonesian nationalism and in August 1945 met with **Sukarno** and **Mohammad Hatta** in Taiping at which an abortive agreement was reached that Malaya would be incorporated within a greater independent Indonesia.

After the Pacific War, Dr Burhanuddin helped to found the Malay Nationalist Party which he was willing to associate with the anti-colonial and multiracial **All-Malaya Council of Joint Action**. He was arrested after the **Maria Hertogh**

riots in Singapore in 1950 and withdrew from politics for several years until the mid-1950s, when he became identified with Malay opposition to **UMNO** (United Malays National Organization). He was invited to assume the presidency of PAS in late 1956 and as its leader drew on the nationalist example of Sukarno rather than on Islamic virtues. His political career was broken as a result of his arrest in January 1965 for allegedly plotting to assist Indonesia in its **Confrontation** of Malaysia. He was released in the following year because of ill-health but ceased to play any further part in political life. He died in October 1969.

see also: All-Malaya Council of Joint Action; Confrontation; Hatta, Mohammad; Hertogh, Maria; *Parti Islam Se-Malaysia*; Sukarno; UMNO.

## Burma Socialist Programme Party (BSPP) (Burma/Myanmar)

On 2 March 1962 a military-based Revolutionary Council led by General **Ne Win** seized power in Burma. The Revolutionary Council then published an ideological document entitled the **'Burmese Way to Socialism'**, which sought to justify the coup against the democratically elected government and to chart the future course of the state. On 4 July the Revolutionary Council announced the establishment of a new Burma Socialist Programme Party (*Lanzin* in Burmese) charged with the task of guiding the country along the so-called way to socialism. All other parties were declared illegal. Comprising initially members of the Revolutionary Council only, the Burma Socialist Programme Party (BSPP) was modelled on Communist counterparts but, in effect, served as a political instrument at the personal disposal of Ne Win and his clients in the armed forces for only as long as it was necessary.

The BSPP was changed from a cadre to a mass party in 1971; membership became essential for any kind of preferment in society. Of the 1 million full and candidate members, over half were drawn from serving or retired military or police, while around 80 per cent of the active armed forces belonged to the patronage network. A new constitution promulgated in January 1974, which inaugurated the Socialist

Republic of Burma, made no difference to the power structure with which Ne Win through the armed forces controlled the BSPP and its mass organizations. For example, Ne Win stepped down as head of state in November 1981 but continued as chairman of the BSPP. In the mean time, through a dogmatic and highly bureaucratized system of economic planning compounded by an isolationist foreign policy, the Burmese people experienced a steady decline in their standard of living. The party and the army, however, maintained a position of privilege, generating a growing popular alienation which came to a head in the late 1980s.

Popular dissent began to manifest itself in a politically significant way from September 1987 after an arbitrary act of demonetization to cope with economic collapse removed some 80 per cent of banknotes in circulation. In March 1988 a clash involving students in a teashop in a Rangoon suburb sparked off sustained protests which were put down by the military with great loss of life. The BSPP convened an extraordinary congress in July at which Ne Win announced his intention to retire as chairman. After a bloody confrontation in the streets of Rangoon in August, the BSPP convened a second extraordinary congress in September at which multi-party elections were promised. Shortly after, the government revealed that all members of the armed forces had given up membership of the BSPP. On 18 September 1988 the minister of defence, General Saw Maung, announced that the military had set up a **State Law and Order Restoration Council** (SLORC) which, in effect, marked the end of the BSPP as the main political instrument of Ne Win's rule.

On 26 September 1988 the BSPP changed its name to the **National Unity Party**. It took part in elections for a constituent assembly in May 1990, losing heavily to the **National League for Democracy** led in effect by an incarcerated **Aung San Suu Kyi**, the daughter of nationalist martyr **Aung San**. The military authorities refused to recognize the results of the elections and employed SLORC as the principal vehicle for exercising power, having lost all use for the BSPP in its revised form. In November 1997, SLORC was succeeded by the **State Peace and Development Council** (SPDC).

*see also:* Aung San; Aung San Suu Kyi; Burmese Way to Socialism; National League for Democracy; National Unity Party; Ne Win; San Yu; State Law and Order Restoration Council; State Peace and Development Council.

## Burmese Way to Socialism (Burma/ Myanmar)

In April 1962, a month after seizing power, the Revolutionary Council led by General **Ne Win** promulgated an ideological document called the 'Burmese Way to Socialism'. This creed set out the basis on which the political economy of Burma would be transformed essentially through national self-help. The document sought to blend Marxist and Buddhist tenets as a way of lending legitimacy to the new order established by the armed forces through the vehicle of its **Burma Socialist Programme Party** (BSPP). The syncretic ideology failed to provide a practical guide for human welfare to be demonstrated by a continuous economic decline which led to political violence at the end of the 1980s. With the establishment of the **State Law and Order Restoration Council** (SLORC) in September 1988, the Burmese Way to Socialism disappeared from the political lexicon.

*see also:* Burma Socialist Programme Party; Ne Win; State Law and Order Restoration Council.

## Buy British Last Policy (Malaysia)

The Buy British Last Policy was an act of open discrimination against the purchase of British goods and services which was first announced by Malaysia's prime minister, Dr **Mahathir Mohamad**, in October 1981 within three months of his assumption of high office. He explained: 'We will buy British when it is absolutely necessary, when your prices and services are way ahead, but otherwise I think we will show a definite preference for non-British sources.' The Buy British Last Policy was precipitated by the decision of the London Stock Exchange to adjust its rules in order to make 'dawn raids' or surprise takeover bids more difficult to execute. In September 1981 Malaysia's National Investment Corporation, acting through British agents, had secured control of Guthrie, which owned large plantations in the Federation, by such means.

Dr Mahathir construed the decision by the Stock Exchange as a deliberate attempt to frustrate his government's policy of securing control of national assets. He was angered also by the British government's decision to oblige its universities to charge higher fees for overseas students, of whom Malaysians constituted the largest number, as well as resistance to additional flights into London for his country's national airline. In employing the policy, Dr Mahathir was giving public vent to a deep-seated personal resentment arising from his experiences during the colonial period as well as securing political advantage from his open confrontation of Britain.

The Buy British Last Policy was sustained until April 1983 when Dr Mahathir withdrew his directive to government departments which required all contracts with British firms to be scrutinized by his office to see whether or not there was a better alternative source. His change of political heart had been prompted by discussions with Britain's prime minister, Mrs Margaret Thatcher, during a visit to London in the previous month. Anglo-Malaysian rapprochement was sealed during a visit to Malaysia by Mrs Thatcher in April 1985 but an understanding on aid and trade reached during that visit sowed the seeds for future acrimony between the two governments.

A confidential Anglo-Malaysian memorandum of understanding was concluded in September 1988 for Malaysia's purchase of British defence exports. An earlier draft of that memorandum had linked aid provision and defence sales. The matter became public knowledge in Britain following a report from the National Audit Office in October 1993 which was highly critical of aid provided for a hydroelectric dam on the Pergau River in the state of Kelantan. During the course of an extensive press investigation and hearings by the House of Commons Public Accounts Committee and its Select Committee on Foreign Affairs, the memorandum of understanding was leaked to a British newspaper, to the embarrassment of the two governments. In addition, a report in *The Sunday Times* in February 1994 alleged that a leading British construction company had been involved in negotiating 'special payments' at the highest level in Malaysia in order to secure a contract. The Malaysian government reacted angrily on 25 February 1994 when the deputy prime minister, **Anwar Ibrahim**, announced a boycott of all British companies bidding for official contracts. Malaysia's decision was prompted by the personal fury of the prime minister, Dr Mahathir, at allegations of his personal financial impropriety set against a domestic background of political challenges and set-backs after nearly thirteen years in high office. He may well have resented also the unwillingness of Britain's prime minister, John Major, to defend publicly his personal probity. The prospect of the boycott being rescinded early through private diplomacy was dashed with further British press allegations. Dr Mahathir wrote to the *Financial Times* in March 1994 to say: 'For Malaysia, the die is cast. No contracts in exchange for British press freedom to tell lies.' Reconciliation became more likely in mid-year, when it was announced that Andrew Neil, the editor of *The Sunday Times*, was transferring to an American television station. The ban was rescinded in September 1994. A revival of Anglo-Malaysian tensions seemed likely in November 1994 when the High Court in London ruled that the British government had acted unlawfully by offering a loan on concessional terms from its foreign aid budget to assist in the construction of the Pergau Dam. That prospect abated, however, when the foreign secretary, Douglas Hurd, affirmed that Britain would meet its commercial obligations.
see also: Anwar Ibrahim; Mahathir Mohamad, Datuk Sri.

# C

**Cam, Nguyen Manh** (Vietnam) *see* Nguyen Manh Cam.

**Cam Ranh Bay** (Vietnam)

Cam Ranh Bay is situated on the central coast of Vietnam some twenty miles to the south of Nha Trang. It provides good natural anchorages and was used in 1905 by the ill-fated Russian fleet on their way to engage the Japanese. It assumed more than local significance from the mid-1960s, when it was developed into a major military logistical facility for both aircraft and naval vessels by the United States then assuming the prime burden in military confrontation with the Vietnamese Communists. In the **Vietnam War** the base was subject to rocket attack during the **Tet Offensive** in 1968 and was taken over by the government in Hanoi following its ultimate military success in 1975. Soviet interest in replacing the United States as the tenant of the base was resisted by Hanoi until early 1979, when relations with the People's Republic of China had deteriorated dramatically over Cambodia. A **Treaty of Friendship and Cooperation** signed with the Soviet Union in November 1978 provided the basis for the deployment of its aircraft and naval vessels at Cam Ranh Bay from March 1979. That deployment never had a tangible military role; Soviet forces were never engaged in any military action from the base. Intelligence-gathering and showing the flag constituted the main purpose of the exercise, which aggravated Vietnamese and Soviet relations with China and caused suspicion within South-East Asia. The Soviet presence was directly affected by the attempt by Mikhail Gorbachev from his assumption of power in March 1985 to improve relations with both China and the United States.

In January 1990 it was announced in Moscow that in line with an overall reduction in overseas commitments that the Soviet Union had begun withdrawing most of its aircraft from Cam Ranh Bay from the end of 1989. In October 1990 the Soviet ambassador to Vietnam announced that his country had begun withdrawing its troops from the base. With the break-up of the Soviet Union, Russia assumed responsibility for the residual military presence in Vietnam and it was announced in January 1992 that the last major warship had returned to Vladivostok in December 1991. A vestigial presence of neither military nor political significance has remained which Russia has sought to retain, while the Vietnamese have begun to explore alternative commercial possibilities for the facility. After a visit by Russia's foreign minister in July 1995, it was announced that its fleet would continue to enjoy access to the military base. Continued Russian use was discussed during a visit to Vietnam in October 1998 by the defence minister, Igor Sergeyev.

*see also:* Tet Offensive 1968; Treaty of Friendship and Cooperation 1978; Vietnam War.

## Cambodian People's Party (CPP) (Cambodia)

The Cambodian People's Party is the dominant party in the coalition government, which was formed in November 1998 after elections in the previous July. With 64 seats, it secured a majority in the National Assembly but was 18 seats short of the two-thirds required under the constitution to form an administration. Public protests organized by less successful parties at the flawed conduct of the elections delayed the establishment of a new government. By its formation in November, prime minister Hun Sen of the CPP was in effective political control.

The Cambodian People's Party (CPP) is the direct lineal successor of the **Kampuchean People's Revolutionary Party** (KPRP), which was established in January 1979 in the wake of Vietnam's invasion and occupation of Cambodia. The change in nomenclature, together with a disclaimer of Marxist identity and Vietnamese links, took place at an extraordinary congress on 17–18 October 1991 just before the **International Conference on Cambodia** reconvened in Paris. The CPP was a signatory to the political settlement reached in the French capital, which left its administration of Cambodia intact during the transitional period before elections held under **United Nations** auspices. The CPP, headed by **Chea Sim**, president of the National Assembly, and **Hun Sen**, the prime minister, cooperated up to a point with **UNTAC** (United Nations Transitional Authority in Cambodia) but employed its internal security apparatus to intimidate its noncommunist electoral opponents. In the event, it came second with 51 seats to FUNCINPEC led by Prince **Norodom Ranariddh** with 58. The CPP contested the outcome vociferously and, for a time, threatened secession in the country's eastern provinces as a gambit to ensure its participation in government. In the event, it joined a fragile coalition at the end of October in which Hun Sen assumed the office of Second Prime Minister to Prince Ranariddh, while Chea Sim maintained his National Assembly position.

The coalition government existed more in form than substance and was flawed by the refusal of the CPP to share power within the army, police and the provincial administration where its hold was tightly maintained. Political polarization within the coalition came to a head over the competing ambitions of Hun Sen and Prince Ranariddh and their attempts to recruit defectors from the **Khmer Rouge** for their bitter struggle. In April 1997, Hun Sen had engineered the defection to the CPP of sufficient FUNCINPEC members of the National Assembly to overturn its majority. In July 1997, Hun Sen ousted Prince Ranariddh in a bloody coup and established his political dominance, while still holding the office of Second Prime Minister. After elections in July 1998, a new coalition government was established in November based on a new power-sharing agreement between the CPP and FUNCINPEC, which barely masked political realities. Hun Sen became the sole prime minister, while Prince Ranariddh assumed the office of president of the National Assembly. By that juncture, the CPP had long shed its Vietnamese provenance and had become a vehicle for the personal political ambitions of Hun Sen.
*see also:* Chea Sim; FUNCINPEC; Hun Sen; International Conference on Cambodia, Paris 1991; Khmer Rouge; Kampuchean People's Revolutionary Party; Ranariddh, Prince Norodom; United Nations: Cambodia 1991–3; UNTAC.

## *Cao Dai* (Vietnam)

The *Cao Dai* is a quasi-religious sect which sprung up in southern Vietnam after the First World War. It originated from psychic experiments conducted by clerks in Saigon-Cholon who claimed to have established contact with Cao Dai, the all powerful master of the universe. Attracting funds for the purchase of land near Tay Ninh, a holy see of a kind was established centring on a church-like temple which became the centre of successful missionary activity. The appeal of *Cao Dai* was that it claimed to represent the synthesis of the main religions, except **Islam**. Its pantheon of saints included Jesus Christ, Buddha, Joan of Arc, Victor Hugo and Sun Yat Sen. At the outbreak of the Second World War, the sect had attracted some 300,000 adherents, rising to four times that number at its end. Members received military training as auxiliaries to the Japanese and after the war clashed with the Communists led by the **Viet Minh**. In opposition to the Communists and subsidized by the French, they operated as a state within a state. The *Cao Dai* joined with other dissident groups to challenge the government of **Ngo Dinh Diem** after the **Geneva Agreements on Indochina** in 1954. They were defeated with US assistance and disintegrated as a coherent movement, losing members to the Communist insurgency. With Communist military success in April 1975 and the subsequent unification of the country as the Socialist Republic of Vietnam, the *Cao Dai* now enjoys a constrained vestigial existence.
*see also:* Diem, Ngo Dinh; Viet Minh; Vietnam War.

## Cham (Cambodia/Vietnam)

The Cham are a distinct ethno-cultural group to be found in both Cambodia and Vietnam. They trace their origins to the ancient Kingdom of Champa once located in central Vietnam, which was overwhelmed and its inhabitants dispersed in the fifteenth century by Vietnam's relentless expansion to the south. By that time, **Islam** had been adopted as the religious faith, which has been more rigorously maintained in the Cambodian diaspora, while a form of Malay has become the common language. Cham in Cambodia, who numbered fewer than 100,000, sustained a distinct identity under French rule which began to be challenged by Prince **Norodom Sihanouk**'s regime. They suffered cruelly from the **Khmer Rouge**, however, who sought to extinguish their separate cultural existence, decimating their communities in the process. Since Vietnam's overthrow of **Pol Pot**'s government, the Cham have maintained a vestigial existence, although a significant number have been accepted as refugees in Malaysia.

see also: Islam; Khmer Rouge; Pol Pot; Sihanouk, Norodom.

## Chamlong Srimuang, General
(Thailand)
Chamlong Srimuang played a critical role in mobilizing popular protest against the former army commander-in-chief General **Suchinda Krapayoon** in May 1992 after he had assumed the office of prime minister of Thailand without having stood in general elections in March 1992. Chamlong Srimuang was born on 5 July 1935 in Thonburi of Chinese immigrant parents and was educated at the Chulachomklao Royal Military Academy, after which he began his career as a signals officer. He served in Vietnam and received postgraduate training in public administration in the United States. He was a prominent member of the **Young Turks** faction of the military, which was responsible for replacing General **Kriangsak Chomanan** with General **Prem Tinsulanond** as prime minister in 1980. He served as secretary-general to Prem but resigned this post after an abortive coup in April 1981 mounted by his military contemporaries. Chamlong had joined the radical Buddhist *Santi Asoke* sect in 1979 and became an open advocate of its regime of personal self-denial. In 1985, he resigned from the army with the rank of major-general and in November stood as an independent candidate in elections for the office of governor of Bangkok, which he won comfortably. In 1988 he established the *Palang Dharma* (Moral Force party), which had only limited success in general elections in July. Chamlong won a second term as governor of

Bangkok in January 1990 but resigned in January 1992 to stand in national elections in March. His party fared much better this time and after General Suchinda assumed the office of prime minister, Chamlong led the popular confrontation in the streets against the military which resulted in not only great loss of life but in Suchinda's political downfall. Chamlong was re-elected to Parliament in September 1992 and his party became a member of the ruling coalition. Chamlong refused to hold office, however, and announced in January 1993 that he was giving up the leadership of *Palang Dharma*. He continued to be politically active however. In April 1994 he made a crude bid for cabinet office, which was resisted by the prime minister, **Chuan Leekpai**. He then secured re-election as leader of *Palang Dharma* and in October 1994 entered the cabinet as deputy prime minister. He gave up the leadership of his party just before parliamentary elections in July 1995 in favour of Thaksin Shinawatra, reflecting the tension between religious and business-oriented factions and also announced his withdrawal from political life. However, in June 1996, he stood unsuccessfully for governor of Bangkok. Chamlong has enjoyed a mixed reputation. His role in challenging military autocracy has been acknowledged but together with a ruthless personal ambition and an authoritarian disposition.

see also: Chuan Leekpai; Kriangsak Chomanan; *Palang Dharma*; Prem Tinsulanond; *Santi Asoke*; Suchinda Krapayoon; Young Turks.

## Chang Shee-fu (Burma/Myanmar) see Khun Sa.

## Chart Pattana Party (Thailand)
The Chart Pattana (National Development) Party was set up in July 1992 as the political vehicle of former prime minister, **Chatichai Choonhavan**, who defected from the **Chart Thai** Party of which he had been leader. It enjoyed modest electoral success in September 1992 and was in opposition until December 1994 when it entered the **Democrat Party**-led coalition but without Chatichai assuming ministerial office. It returned to opposition after elections in July 1995 but then joined the government headed by the **New**

Aspiration Party after elections in November 1996. In November 1997, with a political realignment induced by economic adversity, and after an abortive bid by Chatichai to become prime minister, the Democrat Party replaced the New Aspiration Party as the core of the ruling coalition and Chart Pattana returned to opposition. Chatichai died in May 1998 but, despite expectations of the party's likely demise, it entered the Democrat-led ruling coalition in October 1998 in the face of some resistance because of its reputation for corruption.

*see also:* Chatichai Choonhavan; Chart Thai Party; Democrat Party; New Aspiration Party.

## Chart Thai Party (Thailand)

The Chart Thai (Thai National) Party served as a junior member of the **Democrat Party**-led ruling coalition which assumed office in November 1997. It had been the core party in government between July 1995 and November 1996, when a poor electoral showing led to a period in opposition. The Chart Thai Party has its origins in a military–business family network in direct lineal descent to Field Marshal Pin Choonhavan, a political strongman during the 1950s. It was founded in 1974 by close relatives of Field Marshal Pin, including his son-in-law, General Adireksan, who became its leader. He was succeeded in 1986 by Pin's son, General **Chatichai Choohavan** who was prime minister between 1988 and 1991. The Chart Thai Party has participated in a series of coalition governments since 1975 primarily as a political vehicle for a set of business interests with military links, which have disposed of great wealth in election campaigns. Like virtually all Thai parties, it has experienced recurrent defections from its ranks, including its former leader, Chatichai Choonhavan, who established the **Chart Pattana** (National Development) Party just before elections in September 1992. Despite factional tensions, the Chart Thai Party has sustained its institutional identity. It was led nominally by retired Air Chief Marshal Sombun Rahong until May 1994, when he was succeeded by provincial businessman **Banharn Silpa-archa** who took the party to electoral success in July 1995 when it secured 92 seats in a Parliament of

391 and assumed the office of prime minister. It lost office in elections in November 1996 but returned to government as a junior partner in November 1997. In coalition, Banharn has retained tight control over the party without assuming ministerial office.

*see also:* Banharn Silpa-archa; Chart Pattana; Chatichai Choonhavan; Democrat Party.

## Chatichai Choonhavan, General (Thailand)

Chatichai Choonhavan was a flamboyant political figure who served as prime minister of Thailand from August 1988 until his removal from office through a military coup in February 1991. As leader of the **Chart Thai Party** (Thai National Party), with the largest number of members in the Parliament, he succeeded **Prem Tinsulanond** on his resignation. As the first elected prime minister for twelve years, Chatichai Choonhavan made an immediate impact in foreign policy by softening his country's stance towards Cambodia and Vietnam and announcing his intention of turning Indochina from a battleground into a trading market. In domestic policy he departed from the cautious technocratic culture of his predecessor to provide a more direct business orientation. In the event, his administration's reputation for corrupt practice softened the public response to his overthrow, which was precipitated by suspicion within the military establishment that he intended to purge its serving hierarchy. Chatichai Choonhavan was born in Bangkok on 5 April 1922. His father was Field Marshal Pin Choonhavan, who was a powerful political figure during the 1950s until displaced by Marshal **Sarit Thanarat**. He was educated at the Chulachomklao Royal Military Academy in Bangkok and served with Thai units in Burma and southern China during the Pacific War and also saw action in the Korean War. With his father's political fall, he was sent, in effect, into exile serving as ambassador in Europe and Latin America. After the death of Sarit, he returned to Thailand and worked in the Foreign Ministry; in 1972 he distinguished himself for his bravery in rescuing Israeli hostages seized by the Palestinian Black September organization. He was a founder member of the Chart Thai Party in

1974. As a leading member of that alliance between the military and business, he held a number of government offices including that of foreign minister. Following his removal from power, he spent time in exile in Britain but returned to political life in 1992. He led a defection from the Chart Thai Party to form the **Chart Pattana** Party (National Development Party), which took part in elections in September 1992 to win sixty seats but without securing membership of the coalition government led by **Chuan Leekpai**. His new party entered the ruling coalition in December 1994 but without Chatichai assuming ministerial office. It returned to opposition after elections in July 1995 but re-entered government after further elections in November 1996 but again without Chatichai. In November 1997, when prime minister **Chavalit Yongchaiyuth** was obliged to give up office against a background of economic crisis, Chatichai made an abortive bid to succeed him. He died in May 1998.

*see also:* Chart Pattana; Chart Thai Party; Chavalit Yongchaiyuth; Chuan Leekpai; Prem Tinsulanond; Sarit Thanarat.

## Chavalit Yongchaiyuth, General
(Thailand)

General Chavalit Yongchaiyuth was prime minister of Thailand between November 1996 and November 1997 when he was obliged to resign office against a background of economic crisis. Chavalit Yongchaiyuth was born on 15 May 1932 in Nonthaburi Province and began his career as a professional soldier on entering the Chulachomklao Royal Military Academy in 1953. He received staff training in Thailand and also at Fort Leavenworth in the United States. He developed strong ideas from Communist defectors about the need to promote rural economic development as a counter to insurgency and was associated with the influential **Democratic Soldiers** faction. He put such ideas into practice when he rose to become army commander-in-chief in 1986. In that position, he indicated clear political ambition but his crude ideological formulations aroused hostility from the royal family, who suspected him of republican leanings. He was never tempted to realize his ambition through direct military means but

was attracted by an offer of political preferment by the prime minister, **Chatichai Choonhavan**. He retired from active command in March 1990 to be directly appointed deputy prime minister and minister of defence. His first spell in politics as an unelected minister proved to be frustrating and in June he resigned from the government, ostensibly because of allegations of corruption by a cabinet colleague. In October 1990 General Chavalit founded the **New Aspiration Party** with military and bureaucratic support. He was out of office when the military coup of February 1991 took place. His party contested the elections held in March 1992 and won seventy-two seats but was not made a member of the governing coalition which nominated the non-elected former army commander, General **Suchinda Krapayoon**, as prime minister. General Chavalit was not tainted by the bloodshed which occurred in May when mass protests at General Suchinda's appointment took place in Bangkok. In the fresh elections which were held in September 1992, the New Aspiration Party secured only fifty-one seats but was included in the ruling coalition led by **Chuan Leekpai**. After elections in July 1995, he became a deputy prime minister and minister of defence in the ruling coalition formed by **Banharn Silpa-archa** and demonstrated his political influence in September that year when he secured the appointment of his nominee as army commander against the wishes of the retiring incumbent. In elections in November 1996, his New Aspiration Party won 125 seats in the Parliament to form a new coalition government under his leadership. That realization of political ambition turned sour within a year as Thailand was confronted with economic adversity, which brought his government down. In opposition, he has been combative but has been unable to live down his close association with economic failure.

*see also:* Banharn Silpa-archa; Chatichai Choonhavan; Chuan Leekpai; Democratic Soldiers; New Aspiration Party; Suchinda Krapayoon.

## Chea Sim　(Cambodia)

Chea Sim became the president of a newly-constituted appointed Senate in November 1998 with the additional responsibility for serving as acting head of state during the absence abroad of King **Norodom Sihanouk**. He was born on 15 November 1932 into a peasant family in Svay Rieng Province. His revolutionary activity is believed to date from the early 1950s and two decades later he was secretary of a district committee of the Communist Party of Cambodia under the **Khmer Rouge**. After they came to power in April 1975, he was elected to the National Assembly but then became disaffected and was one of the leaders of a rebellion in eastern Cambodia against **Pol Pot**'s rule. That rebellion provided the Vietnamese with an opportunity to invade through a united front of Cambodians. Chea Sim rose in the hierarchy of the Vietnamese-sponsored **Kampuchean People's Revolutionary Party** (KPRP) as well as holding ministerial portfolios in the **People's Republic of Kampuchea** and the chairmanship of the National Assembly from its establishment in 1981. He has enjoyed a reputation as a party hardliner and asserted his position against the younger, more moderate prime minister, **Hun Sen**. Chea Sim assumed the leadership of the **Cambodian People's Party**, established in succession to the KPRP when it was set up at an extraordinary congress on 17–18 October 1991, shortly before the **International Conference on Cambodia** was reconvened in Paris. After the formation of a coalition government in October 1993 following elections conducted by the United Nations, he became the President of the National Assembly until November 1998. Although he remains chairman of the Cambodian People's Party, effective power has been assumed by Hun Sen.

*see also:* Cambodian People's Party; Hun Sen; International Conference on Cambodia, Paris 1991; Kampuchea, People's Republic of; Kampuchean People's Revolutionary Party; Khmer Rouge; Pol Pot; Sihanouk, Norodom.

## Chin (Burma/Myanmar)

The Chin are an indigenous minority group of Tibeto-Burman origin who are to be found in a stretch of mountainous terrain extending southwards along the borders with India and Bangladesh and then into the heart of the Arakan region. Mixed culturally in attachment to Hindu, Christian and folk religions, the Chin

have never assimilated to Burmese **Buddhism** and during the colonial period were recruited by the British into the local army. Their leaders welcomed independence in 1948 but sought political autonomy within the Union of Burma beyond the special territorial division which they were accorded. The Chin, like other ethnic minorities in Burma, have long been in a state of armed rebellion against the government in Rangoon. They found increasing difficulty in sustaining their military campaign during the 1990s, however, as the ruling **State Law and Order Restoration Council** (SLORC) and its successor, the **National Peace and Development Council** (NPDC), were able to disrupt their lines of logistical support as well as to reinforce their own counter-insurgency capabilities.

*see also:* Kachin; Karen; National Peace and Development Council; Shan; State Law and Order Restoration Council.

## Chin Peng (Malaya/Malaysia)

Chin Peng, whose real name is believed to be Ong Boon Hua, became general secretary of the Communist Party of Malaya in March 1947 in succession to **Loi Tack**, who was revealed as a double agent after he had absconded with party funds. Chin Peng, who was born in Malaya in 1922, had been a wartime guerrilla commander decorated with the OBE by the British for his role against the Japanese. He assumed the leadership of the Communist Party of Malaya at the outset of the Cold War and, when confirmed in office by its central committee in March 1948, the party announced a programme of mass struggle against British imperialism. Under his leadership, an insurrection was launched from June after the colonial government had declared a state of emergency in response to growing acts of Communist violence. By the mid-1950s, that insurrection had been well contained with its fighting remnant regrouped along the border with Thailand. In November 1955 Chin Peng indicated a willingness to negotiate with the elected governments of Malaya and Singapore. The **Baling Talks** with the chief minister of Malaya, **Tunku Abdul Rahman**, and that of Singapore, **David Marshall**, took place near the border with Thailand in the following month but without success. Chin Peng's offer to end the insurrection in return for the legalization of the Communist Party met with a blank refusal. He returned to the jungle but the insurrection continued to lose momentum and the state of **Emergency** was rescinded in 1960 by the government of an independent Malaya. There were no further confirmed sightings of Chin Peng, who was alternately reported to be in southern Thailand and in China. His voice was heard, however, on the clandestine radio station, the Voice of the Malayan Revolution, whose transmitter was located in southern China. During the 1970s, when the Communist Party of Malaya split into three factions concurrent with a revival of guerrilla activities, he was rumoured to have been replaced as general secretary. On 2 December 1989 Ching Peng appeared in public for the first time since 1955 at a hotel in the southern Thai town of Hat Yai dressed in a business suit and in apparent good health. On behalf of the Communist Party he signed two peace agreements with the governments of Thailand and Malaysia which, in effect, constituted acts of surrender but without indicating the party's disbandment. He then appeared to return to the jungle but in the following decade has been known to engage in business in Thailand and also to give media interviews about his experience as an insurgent leader with a view to publishing his memoirs.

see also: Baling Talks 1955; Emergency 1948–60; Loi Tack; Marshall, David; Rahman, Tunku Abdul.

## Chinh, Truong  (Vietnam) see Truong Chinh.

## Christmas Bombing 1972  (Vietnam)

The blunting of their spring offensive in 1972 by the force and accuracy of US aerial firepower caused the Vietnamese Communists to revive interest in a negotiated solution to the **Vietnam War**, especially with a presidential election pending in the United States. In early October in private in Paris, **Le Duc Tho** presented the US national security adviser, Dr Henry Kissinger, with a draft peace agreement which became the basis for an ultimate accord and the United States' military disengagement. Although the Vietnamese Communists no longer demanded that the Americans remove President **Nguyen**

**Van Thieu** from office, he initially refused to accept the agreement in part because the prospect of a coalition government with the Communists could not be tolerated. In response, the Vietnamese Communists disclosed the terms of the draft agreement towards the end of October. Renewed talks in November and into December proved inconclusive. On 18 December 1972 US President Richard Nixon, who had been re-elected in the previous month, authorized the aerial bombardment of Hanoi and Haiphong, which took place over twelve days with surprisingly limited casualties given the scale of the operation. This deliberate act of intimidation provoked international protest as well as leading to the loss by the Americans of a large number of aircraft. The peace negotiations resumed on 8 January 1973 and the final **Paris Peace Agreements** were signed before the end of the month by all parties, including the government in Saigon, but without any fundamental difference in the text compared to the initial draft. Among the explanations for US conduct, the most convincing is that the Christmas bombing was a deliberate demonstration of power by President Nixon to impress President Thieu that he was not being abandoned by his long-standing ally and to ensure that he endorsed the Paris accords.

see also: Le Duc Tho; Paris Peace Agreements 1973; Thieu, Nguyen Van; Vietnam War.

## Chuan Leekpai  (Thailand)

Chuan Leekpai, as leader of the **Democrat Party**, was prime minister of Thailand from September 1992 until July 1995 and then, after more than two years in opposition, resumed that high office from November 1997. He was the first truly civilian prime minister since the mid-1970s and has maintained a reputation for personal probity and integrity. He came to power through elections in September 1992, which were held in the wake of a bloody confrontation on the streets of Bangkok in the previous May. Civilian demonstrators had challenged the right of former army commander, General **Suchinda Krapayoon** to become prime minister without election to Parliament. The Democrat Party secured 79 seats, the largest number in the Parliament, and provided the core of a new coalition government.

Chuan Leekpai was born on 28 July 1938 in Trang Province. He studied law at Thammasat University in Bangkok and entered Parliament at the age of 31, when Thailand was still under military rule. He has been a member of Parliament continuously ever since and first held government office as deputy minister of justice in 1975. He was speaker of the lower house during 1986-8 as well as a deputy prime minister between the end of 1989 and August 1990, which is when he became leader of the Democrat Party on the resignation of Bhichai Rattakul. During his first term of high office, Chuan Leekpai ruled at the head of a discordant coalition without demonstrating inspired or decisive leadership. For example, in early 1994, he failed to secure the passage of amendments designed to revise the constitution imposed by the military after they seized power in 1991. This failure indicated his inability then to overcome a structural tension in Thai politics between civilian and military interests. He was also embarrassed by the residual support of the military for the **Khmer Rouge**, despite his government's commitment to good relations with its counterpart in Phnom Penh. He lost office in July 1995 after elections, which had been precipitated by the defection of a coalition partner. The Democrat Party won 86 seats compared to 96 by the **Chart Thai Party**, which provided the core of a new coalition from which the Democrat Party was excluded.

Chuan Leekpai returned to high office in November 1997 when **Chavalit Yongchaiyuth** lost national confidence and was obliged to resign as prime minister after the devastating onset of an acute economic crisis. A political realignment allowed Chuan to form a new coalition government, although initially with only a limited parliamentary majority, which was not augmented until October 1998. There was no resistance from the armed forces to his return to power, while he enjoyed critical support from King **Bhumiphol Adulyadej**. On taking office, he put together a credible economic team that inspired confidence among international financial institutions as well as the approval of the United States. Under Chuan's leadership, Thailand was set on the path to economic recovery, while the ruling coalition overcame recurrent opposition attempts to split

it through parliamentary motions of no confidence. Although not an inspiring political figure, Chuan has commanded popularity and confidence because he is trusted as an honest man committed to democratic reforms and the eradication of corruption under a new constitution promulgated in September 1997.

*see also:* Bhumiphol Adulyadej; Chart Thai Party; Chavalit Yongchaiyuth; Democrat Party; Khmer Rouge; Suchinda Krapayoon.

## Clark Air Base (Philippines)

Clark Air Base on the island of Luzón was one of the major military facilities to which the United States acquired leasehold title, initially for ninety-nine years, under an agreement concluded with the government of the Philippines on 17 March 1947. That tenure was reduced to twenty-five years under a revised agreement of 16 September 1966. Under a further agreement concluded with the Philippine government on 27 August 1991, designed to extend US tenure at **Subic Bay Naval Base** for ten years, the United States agreed to transfer jurisdiction over Clark Air Base by September 1992 but by then it had lost its operational value because of the damaging effect of the volcanic eruption of neighbouring Mount Pinatubo. Also, the Philippine Senate repudiated the overall package in September 1991. Clark Air Base had been the site for the only major US tactical air force deployment in South-East Asia with fighter and airlift wings. It had also been the air logistics centre for all US forces in the western Pacific, while the Crow Valley Weapons Range provided the only facility for live tactical training west of California. The base lost its former military significance with the end of the Cold War and tactical fighter aircraft were withdrawn early in 1991. In June 1991 the volcanic eruption of nearby Mount Pinatubo caused irreparable damage to the base, which was completely evacuated by United States personnel.

*see also:* Subic Bay Naval Base.

## (Central Limit Order Book) CLOB
(Malaysia/Singapore)

The Central Limit Order Book (CLOB) is the name given to an arrangement whereby Malaysian company shares could be traded through the Singapore Stock Exchange. At the beginning of September 1998, however, concurrent with economic crisis and the imposition of exchange controls in Malaysia, such trading was declared illegal. Shares to the value of around US$4.2 billion, and held mainly by Singaporeans, were frozen. An agreement between agencies of both stock exchanges later in the month bound Malaysia to effect the transfer of all CLOB securities into the individual securities accounts of CLOB investors by the end of 1999. That obligation was not met, while Malaysia's Finance Ministry threatened to transfer the frozen shares to its custody from a nominee account if a derisory offer for them was not accepted. Although Malaysia intimated that releasing such a volume of illegally-traded shares would pose a threat to other stock values, Malaysian shares could still be traded legally in Copenhagen, London and Tokyo. The impasse was sustained by the structural alienation between Kuala Lumpur and Singapore aggravated by regional economic crisis and domestic political difficulties faced by Prime Minister Dr **Mahathir Mohamad**, which arose from his attempt to destroy the reputation and career of his former deputy, **Anwar Ibrahim**. In February 2000, an agreement between the Kuala Lumpur and Singapore stock exchanges offered investors a choice of two options involving limited premium fees through which to recover their shares. Their release over thirteen months began in July. At issue for Malaysia was an interest in having Morgan Stanley Capital International return the Kuala Lumpur Stock Exchange to its stock-market indices so as to counter selling pressure from the release of CLOB shares.

*see also:* Anwar Ibrahim; Mahathir Mohamad.

## Cobbold Commission 1962 (Malaya/ Malaysia)

A commission of inquiry was appointed by the British and Malayan governments on 16 January 1962 to ascertain whether or not the inhabitants of Britain's colonies of Sarawak and North Borneo wished them to become constituent parts of the projected Federation of Malaysia. Comprising five members and chaired by Lord Cobbold, governor of the Bank of England, the commission issued its report in July 1962. Its members concluded that about one-third of the population in each territory strongly favoured an early realization of Malaysia; another third, many of whom favoured the project, had asked for conditions and safeguards of a varying nature; the remaining third was divided between those who insisted on independence before Malaysia was considered and those who strongly preferred British rule to continue. The report had the effect of reinforcing the momentum for the new Federation which enjoyed the explicit support of the Malayan and British governments. At the time, Brunei was a candidate for membership but was not included within the Cobbold Commission's remit.

## Cobra Gold Military Exercises (Thailand)

Cobra Gold is the name given to combined exercises between Thai and US forces which have been held on an annual basis from 1982, with an interruption in 1991, from the early 1980s. After the end of the **Vietnam War** in April 1975, Thailand moved quickly to distance itself from a close military relationship with the United States. The civilian government brought about the withdrawal of all US military bases and troops by July 1976. However, a military coup in October restored an earlier strategic perspective in Bangkok, which was reinforced after Vietnam's invasion of Cambodia at the end of 1978 in the third phase of the **Indochina Wars**. The exercises, involving troops from both countries, were intended to signal the continued commitment of the United States to the territorial integrity of a Thailand seemingly under threat from an expansionist Vietnam. Following the end of the Cold War and Vietnam's withdrawal from Cambodia, the United States had no compunction in suspending the exercises after the military removed the elected government of **Chatichai Choonhavan** by a coup in February 1991. Political violence in May 1992 by the military in an attempt to hold on to power served to maintain that suspension. The appointment of a civilian prime minister, **Chuan Leekpai**, after elections in September 1992 led to a decision to revive Cobra Gold, which resumed in northern Thailand in May 1993. It was announced in January 2000 that forces from Singapore would participate in the annual exercise; the first country to be so invited, although it had provided observers for a number of years.

see also: Chatichai Choonhavan; Chuan Leekpai; Indochina Wars; Vietnam War.

## Collective Security in Asia: Soviet Proposal 1969

A proposal for a system of collective security was advanced by Leonid Brezhnev on 7 June 1969 at a Conference of Communist and Workers Parties in Moscow. It was put forward almost as an afterthought to a speech on peaceful coexistence and was expressed in a single sentence: 'We think that the course of events places on the agenda the task of creating a system of collective security in Asia.' Although deficient in detail, the proposal was generally interpreted as an attempt to mobilize countervailing power against the People's Republic of China both in the light of a deteriorating bilateral relationship and the prospect of Sino-US rapprochement. The proposal was symptomatic of the changing pattern of global alignments but failed to attract any regional support, even from close affiliates of the Soviet Union such as Vietnam.

## Commonwealth Strategic Reserve
(Malaya/Malaysia)

The Commonwealth Strategic Reserve was a deployment of British, Australian and New Zealand forces based in Malaya under British command established in December 1955. The joint deployment served as a supplement for counter-insurgency operations in Malaya but was conceived as a support for regional defence under the terms of the **Manila Pact** of 1954 to which Malaya refused to adhere on independence in August 1957. Under the terms of the **Anglo-Malayan Defence Agreement** concluded in October 1957, the Federation of Malaya granted the United Kingdom the right to maintain naval, land and air forces 'including a Commonwealth Strategic Reserve . . . for the fulfilment of Commonwealth and international obligations'. That right was carried over with the establishment of Malaysia in September 1963 but lapsed when the Anglo-Malaysian Defence Agreement was superseded by the **Five Power Defence Arrangements** in November 1971.

see also: Anglo-Malayan/Malaysian Defence Agreement 1957–71; Five Power Defence Arrangements 1971–; Manila Pact 1954.

## Communism in South-East Asia

Communism in South-East Asia has attained and maintained positions of power only in Vietnam and Laos.

The Communist Party of Vietnam, established originally as the Communist Party of Indochina in 1930, came to power in two stages. In July 1954, after a period of armed revolution from 1945 when it seized power briefly in Hanoi, it formed the government north of the 17th parallel of latitude in the name of the *Lao Dong* (Workers Party). It then inspired and supported the insurgency to the south of that latitude led nominally by the **National Liberation Front of South Vietnam**. In April 1975 its armed forces seized power in the southern part of Vietnam, which was formally reunified in July 1976 as the Socialist Republic of Vietnam. At its fourth national congress in December 1976, the name Communist Party of Vietnam was adopted. The **Lao People's Revolutionary Party**, which was created from the Communist Party of Indochina, consolidated its power in the wake of the Communist victory in Vietnam. In December 1975 it established the Lao People's Democratic Republic, displacing the Kingdom of Laos.

A Communist government came to power in Cambodia in April 1975 through the revolutionary success of the **Khmer Rouge**. In the name of the State of **Democratic Kampuchea**, it achieved notoriety through its brutal and bloodthirsty collectivism. It was overthrown by a Vietnamese invasion in December 1978 and in January 1979 an alternative Marxist regime was established under Vietnamese aegis in the name of the **People's Republic of Kampuchea** (PRK). That regime was superseded in September 1993 when a royalist constitution was reinstated in the wake of the political settlement of the Cambodian conflict concluded by an **International Conference on Cambodia** in Paris in October 1991. The former ruling **Kampuchean People's Revolutionary Party** (KPRP), in the name of the **Cambodian People's Party** (CPP), which had repudiated Marxist ideology, then shared power in a coalition government from

October 1993. After mounting a violent coup in July 1997, the Cambodian People's Party consolidated its position, which was validated by elections a year later. The insurgent Khmer Rouge had begun to disintegrate as a fighting force from the establishment of the coalition government and also suffered political defections. With the death of its leader **Pol Pot** in April 1998, it ceased to exist as a viable organization and to inspire the awesome fear that had been generated during its murderous rule between 1975 and 1978.

Elsewhere in South-East Asia, Communism has come close to seizing power but has experienced declining fortunes from the mid-1960s. Communism in the region has its origins in the colonial connection and through **Overseas Chinese** links.

The first party to be established was in the Netherlands East Indies where a Dutch Marxist, Franciscus Marie Sneevliet, set up the Indies Social Democratic Association on 9 May 1914. It was transformed into the Communist Party of Indonesia (*Partai Komunis Indonesia*: PKI) on 23 May 1920, the first such organization to be set up in Asia outside of the former Russian empire. Under an indigenous leadership in the mid-1920s the party launched an uprising, which was crushed. It also failed to put its political stamp on the nascent republic through involvement in an abortive uprising, the **Madiun Revolt**, in east Java in 1948. After international recognition of independence in December 1949, a younger generation of cadres led by D. N. Aidit secured a legitimate place for Communism within the parliamentary system by stressing its nationalist credentials. During the period of **Guided Democracy**, the PKI established a close relationship with President **Sukarno** and raised its membership to 3 million, which made it the largest party outside of the Communist commonwealth. By the mid-1960s, the PKI seemed to be on the threshold of power but an abortive coup (*see* **Gestapu**) in October 1965, in which it was implicated, provided an opportunity for the armed forces to destroy and outlaw it. The Communist Party of Indonesia has never recovered from that act of repression in which its leadership was liquidated and its membership decimated.

Communism in the Philippines has also had a colonial connection in its provenance. Harrison George, a leader of the Communist Party of the United States, took the initiative to induct Filipinos into the international movement. The Communist Party of the Philippines was founded on 26 August 1930 by Cristanto Evangalista, who was a trade union leader. It began to make an impact during the Japanese occupation when it organized the insurgent *Hukbo ng Bayan Laban sa Hapon*, in abbreviation **Hukbalahap**, which translates as People's Anti-Japanese Army. Mixed success in harassing the Japanese led to the establishment of local territorial positions of power prior to liberation which were not recognized by the United States. A period of legal struggle followed, with the Democratic Alliance Party serving as an electoral vehicle in April 1946 just before independence. Its six successful candidates were then denied seats in the Congress and its demands for land reform were rejected. The *Hukbalahap* took up armed struggle in January 1950 under the banner of the *Hukbong Mapagpalaya ng Bayan* (People's Liberation Army). During the course of the year a series of military challenges was posed to the government in Manila; these were overcome in October only when virtually the entire party Politburo was arrested in Manila. From that juncture, and with the subsequent surrender of their military commander, Luis Taruc, they went into decline despite the failure of the government to address fundamental economic and social ills.

The Communist Party then degenerated into an armed banditry although a fraternal affiliation of a kind was maintained with the Soviet Union. Under the intellectual guidance of José María Sisón, the party was reconstituted at the end of 1968, inspired by Chinese revolutionary experience, when a **New People's Army** was established in March 1969 as its military wing. Adopting a strategic doctrine which exploited the archipelagic condition of the Philippines as well as economic distress in the rural areas, the Communist Party was able to make dramatic gains from the mid-1970s as the rule of President **Ferdinand Marcos** began to decay. The prospect of political victory slipped away after the downfall of President Marcos and his succession by Mrs **Corazón Aquino**. A miscalculation of the popular mood followed and unrealistic demands of government in Manila were met with military repression, which took its toll of insurgent strength. By 1992 President **Fidel Ramos**, who had succeeded Mrs Aquino, felt sufficiently confident to persuade the Congress to make the Communist Party a legal organization. Subject to internal cleavage and a loss of morale from the failure of communism as a practical ideology, the party enjoys only a vestigial existence despite continuing gross inequalities within Philippine society. It continues to be represented by the **National Democratic Front**, whose leadership has been bitterly divided. In November 1999, however, Philippines Defence Secretary Orlando Mercado warned of a revival in the strength and activities of the New People's Army marked by kidnapping and attacks on police stations in Quezon Province. NPA ambushes of police and the military continued into 2000.

Chinese influence was more direct and continuous in the case of Communist parties in Malaysia, Singapore and Thailand, although their achievement has been even less than that of comrades in the Philippines. The Chinese Communist Party was instrumental in organizing in Singapore in January 1928 the Nanyang or South Seas Communist Party, which was succeeded in April 1930 by the Communist Party of Malaya, which incorporated Singapore within its revolutionary jurisdiction. The party engaged in trade union agitation but built up its following through anti-Japanese activity in the late 1930s. With the outbreak of the Pacific War, British assistance was provided for military training for the insurgent Malayan People's Anti-Japanese Army, which engaged in jungle warfare after the surrender of Singapore. Only limited demobilization took place after the defeat of the Japanese and peaceful struggle was replaced by armed struggle against the colonial government in June 1948. During the **Emergency** declared by the colonial administration, the Communist Party drew on support almost exclusively from the Chinese community and appeared to have seized the military initiative by 1951, when they assassinated the British high commissioner, Sir Henry Gurney. However, by that juncture, the balance of military advantage

had already begun to turn against the Communist Party, which had sought to revise its militant strategy in order to widen its political appeal. The **Baling Talks** between its leader, **Chin Peng**, and the chief ministers of Malaya and Singapore in December 1955 were inconclusive, because the latter refused to countenance the legality of the party. Chin Peng refused to give up armed struggle, which continued in a sporadic manner from redoubts established along the border with Thailand. The reduction in military activity enabled the independent government of Malaya to announce an end to the Emergency in 1960. The Communist Party was afflicted by splits within its ranks during the late 1960s but revived its military activities at the end of the **Vietnam War** without any political advantage. In Singapore, the Communist movement had been effectively crushed by the time the island became independent in 1965. In December 1989 Chin Peng appeared along the border with Thailand to sign two ceasefire agreements with the Malaysian and Thai authorities, which amounted to a virtual surrender after forty years of fruitless struggle. A Communist movement developed in Sarawak in northern Borneo during the wartime Japanese occupation with a constituency among the Chinese community. It enjoyed a measure of success during Indonesia's **Confrontation** of Malaysia but was crushed after their reconciliation.

The Communist Party of Thailand originated from the same source as the Communist Party of Malaya in the form of a Siam Special Committee, which was set up by the South Seas Communist Party in the late 1920s. Although a fully fledged Thai party was established in July 1929, its first congress is believed to have convened only in 1942 with a predominantly Chinese membership. Significant activity by the party dates only from the 1960s, concurrent with the United States' growing military involvement in Vietnam with a clandestine radio station, the Voice of the People of Thailand, operating from March 1962. Armed struggle, which began only in August 1965 in the economically deprived north-eastern province of Nakhon Phanom, spread during the decade to the north and south of the country. The overthrow of the military regime in October 1973 provided an opportunity for the party to extend its support to a student constituency which was strengthened with the **Thammasat University Massacre** in October 1976 and the return to power of the armed forces. The ranks of the party were augmented by students seeking refuge in the jungles but tension developed between an ethnic Chinese leadership and the younger generation of Thai members. The opportunity to pose a challenge of substance to the government in Bangkok was frustrated by the development of civic action programmes by the armed forces as well as by the alienation that developed between the Vietnamese and Chinese Communists. With the onset of the Cambodian conflict, the Thai Communists were driven out of sanctuaries in Laos and their cause was sacrificed by China to the need to align with Thailand to challenge Vietnam's occupation of Cambodia. From that juncture, the Thai Communist movement began to collapse until it had ceased to exist as a viable entity by the end of the Cold War.

Communism in Burma has had a more indigenous source arising from the Marxist stream of the nationalist movement against the colonial administration. At the end of the Pacific War, Communist rebellion challenged the government in Rangoon together with ethnic-minority uprisings. The party then split into two factions which aligned in time with Moscow and Beijing. The White Flag faction which looked to China was provided with a measure of material support and served as a point of leverage for Beijing but without ever enabling the party to pose an effective military threat. The Burmese army was successful in driving the Communists from the Pegu Yoma heartland in the 1970s and the party continued its insurgency with support from Wa tribesmen in the north adjacent to the border with China. A revolt by these tribesmen in 1989 dispossessed an ethnic Chinese leadership, which had the effect of emasculating the party as a viable political entity.

Communism has enjoyed its greatest success in Indochina. Under the original inspiration and leadership of **Ho Chi Minh** acting for the Comintern, rival revolutionary groupings were amalgamated into the Communist Party of

Indochina at a unity conference in Hong Kong in 1930. The Communist Party of Indochina provided the core of the **Viet Minh**, a national front which challenged French rule at the end of the Pacific War in the **August Revolution 1945**. The party divided formally into three national components in 1951, with the *Lao Dong* assuming responsibility for revolution in Vietnam. Corresponding parties were set up for Laos and Cambodia under Vietnamese patronage, but in the case of Cambodia an alternative leadership emerged in the 1960s, which rejected lineal descent from the Communist Party of Indochina and became known as the Khmer Rouge.

The ruling parties in Hanoi and Vientiane have maintained their monopoly of power but have been obliged to compromise their socialist doctrine in order to practise market economics. The lead was taken by Vietnam's Communist Party at its sixth national congress when it adopted a policy of ***Doi Moi*** (economic renovation) followed by its Laotian counterpart. Both parties have resisted demands for liberalization and have maintained a tight control over their respective political systems.

*see also:* Aquino, Corazón; August Revolution 1945; Baling Talks 1955; Cambodian People's Party; Chin Peng; Confrontation; Crocodile Hole; Democratic Kampuchea; *Doi Moi*; Emergency 1948–60; *Gestapu*; Guided Democracy; Ho Chi Minh; *Hukbalahap* Movement; International Conference on Cambodia, Paris 1991; Kampuchea, People's Republic of; Kampuchean People's Revolutionary Party; Khmer Rouge; *Lao Dong*; Lao People's Revolutionary Party; Madiun Revolt 1948; Marcos, Ferdinand; National Democratic Front; National Liberation Front of South Vietnam; New People's Army; Overseas Chinese; Pol Pot; Ramos, Fidel; Sisón, José María; Sukarno; Thammasat University Massacre 1976; Viet Minh; Vietnam War.

## Confrontation  (Indonesia/Malaysia)

Confrontation (*Konfrontasi* in Indonesian) was a term first employed by President **Sukarno** in June 1960 to register his country's militant stance towards the Netherlands in pursuing its claim to the western half of the island of

New Guinea, now **Irian Jaya**. The term was subsequently employed in January 1963 by the foreign minister, Dr **Subandrio**, to register a corresponding stance towards the advent of the Federation of Malaysia, whose legitimacy was thereby challenged. Described by Sukarno as a contest of power in all fields, Confrontation amounted to a practice of coercive diplomacy, employing military measures stopping short of all-out war, which was designed to create a sense of international crisis in order to provoke diplomatic intervention in Indonesia's interest. The campaign of Confrontation to recover West New Guinea from the Dutch, who had retained the territory after according independence to the rest of the Netherlands East Indies, reached a successful conclusion in August 1962. US mediation, driven by fear of Communist advantage, produced a negotiated settlement which provided for the transfer of the territory to Indonesia, via the United Nations' temporary administration in May 1963. In the case of Malaysia (a British-backed Malayan proposal to merge the Federation of Malaya, the self-governing island of Singapore, the British colonies of Sarawak and North Borneo and the British protected Sultanate of Brunei), Confrontation failed in its purpose (*see* **Anglo-Malayan/ Malaysian Defence Agreement 1957–71; Brunei Revolt 1962**). Indonesia was not able to press its anti-colonial claim with the same legitimacy as in the case of Irian Jaya and proved unable to mobilize corresponding international support. President Lyndon Johnson did dispatch the US attorney-general, Robert Kennedy, to engage in seeming mediation in January 1964 but was not disposed to bring pressure to bear on Malaysia in the way that the late President John F. Kennedy had coerced the Dutch. Britain honoured its treaty commitment and with Australian, New Zealand and Malaysian military support, fended off armed incursions in northern Borneo and peninsular Malaysia and also deterred more substantial military intervention. After the political downfall of Sukarno in 1966, Indonesia became reconciled to Malaysia with which it established diplomatic relations in August 1967. The term Confrontation disappeared from Indonesia's political lexicon with the consolidation of President **Suharto's New Order**.

*see also:* Anglo-Malayan/Malaysian Defence Agreement 1957–71; Brunei Revolt 1962; Irian Jaya; New Order; Subandrio; Suharto; Sukarno.

## Constitutional Crises (Malaysia)

In 1983 and in 1992, the popularly elected government of the Federation of Malaysia came into conflict with the country's constitutional monarchy comprising the king and the hereditary sultans or rulers of the peninsular Malaysian states. The king, known in Malay as *Yang di-Pertuan Agong*, holds an elected five-year term of office which rotates among the nine rulers in an agreed order of seniority. The initial conflict was precipitated when a package of constitutional amendments was rushed through the federal Parliament in August 1983. The most significant measure provided for any Bill to become law automatically fifteen days after it had been presented to the king for his assent, with a corresponding application to states' legislatures and sultans. In addition, the formal right of the king to proclaim a state of emergency was transferred to the prime minister. The particular motive for the legislation was concern on the part of the government at the likely interventionist political role of a future king. An underlying complementary factor was the attitude towards the rulers and the monarchy on the part of the prime minister, Dr **Mahathir Mohamad**, whose social background disposed him against the idea of royal prerogative. The constitutional crisis arose when the king – then the Sultan of Pahang – refused his assent to the package of amendments with unanimous support from all the other hereditary rulers. After a period of political tension, a basis for compromise was reached at the end of the year. In mid-December during the indisposition of the king, who had suffered a stroke, his deputy signed the Constitution (Amendment) Bill on the understanding that a special session of Parliament would be called to introduce new legislation restoring the monarch's right to proclaim a state of emergency on the advice of the prime minister. The right of the king to refuse his assent to any federal legislation was not restored but his power of delay was extended to thirty days in the case of non-money Bills; the states' rulers retained such a right in principle. The compromise package was approved by the federal Parliament in January 1984, with the prime minister judged to have made important concessions.

A second constitutional crisis arose at the end of 1992 when the federal Parliament, in a unanimous and unprecedented measure, approved a motion censuring the Sultan of Johor, and former king, for having (allegedly) assaulted a college field-hockey coach. Parliament convened in a special session in January 1993 and proceeded to amend the constitution so as to remove the immunity from criminal prosecution enjoyed by the hereditary rulers. The rulers initially refused to grant their assent to the legislation as required under the constitution, which prompted an inspired press campaign against their self-indulgent lifestyles. Compromise was reached in March when a revised Bill was passed which made provision for a special court to hear criminal cases which might be brought against any of their number. In May 1994 a further constitutional amendment was passed whereby all Acts of Parliament would be deemed to have been assented to by the *Yang di-Pertuan Agong* after thirty days following approval by both houses, even if not formally granted. Dr Mahathir was still prime minister and had not relented in his determination to bring the monarchy within the rule of law on his terms.

*see also:* Mahathir Mohamad, Datuk Sri; *Yang di-Pertuan Agong.*

## Contemplacion, Flor: Hanging 1995
(Philippines/Singapore)

In March 1995, a diplomatic rift occurred between the governments of the Philippines and Singapore over the execution of Flor Contemplacion, a Filipina maid working in the republic who had been convicted of murder. The episode demonstrated how easily domestic issues could enter into and test longstanding cordial relationships within **ASEAN**, of which the Philippines and Singapore are founder members.

Flor Contemplacion was hanged in Singapore on 17 March 1995. She had been sentenced to death by its High Court in January 1993 for the murder in May 1991 of another Filipina maid,

Della Marga, and a 4-year-old Singaporean boy in the latter's charge. An appeal led to a further trial in April 1994 at which she was again sentenced to death, while a further appeal was dismissed in October 1994. In January 1995, President **Fidel Ramos** wrote to President **Ong Teng Cheong** requesting clemency on humanitarian grounds, which was refused in the absence of special circumstances. He wrote again in March, six days before the scheduled hanging, asking for a stay of execution in the light of alleged new evidence forthcoming from another Filipina maid but once again his plea was refused, this time on the grounds that the so-called new evidence had no basis in fact.

The execution of Flor Contemplacion went ahead as scheduled but aroused an immediate emotional outrage among Filipinos, which had an adverse effect on relations with Singapore. That popular outrage, which was fanned by the press and exploited by opponents of President Ramos in the run-up to mid-term congressional elections in May, caught his government by surprise. In addition to the element of political opportunism, the outrage expressed a strong sense of national guilt and anguish that it was necessary for so many Philippines women to work overseas in trying circumstances in order to support their impoverished families. The government in Manila was charged with not doing enough for such workers, who number around 2 million, while Flor Contemplacion was portrayed as a heroine and martyr in their cause. Singapore was depicted as arrogant and insensitive in its handling of the case and not acting as a friendly regional partner.

The Philippines government immediately postponed a visit to Manila by Singapore's prime minister, **Goh Chok Tong**, and also downgraded its representation in the island-state to that of charge d'affaires, which was reciprocated. President Ramos then set up a special commission to investigate the case and threatened to break off diplomatic relations should it find that Flor Contemplacion had been the victim of injustice. By the end of March, however, President Ramos was making conciliatory noises out of concern at the damage that might be caused both to relations with Singapore and to ASEAN. Singapore responded by indicating a willingness to accept his proposal for an independent autopsy but in early April the Philippines commission found that Flor Contemplacion had been mistakenly blamed and hanged for the two murders and that Della Marga had been severely beaten before she died and therefore could have been killed only by a man. President Ramos then acted to contain domestic anger by suspending nine diplomats and labour officials allegedly remiss in their duties in connection with Flor Contemplacion's hanging, including the ambassador to Singapore. The two governments then agreed to a re-examination of Della Marga's remains by forensic experts of both countries but President Ramos still found it necessary to force the sacrificial resignation of his foreign secretary, **Roberto Rómulo**, on 17 April two days before an inconclusive joint autopsy attended by American forensic experts, who supported the initial Singaporean conclusion. Both parties then recognized the value of a cooling-off period before seeking a further fully independent autopsy in a neutral location. That autopsy was not held until after the mid-term congressional elections in May in which President Ramos' coalition overcame the burden of the Flor Contemplacion issue to secure command of the Senate. The diplomatic rift did not affect working relations between Singapore and the Philippines, with the former offering strong support for the latter in its dispute with China over its seizure of Mischief Reef in the **Spratly Islands**. Tourist traffic and much needed Singaporean investment in the Philippines suffered, however. Moreover, within the Philippines, the making of a film about the life and death of Flor Contemplacion sustained popular interest in the alleged miscarriage of justice. In July 1995, an independent panel of American pathologists examined the remains of Della Marga in the presence of medical observers from the Philippines and Singapore and upheld the original findings of Singapore's pathologists that her death was due to strangulation. Those findings were accepted as final by the government of the Philippines. President Ramos then announced that he had taken steps to normalize ties with Singapore. Singapore's new ambassador to Manila presented his credentials in April 1996. *see also:* ASEAN; Goh Chok Tong; Ong Teng

Cheong; Ramos, Fidel; Romulo, Roberto; Spratly Islands.

**Corregidor Affair 1968** (Philippines/ Malaysia)

The Corregidor Affair is the term used to describe an alleged massacre of Filipino Muslims on the island in Manila Bay which was the site of a memorable last stand by Filipino and US troops following Japan's invasion of the Philippines at the outset of the Pacific War. The episode was reported in the Philippine press from 21 March 1968 after a survivor of the alleged massacre presented himself at the residence of the governor of Cavite Province. He claimed to be one of more than a hundred young Muslims recruited in the southern Sulu region in 1967 by an air force major who was head of the Civil Affairs Office of the Department of National Defence. Their role was to train in special forces techniques in preparation for infiltration into Sabah, which had become part of Malaysia in September 1963 in the face of Philippine objections. It was claimed initially that eleven trainees had been killed by their officers when they mutinied over demands for back-pay. The full facts of the episode have never been established but confirmation of the training programme was indicated when the Malaysian government announced that it had arrested twenty-six Filipinos in possession of small arms and explosives on an island belonging to the Federation some thirty miles to the north of Sabah's mainland early in March 1968. The revelations had the effect of reversing the signal improvement in Malaysian–Philippine relations indicated by the official visit to Kuala Lumpur in January 1968 by President **Ferdinand Marcos** accompanied by his wife, **Imelda Marcos**. Malaysian demands that the government in Manila affirm its recognition of the Federation's sovereignty over the territory prompted a revival of the **Philippines' Claim to Sabah** first enunciated in June 1962. The episode led to a suspension of diplomatic relations and imposed a strain on the workings of the recently established **ASEAN** (Association of South-East Asian Nations) of which Malaysia and the Philippines were founder members. It also served as a factor in aggravating Muslim alienation in the Philippines which erupted into revolt in 1972 (*see* **Moro National Liberation Front**).

*see also:* ASEAN; Marcos, Ferdinand; Marcos, Imelda; Moro National Liberation Front; Philippines' Claim to Sabah.

## Crocodile Hole *(Lubang Buaya)*
### (Indonesia)

*Lubang Buaya* (Crocodile Hole) is an area at the edge of Halim Air Base to the south-east of the capital of Indonesia, Jakarta. It acquired notoriety as the scene of the murder on 1 October 1965 of three surviving generals and a lieutenant abducted at the outset of an abortive coup attributed to the Communist Party (*see Gestapu*) which marked a turning-point in Indonesian politics. After the murder, the four corpses together with those of three other generals, including the army commander Lt-General Achmad Yani, who had been killed in the course of abduction, were thrown into a disused well. The discovery of the bodies and their exhumation on 4 October served as an opportunity for Major-General **Suharto**, who had taken charge of the army, to mobilize popular feeling against President **Sukarno** and the Communist Party. The well at Crocodile Hole has been converted into a memorial to those who were dispatched into its depths.

*see also: Gestapu;* Suharto; Sukarno.

# D

## Daim Zainuddin, Tun (Malaysia)

Daim Zainuddin was appointed finance minister of Malaysia for the second time in January 1999. He had held the office previously from July 1984 until resigning to return to the private sector in March 1991. His resumption of high office was precipitated by economic and political crisis. He had returned to the cabinet in June 1998 with the portfolio of minister for special functions in charge of economic development, which was interpreted as an attempt by prime minister Dr **Mahathir Mohamad** to reduce the influence of deputy prime minister and finance minister, **Anwar Ibrahim**. After the imposition of exchange controls and the dismissal and arrest of Anwar Ibrahim, Dr Mahathir assumed the finance portfolio but then transferred it to Daim after his ruling coalition was returned to government in elections in November 1999.

Daim Zainuddin was born on 29 April 1938 in the same village in Kedah as the prime minister, Dr Mahathir. He qualified as a lawyer at Lincoln's Inn in London in 1959. He worked for a while in government legal service before entering private business in the late 1960s. He has enjoyed a long-standing close personal relationship with Dr Mahathir, who was instrumental in appointing him to head of government enterprises, including Fleet Holdings, the investment arm of **UMNO** (United Malays National Organization). Daim was elected to the federal Parliament in 1982 when Dr Mahathir first led UMNO and the ruling *Barisan Nasional* (National Front) coalition at the polls. As finance minister, he managed the scandal which arose over the **Bank Bumiputera Crisis** and was also responsible for guiding Malaysia through a period of economic recession in the mid-1980s to a spectacular recovery by the early 1990s. He remained an economic adviser to the prime minister after giving up office in 1991 and on his return to the cabinet in June 1998 is believed to have been the decisive influence in the change of Malaysia's economic course from the following September in the face of unprecedented adversity. He has also been accused by an incarcerated Anwar Ibrahim of being part of a political conspiracy to discredit and ruin the former deputy prime minister. After elections in November 1999, his relationship with Dr Mahathir became strained over economic appointments and decisions.

see also: Anwar Ibrahim; Bank Bumiputera Crisis; *Barisan Nasional*; Mahathir Mohamad; UMNO.

## Dakwah (Malaysia)

*Dakwah* is the generic name for an Islamic revivalist movement which arose among younger educated Malays in the wake of intercommunal violence in May 1969. *Dakwah*, which translates literally as to call or invite, is best understood as missionary activity among Muslims. It began in moderate form within Malaysia as a dissenting search for identity and challenge to government spearheaded by **ABIM** (Islamic Youth Movement of Malaysia), which had its origins in the University of Malaya. It assumed a more radical expression through the role of students who, returning from higher education in Britain from the mid-1970s, had been subject to the influence of radical Islamic ideas from Egypt and Pakistan. *Dakwah* so dominated university campuses by the end of the 1970s that the government was obliged to launch its own countervailing programme of Islamization but more in form than in substance. Islamic identity in Malaysia had become well entrenched by the 1990s and in the wake of economic crisis towards the end of the decade served as a basis for political challenge to the ruling *Barisan Nasional* (National Front) coalition. That challenge was effectively mounted in elections in November 1999 by *Parti Islam se-Malaysia* (PAS).

see also: ABIM; Al-Arqam; *Barisan Nasional*; Islam; *Parti Islam*.

## Darul Arqam (Malaysia) *see* Al-Arqam.

## Darul Islam (Indonesia)

*Darul Islam*, which translates literally as House of Islam, is the name given to a rebellion launched against the embattled Republic of Indonesia in west Java in 1948 which petered out only in the early 1960s. In west Java, the Hizbullah (a Japanese-inspired Muslim militia) had operated independently of the aspirant republic whose forces had been withdrawn from early 1948 under the terms of the Renville Agreement with the Dutch. *Darul Islam* was set up in March 1948. In August its leader, S. M. Kartosuwirjo, proclaimed *Negara Islam Indonesia*, literally the Islamic State of Indonesia. Because the republic was subject to continuing military pressure from the Dutch, the theologically driven movement was able to extend its presence into central Java. *Darul Islam* refused to acknowledge the authority of the Indonesian state after the transfer of sovereignty from the Dutch in December 1949. Attempts at negotiations were rebuffed and an insurgency was sustained albeit with decreasing effect on Java during the 1950s as the army began to bring its power to bear against the movement. Loose affiliates of *Darul Islam* in north Sumatra and south Sulawesi troubled the central government in the context of widespread regional rebellions in the latter part of the decade. These rebellions were broken by the early 1960s and *Darul Islam* came to an effective end in June 1962 with the capture of Kartosuwirjo, who then ordered his followers to lay down their arms. The impact of the *Darul Islam* movement on Indonesian political life has been profound. Within the armed forces an abiding antagonism was entrenched towards organized **Islam** perceived as a threat to the cohesion and integrity of the culturally diverse Indonesian state. That military disposition became diluted during the 1990s after former President **Suharto** began to promote organized Islam and Islamic officers as a way of controlling the armed forces.
*see also:* ABRI; ICMI; Islam; Suharto.

## Declaration of ASEAN Concord 1976
(Indonesia/Malaysia/Philippines/
Singapore/Thailand)
The Declaration of ASEAN Concord was made on 24 February 1976 on the island of Bali at the first meeting of the heads of government of **ASEAN** (Association of South-East Asian Nations). The **Bali Summit**'s declaration was significant for registering the political identity and goals of ASEAN nearly a decade after the **Bangkok Declaration 1967** claimed that its prime purposes were economic, social and cultural cooperation. Cooperation in pursuit of political stability was identified as the pre-eminent priority, while common threat was defined with reference to subversion. Security cooperation was excluded from the corporate structure of the Association but could be undertaken on 'a non-ASEAN basis'. The open commitment to political cooperation was a direct response to the success of revolutionary communism in Indochina in April 1975. The declaration brought the commitment in November 1971 to a **ZOPFAN**, a Zone of Peace, Freedom and Neutrality, under the formal aegis of the Association as well as recording the agreement to establish an ASEAN Secretariat.
*see also:* ASEAN; Bali Summit 1976; Bangkok Declaration 1967; ZOPFAN.

## Declaration on the South China Sea (ASEAN) 1992 (Brunei/Indonesia/
Malaysia/Philippines/Singapore/
Thailand)
At a meeting of **ASEAN**'s foreign ministers in Manila on 22 July 1992, a joint declaration was issued on the **South China Sea**. Among its members, Malaysia and the Philippines claimed jurisdiction over some of the **Spratly Islands** in that sea, while Brunei claimed jurisdiction over adjacent maritime space. China, including Taiwan, and Vietnam claimed the entire group. The declaration arose from a Philippine initiative, which was supported by Malaysia in return for Manila withdrawing its candidate for the office of secretary-general of ASEAN in favour of that from Kuala Lumpur. ASEAN's interest and apprehension had arisen since 1988 when China had engaged in military action at Vietnam's expense in order to hold some of the Spratly Islands. China had also published a law on its territorial waters and their contiguous areas in February 1992 which proclaimed its maritime rights in a way that suggested a policy of creeping assertiveness. The disturbing effect

of the disintegration of the Soviet Union at the end of 1991 and the impending withdrawal of the United States' military presence from the Philippines later in 1992 on the regional balance of power served to encourage the diplomatic initiative. The declaration emphasized 'the necessity to resolve all sovereignty and juris-dictional issues pertaining to the South China Sea by peaceful means, without resort to force' and also urged 'all parties concerned to exercise restraint with the view to creating a positive climate for the eventual resolution of all dis-putes'. The declaration, which invited all par-ties concerned to subscribe to the declaration of principles, received a positive response from Vietnam, whose foreign minister attended the Manila meeting as an observer. China responded more equivocally and subsequently seized an additional reef in the Spratly Islands. The dec-laration had a moderating effect on the issue at the time but without inducing any ASEAN claimants to modify their own positions on sovereignty. The ASEAN governments invoked the declaration in March 1995 in response to China's maritime assertiveness but without any signal effect. At an informal summit in Manila in November 1999, ASEAN's heads of govern-ment sought to elevate the declaration into a code of conduct binding all member states but without securing China's endorsement.
see also: ASEAN; South China Sea; Spratly
  Islands.

## Democracy Forum (Indonesia) see
*Forum Demokrasi.*

## Democrat Party (Thailand)
The Democrat (*Prachathipat*) Party has enjoyed the greatest continuity of any Thai civilian pol-itical organization. After holding office twice briefly after the Pacific War and then again briefly in the mid-1970s, it enjoyed more sus-tained fortunes during the 1990s and into the next century. In general elections in September 1992, it secured 79 seats, the largest number in the Parliament. In consequence, its leader, **Chuan Leekpai**, became prime minister of a coalition government. The Democrat Party lost power in July 1995 after elections precipitated by the defection of a coalition partner. Its

parliamentary numbers were reduced to 86, 6 less than its main rival the **Chart Thai Party**, which went on to form a new coalition. The Democrat Party returned to government with Chuan again as prime minister in November 1997 after the ruling coalition collapsed because of its failure to cope with economic crisis.

Its success had followed a period of political turmoil after which the military had been obliged to concede a long-standing popular demand for a democratically elected prime minister. The Democrat Party was established in 1946 as a conservative pro-monarchist parliamentary group in opposition to the government of **Pridi Phanomyong** which had replaced the military dictatorship of **Phibul Songkram**, both men having been party to removing the absolute monarchy in 1932. The Democrat Party leader, Khuang Aphaiwong, became prime minister from November 1947 after a military coup and then again after elections in January 1948, but within two months was obliged to give up office by an assertive military. The Democrat Party drew its support in the main from Bangkok and southern Thailand and stood for liberal consti-tutionalism rather than for any coherent social programme. During the course of Thailand's fluctuating political evolution, the Democrat Party has seized every opportunity for parlia-mentary representation. During the democratic interlude, which followed the successful student-led challenge to military rule in October 1973, its political fortunes revived. Under the leader-ship of wartime resistance leader and co-founder **Seni Pramoj**, it initially failed to form a govern-ment. In April 1976, however, fresh elections brought the Democrats to office in a short-lived administration headed by Seni, which was then overthrown by a military coup in October. A poor performance in elections in 1979 was succeeded by a much better one in 1983, with continued minority participation in govern-ment during the decade until a military coup in February 1991 led on to a further turning-point in Thai politics, which after political turbulence in May 1992 saw its return to government in September. The Democrat Party attracted popular support because of its civilian creden-tials but its parliamentary majority was eroded through stress within the ruling coalition over perquisites of office. It suffered also through the inability of the prime minister, Chuan Leekpai, to command the political stage in the face of obstruction of democratic political reforms by the military establishment. On its return to office, the Democratic Party has commanded greater respect because of its degree of success in economic management and also because of its relative freedom of taint from corruption. However, it has been vulnerable to revived charges of corruption, which have damaged its electoral prospects. In March 2000, Sanan Kachornprasart, its secretary-general and minister of the interior as well as a deputy prime minister, was obliged to resign government offices after being charged by the National Counter Corruption Commission with concealing his assets by falsifying documents relating to a loan. He was found guilty by the Constitutional Court in August 2000, thus reducing his party's electoral prospects.

see also: Chart Thai Party; Chuan Leekpai; Phibul Songkram; Pridi Phanomyong; Seni Pramoj.

## Democratic Action Party (DAP)
(Malaysia)

The Democratic Action Party (DAP) is the most important non-Malay opposition party in Malaysia. It consistently captured around 20 per cent of the popular vote in federal elections until April 1995 when it suffered a major reverse with its vote cut to around 12 per cent with only 9 seats out of 192 compared to 20 out of 180 in October 1990. In elections in November 1999, it performed only marginally better winning 10 seats out of 193 with 12.7 per cent of the popular vote. However, its leader, **Lim Kit Siang**, lost his seat, while the DAP gave way to *Parti Islam Se-Malaysia* (PAS) in providing the official leader of the federal parliamentary opposition. The DAP had entered into an electoral pact with PAS and two other Malay-based parties in the June before the elections and this *Barisan Alternatif* (Alternative Front) held together after the Parliament reassembled. Its successor as secretary-general is Kirk Kim Hock.

The Democratic Action Party originated as the peninsular Malaysian branch of Singapore's ruling **People's Action Party** (PAP) while the island was a constituent part of Malaysia. As such, it participated in elections on the mainland in April but secured only one seat out of nine contested. After Singapore separated from Malaysia in August 1965, it became necessary for the PAP branch to assume a different name to avoid deregistration, which it did in March 1966. The name Democratic Action Party and a commitment to a socialist model of society corresponded closely to the declared political identity of its predecessor. The taint of its origins have never been completely overcome, especially given the abiding structural tension between Malaysia and Singapore. The DAP's constituency is non-communal, in principle, and it puts up Malay electoral candidates. In practice, however, voting support has been drawn primarily from non-Malays and in particular urban Chinese frustrated by the denial of educational and career opportunities to their children because of the preference accorded to Malays under the **Bumiputera** policy. The DAP has been outspoken on behalf of the rights of the non-Malays and also in support of civil liberties. It has been a constant thorn in the side of government over constitutionalism, corrupt practice and maladministration. The DAP has been subject to recurrent political constraints with its leading members, including Lim Kit Siang, being detained under the Internal Security Act, as well as being disciplined by the speaker of the federal Parliament for alleged breaches of standing orders. In addition, restrictions have been placed on the circulation of the party's newspaper. In January 2000, the party's deputy leader, Karpal Singh, who had lost his parliamentary seat in the previous November, and the legal representative of former deputy prime minister, Anwar Ibrahim, was charged with sedition for a statement made in court during the latter's trial.

see also: Anwar Ibrahim; *Barisan Alternatif*; *Bumiputera*; Lim Kit Siang; People's Action Party (PAP).

## Democratic Kampuchea (Cambodia)

The **Khmer Rouge** seized power in Cambodia on 17 April 1975 in the name of the Royal Government of National Unification, which had been proclaimed in the People's Republic of

China on 5 May 1970, with Prince **Norodom Sihanouk** as head of state. On 5 January 1976 a new constitution was promulgated in Phnom Penh establishing the State of Democratic Kampuchea, initially with Prince Sihanouk as its head. He resigned on 4 April, to be succeeded by **Khieu Samphan**. On 14 April **Pol Pot** was appointed prime minister but gave up the post between 27 September and 15 October. On 25 December 1978 Vietnamese forces, acting ostensibly as volunteers in support of a Kampuchean National United Front for National Salvation, invaded Cambodia. They ousted the government of Democratic Kampuchea and replaced it on 8 January 1979 with the **People's Republic of Kampuchea**. Representatives of Democratic Kampuchea continued to occupy the Cambodian seat in the United Nations, albeit from 1982 until 1990 as part of a coalition delegation with two non-Communist Khmer factions. From the General Assembly session beginning in 1991, the Cambodian seat was held, in principle, by the **Supreme National Council** comprising representatives of all four Khmer groupings until a coalition government of the restored kingdom of Cambodia, without Khmer Rouge participation, was established in October 1993. The term Democratic Kampuchea is replete with tragic irony because of the bloody tyranny which marked its tenure.

*see also:* Democratic Kampuchea, Coalition Government of; Kampuchea, People's Republic of; Khieu Samphan; Khmer Rouge; Pol Pot; Sihanouk, Norodom; Supreme National Council.

## Democratic Kampuchea, Coalition Government of (CGDK) 1982–90
(Cambodia)

At a meeting in Kuala Lumpur in June 1982, sponsored by **ASEAN** (Association of South-East Asian Nations), representatives of three insurgent Cambodian (Kampuchean) factions challenging Vietnam's occupation agreed to form a coalition government. They comprised the **Khmer Rouge**, led nominally by **Khieu Samphan**, which had retained Cambodia's seat in the United Nations in the name of the ousted government of **Democratic Kampuchea**, the republican-oriented non-Communist **Khmer**

People's National Liberation Front (KPNLF) led by a former prime minister, **Son Sann**, and the royalist **FUNCINPEC** (National United Front for an Independent, Neutral, Peaceful and Cooperative Cambodia) led by the former head of state, Prince **Norodom Sihanouk**. Prince Sihanouk became president, Son Sann became prime minister and Khieu Samphan became vice-president responsible for foreign affairs.

The coalition government did not establish an identifiable territorial seat, while the agreement did not provide for merging the resistance factions. On the contrary, it was stipulated that the coalition partners would retain separate organizational and political identities as well as freedom of operational action. Moreover, the Khmer Rouge insisted on having written into the agreement their proprietary right to the political trademark 'Democratic Kampuchea' and to the United Nations seat should the coalition break up. The accord was an expression of tactical political convenience intended to dilute the bestial identity of Democratic Kampuchea and to refute charges that ASEAN was engaged in an immoral relationship in its diplomatic challenge to Vietnam. The coalition device made it easier to solicit voting support in the United Nations and to justify ASEAN's charge that Vietnam had implanted an illegitimate government in Cambodia. The coalition partners maintained a common diplomatic front over the terms for a political settlement but the relationship among the disparate factions along the Thai border during the 1980s, where they drew on support from concentrations of refugees, was tense, in the main because of unprovoked armed attacks by Khmer Rouge units. Acts of resignation by Prince Sihanouk were justified on that ground, although he insisted on Khmer Rouge participation in a political settlement because of the danger of violent disruption should they be excluded. The coalition changed in nomenclature to the National Government of Cambodia in 1990 as negotiations proceeded between Cambodian factions over the terms of a United Nations peace plan which was approved by an **International Conference on Cambodia** in Paris in October 1991. The so-called coalition lapsed when its members participated in the **Supreme National Council**, which was accorded a symbolic sovereignty so that authority could be delegated to the United Nations to implement the 1991 Paris peace agreement. The coalition broke up in discord when the Khmer Rouge refused to participate in elections in May 1993 to elect a Constituent Assembly. It was superseded when the incumbent **Cambodian People's Party** (CPP) joined with FUNCINPEC and the political successor of the KPNLF to form a coalition government in Phnom Penh in October 1993.

see also: Cambodian People's Party; Democratic Kampuchea; FUNCINPEC; International Conference on Cambodia, Paris 1991; Khieu Samphan; Khmer People's National Liberation Front; Khmer Rouge; Sihanouk, Norodom; Son Sann; Supreme National Council; United Nations: Cambodia 1991–3; UNTAC.

## Democratic Soldiers (Thailand)

Democratic Soldiers is the term applied to a group of middle-ranking Thai officers who were influential from the late 1970s in providing a conceptual social basis for the military's claim to political entitlement. More intellectual than the **Young Turks** faction which changed prime ministers in 1980 by switching support from General **Kriangsak Chomanan** to General **Prem Tinsulanond**, its members were driven by their experience of countering Communist rural insurgency by civic action. Tutored by defectors from the Communist Party of Thailand, they espoused a simplistic state socialism as a way of overcoming rural poverty and a condition of alleged international economic dependence brought about by feckless civilian politicians and Sino-Thai business people. Former Democratic Soldiers sought political expression through the Thai People's Party (Puang Chon Chao Thai) which enjoyed a brief period of coalition government from October 1990 until February 1991. In the next elections in March 1992, it secured only one seat and had lost its political identity by the subsequent elections in September that year. Its leader, General **Arthit Kamlang-ek**, resigned from the party in January 1992 to join another military-based grouping, Sammakkhi Tham. By

the time of the disintegration of the Thai People's Party, the ideas of the Democratic Soldiers had lost their earlier political immediacy as Communist insurgency had effectively ceased.

see also: Arthit Kamlang-ek; Kriangsak Chomanan; Prem Tinsulanond; Young Turks.

## Demokrasi Terpimpin (Indonesia) see Guided Democracy.

## Dhanabalan, Suppiah (Singapore)

Suppiah Dhanabalan served as Singapore's second only foreign minister between June 1980 and September 1988. He carried the main responsibility for an active diplomacy within and on behalf of **ASEAN** over the Cambodian conflict in the third phase of the **Indochina Wars**. A man of strong Christian convictions and simple tastes, Suppiah Dhanabalan has exemplified the dedication and non-corruptibility which has become conventional wisdom about Singapore. He was born in Singapore on 8 August 1937 and received his higher education in economics at the University of Malaya, whose campus was then located in Singapore. He began his career as a civil servant in the Ministry of Finance and then spent ten years in the Development Bank of Singapore, rising to the office of vice-president. He was drawn into politics in the mid-1970s as a member of a new intake into the parliamentary ranks of the ruling **People's Action Party** (PAP). He was given junior office first in the Ministry of National Development in 1978 and then concurrently in the Ministry of Foreign Affairs in 1979. He succeeded **Sinnathamby Rajaratnam** as foreign minister in June 1980, holding that office concurrently in turn with those of culture, community development, and national development. Towards the end of the 1980s, he had to be persuaded to remain in political office, giving up the foreign affairs portfolio to hold only that of national development from September 1988. He gave up that post four years later to return to the private sector but resumed cabinet responsibility in November 1992 as minister for trade and industry after it had been announced that both deputy prime ministers had contracted cancer. At the end of 1993, he returned to the private sector when deputy prime minister Lee Hsien

Loong was pronounced to be in full remission.
*see also:* ASEAN; Indochina Wars; Lee Hsien
Loong; People's Action Party; Rajaratnam,
Sinnathamby.

## Diem, Ngo Dinh  (Vietnam)

Ngo Dinh Diem was president of the Republic
of (South) Vietnam from its proclamation on
26 October 1955 until his assassination on 2
November 1963. Diem was born on 3 January
1901 in Hue in central Vietnam. His family were
traditionally mandarins or public servants and
had been Catholic for more than two centuries.
After a conventional education which culminated with the study of law at the University of
Hanoi, Diem entered the imperial service and
so distinguished himself that he was appointed
minister of the interior by Emperor **Bao Dai** in
1933 but soon resigned in protest at the constraints imposed on his office by French colonial
rule. His nationalist credentials assured, he withdrew from public life in keeping with an early
ambition to become a priest. Ngo Dinh Diem
was a fervent anti-Communist which was an
extension of his religious faith. He refused to
join in cooperation with **Ho Chi Minh** and was
embittered by the Communists' assassination of
his brother Ngo Dinh Khoi, when governor
of Quang Nai Province. He also rejected an
offer to serve in the government of the former
emperor Bao Dai in the late 1940s under French
aegis. He left Vietnam in 1950 and travelled in
Japan, Italy, the Philippines, the United States
and Belgium, enjoying the hospitality of a network of Catholic associates. He went to France
in 1953 and was still there in June 1954 when
Bao Dai, influenced by the Eisenhower administration, invited him to become prime minister.
He returned to Saigon towards the end of the
month in time to oppose the terms of the **Geneva
Agreements on Indochina**: the conference concluded its deliberations on 21 July 1954. Diem
built up his political position with US support
after crushing the criminal Binh Xuyen organization and two religious sects. In October 1955
he held a spurious referendum whose controlled
outcome enabled him to remove Bao Dai as head
of the State of Vietnam and to have himself appointed as president of the Republic of Vietnam.
Committed to celibacy, Diem came under the
powerful influence of his brother (and minister of
the interior) Ngo Dinh Nhu and his formidable
wife. Their authoritarian regime, within which
Diem appeared as a remote figure, failed to contain the revival of Communist insurgency by
the end of the 1950s. US support began to wane
in the wake of Buddhist demonstrations and self-
immolations and the Kennedy administration
became persuaded to countenance a military
coup by dissident army officers. That coup was
mounted on 1 November 1963. Diem and his
brother were captured and then killed the next
day but successive military governments failed
to do any better against the Communist insurgency directed from the northern part of the
country.
*see also:* Bao Dai; Geneva Agreements on
Indochina 1954; Ho Chi Minh.

## Dien Bien Phu, Battle of, 1954
(Vietnam)

Dien Bien Phu (literally seat of the Border County
Prefecture) is the name of a valley in north-
western Vietnam close to the border with Laos
and the site of the most decisive battle of the
First **Indochina War** between the Communist-
led **Viet Minh** and the French colonial army.
The battle took the form of a siege of French military positions established in November 1953.
It began on 13 March 1954 and culminated fifty-
six days later with a Viet Minh victory which
sapped the political will of the French government. The site of the battle was fixed by a
French determination to force a major test of
military strength on the elusive Viet Minh and
because the valley was a practical blocking
point against incursions into Laos. The military
deployment to the valley floor proved to be
a fatal blunder. Against expectations and all
odds, the Viet Minh had transported heavy
artillery to impregnable dominating positions
in the surrounding mountains. Superiority in
firepower determined the outcome of the battle,
which was virtually decided in the first week,
presaged by the suicide of the French artillery
commander, Colonel Charles Piroth. The final
French position surrendered on 7 May 1954
with impeccable timing just one day before an
international conference convened in Geneva to
address the political future of Indochina.

*see also:* Geneva Agreements on Indochina 1954; Indochina Wars; Viet Minh.

## Do Muoi (Vietnam)

Do Muoi served as general secretary of the Communist Party of Vietnam from June 1991 until December 1997. He was elected to that office at the seventh party congress and was re-elected at the eighth congress in June 1996. At the age of 80, he was replaced as general secretary by the party's central committee at its meeting in December 1997 in favour of General **Le Kha Phieu**. He then resigned from the party's politburo but was appointed as an adviser to the central committee. Do Muoi was born on 2 February 1917 in an outer district of Hanoi. He worked as a house painter and became involved in nationalist politics in his late teens. Do Muoi joined the original Communist Party of Indochina in 1939. He was arrested by the French authorities and sentenced to ten years' imprisonment in 1941 but escaped in 1945 and was active as a party official and political commissar during the First **Indochina War**. He then rose steadily within the party hierarchy. In March 1955 he became an alternate member of the Central Committee and a full member in December 1960. Over the next twenty years, he combined governmental office with party position, rising to vice-premier. Do Muoi was elected an alternate member of the Politburo of the Communist Party at its fourth national congress in December 1976 and became a full member at its fifth national congress in December 1986. Over the years, Do Muoi acquired a reputation as a conservative idealogue who only reluctantly agreed to the policy of *Doi Moi* (economic renovation) which had been introduced as a matter of political necessity. In June 1988, when he was elected to the office of chairman of the Council of Ministers (the equivalent of prime minister), it was assumed that he had been chosen to balance the reformist zeal of the new general secretary of the party, **Nguyen Van Linh**. In the event, he showed himself to be a pragmatist willing to encourage Vietnam's economic adaptation in order to overcome adverse circumstances. At the same time, he represented ideological continuity and reaffirmed a commitment to socialism. As general secretary for over six years, Do Muoi stood fast against any concessions to political pluralism and any diminution of the monopoly role of the ruling Communist Party.

*see also:* *Doi Moi*; Indochina Wars; Le Kha Phieu; Linh, Nguyen Van.

## Doi Moi (Vietnam)

The term *Doi Moi* means renovation or renewal of the economy. It was promulgated at the sixth national congress of Vietnam's Communist Party in December 1986 and reconfirmed at the seventh national congress in June 1991. As a direct consequence of the attendant reforms, the material condition of Vietnam has been transformed with a growing engagement with the international economy. The policy of Doi Moi seeks to encourage free market economics while protecting the Communist political system. It was introduced by **Nguyen Van Linh** as a matter of political necessity. The failings of the Communist Party in not fulfilling the promise of the revolution to give the people of Vietnam a better life had brought it into political disrepute and also threatened its regime. *Doi Moi* has been distinguished from *perestroika*, introduced in the former Soviet Union, because the notion of restructuring which it conveyed was regarded in Hanoi as subversive of the leading role of the Communist Party. In consequence, political conservatism induced caution in economic liberalization, which had the effect of retarding the momentum of *Doi Moi* by the turn of the century.

*see also:* Do Muoi; Linh, Nguyen Van.

## Domino Theory (Cambodia/Laos/Vietnam)

Domino theory served as an underlying rationale for the United States' fateful intervention in Vietnam. In the context of the Cold War and US policy of containing a monolithic international communism, the strategic importance of Indochina was represented in terms of an analogy with a line of standing dominoes which would tumble one by one should the first fall. The theory has been most closely identified with President Dwight D. Eisenhower, who argued at a press conference in Washington on

7 April 1954: 'You have a row of dominoes set up, you knock over the first one, and what will happen to the last one is that it will go over very quickly'. He concluded that if Indochina fell to communism, the rest of South-East Asia would go very quickly, with incalculable losses to the free world. That statement was made as French forces, embattled by the communist-led **Viet Minh** at **Dien Bien Phu**, seemed likely to be overcome in the absence of a military intervention. The US government was not prepared then to risk military intervention in the light of recent experience in Korea; nor was its British ally. In the event, Dien Bien Phu fell to the Viet Minh in the first **Indochina War** in May 1954 and at an international conference on Indochina which convened concurrently in Geneva and concluded its deliberations in the **Geneva Agreements on Indochina** in July, Vietnam became subject to a de facto partition with the north in communist hands. Laos was subject to a measure of partition, while only Cambodia remained intact under a non-communist government.

A domino effect did not immediately follow but domino theory remained integral to the United States' strategic rationale expressed in the Collective Defence Treaty for South-East Asia or **Manila Pact** in September 1954 and the establishment of **SEATO** (South-East Asia Treaty Organization) in February 1955. Domino theory was based in part on an interpretation in Washington of Cold War circumstances in which Vietnam's communists were perceived as proxies of a revolutionary China, which was in turn viewed as the Soviet Union's vehicle for expansion in Asia against whom a line had to be drawn and held. Underlying that interpretation was the United States' experience of the outbreak of the Pacific War in which Japan's avenue to spectacular conquest in South-East Asia from December 1941 had been through Indochina, where access had been secured at French expense. In the event, the forcible unification of Vietnam in April 1975 had a domino effect of a kind as political accommodation in neighbouring Laos between communist and non-communist parties crumbled in favour of the former by the end of the year. In neighbouring Cambodia, Vietnamese communist support helped the murderous **Khmer Rouge**

come to power but not as subordinates to the ruling party in Hanoi with whom confrontation ensued. To the extent that China backed the Khmer Rouge against Vietnam, a sort of reverse domino effect occurred. Moreover, the success of revolutionary communism in Indochina during 1975, in the wake of ignominious American withdrawal, did not produce any domino effect within the rest of South-East Asia, which did not succumb to internal communist challenge. At issue and controversial, however, is the extent to which the United States' ill-fated military intervention, prompted by the reasoning of domino theory, was responsible for 'buying time' against the threat of communism for the states of South-East Asia beyond Indochina.

*see also:* Communism in South-East Asia; Dien Bien Phu; Geneva Agreements on Indochina 1954; Indochina Wars; Khmer Rouge; Manila Pact 1954; SEATO; Viet Minh; Vietnam War.

## Dong, Pham Van  (Vietnam) *see* Pham Van Dong.

## Duan, Le  (Vietnam) *see* Le Duan.

## Dwi Fungsi  (Indonesia)
*Dwi Fungsi* translates as Dual Function and is employed in Indonesia to explain and justify the prerogative position of the armed forces. The term originated in the critical role played by them during the National Revolution, especially in the latter stage after the Dutch had captured its political leadership. After independence, that role first received doctrinal expression with the failure of parliamentary democracy and the declaration of martial law in 1957. The army chief of staff, Major-General **Abdul Harris Nasution**, devised the notion of a 'middle way', namely, that the armed forces would neither totally disengage from public life nor totally dominate it. In April 1965 at their first national seminar, the armed forces affirmed their dual role as both a military and a socio-political force. After General **Suharto** had established his **New Order** after March 1966, the concept of dual function became a central legitimizing device. The second armed forces seminar in August 1966 and a Ministry of Defence seminar in November gave content to the concept, which

was adopted as part of military doctrine. It was accorded formal recognition by the People's Consultative Congress in 1978 and then enacted in law in 1982. The claim to a *Dwi Fungsi* has been asserted as a military prerogative and was expressed in the right of the armed forces to hold 100 seats in the 500-member Parliament in return for not voting in national elections. The reduction of that number to 75 seats by former president Suharto for the Parliament elected in May 1997 indicated his intention to limit the remit of dual function. Following President Suharto's resignation in May 1998 and his succession by interim president **Habibie**, that number was further reduced to 38 for the Parliament elected in June 1999. By that juncture, the reputation and national standing of the armed forces had been diminished and the concept of *Dwi Fungsi* was in disrepute. In August 2000, however, the **People's Consultative Assembly** resolved to extend military representation until 2009.

*see also:* ABRI; Habibie, B. J.; Nasution, Abdul Harris; New Order; People's Consultative Assembly; Suharto.

# E

## East Asian Economic Caucus
(Malaysia)

A proposal for an East Asian Economic Grouping, subsequently modified to an East Asian
Economic Caucus, was first put forward
by Malaysia's prime minister, Dr **Mahathir
Mohamad**, at a banquet for China's prime minister, Li Peng, in December 1990. Dr Mahathir
argued that it was necessary for Asian Pacific
countries to form a bloc to protect their trade
share in the face of protectionism in Europe and
North America. A hostile reaction followed from
regional partners within **ASEAN** (Association
of South-East Asian Nations) as well as from
Japan. Its government objected to the very
concept of a trade bloc as well as to the conspicuous exclusion of the United States and
other western states. This response prompted
Dr Mahathir to recast his proposal in less offensive terms as a consultative grouping devoted
to free trade. The issue became one of political
face for Malaysia with the development from
1989 of the Asia-Pacific Economic Cooperation (APEC), a consultative forum arising from
Australian initiative and which also included
the United States, Canada and New Zealand.
Malaysia sought ASEAN's endorsement for
Dr Mahathir's proposal and, at the meeting of
its economic ministers in October 1991, a revised version in the form of an East Asian
Economic Caucus was endorsed in principle.
Malaysia experienced frustration, however,
when the meeting of ASEAN's heads of government in Singapore in January 1992 failed to do
more than agree to have the proposal studied
further. The matter was addressed again at the
annual meeting of ASEAN's foreign ministers
held in Singapore in July 1993, when a face-
saving formula of a kind was found. It was
agreed, with Malaysia's grudging acquiescence,
that the East Asian Economic Caucus should
become a caucus within APEC but without any
indication of how the enterprise might work
in practice. The issue became controversial
again when Dr Mahathir refused to attend an

informal summit of Asia-Pacific leaders in Seattle
in November 1993 called by US President Bill
Clinton after a scheduled ministerial meeting of
APEC, in part because it had put his own proposal in the shadow. Dr Mahathir was the only
Asian leader to boycott the occasion and has
remained unrepentant in advocating the need
for an East Asian Economic Caucus to balance
regional economic groupings elsewhere. He
has been vindicated by the composition of
Asian States represented at a meeting with the
European Union at heads of government level
in Bangkok in March 1996. In addition, heads of
government from China, Japan and South
Korea also attended informal annual ASEAN
summits beginning in Kuala Lumpar in
December 1997. At an informal summit in
Manila in November 1999, a framework was
agreed for East Asian economic cooperation. In
May 2000, finance ministers of ASEAN and
China, Japan and South Korea concluded an
accord on currency swaps as a precaution
against a repetition of the intensive currency
speculation of the late 1990s. The Malaysian
project, however, has not progressed substantially beyond the rhetorical level.
see also: APEC; ASEAN; Mahathir Mohamad,
  Datuk Sri.

## East Timor  (Indonesia) see Timor, East.

## EDSA (Epifanio de los Santos Avenue)
(Philippines)

Epifanio de los Santos Avenue is a major thor-
oughfare in Manila. From 23 to 25 February
1986 it was the setting for a remarkable display
of popular opposition in support of a military
revolt led by **Juan Ponce Enrile** and **Fidel
Ramos** against the regime of President **Ferdinand
Marcos** in the wake of a fraudulently conducted
snap election. Its acronym EDSA was taken as
the name for the civilian-supported military
revolt whose headquarters in Camp Crame
were bordered by the avenue. After an appeal
by Cardinal **Jaime Sin**, the revolt was sustained

by an interposing human wall of passive resistance which prevented Marcos loyalists from crushing it by force. The episode, which was critical in **Corazón Aquino** becoming president of the Philippines, has passed into legend as '**People Power**'.
see also: Aquino, Corazón; Enrile, Juan Ponce; Marcos, Ferdinand; People Power; Reform the Armed Forces Movement; Sin, Jaime.

## Elysée Agreement 1949 (Vietnam)

On 8 March 1949 an agreement was reached between the French government and **Bao Dai**, who had abdicated as Emperor of Vietnam in August 1945 in favour of the Communist-controlled **Viet Minh**. The agreement provided for French recognition of the limited independence of the Associated State of Vietnam within the French Union and included the former colony and so-called Republic of Cochin China, which had been accorded a separate constitutional identity in 1946. The agreement took effect in Vietnam with a ceremony in Saigon on 14 June which led on to the formal establishment of the Associated State on 1 July. It was ratified by the French National Assembly on 29 January 1950. The background to the agreement was France's attempt to engage the United States in its military struggle in the First **Indochina War** to retain its colonial domain in Indochina by representing it as a critical theatre in the global conflict against international communism. The United States had made its support dependent on France being willing to transfer power to nationalist figures who could provide a credible alternative to the Communists. The result was the so-called Bao Dai solution whereby the former emperor returned from exile to become head of state. It was no coincidence that on 4 February 1950, within days of the ratification by the French National Assembly, the United States extended formal diplomatic recognition to the Associated State of Vietnam as well as to Laos and Cambodia, to which corresponding commitments had been made: Laos on 19 July 1949 and Cambodia on 8 November 1949. A formal request from France for US military aid followed on 16 February 1950; this was approved by US President Truman on 1 May to the sum of US$15 million. That commitment marked the beginning of the United States' intervention in what became known as the **Vietnam War**.
see also: Bao Dai; Indochina Wars; Viet Minh; Vietnam War.

## Emergency 1948–60 (Malaya)

The term 'Emergency' was employed to describe the insurrection mounted by the Communist Party of Malaya against the British colonial authorities from 1948. Emergency regulations were promulgated on 18 June 1948 in response to armed attacks against rubber plantations. Those regulations were not rescinded until 31 July 1960. A distinguishing feature of the insurrection was the predominant support provided by the ethnic Chinese community, initially mobilized during the Japanese occupation. Although the colonial authorities were unprepared for the insurrection, the Communist Party was also less than fully ready for armed struggle, feeling obliged to respond to governmental action against its trade union representatives as well as to the call of the Cominform for national liberation revolution. The insurrection reached its peak in 1951 with the assassination of Britain's high commissioner, Sir Henry Gurney. By then, however, the party had admitted the failure of its policy to establish liberated areas and sought to change tack in an attempt to widen its popular base. But it was too late as the security forces had gained the initiative in both the armed struggle and in that for hearts and minds. The Communist guerrillas were driven deeper into the rainforest and from the mid-1950s were obliged to retreat to redoubts along the border with Thailand. Although the Communist Party was able to engage in sporadic military operations after 1960, especially at the end of the **Vietnam War** in 1975, internal dissension and governmental performance effectively confined the insurgency to a nuisance role. On 2 December 1989 in the southern Thai town of Hat Yai, the governments of Thailand and Malaysia and the Communist Party of Malaya issued a joint statement to mark the signing of two peace agreements whereby the three sides would terminate all armed activities. The agreement constituted an act of surrender by the Communist Party of Malaya; it was signed by the party's general secretary, **Chin Peng**, who had not been

seen in public since the **Baling Talks** in 1955.
*see also:* Baling Talks 1955; Chin Peng.

## Enrile, Juan Ponce  (Philippines)

Juan Ponce Enrile, as minister of defence, led a
military mutiny against President **Ferdinand
Marcos** on 22 February 1986 in the wake of
fraudulently conducted elections. He was joined
in revolt by the deputy chief of staff of the
armed forces, **Fidel Ramos**, and encouraged by
the head of the Catholic Church, Cardinal **Jaime
Sin**. Cardinal Sin's appeal for popular support
led to the remarkable political phenomenon of
'**People Power**' whereby residents of Manila
stood between the military dissidents based in
Camp Crame and those units loyal to President
Marcos. President Marcos went into exile later
that month, to be succeeded by his electoral
rival **Corazón Aquino**, who reappointed Enrile
as minister of defence in her first cabinet.

Juan Ponce Enrile was born on 14 February
1924 in Cagayan Province, north of Manila. He
had a legal education at the University of the
Philippines and in the United States at Harvard
University after the Pacific War and began his
career as a corporation lawyer. He assumed
political office as under-secretary of finance
after Ferdinand Marcos became president in
January 1966, rising to minister of defence by
the turn of the decade. As a close confidant of
President Marcos, he helped to mastermind the
introduction and management of martial law
from 1972. When the promise of Marcos's **New
Society Movement** began to sour, he cultivated
a coterie of young military officers, the **Reform
the Armed Forces Movement**, ostensibly in the
cause of reform but essentially to further his
own political ambitions. His act of mutiny in
February 1986 was precipitated by fear of his
impending arrest.

His tenure as minister of defence under
President Aquino was short-lived. Enrile was
removed from office in November 1986 after
coming into conflict with her over policy
towards the insurgent Communist Party, which
expressed his personal frustration that Corazón
Aquino had been the political beneficiary of
the mutiny which he had inspired. He stood as
a successful candidate in elections for the Senate
in May 1987 and was subsequently linked to

a series of abortive coups against President
Aquino's administration. In February 1990 he
was arrested on charges of murder, rebellion
and harbouring criminals. Released on bail in
March, the charges were dismissed by the
Supreme Court in June. Enrile then sought to
pursue his presidential ambitions through the
vehicle of the revived **Nacionalista Party** but
his expectations were dashed with its fragmentation into rival factions. In elections in May
1992, he was successful in his bid for a seat in
the House of Representatives on behalf of
a Cagayan provincial constituency and then
went on to win a Senate seat in May 1995 but
has remained a peripheral figure in national
politics.

*see also:* Aquino, Corazón; Marcos, Ferdinand;
    Nacionalista Party; New Society Movement;
    People Power; Ramos, Fidel; Reform the
    Armed Forces Movement; Sin, Jaime.

## Estrada, Joseph  (Philippines)

Joseph Estrada (known by the nickname *Erap*, a
play on a Tagalog word *pare*, meaning friend)
was elected president of the Philippines in May
1998 with 39 per cent of the vote, which was a
superior performance to that of his predecessor,
**Fidel Ramos**, who had secured only 23 per cent
in the previous elections. In May 1992, Joseph
Estrada had been elected vice-president but
not on the same ticket as Ramos. He had entertained presidential ambitions since entering
national politics in 1987 and had registered as a
candidate on behalf of his own People's Filipino
Party. In March 1992, however, Estrada agreed
to stand as the vice-presidential running mate
of Eduardo Cojuangco, an alienated cousin
of incumbent president, **Corazon Aquino**, on
a ticket representing a combination of old
**Nacionalista Party** and **Liberal Party** interests.
In the event, Cojuangco came third to Ramos in
the presidential contest but Estrada secured 33
per cent of the vote to win the vice-presidential
election. The constitutional limit of one six-year
presidential term put him in an advantageous
position to succeed Ramos.

Joseph Estrada was born on 19 April 1937 in
the Tondo area of Manila. He became a national
figure as a young man through his success as
a movie actor playing dashing action parts,

while his private life mirrored his screen roles. He entered politics in August 1969 when he became Mayor of San Juan, which is within the metropolitan limits of Manila, after a long legal battle in which he successfully challenged the initial outcome of the polls. Estrada was detained twice after President **Ferdinand Marcos** introduced martial law in 1972. He subsequently became a member of President Marcos's **New Society Movement** and secured support for social welfare in his municipality but was not politically disadvantaged by the president's fall from power. He was elected to the Senate in 1987 as one of only two opposition senators together with **Juan Ponce Enrile** and built a political reputation by playing on populist-nationalist issues. He was outspoken in his opposition to US military bases and also called for the repudiation of national debts incurred during Marcos's tenure. As vice-president, he enjoyed an uneasy relationship with President Ramos, with whom he had little in common. However, he was allocated the high-profile office of head of the Presidential Anti-Crime Commission, which attracted extensive media coverage particularly when he led police raids in virtual reruns of his former movie roles. A major asset in Joseph Estrada's successful presidential bid was his strong reputation as a champion of the interests of the poor. Within eighteen months, however, his popularity had declined significantly. Against a background of economic adversity attributed to inept management, he was accused of benefiting the rich and of returning Philippine politics to corruption and cronyism. Moreover, his abortive attempt to amend the 1987 constitution to allow foreigners to purchase land and to own 100 per cent of investments was represented as having the hidden agenda of permitting himself a second term of office. He has also been subject to domestic and international criticism for his hard line in support of the military against the **Moro Islamic Liberation Front**, which is alleged to have prejudiced peace negotiations.

see also: Aquino, Corazón; Enrile, Juan Ponce; Liberal Party; Marcos, Ferdinand; Moro Islamic Liberation Front; Nacionalista Party; New Society Movement; Ramos, Fidel.

# F

## Five Power Defence Arrangements 1971– (Malaysia/Singapore)

On 15–16 April 1971 representatives of Britain, Australia, New Zealand, Malaysia and Singapore met in London to revise provision for the external defence of the two South-East Asian states. A joint air defence council was established to manage an integrated air defence system. Agreement was reached also on deploying a joint ANZUK (Australian, New Zealand and United Kingdom) ground force in Singapore and on an Australian air force contribution in Malaysia. Under these arrangements, an obligation to consult in the event of any form of external attack was substituted for the automatic commitment to respond in the **Anglo-Malaysian Defence Agreement**, which was superseded on 1 November 1971 when the arrangements came into effect. The defence arrangements, promoted by the British Conservative government which assumed office in June 1970, modified the decision of its Labour predecessor to disengage militarily from east of Suez by the end of 1971. The original tripartite military structure was denuded during the 1970s. Australia's battalion was withdrawn from Singapore by February 1974. Britain's ground troops left by the end of March 1976, its naval presence having been removed in September 1975. Joint military cooperation through exercises lapsed for a time but were revived from 1980 through an Australian initiative in the wake of Vietnam's invasion of Cambodia and the Soviet invasion of Afghanistan. In July 1983 Australia withdrew one of its two Mirage fighter squadrons based at Butterworth. The remaining squadron was withdrawn from 1986 but the Australian government committed itself to deploying F–18 fighter aircraft for a minimum of sixteen weeks a year on joint exercises and maritime surveillance for a further five years. In December 1986 New Zealand's government gave notice that it would withdraw its military battalion from Singapore by the end of 1989.

The initial arrangements had been predicated on the indivisibility of the defence of Malaysia and Singapore. They were intended as transitional to prevent a power vacuum in the wake of major military disengagement by Britain and to give Malaysia and Singapore time to develop their armed strength. Above all, they were intended to promote regional stability by engaging Malaysia and Singapore – at odds politically since separation in August 1965 – in a structure of defence cooperation. Despite recurrent tensions in the relationship, that defence cooperation has been sustained. In September 1988 a major five-power military exercise indicated a continuing commitment to uphold the defence arrangements by the original signatories. Limited military exercises have continued on an annual basis but the signatories have never been required to consult in response to the threat of an external attack against either Malaysia or Singapore. In August 1998, however, against the background of deteriorating relations with Singapore, Malaysia announced that it would not participate in that year's Five Power military exercises but then resumed participation in April 1999. Also in August 1998, the Five Power Defence Arrangements Consultative Committee commissioned a policy working group to provide advice to the five defence ministers. It noted the growing tendency towards joint exercises, particularly of a maritime kind and recommended only adjustments to the organization of the Integrated Air Defence System based in Butterworth as well as to exercise and training programmes.

see also: Anglo-Malayan/Malaysian Defence Agreement 1957–71; Sunda Strait.

## Forum Demokrasi (Indonesia)

*Forum Demokrasi* (Democracy Forum) is the name of a discussion group with a political agenda established among a number of well-known Indonesian intellectuals in March 1991. The group attracted public attention in part because of the role in its formation of the charismatic

figure of **Abdurrahman Wahid**, the head of the Islamic *Nahdatul Ulama* (NU). Links were indicated also to members of the dissident **Petition of Fifty**. The Democracy Forum was intended as a political statement in response to the establishment in December 1990 of **ICMI** (Association of Indonesian Muslim Intellectuals) under the sponsorship of President **Suharto**. Abdurrahman Wahid had refused to join this association on the ground that it would encourage sectarianism and religious intolerance. The authorities regarded the Democracy Forum with considerable suspicion and a number of its meetings have been disrupted and banned by an over-zealous police. The Democracy Forum did not seek a mass following but confined its activities to a limited urban constituency that viewed the claim of President Suharto's government that it was prepared to tolerate so-called political openness with a deep scepticism. With economic crisis at the end of the 1990s, which provided the context for President Suharto's resignation, the Democracy Forum *per se* was not in the forefront of political challenge but a number of its participants played an active role; above all, Abdurrahman Wahid who became president of Indonesia in October 1999.
*see also: Nahdatul Ulama;* ICMI; Petition of Fifty; Suharto; Wahid, Abdurrahman.

## Free Papua Movement  (Indonesia)

The Free Papua Movement (*Organisasi Papua Merdeka* – OPM) is the name of an indigenous Melanesian insurgency in **Irian Jaya**, the western half of the island of New Guinea. The OPM posed only limited challenge to Indonesian authority since it was established under United Nations auspices in May 1963. Resistance to Indonesian rule had been encouraged by the Dutch, who withheld the territory from the transfer of sovereignty over the Netherlands East Indies in 1949. They actively promoted local self-government until persuaded to give up their administration through Indonesian intimidation and US pressure. Violent opposition to Indonesian rule was triggered by its even more heavy-handed colonial nature and the clash of cultures involved. The roots of organized opposition are to be found in a Papua Youth Movement established in late 1962 by a student,

Jakob Prai, who was subsequently arrested but then escaped to join a small core of dissidents. An initial uprising in the central highlands in July 1965 among Dutch-trained militia was put down after two years but sporadic armed resistance by poorly armed and trained irregulars was sustained with some support from across the border in Papua New Guinea after the eastern half of the island became independent in 1975. A declaration of independence took place under the name of Seth Rumkorem in 1971 but without any evidence of territorial control. The movement has been beset by factionalism through tribal divisions and many of its leaders have been either killed or driven into exile. The OPM has never attracted the kind of international support mobilized in the case of *Fretilin* in **East Timor**, while the government in Port Moresby has placed good relations with Jakarta before any sense of shared Melanesian identity. A continuing source of local grievance and alienation sustaining separatist sentiment in Irian Jaya has been Indonesia's encouragement of migration from more densely populated islands interpreted as an attempt to change the demographic character and political balance of the territory. In June 1995, a regional military commander admitted that elements of the so-called Security Disturbance Group were active along the border with Papua New Guinea. The arrest, torture and murder of civilians near the Freeport-McMoran mining complex has attracted the condemnation of Indonesia's Human Rights Commission. In January 1996, a unit from the Free Papua Movement led by Kelly Kwalik seized and held hostage a group of Westerners and Indonesians engaged on a scientific expedition in an attempt to secure political recognition and a withdrawal of Indonesian forces. The hostages were not released until May in a military operation with fatalities among them and the OPM. Popular support within Irian Jaya for the OPM was stimulated by the political downfall of President **Suharto** May 1998 with demonstrations and violent confrontations with security forces in the capital Jayapura in July as well as representations in Jakarta. More significant was the example of a referendum in East Timor in August 1999 in which the vast majority of voters opted for independence. In December 1999, in emulation of a popular protest in Aceh, around 10,000 supporters of the OPM assembled in the provincial capital for a ceremonial hoisting of the flag of the separatist movement to mark the anniversary of its formation. The government of President **Abdurrahman Wahid** has refused to concede the OPM's demand for independence and has offered, as an alternative, autonomy and a change in the province's name to West Papua. In June 2000, a people's congress in Jayapura resolved that West Papua was sovereign and independent.

*see also:* Fretilin; Irian Jaya; Suharto; Timor, East; Wahid, Abdurrahman.

## *Fretilin*  (Indonesia/East Timor)

*Fretilin* is an acronym derived from *Frente Revolucionária do Timor Leste Independente*, the Portuguese term for the Revolutionary Front for an Independent East Timor. This political movement was established in its original form in **East Timor**'s administrative capital, Dili, in May 1974 in the wake of the revolutionary Armed Forces Movement in Lisbon which committed Portugal to independence for all of its overseas possessions. *Fretilin* was established by a seminary-trained mestizo elite of intellectuals and civil servants with links to left-wing groups in both Portugal and its African colonies. The title *Fretilin* was devised in August 1974 to replace that of the more innocuous Timorese Social Democratic Association. *Fretilin* possessed an intentional acronymic similarity to *Frelimo* in Mozambique and the radical rhetoric of its leadership alarmed the military government in Indonesia, which ruled the western half of the island of Timor. Indonesia's sponsorship of competing political groups encouraged a seizure of power by its clients in August 1975 which was crushed by *Fretilin* loyalists among Timorese soldiers in the Portuguese garrison. By mid-September, *Fretilin* was in control of Dili and had eliminated all opposition except along the border with West Timor. An Indonesian attempt to intervene through the vehicle of a multinational force failed because of a lack of Australian and Portuguese cooperation. When Portugal conceded Indonesia's right to be a principal party to the conflict, *Fretilin* asserted a

unilateral independence for the territory on 28 November 1975. Timorese clients of Indonesia then declared the integration of the territory into the republic. A brutal invasion by Indonesia, ostensibly by volunteers, followed on 7 December, delayed briefly by a visit to Jakarta by US President Gerald Ford. East Timor was formally integrated into Indonesia as the twenty-seventh province of the republic on 17 July 1976 after a bloody war in which an estimated 100,000 Timorese died.

Despite the lack of external military assistance and repressive rule by Indonesia's army, *Fretilin*'s military arm sustained a sporadic resistance that appeared to have run its course by the end of the 1980s. A massacre of its youthful supporters at a funeral demonstration at a cemetery in Dili in November 1991 aroused international outrage but also thinned the ranks of the movement. A further blow followed in November 1992 when, **Jose 'Xanana' Gusmao**, the commander of *Fretilin*'s military arm, was captured on the outskirts of Dili. He was sentenced to life imprisonment in May 1993, which was commuted to twenty years in the following August. *Fretilin*'s cause received international backing in November 1996 when East Timor's most prominent dissidents, Bishop Carlos Belo of Dili and Jose Ramos Horta, the movement's official observer at the United Nations, jointly received the Nobel Peace Prize. Resistance to Indonesia's rule intensified during 1997, culminating in Indonesian troops storming the campus of the university in Dili. A national convention of East Timorese exiles met in Portugal in April 1998 to establish a National Council of the Timorese Resistance and elected Gusmao as president and Horta as vice-president of its political committee. In June 1998, in the wake of the resignation of President Suharto, interim President Habibie offered the territory a special autonomous status within Indonesia, which was rejected by Gusmao who called for a referendum on independence. In an unanticipated reversal of policy in January 1999, Indonesia offered East Timor the choice between independence and autonomy. The next month Gusmao was released from prison into house arrest and began to take part in negotiations that led to an agreement to hold a referendum under

UN auspices in the following August. Despite brutal intimidation by local militia organized and armed by Indonesia's army, the outcome of the referendum was overwhelmingly in favour of independence. International pressure and domestic political change, rather than action by *Fretilin*, persuaded Indonesia to permit the deployment of an international peace-keeping force sanctioned by the UN and to endorse the result of the referendum. Gusmao returned to East Timor in October and Horta in December 1999. That month, the first meeting of the National Consultative Council convened in Dili with *Fretilin* representatives in the majority. *see also:* Gusmao, Jose 'Xanana'; Timor, East.

## Fuad, Tun Mohammad (Donald Stephens) (Malaysia/Sabah)

Mohammad Fuad, who was born in Kudat in 1920 as Donald Stephens of an Australian father and a Kadazan ethnic-group mother, was the first chief minister of Sabah on its incorporation into Malaysia in September 1963. A successful businessman who owned a local newspaper, he entered politics in the early 1960s, drawing on Kadazan support initially to oppose membership of the Federation of Malaysia. Converted to its cause, in part by the **Philippines' Claim to Sabah**, he became a defender of Sabah's rights as chief minister but was eased from office in December 1964 in exchange for the post of federal minister for Sabah affairs, which he held for only nine months, giving up political life shortly after. He became high commissioner to Australia in 1968 and in 1971 converted to **Islam**, taking the name Mohammad Fuad. He served as Sabah's head of state for nearly two years from September 1973 and then resigned in July 1975 to assume the leadership of a new intercommunal party **Berjaya** (Sabah People's Union), set up with federal support in June 1975 in challenge to the ruling **United Sabah National Organization** (USNO) led by the chief minister, **Tun Mustapha Harun**. He led *Berjaya* to electoral victory in April 1976 and again became chief minister but held office for only fifty-three days. On 6 June he was killed, together with four of his ministers as well as his son, when the light aircraft in which he was travelling crashed into the sea on its approach to Kota Kinabalu airport.

*see also: Berjaya*; Mustapha bin Datuk Harun, Tun; Philippines' Claim to Sabah; United Sabah National Organization.

## FUNCINPEC (Cambodia)

FUNCINPEC is an acronym derived from *Front uni national pour un Cambodge indépendant, neutre, pacifique et coopératif*, the French term for the National United Front for an Independent, Neutral, Peaceful and Cooperative Cambodia, which was established in March 1981 by Prince **Norodom Sihanouk** with a presence on the Thai border. This resistance movement to challenge Vietnam's occupation of Cambodia was encouraged in particular by the **ASEAN** states which were concerned at the prominence of the **Khmer Rouge**'s role. In June 1982 FUNCINPEC joined with another non-Communist movement, the **Khmer People's National Liberation Front** (KPNLF) and the Khmer Rouge in a so-called **Coalition Government of Democratic Kampuchea** (CGDK) with Prince Sihanouk as its head. That coalition maintained an uneasy coexistence until the **International Conference on Cambodia** in Paris reached agreement in October 1991. In the intra-Cambodian negotiations leading to the establishment of a symbolically sovereign **Supreme National Council**, Prince Sihanouk gave up his leadership of FUNCINPEC in order to head the new council, to be succeeded by his son Prince **Norodom Ranariddh**. Prince Ranariddh led FUNCINPEC in the elections conducted in Cambodia in May 1993 by the United Nations and secured a plurality of the seats in the Constituent Assembly. As leader of FUNCINPEC, Prince Ranariddh became First prime minister in the coalition government formed in Phnom Penh at the end of October 1993. Tensions and cleavages emerged with FUNCINPEC as the practice of coalition government confirmed the political dominance of the **Cambodian People's Party**, which had been put in power by the Vietnamese but had come second in the 1993 elections. Those tensions and cleavages were manifested openly with the dismissal of FUNCINPEC member, Sam Rainsy, as finance minister in October 1994 and from the National Assembly in June 1995. They were manifest also with the arrest and exile of former foreign minister, Prince Norodom Sirivudh, who was the party's secretary general, at the end of the year. In April 1996, four FUNCINPEC National Assembly members defected to the Cambodian People's Party overturning the former's narrow majority in the latter's favour. Tension between the two parties rose with competing negotiations with the **Khmer Rouge**. Those tensions came to a head when Second Prime Minister **Hun Sen** mounted a successful coup in July 1997 to oust Prince Ranariddh, who had fled abroad. Elections were held in July 1998, monitored by international observers, in which FUNCINPEC participated. In the event, it took second place behind the Cambodian People's Party which won a plurality of seats but insuf-

ficient to form a government. After extensive negotiations, FUNCINPEC joined in a coalition government headed by Hun Sen in the following November. Prince Ranariddh accepted the post of chairman of the National Assembly and, by implication, the subordinate position of FUNCINPEC in Cambodian politics.

*see also:* Cambodian People's Party; Democratic Kampuchea, Coalition Government of; Hun Sen; International Conference on Cambodia, Paris 1991; Khmer People's National Liberation Front; Khmer Rouge; Ranariddh, Norodom; Sihanouk, Norodom; Supreme National Council.

# G

## Geneva Agreements on Indochina 1954 (Cambodia/Laos/Vietnam)

The Geneva Agreements on Indochina comprise a set of accords which were intended to restore peace and confirm the sovereign independence of Cambodia, Laos and Vietnam. They were concluded at an international conference between 8 May and 21 July in Geneva. Indochina had been subject to violent conflict from the end of the Pacific War when the **Viet Minh** (a Communist-led Vietnamese nationalist movement) took the lead in challenging the restoration of French colonial rule throughout the peninsula in the **August Revolution 1945**. The Viet Minh, headed by **Ho Chi Minh**, had declared the independence of the Democratic Republic of Vietnam in Hanoi on 2 September 1945. Limited political concessions by France as well as US military assistance failed to stem Communist insurgent success. By the end of 1953, French political will had virtually drained away as the colonial conflict and its costs became matters of domestic political contention.

At a meeting of the foreign ministers of the United States, the Soviet Union, Britain and France in Berlin in February 1954, it was agreed that Indochina would be placed on the agenda of a forthcoming international conference in Geneva which had been arranged to address the question of Korea. The Korean phase of the conference was inconclusive. Moreover, the negotiating position of the French was dramatically weakened by the fall of its military fortress in the **Battle of Dien Bien Phu** to Viet Minh forces on 7 May 1954, the day before the Indochina phase of the conference was due to begin. Representatives attended from France, the United States, the Soviet Union, the People's Republic of China, Britain, the Democratic Republic of Vietnam, the French-backed State of Vietnam and the kingdoms of Laos and Cambodia. The conference was chaired jointly by Anthony Eden and Vyacheslav Molotov, the foreign ministers of Britain and the Soviet Union, who rejected a request by the Democratic Republic of Vietnam that representatives from self-styled Laotian and Cambodian resistance governments also be permitted to participate. That decision indicated Soviet and Chinese interest in avoiding contention with the United States. This consideration was also important in arriving at a line of demarcation in Vietnam which did not reflect the full extent of Communist military success. The Viet Minh were thus constrained by their external allies into accepting an accommodation that compromised their political interests.

The Geneva Agreements took the principal form of three accords on the cessation of hostilities in Vietnam, Laos and Cambodia and a final declaration on restoring peace in Indochina. The armistice agreements for Vietnam and Laos were signed between representatives of the French and Viet Minh high commands, while that for Cambodia was signed between military representatives of the Royal government and the Viet Minh. A declaration by the French government affirmed a willingness to withdraw all of its troops from Indochina at the request of the peninsular governments concerned. The provisions for Vietnam were the most important and the failure to implement them led on to further conflict over the unification of the country which was not resolved until the end of the **Vietnam War** in 1975. A provisional line of demarcation was established along the 17th parallel of latitude, on either side of which the two contending sides were to withdraw and regroup their forces. After two years, elections were to be held to determine the political future of the country, conducted by an international commission for supervision and control comprising India, Poland and Canada, with prior responsibility for overseeing the workings of the cease-fire agreements. The cease-fire agreements for Laos and Cambodia made provision for the withdrawal of foreign forces and recognized a single governmental authority in each case but in the case of Laos took account of the separate control by Viet Minh-stiffened insurgents of two provinces adjacent to Vietnam.

The Final Declaration of the Conference, which was not a signed document, encompassed provisions for cease-fire and political order for all three countries, spelling out their political and electoral obligations and the role of international supervision. A formal treaty commitment was not undertaken, only a series of expressions of assent and reservations by the nine representatives on all of the accords, including the Final Declaration. One reason why the Final Declaration of the Conference was not signed was the resistance of the United States, which resented the confirmation of Communist victory as well as the Communist Chinese presence. The US secretary of state, John Foster Dulles, boycotted the conference proceedings after an initial participation. The United States took note of the accords and promised to refrain from the threat of force to disturb them, but maintained that elections set for July 1956 should be supervised by the United Nations. That stand encouraged the Vietnamese government to the south of the 17th parallel to refuse to comply with the provision for national elections.

The Geneva Agreements provided, in effect, for an interlude between two phases of violent conflict in Indochina. They had the unintended consequence of dividing Vietnam into two parts, reflecting in international recognition the pattern of Cold War alignments. The cessation of hostilities broke down when the Democratic Republic of Vietnam (re-established in Hanoi after July 1954) revived its military challenge. In December 1960 the **National Liberation Front of South Vietnam** (NLF) was set up as a vehicle for reunifying Vietnam on Communist terms. In the case of Laos, the two provinces under insurgent control were never integrated under the authority of a central government until the Communists assumed power in December 1975 in the wake of the victory in April 1975 of their counterparts in Vietnam. It was only in Cambodia that the accord reached at Geneva was implemented with endorsement by the International Commission for Supervision and Control of the conduct and outcome of general elections in 1955. Prince **Norodom Sihanouk**'s political order, established by those elections, was overthrown in 1970.

see also: August Revolution 1945; Dien Bien Phu,

Battle of, 1954; Geneva Agreements on Laos 1962; Ho Chi Minh; Indochina Wars; National Liberation Front of South Vietnam; Sihanouk, Norodom; Viet Minh; Vietnam War.

## Geneva Agreements on Laos 1962
(Laos)

On 23 July 1962 an international conference in Geneva attended by fourteen governments reached agreements on political unity and neutralization for Laos. The earlier **Geneva Agreements on Indochina** of July 1954 had failed to bring peace to the country. Laos had not been subject to partition like Vietnam but national integration had been frustrated because the Communist *Pathet Lao*, stiffened by Vietnamese counterparts, had withheld the administration of Phong Saly and Sam Neua provinces from the Royal government in Vientiane. Polarization between Laotian factions aligned competitively with Vietnam and with Thailand and the United States prevented national unity by consensus during the rest of the 1950s. A coup in August 1960 by a young paratroop officer, Captain **Kong Le**, which established an ostensibly neutral government under Prince **Souvanna Phouma**, served only to extend political fragmentation. By this stage, the second phase of the **Indochina Wars** had begun with Vietnam as the main prize. Laos became of increasing importance to the resolution of that conflict because its eastern uplands made up the critical section of the **Ho Chi Minh Trail**.

By 1961, Laos existed as a state in international legal fiction only as three politico-military groupings with external supporters contended for power. At that juncture, a diplomatic initiative by the Soviet Union attracted US interest because of common fears that an escalation of internal conflict would lead to wider confrontation. Agreement on a cease-fire made possible the fourteen-power international conference which convened in Geneva in May 1961. It took until June 1962, however, for a preliminary accord to be concluded between the leaders of the contending factions. A formal agreement on establishing a tripartite coalition and on neutralizing Laos was eventually signed on 23 July 1962. That settlement broke down beyond repair by 1964 and neutralization came to exist only on paper. In the event, competitive military intervention confirmed Laos's role as a subordinate theatre of the **Vietnam War** whose eventual outcome determined its political identity by the end of 1975.

see also: Geneva Agreements on Indochina 1954; Ho Chi Minh Trail; Indochina Wars; Kong Le; *Pathet Lao*; Souvanna Phouma; Vietnam War.

## Gerakan Ra'ayat Malaysia (Malaysia)

*Gerakan Ra'ayat Malaysia* translates from Malay as the Malaysian People's Movement and is most commonly known as *Gerakan*. The party was founded on the island of Penang on 25 March 1968 in the main by intellectually minded Chinese opposition politicians and university teachers as a multiracial and democratic socialist party. In the elections of May 1969, whose outcome provoked the **May 13 Racial Riots**, *Gerakan* won eight seats in the federal Parliament and secured control of the state government in Penang. After an internal split, the party began to cooperate politically with the **Alliance Party** coalition government, which became a formal arrangement in February 1972 further consolidated with the establishment of the *Barisan Nasional* (National Front) in June 1974. *Gerakan* has maintained its multiracial platform but over the years has become primarily a vehicle for urban middle-class Chinese who lack confidence in the **Malaysian Chinese Association** (MCA) to represent their interests within the ruling coalition. In April 1995, it increased its share to 7 seats compared to 30 won by the MCA. In November 1999, it won 6 seats compared to 29 by the MCA. *Gerakan* enjoys minimal representation in the federal government.

see also: Alliance Party; *Barisan Nasional*; Malaysian Chinese Association; May 13 Racial Riots 1969.

## Gestapu (Indonesia)

*Gestapu* is an acronym in Indonesian taken from *Gerakan September Tiga Puluh* (Thirtieth of September Movement). The acronym represents a deliberate attempt to tar an abortive coup with the brush of Nazi-German symbolism. That abortive coup was mounted primarily in the capital Jakarta in the early hours of 1 October 1965 against a background of rising political tension. A group of dissident army and air force officers led nominally by a battalion commander from President **Sukarno**'s palace guard arranged the abduction of six of the country's most senior generals, including the army commander Lt-General Achmad Yani. They were taken to Halim Air Base outside the capital where those not killed during their abduction were murdered at the **Crocodile Hole** and all the bodies thrown down a well. The coup group then broadcast the names of members of a Revolutionary Council set up ostensibly to forestall a plot by the US Central Intelligence Agency (CIA). The council announced that it would carry out the policies of President Sukarno, who was safe under its protection. Major-General **Suharto**, then head of Kostrad, the army's strategic reserve based in west Java, was not on the abduction list. He assumed command and overcame the coup group within two days.

The Communist Party of Indonesia was implicated in the abortive coup and its members and presumed supporters soon became the object of physical attack by security forces and Muslim militants with at least 100,000 fatalities. President Sukarno was politically discredited also because of his patronage of the Communists, his presence at the coup headquarters at Halim Air Base, his failure to denounce the murder of the generals and his description of the coup attempt as an internal affair of the army. The outcome of the abortive coup was a fundamental change in the structure of the political system at the expense of the Communists and President Sukarno and to the advantage of the armed forces as a corporate entity. Its political dominance was asserted on 11 March 1966 when President Sukarno was obliged to transfer executive authority to Suharto, by then promoted to Lt-General (*see* **Supersemar**). The next day, the Communist Party of Indonesia was declared an illegal organization.

see also: Crocodile Hole; Guided Democracy; Sukarno; Supersemar.

## Ghafar Baba, Tun Abdul (Malaysia)

Abdul Ghafar Baba was appointed deputy prime minister of Malaysia in May 1986 following the resignation of **Datuk Musa Hitam**. He held that office until his own resignation in October 1993. He confirmed his political pos-

ition in April 1987 when he narrowly defeated Datuk Musa in the election for the deputy president of **UMNO** (United Malays National Organization). His failure to secure support from party divisions in the face of a challenge by **Anwar Ibrahim** during 1993 for the post of deputy president of UMNO precipitated his resignation from government and party offices. Ghafar Baba was born on 18 February 1925 in Kuala Pilah in the state of Negri Sembilan. He was educated at the Sultan Idris Teachers College and worked for a time as a primary schoolteacher. He entered local politics as a young man and was chief minister of Malacca for twelve years from 1955. He entered federal politics in 1969, going directly into the cabinet as minister of national and rural development drawing on his support among political leaders at the state level. In 1974 he was elected one of the three vice-presidents of UMNO, an office which he held continuously until his further elevation over a decade later. He established a reputation as a traditional power-broker who managed to combine business and political interests. Although of the same generation as the prime minister, Dr **Mahathir Mohamad**, he asserted a right to be regarded as a political successor, despite his problematic health. His inability to hold on to the post of deputy president of UMNO indicated not only a personal failure but the passing of his kind of grass-roots politician. In March 1995, however, he returned to UMNO's ranks to play a role on its behalf in general elections the following month, after which he was honoured with the title *tun*. In an elder statesman role within UMNO, Ghafar Baba indicated grass-roots dissatisfaction after its electoral reverse in November 1999; in particular, over the attempt by Dr Mahathir to ensure that the offices of president and vice-president not be contested in party elections in May 2000.
see also: Anwar Ibrahim; Mahathir Mohamad, Datuk Sri; Musa Hitam, Datuk; UMNO.

## Ghazali Shafie, Tan Sri Mohamad (Malaysia)

Ghazali Shafie transferred from a career in the civil service to political office in the wake of communal violence in the **May 13 Racial Riots** in 1969. He served in turn as minister for special functions and then concurrently as minister of information, minister of home affairs and finally foreign minister of Malaysia. He held the last office from July 1981 until July 1984 in Dr **Mahathir Mohamad**'s first administration and then retired from active politics. Ghazali Shafie was born in Kuala Lipis on 22 March 1922 and was educated at Raffles College in Singapore. During the Japanese occupation, he played a role in British-inspired clandestine resistance. After the Pacific War, he studied law at the University of Wales in Aberystwyth and then spent a year at the London School of Economics. On his return to Malaya, he joined the civil service and then went abroad for training to prepare for a senior position in the country's fledgling Foreign Ministry. On independence in August 1957, he became deputy secretary of the Ministry of External Affairs. In 1958 he assumed the office of permanent secretary, subsequently secretary-general, which he held without interruption until 1970. During that period, he played a key role in advising on foreign policy both over the formation of Malaysia and in countering Indonesia's **Confrontation** of the wider federation during 1963–6. As a flamboyant politician during the 1970s, he acquired a reputation as an ambitious man. After the death of the prime minister, **Tun Abdul Razak**, who was succeeded by **Tun Hussein Onn**, with Dr Mahathir Mohamad becoming deputy prime minister, he used his powers of detention as minister of home affairs to assert his position against political rivals. Dr Mahathir held on to office and when he became prime minister in July 1981, Ghazali Shafie was shifted to the less powerful portfolio of foreign affairs. As foreign minister, he played an active part in **ASEAN**'s collective diplomacy during the early years of the Cambodian conflict.
see also: ASEAN; Hussein Onn, Tun; Mahathir Mohamad, Datuk Sri; May 13 Racial Riots 1969; Razak, Tun Abdul.

## Giap, General Vo Nguyen  (Vietnam)

General Giap is regarded as the founding father of the People's Army of Vietnam. He achieved renown as his country's leading military thinker and as the architect of historic victories against France and the United States in the **Indochina Wars** and the **Vietnam War**. General Giap was born in August 1911 to a peasant family in a village in Quang Binh Province north of Hue. A nationalist in his teens, he was detained in 1930 by the French colonial authorities for leading a student protest. He graduated in law from Hanoi University in 1937 and in political economy the following year, by which time he had joined the Communist Party of Indochina founded by **Ho Chi Minh**. Following the outbreak of the Second World War in 1939, he evaded police arrest and made his way to southern China, where he first met the Vietnamese Communist leader. Giap's wife and child remained in Hanoi, both dying in prison. He returned to the border region of Vietnam early in 1941 as one of Ho's closest advisers, with responsibility for training a fledgling guerrilla army. In May 1941 he participated in establishing the **Viet Minh** (League for the Independence of Vietnam) which nominally led the nationalist struggle against French colonial rule. After the proclamation of the Democratic Republic of Vietnam in Hanoi in September 1945, Giap became minister of the interior as well as commander-in-chief of the armed forces and then minister of defence in 1947. He always upheld the primacy of politics in war. He displayed logistical genius at the **Battle of Dien Bien Phu** in 1954, planning the decisive deployment of heavy artillery in the mountains surrounding the valley where the French had established their military positions.

After that dramatic victory, the partition of Vietnam and the establishment of a Communist government north of the 17th parallel of latitude, Giap led its armed forces continuously against the government in Saigon and US military intervention until final victory and national unification in 1975. He gave up his post as commander-in-chief in 1976 and was removed as minister of defence in 1980 and then from the Politburo in 1982, possibly for opposing the invasion of Cambodia. He retained office as a deputy prime minister to which he was appointed in 1979 until leaving office in August 1991, but devoted much of his time to a commission responsible for training scientists and technicians. When Vietnam and China began to engage in serious rapprochement in the late 1980s, General Giap played a role in the personal diplomacy. In September 1989 he led the Vietnamese delegation to the Asian Games in Beijing, the highest rank-

ing Vietnamese to visit the Chinese capital openly for over a decade. He also played a personal role in reconciliation with the United States through participating in historical seminars in Hanoi on the Vietnam War.

*see also:* August Revolution 1945; Dien Bien Phu, Battle of, 1954; Ho Chi Minh; Indochina Wars; Viet Minh; Vietnam War.

## Goh Chok Tong (Singapore)

Goh Chok Tong is only the second person to have held the office of prime minister of Singapore, succeeding **Lee Kuan Yew** on 28 November 1990. Goh was born on 20 May 1941 in Singapore; he read economics at the University of Singapore and then entered the government's Economic Planning Unit. In 1969, after postgraduate studies at Williams College in the United States, he was seconded to Neptune Oriental Lines as planning and projects manager, rising to managing director in 1973. He was persuaded to enter politics by the finance minister, Hon Sui Sen, and stood successfully as a candidate for the ruling **People's Action Party** (PAP) in the parliamentary elections of December 1976. Goh was appointed senior minister of state in the Ministry of Defence in September 1977 and then minister for trade and industry in March 1979. As a leading member of the second generation of politicians whom Lee Kuan Yew was training to succeed the founding fathers of the republic, he was also given experience in the portfolios of health and defence.

After general elections in December 1984 in which there was a notable swing against the ruling party, Goh was made First deputy prime minister, having been picked by his cabinet colleagues, although Lee Kuan Yew let it be known that he had not been his first choice. Goh succeeded Lee in November 1990 after a long apprenticeship which was not really over even after he became prime minister, because his predecessor remained in the cabinet with the office of senior minister, also retaining initially the post of secretary-general of the PAP. Goh is distinguished from Lee by his softer political style, more in tune with the aspirations of a younger, more affluent generation of Singaporeans. In political practice, however, he represents a continuity of philosophy based on the shared conviction of the essential vulnerability of the island-state and the need to demonstrate resoluteness of mind and action. He has led the PAP to resounding electoral victories in August 1991 and in January 1997. After the latter success, he claimed that Singapore's voters had rejected Western-style Liberal Democracy.

*see also:* Lee Kuan Yew; People's Action Party.

## Goh Keng Swee  (Singapore)

Goh Keng Swee was active as a leading political figure in Singapore for twenty-five years, playing a key role in promoting both the island-state's economic development and its defence capability. He was born in Malacca in colonial Malaya on 6 October 1918 and was educated at Raffles College in Singapore and after the Pacific War in England at the London School of Economics, returning to join the local civil service. In London, he was a founder and first chairman of the nationalist Malayan Forum, whose alumni included **Lee Kuan Yew** and **Tun Abdul Razak**. He resigned from the civil service to stand as a candidate for the **People's Action Party** (PAP) in May 1959 and was appointed minister of finance in the government formed after its electoral victory. On Singapore's expulsion from the Federation of Malaysia in August 1965, he was the first defence minister in the independent state and then became deputy prime minister in 1972, a post which he held until he retired from politics in 1984. He enjoys the reputation of being one of the few intellectual peers of Lee Kuan Yew. In retirement, he served for a time as deputy chairman of the Monetary Authority of Singapore, an economic adviser to the government of China and head of the Racecourse Totalizer Board.

*see also:* Lee Kuan Yew; People's Action Party; Razak, Tun Abdul.

## *Golkar*  (Indonesia)

*Golkar* is an acronym drawn from the Indonesian *Golongan Karya*, meaning Functional Groups. *Golkar* is a political organization which was employed primarily to generate electoral support for the administration of President **Suharto**. It was established in October 1964 by senior army officers under the extended acronym of *Sekber Golkar* from *Sekretariat Bersama Golongan Karya* (Joint Secretariat of Functional Groups). Their object was to use the organization to counter the influence of the Communist Party within the National Front set up by President **Sukarno** as a vehicle for mass mobilization in his own political interest. *Sekber Golkar* failed to make any political showing and was then overtaken by events with the abortive coup (see *Gestapu*) of October 1965 and its far-reaching political consequences. Nothing was heard of the organization until 1971 when it was revived to serve the electoral interests of the Suharto administration, which had made a formal commitment to constitutionalism.

Under the independence constitution of 1945, Indonesia is governed by an executive president chosen every five years by the **People's Consultative Assembly**. That Congress is made up in part of an elected Parliament with legislative powers. *Golkar* was rehabilitated in 1971 for the specific purpose of demonstrating electoral support for President Suharto's rule without risking a change of government. Golkar was first so employed in elections in July 1971 and secured 62.8 per cent of the vote with the evident support of the armed forces and the civil service. That figure was raised to 64.3 per cent in May 1977 and approximately held in May 1982. In April 1987 *Golkar* received a somewhat embarrassing 72.9 per cent of the vote, which was reduced to 68 per cent in elections in June 1992. In parliamentary elections in May 1997, it polled 74 per cent of the vote and secured 325 of the 425 elective seats. This overwhelming majority served to provide a mandate for President Suharto's successful bid for a seventh consecutive term of office in March 1998. *Golkar's* political fortunes waned dramatically with President Suharto's resignation in the following May against a background of economic crisis. Interim-President **Habibie** led the much discredited party into fresh parliamentary elections in June 1999 in which *Golkar* secured 20.9 per cent of the vote with 120 seats behind the *Partai Demokrasi Indonesia* (PDI-P), which secured 37.4 per cent and 154 seats. Moreover, after a banking scandal over financing his campaign and resentment over his handling of **East Timor** and evident divisions within the party, Dr Habibie withdrew from the presidential contest within the **People's Consultative Assembly** (MPR) in October 1999, which was won by **Abdurrahman Wahid**. However, a number of members of the liberal wing of *Golkar* were included in the new cabinet announced at the end of the month, while Akbar Tanjung became speaker of the Parliament. *Golkar* has sustained a political identity as part of an opposition coalition seeking greater accountability from President Wahid. Its opposition role was reinforced with its exclusion from a reconstituted cabinet in August 2000.

*see also:* Crocodile Hole; *Gestapu*; Habibie, B. J.; *Partai Demokrasi Indonesia*; People's Consultative Assembly; Suharto; Sukarno; Timor, East; Wahid, Abdurrahman.

## Guided Democracy (Indonesia)

Guided Democracy is the name for the authoritarian political system inaugurated by decree by President **Sukarno** on 5 July 1959 when he dissolved the elected Constituent Assembly and reinstated the independence constitution of 1945. Known in Indonesian as *Demokrasi Terpimpin*, its inauguration marked the final failure of Indonesia to practise parliamentary democracy against a tempestuous background of political and military factionalism, religious and regional dissension and economic decline. Guided Democracy gave rise to a myriad of radical and romantic political symbols which Sukarno wielded to his short-term advantage to the neglect of economic priorities. Although Guided Democracy was represented as an authentically Indonesian alternative to an alien political tradition, it was an intensely competitive system. The personal dominance of President Sukarno barely masked the bitter contention between the conservative armed forces and the radical Communist Party. Sukarno's political balancing act between the two rivals came to an end after an abortive coup (see *Gestapu*) in October 1965 which discredited him and the Communist Party. A military initiative in March 1966 led by Lt-General **Suharto** which removed Sukarno from effective power and also proscribed the Communist Party marked the dissolution of Guided Democracy and its replacement by a more constructive developmental authoritarianism.

*see also:* Crocodile Hole; *Gestapu*; Suharto; Sukarno.

## Gulf of Tonkin Incident 1964

(Vietnam) *see* Tonkin Gulf Incident.

## Gusmao, José 'Xanana' (Indonesia/East Timor)

Jose 'Xanana' (Alexandre) Gusmao has been the leader of East Timorese resistance to Indonesian rule and is the most likely head of government of an independent **East Timor**. He was born in 1946 in Dili and was educated at a Jesuit seminary. He then worked in the Department of Forestry and Agriculture during Portuguese rule until 1974. After Indonesia's invasion in December 1975, he rose to prominence as a *Fretilin* resistance leader. He succeeded Nicolau Lobato as commander of its military wing in 1979 and helped to sustain its armed struggle against superior odds during the 1980s. He was captured in Dili in 1992 and sentenced to life imprisonment in the following year, which was subsequently commuted to twenty years. In April 1998, he was elected as President of the National Council for Maubere (East Timorese) Resistance at a convention of exiles in Portugal. After the overthrow of President **Suharto** in May 1998, he became the interlocutor for the East Timorese cause and was released into house arrest in February 1999 in the month after the decision by President **Habibie** to permit the East Timorese to choose between autonomy within Indonesia or full independence. He returned to East Timor in October 1999, after the United Nations-sanctioned International Force for East Timor had begun to restore order following the orchestrated anarchy in the wake of the UN-conducted referendum in which the vast majority of voters had opted for independence. Gusmao is a mild-mannered man with a poetic disposition and considerable personal appeal. He has no illusions about the gigantic task involved in reconstructing East Timor into an independent state and has also adopted a conciliatory position towards the Indonesia of President **Abdurrahman Wahid**. In August 2000, he relinquished his military command prior to assuming civilian political office.

*see also: Fretilin*; Habibie, B. J.; Suharto; Timor, East; United Nations: East Timor; Wahid, Abdurrahman.

# H

## Habibie, Dr B. J. (Indonesia)

Dr B. J. Habibie became President of Indonesia on 21 May 1998 on the resignation of President **Suharto** against a background of economic crisis and political turbulence. As vice-president, elected by the **People's Consultative Assembly** (MPR) in the previous March, he succeeded to high office for the remainder of the presidential term under article eight of Indonesia's constitution. As a protégé and close confidant of former President Suharto, he represented political continuity as a symbol of a discredited order. Nonetheless, he did not abdicate presidential ambitions. He pursued them through promoting a liberal agenda whereby political prisoners were released and freedom of the press was restored. He authorized fresh parliamentary and presidential elections but failed to overcome the political taint of the Suharto era, which was demonstrated in the poor performance of *Golkar*, the government's party in parliamentary elections in June 1999. He lost the support of the armed forces through his seemingly precipitate willingness to countenance the independence of **East Timor** in an offer of a referendum made unexpectedly in January 1999. A scandal over campaign financing further diminished his presidential chances, while he was opposed by a liberal faction within his own party. In the event, he withdrew from the presidential contest and gave up office on 20 October when the People's Consultative Assembly elected **Abdurrahman Wahid**.

Bacharuddin Jusuf Habibie was born on 25 June 1936 in Pare-Pare in south Sulawesi. He was educated at the Technical University in Bandung and then at the Technical University in Aachen, Germany, from which he graduated with a doctorate in engineering. He became a member of the faculty and then director for research and development for Messerschmitt, the German aircraft corporation. He was well known to President Suharto through a family connection established during a military posting in Sulawesi. Indeed, President Suharto took the personal initiative to bring Dr Habibie back to Indonesia in 1974, where he worked initially for Pertamina, the state oil corporation. In 1978, he was appointed minister of state for research and technology holding that portfolio continuously until becoming vice-president in 1998. In that portfolio, he made a dubious mark by establishing an aircraft manufacturing industry in Bandung as part of a grand design to make Indonesia a regional centre of modern technology. In this costly and unsuccessful enterprise, he enjoyed President Suharto's full backing. Dr Habibie began to engage in political activities from December 1990 when, again with President Suharto's support, he was instrumental in establishing **ICMI** (Association of Indonesian Muslim Intellectuals) as a counter to the influence of the armed forces. Before elections in March 1993, he intimated that he was interested in becoming vice-president. That ambition was realized in 1998 when he was hand-picked by President Suharto in a political initiative interpreted as an attempt to ensure that his running mate was not a credible successor. Dr Habibie had by then secured a reputation for eccentricity in economic judgements as well as displaying an excessively egocentric disposition.

*see also:* East Timor; *Golkar*; ICMI; People's Consultative Assembly (MPR); Suharto; Wahid, Abdurrahman.

## Hanoi Summit (ASEAN) 1998 (Burma (Myanmar)/Brunei/Cambodia/Indonesia/Laos/Malaysia/Philippines/Singapore/Thailand/Vietnam)

The sixth meeting of ASEAN's heads of government convened in the Vietnamese capital in mid-December 1998. The venue of the meeting was significant as further evidence of reconciliation between Vietnam and those founding members of ASEAN, which had challenged its invasion and occupation of Cambodia. The declared purpose of the meeting was to devise a corporate strategy that would enable ASEAN's governments to address the regional economic crisis whose devastating impact had diminished the standing of the Association. To that end, a Hanoi Plan of Action was promulgated in an attempt to strengthen regional cooperation but without any tangible effect on economic circumstances. In the event, the main business of the meeting was the problem of Cambodia's membership, which had been postponed in July 1997 after a violent coup in Phnom Penh displacing First Prime Minister Prince **Norodom Ranaridh** to the political advantage of Second Prime Minister **Hun Sen**, who attended the Hanoi meeting as an observer. Vietnam used its position as host to press for Cambodia's immediate entry and was supported by Indonesia and Malaysia, while the Philippines, Singapore and Thailand insisted that its entry be delayed until the coalition government formed in the previous month headed by Hun Sen had demonstrated its durability. Vietnam's prime minister, **Phan Van Khai**, had his way in announcing that a consensus had been reached on Cambodia's membership and that a ceremony to mark its entry would take place in Hanoi at an unspecified date. That ceremony took place in April 1999.

see also: ASEAN; Hun Sen; Phan Van Khai; Ranariddh, Norodom.

## Harris Mohamad Salleh, Datuk
(Malaysia/Sabah)
Datuk Harris Mohamad Salleh was chief minister of Sabah from June 1976 until April 1985. He had been instrumental in helping to form *Berjaya* (the Malay acronym for the Sabah People's Union) in July 1975 as a challenge to the government of chief minister **Tun Mustapha Harun** but gave up the leadership to **Tun Mohammad Fuad** on his resignation as head of state. He became deputy chief minister to Tun Mohammad Fuad after *Berjaya* won the state elections in April 1976 but then succeeded Fuad after his death in an air crash in June. Datuk Harris was born in Brunei on 4 November 1930 and initially received only a secondary education. He worked as a teacher, a government clerk and then as an assistant district officer, which gave him the opportunity to pursue a qualification in public administration at the University of Melbourne. His career blossomed

as political opportunities opened up with decolonization and Sabah's membership of Malaysia. He was vice-president of the **United Sabah National Organization** (USNO) led by Tun Mustapha and held a number of senior cabinet portfolios until his resignation in July 1975. His defection from USNO was encouraged by the federal government, which had become alarmed at Tun Mustapha's separatist disposition. As chief minister, he failed to live up to expectations of good government generated by his initial criticism of Tun Mustapha's administration and was neglectful of non-Muslim interests. In February 1985 a new party was formed in Sabah based on an alliance of Christian Kadazans and Chinese. This *Parti Bersatu Sabah* (**Sabah United Party**) was carried to office by the same kind of popular wave which had benefited *Berjaya* nearly ten years previously. After his electoral defeat, Datuk Harris retired from political life.

see also: Berjaya; Fuad, Mohammad; Mustapha bin Datuk Harun, Tun; Sabah United Party; United Sabah National Organization.

## Hatta, Mohammad  (Indonesia)
Mohammad Hatta, who proclaimed the independence of Indonesia jointly with **Sukarno** on 17 August 1945, was the republic's first vice-president. He played a critical role in the concurrent office of prime minister from January 1948 in guiding the embryonic state during the struggle for independence from the Dutch during which he also articulated the ideal of an 'independent and active' foreign policy for the republic. He led the Republic of Indonesia's delegation at the Round Table Conference in the Hague from August 1949, which concluded with an agreement on independence in the following December. After independence, he continued as prime minister of the United States of Indonesia until its replacement by a unitary republic in August 1950. His attempt to steer Indonesia in the direction of economic development was thwarted by the political radicalism of President Sukarno. He resigned as vice-president in July 1956 out of a sense of frustration. Although he continued to command wide respect, he never again held public office.

Mohammad Hatta was born in western Sumatra on 12 August 1902. As a young man, he was exposed to Islamic modernism, while as a student of economics in Rotterdam he was attracted to Marxist ideas and became an active nationalist. On his return to the then Netherlands East Indies in 1932, he came into conflict with the colonial authorities who sent him into internal exile in West New Guinea and Banda. He cooperated with the Japanese during their occupation in the nationalist cause, advocating negotiation as the prime means of its fulfilment. During the end of his life, Mohammad Hatta was drawn into an abortive attempt by a Javanese mystic, Sawito Kartwibowo, to persuade President **Suharto** to give up power on the ground that he had abused it (*see* **Sawito Affair**). Mohammad Hatta, who died in 1980, was never able to translate his ideal role as the social and political conscience of Indonesia into practical politics.

*see also:* Sawito Affair; Suharto; Sukarno.

## Heng Samrin  (Cambodia)

Heng Samrin came to international attention when he was appointed from obscurity as president of the National United Front for National Salvation in whose name Cambodia was invaded by Vietnam in December 1978. In January 1979 he became president of the ruling People's Revolutionary Council of the **People's Republic of Kampuchea** and in the following month president of the Council of State. Heng Samrin has served as a political front man without a power base of his own. He is believed to have been born in 1934 in Prey Veng Province but apart from an association with **Khmer Rouge** insurgency, little more is known of his early life. Between 1976 and 1978 he was a political commissar and commander of its fourth infantry division deployed in the eastern region. In May 1978 Heng Samrin was involved in that region's rebellion against **Pol Pot**'s leadership, finding refuge in Vietnam where he was given a political role. He became general secretary of the ruling **Kampuchean People's Revolutionary Party**'s central committee in December 1981 after Vietnam's initial nominee had proved unreliable. He remained in that position for nearly a decade until a political settlement came

into sight, although real leadership was shared between the prime minister, **Hun Sen**, and the speaker of the Parliament, **Chea Sim**. With the adoption of the title State of Cambodia in place of People's Republic of Kampuchea in April 1989, Heng Samrin's role began to diminish. In October 1991 the Kampuchean People's Revolutionary Party changed its name to the **Cambodian People's Party**, dropping Heng Samrin as general secretary for Chea Sim. He was replaced as head of state by Prince **Norodom Sihanouk** when he returned to Cambodia in November 1991, enjoying no more than a nominal role as honorary president of the Cambodian People's Party.

*see also:* Cambodian People's Party; Chea Sim; Hun Sen; Kampuchea, People's Republic of; Kampuchean People's Revolutionary Party; Khmer Rouge; Pol Pot; Sihanouk, Norodom.

## Hertogh, Maria: Riots 1950
(Singapore)

Maria Hertogh was a Dutch girl who had been given over by her parents at the age of 4 to a local foster mother for safe-keeping just prior to Japan's occupation of the Netherlands East Indies. After the end of the Pacific War, her parents located their daughter in Malaya where she was living as a Muslim and speaking only Malay. They commenced proceedings in Singapore's High Court to regain custody but in the mean time their daughter was married to a Malay. The decision of the court to revoke the marriage, the removal of the girl to a Roman Catholic convent and from there to Holland, and then a Malay newspaper's publication of her photograph in the convent sparked off violent demonstrations in Singapore by Malays in December 1950. They felt aggrieved that their faith had been publicly insulted. Violence was directed primarily against Europeans and Eurasians, leaving sixteen people dead.

## Herzog Affair 1986  (Singapore)

An official visit to Singapore in November 1986 by President Chaim Herzog of Israel prompted diplomatic protests from the governments of Brunei, Indonesia and Malaysia. In addition, Indonesia and Malaysia withdrew their heads of mission for the duration of the visit. Greatest strain occurred in the relationship between Singapore and Malaysia, whose prime minister, Dr **Mahathir Mohamad**, interpreted the visit as a personal slight. It had been announced, without consultation or notice, coincident with his public denunciations of Zionism provoked by allegations in the *Asian Wall Street Journal* that his finance minister had been manipulating the stock market. Singapore's invitation was also resented because it touched Dr Mahathir's political authority, then subject to challenge by rivals within **UMNO** (United Malays National Organization). Dr Mahathir's evident displeasure provided an opportunity for an *ad-hoc* coalition of political forces to agitate against the visit, with the ulterior motive of embarrassing Malaysia's prime minister. In Singapore, Malaysian ministerial and journalistic protests were treated as a test of national sovereignty, while the willingness of the Malay-Muslim community of Singapore to take their lead from Malaysia in opposing the Israeli president's visit caused serious concern. In the event, the domestic repercussions of the affair in both states brought home to their respective prime ministers that they could not afford to allow the quarrel to fester. After an apology of a kind from Singapore's prime minister, **Lee Kuan Yew**, and despite a revival of tension because of a remark about the role of Malays in the republic's armed forces by the defence minister, **Lee Hsien Loong** (the prime minister's elder son) serious attempts were made to repair relations. Lee Kuan Yew and Dr Mahathir talked in October 1987 at the Commonwealth heads of government meeting in Vancouver and set in train a process of reconciliation, expressed in subsequent agreements on the sale of water and gas by Malaysia to Singapore and in defence cooperation. Symbolic reconciliation was marked in July 1988 by the first official visit to Singapore by a reigning king of Malaysia. In October 1993 a brief visit to Singapore by Israel's prime minister, Yitzhak Rabin, which followed on a stop-over in Indonesia, passed off without comment from Malaysia, while Lee Kuan Yew paid his first visit to Israel in May 1994.

*see also:* Lee Hsien Loong; Lee Kuan Yew; Mahathir Mohamad, Datuk Sri; UMNO.

## *Hmong*  (Laos)

The *Hmong* are an ethnic minority identified with mountain settlement in Laos who were known at one time by the pejorative *Meo* (savage). Because of clan rivalries, *Hmong* were to be found on both sides of the internal conflict which afflicted Laos for three decades after the end of the Pacific War (*see* **Indochina Wars; Vietnam War**). The *Hmong* are not indigenous to Laos but migrated from southern China from the early nineteenth century; they have been identified with slash-and-burn agriculture and the cultivation of opium. A French-inspired attempt to administer the *Hmong* in 1938 led to the split within the minority which enabled both the ***Pathet Lao*** and the Royal Lao government to recruit them for their military purposes. Many thousands of *Hmong* were recruited into a fighting force by General **Vang Pao**, who was funded by the US Central Intelligence Agency (CIA). Many of them fled Laos after the *Pathet Lao* achieved power in 1975. From exile in Thailand, France, Australia and the United States, there have been recurrent abortive attempts to mobilize resistance to the government in Vientiane which has been unsympathetic to demands for *Hmong* political autonomy. That resistance revived in the form of a limited insurgency from the late 1990s, especially in the central province of Xiang Khouang.

*see also:* Indochina Wars; *Pathet Lao*; Vang Pao; Vietnam War.

## Ho Chi Minh  (Vietnam)

Ho Chi Minh is a legendary figure in Vietnamese and international communism. As a thinker, he combined an attachment to Marxist principles with a fervent nationalist commitment. As a revolutionary leader, he was distinguished as a practitioner rather than as a theoretician. In his later years, he was portrayed as an ascetic and benign father figure as a role model for the Vietnamese people. For youthful dissenters in the west during the **Vietnam War**, he served as a symbol of revolutionary dedication to a just cause. Ho Chi Minh was born Nguyen Tat Thanh in Nghe An Province in central Vietnam on 19 May 1890. His father was an official at the imperial court in Hue who had also worked as an itinerant teacher. Ho is believed to have been expelled from the French Lycée at Vinh as a teenager for nationalist activities. In September 1911 he began work as a mess boy on a French liner, so beginning a long period of travel outside of Vietnam. During the First World War he settled in France, where he began to involve himself in the Vietnamese nationalist cause, taking the name Nguyen Ai Quoc (Nguyen the Patriot). In 1920, influenced by Lenin's writings, Ho became a founder member of the French Communist Party. He went to Moscow in the early 1920s and began to work for the Comintern, whose agent he became in South-East Asia later in the decade. It was in this capacity that in 1930 he reconciled competing factions to establish the Communist Party of Indochina whose direct lineal successor is the ruling Communist Party of Vietnam. In May 1941 he set up the **Viet Minh** (League of the Independence of Vietnam) which was a Communist-led national united front which successfully challenged French colonial rule after the end of the Pacific War in the **August Revolution 1945**. Ho Chi Minh took the full pseudonym (meaning Ho who brings enlightenment) to avoid arrest on entering China in 1942. Ho engaged in fruitless negotiations with France in 1946 and then led the Viet Minh to victory in the First **Indochina War**, which secured the country north of the 17th parallel for Communist Party rule in 1954. He inspired the insurgent challenge to the government in Saigon after 1960 but did not live to see Vietnam's unification. He died on 2 September 1969 at the age of 79. His party colleagues announced his death as having occurred a day later because they did not want it known that he had passed away on the anniversary of national independence, which he had declared in Hanoi on 2 September 1945.

see also: August Revolution 1945; Indochina Wars; National Liberation Front of South Vietnam; Viet Minh; Vietnam War.

## Ho Chi Minh Trail  (Vietnam)

The Ho Chi Minh Trail was the name given in the west to the network of infiltration routes extending from North Vietnam through southern Laos and eastern Cambodia into the highlands of South Vietnam which bypassed the effective political boundary of the 17th

parallel of latitude created by the **Geneva Agreements on Indochina** in 1954. These routes were employed from the early 1960s during the **Vietnam War** by the People's Liberation Army to channel personnel and supplies first to the southern insurgency and then to the conventional military challenge to the government in Saigon, which was defeated in April 1975. The trail ran through mountainous and jungle terrain and took a heavy toll on the flow of Vietnamese forces who were subjected to military interdiction (see **Lam Son 719**) on their way south. In February 2000, Prime Minister **Phan Van Kai** approved a plan to turn part of the trail into a 1,690-kilometre modern highway linking northern and southern parts of Vietnam.

see also: Geneva Agreements on Indochina 1954; Indochina Wars; Lam Son 719; Phan Van Kai; Vietnam War.

## Hoa Hao  (Vietnam)

The Hoa Hao is a reformist Buddhist sect which was established at the outbreak of the Second World War as a result of the mystical experiences of Huynh Phu So, who lived in Hoa Hao village in southern Vietnam near the Cambodian border. He claimed to be the apostle of a famous Buddhist monk and attracted thousands of adherents through his faith-healing skills. He was detained by the French and then protected by the Japanese. His supporters raised a military force but failed to make common cause with the **Viet Minh**, who massacred hundreds of Hoa Hao followers in September 1945 and were also responsible for the murder of Huynh Phu So in April 1947. The Hoa Hao then rallied to the French, who paid for their military services in the **Indochina Wars**. After the **Battle of Dien Bien Phu** and then the **Geneva Agreements on Indochina** in July 1954, they joined with other dissident forces in challenging the US-supported government of **Ngo Dinh Diem** but were crushed. The movement went into speedy decline to the benefit of the Communist insurgency, which recruited Hoa Hao members into its ranks.

see also: Buddhism; Diem, Ngo Dinh; Dien Bien Phu, Battle of, 1954; Geneva Agreements on Indochina 1954; Indochina Wars; Viet Minh.

## Hor Namhong (Cambodia)

Hor Namhong was appointed Minister of Foreign Affairs and International Cooperation of the Kingdom of Cambodia in November 1998 having been foreign minister of the defunct State of Cambodia between 1990 and 1993. Hor Namhong was born in Phnom Penh in 1935 where he was educated at the Royal National School of Administration before studying at the University of Paris. He then entered the foreign service and was appointed first secretary in Paris in 1967 where he was serving when Prince **Norodom Sihanouk** was overthrown in March 1970. He joined Sihanouk's united front with the **Khmer Rouge** and was made ambassador to Cuba of his government in exile in 1973. He was recalled to Phnom Penh in 1975 after the Khmer Rouge had assumed power and was subsequently interned but survived. After Vietnam's invasion of Cambodia in December 1978, he joined the administration of the **People's Republic of Kampuchea**. He was deputy foreign minister during 1981–2 and ambassador to Moscow during 1982–90. After the State of Cambodia gave way to the Kingdom of Cambodia in 1993, he became ambassador to Paris until 1998. He is believed to be close to Prime Minister **Hun Sen**.

*see also:* Hun Sen; Kampuchea, People's Republic of; Khmer Rouge; Sihanouk, Norodom.

## Horsburgh Lighthouse (Malaysia/ Singapore)

The Horsburgh Lighthouse is situated on the tiny island of Pedra Branca (White Rock); it is known in Malay as Pulau Batu Puteh. The island is located at the eastern entrance to the **Singapore Strait** between the opposite coasts of Malaysia and Indonesia. The lighthouse was constructed by the British Straits Settlements colonial administration in 1850 and began operating a year later. The lighthouse has always been administered and maintained from Singapore, even though it is located some eighteen nautical miles beyond the republic's territorial waters limit of three miles. The basis for the republic's claim to jurisdiction over the island as well as adjacent waters and sea-bed is a series of treaties between the Honourable East India Company and the Sultanate of Johor and an Anglo-Dutch Treaty of 1824 which demarcated colonial dominion. Singapore's jurisdiction over Pedra Branca has been the subject of dispute by the government of Malaysia. A claim was first signalled in December 1979 when Malaysia published a map including the island within its territorial waters. Singapore responded with a protest note. It has been argued in Kuala Lumpur that although the lighthouse had been built and operated from Singapore, it was not a sufficient basis for ownership of the island, which was part of the domain of Johor inherited by Malaysia. The dispute is symptomatic of an underlying tension which has been a persistent feature of the bilateral relationship ever since Singapore was separated from the Federation of Malaysia in August 1965 to become an independent state. It has also been a product of the need of the federal government in Kuala Lumpur to respond to domestic political pressures. The dispute became a matter of public contention from the late 1980s when fishing vessels from Johor were discouraged from sailing close to the island. In September 1991 the chief minister of Johor endorsed the claim publicly. There was an abortive attempt in 1992 by members of the youth wing of the opposition *Parti Islam Se-Malaysia* (PAS) to plant the Malaysian flag on the island. The issue has been addressed without resolution through the diplomatic process, including exchanges of documents, as well as at the ministerial level. Singapore is in the advantageous position of being able to demonstrate that in 1974 Malaysia had published a map of south-eastern Johor on which Pulau Batu Puteh/Pedra Branca is shown as lying within the republic's jurisdiction. In September 1994 at a meeting in Malaysia, Dr Mahathir Mohamad and Goh Chok Tong agreed to resolve the dispute through reference to a third party, including the International Court of Justice (ICJ). Although both states have indicated a willingness, in principle, to take the matter before the ICJ, they have failed to reach a working accord on the matter against a background of recurrent bilateral tensions.

*see also:* Goh Chok Tong; Mahathir Mohamad; *Parti Islam Se-Malaysia*; Singapore Strait.

## Horta, Jose Manuel Ramos (Indonesia/ East Timor)

Jose Ramos Horta was the external representative of East Timorese resistance during the period of Indonesian occupation between 1975 and 1999. He was in Australia at the time of the invasion of **East Timor** and took *Fretilin*'s case to the United Nations acting as a vigorous and persistent advocate of its cause as well as lobbying intensively around the world in order to keep it alive. In recognition of his activities, he shared the Nobel Peace Prize with Bishop Carlos Belo in November 1996. Jose Ramos Horta was born in Dili in December 1949 of mixed Portuguese and Timorese parentage. He was involved from the outset with the Timorese Social Democratic Association, the forerunner of *Fretilin*. During his long period of exile, he spent much time in Australia where he found political and financial support. He also developed notable diplomatic skills and is likely to become an independent East Timor's first foreign minister. He returned to Dili in December 1999.
*see also: Fretilin*; Timor, East.

## Hukbalahap Movement (Philippines)

*Hukbalahap* is a contraction of the Tagalog term *Hukbo ng Bayan laban sa Hapon*, which translates as People's Anti-Japanese Army. The *Huk* Movement, as it became known, had its origins in the establishment in March 1942 of an anti-Japanese resistance by a group of Communist and Socialist Union leaders who had organized armed uprisings by tenant farmers in sugar-producing provinces of central and southern Luzón during the 1930s. Consolidating their position during the Pacific War, they sought to engage in electoral politics after its conclusion, backing the Democratic Alliance in opposition to established parties which had collaborated with the Japanese. Despite notable success in central and southern Luzón, the new Congress elected in April 1946 refused to seat the Democratic Alliance candidates. Frustrated in their attempt to act through the political process, the *Huk* Movement resorted to military action, confronting the private armies of landlords as well as government forces. Full-scale rebellion was signalled in February 1950 when the movement changed its name to *Hukbong Mapagpalaya ng*

*Bayan* (People's Liberation Army) and called for the overthrow of the government in Manila. At their peak, the *Huks* claimed a following of 30,000 armed insurgents and were able to take temporary charge of the provincial capitals in central Luzón, giving the impression of imminent revolutionary success.

The revolutionary challenge from the *Huks* was repelled after **Ramón Magsaysay** was appointed secretary of national defence in August 1950. The turning-point came when the entire Communist Politburo was captured during raids in Manila in October. Magsaysay was able to revive the morale of a dispirited army with US backing as well as detaching peasant support from the insurgents through a skilful combination of personal public relations and governmental benefaction in the rural areas. Magsaysay, who went on to become president in 1953 with US assistance, conveyed a charismatic appeal which the urban intellectual leadership of the peasant insurgency could not match. By 1954 the *Huk* Movement had been crushed and reduced to a desultory banditry which it remained until it was revived in a different form and with a different leadership from the late 1960s.
*see also:* Magsaysay, Ramón.

## Hun Sen (Cambodia)

Hun Sen became prime minister of the Kingdom of Cambodia in October 1998 as head of a revamped coalition government dominated by his **Cambodian People's Party** (CPP), which had secured a plurality of seats in elections in the previous July. Hun Sen's assumption of high office reflected the effective balance of power in the country, which had been evident from July 1997 when he had mounted a violent coup displacing his senior partner in a coalition government established in October 1993.

Hun Sen was born on 4 April 1952 in Kompong Cham Province into a peasant family. He joined the **Khmer Rouge** in 1970 after Prince **Norodom Sihanouk** had been overthrown by a right-wing coup. With their seizure of power in April 1975, he rose in the military hierarchy of the country's eastern zone to become a deputy regimental commander but defected to Vietnam in 1977 as an internecine purge spread within the Cambodian revolutionary party. He became a member of the central committee of the Kampuchean National Front for National Salvation, which served as Vietnam's vehicle for invading Cambodia in December 1978. Hun Sen was made foreign minister of the **People's Republic of Kampuchea** on its establishment in January 1979 and a deputy prime minister in June 1981. From an untutored base, Hun Sen demonstrated a growing aptitude for political organization but also became involved in factional rivalries with an older generation of party cadres. He was appointed prime minister in January 1985 but gave up his concurrent office of foreign minister between December 1986 and December 1987. He then resumed the additional foreign affairs portfolio to lead negotiations with Prince Norodom Sihanouk which paved the way to the **International Conference on Cambodia** in Paris in 1989 and then to an eventual settlement of the Cambodian conflict, also in Paris, in October 1991. In April 1989, the People's Republic of Kampuchea had been renamed the State of Cambodia with Hun Sen continuing as prime minister. Early in October 1991, the ruling **Kampuchean People's Revolutionary Party** was renamed the Cambodian People's Party and Hun Sen led its campaign in UN-supervised elections in May 1993. The party was bitterly disappointed at coming second in those elections to FUNCINPEC (the National United Front for an Independent, Neutral, Peaceful and Cooperative Cambodia) headed by Prince Norodom Ranariddh. A threat of force served to give the CPP a place in coalition government in which Hun Sen became Second Prime Minister to Prince Ranariddh. The political partnership was strained from the outset over the issue of power-sharing, while Hun Sen displayed great skill in marginalizing Prince Ranariddh and his allies as well as considerable ruthlessness in deploying intimidating violence against all opponents. On becoming sole prime minister in 1998, he also assumed the office of President of the Throne Council, which has the responsibility for authorizing monarchical succession.

*see also:* Cambodian People's Party (CPP); International Conference on Cambodia, Paris 1989; FUNCINPEC; Kampuchea, People's Republic of; Kampuchean People's Revolutionary Party; Khmer Rouge; Ranariddh, Norodom; Sihanouk, Norodom.

## Hussein Onn, Tun  (Malaysia)

Hussein Onn was Malaysia's third prime minister and held office from January 1976 until July 1981. He was a reluctant politician who was persuaded to return to public life by his brother-in-law, the incumbent prime minister, **Tun Abdul Razak**, whom he succeeded following Abdul Razak's death from leukaemia. Hussein Onn was born on 12 February 1922, the son of a Johor state official. Trained as a soldier, he served in the Indian army during the Second World War. After hostilities, he joined with his father, Dato Onn bin Ja'afar, then chief minister of Johor, in founding **UMNO** (United Malays National Organization) to challenge the **Malayan Union Proposal** by the British. When his father was rejected by UMNO for attempting to make it multiracial, Hussein Onn withdrew from active politics out of a sense of filial piety and took up the study and practice of law. He returned to public life after the **May 13 Racial Riots 1969**, when Malaysia had experienced unprecedented racial violence, and held ministerial office for only five years before becoming prime minister. His tenure was not marked by strong government or imaginative leadership. He was responsible for appointing Dr **Mahathir Mohamad** as his deputy prime minister, which precipitated a period of intra-party strife. He gave up office in July 1981 because of ill-health but regretted his successor's style of government and openly indicated his support for an alternative splinter party which challenged UMNO for the leadership of the Malay community. He died on 28 May 1990 at the age of 68, retaining intact his reputation as an honest politician.

*see also:* Mahathir Mohamad, Datuk Sri; Malayan Union Proposal 1946; May 13 Racial Riots 1969; Razak, Tun Abdul; UMNO.

# I

## ICMI (Indonesia)

*Ikatan Cendekiawan Muslim Indonesia*, abbreviated in Indonesia to ICMI, translates as the Association of Indonesian Muslim Intellectuals, which was established in December 1990 in the east Javanese town of Malang. The inaugural meeting was attended by President **Suharto**, who had cultivated the Islamic community from the late 1980s in order to give himself greater political leverage with the armed forces. The military establishment, which had been his power base from the outset, had become less enthusiastic in supporting him in high office, in part because of the way in which his family had enriched themselves. President Suharto therefore turned to the Muslims in order to bolster his position for the elections of March 1993, in which he was again returned unopposed. President Suharto's apparent shift towards orthodox **Islam** stood in contrast to his Javanese cultural identity and took place in the face of the long-standing opposition of the armed forces to any concessions that might open the way to an Islamic state. It also attracted the opposition of **Abdurrahman Wahid**, the leader of the Islamic *Nahdatul Ulama* (NU), on the ground that it would encourage confessionalism in politics; in March 1991 he was involved in the formation of *Forum Demokrasi*. The military establishment was outraged by the formation of ICMI and by the role in the Association of Dr **B. J. Habibie**, the influential minister of state for technology and research and boycotted the inaugural meeting. The concern of the military establishment was reinforced when the president made his first pilgrimage to Mecca in June 1991 close to his seventieth birthday accompanied by an entourage of family and loyalists.

Although ICMI was intended to serve as an instrument of political management for President Suharto, it evolved into more than just a religious body for its members. Its formation provided a new focal point for Muslims of a modern outlook with a nationalist economic agenda who had lost their political locus with the disbanding of the *Masyumi* Party in 1960. ICMI established its own newspaper, *Republika*, and a think-tank, the Centre for Information and Development Studies (CIDES). Dr Habibie enjoyed support within ICMI as the champion of *Pribumi* interests and as a candidate for president after Suharto. It became very influential in government following Dr Habibie's assumption of high office in May 1998. Its support drained, however, because of the political taint of the post-Suharto administration and its ties to *Golkar*. Moreover, the establishment of the opposition **National Mandate Party** headed by Amien Rais, a former ICMI luminary and head of *Muhammadiyah*, an urban-based Islamic organization with educational and social goals, provided a competing locus. ICMI ceased to enjoy an active political role after interim President Habibie withdrew from the presidential contest in October 1999 to be succeeded in office by Abdurrahman Wahid. The newspaper *Republika* has remained a vehicle for Islamic interests.

*see also: Forum Demokrasi; Golkar*; Habibie, B. J.; *Masyumi; Muhammadiyah; Nahdatul Ulama*; National Mandate Party; Pribumi; Suharto; Wahid, Abdurrahman.

## Ieng Sary (Cambodia)

Ieng Sary was a deputy prime minister in the government of **Democratic Kampuchea** between 1975 and 1978. He had been a leading figure in the **Khmer Rouge** until the withdrawal of Chinese support after the **International Conference on Cambodia** in Paris in October 1991 led to his political demotion. The early life of Ieng Sary is obscure, with his date of birth probably in the second half of the 1920s and his place of birth in Tra Vinh Province i n southern Vietnam. He is believed to have befriended Saloth Sar, later **Pol Pot**, when they were both students at the Lycée Sisowath in Phnom Penh at the end of the war. Like Pol Pot, he secured a government scholarship to study in France, where he arrived in October 1950 and where formative social bonding and political commitment took place. His wife, Ieng Thirith, was the sister of Pol Pot's wife, Khieu Ponnary. On his return to Cambodia in the mid-1950s, Ieng Sary became a teacher and an active participant in clandestine revolutionary activity. In September 1960 he was present at a secret meeting of the Communist Party of Cambodia which set it on the road to revolutionary struggle and at which he was elected to its central committee. In May 1963, after his name had been included in a list of subversives announced by Prince **Norodom Sihanouk**, together with Pol Pot he left the capital for the forests of eastern Cambodia. His movements until 1971 are not well known but he is believed to have assumed responsibility for contacts with both Vietnamese and Chinese Communist parties. In August 1971 his presence was announced in Beijing, ostensibly as special envoy from the liberated area of Cambodia, but he acted as watch-dog to Prince Norodom Sihanouk, who was then head of a government in exile. He accompanied Prince Sihanouk on visits abroad, in particular to the Non-Aligned Conference in Algeria and to the liberated area of Cambodia in 1973. He held high office with responsibility for foreign affairs during the period of Khmer Rouge rule; in the negotiations with Thailand he demonstrated a clear preference for the finer qualities of life, including expensive cigars and brandy. He escaped from Phnom Penh by train to Thailand before the city was occupied by the Vietnamese in January 1979. He travelled on to Beijing and was subsequently for a time a member of the Democratic Kampuchean delegation at the United Nations, being confirmed as deputy prime minister in charge of foreign affairs for the government in exile at the end of 1979. After the formation of the tripartite Coalition Government of Democratic Kampuchea (CGDK) in June 1982, he gave up formal responsibility for foreign affairs to his Khmer Rouge colleague, **Khieu Samphan**. He ceased to hold any official position within the Khmer Rouge hierarchy but established a personal stronghold in the gem-rich Pailin district in western Cambodia. In August 1996, he defected to the government in Phnom Penh and was granted an amnesty by King Norodom Sihanouk

in the following month from the death sentence passed on him *in absentia* in August 1979 for his complicity in mass murder. His defection, together with the forces under his command, marked the effective disintegration of the Khmer Rouge. He integrated those forces nominally into the Cambodian army in November 1996 and returned to Phnom Penh in November 1997 for a meeting with Second Prime Minister **Hun Sen**, which was his first visit to the capital for nearly eighteen years. He has continued to run Pailin like a private fiefdom generating a substantial income from gambling, prostitution and the sale of precious stones and hardwoods.

*see also:* Democratic Kampuchea; Democratic Kampuchea, Coalition Government of; Hun Sen; International Conference on Cambodia, Paris 1991; Khieu Samphan; Khmer Rouge; Pol Pot; Sihanouk, Norodom.

## Independence of Malaya Party (IMP)
(Malaya)

The Independence of Malaya Party (IMP) was set up in 1951 in an abortive attempt to establish a non-communal political organization to encourage Britain to speed up the process of independence. Its founder was Dato Onn bin Ja'afar, who had been the key figure in arousing Malay nationalism after the Pacific War and who became the first president of **UMNO** (United Malays National Organization) on its establishment in 1946. In the late 1940s, in the light of the challenge posed by Communist insurrection, he sought to open UMNO to non-Malays but was rebuffed by his coreligionists, who were concerned at the possible challenge to Malay political prerogative. In August 1951 Dato Onn left UMNO to found the new party, which would be open to all Malayans, but failed to attract anticipated cross-communal support. In municipal elections in Kuala Lumpur in 1952, the IMP won only two seats, compared to nine secured by the **Alliance Party**, an intercommunal electoral pact between UMNO and the Malayan (subsequently **Malaysian**) **Chinese Association** (MCA). In desperation in February 1954, Dato Onn disbanded the IMP and reverted to an exclusive Malay constituency by launching the Party *Negara* (National Party) but did not succeed in restoring his original political support or standing. It remained, in effect, a one-man party and after Dato Onn's death in 1962 became moribund, leading to its deregistration in 1967.

see also: Alliance Party; Emergency 1948–60; Hussein Onn, Tun; Malaysian Chinese Association; UMNO.

## Indochina Wars  (Cambodia/Laos/Vietnam)

Three successive wars of international significance have afflicted the three states of Indochina, Cambodia, Laos and Vietnam, between 1946 and 1991.

*The First Indochina War* took place primarily between French forces seeking to restore colonial dominion and the insurgent Democratic Republic of Vietnam, which had been declared an independent state by the legendary Communist leader, **Ho Chi Minh**, on 2 September 1945 following the **August Revolution**. It was triggered by a dispute over control of customs in the port of Haiphong in November 1946 following the failure of a conference in Fontainebleau in the previous summer to resolve political differences. The escalating violence which spread to Laos and Cambodia became a major factor in the Cold War, with the formation in October 1949 of the People's Republic of China, seen by the United States as the aggressive ally of the Soviet Union. China provided military support for the fraternal Communist movement across a common border, while corresponding assistance for France came from the United States. The war culminated in France's defeat in May 1954 in the **Battle of Dien Bien Phu**, which destroyed the political will of the government in Paris. The Communist victory coincided with the opening of an international conference on Indochina, which resulted in the **Geneva Agreements on Indochina** (July 1954) to demarcate Vietnam provisionally along the line of the 17th parallel of latitude prior to countrywide elections two years later. The Communist Democratic Republic of Vietnam assumed power north of that line; the residual State of Vietnam to its south came under the control of an anti-Communist government headed by a returned exile, **Ngo Dinh Diem**, who enjoyed the support of the United States

for his decision not to take part in countrywide elections.

Both Laos and Cambodia were accorded an intact independence under royal governments, although two Laotian provinces bordering Vietnam remained effectively under the control of the insurgent *Pathet Lao* which was, in effect, a branch of the Vietnamese Communist movement.

*The Second Indochina War* was very much a continuation of the first. At issue was the unity and political identity of a divided Vietnam but again Laos and Cambodia were drawn into the fray. Although a northern-inspired insurgency had revived in the south from the late 1950s, the lines of conflict became clearly drawn from 20 December 1960 with the establishment of the **National Liberation Front of South Vietnam** (NLF) which was the irredentist vehicle of the northern Communist government. Cold War considerations dominated the conflict. The United States, committed to containing international communism, became increasingly involved in military support of the government in Saigon from the mid- to late 1960s until its forces were shouldering the main responsibility for the war. Aerial bombardment of the north and the deployment of half a million combat troops failed to break a military stalemate. The ability of the Vietnamese Communists to launch a series of coordinated attacks on urban centres at the end of January 1968 produced a devastating political impact within the United States. The historic **Tet Offensive** demonstrated to an American public sickened by continuing heavy casualties in the **Vietnam War** that a military solution was unlikely, which convinced President Lyndon Johnson of the need to enter into negotiations, which began formally in Paris in January 1969. By this juncture, Laos and Cambodia had become part of the theatre of war as the Vietnamese Communists used their territories to transship troops and supplies along the **Ho Chi Minh Trail** from the north to battlefields in the south. Johnson's successor, President Richard Nixon, began a process of military disengagement facilitated by a rapprochement with China. After the failure of a major offensive by the Communist forces across the 17th parallel of latitude in March 1972 in an abortive attempt to break the military stalemate, negotiations led to the **Paris Peace Agreements** in January 1973. The United States agreed to withdraw all of its forces in return for the repatriation of prisoners of war but without removing the Saigon government, which had been a long-standing demand of the National Liberation Front of South Vietnam (NLF). A weakened southern government resisted for just over two years until overwhelmed by a northern military attack, the **Ban Me Thuot Offensive**, launched in March 1975, which culminated in the seizure of Saigon at the end of April and the effective unification of the country under Communist rule. Formal unification as the Socialist Republic of Vietnam occurred in July 1976. A corresponding peace agreement for Laos, the **Vientiane Agreement on the Restoration of Peace and Reconciliation in Laos**, was concluded in February 1973. The military victory in Saigon at the end of April 1975, however, led to the political collapse of the ostensibly neutral government in Vientiane, with the Communist *Pathet Lao* removing the monarchy to establish the Laotian People's Democratic Republic at the end of the year. In Cambodia, the head of state, Prince **Norodom Sihanouk**, had been removed in a right-wing coup in March 1970 which received US support. A civil war followed in which Vietnamese military intervention to protect lines of communication served as the initial vanguard for the eventual victory in mid-April 1975 of the politically fundamentalist **Khmer Rouge** insurgents. Their state of so-called **Democratic Kampuchea**, headed by the notorious **Pol Pot**, rejected the concept of a special relationship with Vietnam and subsequently engaged it in armed confrontation, which provoked a full-scale war from the end of 1978.

*The Third Indochina War* began in December 1978 when Vietnamese forces invaded and occupied Cambodia. The conflict registered the radical revision of international alignments arising from Sino-Soviet antagonism and Sino-US rapprochement. Relations between former allies Vietnam and China had deteriorated, with the former resentful of the act of betrayal of the latter in coming to terms with their US adversary. For its part, China came to view Vietnam

as the willing proxy for the interests of its Soviet antagonist, to which Vietnam had turned through a **Treaty of Friendship and Cooperation** in November 1978 for countervailing support. The paranoid Khmer Rouge regime had earlier aligned itself with China, which convinced the government in Hanoi that Vietnam was being trapped in a strategic vice from which it had to break free. Vietnam overwhelmed Khmer Rouge military resistance, driving their forces to the Thai border. A **People's Republic of Kampuchea** was established in January 1979 but failed to attract international recognition other than from the Soviet Union and its allies. Moreover, China launched a punitive military expedition into northern Vietnam in February 1979. Vietnam's stalwart military defence was not sufficient to diminish the political significance of China's action, which pointed up the permanent geopolitical relationship between the two neighbouring countries. Vietnam was then obliged to face an international alignment comprising China, the United States and the members of **ASEAN**, which together brought military, economic and diplomatic pressure to bear on Vietnam. The alignment was also responsible for mobilizing Cambodian military resistance to Vietnam's occupation and the government in Phnom Penh, making it possible in particular for the Khmer Rouge to regenerate as a fighting machine. The failure to crush an externally supported Cambodian insurgency together with economic failure and the loss of Soviet patronage eventually obliged Vietnam to accept a United Nations political settlement endorsed at the **International Conference on Cambodia, Paris 1991** (October). It had withdrawn its main force units from Cambodia by September 1989 and had left the government implanted there to fend for itself in part through a reversion in nomenclature to the State of Cambodia. Vietnam's military intervention in Cambodia was of major international significance in the context of the so-called Second Cold War, which reached its peak with the Soviet invasion of Afghanistan. The settlement of the Cambodian War as an international problem was a direct consequence of the end of the Cold War, which required Vietnam to come to terms with China in the absence of access to any credible source of external countervailing power. Within Cambodia, the United Nations was able to conduct countrywide elections which produced a coalition government in October 1993. But it proved unable to implement the critical military terms of the Paris agreement of October 1991 because of the recalcitrance of the Khmer Rouge. The continuing civil war has lost its earlier strategic significance, however, because Indochina has lost its former place as a point of reference for global rivalry.

see also: ASEAN; August Revolution 1945; Ban Me Thuot Offensive 1975; Diem, Ngo Dinh; Dien Bien Phu, Battle of, 1954; Democratic Kampuchea; Geneva Agreements on Indochina 1954; Geneva Agreements on Laos 1962; Ho Chi Minh; Ho Chi Minh Trail; International Conferences on Cambodia, New York 1981, Paris 1989, 1991; Kampuchea, People's Republic of; Khmer Rouge; National Liberation Front of South Vietnam; Paris Peace Agreements 1973; *Pathet Lao*; Pol Pot; Sihanouk, Norodom; Tet Offensive 1968; Treaty of Friendship and Cooperation 1978; Vientiane Agreement on the Restoration of Peace and Reconciliation in Laos 1973; Vietnam War.

## Indo-Chinese People's Conference 1970 (Cambodia/Laos/Vietnam)

On 24 and 25 April 1970 the People's Republic of China acted as host to four delegations from Indochina, who met at an undisclosed venue close to the Lao and Vietnamese borders. Heading the delegations were Prince **Norodom Sihanouk** of the National United Front of Kampuchea (Cambodia), Prince **Souphanouvong** of the Laotian Patriotic Front, Nguyen Huu Tho, president of the Advisory Council of the **Provisional Revolutionary Government of the Republic of South Vietnam** (PRG), and **Pham Van Dong**, prime minister of the Democratic Republic of (North) Vietnam. The delegations were also addressed by China's prime minister, Zhou En-lai. The conference had been convened in response to the overthrow of Prince Sihanouk in the previous month by a right-wing coup which had received immediate support from the United States. The occasion marked the formation of a united front to

challenge US policy in Indochina, which seemed to have entered a new assertive phase despite the promulgation of the **Nixon Doctrine** on the island of Guam in July 1969. It also marked a less public coalition between Prince Sihanouk on the one hand and the **Khmer Rouge** on the other, with the latter able to exploit the legitimacy of the former to advance their revolutionary cause. A previous Indo-Chinese People's Conference had been convened in Phnom Penh in March 1965 at the initiative of Prince Sihanouk in an attempt to secure international guarantees for Cambodia's neutrality and territorial integrity.

see also: Khmer Rouge; Nixon Doctrine 1969; Pham Van Dong; Provisional Revolutionary Government of the Republic of South Vietnam; Sihanouk, Norodom; Souphanouvong.

## Indonesia–Australia Mutual Security Agreement, 1995–99 (Indonesia)

An Agreement on Maintaining Security with the status of a treaty was signed in Jakarta on 18 December 1995 by the foreign ministers of Indonesia and Australia in the presence of their respective heads of government, President **Suharto** and Prime Minister Paul Keating, the leader of the Labour Party. The terms of the agreement indicated the spirit of an alliance. They stated *inter alia* that the two states would consult 'in the case of adverse challenges to either party or to their common security interests and, if appropriate, consider measures which might be taken individually and jointly and in accordance with the processes of each party'. The agreement had been negotiated in utmost secrecy and caused consternation among some **ASEAN** partners, when news of the accord was revealed days in advance of signature at ASEAN's fifth summit in Bangkok. The agreement was one between two leaders and a motivating factor on the part of President Suharto was apprehension over China's newfound strategic latitude in the wake of the Cold War, exemplified by its prior seizure of Mischief Reef in the **Spratly Islands** and its claim to some of the resource-rich waters of Indonesia's Natuna Islands. The agreement not only disavowed Australia's strategic concern about Indonesia but marked a significant break with the non-aligned tenet of the republic's foreign policy, especially given Canberra's close defence links with Washington.

The relationship between Indonesia and Australia deteriorated after the political downfall of President Suharto in May 1998 and his succession by Vice-President **Habibie**. By then, Paul Keating had been succeeded by John Howard, the leader of the Liberal–National coalition. At issue was the status of **East Timor**, which Australia had recognized as subject to Indonesia's jurisdiction in 1978, which was exceptionable among Western states. However, in mid-January 1999, its government announced that it might be prepared to support self-determination for the territory. The prospect of this change in Australian policy is believed to have been a factor in President Habibie making a surprising offer towards the end of the month of independence for East Timor should its inhabitants reject special autonomy status. In the event, Indonesia agreed to a referendum on either autonomy or independence for the territory under United Nations auspices but with security subject to its authority. The referendum took place on 30 August 1999 with an overwhelming vote for independence but against a breakdown in law and order fomented by Indonesia's army and police. The scale of violence and destruction prompted the United Nations to press Indonesia to accept an international force to restore peace, which was authorized by the Security Council on 15 September. Australia, which had already placed its armed forces on alert in Darwin, provided the largest contingent and the leadership of the International Force East Timor (INTERFET). The very next day, Feisal Tanjung, Indonesia's coordinating minister for political and security affairs, announced that the Security Agreement with Australia had been revoked because Australia's role in the peacekeeping operation constituted interference in Indonesia's internal affairs. Anti-Australian feeling was strong in Jakarta for a while, partly because of the way its intervention had reinforced a sense of national humiliation over Indonesia's ignominious exit from East Timor. Relations with Australia remained uneasy after the assumption to office of President **Abdurrahman Wahid** in October 1999 and the

replacement of INTERFET by a United Nations Peacekeeping Force (UNPKF) headed by a Filipino general in February 2000.

*see also:* East Timor; Habibie; Spratly Islands; Suharto; United Nations: East Timor 1999; Wahid, Abdurrahman.

## Indonesian Democratic Party-Struggle (PDI-P) (Indonesia) *see Partai Demokrasi Indonesia.*

## International Conference on Cambodia, New York 1981
(Cambodia)

In July 1981 an international conference on Kampuchea (as Cambodia was then known) convened in New York under the auspices of the secretary-general of the United Nations. The meeting was a diplomatic success of a kind for **ASEAN** (Association of South-East Asian Nations), which had pressed for it from 1979 in the wake of Vietnam's invasion of Cambodia (*see* **Indochina Wars**). That success was one of form rather than of substance, however, because of the absence in particular of representation from Vietnam and the Soviet Union. Their governments had objected to the ousted **Khmer Rouge** regime occupying the Cambodian seat in the world organization in place of the incumbent administration in Phnom Penh. The conference convened, therefore, as a group of states opposed to Vietnam's position rather than as a forum for negotiations. Moreover, its sessions exposed major differences of interest between the ASEAN states and the People's Republic of China over terms for a political settlement. An ASEAN proposal for an interim administration before elections to be conducted under United Nations supervision foundered on the rock of Chinese opposition with tacit US support. In the event, the conference reiterated bland General Assembly resolutions, while a semblance of institutional continuity was maintained through the mediatory role of its Austrian chairman but without any tangible result. A decade would have to pass together with a change in strategic context before the Cambodian conflict became susceptible to solution through an international conference. Ironically, the formula adopted for a political settlement at the **International Conference on Cambodia** in Paris in October 1991 was much the same as that rejected in New York in July 1981.

*see also:* ASEAN; Indochina Wars; International Conferences on Cambodia, Paris 1989, 1991; Khmer Rouge.

## International Conference on Cambodia, Paris 1989 (Cambodia)

At French initiative, a second international conference on Cambodia convened in Paris at the end of July 1989 with Indonesia as co-chairman. Unlike the **International Conference on Cambodia** held in New York in July 1981, it was attended by all the internal and external parties to the conflict as well as the foreign ministers of all permanent members of the United Nations Security Council and a representative of the secretary-general. The conference had been preceded by a series of abortive negotiations among Cambodian and regional parties in the previous twelve months. The incentive for organizing a meeting in Paris had been the announcement in April 1989 by the governments of Hanoi, Vientiane and Phnom Penh that all Vietnamese troops would be withdrawn from Cambodia by the end of September that year, irrespective of a political solution. The conference devolved into four working committees. The first was charged with drawing up cease-fire terms and defining the mandate of an international control mechanism or institution to oversee a settlement. The second was required to construct a system of guarantees for the neutrality and independence of Cambodia. The third was set the task of working out arrangements for repatriating refugees from the Thai border. Finally, an *ad-hoc* committee consisting of France, Indonesia and the four Cambodian factions was established to address the internal aspects of the conflict, including provision for power-sharing prior to internationally supervised elections, which would mark the final stage of political settlement. The four committees concluded their deliberations on 28 August without constructive outcome and the conference suspended its deliberations in the absence of the foreign ministers of the permanent members of the United Nations Security Council (with the exception of France). Several problems

obstructed a successful outcome, including the role of the United Nations in supervision and control of the process of settlement. Primarily at issue, however, was the failure of the Cambodian parties and their external patrons to reach an accord on the status and composition of an interim administration for the period between a political accord and the outcome of general elections to decide the future of the country. The incumbent administration in Phnom Penh refused to be dismantled and to tolerate the **Khmer Rouge** as a legitimate party to a settlement. The failure in August 1989 indicated that those changes in international relations marking the end of the Cold War had not had sufficient regional effect to enable the Cambodian conflict to be resolved.

*see also:* Indochina Wars; International Conferences on Cambodia, New York 1981, Paris 1991; Khmer Rouge.

## International Conference on Cambodia, Paris 1991 (Cambodia)

The **International Conference on Cambodia** in Paris, which had suspended its deliberations in August 1989, reconvened in Paris on 21 October 1991 and two days later approved a comprehensive political settlement which was signed by nineteen governments as well as by four Cambodian factions. The Final Act of the conference comprised three documents:

1   An Agreement on a Comprehensive Political Settlement of the Cambodia Conflict together with five annexes dealing with (a) the mandate of UNTAC (United Nations Transitional Authority in Cambodia); (b) withdrawal, cease-fire and related measures; (c) elections; (d) repatriation of Cambodian refugees and displaced persons; and (e) principles for a new constitution for Cambodia.

2   An Agreement concerning the sovereignty, independence, territorial integrity and inviolability, neutrality and national unity of Cambodia.

3   A Declaration on rehabilitation and reconstruction of Cambodia.

The road back to Paris following the abortive conference in 1989 had been pioneered through an initiative by US Congressman Stephen Solarz to overcome the persisting obstacle of power-sharing through having the United Nations assume the transitional administration of Cambodia before the outcome of general elections. The government of Australia took up this proposal and commissioned a feasibility study of the peacekeeping exercise. The plan then attracted the serious attention of the permanent members of the United Nations Security Council whose officials drafted a framework agreement which was adopted at the end of August 1990. The persisting deadlock over power-sharing was addressed through the vehicle of a **Supreme National Council** on which all Cambodian factions would be represented. The Council, envisaged as a symbol and repository of Cambodian sovereignty rather than as a government, would authorize a ring-holding role for the United Nations. Executive powers would be delegated to UNTAC (United Nations Transitional Authority in Cambodia) comprising civilian and military components with responsibility for supervising key ministries and conducting elections in a secure and neutral environment. In the event, this framework agreement provided the basis for the accord reached in October 1991.

The course of preliminary negotiations was chequered. **Khmer Rouge** participation in a political settlement was accepted at the first meeting of the Supreme National Council in Indonesia in September 1990. However, serious disagreement persisted over the role of UNTAC, the status of the incumbent government in Phnom Penh, provision for demobilization and disarmament of contending Cambodian forces and the chair of the Council. A political breakthrough occurred at the end of June 1991 as a direct consequence of an improvement in relations between the People's Republic of China and Vietnam whose antagonism had been at the heart of the Cambodian conflict from the outset. In effect, an enfeebled and vulnerable Vietnam had been obliged to defer to Chinese priorities in Indochina and withdrew its long-standing patronage of the government which it had imposed by its force of arms in January 1979. As a result of an initiative by Prince **Norodom Sihanouk**, sanctioned by China, the process

of negotiations was accelerated. Within less than four months, outstanding issues such as a cease-fire, demobilization and disarmament of contending forces were resolved, making possible the final accord in Paris. Although the incumbent government in Phnom Penh was not dismantled in advance of general elections, a power-sharing arrangement of a kind was worked out in cooperation between the Supreme National Council chaired by Prince Sihanouk and the United Nations preliminary to general elections scheduled for early 1993. The peacekeeping operation was the most ambitious and difficult undertaken since the UN's formation in 1945. It ran into major difficulty from June 1992, when the Khmer Rouge refused to cooperate in the critical second phase which required the warring factions to regroup their forces into cantonments for disarmament. Elections were conducted, nonetheless, in May 1993 without notable disruption and were endorsed by the United Nations Security Council as free and fair. A new constitution was ratified on 21 September which ended, in effect, the UN mandate as recommended by the Paris conference.

see also: Indochina Wars; International Conferences on Cambodia, New York 1981, Paris 1989; Khmer Rouge; Sihanouk, Norodom; Supreme National Council; United Nations: Cambodia 1991–3; UNTAC.

## Irian Jaya  (Indonesia)

Irian Jaya is the Indonesian name for the western half of the island of New Guinea. This mountainous territory with a population of less than 2 million became an object of contention between Indonesia and Holland for more than a decade after the republic attained independence in 1949. Indonesia's administration has been in place since May 1963 but has been resisted by a local insurgency known as the **Free Papua Movement**. Although of limited military significance, it has attracted sympathy and support from fellow Melanesians in neighbouring Papua New Guinea. At the time of Indonesia's proclamation of independence, the western half of New Guinea was part of the Netherlands East Indies. During negotiations at The Hague in 1949 over the transfer of sovereignty, the Dutch insisted on retaining control of the territory, subject to further talks within a year. These talks proved to be inconclusive and the dispute which followed strained the post-colonial relationship. President **Sukarno** took the major initiative in prosecuting the nationalist claim through a practice of coercive diplomacy self-styled as **Confrontation**. The dispute was resolved eventually through US diplomatic intervention from a concern that further denial of Indonesia's claim would provoke its adherence to the Communist camp. An agreement between Indonesia and Holland was concluded on 15 August 1962. It provided for an initial transfer of administration to United Nations authority from 1 October 1962 and then an ultimate transfer to Indonesia from 1 May 1963. In addition, it was stipulated that an 'act of free choice' with United Nations advice, assistance and participation would take place before the end of 1969 in order to determine whether or not the inhabitants wished to remain subject to Indonesian jurisdiction. That exercise took place in July and August 1969 but was conspicuously a form of political stage-management.

Nonetheless, the **United Nations** endorsed the transfer of the territory, which was incorporated into the republic as its twenty-sixth province on 17 September 1968. Indonesia's jurisdiction has not been matched by popular acceptance. Indigenous resentment of its rule has been aggravated by Jakarta's policy of trans-migration whereby around 200,000 settlers, primarily from overcrowded Java, have been dispatched to the province, while the local population has felt discriminated against in employment opportunities. Moreover, human rights abuses by the armed forces have also alienated the indigenous people. Organized resistance has been mounted by the Free Papua Movement (*Organisai Papua Merdeka*) with limited effect, which appeared to have petered out by the 1990s. The momentum of separatism revived with the political downfall of President **Suharto** in May 1998. Demonstrations in favour of independence were mounted in Jakarta as well as within Irian Jaya where violent clashes occurred with security forces. Developments in **East Timor**, where a referendum offering a choice between autonomy and independence was held in August 1999, encouraged demands

for comparable treatment. In December 1999, over 10,000 pro-independence supporters demonstrated in the central square of the province's capital Jayapura, where they raised the separatist Morning Star flag. Such protests have not brought any substantive concessions from the government in Jakarta concerned to uphold the integrity of Indonesia, after East Timor, as well as to retain control of Irian Jaya's rich natural resources. During a visit to the province in January 2000, President **Abdurrahman Wahid** was only prepared to offer autonomous status and a change in the name of the province to West Papua. He reiterated that position in a meeting in Jakarta with members of a delegation from the province in May 2000. In June 2000, a people's congress in Jayapura resolved that West Papua was sovereign and independent but without formally declaring independence.
*see also:* Confrontation; East Timor; Free Papua Movement; Suharto; Sukarno; United Nations: Irian Jaya 1962–9; Wahid, Abdurrahman.

## Islam   (Brunei/Burma (Myanmar)/ Cambodia/Indonesia/Malaysia/ Philippines/Singapore/Thailand)

The Islamic faith requires complete submission to the will and obedience to the law of a single god. Its adherents believe that the precepts of their faith were revealed in the seventh century AD to his messenger, the Prophet Muhammad, who incorporated them into the *Qur'an* to provide a comprehensive and superior way of life. Islam did not take root within South-East Asia until around the beginning of the fourteenth century, when port cities began to adopt the Sunni faith of Arab and Indian maritime traders. This conversion extended northwards through the Malay peninsula into southern Thailand and south and east through the northern coasts of the Indonesian archipelago and then northwards from Borneo to the island of Luzón in the Philippines. In the case of Burma, Islam spread to the Arakan region overland from India.

Islam became identified with state power in South-East Asia from the fifteenth century shortly after the foundation of the trading empire of Malacca based on the west coast of the Malay peninsula. But after the fall of Malacca to the Portuguese in the early sixteenth century, its adherents dispersed to other parts of the Indonesian archipelago where their faith became most deeply accepted among coastal trading communities. In Java, Islam was later adopted by local princes to underpin their mystical power but primarily as a cultural veneer on entrenched animist and Hindu-Buddhist beliefs whose syncretic legacy is to be found in eastern and central parts of the island. The Islamic faith was also employed to mobilize opposition to Dutch colonial control.

Within South-East Asia, the most significant Islamic communities are to be found in Indonesia, Malaysia and Brunei.

In *Indonesia*, Muslims number around 90 per cent of a population of some 190 million but do not constitute a homogeneous community. A division between devout (*Santri*) and nominal (**Abangan**) adherents of the faith is a consequence of the uneven pattern of conversion. Islam played an important part in the rise of nationalism against the Dutch but attempts to promote an Islamic state were denied before the proclamation to independence in August 1945. The authorized state philosophy *Pancasila* enjoins all Indonesians to believe in a single deity but accords them the right to believe in any god of their own choosing. It was conceived in June 1945 by President **Sukarno** to prevent the political pretensions of Islam from provoking civil strife and has been accorded an even greater political sanctity by President **Suharto**. From independence, Islam was not accorded a special status but has been one of several recognized faiths under the auspices of the Ministry of Religious Affairs. After independence, the government of Jakarta faced insurgent challenge from the **Darul Islam** movement based primarily in northern Sumatra and western Java which was crushed by the 1960s with a limited recurrence by a so-called *Komando Jihad* (Holy War Command) in the early 1980s. Under the rule of President Suharto, a policy of draining Islam of political content has been pursued especially after its global resurgence had been registered by the revolution in Iran. All Muslim political parties have been brigaded within one umbrella organization, the **United Development Party**, which has been obliged to acknowledge *Pancasila* as its sole ideology.

Personal devotion to Islam has increased, however, in response to the materialism unleashed by successful economic development. President Suharto encouraged the formation of **ICMI** (Association of Indonesian Muslim Intellectuals) as an instrument to counter the influence of the armed forces and to generate greater support for his retention of high office. Under the leadership of Dr B. J. **Habibie**, ICMI served as the political vehicle of modern Islam with a nationalist economic agenda. Islam took on a more conspicuous, albeit diverse, political expression after Dr Habibie, as vice-president, succeeded Suharto in May 1998. In the event, a so-called central axis of Muslim-based parties collaborated to deny the presidency to **Megawati Sukarnoputri**, regarded as a representative of Christian and secular forces. The beneficiary of this manoeuvre was **Abdurrahman Wahid**, the leader of the Muslim-based **National Awakening Party** and also of the *Nahdatul Ulama* (Religious Scholars), whose commitment to religious pluralism and opposition to an Islamic state made him the natural political partner of Megawati, who became vice-president. He has sought to keep political Islam to the margins of public life. However, sectarian violence between Muslims and Christians has caused considerable loss of life and devastation in the Moluccan Islands and also in Sulawesi and Lombok. In Aceh, in north Sumatra, an independence movement driven by Islamic priorities has long been engaged in insurgency but concluded a ceasefire with the government in Jakarta in May 2000.

In *Malaysia*, Islam provides a common orthodoxy for half of the population of around 19 million. Adherents are concentrated mainly in the Malay peninsula with only a minority position in Sarawak and Sabah. Islam has been the official religion since independence and is an essential criterion for defining identity on the part of indigenous Malays, who have long felt their political birthright threatened by the large and commercially successful ethnic-Chinese community of migrant origin (**Overseas Chinese**). Malay and not Islamic symbolism, however, served as the vehicle for nationalist assertion after the Pacific War in response to a British attempt to create a common citizen to include Chinese and Indians and to dethrone the Malay sultans. In political life, Islam has been associated primarily with Malay opposition to **UMNO** (United Malays National Organization), which has governed in coalition with Chinese and Indian-based parties since before independence. Malaysia also experienced the effects of Islamic resurgence from the 1970s as economic modernization disturbed the values and orientation of a younger generation of Malays, especially from a rural environment. UMNO has sought to contain the political impact of Islam by championing its virtue and causes and for a time accommodating the opposition *Parti Islam Se-Malaysia* (PAS) within the ruling coalition. Apart from an alternating control of the state government of Kelantan, PAS has remained a secondary factor in Malaysian politics. But Islam has become central to national political and cultural life because of the need of UMNO to compensate for a vulnerability arising from its long-standing practice of intercommunal coalition politics. The revivalist *Al-Arqam* movement was banned in Malaysia in August 1994 and disbanded formally in the following November. PAS was able to mount a political challenge to UMNO in the wake of the political crisis generated by the dismissal from office, detention, trial and imprisonment of former deputy prime minister, **Anwar Ibrahim**. It demonstrated its electoral appeal in November 1999 not only on the basis of its Islamic credentials among the rural Malays but also from the example of probity in the public and personal lives of its leadership. Although *Parti Islam* is committed to establishing an Islamic state, it has found it politic to enter into an opposition alliance with the primarily ethnic-Chinese Democratic Action Party in recognition of the fact that to achieve political power in Malaysia, the support of the non-Malay and non-Islamic communities is required. In July 2000, members of an Islamic cult, *Al Ma'unah* (Brotherhood of Inner Power) raided two military arms depots and seized heavy weapons. Anti-terrorist commandos then overran their jungle camp.

In *Brunei*, Islam is the faith of some 200,000 Malays out of a population of around 270,000. Brunei is unique in South-East Asia as the sole ruling monarchy. The sultan, **Hassanal Bolkiah**, is the head of the faith combining temporal and spiritual powers in one person in the classical Muslim tradition. The authoritarian system which pivots on a materially self-indulgent royal family has been rationalized as a *Melayu Islam Beraja* (Malay Islamic Monarchy) in an attempt to perpetuate a regional political anachronism. In a conscious attempt also to fend off external Islamic influences, the government has introduced a superficial austerity by banning the sale of alcohol and preventing the celebration of the religious festivals of other faiths, such as Christmas. Unlike the experience of Indonesia and Malaysia, Brunei has never faced political challenge through the vehicle of Islam.

Islam is in a minority position in Cambodia, Burma, the Philippines, Singapore and Thailand. With the exceptions of Cambodia and Singapore, heightened ethno-religious identity in the face of discrimination by the dominant culture has led to abortive separatist violence which has been met with repressive reaction.

The **Cham** Islamic minority in *Cambodia* are the displaced survivors of the Kingdom of Champa (once located in central Vietnam), which was extinguished by the drive southwards of the Vietnamese in the fifteenth century. They enjoyed a tolerated existence after independence until they became victims of civil war and the bestiality of the **Khmer Rouge** during the 1970s. A significant number escaped as refugees to Malaysia; since the downfall of the Khmer Rouge regime in 1979, the Cambodian Cham have virtually disappeared as a separate community.

Muslim separatist activity has not enjoyed any success in *Burma/Myanmar* despite participation in challenge to government in Rangoon with other ethnic minority groups from independence in 1948. Since the advent of rule by the military **State Law and Order Restoration Council** (SLORC) in September 1988, the **Rohingya** minority in Arakan has been driven in tens of thousands as refugees into neighbouring Bangladesh.

In *Thailand*, Muslims number around 2 million out of a population of 56 million. Over half are concentrated in the four southern provinces of Narathiwat, Pattani, Satun and Yala, close to the northern border of Malaysia which was determined by Anglo-Thai agreement in 1909. Muslim alienation had been generated by a policy of

Buddhist cultural assimilation by Bangkok in the late 1930s and then the success of Malay nationalism across the southern border after the Pacific War, while malign administration also made a continuous contribution. Armed separatism has been a recurrent activity from the late 1940s with the best-known exponent being the **Pattani United Liberation Organization** (PULO). Apart from sporadic bombings in Bangkok and the south of the country, the challenge to central government has been limited.

In the *Philippines*, Muslims number around 3 million out of a population of some 65 million. They are concentrated in the southern islands of Basilan, Mindanao, Palawan, Sulu and Tawi Tawi. Subject to religious and administrative discrimination under Spanish colonial rule, the Muslims have long been a deprived community. Political alienation became acute after the Pacific War. Christian settlers moved south to appropriate Muslim land and to transform the demographic pattern. Political alienation was expressed organizationally by the **Moro National Liberation Front** (MNLF) which began armed struggle against the government of President **Ferdinand Marcos** in 1972 after it had declared martial law. Violent conflict reached a peak in the mid-1970s, but has diminished ever since a provisional settlement was negotiated through the good offices of Colonel Gadaffi of Libya in 1976 and the Marcos government began to play on tribal divisions within the Muslim community. A political solution remained elusive for two decades, while a split developed in the Muslim separatist movement giving rise to the **Moro Islamic Liberation Front**. In 1996, with Indonesia in the role of broker, the MNLF agreed to a cessation of armed struggle in return for the establishment of an

Autonomous Region of Muslim Mindanao with its leader, **Nur Misuari**, as its governor together with a key role in a Southern Philippines Council for Peace and Development. The Moro Islamic Liberation Front together with the insurgent **Abu Sayyaf** group have continued with Islamic rebellion in support of a separate state. The latter has degenerated, however, into a criminal organization noted for armed abduction of hostages for ransom, especially after the seizure of tourists from Malaysian Borneo in April 2000.

In *Singapore*, with an overwhelming Chinese majority, the Muslim community of around 400,000 has close links with peninsular Malaysia. Their politically suspect orientation was pointed up by reaction to the visit to the republic by Israel's president Chaim Herzog in 1986. At one time, they were excluded from national service but greater efforts have been made by the government to promote their integration.

*see also: Abangan*; Abu Sayyaf; *Al-Arqam*; Anwar Ibrahim; Bolkiah, Hassanal; Cham; *Darul Islam*; Habibie, B. J.; Herzog Affair; ICMI; Khmer Rouge; Marcos, Ferdinand; Megawati Sukarnoputri; *Melayu Islam Beraja*; Moro Islamic Liberation Front; Moro National Awakening Party; *Nahdatul Ulama*; National Liberation Front; Nur Misuari; Overseas Chinese; *Pancasila*; *Parti Islam Se-Malaysia*; Pattani United Liberation Organization; Rohingyas; *Santri*; State Law and Order Restoration Council; Suharto; Sukarno; UMNO; United Development Party; Wahid, Abdurrahman.

## Islamic Youth Movement (Malaysia)
*see* ABIM.

# J

## Jakarta Conference on Cambodia 1970 (Cambodia/Indonesia)

The government of Indonesia convened an international conference on Cambodia in Jakarta on 16 May 1970. It acted out of concern for the possible impact on national security of the extension of the **Vietnam War** to Cambodia after the deposition of its head of state, Prince **Norodom Sihanouk** in March 1970. The motivation was complex, however. Some military officers sought to exploit the conflict by transferring a stock of outmoded rifles to Cambodia in return for the United States replacing them with modern weapons. In addition, a proposal to dispatch an expeditionary force to help the vulnerable **Lon Nol** government was put to President **Suharto**. Suharto had a special interest in Cambodia, viewed previously as a model non-aligned state which he had visited for that very reason during his first overseas tour in 1968. However, his foreign minister, **Adam Malik**, persuaded Suharto of the risks of any military involvement and of the greater political utility of a conference which could demonstrate Indonesia's resumption of an independent and active foreign policy.

The conference, which was called with the approval of the secretary-general of the United Nations, was intended as a representative Asian diplomatic gathering. A major obstacle was Indonesia being identified with demands for the withdrawal of foreign troops and the restoration of Cambodia's neutrality, which appeared to endorse the authority of Lon Nol. In the event, the Jakarta Conference convened as a partisan assembly, attended only by western-aligned states. Communist invitees refused to participate, as did notable Asian neutrals such as India and Burma. Moreover, military incursions into Cambodia at the beginning of May by combined US and South Vietnamese units constituted a major political embarrassment. The conference was called 'to find a constructive formula on how to stop the deteriorating situation in Cambodia and restore peace and security to that country'

but failed to accomplish anything. A pious resolution calling for the withdrawal of all foreign troops was placed in the charge of a three-man mission from Indonesia, Malaysia and Japan, which then engaged in a fruitless perambulation to solicit cooperation from members of the Security Council of the United Nations.

see also: Malik, Adam; Nol, Lon; Sihanouk, Norodom; Suharto; Vietnam War.

## Jayakumar, Professor S. (Singapore)

Professor S. Jayakumar assumed the office of minister of foreign affairs in Singapore on 2 January 1994. By then, he had been engaged in Singapore's political life for more than a decade, having entered Parliament for the ruling **People's Action Party** (PAP) in 1980. Shunmugan Jayakumar was born on 12 August 1939 in Singapore and was educated at the elite Raffles Institution and then at the Law Faculty of the University of Singapore before pursuing postgraduate studies in the United States at Yale University. He joined the Law Faculty of the University of Singapore in 1964 and became its dean ten years later. He specialized in constitutional and public international law. In 1971 he was seconded to serve as Singapore's permanent representative to the United Nations and then from 1974 until 1979 was a member of Singapore's delegation to the United Nations Conference on the Law of the Sea. Professor Jayakumar was appointed minister of state for both law and home affairs in 1981. When he was appointed minister of foreign affairs, he was holding full portfolios in these two ministries and retained that of law with his new responsibility. He continued to hold both offices in the cabinet formed after elections in January 1997.

see also: People's Action Party.

## Jeyaretnam, J. B. (Singapore)

Benjamin Jeyaretnam became the first opposition Member of Parliament in Singapore for over a decade when, standing for the **Workers**

**Party**, he defeated the **People's Action Party** (PAP) candidate in a by-election on 31 October 1981. He was born in 1926 in Jaffna, Ceylon (now Sri Lanka), and trained as a lawyer in London. As a loquacious opposition Member of Parliament, he became a thorn in the flesh of the prime minister, **Lee Kuan Yew**, who appeared determined to drive him from political life. Jeyaretnam was returned to Parliament in 1984 but in 1986 he was found guilty of making a false declaration of his party's accounts and fined a sum which made him liable to expulsion from the legislature. He was disqualified from holding a seat until November 1991 and also disbarred from legal practice. In October 1988 the judicial committee of the Privy Council ruled that he had been wrongly disbarred and that the court decision was 'a grievous injustice'. The Workers Party won a single seat in general elections in August 1991 but Jeyaretnam did not take the opportunity to stand in a by-election in December 1992 after his disqualification had expired and lost political credibility as a consequence. However, in January 1997, he stood again for election this time with party colleagues in the five-member Group Representation Constituency of Cheng San. The Workers Party ran the PAP sufficiently close for J. B. Jeyaretnam, as its secretary-general, to assume the third opposition seat in the Parliament as a non-constituency member without voting rights. In the following August, he was tried before the High Court on the charge of having defamed Prime Minister **Goh Chok Tong** and ten other senior members of the PAP in remarks made at an election rally concerning fellow Workers Party candidate Tang Liang Hong, who subsequently fled Singapore. In September, the court found in favour of the prime minister but awarded damages of S$20,000, only one-tenth of that demanded and imposed only 60 per cent of the costs on Jeyaretnam. On appeal in July 1998, the damages were increased to S$100,000 and full costs imposed. In the following October, Jeyaretnam agreed to pay the damages in instalments to avoid bankruptcy proceedings and prejudicing his parliamentary status. In his declining years, and despite attracting a measure of public sympathy, he has ceased to be a thorn in the flesh of the government. In May 2000, he was declared bankrupt by the High Court for failing to keep up payments for damages in another libel case.

*see also:* Goh Chok Tong; Lee Kuan Yew; People's Action Party; Workers Party.

## Johor, Strait of (Malaysia/Singapore)

The Strait of Johor separates peninsular Malaysia from Singapore. Maritime traffic cannot pass through it because of the road and rail links across a causeway linking the two states. The strait varies in width from between three-quarters of a mile to two miles; the boundary between the two states has its origins in a treaty of 1824 between the British East India Company and the Sultan of Johor from whom Sir Stamford Raffles acquired Singapore in 1819. That treaty ceded to the company and its successors 'the island of Singapore, situated in the Straits of Malacca, together with the adjacent seas, straits and islets, to the extent of ten geographical miles from the coast'. A subsequent treaty of 1828 retroceded some islets and areas of territorial water within three nautical miles of the Johor coast and also employed the principle of an imaginary line following the centre of the deep-water channel in the strait to establish the maritime boundary which still obtains. In March 1994 the governments of Singapore and Malaysia signed an agreement to build a second land-link to the west of the existing causeway. That bridge was opened in April 1998.

*see also:* Malacca Strait; Singapore Strait.

# K

## Kachin  (Burma/Myanmar)

The Kachin are a minority tribal group of Tibeto-Burman linguistic affiliation who inhabit the north-eastern uplands of Burma adjacent to India and the People's Republic of China. They have been party to rebellion against the central government in Rangoon since the early 1960s. Before independence, their sense of separate cultural identity was reinforced by the influence of Christian missionaries and by recruitment into the colonial army. Their leaders agreed to join the Burmese state at a meeting in Panglong in early 1947 and supported the central government for the first ten years of independence. However, after the first assumption of power by the military led by General **Ne Win**, they launched a rebellion under the auspices of the Kachin Independence Organization which in time forged cooperative links with eleven other dissident ethnic minorities within a National Democratic Front. The Kachin rebellion was sustained over three decades but lost its momentum when the central government was able to interdict their sources of material support. On 1 October 1993 a peace agreement was signed between the Kachin leader, Major-General Zau Mai, and Burma's intelligence chief, Lt-General **Khin Nyunt**, bringing to an end the most significant insurgent challenge to the government in Rangoon. That accord was consolidated by a subsequent meeting and a formal cease-fire between the two sides in Myitkyina in Kachin state in February 1994.

*see also:* Chin; Karen; Khin Nyunt; Ne Win; Rohingyas; Shan.

## Kampuchea, People's Republic of (PRK)  (Cambodia)

The People's Republic of Kampuchea (PRK) was proclaimed on 8 January 1979, the day after Phnom Penh fell to Vietnamese forces acting on behalf of a so-called Kampuchean National United Front for National Salvation (KNUFNS). The new state was very much a Vietnamese creation. Its leading personnel comprised a mixture of **Khmer Rouge** defectors, survivors of the terror between 1975 and 1978 who had served both the **Lon Nol** and **Norodom Sihanouk** regimes, as well as Cambodian Communists long in political communion with Vietnam. A constitution was promulgated in June 1981 in which the PRK was described as an independent sovereign state moving step by step towards socialism. Elections were held only once, in May 1981, when 117 seats in the National Assembly were contested by 148 KNUFNS members. Power was exercised by the leadership of the **Kampuchean People's Revolutionary Party** (KPRP), the only political organization permitted. The administration was built up with Vietnamese advisers but by the end of the 1980s with the withdrawal of its main force units, the PRK had become relatively autonomous, albeit politically isolated and fragile. It enjoyed very limited diplomatic recognition, primarily from Vietnam and its political friends, and failed to secure United Nations endorsement. In April 1989, in an attempt to attract international sympathy, the name of the PRK was changed to the State of Kampuchea, readily transliterated as Cambodia. The country's national flag, national anthem and coat of arms were altered to remove any offending political symbolism, while **Buddhism** was re-established as the national religion. In October 1991 the ruling party changed its name to the **Cambodian People's Party** (CPP) and also discarded its Marxist political identity. The People's Republic of Kampuchea was effectively superseded on 21 September 1993 when a new constitution was ratified which re-established the Kingdom of Cambodia.

*see also:* Cambodian People's Party; Kampuchean People's Revolutionary Party; Khmer Rouge; Nol, Lon; Sihanouk, Norodom.

## Kampuchean People's Revolutionary Party (KPRP)  (Cambodia)

The Kampuchean People's Revolutionary Party (KPRP) was the ruling and sole legal party in the **People's Republic of Kampuchea** (PRK) established on 8 January 1979. The party's existence was revealed only at its claimed fourth congress in May 1981. The date of its foundation was given as 1951 in order to demonstrate a direct lineal descent from the Vietnamese-dominated Communist Party of Indochina founded by **Ho Chi Minh** in 1930. Its first secretary-general was Pen Sovan, who was replaced by **Heng Samrin** in December 1981. His role (held concurrently with that of head of state) was primarily ceremonial. The two dominant political figures have been Politburo members, **Hun Sen** and **Chea Sim**, who were respectively prime minister and chairman of the National Assembly. On 17–18 October 1991, just prior to the reconvening of the **International Conference on Cambodia** in Paris, the People's Revolutionary Party held an extraordinary congress. In a dramatic initiative, the word 'revolutionary' was dropped from the party's name and in translation the word 'Cambodian' was substituted for 'Kampuchean'. Heng Samrin was removed as formal leader in favour of Chea Sim and an exclusive Marxism was repudiated for political pluralism, while Prince **Norodom Sihanouk** was endorsed as head of state in succession to Heng Samrin. The change in nomenclature and the decision to opt for a multi-party system and political realignment in order to be identified with Prince Sihanouk served to demonstrate the shallow political base of the party and the extent to which it had been a creation of the Vietnamese invasion and a career vehicle for its leadership. The **Cambodian People's Party** (CPP) took part in elections in May 1993 conducted under United Nations auspices, securing second place overall, and then joined a coalition government in October in which Hun Sen became Second prime minister.

*see also:* Cambodian People's Party; Chea Sim; Heng Samrin; Ho Chi Minh; Hun Sen; International Conference on Cambodia, Paris 1991; Kampuchea, People's Republic of; Sihanouk, Norodom.

## Karen (Burma/Myanmar)

The Karen are a substantial but less than homogeneous ethnic minority in Burma who have long resisted domination by the government in Rangoon through armed struggle. Numbering some 1.5 million, the Karen are concentrated

from south of Mandalay in three mixed geographic zones of deltas, mountain ranges and plateaux which extend in a south-easterly direction parallel to the border with Thailand. The separate identity of the Karen was strengthened during British rule when a good number were converted to denominations of Christianity and also recruited into the ranks of the colonial army. Karen were involved in helping to crush an anti-colonial rebellion in the early 1930s and in conducting armed resistance against the Japanese in 1942 to cover the British retreat into India. Ethnic-Burmans within the Japanese-sponsored Burma Independence Army took a savage revenge against the Karen civilian population, which left a bitter legacy of political alienation after independence in 1948.

In February 1947 a meeting in Panglong between the provisional government in Rangoon and representatives of a number of ethnic minorities came to an agreement on the constitutional basis of a federal Union of Burma. The Karen, organized in the Karen National Union, rejected this accord and boycotted elections to a constituent assembly in April 1947. Independence in January 1948 was followed by civil war in which the Karen played a major role in challenging the authority of Rangoon. By January 1949, the Karen rebellion had penetrated the northern suburbs of the capital and posed an acute threat to the integrity of Burma, until in August 1950 when good fortune enabled a unit of the national army to eliminate two of their key leaders. The Karen were pushed back into their traditional areas of settlement but have continued to resist the central government since the early 1950s. The Karen National Union has continued to demand political autonomy within a multi-minority National Democratic Front, which in 1988 transformed itself into the Democratic Alliance of Burma with dissident student and religious groups who had been alienated by the bloody repression of the military regime. An opposition National Coalition Government of the Union of Burma was established in December 1990 in the town of Manerplaw (close to the Thai border) which housed the headquarters of the Karen National Union. Manerplaw had been under recurrent attack by the Burmese army and in 1992 its troops advanced to within six miles of the town before being repulsed with heavy casualties. The Karen position crumbled in December 1994 with the defection of a Buddhist faction which allied with the Rangoon government. Manerplaw fell in January 1995 after being held by the Karen for forty-seven years. The Karen National Union entered into talks with the Rangoon authorities from December 1995 but they failed to produce an accord and collapsed in January 1997. Fighting then resumed, which was spearheaded by the disaffected Democratic Karen Buddhist Army giving rise to a flow of refugees into Thailand and a further deterioration of the Karen position. In October 1999, a Karen splinter group, known as God's Army, seized Burma's Embassy in Bangkok and then negotiated their release by helicopter to the Thai border. In January 2000, the same splinter group seized Ratchaburi hospital along Thailand's western border in an attempt to stop the Thai army from shelling its positions and also to secure permission for its unarmed fighters to receive medical treatment. In the event, the hospital was stormed by Thai commandos who killed all the Karen insurgents and released all hostages. The net effect was to turn Thai public sentiment against the Karens. The Karen National Union, which denounced the hospital seizure, then announced the removal from military command of General Bo Mya, its long-time leader.

*see also:* Chin; Kachin; Rohingyas; Shan.

## Kaysone Phomvihan (Laos)

Kaysone Phomvihan was the most powerful figure in the Laotian Communist movement from its formation at the end of the Pacific War for almost half a century. He was born on 13 December 1920 near the southern town of Savannakhet to a Laotian mother and a Vietnamese father who was an official in the French colonial administration. His parents sent him to be educated in Hanoi, where he studied law and also became drawn into the anti-colonial movement which was subject to the strong influence of the Communist Party of Indochina (and subsequently of Vietnam) which he joined. At the end of the Pacific War, the party dispatched him back to his home town in an abortive attempt to seize power from the

Japanese in order to pre-empt the return of the French.

In his political career, Kaysone appeared guided by the judgement that independence for landlocked Laos could be secured only through the patronage of the Communist Party of Vietnam. In January 1949 he founded a fighting unit which was the precursor of the Lao People's Liberation Army. In August 1950 he became minister of national defence in the Vietnamese-sponsored Lao Resistance government, more commonly known as *Pathet Lao* (translated as Lao Nation or State). This so-called government failed to secure representation at the conference leading to the **Geneva Agreements on Indochina** in 1954, which recognized the independence of the Kingdom of Laos from France. Kaysone then devoted his organizational skills to challenging the Royal government in Vientiane, serving as general secretary of the clandestine **Lao People's Revolutionary Party** founded in March 1955. The open instrument of challenge was the *Neo Lao Hak Sat* (Lao Patriotic Front) led nominally by Prince **Souphanouvong** but with Kaysone always in a commanding position able to draw on Vietnamese military stiffening. The political future of Laos was determined by the outcome of revolutionary struggle in neighbouring Vietnam. The fall of Saigon in April 1975 led to a progressive collapse of the coalition government in Vientiane by the end of the year. On 2 December 1975 the monarchy was abolished and the Lao People's Democratic Republic was proclaimed with Kaysone Phomvihan as prime minister. He combined the office with that of general secretary of the Lao People's Revolutionary Party.

Initially, Kaysone followed Vietnamese doctrine and practice in managing the economy which led to a dramatic failure in performance. He also allied Laos with Vietnam in the conflict over Cambodia in the third of the **Indochina Wars**, early in the course of which relations with the People's Republic of China became strained, while those with the Soviet Union were reinforced. Under Kaysone's leadership and again following Vietnam's lead, Laos changed economic course and adopted market-driven principles, while retaining an authoritarian political system. Correspondingly, relations were repaired with China and improved with Thailand and the United States. With the end of the Cold War, Laos under Kaysone still acknowledged a special relationship with Vietnam but sought a more balanced international position to compensate for the loss of benefaction from both Vietnam and the former Soviet Union. Despite the fluctuations of policy which distinguished his rule, Kaysone never appeared to be subject to serious political challenge. At the fifth congress of the Lao People's Revolutionary Party in March 1991, the Secretariat was abolished and Kaysone was elected to a new office of party president. In August 1991, with the promulgation of a new constitution, he gave up the office of prime minister for that of president. On his death on 21 November 1992, his offices were shared out among senior colleagues. The prime minister, **Khamtay Siphandon**, became party leader, while **Nouhak Phoumvasan** became head of state.

*see also:* Geneva Agreements on Indochina 1954; Geneva Agreements on Laos 1962; Indochina Wars; Khamtay Siphandon; Lao People's Revolutionary Party; *Neo Lao Hak Sat*; Nouhak Phoumvasan; *Pathet Lao*; Souphanouvong.

## Ketahanan Nasional (Indonesia) *see* National Resilience.

## Khamtay Siphandon (Laos)

Khamtay Siphandon became head of state in February 1998 concurrently with his tenure of the office of chairman of the **Lao People's Revolutionary Party**, which he had assumed in November 1992 on the death of **Kaysone Phomvihan**. He had been a close associate of Kaysone for over three decades, having succeeded him as head of the *Pathet Lao* armed forces in 1962. Khamtay was born on 8 February 1924 in Champassak Province in humble circumstances. He worked as a postman under French rule but became involved in revolutionary nationalism under Vietnamese sponsorship at the end of the Pacific War. By the late 1940s, he had made his mark as a political cadre and military leader. He attended the meeting in August 1950 of the Free Laos Front, which gave the name *Pathet Lao* to the pro-Communist insurgency against the government in Vientiane.

He became a member of the central committee of the Lao People's (subsequently Revolutionary) Party in 1957 and following on his military leadership of the *Pathet Lao* in 1962, he was appointed commander-in-chief of the Lao People's Liberation Army in 1966. He became a member of the Politburo of the Lao People's Revolutionary Party in 1972 and played a leading role in the seizure of power during 1975. After the creation of the Lao People's Democratic Republic, Khamtay was appointed minister of defence and deputy prime minister. By the early 1990s, he had risen to third place in the Politburo and in August 1991 succeeded Kaysone as prime minister. He gave up that office on becoming head of state in succession to **Nouhak Phoumvasan**.

*see also:* Kaysone Phomvihan; Lao People's Revolutionary Party; Nouhak Phoumvasan; *Pathet Lao*.

## Khieu Samphan (Cambodia)

Khieu Samphan has been the best-known intellectual voice among the **Khmer Rouge** as well as acting as their official representative and spokesman with consistent servile loyalty to **Pol Pot**'s leadership. Khieu Samphan is believed to have been born in 1931 in Svay Rieng Province, the son of a local judge. He was a promising student and won a scholarship to study economics in Paris, where he became secretary-general of the Communist-dominated Union of Cambodian Students. In 1959 he was awarded a doctorate for his thesis on Cambodia's economy; this advocated an autonomy from market capitalism which corresponded to policies implemented by the Khmer Rouge when they were in power. On his return to Cambodia, he entered left-wing journalism and was subsequently elected to the National Assembly in 1962 and again in 1966, where he acquired a popular reputation for political integrity and incorruptibility. He was coopted into government by Prince **Norodom Sihanouk** but broke with him and in 1967 fled the capital with two other dissident colleagues to join Pol Pot in the jungle, although at the time it was widely rumoured that they had been murdered by the secret police. Khieu Samphan did not make a public reappearance until 1973 after the deposition of Prince Sihanouk, who made a clandestine visit to Cambodia from the People's Republic of China where he was in exile. Khieu Samphan was then commander-in-chief of the Khmer Liberation Armed Forces, despite a lack of military experience. After the Khmer Rouge seized power, he succeeded Prince Sihanouk as head of state in April 1976 and survived in that position until the Vietnamese invasion in December 1978. He was evacuated through Beijing and assumed a major diplomatic role on behalf of the ousted government of so-called **Democratic Kampuchea**, which still retained the Cambodian seat in the United Nations. When the **Coalition Government of Democratic Kampuchea** (CGDK) was formed in June 1982 with non-Communist participation under Prince Sihanouk's leadership, he became vice-president in charge of foreign affairs. In August 1985 he assumed formal responsibility for the Democratic Kampuchean faction on the ostensible retirement of Pol Pot. In that role, he took part in negotiations which led ultimately to a political settlement for Cambodia under United Nations auspices reached at the **International Conference on Cambodia** in Paris in October 1991. He became the senior Khmer Rouge representative on the **Supreme National Council**, returning to Cambodia in the following month, when he was almost lynched by a mob organized by the incumbent government. As a member of that Council, he registered Khmer Rouge obstructionism to implementing the Paris accords and in April 1993 withdrew from Phnom Penh as an act of defiance before general elections which were boycotted by the Khmer Rouge. With the successful holding of those elections in May and the formation of a coalition government in October, from which the Khmer Rouge were excluded, Khieu Samphan made an abortive attempt to secure an advisory place for his faction. He refused to return to Phnom Penh on the grounds that adequate provision could not be made for his protection. In July 1994, he was named prime minister in a provisional government proclaimed by the Khmer Rouge and served as its nominal leader. In July 1997, he was involved in abortive negotiations with representatives of Cambodia's First Prime Minister **Norodom Ranariddh**, which precipitated a suc-

cessful coup mounted by Second Prime Minister **Hun Sen** the following month. Although Pol Pot died in April 1998, Khieu Samphan only surrendered to the authorities in Phnom Penh in December that year. He was flown in a helicopter to the capital where he was received by Prime Minister Hun Sen, who initially promised him an amnesty in return for pledging allegiance to his government. Domestic and international protest caused Hun Sen to reverse himself but he subsequently provided assurances that Khieu Samphan would not be subject to legal action originating in France. Khieu Samphan has settled without restraint in the Pailin region controlled by former Khmer Rouge forces loyal to **Ieng Sary**.

*see also:* Democratic Kampuchea, Coalition Government of; Hun Sen; Teng Sary; International Conference on Cambodia, Paris 1991; Khmer Rouge; Pol Pot; Ranariddh, Norodom; Sihanouk, Norodom; Supreme National Council.

# Khin Nyunt (Burma/Myanmar)

Lt-General Khin Nyunt became First Secretary of the **State Peace and Development Council** (SPDC) on its formation in November 1997, which was the same position he had held within its predecessor, the **State Law and Order Restoration Council** (SLORC) from its formation in September 1988. After the removal of its chairman, General Saw Maung, in April 1992, he reinforced a reputation for being the most powerful man in the country, albeit still deferential to his patron **Ne Win**. Khin Nyunt was born on 11 October 1936 and studied psychology at the University of Rangoon before entering the armed forces. He began his career in the infantry and rose to command a division before moving to military intelligence. He was appointed as head of the Directorate of Defence Services Intelligence, with a secret police role, in 1983. He is believed to have been the prime influence in managing the country's burgeoning relationship with the People's Republic of China as well as responsible for sustaining military pressure against dissident ethnic minorities, such as the **Kachin**. In late 1992 he was reported to have overcome an attempt to remove him by a group of military officers opposed to his policy of a close relationship with China. Khin Nyunt's dominant position is believed to be dependent on continuing support from an ailing Ne Win in the face of resentment of his role by mainstream field commanders. That position appeared to have been consolidated with the establishment in September 1998 of a political affairs committee with Khin Nyunt as its chairman.

see also: Kachin; Ne Win; State Law and Order Restoration Council; State Peace and Development Council.

## Khmer People's National Liberation Front (KPNLF)  (Cambodia)

The Khmer People's National Liberation Front (KPNLF) was a non-Communist resistance organization set up in October 1979 in order to challenge the government imposed in Cambodia by Vietnamese force of arms in January 1979. The principal role in its formation was played by **Son Sann**, who had served as prime minister under Prince **Norodom Sihanouk**. The KPNLF drew support from an educated constituency of a republican disposition which had supported the overthrow of Prince Sihanouk in 1970. In June 1982 it joined in a so-called **Coalition Government of Democratic Kampuchea** (CGDK) with the **Khmer Rouge** and Prince Sihanouk's **FUNCINPEC** (National United Front for an Independent, Neutral, Peaceful and Cooperative Cambodia) in which Son Sann was named prime minister. The KPNLF suffered from problems of divided leadership and internal cohesion and also enjoyed very mixed military fortunes. Despite misgivings about direct negotiations with the government in Phnom Penh, the KPNLF became a party to the dialogue, initially at regional level, which led on to the United Nations-sponsored peace accord concluded at the **International Conference on Cambodia** in Paris in October 1991. When the United Nations presence in Cambodia charged with conducting elections began to register political parties (*see* **UNTAC**), the KPNLF changed its name to the **Buddhist Liberal Democratic Party**. It participated in those elections in May 1993, winning 10 seats in a Constituent Assembly of 120 members and then secured minimal representation in the coalition

government established at the end of October 1993.

see also: Buddhist Liberal Democratic Party; Democratic Kampuchea, Coalition Government of; FUNCINPEC; International Conference on Cambodia, Paris 1991; Khmer Rouge; Sihanouk, Norodom; Son Sann; United Nations: Cambodia 1991–3; UNTAC.

## Khmer Republic  (Cambodia)

The Khmer Republic was proclaimed in Phnom Penh on 9 October 1970 in succession to the monarchy which had been terminated with the overthrow of Prince **Norodom Sihanouk** in March 1970. The Khmer Republic, which was inspired by Marshal **Lon Nol**, who led the coup against Prince Sihanouk, lasted only until 17 April 1975, when the **Khmer Rouge** seized power. The Khmer Republic was distinguished by feckless political leadership and corrupt practice which led to an initial popular welcome to the end of the civil war won by the Khmer Rouge.

see also: Khmer Rouge; Nol, Lon; Sihanouk, Norodom.

## Khmer Rouge  (Cambodia)

The pejorative term Khmer Rouge (Red Cambodians) was originally applied to the country's Communist movement in the 1960s by the head of state, Prince **Norodom Sihanouk**, to differentiate them from the right-wing Khmer Bleu. That movement had by then become dominated by an indigenous intellectual leadership which had been converted to Marxism while students together in Paris. By the late 1960s, it had mounted an insurgency which exploited rural discontent. In March 1970 Prince Sihanouk was overthrown by a right-wing coup while out of the country. In exile in the People's Republic of China, he joined a united front with his Communist adversaries against the government in Phnom Penh headed by General **Lon Nol**. The term Khmer Rouge stuck, nonetheless. Its revolutionary army, initially spearheaded by Vietnamese intervention, achieved military victory in April 1975. A reign of collectivist terror was then launched under the leadership of party leader **Pol Pot** in an attempt to create an ideal socialist society, which led to up to 1 million deaths. All members of the Lon Nol administration and army were executed. The cities were emptied of their populations, who were set to work in agricultural communes, many to die from malnutrition and disease. Family life was abolished and the Buddhist religion erased. Economic failure aggravated a paranoid tendency expressed in intra-party purges against alleged Vietnamese agents, while armed raids were conducted across the eastern border. In December 1978 invading Vietnamese forces drove the Khmer Rouge from Cambodia. Provided with territorial sanctuary by Thailand and military supplies by China, the Khmer Rouge was revived and able to launch an insurgency against the government installed in Phnom Penh by Vietnam in January 1979. In June 1982 the Khmer Rouge joined in a fragile **Coalition Government of Democratic Kampuchea** (CGDK) with two non-Communist Cambodian factions in a united challenge to Vietnam's military occupation and the Phnom Penh government under the nominal leadership of Prince Sihanouk. As a party to that coalition, they engaged in negotiations which culminated in a political settlement for Cambodia at the **International Conference on Cambodia** in Paris in October 1991. That settlement provided for **UNTAC** (United Nations Transitional Authority in Cambodia) with a peacekeeping role and a mandate to conduct free and fair elections to resolve the political conflict. Although a signatory to the Paris accord, the Khmer Rouge refused to accept its military provisions and then boycotted the elections, which were held in May 1993 without significant disruption. The elections led to a new coalition government in October 1993 between the two non-Communist factions and the prior incumbent administration in Phnom Penh. The Khmer Rouge then sought an advisory position within the new government, while continuing their insurgency. The Phnom Penh government conducted armed operations against Khmer Rouge base camps in the north and west of the country in early 1994 but after initial successes experienced military reverses at heavy cost. The effect was to demonstrate the military resilience of the Khmer Rouge, leaving them with greater territorial control. The Khmer Rouge have maintained a coherent political identity and a viable military

organization with a younger generation of commanders assuming leadership roles. Although Pol Pot formally retired from all leadership positions in September 1985, informed sources have maintained that he has continued in overall control of the Khmer Rouge. A photograph of him taken in 1986 in the company of other leaders of the organization came to light following the initially successful assault on Khmer Rouge headquarters in Pailin in March 1994. In July 1994, the Khmer Rouge proclaimed a provisional government headed ostensibly by **Khieu Samphan** in reaction to their being outlawed by Cambodia's parliament.

Although able initially to resist military challenge by the government in Phnom Penh, the Khmer Rouge failed to demonstrate an ability to challenge its national power. Moreover, it began to experience a revival of self-destructive internal strife, which led on to its effective disintegration as a viable political–military entity signalled first by the defection of **Ieng Sary** in August 1996. Moreover, the two rival first and second prime ministers in Phnom Penh competed to inspire further defections. It was in this context in June 1997, that Pol Pot ordered the murder of former defence minister, **Son Sen**, his wife and sixteen members of his family. Pol Pot then fled into the jungle with a small band of loyalists with other Khmer Rouge leaders as hostages. Pol Pot was captured by **Ta Mok**, the one-time chief of staff, and returned to the redoubt of Anlong Veng where, in July 1997, he was sentenced to life imprisonment by a 'people's court' for the murder of Son Sen. The trial was witnessed by an American journalist, Nate Thayer, who interviewed an unrepentant Pol Pot in October. Pol Pot died in April 1998 in a remote jungle retreat, apparently from a heart attack, although his body was cremated before a post-mortem examination could be conducted. Desultory armed confrontation continued between government forces and Khmer Rouge bands but several hundred insurgents surrendered nominally to the government in a ceremony near the Thai border in December 1998, leaving just a small number led by Ta Mok under arms. At the end of the month, Khmer Rouge leaders, Khieu Samphan and Nuon Chea, were flown by helicopter to Phnom Penh where they were met by **Hun Sen** who received their pledge of allegiance to his government. The surrender of the last main fighting units and of the political leaders brought an effective end to over three decades of civil war, which had drawn Cambodia into a living hell. Ta Mok was captured in March 1999. In May, security forces apprehended Kang Kek Leu, alias Duch, the commandant of the notorious prison and interrogation centre, **Tuol Sleng**. They were both charged with genocide in September 1999 but their trial was delayed by a dispute with the United Nations over the composition of the judicial tribunal and the appointment of prosecutors, which was resolved through a compromise agreement in May 2000. The Khmer Rouge period in Cambodian history was a murderous experience; its historical lesson is that evil practice may be readily justified in the name of a noble ideal. Moreover, a significant remnant of the Khmer Rouge live unmolested in the town of Pailin to the south-west of Battambang, which is a centre of gem-trading, gambling and prostitution.

see also: Democratic Kampuchea, Coalition Government of; Hun Sen; Ieng Sary; International Conference on Cambodia, Paris 1991; Khieu Samphan; Nol, Lon; Pol Pot; Son Sen; Sihanouk, Norodom; Ta Mok; Tuol Sleng; United Nations: Cambodia 1991–3; UNTAC.

## Khun Sa  (Burma/Myanmar)

Khun Sa enjoyed notoriety as the leader of a major heroin production and distribution network in eastern Burma, close to the border with Thailand. Khun Sa's headquarters were located in the town of Homong, where he attracted strong support for his advocacy of ethnic-**Shan** autonomy through command of the Mong Tai Army and his role as president of the Shan State Restoration Council. Khun Sa was born in 1934 in the northern Shan state to a Chinese father and a Shan mother; his Chinese name is Chang Shee-fu. He was a shiftless youth with a criminal disposition who embarked on the opium trade in the early 1960s, when head of a local militia under the command of the Burmese army. His career came to a temporary halt between 1969 and 1974, when he was placed in detention. His release was secured by his supporters in

exchange for two Soviet doctors whom they had abducted. Khun Sa then set up a base in north-western Thailand in coalition with elements of the Kuo Ming Tang, who had retreated overland from China in 1949. He enjoyed Thai support because of his anti-Communist credentials until a change of political circumstances led to his forces being driven back into Burma in January 1982. His position came under increasing challenge because of alternative sources of heroin production within Burma and also because the Burmese army embarked on a major military campaign against his territory from the end of 1993. It was effectively undermined from June 1995 when a mutiny within his Mong Tai Army split it into Shan and ethnic-Chinese components. Khun Sa stepped down as its leader in November. In December 1995, he surrendered with his remaining forces to the Burmese army in Homony under the terms of a suspected deal whereby he bought his way to a peaceful retirement. In retirement, he has changed his name to U Htet Aung and lives in a house on Inya Lake in Rangoon. It is reported that he has been given licences to operate transport companies, trade in real estate and to direct a mineral concession. In return, he was obliged to repatriate funds from Thailand to Burmese state banks and to hand over control of his Homong fiefdom to the military who have established opium farms manned by forced labour as well as benefiting from the laundering of drug profits. In May 2000, a Thai-based news agency reported that Khun Sa was terminally ill and semi-paralysed. One of his sons, Chang Weikang, was reportedly building an alternative power base in Shan state.

see also: Shan.

## Kiet, Vo Van  (Vietnam) see Vo Van Kiet.

## Kilusang Bagong Lipunan  (Philippines) see New Society Movement.

## Kit Sangkhom  (Thailand) see Social Action Party.

## Kitingan, Datuk Joseph Pairin (Malaysia/Sabah)

Until his resignation on 17 March 1994, Joseph Pairin Kitingan had been chief minister of the north Bornean state of Sabah from April 1985 when he lead the newly formed **Sabah United Party** (*Parti Bersatu Sabah* – PBS) to electoral victory. He was born on 17 August 1940 in Papar in British North Borneo, the son of a police sergeant of the Kadazan ethnic group and of the Roman Catholic faith. Datuk Kitingan studied law at the University of Adelaide in South Australia and was the first Kadazan to qualify as a lawyer. On his return to Sabah, he joined the state legal service but left to go into private practice three years later. He was a founder member of *Berjaya* (Sabah People's Union) and entered the state legislature in April 1976. In July that year, he was appointed minister of local government and then to the portfolios of manpower and of resources development until resigning from the latter post in August 1982. He resigned from *Berjaya* in August 1984 and also from his parliamentary seat in protest at the deviation of the party from its ostensibly multiracial identity to a preference for the Muslim community. He was re-elected as an independent in December and in March 1985 agreed to join the minor party *Pasok* as its leader but within a week he quit to establish the Sabah United Party which draw support from the Kadazans and the Chinese community in the elections in April 1985.

The former chief minister **Tun Mustapha Harun**, in collusion with the state governor, made an abortive attempt to prevent Datuk Kitingan's appointment as chief minister, which was followed by a protracted court case. Kitingan dissolved the state assembly in February 1986 after a series of defections from his ruling party to the opposition **United Sabah National Organization** (USNO). A wave of bombings, riots and arson followed in a deliberate attempt to prevent the Elections Commission from fixing a polling date. Elections were held again in May, when Datuk Kitingan led PBS back to office with an increased majority. The next month, his party was admitted to the federal *Barisan Nasional* (National Front) coalition which marked an acceptance of the legitimacy of a non-Muslim party and leader in the Malaysian state. Datuk Kitingan's relationship with the federal prime minister, Dr **Mahathir Mohamad**, proved to be uneasy, however. That relation-

ship was ruptured in October 1990 when Kitingan took PBS out of the *Barisan Nasional* to join the opposition coalition only five days before the federal elections. That decision proved to be a major miscalculation when the *Barisan Nasional* was returned to federal office.

Datuk Kitingan and his party were then subject to political challenge, with Sabah deprived of development funds. In January 1991 he was arrested on charges of corruption but was allowed to continue in office while on bail. The High Court returned a verdict of guilty in January 1994 but the fine imposed did not disqualify him from contesting state elections in February, which had been called before the verdict had been announced. Despite a major effort by the federal government, Datuk Kitingan led the PBS to a further electoral victory with a narrow majority. He had just prevailed politically because he represented communal and state interests which resented the dominance of a federal centre, which had starved the state of development funds and which was identified with an Islamic agenda. Before he was sworn in again as chief minister, he found it necessary to camp outside the state governor's mansion for thirty-six hours. The governor had claimed that he was unwell but Datuk Kitingan feared a repeat of the episode in 1985 when there was an abortive attempt to deny him office, even though his party had won the elections. By the middle of March, however, sufficient defections had been inspired from PBS to cause it to lose its majority in the state legislature, which led Datuk Kitingan to resign office on 17 March 1994. He was succeeded by the leader of the *Barisan Nasional* in Sabah, Tan Sri Sakaran Dandai. Following his resignation, Kitingan's political party virtually collapsed under him but revived after federal elections in April 1975. The PBS won eight out of twenty seats contested, with Datuk Kitingan retaining his constituency. His political fortunes did not improve, however. In state elections in March 1999, his party won 17 out of 48 seats, while in federal elections in the following November, its representation was reduced to 3 seats. A further blow was the defection in April 2000 of six Sabah United Party members of the state legislature to the *Barisian Nasional*.

*see also: Barisan Nasional*; *Berjaya*; Mahathir Mohamad, Datuk Sri; Mustapha bin Datuk Harun, Tun; Sabah United Party; United Sabah National Organization.

## Konfrontasi (Indonesia/Malaysia) *see* Confrontation.

## Kong Le, Captain (Laos)

Kong Le played an important part in Laotian politics during the 1960s. On 9 August 1960 Kong Le, who was then a paratroop captain, mounted a coup in Vientiane on behalf of neutralist interests against the right-wing government led nominally by Prince Somsanith. He was instrumental in securing the return of Prince **Souvanna Phouma** as prime minister and assumed the position of commander-in-chief of the neutralist armed forces. His military initiative prompted negotiations that led to the abortive **Geneva Agreements on Laos** in July 1962. By then, political naivety had led him into a short-lived coalition with the Communist *Pathet Lao*. When that coalition fell apart, Kong Le was obliged to come to terms with the conservative government in Vientiane, returning his troops to the command of the Royal Lao Army. Kong Le was born in Savannakhet Province on 6 March 1934 and joined the Royal Lao Army in 1952. He received military training in Thailand and the Philippines and was engaged in operations in northern Laos before achieving the rank of captain and appointment as deputy commander of the Second Parachute Battalion. He justified his action in 1960 on the ground that he wished to stop Laotians fighting one another. After his accommodation with the military establishment, he became the object of a number of assassination attempts, leaving the country in 1967 for exile in France. With t he victory of the *Pathet Lao* in 1975, he sought to organize resistance to their rule and benefited briefly in the early 1980s from a convergent Chinese interest but failed to employ it to advantage. He moved to the United States in the late 1980s where, as a stateless alien, he lives a nomadic existence trying to persuade communities of Laotian exiles that the fight against the communist government in Vientiane is not over.

*see also:* Geneva Agreements on Laos 1962; *Pathet Lao*; Souvanna Phouma.

## KOPKAMTIB (Indonesia)

*KOPKAMTIB*, which is the acronym for *Komando Operasi Pemulihan Keamanan Dan Ketertiban*, (Operational Command for the Restoration of Security and Order), was a military command set up by General **Suharto** on 10 October 1965 to give himself the power to crush all parties to a coup attempt that had been mounted ten days before (*see* **Gestapu**). With its initial failure, President **Sukarno** had given authority to Suharto as head of the army's strategic reserve to restore order and security. However, Sukarno displayed an evident ambivalence about Suharto's role and had appointed the politically malleable General Pranoto to replace the army commander, Lt-General Achmad Yani, who had been murdered during the abortive coup. In the event, Suharto succeeded Pranoto on 16 October and Sukarno formally recognized *KOPKAMTIB* under Suharto's control on 1 November 1965. The original security function of the command was to seek out and eliminate supporters of the Communist Party, which was charged with responsibility for mounting the coup. Its role expanded as an instrument for consolidating General Suharto's so-called **New Order** in Indonesia. Employing virtually unlimited powers, it acted as the main agency for maintaining political control against all dissidents and from 1971 policed election campaigns. Executive control of *KOPKAMTIB* rested initially with Suharto. However, he delegated authority to military subordinates according to political circumstances. The command was eventually abolished on 5 September 1988, to be replaced by a new security organization *BAKORSTANAS* (an acronym translating as Coordinating Agency for the Enforcement of National Stability) under the control of the armed forces commander, General Try Sutrisno. By then, *KOPKAMTIB* had outlived its political usefulness, while President Suharto had become concerned that its powers might be used against his interest by the previous armed forces commander and minister of defence, General **L. B. Murdani**, from whom he had become estranged.

*see also:* BAKORSTANAS; Crocodile Hole; *Gestapu*; Murdani L. B.; New Order; Suharto; Sukarno.

## Kriangsak Chomanan, General
(Thailand)
General Kriangsak held the office of prime minister of Thailand from November 1977 until February 1980. In the wake of a coup that removed prime minister **Thanin Kraivichian**, he was appointed as a compromise candidate of the military with the conditional support of a **Young Turks** faction. He initiated a policy of reconciliation with Vietnam and Laos and then authorized its reverse in response to the challenge posed by Vietnam's occupation of Cambodia from December 1978 in the third phase of the **Indochina Wars**. He was obliged to resign office in favour of the army commander, General **Prem Tinsulanond**, after losing the support of young military officers represented in the Parliament. Kriangsak Chomanan was born in 1917 and educated at Chulachomklao Royal Military Academy and the American Army Staff College. He saw service during the Korean War and by the 1970s had assumed a series of senior staff posts. In October 1977 he held the honorific office of supreme commander of the armed forces. He was the first prime minister drawn from the ranks of the military in forty-six years who had not previously been a first army area commander and commander-in-chief of the army. After losing office, he stood successfully for Parliament in August 1981 but was implicated in an abortive military coup in September 1985 and was placed under arrest. He was granted bail in February 1986 and went on trial in 1987. He benefited from a general amnesty in 1988 and has ceased to play any part in public life, with the exception of assisting in restoring relations with Laos.
*see also:* Prem Tinsulanond; Thanin Kraivichian; Young Turks.

## Kuala Lumpur Declaration 1971
(Indonesia/Malaysia/Philippines/Singapore/Thailand)
A meeting of foreign ministers of **ASEAN** (Association of South-East Asian Nations) states in Kuala Lumpur issued a declaration on 27

November 1971 which expressed their governments' determination 'to exert initially necessary efforts to secure the recognition of, and respect for, South-East Asia as a Zone of Peace, Freedom and Neutrality, free from any form or manner of interference by outside Powers'. The meeting had been arranged at the United Nations in New York at the beginning of October in the expectation that the People's Republic of China would assume China's seat in place of Taiwan. The realization that such a change would have an impact in South-East Asia brought the five representatives to the Malaysian capital to find an acceptable formula for regional order. At issue was whether to endorse an earlier Malaysian proposal that South-East Asia be neutralized with guarantees from major powers. Indonesia, in particular, took exception to this prescription, which appeared to accord virtual policing rights to extra-regional states. The final declaration reflected Indonesia's priority that regional order should be managed on an autonomous basis rather than be determined through the intervening role of external powers. Accordingly, only lip-service was paid to the desirability of neutralization. In November 1971 ASEAN was not yet ready to declare a corporate political role. Consequently, the foreign ministers met on an *ad-hoc* basis and not in a corporate capacity. In February 1976, however, at the **Bali Summit**, the first meeting of heads of government of ASEAN, the Kuala Lumpur Declaration was incorporated in the **Declaration of ASEAN Concord** which registered political goals. Subsequently the formula for a **ZOPFAN** (Zone of Peace, Freedom and Neutrality) became a part of the common declaratory policy of ASEAN but without any practical operational utility, despite the measure of success in December 1995 in concluding a treaty on a regional nuclear weapon-free zone.
*see also:* ASEAN; Bali Summit 1976; Declaration of ASEAN Concord 1976; South-East Asia Nuclear Weapon-Free Zone (SEANWFZ); ZOPFAN.

## Kuala Lumpur Summit (ASEAN) 1977
(Indonesia/Malaysia/Philippines/Singapore/Thailand)
The tenth anniversary of the formation of

**ASEAN** (Association of South-East Asian Nations) was celebrated with a meeting of heads of government in the Malaysian capital on 3–4 August 1977. Although the first summit had taken place only in February 1976, the meeting was convened in order to reaffirm the corporate solidarity of ASEAN within a South-East Asia which had not long partly fallen prey to successful revolutionary forces. In addition, there was some expectation that proposals for trade liberalization among members which had proven abortive at the **Bali Summit** might be revived. In the event, little of substance was achieved by way of new forms of economic cooperation, while a Thai initiative for greater security cooperation came to nought. ASEAN did achieve an important measure of diplomatic success, however. Any disappointment experienced at Vietnam's refusal to be represented at the inaugural ceremony was more than compensated for by the presence in Kuala Lumpur of the prime ministers of Japan, Australia and New Zealand, who took part in post-summit discussions with their ASEAN counterparts. Of special significance was the presence of the Japanese prime minister, Takeo Fukuda, indicating a major Japanese reappraisal of ASEAN. The Kuala Lumpur Summit provided the opportunity for Japan to communicate its visible approval of ASEAN. Moreover, it inaugurated a wider process of institutionalized dialogue between ASEAN as a corporate entity and industrialized states which served to enhance the Association's international standing. The practice of wider dialogue was inaugurated in September 1977 with a meeting in Manila with a US delegation led by an under-secretary of state for economic affairs.
see also: ASEAN; Bali Summit 1976.

## Kuantan Statement 1980 (Indonesia/Malaysia)

At a meeting in March 1980 in the east coast town of Kuantan in peninsular Malaysia, the prime minister, **Datuk Hussein Onn**, and Indonesia's President **Suharto** issued a joint statement indicating concern over **ASEAN**'s policy of confronting Vietnam following its invasion and occupation of Cambodia in December 1978 in the third phase of the **Indochina**

**Wars**. A particular anxiety was the way in which that policy had arisen from Thailand's burgeoning association with the People's Republic of China, which both Indonesia and Malaysia regarded as a greater source of external threat than Vietnam. Moreover, they were disturbed at the penetration of South-East Asia by the Soviet Union and at the way in which the persistence of regional conflict over Cambodia had drawn in Sino-Soviet rivalry. Accordingly they issued a statement that envisaged Vietnam free of the influence of both China and the Soviet Union and which also took account of Vietnam's security interests in Indochina. That statement was virtually stillborn because the implicit acceptance of Vietnam's hegemonial role in Indochina was totally unacceptable to Thailand. The Thai prime minister, **Prem Tinsulanond**, made the matter a test of ASEAN's solidarity which his Malaysian and Indonesian partners did not wish to prejudice. It also proved unacceptable to Vietnam, because the statement failed to take account of the asymmetry in its relations with China and the Soviet Union. As a result, the Kuantan Statement was allowed to lapse. Nonetheless, it reflected long-standing interests by both Indonesia and Malaysia in persisting with the proposal to make South-East Asia a **ZOPFAN** (Zone of Peace, Freedom and Neutrality) promulgated by ASEAN's foreign ministers in the **Kuala Lumpur Declaration** of November 1971.
see also: ASEAN; Hussein Onn, Tun; Indochina Wars; Kuala Lumpur Declaration 1971; Prem Tinsulanond; Suharto; ZOPFAN.

## Kukrit Pramoj (Thailand)

Kukrit Pramoj was prime minister of Thailand between March 1975 and April 1976 during the democratic interlude after the student-inspired removal of the military regime in 1973. He led a minority government as head of the progressive **Social Action Party** (*Kit Sangkhom*). In January 1976 he dissolved the Parliament; in elections in April he lost his seat in a Bangkok constituency which contained a high proportion of military voters. Kukrit Pramoj was born in Bangkok on 20 April 1911 into a junior branch of the royal family and is the younger brother of the former prime minister, **Seni Pramoj**. He completed his higher education in England at the Queen's College, Oxford, and on his return to Thailand made an initial career in the Ministry of Finance. After the Pacific War, he became active in the **Democrat Party** and then made a reputation as the publisher of the newspaper *Siam Rath* (Thai State). After the fall of the military regime in 1973, he was instrumental in helping to form the liberal conservative Social Action Party, which remained a continuing factor in Thai politics after Kukrit ceased to be prime minister. He stayed in politics on losing high office but played only an elder statesman role, being especially critical of military inter-

vention and opposed to the unelected prime minister, **Prem Tinsulanond**, who initially took that position when army commander. He gave up the leadership of the Social Action Party in December 1985 to the foreign minister, **Siddhi Savetsila**, to retire from public life. He died on 9 October 1995 aged 84.

*see also:* Democrat Party; Prem Tinsulanond; Seni Pramoj; Siddhi Savetsila; Social Action Party.

**Kwam Wang Mai** (Thailand) *see* New Aspiration Party.

# L

## Laban ng Demokratikong Pilipino
(LDP) (Philippines)

*Laban ng Demokratikong Pilipino* (LDP), the Philippine Democratic Struggle, is a coalition of political groups, not a coherent party. Its origins lie in the formation in 1978 of *Lakas ng Bayan* (*Laban*), the People's Struggle Movement, by the late **Benigno Aquino**, while in detention. In 1983, after his assassination, *Laban* was merged with the *Partido Demokratiko Pilipino* (Philippine Democratic Party – PDP) as PDP-*Laban* by José Cojuangco, the younger brother of Mrs **Corazón Aquino**. It served as the vehicle for challenge to President **Ferdinand Marcos** by Mrs Aquino, who ran for election in February 1986 under its banner. After her success, it became the governing party but was joined in a wider coalition in June 1988 to become the LDP. The enlarged grouping began to fracture, as it was employed as an instrument for the presidential ambitions of the speaker of the House of Representatives, Ramon Mitra. The LDP secured seventeen seats in the Senate and eighty-nine seats in the House of Representatives in the legislative elections in May 1992, making it the largest party in the Congress. But with Ramon Mitra's failure in the concurrent race for president, it progressively lost sixty-four of its members through defection to *Lakas*-**NUCD**, the party of President **Fidel Ramos**. Fidel Ramos had himself left the LDP after it had failed to nominate him for the presidency. The party revived during 1994 as popular alienation with President Ramos over his taxation policy prompted political realignments in the Congress. The LDP then moved from opposition into a coalition with President Ramos' Lakas-NUCD to contest mid-term elections in May 1995. Success in that venture reinforced the congressional position of the LDP. In February 1996, the LDP broke with *Lakas*-NUCD, ostensibly over taxation policy but driven by the presidential aspirations of its leader in the Senate, Edgardo Angara. In October, it forced a change in the Senate presidency in order to pre-empt the tabling of a constitutional amendment, which would have permitted President Ramos to stand for a second term. In June 1997, however, the LDP merged with the **Struggle of the Nationalist Filipino Masses** (LMMP) headed by Vice-President **Joseph Estrada**, which served as the vehicle for his successful bid for presidential office in May 1998. Angara stood as the LMMP's unsuccessful candidate for vice-president but was appointed agriculture minister in the new administration.

*see also:* Aquino, Benigno; Aquino, Corazón; Estrada, Joseph; *Lakas*-NUCD; Marcos, Ferdinand; Ramos, Fidel; Struggle of the Nationalist Filipino Masses (LMMP).

## Lakas-NUCD (Philippines)

*Lakas*-NUCD is a mixed acronym for the ruling coalition in the Philippines during the incumbency of President **Fidel Ramos**. Lakas is the shortened form for *Lakas ng Edsa* (People's Power Party) which harks back to the overthrow of **Ferdinand Marcos** in 1986 (*see* **EDSA**; **People Power**), while NUCD stands for National Union of Christian Democrats. *Lakas* was formed in January 1992 as the vehicle for the presidential ambitions of the former defence minister, Fidel Ramos, who had left the **Laban ng Demokratikong Pilipino** (LDP) after he had failed to secure its nomination. It formed a partnership with the minor liberal-centre NUCD headed by Mrs **Corazón Aquino**'s foreign minister, **Raul Manglapus**. Fidel Ramos stood under its banner in May 1992 to win the presidential elections with 23.6 per cent of the vote. *Lakas*-NUCD failed to make much of a showing in the elections to the Congress. It subsequently attracted the largest number of members to its parliamentary ranks through defections from other parties but without any deep political loyalty. Opposition within the Congress was overcome through a pact with the LDP to contest mid-term elections in May 1995. Success in nine out of twelve seats in the Senate and in the House of Representatives enabled President Ramos to claim a fresh mandate for his economic reform programme, but *Lakas*-NUCD remained in a minority position in the Congress. That minority position was exposed again when its coalition with LDP broke up in February 1996. In December 1997, after the failure of his attempt to secure a second term, Fidel Ramos endorsed Jose de Venecia, speaker of the House of Representatives, as his party's preferred presidential candidate. In May 1998, Venecia polled badly well behind the successful **Joseph Estrada**. A significant consolation for *Lakas*-NUCD was the election of its candidate **Gloria Macapagal-Arroyo** to the office of vice-president. She was appointed to the portfolio of social welfare in the new cabinet. Her presidential prospects for 2004 have served to keep the party viable.

see also: Aquino, Corazón; Estrada, Joseph; Laban ng Demokratikong Pilipino; Macapagal-Arroyo, Gloria; Manglapus, Raul; Marcos, Ferdinand; Ramos, Fidel.

## Lam Son 719  (Laos/Vietnam)

Lam Son 719 was the codename for a military operation launched into eastern Laos from South Vietnam by forces of the Saigon government with US logistical support on 8 February 1971. The operation, whose name commemorated an historical triumph over China, had two purposes. The first was to interdict the **Ho Chi Minh Trail** to deny a Communist build-up of military supplies which could support a major offensive in South Vietnam in the United States election year of 1972. The second was to demonstrate the efficacy of **Vietnamization** and so make a virtue of necessity because the US Congress had prevented US ground troops from entering Laos and Cambodia. The military operation proved to be ill conceived and a major disaster. Some 30,000 inexperienced troops were deployed with US air support to seize the town of Tchepone, some twenty miles from the Vietnamese border. The heavily bombed target was reached only after the invading force had suffered heavy casualties, having been trapped by surrounding Communist units. By the end of the month, the operation had become a rout, with some survivors being brought out on the skids of US helicopters. The collapse of the operation was significant above all for the failure of Vietnamization, the policy of transferring the burden of fighting the **Vietnam War** from United States to South Vietnamese forces.

see also: Ho Chi Minh Trail; Vietnam War; Vietnamization.

## *Lanzin*  (Burma/Myanmar) *see* Burma Socialist Programme Party.

## Lao Dong  (Vietnam)

*Dang Lao Dong Viet Nam* (Vietnam Workers Party) was the name adopted by the Communist Party of Indochina in February 1951 when concurrently separate revolutionary parties were established for Laos and Cambodia, partly in order to accommodate nationalist feelings in the peninsula. The term *Lao Dong* continued to be employed by the party during the course of the **Vietnam War** against France and the United States. After formal unification of the country in July 1976, the title Communist Party of Vietnam was adopted in replacement at its fourth national congress in December that year. It incorporated also the People's Revolutionary Party which had been established in southern Vietnam in 1962 as a branch of the northern organization.

see also: Communism in South-East Asia; Indochina Wars; Provisional Revolutionary Government of the Republic of South Vietnam; Vietnam War.

## Lao Patriotic Front  (Laos) *see Neo Lao Hak Sat.*

## Lao People's Revolutionary Party  (Laos)

The Lao People's Revolutionary Party is the title adopted by the ruling Communist Party in Laos. It traces its origins in direct lineal descent to the Communist Party of Indochina set up by **Ho Chi Minh** in 1930 and has always modelled itself on its Vietnamese mentor. When the Communist Party of Indochina was dissolved in 1951, successor parties for the three Indochinese states were established but in the case of Laos it took the initial form of a committee for the preparation of the party. The Lao People's Party was subsequently set up in March 1955 as the clandestine core organization within the *Neo Lao Hak Sat* (Lao Patriotic Front) designed to attract popular support for the *Pathet Lao* (Lao Nation or State) revolutionary movement. At the second congress of the party in 1972, its name was changed to Lao People's Revolutionary Party, which was revealed after the Communists had consolidated their seizure of power in December 1975 and proclaimed the Lao People's Democratic Republic. The distinguishing feature of the party, apart from its monopoly political role, has been the continuity in high office of a limited number of members whose association dates from the initial struggle against French rule at the end of the Pacific War. **Kaysone Phomvihan** served as its leader from the formation of the Lao People's Party in 1955 until his death in November 1992. He was succeeded by **Khamtay Siphandon**, also a veteran party member, who had followed Kaysone as commander of the *Pathet Lao* armed forces and as prime minister in August 1991. In February 1998, he exchanged the office of prime minister for that of head of state, while continuing as party chairman.

*see also:* Ho Chi Minh; Kaysone Phomvihan; Khamtay Siphandon; *Neo Lao Hak Sat*; *Pathet Lao*.

## Le Duan  (Vietnam)

Le Duan held the office of general secretary of the Communist Party of Vietnam from September 1960 until his death in July 1986 and was its most important leader after the death of **Ho Chi Minh** in 1969. He was born in 1908 in Quang Tri Province, where his father was a railway clerk. Twenty years later, he joined Ho Chi Minh's revolutionary movement and in 1930 became a founding member of the Communist Party of Indochina. He spent ten of the next fifteen years in prison, including the period of the Pacific War. After his release in 1945, he assumed responsibility for organizing revolutionary activity in the south of the country where he remained until after the **Geneva Agreements on Indochina** in 1954. He was brought to Hanoi in 1957 to join the Politburo and after Ho Chi Minh's death presided effectively over a collective leadership and the revolutionary struggle which culminated in the unification of Vietnam in 1975. That success was followed by bitter years. Le Duan is believed to have been responsible for the dogmatic application of socialist economic doctrine as

well as implicated in the ill-fated military intervention into Cambodia which together brought Vietnam virtually to its knees. He was also identified with the country's alignment with the Soviet Union (the **Treaty of Friendship and Cooperation 1978**) which aggravated relations with the People's Republic of China. After he died in July 1986, he was succeeded initially by another reputed hardliner **Truong Chinh**. But in December, at the Communist Party's sixth national congress, Vietnam embarked on a radical reversal of the economic policy associated with his leadership, with **Nguyen Van Linh** appointed as a reformist general secretary.

*see also:* Geneva Agreements on Indochina 1954; Ho Chi Minh; Linh Nguyen Van; Treaty of Friendship and Cooperation 1978; Truong Chinh; Vietnam War.

## Le Duc Anh, General  (Vietnam)

General Le Duc Anh was president of the Socialist Republic of Vietnam between September 1992 and September 1997. On his election by the National Assembly, he was the second-ranking member of the Politburo of the ruling Communist Party, which indicated his national political standing. Le Duc Anh was born near the central Vietnamese city of Hue in 1920. He was a factory worker as a young man, joining the Communist Party in his late teens and then assuming a military career during the long period of armed struggle. He held the rank of Lt-General at the time of unification in 1975 and in 1980 became vice-minister of defence, having played a key role in the invasion of Cambodia. Le Duc Anh was admitted to the Politburo in 1981 and became full minister of defence in 1986. He assumed a special responsibility for managing relations with the People's Republic of China. He was the first senior party official to make an official visit to China after key changes in the leadership following the seventh national congress in June 1991. In November 1993 he was also the first president of Vietnam to visit China since **Ho Chi Minh** in 1959. His election as president was interpreted as an assurance to the party faithful that economic reform would not be allowed to infect the conservative communist political system.

*see also:* Ho Chi Minh; Vietnam War.

## Le Duc Tho  (Vietnam)

Le Duc Tho was a senior member of the Communist Party of Vietnam who is best known for his role in leading the negotiations for the **Paris Peace Agreements** which ended the United States' military intervention in the **Vietnam War** and also for turning down the joint award of the Nobel Peace Prize with Dr Henry Kissinger. He was born in Mam Ha Province on 14 October 1911, the son of an official in the French colonial administration. Inducted into the anti-French revolutionary movement as a teenager, he was a founder member of the Communist Party of Indochina and spent many years in the 1930s and early 1940s in French prisons. He was released in time to join **Ho Chi Minh** for the declaration of Vietnam's independence in Hanoi in September 1945 following the **August Revolution** and the beginning of military confrontation with France in the first of the **Indochina Wars**. By the early 1950s he had become a member of the Politburo of the Communist Party. In that capacity, he held a special responsibility for its southern branch and proved to be a guardian of ideological rectitude, especially after unification in 1975. He is believed to have been jointly responsible for Vietnam's decision to invade Cambodia in December 1978 and also for resisting the pace of economic reform intended to overcome the country's attendant international isolation. He was obliged to step down from the Politburo at the Communist Party's sixth national congress in December 1986 but continued to exercise political influence, supporting the position of his equally conservative younger brother Mai Chi Tho, who had become minister of the interior. His death at the age of 79 on 13 October 1990 is believed to have paved the way for a softening of Vietnam's position on Cambodia and a greater concentration on internal priorities.
*see also:* August Revolution 1945; Ho Chi Minh; Indochina Wars; Paris Peace Agreements 1973; Vietnam War.

## Le Kha Phieu, General  (Vietnam)

General Le Kha Phieu, then senior political commissar in the armed forces, was elected general secretary of the Communist Party of Vietnam in December 1997. He was born on 27 December 1931 in Thanh Hoa province. He joined the Communist Party in 1949 and took part in the military struggle against the French. He graduated from the military college and subsequently transferred into the army's political wing receiving his higher military education in the Soviet Union. He spent his army career as a political officer and saw service in Cambodia between 1984 and 1988. He was elected to the party's central committee in June 1991 and to its politburo in January 1994 joining its inner-core Standing Board in July 1996. He has been identified as a hard-line conservative with misgivings about the political implications of market-based economic reforms. However, he has held the middle-ground in the debate about their continued pace in the face of economic adversity during the late 1990s. He has also been publicly identified as a strong opponent of corruption.

## Lee Hsien Loong  (Singapore)

Lee Hsien Loong is one of Singapore's two deputy prime ministers having been appointed in November 1990 in the cabinet reshuffle after his father **Lee Kuan Yew** had stepped aside as prime minister in favour of **Goh Chok Tong**. He was then only 38, having enjoyed a meteoric rise in politics. Lee Hsien Loong was born on 10 February 1952 in Singapore and educated in England and the United States; in mathematics and computer sciences at the University of Cambridge and in public administration at Harvard University on scholarships awarded to him as a serving officer in Singapore's armed forces. His intellectual attainment at university was distinguished. In September 1984, shortly after having been promoted to the rank of brigadier general, he retired from military service and stood successfully as a parliamentary candidate for the ruling **People's Action Party** (PAP). Within two years, Lee Hsien Loong had become minister for trade and industry and had begun to acquire a reputation for administrative ability and also for an abrasive assertiveness in the style of his father. His position as heir apparent to Goh Chok Tong was placed in doubt with the announcement in November 1992 that he was suffering from cancer of the lymphatic system and that he was temporarily relinquishing his trade and industry portfolio. The next month, however, he was elected First assistant secretary-general of the ruling PAP when Goh Chok Tong succeeded Lee Kuan Yew as secretary-general. In December 1993, as part of a cabinet reshuffle, the prime minister, Goh Chok Tong, confirmed Lee Hsien Loong's position as sole deputy prime minister and also that he was in full remission from cancer. He was appointed to oversee the Ministry of Trade and Industry from January 1994 and from mid-1994 the Ministry of Defence, without holding either portfolio. The return to the cabinet in August 1995 of **Tony Tan** as deputy prime minister and as minister of defence revived speculation about his health and his political future. In the event, such speculation proved to be ill-founded. Lee Hsien Loong assumed a vigorous role in managing Singapore's response to economic crisis in the late 1990s. In December 1997, he was appointed chairman of its Monetary Authority. He had also begun to assume a more appropriate public persona for advancing his political career. *see also:* Goh Chok Tong; Lee Kuan Yew; People's Action Party; Tan, Tony.

## Lee Kuan Yew  (Singapore)

Lee Kuan Yew was prime minister of Singapore from June 1959 until November 1990, when he relinquished that office voluntarily. He has enjoyed an international reputation as a politician of singular intellectual ability and fearsome personality. His principal legacy is the remarkable economic achievement and environmental quality of Singapore, which under his leadership was transformed from a declining regional entrepôt into a renowned international centre for manufacturing, technology and financial services. As a politician, he has commanded more respect than affection, acting ruthlessly to crush dissent whenever it was deemed necessary. He has been guided by the conviction that Singapore is afflicted by an innate vulnerability and that its government's margin for error is minimal. He has been an unrepentant elitist believing in the virtues of good government and civic discipline, which in Singapore's case are said to require limiting western-style democracy.

Lee Kuan Yew was born in Singapore on 16 September 1923 to a Straits Chinese family. He received his secondary education at Raffles Institution. He was in his second year at Raffles College when his studies were interrupted by the outbreak of the Pacific War. During the Japanese occupation, he worked for a time as a cable editor for a propaganda agency. At the end of hostilities, he made himself useful to the returning British military authorities by procuring supplies and in return secured passage on a troopship to Britain where he had obtained a place to study law at the London School of Economics. Lee found postwar London a trying place and moved to Cambridge, where he studied law at Fitzwilliam House with great distinction. He completed his professional legal studies at the Middle Temple in London and became involved in the Malayan Forum, a political club comprising students from Malaya and Singapore who sought an early end to colonial rule.

On returning to Singapore, Lee entered legal practice and his skill as an advocate took him into politics through becoming an adviser to a number of radical trade unions subject to Communist influence. In November 1954 he played a leading role in founding the **People's Action Party** (PAP), a self-styled democratic socialist body committed to the political union of Singapore and Malaya. Lee Kuan Yew bid deliberately for the Chinese-educated vote in an island whose population was then more than three-quarters ethnic-Chinese and won election as one of three PAP members in 1955. He also skilfully played the anti-colonial card and secured support from the Communist Party of Malaya while fending off their control of the PAP, of which he was secretary-general. In May 1959 Lee led the PAP to an impressive victory at the polls, becoming in June prime minister of a self-governing but not fully independent Singapore. One of his early successes was to convince Malaya's prime minister, **Tunku Abdul Rahman**, of the urgency of proceeding with a political merger, albeit in a wider context incorporating British North Borneo. The terms of union for a Federation of Malaysia announced in 1961 provoked a split within the PAP, with a left-wing faction moving into opposition as the *Barisan Sosialis* (Socialist Front). Lee's government held on to office with the support of right-wing opponents and won the day pol-

itically through successfully managing a referendum on Singapore's entry into Malaysia. On
the formation of the new federation in September
1963, which had been opposed externally by
Indonesia, Lee led his truncated party to a second victory at the polls.

Singapore's membership of Malaysia was
short-lived. The island with its Chinese majority had been accepted into the new federation
only as a matter of political necessity. Tunku
Abdul Rahman pointedly described Singapore
as the New York of Malaysia by contrast with
Kuala Lumpur, which was represented as its
Washington. Lee Kuan Yew and the PAP did
not keep their political place, however. In April
1964 the PAP contested nine constituencies
in elections in mainland Malaya in a declared
attempt to attract the vote of the ethnic-Chinese
and secure a place in the federal cabinet. Although the PAP won only one seat, Lee Kuan
Yew continued to press his party's claim to be
more representative of the interests of the non-
Malays than the peninsular-Chinese **Alliance
Party** partners of the **UMNO** (United Malays
National Organization) led by Tunku Abdul
Rahman. His perceived headstrong approach,
including speeches in the federal legislature,
provoked racial tension which Tunku Abdul
Rahman decided could be contained only by
Singapore's separation from Malaysia, which
took place in August 1965. Lee's public expression of disappointment was tearful but he was
quick to recover and he and his cabinet colleagues demonstrated remarkable resoluteness
and resilience as they tackled the unanticipated
problem of governing an independent Singapore.

Deprived of a natural hinterland, Singapore
under Lee's leadership set out to extend national
economic horizons by transcending the island-
state's regional environment to make the world
its market-place. In that endeavour, his success
has been quite remarkable. Lee Kuan Yew has
been distinguished among politicians by always
thinking ahead, driven in Singapore's context
by an acute sense of the innate vulnerability of
the island because of its scale, locale, predominantly ethnic-Chinese identity and economic
role. He began to make provision for orderly
political succession early on by promoting a
second generation of leadership. Concern that

they were not steeled sufficiently in political
combativeness reinforced a natural intolerance
towards organized dissent expressed in the use
of the Internal Security Act, especially in the
late 1980s. When he gave up office as prime
minister, he remained in the cabinet as senior
minister and also held on for a time to the
post of secretary-general of the PAP. He over
shadowed his successor, **Goh Chok Tong**, early
on by chairing informal cabinet sessions and
by some of his public comments. However,
after his elder son and deputy prime minister
**Lee Hsien Loong** had been diagnosed as suffering from cancer of the lymphatic system,
he resigned as secretary general of the PAP
in favour of Goh Chok Tong and took more of
a political back-seat. Regionally within South-
East Asia, Lee Kuan Yew played an important
part in helping to consolidate the viability
of **ASEAN** (Association of South-East Asian
Nations). Initially suspicious of the Association
as an Indonesian vehicle for regional dominance,
he soon recognized its utility as a diplomatic
community which could protect Singapore's
interests through encouraging the habit of bureaucratic and ministerial consultation. More
widely in Asia, he has enjoyed the confidence
of governments both in Beijing and Taiwan and
after his retirement as prime minister travelled
on invitation to Vietnam, where his advice on
economic development has been eagerly sought.
As an international statesman, Singapore has
provided a limited base for Lee Kuan Yew's
talents. At one stage, he was talked of as a possible secretary-general of the United Nations
but the permanent members of the Security
Council were unenthusiastic about having
such a dynamic and cerebral figure in that
office. In his later years, Lee Kuan Yew has been
a vigorous advocate of authoritarian 'good government' as a visible alternative to the failings
of Western liberal democracy. In September
1998, on his seventy-fifth birthday, he published
the first volume of his memoirs dealing with
his life experience up to separation in 1965. Its
appearance served to aggravate relations with
Malaysia but Lee Kuan Yew was unperturbed
having pointed out in the preface that he thought
that the people of Singapore should understand
how vulnerable Singapore was and is.

*see also:* Alliance Party; ASEAN; *Barisan Sosialis*; Goh Chok Tong; Lee Hsien Loong; People's Action Party; Rahman, Tunku Abdul; UMNO.

## Liberal Party (Philippines)

The Liberal Party has held a marginal place in Philippine politics ever since President **Ferdinand Marcos** suspended the constitution and proclaimed martial law in 1972. Its political heyday was in the period immediately after the Pacific War when the defecting so-called 'Liberal Wing' of the long-dominant **Nacionalista Party** was employed as the vehicle for the electoral ambitions of **Manuel Roxas**. Roxas was elected president in April 1946 with evident United States backing under the banner of the Liberal Party. From that juncture until the introduction of martial law, the Liberal Party was one of the two principal national political constellations. There was nothing, however, to differentiate the Liberal and Nacionalista parties, which served as competing electoral and patronage machines for a national elite linked by family and provincial ties. The Liberal Party continued to hold the presidency under Elpidio Quirino in 1949, after Roxas had died from a heart attack. He was defeated in 1953 when **Ramón Magsaysay** defected to join the Nacionalistas, who held on to power after Magsaysay's death in a plane crash, when Carlos García won election in 1957. The Liberal Party recaptured the presidency in 1961 with **Diasdado Macapagal**, who was then defeated in 1965 by Ferdinand Marcos who had defected to the Nacionalista Party. The Liberal Party has never again held power. It was revived after **Corazón Aquino** became president but failed to make a significant impact because its association with an era of corrupt politics did not fit well with a new-found left-leaning nationalism. In May 1992 it was employed as the electoral vehicle for the presidential ambitions of Jovito Salonga but he secured only 10 per cent of the vote, which then led to defections from its congressional ranks as provincial politicians accommodated themselves to the regime of **Fidel Ramos**.

*see also:* Aquino, Corazón; Macapagal, Diasdado; Magsaysay, Ramón; Marcos, Ferdinand; Nacionalista Party; Ramos, Fidel; Roxas, Manuel.

## Lim Kit Siang (Malaysia)

Lim Kit Siang was the leader of the opposition **Democratic Action Party** (DAP) for over thirty years until his resignation in December 1999 following his failure to hold both state and federal seats in elections in the previous month. He had also been leader of the federal parliamentary opposition and in that role was the most vocal critic of the ruling *Barisan Nasional* (National Front) coalition. He was born on 20 February 1941 in Batu Pahat in the state of Johor. After finishing his secondary education in 1959, he worked as a temporary teacher and then as a journalist in Singapore. He returned to Malaysia after Singapore had been expelled from the Federation to work for the *Rocket*, the newspaper of the newly registered DAP. Lim Kit Siang was first elected to the federal Parliament for a Malacca constituency in May 1969 but was detained for almost a year and a half under the Internal Security Act after the **May 13 Racial Riots** that followed the elections. He returned to active politics after October 1970 and also stood successfully for the DAP for the Malacca state legislature. During the 1970s Lim Kit Siang found time to pursue a career as a lawyer, qualifying from Lincoln's Inn in London in 1977. He spent a second period in detention from October 1987, when the prime minister, Dr **Mahathir Mohamad**, seized the opportunity to detain a large number of political opponents in response to a rise in racial tension over the issue of Chinese education. He was made subject to a two-year detention order in December together with his son, Lim Guan Eng. In April 1989 Lim Kit Siang and his son became the last of 106 people detained without trial in October 1987 to be released. Lim Kit Siang has remained a forceful and resilient opponent of government, paying special attention to malpractice and abuses of power but with a limited audience because of the firm controls on media and press freedom in Malaysia. The humiliating defeat of the DAP in elections in April 1995 raised doubts about his political future. In June 1999, however, he took the DAP into the *Barisan Alternatif* (Alternative Front), an inter-racial electoral pact. In the elections in the following November, his party improved its federal position only marginally, while his personal political standing was diminished with his failure at the polls.

see also: *Barisan Alternatif; Barisan Nasional;* Democratic Action Party; Mahathir Mohamad, Datuk Sri; May 13 Racial Riots 1969.

## Lim Yew Hock  (Malaysia/Singapore)

Lim Yew Hock served as chief minister of Singapore between June 1956 and June 1959 before the colony acquired self-governing status. He was born in 1914 in Singapore and from a lowly occupation as a clerk moved into politics through the trade union movement. As secretary-general of the Singapore Clerical and Administrative Workers Union, he was nominated to the Legislative Council in 1948. As president of the Singapore Labour Party in 1949, he went on to form the Labour Front coalition to participate in elections to the more representative Legislative Assembly in 1955. He succeeded **David Marshall** as chief minister in June 1956 against a background of Communist-inspired political violence and went on to reach an understanding with the British government for Singapore's self-rule. His wider coalition, the Singapore People's Alliance, lost to **Lee Kuan Yew's People's Action Party** (PAP) in 1959 and Lim Yew Hock lost his parliamentary seat in elections in 1963. He moved to Kuala Lumpur under the patronage of Malaysia's prime minister, **Tunku Abdul Rahman**, and became high commissioner to Australia but was obliged to resign in embarrassing circumstances. Lim Yew Hock then converted to **Islam** and moved to Saudi Arabia as an official of the Islamic Conference, dying there in November 1984.

see also: Lee Kuan Yew; Marshall, David; People's Action Party; Rahman, Tunku Abdul.

## Limbang Claim  (Brunei/Malaysia)

Limbang is a tongue of territory under the jurisdiction of the Malaysian state of Sarawak in northern Borneo which interposes between the two enclaves of land that comprise the Sultanate of Brunei. Limbang had at one time been a constituent part of Brunei but had been annexed in March 1890 by Sarawak, then under the rule of Raja Charles Brooke. That final dismemberment of the once extensive Brunei state has long rankled its ruling royal family because it occurred

after British protection had been established in 1888. In the wake of some acrimony over Brunei's decision not to merge with Malaysia, Sultan Sir Omar Ali Saifuddin revived the claim to Limbang in the late 1960s. Although relations between Brunei and Malaysia improved substantially from the late 1970s and especially after the sultanate became independent and joined **ASEAN** (Association of South-East Asian Nations) in January 1984, the claim has not been withdrawn. In 1986 a meeting in Brunei between the current sultan, **Hassanal Bolkiah**, and Malaysia's prime minister, Dr **Mahathir Mohamad**, prompted press speculation about the retrocession of Limbang in return for financial compensation. In April 1994, a joint commission involving the foreign ministers of Brunei and Malaysia agreed to address the Limbang claim through bilateral dialogue and not through litigation but without making any headway towards resolving the dispute.

see also: ASEAN; Bolkiah, Hassanal; Mahathir Mohamad, Datuk Sri.

## Linh, Nguyen Van  (Vietnam)

Nguyen Van Linh held the office of general secretary of the Communist Party of Vietnam from its sixth national congress in December 1986 until its seventh national congress in June 1991. In that office, he was responsible for promoting the policy of *Doi Moi* (economic renovation) as well as initiating Vietnam's military withdrawal from Cambodia. His appointment to succeed **Truong Chinh** came as a surprise. Nguyen Van Linh had suffered politically in the late 1970s for his resistance to doctrinaire economic policies for southern Vietnam, losing his Politburo seat in 1982 as a consequence. Nguyen Van Linh was born in Hanoi on 1 July 1915 with the original name of Nguyen Van Cuc which was changed to avoid arrest by the South Vietnamese authorities after 1954. He grew up in the south of the country where he joined the revolutionary movement as a young man. He was imprisoned by the French and spent the Pacific War years in incarceration. After the war, he worked under party luminary **Le Duan**, rising to direct the Central Office for South Vietnam (COSVN) which was the headquarters for Communist revolutionary activity against the Saigon administration. After Vietnam's unification, he was made a member of the party's Politburo and headed its committee for Ho Chi Minh City (formerly Saigon). He fell out of political favour from the late 1970s for his objections to so-called socialist reconstruction in the south. Shortly after losing his Politburo seat, he was returned as party chief in Ho Chi Minh City and then extraordinarily reinstated to the Politburo in July 1985 without the sanction of a party congress when it had become evident that without economic reform, Vietnam faced a major crisis. In retirement, he was an outspoken critic of inefficiency and corruption. He died on 27 April 1998 aged 87.

*see also: Doi Moi*; Le Duan; Truong Chinh; Vietnam War.

## Loi Tack  (Malaya)

Loi Tack was general secretary of the Communist Party of Malaya between 1939 and 1947. He disappeared with its funds after having served as a prime source of intelligence for British Special Branch in Singapore. Although posing as a Chinese, he was born in Vietnam and had worked for French Intelligence in Indochina. British Special Branch had arranged for him to move to Singapore in the early 1930s ostensibly as a representative of the Comintern. He worked for the Japanese during the occupation and organized the liquidation of leading party members in an ambush in the Batu Caves outside of Kuala Lumpur in September 1942. After the war, he resumed his work for British Intelligence until he came under suspicion in March 1947, leaving first for Hong Kong and then on to Thailand, where he was assassinated, probably by a Communist hit-squad.
*see also:* Emergency 1948–60.

## Lon Nol  (Cambodia) *see* Nol, Lon.

## *Lubang Buaya*  (Indonesia) *see* Crocodile Hole.

## Luong, President Tran Duc  (Vietnam)

Tran Duc Loung was elected President of Vietnam in September 1997. He was born on 5 May 1937 in Quang Ngai Province. He trained as a geologist and also studied economic management in Moscow. He rose to the post of general director of the Mining and Geology General Department in 1982. He was then made an alternative member of the central committee of the Communist Party. He became a full member in 1986 and a deputy prime minister in the following year with industrial and technological responsibilities. He held that position until being elevated to presidential office but was elected to the party's politburo in 1996. Without military experience and a personal power base, he is regarded as a compromise choice for president without strong views either for or against economic reform.

# M

## Macapagal, Diasdado (Philippines)

Diasdado Macapagal was president of the Philippines for a single term between January 1961 and January 1965, having served for the previous four years as vice-president. He was born on 28 September 1910 into a peasant family in Pampanga Province and in his youth had ambitions to become an actor. A benefactor financed his legal education at Santo Tomas University in Manila, after which he went into a United States law firm. After the Pacific War he served in his country's foreign service where he developed an interest in reclaiming territory which had once been part of the domain of the Sultanate of Sulu and had then been incorporated into British North Borneo. He entered politics in 1949, winning a place in the House of Representatives on behalf of the **Liberal Party**. He established himself as a fine orator and was skilful at securing financial support for agriculture and rural health projects. In 1957 he was elected as vice-president to Carlos García from the **Nacionalista Party**, who treated him as a non-person. Macapagal exploited his humble origins and exposed governmental graft and corruption to succeed to highest office in 1961 aided by strong United States support. As president, he failed to make a real impact on fundamental economic and social ills, giving considerable attention to rousing nationalist feelings as a distraction. He changed the date of the anniversary of national independence from 4 July, when sovereignty had been transferred from the United States in 1946, to 12 June, when Emilio Aguinaldo had declared independence from Spain in 1898. He also prosecuted the **Philippines' Claim to Sabah** and in the process challenged the formation of Malaysia in the company of President **Sukarno**'s Indonesia (*see* **Confrontation**). As an alternative, he proposed the formation of a confederation called in acronym **Maphilindo** (comprising the first parts of the names of Malaya, the Philippines and Indonesia) but it foundered from the outset (*see* **Manila Agreements**). He was defeated in his attempt to retain office by **Ferdinand Marcos**, who had defected from the Liberal Party to the Nacionalista Party after Macapagal had reneged on a promise to stand down from the presidency after only one term. He died on 21 April 1997.

*see also:* Confrontation; Liberal Party; Manila Agreements 1963; Maphilindo; Marcos, Ferdinand; Nacionalista Party; Philippines' Claim to Sabah; Sukarno.

## Macapagal-Arroyo, Gloria (Philippines)

Gloria Macapagal-Arroyo was elected vice-president of the Philippines in May 1998 as running-mate of Jose de Venecia, the unsuccessful presidential candidate of the ruling *Lakas*-NUCD, with more than 50 per cent of the vote. She was then appointed secretary for social welfare and development by President **Joseph Estrada**. Gloria Macapagal-Arroyo was born in Manila on 5 April 1947 and is the daughter of the late president, **Diasdado Macapagal**. She was educated at the Ateneo de Manila and at Georgetown University in Washington, where she was a contemporary of President Bill Clinton. She returned home to take a doctorate in economics at the University of the Philippines after which she pursued an academic career. She was drawn to politics through her opposition to the late president, **Ferdinand Marcos**. After his overthrow in 1986, she received junior office in the government of President **Corazón Aquino**. She stood successfully for the Senate in June 1992, where she established a reputation for championing economic reform legislation. She also established her own party as a vehicle for pursuing presidential ambitions but judged such a bid premature and settled successfully for vice-presidential office. Given the constitutional limitation of one term on an incumbent president, she has become the front-runner to succeed President Estrada in elections in 2004. As a member of his administration, she has skilfully reconciled collective responsibility with her evident role as a focus of opposition to a president who has failed to live up to his populist promise.

see also: Aquino, Corazón; Estrada, Joseph; Macapagal, Diasdado; Marcos, Ferdinand.

## Madiun Revolt 1948 (Indonesia)

Madiun is a town in east Java where in late September 1948 armed clashes between dissident military units and forces loyal to the government of the revolutionary Republic of Indonesia escalated into an uprising on the part of the Communist Party of Indonesia. The uprising, which received retrospective endorsement from Moscow Radio, was crushed by the end of the month and the principal leaders of the party were killed. A factor in the uprising had been the disguised return to Indonesia in early August 1948 of Musso, the prewar Communist leader, who was believed to have been in exile in the Soviet Union. His return and resumption of party leadership encouraged the radical left-wing of the nationalist movement to challenge the policy of the Republican government of seeking independence from the Dutch by diplomacy rather than by armed struggle. They attracted support from irregular forces resentful of a programme of rationalization intended to ensure central military control as well as of the terms of an agreement with the Dutch reached in January 1948. In the event, Musso found himself drawn into an abortive physical challenge to the government of the republic at a time when it was still subject to acute menace from the Dutch. The Communist Party was accordingly discredited with its leadership eliminated, but the embryonic republic attracted favourable interest in Washington, where foreign policy had come to be dictated by Cold War priorities. Madiun marked a turning-point in Indonesia's national revolution, leaving not only a legacy of political bitterness but one of communal hatred. Armed confrontation in the villages around Madiun tended to correspond with a fundamental cultural- religious division in Java between observant Muslims (*Santri*) and those who combined a nominal observance of **Islam** with attachment to Hindu-**Buddhism** and mystical practices (*Abangan*). That division, with a repetition of bloodletting,

was revealed again after the abortive coup (see **Gestapu**) in Indonesia in October 1965. A notable party to and casualty of the uprising, besides Musso, was Amir Syarifuddin, a former socialist party prime minister, who was captured and executed in December 1948 by republican forces.

see also: *Abangan*; *Gestapu*; Islam; *Santri*.

## Magsaysay, Ramón (Philippines)

Ramón Magsaysay was president of the Philippines from January 1953 until his premature death in an air crash on 16 March 1957 on the island of Cebu. He was a man of considerable personal magnetism whose honesty and close affinity with the mass of the people as well as a reputation for having been instrumental in crushing the 'Huk' (**Hukbalahap Movement**) insurgency made him a national hero and then a martyr. Ramón Magsaysay was born in 1907 in Zimbales Province into a wealthy family of part Chinese descent. He was an indifferent student and became a bus mechanic before taking over the management of the bus company. During the Japanese occupation, he joined a US-led guerrilla group and at the end of the war was made provincial military governor. He stood successfully for Congress in 1946 and made a name for himself as a lobbyist in Washington on behalf of Filipino war veterans. This activity brought Magsaysay to the attention of Colonel Edward Landsdale of the US Central Intelligence Agency (CIA) who saw him as the ideal candidate to lead the fight against the Communist insurgency in the Philippines. Through Landsdale's intervention with the US State Department, President Elpidio Quirino was persuaded to appoint Magsaysay as secretary of national defence in August 1950. In that office, he became identified with land reform and clean elections and received the credit for the collapse of the insurgency which failed for a variety of reasons without any fundamental change to the Philippine pattern of land tenure. With United States funding and public relations support, Magsaysay won a landslide victory in contesting the presidency against the incumbent Quirino in 1953. This moment of glory was followed by several years of political anti-climax until his death as he never came to grips with fundamental problems of governance

and administration which required more than public relations for their solution.
*see also:* Hukbalahap Movement.

## Mahathir Mohamad, Dr Datuk Sri
(Malaysia)

Dr Mahathir Mohamad has held the office of prime minister of Malaysia since July 1981 on the retirement of **Tun Hussein Onn**. He has left his political mark on Malaysia as a strong testy-minded and successful leader determined to bend all independent institutions, such as the press and the judiciary, to his will. He has also assumed a strident role as a spokesman for post-colonial states revealing a deep resentment of British attitudes and policies. Mahathir Mohamad was born on 20 December 1925 in Alor Setar, Kedah. His father was a schoolteacher who had migrated from southern India. He qualified in medicine at the University of Malaya, then located in Singapore. Dr Mahathir entered politics in April 1964 as a Member of Parliament for **UMNO** (United Malays National Organization). He was expelled from the party in July 1969 after losing his seat in elections in May and then writing a bitterly critical letter to the prime minister, **Tunku Abdul Rahman**, accusing him of betraying the Malay community. In the political wilderness, he wrote a controversial book entitled *The Malay Dilemma*, which addressed the economic backwardness of the indigenous people. Dr Mahathir was re-admitted to UMNO after **Tun Abdul Razak** became prime minister. He was re-elected to parliament in August 1974 and then appointed minister of education. In March 1976, after Hussein Onn had succeeded Tun Razak as prime minister, he appointed Dr Mahathir as deputy prime minister. On assuming high office, Dr Mahathir sought to transform the national work ethic, encouraging his countrymen to look east to Japan for economic example. He led UMNO to resounding electoral victories in April 1982 and August 1986 but his strong-minded style of leadership together with scandal in public life provoked dissension within the party. In April 1987 he was challenged for UMNO's leadership by **Tengku Razaleigh Hamzah**, the minister for trade and industry, and retained office only by a narrow margin of forty-three votes. In

February 1988, after a High Court decision declaring UMNO to be an illegal organization because some of its branches were not validly registered, Dr Mahathir set up UMNO *Bahru* (New UMNO) with majority support in Parliament. Faced with a major political challenge by an alternative Malay party, *Semangat '46* (Spirit of 1946), headed by Tengku Razaleigh, he consolidated his leadership by taking UMNO to a further victory in general elections in October 1990, retaining a two-thirds majority for the *Barisan Nasional* (National Front) coalition in which UMNO was the dominant party. The political rise of his protege and finance minister, Anwar Ibrahim, who became deputy prime minister in December 1993, aroused speculation about his future. However, a resounding success in elections in April 1995, in which the ruling Barisan Nasional secured 162 seats in an enlarged federal Parliament of 192, registered Dr Mahathir's continuing dominance of Malaysian politics.

Although he announced in November 1995 that he would soon hand over office to Anwar, relations with his deputy and finance minister became uneasy, especially with the impact of economic crisis from late 1997. Differences over economic policy reinforced a growing personal rivalry. Matters came to a head after the political downfall of President Suharto of Indonesia when Dr Mahathir concluded that Anwar was trying to force him from office and that his historical reputation as a successful economic modernizer would be placed in jeopardy. In September 1998, Dr Mahathir dismissed Anwar from government office and also had him removed as deputy president and as a member of UMNO. He was then detained and charged with abuse of power in connection with allegations of sodomy on which he was subsequently tried and convicted. Anwar was sentenced to six years' imprisonment and Malaysian politics was thrown into turmoil. In the event, Dr Mahathir led the *Barisan Nasional* to an overwhelming federal electoral victory in November 1999. That outcome was mixed with major disappointment because of UMNO's poor showing in Malay constituencies to the advantage of *Parti Islam Se-Malaysia* (PAS), which also gained control of the state legislature in

Terengganu. On forming his new cabinet, Dr Mahathir announced that it would be his last term of office. He was re-elected president of UMNO unopposed in May 2000 and has devoted his energies to ensuring that his new deputy, **Abdullah Ahmad Badawi**, a long-standing political rival of Anwar's, succeeds him so as to ensure that he is not depicted in historical revision as a failed ageing leader. In his seventies, Dr Mahathir has sustained the combative qualities and authoritarian disposition which have distinguished his political style and career.

In foreign policy, Dr Mahathir gained attention during the early 1980s by denigrating the Commonwealth and by his **Buy British Last Policy**, prompted by a belief that the former colonial power had deliberately acted against Malaysia's interests. He enhanced Malaysia's standing with initiatives on international control of drugs and in promoting South-South cooperation and also took a strong stand on the Palestinian issue in which his anti-Zionism was at times difficult to distinguish from anti-semitism. He has enjoyed an uneasy position within **ASEAN** (Association of South-East Asian Nations), creating tension within the Association by his proposal for an **East Asian Economic Caucus** which was put forward publicly without consultation. His anger at US President Bill Clinton's neglect of his proposal led him to boycott an informal summit of Asian-Pacific leaders called by the president in Seattle in November 1993 at the end of an Asia-Pacific Economic Cooperation (APEC) ministerial meeting. In February 1994 Dr Mahathir announced that British firms would cease to be eligible to bid for Malaysian government contracts because of allegations in the British press of his financial impropriety. The ban, which was rescinded in September 1994, was a matter of some embarrassment to his ASEAN partners. Among South-East Asian leaders, Dr Mahathir has been prominent in arguing that China does not represent a threat to regional security, while the presence of the United States is unnecessarily intrusive.

*see also:* Anwar Ibrahim; ASEAN; Badawi, Abdullah Ahmad; Barisan Nasional;   Buy British Last Policy; Constitutional Crises; East Asian Economic Caucus; Hussein Onn, Tun; *Parti Islam*; Rahman, Tunku Abdul; Razak, Tun Abdul; Razaleigh Hamzah, Tengku; UMNO; Yang di-Pertuan Agong.

## Malacca Strait (Indonesia/Malaysia/ Singapore)

The Malacca Strait is located between the eastern coast of the Indonesian island of Sumatra and the western coasts of Thailand and peninsular Malaysia. It extends for more than 500 miles to join up with the **Singapore Strait**, which is located south of the island-republic and the south-eastern tip of peninsular Malaysia and north of Indonesia's Riau Islands. Together the linked straits extend for some 600 miles and have provided the shortest and most important maritime passage between the Indian and Pacific Oceans since the Suez Canal was opened in 1869 (*see* **Sunda Strait**). The straits are constricted and heavily congested and had experienced a number of serious collisions and groundings involving oil tankers before a traffic separation scheme was instituted in 1977. Close to where the Malacca and Singapore straits merge, the land width narrows to 3.2 miles and the navigable channel reduces to 1.8 miles. Indonesia had extended the breadth of its territorial waters to 12 miles in a historic **Archipelago Declaration** in December 1957 (subsequently enacted in law in February 1960) so extending its jurisdiction in the Malacca Strait. In August 1969 Malaysia followed suit. On 17 March 1970 a treaty was concluded which delimited the territorial sea boundary between Indonesia and Malaysia in the Malacca Strait, south of One Fathom Bank, reflecting the improved bilateral relationship since the end of **Confrontation**. Maritime cooperation continued with both safety of navigation and security in mind. On 16 November 1971, in response to a Japanese attempt to institutionalize international responsibility for safety of navigation through the linked straits, the governments of Indonesia, Malaysia and Singapore issued a dissenting joint declaration. That declaration maintained that safety of navigation was the exclusive responsibility of the three coastal states. Controversy arose from a part of the statement, to which Singapore only took note, by which Indonesia and Malaysia challenged the customary legal status of passage through the linked straits. This attempt to substitute a regime of innocent for that of free passage was resolved ultimately during the course of the Third United Nations Conference on the Law of the Sea and embodied in the Convention promulgated on 10 December 1982. In that Convention, the linked straits of Malacca and Singapore were to be encompassed by a new regime of transit passage applying to all straits used for international navigation. As a preliminary to this accord, the three coastal states had come to an agreement on 24 February 1977 on provision for safety of navigation incorporating a traffic separation scheme which received international recognition. However, by the early 1990s, a series of collisions in the Malacca Strait with loss of life and spillage of oil had led to calls by Malaysia and Indonesia that the self-policing traffic separation scheme should be replaced by a new regime corresponding to that employed in trans-oceanic canals. An additional hazard to navigation, life and property has been the growing incidence of piracy.

see also: Archipelago Declaration 1957; Singapore Strait; Sunda Strait.

## Malari Affair 1974 (Indonesia)

On 15 January 1974 serious rioting broke out in Jakarta during a visit by Japan's prime minister, Kakuei Tanaka, which cast doubt on the stability of the government of President **Suharto**. The episode came to be described in Indonesian as *Malapetaka Januari* (January Disaster) and in Indonesian acronym as *Malari*. The Japanese prime minister's visit provided the occasion for public disturbances against a background of growing criticism of Japanese investment and the government's approach to development based on foreign capital and the role of the local Chinese community. The riots were consequently represented as an organized attempt by civilian opponents of the military-based administration to overthrow it, especially those connected with the Socialist Party, which had been banned by President **Sukarno** in 1960. Trials of student leaders and civilian critics were informed by this charge as was proscription of critical newspapers. That charge was, in effect, grossly mis-

leading because *Malari* had been precipitated by a faction fight within the armed forces. Tension obtained in particular between a small group of personal military assistants to President Suharto who performed financial and political services and a number of senior officers in active professional posts. The most prominent of the personal assistants (known as *Aspri*) was Major-General **Ali Murtopo**; his principal professional rival was General Sumitro, the deputy commander of the armed forces and commander of the internal security organization *KOPKAMTIB* (Operational Command for the Restoration of Order). Intra-elite jostling for President Suharto's political favour and possibly for succession took place against a background of growing popular agitation on the part of both Muslim and student groups exercised by a controversial marriage law and the fall of the military regime in Thailand in October 1973. In the weeks before the visit to Jakarta by Kakuei Tanaka, General Sumitro had adopted a conciliatory approach to Muslim and student agitation, giving the impression that he was mobilizing these groups against his *Aspri* rivals. In the event, protest got out of hand, probably exploited by General Sumitro's rivals, with Jakarta's slum dwellers looting and burning Japanese and local Chinese property. The riot was put down with eleven people shot dead. In its wake, General Sumitro was replaced as commander of *KOPKAMTIB* and then resigned as deputy commander of the armed forces, while his close military allies were moved to nominal positions. The *Aspri* were officially disbanded but Ali Murtopo was subsequently promoted to Lt-General and became deputy head of *Bakin*, the body responsible for military intelligence. The intra-elite struggle was resolved to the apparent advantage of President Suharto's political fixers and certainly in his own interest.

see also: KOPKAMTIB; Murtopo, Ali; Suharto; Sukarno.

## Malayan Democratic Union (Malaya/Singapore)

The Malayan Democratic Union was a radical left-wing party established in Singapore in December 1946 by middle-class English-educated non-Malays who were opposed to Britain's

**Malayan Union Proposal** from which the island colony had been excluded. After Britain withdrew that controversial proposal, the Malayan Democratic Union become the core of a wider left-wing united front which challenged unsuccessfully a subsequent proposal for a Federation of Malaya also excluding Singapore. Its members disbanded in June 1948, within weeks of the declaration of a state of **Emergency** to cope with the Communist insurrection.

see also: All-Malaya Council of Joint Action; Emergency 1948–60; Malayan Union Proposal 1946.

## Malayan Union Proposal 1946
(Malaya)

The Malayan Union was an abortive scheme for constitutional change in Malaya promulgated by Britain on 1 April 1946. Restricted territorially to the Malay peninsula (that is including Penang but excluding Singapore), it entailed transferring the formal sovereignty of the sultans or rulers of the Malay states to the British Crown and establishing a common citizenship to the advantage of Chinese and Indian residents of migrant origin. The initial objectives were political integration of a plural society and the rationalization of colonial administration within a unitary form of government. However, the coercive manner in which the rulers were relieved of sovereign status confirmed for the indigenous Malays that their political birthright was at serious risk. The scheme provoked an unprecedented expression of Malay nationalism but not a demand for independence from colonial rule, given the growing threat from the predominantly ethnic-Chinese Communist Party of Malaya. In March 1946 a Pan Malayan Malay Congress was convened in Kuala Lumpur in a protest which led on to the formation in May of **UMNO** (United Malays National Organization), the first effective Malay political party. Led by Dato Onn bin Ja'afar, a senior civil servant from Johor, it campaigned successfully for the Malayan Union to be rescinded, touching a British political nerve at the prospect of mass violence of the kind in train in neighbouring Indonesia. The Malayan Union was set aside on 25 July 1946 in favour of a Federation of Malaya under colonial aegis with the position

of the rulers restored and citizenship made more difficult for non-Malays to acquire. Sovereignty was transferred ultimately to an independent Federation of Malaya (still excluding Singapore) on 31 August 1957.

see also: Malayan Democratic Union; UMNO.

## Malaysian Chinese Association (MCA)
(Malaya/Malaysia)

The Malaysian Chinese Association (MCA) was established originally in 1949 as the Malayan Chinese Association, ostensibly as a welfare organization in an attempt to counter the appeal of Communist insurgency among the Chinese community. In February 1952 its Selangor branch took a historic political initiative by entering into an electoral pact with the local branch of **UMNO** (United Malays National Organization) in contesting municipal elections in Kuala Lumpur. Success in this enterprise paved the way for an intercommunal partnership with UMNO and the Malayan (subsequently **Malaysian**) **Indian Congress** (MIC) in federal elections in July 1955. This intercommunal **Alliance Party** provided the political model for a ruling coalition which has been continuously in power since before independence.

The MCA has always occupied the role of principal communal partner of UMNO within the ruling coalition which in the early 1970s became known as the *Barisan Nasional* (National Front). That position has never reflected its true standing within the Chinese community. The MCA has been primarily identified with a wealthy elite prominent within Chinese chambers of commerce who have been content to appease Malay political partners in a narrow economic interest. As such, it has found it difficult to command a majority of the Chinese vote in competition with the opposition **Democratic Action Party** (DAP), which attracts lower-income support. The MCA has always suffered from never having been able to satisfy adequately its senior political partner and its communal constituency at the same time. A humiliating electoral failure in May 1969 was a factor in a political crisis brought to a head by the **May 13 Racial Riots**. In its wake, and with the introduction of a **New Economic Policy** designed to revise the balance of advantage in the Malay interest, the MCA was downgraded as a political partner. While it had to give up key economic portfolios in cabinet, the primarily Chinese-based *Gerakan Ra'ayat Malaysia* (Malaysian People's Movement) was brought into the ruling coalition. The problem for the MCA from that juncture has been that the more its leaders have attempted to cultivate the separate interests of the Chinese community, the greater the political alienation exhibited by UMNO. For example, after a period of internal factionalism, an attempt to take up the emotive issue of Chinese education led in October 1987 to the detention of eight party members. The MCA has survived politically because its place in politics and government serves UMNO's interests and also because Malaysia has prospered since the mid-1970s. The New Economic Policy has caused alien-ation among the Chinese community but they have also shared in the fruits of development. During the 1980s, the MCA did little more than hold its own politically, however, because of the contradiction in representing Chinese interests, while at the same time subordinating those interests to Malay priorities. In national elections in October 1990, the MCA marginally improved its position by winning 18 seats in the 180-member federal Parliament compared to 17 seats in 1986 in a 177-member chamber. In April 1995, however, it made a major political break-through in securing a majority of Chinese votes at the expense of the Democratic Action Party. The MCA won thirty seats out of thirty-four contested in the federal Parliament, its best ever electoral performance. The number was reduced to twenty-nine in elections in November 1999. However, the MCA has never recovered its pre-1969 role in government. After the November 1999 elections, its representatives held four lesser portfolios in a cabinet of twenty-eight members. In May 2000, however, its leader and transport minister, Dr Ling Liong Sik, threatened to resign from the cabinet in an apparent protest at the limited MCA representation after it had helped the *Barisan Nasional* to retain its two-thirds federal parliamentary majority.

see also: Alliance Party; *Barisan Nasional*; Democratic Action Party; Emergency 1948-60; *Gerakan Ra'ayat Malaysia*; Malaysian Indian Congress; May 13 Racial Riots 1969; New Economic Policy; UMNO.

## Malaysian Indian Congress (MIC)
(Malaya/Malaysia)

The Malaysian Indian Congress (MIC), fomerly the Malayan Indian Congress, is one of the core communal components of the *Barisan Nasional* (National Front) ruling coalition. The MIC was founded in 1946 to represent peninsular Malayan residents of sub-continental origin. Its initial orientation was as much Indian as Malayan with the name taken from the Indian National Congress. A leftist disposition was discarded with the onset of the **Emergency** in 1948. After the success of Malay-Chinese political cooperation in municipal elections in Kuala Lumpur in 1952, the MIC participated within the tripartite inter-communal **Alliance Party**, which won every seat but one in national elections the following year. The MIC has always been the most junior partner in this successful governing relationship, which was carried over with the formation of the Federation of Malaysia in 1963 and then in the wider *Barisan Nasional* in the early 1970s. Indians comprise only around 11 per cent of the population of peninsular Malaysia and their geographic distribution means that they command very few natural constituencies, leaving the MIC to secure representation through receiving a small quota of state and federal seats as well as minimal representation in the cabinet. Indian political clout is limited also because of Hindu-Muslim divisions and because Indian rural workers in the rubber industry have never felt that their interests have been represented by the small group of business people and professionals of Tamil origin who have always dominated the MIC. In federal elections in April 1995, it won all seven seats contested. The same number of seats were retained in elections in November 1999. Its sole cabinet representative holds the works portfolio.

see also: Alliance Party; *Barisan Nasional*; Emergency 1948–60; Malaysian Chinese Association; UMNO.

## Malik, Adam  (Indonesia)

Adam Malik served continuously with distinction as foreign minister of Indonesia from March

1966 to May 1977. He was appointed by General **Suharto**, who had assumed executive authority in the wake of an abortive coup (*see* ***Gestapu***) in October 1965 which politically discredited President **Sukarno**. Adam Malik played a key role in the regional and international rehabilitation of Indonesia after an assertive and exhibitionist phase of foreign policy. He was instrumental in promoting reconciliation with Malaysia and in helping to found **ASEAN** (Association of South-East Asian Nations) as well as repairing economic relations with western states. Indonesia's reintegration into international society was registered by his election as president of the United Nations General Assembly in September 1971. Adam Malik was born on 22 July 1917 in Pematang Siantar in northern Sumatra. He combined an early interest in nationalism with that of journalism; at the age of 20 he founded the Antara press agency which after independence became the national news agency. At the end of the Pacific War, Adam Malik was a leading member of a group of young radical nationalists who wished to wrest independence from Japan rather than acquire it under their auspices. During the period of national revolution, he became involved in a plot against the socialist prime minister, **Sutan Syahrir**, and was imprisoned until late 1948. His radical record prevented Adam Malik from playing a political role during the period of parliamentary democracy in the 1950s. Shortly after President Sukarno had instituted his system of **Guided Democracy** in July 1959, he was sent as ambassador to the Soviet Union, which proved to be a disillusioning experience. In November 1963 he was appointed minister of trade but became progressively alienated from the Sukarno regime. He was an appropriate civilian choice for foreign minister in the military-dominated administration which replaced that of President Sukarno. Indeed, he ensured that Indonesia's conduct of foreign policy reflected an independent tradition and was not merely a crude expression of military priorities. After serving as foreign minister for eleven years, Adam Malik became briefly speaker of the country's **People's Consultative Assembly** and then in March 1978 was elected vice-president of the republic. He retired from public life in March 1983 and died on 5 September 1984.

*see also:* ASEAN; Crocodile Hole; *Gestapu*; Guided Democracy; People's Consultative Assembly; Suharto; Sukarno; Syahrir, Sutan.

## Manglapus, Raul (Philippines)

Raul Manglapus served as secretary for foreign affairs from October 1987 until June 1992. He was appointed by President **Corazón Aquino** following the disaffection of vice-president Laurel, who resigned the foreign affairs portfolio. Raul Manglapus assumed prime responsibility for trying to negotiate satisfactory terms for a continuing US military presence. He was thwarted by the Philippines Senate, which in September 1991 rejected the bilateral accord extending the United States' tenure. Raul Manglapus was born in Manila on 20 October 1918 and trained in law at the universities of Santo Tomas and Georgetown. He spent part of the Japanese occupation in prison, after which he became a teacher of constitutional law. For three years from 1954, he served as an undersecretary for foreign affairs and then briefly held full responsibility for the portfolio. As a politician, he sought to find an alternative to the mirror images of the **Nacionalista Party** and **Liberal Party**. He was instrumental in founding in 1957 the Party for Philippine Progress, which became the Grand Alliance Party two years later but then merged with the Liberal Party in 1961. He was elected to the Senate in 1961 where he served until 1967. He became an active member of the Philippine Constitutional Convention from 1970 and when President **Ferdinand Marcos** declared martial law in September 1972, Raul Manglapus found political asylum in the United States. Until President Marcos went into exile in February 1986, Raul Manglapus held a series of temporary academic appointments. During this period, he became resentful of US administrations which had tolerated the tyranny of President Marcos for reasons of strategic interest, such as the **Clark Air Base** and **Subic Bay Naval Base**, for nearly a decade and a half. On his return to the Philippines, Raul Manglapus was elected to the Senate, where he displayed an anti-American disposition before his appointment by President Aquino to the foreign affairs portfolio, which lent considerable irony to his main responsibility and abortive purpose. He died on 25 July 1999.

*see also:* Aquino, Corazón; Clark Air Base; Liberal Party; Marcos, Ferdinand; Nacionalista Party; Subic Bay Naval Base.

## Manila Agreements 1963 (Indonesia/Malaya/Philippines)

At the end of July 1963, Prime Minister **Tunku Abdul Rahman** of Malaya, President **Diasdado Macapagal** of the Philippines and President **Sukarno** of Indonesia met in Manila in an attempt to resolve strong differences over the impending establishment of the Federation of Malaysia to include Malaya, Singapore and two British Borneo territories. The immediate outcome was a set of agreements which addressed the advent of Malaysia and also the management of regional order in South-East Asia but which failed to survive the eventual establishment of Malaysia on 16 September 1963. A preliminary meeting of ministers in Manila in early June had worked out the general terms of an accord for subsequent discussion between the heads of government. In that accord, the governments of Indonesia and the Philippines stated that they would welcome the formation of Malaysia, provided that the support of the people of the Borneo territories was ascertained by an independent and impartial authority - the secretary-general of the United Nations or his representative. In addition, the government of the Philippines reserved its position on the inclusion of Sabah (British North Borneo) within Malaysia subject to the outcome of its territorial claim which had been formally presented in 1962. On 9 July, however, representatives of Britain, Malaya, Singapore and the Borneo territories reached a final agreement in London on terms for the formation of Malaysia, whose inauguration was set for 31 August. The Manila summit was placed in immediate jeopardy with President Sukarno accusing Malaya's prime minister of a breach of faith as well as renewing his open opposition to the new federation. The meeting went ahead at the end of July, nonetheless, because Sukarno believed he would be able to frustrate Malaysia's formation. It was marked by hard bargaining over the terms of the preliminary ministerial accord but in the event the three leaders agreed that a United Nations mission should make a determination of opinion in Borneo rather than conduct a formal plebiscite. A proposal by President Macapagal for a confederation of nations of Malay origin was endorsed together with initial steps towards its establishment through an association of the three states described in acronym as **Maphilindo**. In addition, a statement on regional security identified the primary responsibility of regional states and also committed the three heads of government, in principle, to removing foreign military bases. That section of the Manila Agreements which addressed the advent of Malaysia was implemented but failed to resolve the differences between the three governments. When it became known that the United Nations mission would not be able to complete its work before the date set initially for the inauguration of Malaysia (i.e. 31 August 1963), the Malayan government set an alternative date. Justifying its action on legal grounds and on advice that the findings of the United Nations mission would be made known by 14 September, it annouced that, irrespective of those findings, the new federation would be established on 16 September. Both Indonesian and Filipino reaction was muted. The UN secretary-general published his report on 14 September and found in favour of Malaysia, while indicating displeasure that the new date for its inauguration had been announced before his conclusions had been reached and made known. That pointed admonition then served as the basis for both Indonesia and the Philippines to refuse to recognize the new federation, which prompted a rupture of diplomatic relations between Kuala Lumpur, on the one hand, and Jakarta and Manila, on the other. The Maphilindo enterprise failed to take institutional form.

*see also:* Confrontation; Macapagal, Diasdado; Maphilindo; Philippines' Claim to Sabah; Rahman, Tunku Abdul; Sukarno.

## Manila Pact 1954 (Cambodia/Laos/Philippines/Thailand/Vietnam)

The South-East Asia Collective Defence Treaty, known as the Manila Pact, was concluded in Manila on 8 September 1954 between the governments of the United States, Britain, France, Australia, New Zealand, Pakistan, Thailand and the Philippines. The alliance was inspired by the United States, whose secretary of state, John Foster Dulles, had failed to mobilize united action in April 1954 to prevent the Vietnamese Communist victory at the **Battle of Dien Bien Phu**. As part of a global policy of containing international communism, the alliance was directed at the People's Republic of China and North Vietnam and designed to shore up the provisional territorial settlement reached in the **Geneva Agreements on Indochina** in July 1954. That settlement had divided Vietnam temporarily along the line of the 17th parallel of latitude and had recognized the independence of Laos and Cambodia. The obligations of the signatories of the Manila Pact to act under the central Article IV was extended through a separate protocol to 'the states of Cambodia and Laos and the free territory under the jurisdiction of the State of Vietnam'. The treaty took an institutionalized form from February 1955 when its council meeting in Bangkok approved the establishment of **SEATO** (South-East Asia Treaty Organization) with headquarters in the Thai capital.

The alliance, which required unanimity for common action, was never effective because its members differed over security priorities from the outset. Only two of them were resident regional states. The Cambodian leader, Prince **Norodom Sihanouk**, repudiated the protection of the treaty in February 1956, while Laos was excluded from it in July 1962 under the terms of a neutralization agreement (see **Geneva Agreements on Laos**). South Vietnam never made an explicit appeal for assistance under the protocol. In March 1962 in a joint statement by Thailand's foreign minister, **Thanat Khoman**, and the US secretary of state, Dean Rusk, the latter asserted that his country's obligation did not depend upon the prior agreement of all other parties to the treaty since that obligation was individual as well as collective. However, the most that the alliance ever managed was a limited show of force in Thailand in May 1962 by some of its members in response to a crisis in Laos. Pakistan had become alienated early on because of a failure to attract support against India. France openly opposed the United States' military intervention in Vietnam, while Britain withheld military cooperation, announcing

disengagement from east of Suez initially in July 1967. Apart from the United States, of the original signatories only Australia, New Zealand, the Philippines and Thailand dispatched troops to Vietnam, but not collectively under the terms of the Manila Pact. The alliance lost its original *raison d'être* after US President Richard Nixon's historic visit to Beijing in February 1972, which confirmed Sino-US rapprochement.

A truncated Pakistan withdrew from the alliance in November 1972, following the secession of Bangladesh at the end of 1971. A Council meeting in September 1973, in the wake of the **Paris Peace Agreements** on Vietnam in January 1973, abolished the military structure of SEATO from February 1974. After Communist victories in Cambodia and South Vietnam in April 1975, Thailand's prime minister, **Kukrit Pramoj**, and Philippine's President **Ferdinand Marcos** agreed informally to abolish SEATO during a meeting in Manila in July. That agreement was confirmed at a Council meeting in New York in September 1975 when it was decided that SEATO would be dissolved completely on 30 June 1977. The Collective Defence Treaty has never been revoked, however, primarily because it provides the only formal defence link between Thailand and the United States. In February 1979, following Vietnam's invasion of Cambodia, the US President Jimmy Carter reaffirmed to Thailand's prime minister, **Kriangsak Chomanan**, the validity of the United States' commitment to his country under the Manila Pact. US defence cooperation with Thailand has been sustained but the Collective Defence Treaty survives only as a redundant vestige of the Cold War in Asia.

see also: Dien Bien Phu, Battle of, 1954; Geneva Agreements on Indochina 1954; Geneva Agreements on Laos 1962; Kriangsak Chomanan; Kukrit Pramoj; Marcos, Ferdinand; Paris Peace Agreements 1973; SEATO; Sihanouk, Norodom; Thanat Khoman.

## Manila Summit (ASEAN) 1987
(Brunei/Indonesia/Malaysia/Philippines /Singapore/Thailand)
In December 1987 the six heads of government of **ASEAN** (Association of South-East Asian Nations) met for two days in Manila. It was only

the third such meeting in its history: the first was the **Bali Summit** in February 1976 and the second was the **Kuala Lumpur Summit** in August 1977. The Manila Summit was held amid tight security because of the series of abortive coups mounted against the administration of President **Corazón Aquino**, which had replaced that of **Ferdinand Marcos** in Febraury 1986. The meeting was not significant for any initiatives in political or economic cooperation. Nor did it lead to reconciliation between the Philippines and Malaysia over the **Philippines' Claim to Sabah**. The fleeting gathering was intended, above all, as a display of corporate solidarity for President Aquino's embattled administration on the understanding that failure to have so acted would have reflected adversely on the credibility of ASEAN.

*see also:* Aquino, Corazón; Bali Summit 1976; Kuala Lumpur Summit 1977; Philippines' Claim to Sabah.

## Maphilindo (Indonesia/Malaya/Philippines)

Maphilindo is an acronym taken from the first parts of Malaya, the Philippines and Indonesia which was coined by Indonesia's foreign minister, Dr **Subandrio** in June 1963. The term had its origins in regional contention (**Confrontation**) over the proposal for a Federation of Malaysia with Malaya as its political core. Both Indonesia and the Philippines objected, the latter because of its claim to part of northern Borneo included in the proposal (*see* **Philippines' Claim to Sabah**). As a blocking alternative, the Philippines' president, **Diasdado Macapagal**, advanced a plan for a confederation of nations of Malay origin predicated implicitly on a common anti-Chinese sentiment. At a meeting of senior ministers from the three states, which convened in Manila in June 1963, Dr Subandrio supported the Maphilindo scheme as a flattering gesture to the Philippine president. Malaya's deputy prime minister, **Tun Abdul Razak**, endorsed the concept in an attempt to encourage Indonesia and the Philippines to accept Malaysia. A meeting of heads of government followed at the end of July which upheld the scheme but apparent reconciliation did not last. Maphilindo foundered with the advent of Malaysia on 16 September 1963. Neither Indonesia nor the Philippines accorded recognition to the expanded state and diplomatic relations were broken between the government of Kuala Lumpur and those in Jakarta and Manila. Maphilindo never progressed beyond its declaratory establishment and failed to assume any institutional form.

*see also:* Confrontation; Macapagal, Diasdado; Manila Agreements 1963; Philippines' Claim to Sabah; Razak, Tun Abdul; Sub-andrio.

## Marcos, Ferdinand (Philippines)

Ferdinand Marcos was the most powerful political figure in the post-independence history of the Philippines. He held the office of president from January 1966 until February 1986. Ferdinand Edralin Marcos was born on 17 September 1917 in Ilocos Norte Province on the main island of Luzón. He came to national prominence when he was placed first in the bar finals after sitting the examinations in prison, prior to a successful appeal against a conviction for murdering a political rival of his father. After the Pacific War and national independence, his career was advanced by his claim to have been a distinguished guerrilla war commander. He entered politics in 1949, moving from the House of Representatives to the Senate in 1959. He was elected president in November 1965 and re-elected in November 1968. In the face of rising political dissension and a constitutional impediment to a third term of office, Marcos declared martial law in September 1972. The break with constitutional legality was welcomed initially as a brave attempt to regenerate political and economic life. Within a decade, the promise of Marcos's **New Society Movement** had turned sour. Personal abuse of power undermined all independent institutions, while his family and business circle accumulated great wealth through corrupt practice. His wife **Imelda Marcos** attracted fierce animosity for her regal pretensions. Against a background of economic decline and burgeoning Communist insurgency, his personal authority crumbled visibly from August 1983 when his principal political rival, **Benigno Aquino**, was shot dead while in military custody at Manila airport on his return from exile in the United States. Unable to throw off the stigma of Aquino's assassination, stricken by illness and unable to reverse economic failure, Marcos gambled on re-establishing his political authority through holding a snap election in February 1986. The opposition closed ranks around the popular widow of his assassinated rival, Mrs **Corazón Aquino**. Conspicuous electoral fraud, a military revolt led by the minister of defence, **Juan Ponce Enrile**, and the deputy chief of staff of the armed forces, **Fidel Ramos**, together with a massive display of popular support (**People Power**) for Mrs Aquino backed by Cardinal **Jaime Sin** and the Catholic Church, persuaded the US government to advise Marcos to leave the country. He was flown with his family via Guam to Hawaii where he remained in exile. After inspiring a number of feckless abortive attempts to promote a coup against Mrs Aquino's government, recurrent ill-health (and the warning of his host government) reduced him to a pathetic figure. He was refused permission to return to the Philippines and died in Hawaii on 28 September 1989. It was not until four years later that his family was granted permission by the government of President Fidel Ramos for his remains to be returned to be entombed in a mausoleum in his home town of Batac in the Ilocos region of Luzón. His persisting ill-repute was demonstrated in June 1998, when president-elect **Estrada** revealed that he would permit Marcos's body to be buried in the country's Heroes Cemetery in Manila. The display of public outrage caused his widow, Imelda, to announce that the plan to bury her late husband would be postponed. It was only in February 1999, that the family of the late president agreed to pay substantial damages to victims of human rights abuses during his despotic and corrupt rule.

*see also:* Aquino, Benigno; Aquino, Corazón; Enrile, Juan Ponce; Estrada, Joseph; Marcos, Imelda; New Society Movement; People Power; Ramos, Fidel; Sin, Jaime.

## Marcos, Imelda (Philippines)

Imelda Marcos achieved political notoriety as the venal and controversial consort of President **Ferdinand Marcos** of the Philippines. She was born on 2 July 1929 to an impoverished branch of the wealthy Romuáldez family from Leyte in the central Visayan Islands. Much of her life was spent trying to overcome early social disability and material deprivation. She grew up to become an exceptionally beautiful woman with a sweet soprano voice, subsequently put to her future husband's political service at election rallies. Ferdinand Marcos was attracted to her after Imelda had won the title Muse of Manila at the Philippines International Fair in 1953. In May 1954, after a whirlwind courtship, she married the up and coming Congressman. Imelda proved to be a political asset to the future president but confined herself to only a ceremonial role during his first two terms of office.

After the introduction of martial law in September 1972, Mrs Marcos began to display personal political ambition and at one time came to be regarded as a likely successor to her ailing husband. Her formal political career began in 1975 when she was appointed governor of Metropolitan Manila. She entered the National Assembly in 1978, assuming the portfolio of human settlements later in the year. In 1982 she became a member of the Executive Council charged with responsibility for interim government in the event of the president's death or incapacity. In her political role, she exercised considerable patronage and acted as a plenipotentiary for her husband overseas. Mrs Marcos was an impulsive woman of boundless energy who was obsessed with grandiose schemes, material acquisition and cultivating a coterie of international celebrities. Her facility for political theatre served her and her husband well for a time. However, dynastic pretensions and insatiable greed had an alienating political effect nationally, especially after the blatant murder of opposition leader **Benigno Aquino**, which marked a political turning-point. In February 1986, after military and popular reaction to fraudulently conducted elections had precipitated political change, she left for exile in Hawaii with her discredited husband. In exile, she continued to hold court among a small circle of émigrés and plotted Ferdinand Marcos's political return to the Philippines until thwarted by his death in September 1989. She was denied the right to bring her husband's body back in state to the Philippines. However, in November 1991 she returned to Manila with her son Bombong ostensibly to face civil and criminal charges relating to the expropriation of public funds. Her prime purpose was political vindication and ambition but she received only limited popular acclaim and did not pose a threat to the widow of the murdered Benigno Aquino, Mrs **Corazón Aquino**, who had succeeded Ferdinand Marcos as president. Imelda Marcos stood as a candidate in presidential elections in May 1992, but secured only just over 10 per cent of the national vote, coming fifth behind **Fidel Ramos**, who as deputy chief of staff had led the military revolt which precipitated her husband's political downfall. In September 1993 she was sentenced in Manila to eighteen to twenty-four years in prison for criminal graft in the first court conviction since she and her late husband had been forced into exile in 1986 but was released on bail pending appeal. The same month, she was able to have Ferdinand Marcos's remains entombed in a mausoleum in his home town of Batac in what proved to be an abortive attempt to establish their son Bombong as his political successor. Further charges of embezzlement were brought against her in April 1994 and in September 1995. In May 1995, she secured election to the House of Representatives for a constituency in her home province of Leyte. In January 1998, the Supreme Court upheld the 1993 decision sentencing her to twelve years' imprisonment but she was freed pending an appeal. Mrs Marcos then announced her candidacy for the presidential elections in May but withdrew at the end of April after opinion polls showed that she would secure only around 2 per cent of the vote. In October 1998, the Supreme Court upheld her appeal overturning the only conviction, so far, on charges of graft relating to her late husband's despotic and corrupt rule.

see also: Aquino, Benigno; Aquino, Corazón; Marcos, Ferdinand; Ramos, Fidel.

## Marhaenism  (Indonesia)

Marhaenism was a term coined by President **Sukarno** which was given special prominence in a speech delivered in Bandung on 3 July 1957 to commemorate the thirtieth anniversary of the Indonesian Nationalist Party. It repres-ented an attempt to define an ideology of Indonesian socialism with reference to indigenous experience. According to Sukarno, he had employed the term first during a course of lectures in 1927 in which he sought to explain why the term 'proletarian' was not fully appropriate in identifying the whole of Indonesia's poor. He explained that he used the word Marhaen, from which Marhaenism was derived, because it expressed the condition of a small farmer of that name whom he had once met in a rice field. This man barely made a living even though he owned his own land and implements. Sukarno claimed that he was inspired to use the name Marhaen 'to describe the destitute People of Indonesia'. There has never been any confirmation of Sukarno's reported meeting, which may have taken place only in his fertile imagination. In the event, Marhaen and Marhaenism (the ideology of promoting the interests of the little man) served as Indonesian counterparts and alternatives to Marx and Marxism in the lexicon of the authoritarian political system of **Guided Democracy** which Sukarno instituted by decree in July 1959. The terms disappeared in the wake of an abortive coup (see **Gestapu**) in October 1965 which led to the downfall of Sukarno and the political system which he inspired.

see also: Crocodile Hole; Gestapu; Guided Democracy; Sukarno.

## Marshall, David  (Singapore)

David Marshall was the first chief minister of Singapore, holding the office for fourteen months during 1955–6 in the initial phase of the island's decolonization. He was born in Singapore on 12 March 1908 to an Orthodox Jewish family from Iraq; his father was a successful trader. After failing to settle to a career in business, David Marshall trained in law as a barrister at the Middle Temple in London. His career as a criminal lawyer was interrupted by the Pacific War during which he was interned and then dispatched to Japan to work in coal-mines. After the war, he established a reputation as an outstanding advocate. He also began to involve himself in Singapore's politics. In 1954 David Marshall founded the Singapore Socialist Party, which he took into an alliance with the Labour Party as the Labour Front to make a strong showing in elections in 1955.

His period of office was turbulent, partly as a consequence of industrial unrest fomented by the Communist Party of Malaya and because of his own headstrong temperament. It was also short-lived, as he resigned when talks with the British government over self-government broke down; he was succeeded as chief minister by **Lim Yew Hock**. David Marshall then resigned his parliamentary seat and went on to found the **Workers Party**, which attracted Communist support, enabling him to win a by-election in 1962 which he then lost in general elections the following year. David Marshall returned to legal practice but came into conflict with the government of **Lee Kuan Yew**, which was intolerant of dissent. In October 1972 he was suspended from legal practice for six months because he had breached an undertaking to the attorney-general not to part with affidavits in *habeas corpus* proceedings, which were subsequently released at a conference of the International Press Institute. Reconciliation took place in 1978, however, when the foreign minister, **Sinnathamby Rajaratnam**, asked him to become Singapore's ambassador to France, a post which David Marshall held continuously with distinction until his retirement in 1993. On his return to Singapore, he worked as a legal adviser, but became outspoken against the authoritarianism of the government whose achievements were also applauded. He died on 12 December 1995 aged 87.

see also: Lee Kuan Yew; Lim Yew Hock; Rajaratnam, Sinnathamby; Workers Party.

## *Masyumi* (Indonesia)

*Masyumi* is an Indonesian acronym drawn from *Majelis Syuro Muslimin Indonesia*, which translates as Consultative Council of Indonesian Muslims. It was established by the Japanese as an umbrella organization in October 1943. They conceived of the council as an instrument to serve their own wartime political purpose. After the proclamation of independence in August 1945, *Masyumi* became a part of the nationalist movement but with its own agenda of entrenching the values of **Islam** in the constitution of the republic. Divisions between radical, traditional and modernist wings of the party led to successive defections. After the departure from party

ranks of *Nahdatul Ulama* (Religious Scholars) in 1952, the modernist wing, drawn from the cultural and educational movement *Muhammadiyah* (Followers of the Prophet Muhammad), predominated but its political fortunes went into decline. *Masyumi* enjoyed representation in the early coalition cabinets which failed to address the country's economic problems. In the country's first general elections in 1955, *Masyumi* secured just under 21 per cent of the vote, drawn primarily from the outer islands. That disappointing result undermined its claim to share office, from which it was excluded as parliamentary democracy gave way to **Guided Democracy** through the machinations of President **Sukarno**. Some of its leading members were implicated in abortive regional uprisings in 1958 which led to the party being banned in 1960.

After President **Suharto** established his **New Order** from 1966, an attempt was made to reform the party in February 1968 through creating a legal successor as *Partai Muslimin Indonesia* (in acronym *Parmusi*). However, it was excluded from government. Following a weak showing in elections in 1971, it was merged with other Islamic parties into *Partai Persatuan Pembangunan* (PPP) or **United Development Party** in January 1973. In this form, it served to provide legitimacy for an electoral process whose main function was to lend legitimacy to President Suharto's authoritarian rule, which came to an end in May 1998.

see also: Guided Democracy; Islam; *Muhammadiyah*; *Nahdatul Ulama*; New Order; Suharto; Sukarno; United Development Party.

## May 13 Racial Riots 1969 (Malaysia)

On 13 May 1969 communal violence erupted between Malays and non-Malays (mainly Chinese) in Kuala Lumpur, which took a toll of 196 lives, according to official figures. The violence occurred after a significant electoral reversal for the governing intercommunal **Alliance Party** coalition which had ruled Malaya and then Malaysia continuously from before independence in August 1957. The Alliance retained its parliamentary majority in the elections of 9 May but its Chinese component, the **Malaysian Chinese Association** (MCA) lost fourteen out of twenty-seven seats held previously, while **UMNO** (United Malays National Organization), the dominant party in the coalition, lost a high percentage of votes to its principal Malay opponent, *Parti Islam Se-Malaysia* (PAS), albeit not accurately reflected in seats retained.

Racial tension with a primary source in Malay political insecurity had been a striking feature of the election campaign. It had been heightened by the results for the federal Parliament and also by the uncertain outcome of the concurrent state elections in the case of Selangor, within which the national capital was situated. Selangor had long been assumed to be an exclusive Malay preserve, reflected in the constitutional provision that the chief minister had to be a Malay. The election produced a deadlocked state legislature and Malay anxieties were reinforced by the provocative nature of celebratory processions by supporters of successful non-Malay opposition parties in Kuala Lumpur. A counter-victory procession organized by Selangor UMNO for the evening of 13 May began with a huge gathering at the residence of the chief minister, Datuk Harun Idris. Communal violence at its fringes expanded in an orgy of killing by Malays, which was not fully contained for five days.

The riots proved to be the most significant event in the post-independence history of peninsular Malaysia. Parliamentary democracy was suspended until January 1971. The government was replaced temporarily by a National Operations Council headed by the deputy prime minister, **Tun Abdul Razak**. The format of politics in Malaysia was modified to ensure that the constitutional special position of the Malays was entrenched as one of dominance. A **New Economic Policy** foreshadowed on 1 July 1969 was later given content to shift the balance of material advantage more equitably in the Malay interest. The riots also demonstrated the Malays' loss of confidence in the prime minister, **Tunku Abdul Rahman**, who was obliged to resign in favour of his deputy Tun Razak in September 1970.

*see also:* Alliance Party; Malaysian Chinese Association; New Economic Policy; *Parti Islam Se-Malaysia*; Rahman, Tunku Abdul; Razak, Tun Abdul; UMNO.

## Mayaguez Incident 1975  (Cambodia)

On 12 May 1975 the US freighter *Mayaguez*, en route from Hong Kong to Thailand, was seized by a Cambodian (**Khmer Rouge**) patrol boat off Wai Island in the Gulf of Siam. A mayday call was answered by US President General Ford, who ordered a helicopter-borne attack by marines to rescue the ship and her thirty-nine crew. In the mean time, the *Mayaguez* had been anchored offshore at Koh Tang Island, while the crew had been moved to the country's main port of Kompong Som. The marines' mistaken attempt to storm Wai on 15 May was met with very heavy and costly resistance. The United States responded with a fierce display of firepower from aircraft based in Thailand and from ships of the US Seventh Fleet. After more than a day of bombardment with Kompong Som and the neighbouring Ream Naval Base targeted, Cambodia's only oil refinery had been destroyed together with its small air force and much of its navy. In the face of this show of force, the Khmer Rouge released the vessel and the crew, which was greeted in the United States as a great victory serving to compensate for the double humiliation in April 1975 when Phnom Penh and Saigon fell in turn to revolutionary communism. In attaining this end, however, thirty-eight US marines lost their lives, most of them after the crew of the *Mayaguez* had been released.

The *Mayaguez* Incident came about through a combination of accidental circumstances. First, Khmer Rouge vigilance to protect Cambodian territorial waters was a direct product of clashes with Vietnam and not the United States over maritime jurisdiction. Moreover, the decision to seize the vessel was taken by the Southwestern Zone Command without authorization from Phnom Penh, whose officials learned of the event after their counterparts in Washington. Second, the US response was an attempt to demonstrate that despite the retreat from Indochina, military force would be used to protect national interests. In the United States, the *Mayaguez* Incident was soon forgotten, with President Ford securing a measure of domestic political benefit from the manufactured crisis. In Cambodia, the incident reinforced a pathological view of United States imperialism as well as weakening the capability of the Khmer Rouge regime to challenge Vietnamese claims to offshore islands.

*see also:* Khmer Rouge.

## Megawati Sukarnoputri (Indonesia)

Megawati Sukarnoputri was elected vice-president of Indonesia by the **People's Consultative Assembly** (MPR) on 21 October 1999. She had failed to secure the presidency the day before having been the front-running candidate since the previous June when her *perjuangan* (struggle) faction of the *Partai Demokrasi Indonesia* (PDI) had won a plurality in parliamentary elections. She lost the political advantage through her reluctance to engage in coalition building with the highest office going to **Abdurrahman Wahid**, with whom she became quickly reconciled. Megawati was born on 23 January 1947 in Yogyakarta, then the revolutionary capital of the republic of which her father was president. She was educated at Padjajaran University in Bandung but suffered personally from President **Sukarno**'s fall from political grace from the mid-1960s. Two broken marriages saw her in her forties entering politics in 1987 as a parliamentary representative of the PDI but without displaying much interest in its proceedings. In July 1993, in reaction to an attempt by President **Suharto** to manipulate the choice of party leader, she was nominated as chairman capitalizing on her parentage to secure election to that office in December that year. She was removed from office at a stage-managed party conference in Medan in June 1996, which was followed in July by the violent ejection of her supporters from the PDI headquarters in Jakarta by police and army, which provoked rioting in the capital. Her faction had been excluded from participation in parliamentary elections in May 1997. Moreover, she was not in the forefront of agitation prior to the political downfall of President Suharto in May 1998. With the restoration of the democratic process, Megawati appeared as a symbol of political reform because of her persecution by the previous regime. Although she attracted substantial support as leader of the PDI-P in parliamentary elections, she failed to impress as a potential leader with a concrete agenda for Indonesia's economic and political rehabilitation and also alienated the Islamic constituency by the large number of Christians on her party list. As vice-president, she has played a marginal role to an ailing president and has not registered a commanding political style. She has become more credible as a political alternative as President Abdurrahman Wahid's leadership has alienated domestic and international support. In August 2000, Megawati was accorded responsibility for chairing the cabinet but without assuming any executive powers.

*see also: Partai Demokrasi Indonesia* (PDI); People's Consultative Assembly (MPR); Suharto; Sukarno; Wahid, Abdurrahman.

## Mekong River Project (Burma (Myanmar)/Cambodia/Laos/ Thailand/Vietnam)

The River Mekong rises in Tibet and flows south through southern China. It then continues in the same direction serving as the boundary between Burma/Myanmar and Laos and most of that between Laos and Thailand before passing through Cambodia and then southern Vietnam from where it empties into the **South China Sea** at the end of a course of some 2,600 miles. The lower Mekong River Basin, including Thailand, Laos, Cambodia and Vietnam, attracted the attention of the United Nations Economic Commission for the Far East (ECAFE) in the early 1950s as offering great potential for harnessing its resources for irrigation and energy purposes. The Committee for the Coordination of Investigations of the Lower Mekong Basin was set up in September 1957. Some progress was made during the 1960s, when a consortium of states began to collaborate in planning under United Nations aegis with ECAFE subsequently becoming the Economic and Social Commission for Asia and the Pacific (ESCAP). The progress of the undertaking was obstructed by the **Indochina Wars**, with the government in Saigon presuming to speak for Vietnam. Cambodia withdrew from the undertaking when the Khmer Rouge seized power in 1975, while after its invasion by Vietnam in 1978, the government in Phnom Penh was excluded from the Mekong Committee. The project was revived after the political

settlement of the Cambodian conflict had been signed at the **International Conference on Cambodia** in Paris in October 1991. Acrimony then arose because of unilateral measures by Thailand to dam the river upstream but a joint communiqué was signed between the four riparian states on 5 February 1993. The terms of that communiqué committed the signatories to continued cooperation in the exploitation of the Mekong River and to the establishment of a Mekong Working Group with the task of drafting a framework agreement for future cooperation on the Mekong River based on an equitable and reasonable utilization of mainstream water. That agreement was concluded among the riparian states at a meeting in Thailand in April 1995 which set up a River Mekong Commission with a regulatory mandate replacing an interim secretariat. The first official meeting of the Commission was convened in Phnom Penh in August 1995 to which Burma and China, as riparian states, were invited. A key role in promoting the cooperative endeavour has been played by the United Nations Development Programme but, in June 1996, ASEAN launched a complementary Mekong Basin Development Cooperation (AMBDC) programme with a second ministerial meeting convening in Hanoï in July 2000. Plans are advanced for dams for hydro-electric power, irrigation and flood control. However, in some riparian states, especially in China and Laos, these dams have not always been established in consultation with downstream counterparts. In consequence, upstream reservoirs hold back vital waters in the dry season with serious environmental consequences such as silting up Cambodia's Tonle Sap Lake and the intrusion of salt water into Vietnam's delta region.
*see also:* ASEAN; Indochina Wars; International Conference on Cambodia, Paris 1991.

## Melayu Islam Beraja (MIB)  (Brunei)

*Melayu Islam Beraja* (MIB) is a Brunei-Malay term which translates as Malay Islamic Monarchy. When Brunei resumed independence in January 1984 and joined the United Nations, Sultan **Hassanal Bolkiah** described his country in those terms in his address to the General Assembly. The concept of a Malay Islamic Monarchy was subsequently elevated into a national ideology by the sultan in July 1990 on his forty-fourth birthday. The ideology, which has been explained by the sultan as an attempt to return to national roots, has mixed functions. It serves to fend off any appeal from externally inspired Muslim fundamentalism. It also serves to legitimize the royal absolutism of Brunei by linking conservative values of **Islam** and traditional Malay culture with the unifying role of monarchy. MIB, which has become a compulsory subject in the university and schools, has been accompanied by a number of Islamic prohibitions within Brunei giving rise to social tensions.
*see also:* Bolkiah, Hassanal; Islam.

## Memali Incident 1985  (Malaysia)

On 19 November 1985 members of the Malaysian Federal Reserve Unit (the elite anti-riot squad) and of the paramilitary Field Force became engaged in a violent confrontation with armed villagers while seeking to arrest an Islamic religious teacher and thirty-six other men in Kampung (village) Memali near Baling in the state of Kedah. Ibrahim Mahmud had been an official and a parliamentary candidate of the Malay opposition *Parti Islam Se-Malaysia* (PAS) and had refused to surrender to an arrest warrant issued in September 1984 under the Internal Security Act. He had studied for a time in Tripoli and was commonly known as Ibrahim Libya. During the exchange of fire, which lasted for five hours, eighteen people were killed, including Ibrahim Mahmud and four policemen. After the event, the prime minister, Dr **Mahathir Mohamad**, claimed that all thirty-seven wanted men had concentrated in Ibrahim Mahmud's house prior to the attempt by the security forces to arrest them. A curfew was imposed on the entire Baling area and the government took steps to control religious feelings from being further inflamed. However, the villagers of Kampung Memali insisted on burying the dead according to the rights due to those who had died as martyrs for the sake of Islam. In the event, the bloody incident proved to be an isolated one. At the time, there was deep concern that it might spark off further violent challenges to government by Islamic activists, especially in the rural areas where there were economic grievances.

*see also:* Islam; Mahathir Mohamad, Datuk Sri; *Parti Islam Se-Malaysia.*

## Missing in Action (MIA) (Cambodia/Laos/Vietnam)

The term missing in action (MIA) refers to US servicemen who have not been accounted for in Indochina since the **Paris Peace Agreements** of 1973 and the attendant release of prisoners of war by the government in Hanoi. The US Department of Defense (Pentagon) has listed up to 2,207 Americans as officially missing in Indochina since the end of the **Vietnam War**. Of that number, 1,619 have been listed as missing in Vietnam, 505 in Laos and 77 in Cambodia. Some 80 per cent of all MIAs were airmen. A limited number of these crashed across the Chinese border, which has complicated the reconciliation of numbers. The MIA issue has been a potent factor both in domestic politics in the United States and also in relations between the United States and Vietnam. Until the early 1990s, there had been a strong belief in Washington that the government in Vietnam had not provided an adequate accounting for US soldiers who had been missing in action and in particular for prisoners of war. That belief was fed by recurrent false allegations of sightings of caucasians living in Vietnam together with the appearance of fake photographs. This belief, combined with a view held by a strong lobby acting on behalf of families of missing servicemen that there had been neglect of their fate and a cover-up in Washington, obstructed the process of normalization with Hanoi. By early 1994, after a congressional investigation, it had become evident that the Vietnamese government was providing considerable cooperation in the joint search for the remains of Americans missing in action begun in 1988. By then some 600 cases had been resolved through the identification of remains through forensic examination in Hawaii. Another 50 had been resolved in Laos. Progress in this endeavour made it possible for US President Bill Clinton to rescind a longstanding trade and investment embargo on Vietnam in February 1994, to agree in May 1994 to establish liaison offices in respective capital cities, and finally to establish diplomatic relations in August 1995. By the end of that year, 1618 cases had been accounted for. By mid-1997, 2,124 Americans were still listed as missing in action in Indochina, 1,585 of them in Vietnam.

*see also:* Indochina Wars; Paris Peace Agreements 1973; Vietnam War.

## Misuari, Nur (Philippines)

Nur Misuari was the leader of the **Moro National Liberation Front** (MNLF) ever since it took up arms against the government of President **Ferdinand Marcos** in 1972. He has spent decades since in exile, primarily in Libya where he has enjoyed the patronage of Colonel Gadaffi. Although his movement made a military impact in the mid-1970s, they failed to sustain their initial success because of tribal differences and the ability of the Philippine government to exploit them and to neutralize external Islamic support. Nur Misuari was born in 1940 in the southern island of Sulu. He won a scholarship to the University of the Philippines and after graduating in arts worked as an instructor in Asian philosophies in the Institute of Asian Studies. At the University of the Philippines, he was drawn towards both Islamic and left-wing causes and in the late 1960s secured funding from traditional leaders on Sulu to enable him and other like-minded young Muslims to travel abroad for military training. He was party to an abortive agreement on Muslim autonomy negotiated by Mrs **Imelda Marcos** on behalf of the government in Manila. This **Tripoli Agreement** was concluded in December 1976. Nur Misuari has always maintained that President Marcos and his successors have never kept to their side of the bargain. After the political downfall of President Marcos, he resumed negotiations with representatives of President **Corazón Aquino** and signed a new accord in Jeddah in January 1987 but it failed to hold. From October 1993, he began negotiations with the government of **Fidel Ramos**, which were facilitated by Indonesian mediation. A political breakthrough was reached in June 1996 leading to an agreement signed by Nur Misuari for the MNLF on 2 September in Manila, which established the Southern Philippines Council for Peace and Development (SPCPD) to supervise the peace process in those provinces with significant Muslim populations to be established as a Special Zone for Peace and Development (SZPD) to be funded from presidential funds. It also confirmed the retention of a controversial four-province Autonomous Region of Muslim Mindanao (ARMM), previously opposed by Misuari. On 9 September, he stood unopposed for the office of Governor of the Autonomous Region and was sworn in at the end of the month. In October 1996, Misuari was appointed chairman of the SPCPD. In July 1997, he assumed a mediatory role leading to a temporary cease-fire in government talks with the rival **Moro Islamic Liberation Front** (MILF), which had not endorsed the peace agreement of September 1996. He has also been involved in negotiations following the abduction of foreign tourists from a Malaysian-held resort by members of the **Abu Sayyaf**.

see also: Abu Sayyaf; Aquino, Corazón; Islam; Marcos, Ferdinand; Marcos, Imelda; Moro Islamic Liberation Front; Moro National Liberation Front; Ramos, Fidel; Tripoli Agreement 1976.

## Mochtar Kusumaatmadja, Professor
(Indonesia)
Professor Mochtar Kusumaatmadja was foreign minister of Indonesia from 1978 to 1988, having held the office in an acting capacity from May 1977. In that office, he played a leading role as interlocutor on behalf of **ASEAN** (Association of South-East Asian Nations) in seeking to negotiate an end to the Cambodian conflict with Vietnam in the third phase of the **Indochina Wars**. He also paved the way for Indonesia's ultimate assumption of the chair of the Non-Aligned Movement. Mochtar Kusumaatmadja was born on 17 February 1929 in Jakarta. After independence, he graduated from the Faculty of Law of the University of Indonesia and then spent a period of postgraduate study in the United States at the universities of Yale, Harvard and Chicago. He joined the Faculty of Law at Padjajaran University in Bandung, where he received his doctorate and eventually became its rector. He took a special interest in the law of the sea, representing Indonesia at the early United Nations conferences. Professor

Mochtar made a notable contribution to extending Indonesia's maritime jurisdiction by pioneering the concept of an archipelagic state which was ultimately accepted by the United Nations Conference on the Law of the Sea in 1982. Before becoming foreign minister, he served from 1974 to 1977 as minister of justice. On his retirement from high office in March 1988, he returned to private law practice but retained an advisory role to the government on law of the sea matters.

see also: Archipelago Declaration 1957; ASEAN.

## Mok, Ta  (Cambodia) see Ta Mok.

## Moro Islamic Liberation Front (MILF)
(Philippines)
The Moro Islamic Liberation Front is a Muslim insurgency with religious-separatist goals based in the centre of the southern island of Mindanao. It established a distinct political identity in 1980 as a result of a split in 1978 within the **Moro National Liberation Front** (MNLF) which up to then had been the sole vehicle seeking Muslim political autonomy in the south of the country from the government of the Philippines. The MNLF had drawn its initial support from two main tribal constituencies among the Islamic community - the Tausugs in the Sulu islands and the Maguindanaos from central Mindanao. The MNLF leader was **Nur Misuari**, a Tausug. He was challenged by his deputy, Salamat Hashim, who was not only a Maguindanao but also an Islamic scholar who had been trained at Al-Azhar University in Cairo. Nur Misuari had a secular background and also links with the Communist movement which counted against him in the struggle to keep the MNLF intact; this was decided primarily on tribal-territorial grounds with support being attracted to the MILF from the other major Islamic tribal group on Mindanao, the Maranaos.

The agreement in September 1996 on limited political autonomy between the Philippine government and the MNLF was opposed by the MILF, which continued to demand an independent Islamic state. By that juncture, it had established a territorial redoubt with a military headquarters in central Mindanao. Moreover, a modus vivendi had been worked out with elected provincial and municipal authorities. The military wing of the MILF, which is larger and better armed than the MNLF, has assumed a warlord role providing 'protection' in return for contributions from foreign companies and has engaged in kidnapping to ensure compliance. Recruitment to its ranks has been facilitated by local unemployment. According to Philippine military estimates, it has a standing force of 15,000 guerrillas. The MILF combines a political with a religious agenda and has been able to attract external assistance in the form of funds and manpower. In January 1997, however, the MILF entered into peace talks with the government and signed a cease-fire. Those talks and cease-fire have been interrupted with recurrent hostilities, partly as a result of the MILF attempting to expand its territorial base and the determination of the security forces to reduce its operational zone. In clashes in the late 1990s, the MILF suffered heavy casualties, which may have provoked its announcement that its insurgents would come to the aid of the communist **New People's Army** should it be hard pressed by army attacks. It has disavowed any connection, however, with the fundamentalist-Muslim **Abu Sayyaf** group responsible for murderous raids against civilian settlements and hostage taking in the southern Philippines. Formal peace talks were resumed in October 1999 but were interrupted by cease-fire violations. In March 2000, the MILF launched a major offensive against six military bases in Lanao del Norte Province in Mindanao, which was countered by a ground and air assault by government forces in April. The intensity of the fighting produced over 100,000 refugees, while the MILF demonstrated its ability to set off bombs, grenades and rockets in several towns in Mindanao. In April 2000, Hashim Selamat, the leader of the MILF, reiterated his opposition to the settlement reached with the rival MNLF in 1996 and called for a referendum among all the Muslims in the southern Philippines to endorse any negotiated agreement with the government in Manila. In July 2000, government forces overran Camp Abubakar, the MILF headquarters, but without bringing an end to Islamic insurgency.

*see also:* Abu Sayyaf; Moro National Liberation Front; New People's Army; Nur Misuari.

## Moro National Liberation Front (MNLF) (Philippines)

The Moro National Liberation Front (MNLF) was set up in 1969 with the object of securing a separate state for Muslims concentrated in the southern islands of the Philippines. Muslims comprise around 4 million of the total population of some 73 million. **Islam** had spread to the northern island of Luzón through conversion from the fourteenth century but under Spanish colonial domination the Muslims were driven to the south of the country. The Spanish viewed the Muslims as traditional enemies, associating them with the epic struggle in the Iberian peninsula against the Moors from which the pejorative term Moro is derived. Under Spanish and then United States rule, the Muslims of the south existed as a deprived, resentful and never completely pacified minority. Christian settlement from the north of the archipelago, which accelerated after independence in 1946, led not only to the alienation of traditional lands but to fundamental demographic change. The ultimate result of such settlement has been to leave the Muslims a majority in only four of the twenty-two southern provinces deemed to be their heartland.

Underlying Muslim alienation was acutely reinforced in the late 1960s after the **Corregidor Affair**, an alleged massacre of recruits in training for armed infiltration into Malaysia's state of Sabah, became public knowledge. Additional causes of grievance were acts of violence by Christian gangs acting on behalf of landed interests which culminated in bloodletting in a mosque in 1971 in Cotabato. The Moro National Liberation Movement was founded by a group of young secular Muslims who had become disillusioned with a traditional elite who had set up a Mindanao Independence Movement in 1968 without notable effect. They received some military training in Malaysia, whose government was determined to retaliate against the seeming bad faith of President **Ferdinand Marcos**. Their leader was **Nur Misuari**, who had been an instructor in Asian philosophies at the University of the Philippines and a one-time member of the radical Marxist *Kabataan Makabangan* (Patriotic Youth). The pejorative term Moro was included in the name of the separatist movement as a deliberate gesture of defiance. A central committee was established in Libya and produced a manifesto in April 1974 calling for political independence for the southern islands of Mindanao, Sulu, Palawan, Basilan and Tawi Tawi. Formal recognition from the Organization of the Islamic Conference was accorded in July 1975.

The Moro National Liberation Front began armed rebellion in October 1972 with an attack on the headquarters of the Philippine Constabulary in Marawi City in the wake of President Marcos's proclamation of martial law the month before. That proclamation had required all unregistered firearms to be handed in to the authorities and was construed in the south of the Philippines as a deliberate attempt to place the Muslims in a defenceless position against armed gangs of Christian settlers. Within twenty-four hours, the insurrection had spread with extensive violence and considerable loss of life, especially on the island of Sulu, where a major confrontation took place with security forces.

Negotiations in Tripoli took place under Libyan auspices in 1976 between Nur Misuari and **Imelda Marcos**, representing her husband. A compromise **Tripoli Agreement** was reached on Muslim political autonomy in thirteen provinces and nine cities but was never implemented because of charges of bad faith at the way a facilitating plebiscite had been conducted. The insurrection revived in 1977 but by that juncture, its momentum had passed its peak and President Marcos was able to play on tribal and regional divisions among the Muslim community to contain their challenge. He was able also to attract international Islamic diplomatic and financial support for alternative ways of providing for Muslim needs. It became evident that the Moro National Liberation Front was a loosely knit entity with the emergence of contending alternative leaderships. Indeed, in 1978 Nur Misuari's main rival Salamat Hashim set up the Moro Islamic Liberation Front. Muslim insurrection rumbled on without any attempt at resolution until Mrs **Corazón Aquino** succeeded Ferdinand Marcos in 1986. Nur Misuari returned to the Philippines in September 1986 to begin negotiations on Muslim autonomy.

In January 1987 an agreement was signed in Jeddah between President Aquino's brother-in-law, Agapito Aquino, and Nur Misuari but once again implementation with the cooperation of both parties was frustrated. President Aquino insisted that political autonomy be made conditional on a plebiscite by all inhabitants of the thirteen provinces, irrespective of religion. In addition, the cleavages within the Muslim community served to undermine Nur Misuari's claim to speak on behalf of all Filipino Muslims.

The Philippine government went ahead with the plan for political autonomy through a plebiscite in November 1989 in the thirteen provinces identified in the Tripoli Agreement in 1976. The outcome was the establishment in 1990 of an Autonomous Region of Muslim Mindanao in four provinces only - Maguindanao, Lanao del Sur (on the island of Mindanao), Sulu and Tawi Tawi. Elections were held in that region in February 1990 and a governor appointed to whom limited executive powers were accorded. The Moro National Liberation Front continued to oppose the new constitutional arrangement but with minimal effect. At the end of 1993, Indonesian good offices were employed for direct negotiations, which were transferred to the southern Philippines in early 1994. At the end of January 1994, the Philippine government and the MNLF signed a cease-fire agreement as a basis for proceeding with an accord on political autonomy in the southern islands. In September 1996, a compromise agreement was reached whereby the MNLF came to terms with the Autonomous Region of Muslim Mindanao (ARMM) with Nur Misuari as its governor and also endorsed the establishment of a Southern Philippines Council for Peace and Development (SPCPD) with Misuari as its chairman. As a result, hundreds of MNLF guerillas were incorporated into the Philippines National Police and into its armed forces, which marked the transformation of the Front into a legitimate political entity. In the event, however, the agreement has not lived up to expectations. Economic crisis held up promised development assistance, while investors have been deterred by a lack of infrastructure and the revival of military activity in the south of the Philippines.

*see also:* Aquino, Corazón; Corregidor Affair 1968; Islam; Marcos, Ferdinand; Marcos, Imelda; Misuari, Nur; Moro Islamic Liberation Front; Tripoli Agreement 1976.

## Muhammadiyah (Indonesia)

*Muhammadiyah* (which translates as Followers of the Prophet Muhammad) is an urban-based religious organization which was set in the Javanese city of Yogyakarta in 1912 by a mosque official. He was inspired by the ideas of the Egyptian theologist Mohammed Abduh, who had urged a cleansing of Islamic thought through a return to original texts. This enterprise in renewal was an attempt through education and social welfare to reconcile **Islam** with the modern world. *Muhammadiyah* was not engaged in politics under the Dutch, but with the proclamation of independence in 1945, it became a constituent part of *Masyumi* (Consultative Council of Indonesian Muslims) and aspired to create an Islamic state. *Masyumi* was banned in 1960 because of its implication in the regional revolts of the late 1950s. *Muhammadiyah* had continued in existence in pursuit of its original purposes, with an overlapping connection with the **United Development Party** founded in 1973 by merging all Islamic parties. During the **Suharto** era, the *Muhammadiyah* was obliged to dilute its Islamic identity by adhering to the state philosophy of *Pancasila* as its sole philosophy. In the wake of Suharto's political downfall, its leader, Dr Amien Rais, established the **National Mandate Party** (*Partai Amanat Nasional*–PAN) with a reformist agenda directed beyond a narrow Islamic constituency, which secured some 7 per cent of the vote and 35 out of 462 elective seats in parliamentary elections in June 1999. Through forging a coalition of Islamic-based parties, Dr Rais was elected speaker of the constitutionally supreme **People's Consultative Assembly** (MPR) in the following October.

*see also:* Islam; *Masyumi*; National Mandate Party; *Pancasila*; People's Consultative Assembly; Suharto; United Development Party.

## Muoi, Do (Vietnam) *see* Do Muoi.

## Murdani, General L. B. (Indonesia)

General Benny Murdani was commander of Indonesia's armed forces between March 1983 and February 1988 and then minister of defence between March 1988 and March 1993, when he was retired from public life. Leonardus Benjamin Murdani was born on 2 October 1932 in Cepu, central Java, to Catholic parents. He was literally a boy soldier during the national revolution, beginning his professional military training as a student reserve officer only after independence. As a young infantry officer with paracommando training, he distinguished himself in operations against regional rebels in Menado in northern Sulawesi and then survived a parachute drop into the jungles of Dutch-held West New Guinea (now **Irian Jaya**) which brought him to the attention of the regional commander and future president, General **Suharto**. He then began a career in military intelligence working directly for Colonel (later Lt-General) **Ali Murtopo** in clandestine negotiations to bring an end to Indonesia's ill-fated **Confrontation** of Malaysia. Diplomatic postings in Kuala Lumpur and Seoul were followed in 1974 by a series of senior military intelligence positions in Jakarta in which he served directly as security adviser to President Suharto, whose confidence he enjoyed for his personal loyalty and his dynamic style of leadership. As commander of the armed forces, he was responsible for revising its military doctrine and enhancing its professionalism. However, his relationship with President Suharto became subject to strain, in part because of attempts to restrict the business activities of the president's children, which were causing political alienation, together with his support for *Partai Demokrasi Indonesia* (Indonesian Democratic Party). General Murdani was removed from military office in February 1988 shortly after his period of active service had been renewed in a calculated act of public humiliation by the president. He was subsequently appointed minister of defence in March 1988 without any powers of command in an evident attempt by the president to control any maverick political ambitions. With his removal from high office, his influence within the armed forces was undermined deliberately by President Suharto through loyalist senior military appointments. However, with Suharto's fall from political grace, Murdani re-established close links with the former president.

*see also:* Confrontation; Irian Jaya; Murtopo, Ali; *Partai Demokrasi Indonesia*; *Petrus*; Suharto.

## Murtopo, General Ali (Indonesia)

General Ali Murtopo played a key role as an adviser to President **Suharto** in helping him to consolidate his power in the **New Order** of the late 1960s and early 1970s. He was responsible for the manipulation of the political system and also for the management of the so-called 'act of free choice' in **Irian Jaya**, which confirmed Indonesia's entitlement to the former Dutch possession. Among his other achievements was the establishment of the Centre for Strategic and International Studies (CSIS), which became the leading think-tank in the republic. Ali Murtopo was born on 23 September 1923 in Blora, central Java. He was a student member of the revolutionary army from August 1945 and after independence continued as a professional soldier. He was educated in part at the Army Command and Staff School in Bandung, rising to battalion commander by the end of the 1950s. His career became entwined with that of the future president when General Suharto was in command of the central Javanese Diponegoro Division. Ali Murtopo was active as an intelligence officer in the operations to recover Irian Jaya and more significantly played a key clandestine role in negotiating an end to Indonesia's **Confrontation** of Malaysia in the mid-1960s. He was appointed minister of information in March 1978 but three months later suffered a heart attack during a visit to Malaysia. He never fully recovered and in March 1983 was relieved of his portfolio and made a member of the ceremonial Supreme Advisory Council. He died after a further heart attack on 18 May 1984.

see also: Confrontation; Irian Jaya; New Order; Suharto.

## Musa Hitam, Tan Sri (Malaysia)

Datuk Musa Hitam was deputy prime minister and minister of home affairs of Malaysia between July 1981 and February 1986, when he resigned after a personal conflict with the prime minister, Dr **Mahathir Mohamad**. He then became engaged in an abortive challenge to Dr Mahathir's leadership with a former political rival, **Tengku Razaleigh Hamzah**. Musa Hitam was born on 18 April 1934 in Johor. He was educated at the University of Malaya in Singapore and came into politics through involvement in international student affairs. After a short

period in the civil service, he became executive secretary of **UMNO** (United Malays National Organization), entering Parliament in May 1969. Together with Dr Mahathir, he was publicly identified with criticism of the prime minister, **Tunku Abdul Rahman**, in the wake of intercommunal violence (**May 13 Racial Riots**) which followed the 1969 elections. He then spent a year in virtual exile at the University of Sussex in England, but was able to return to political life and achieve ministerial office when **Tun Abdul Razak** became prime minister. After the failure to unseat Dr Mahathir in 1987, Musa resigned his parliamentary seat in October 1988. He rejoined UMNO in January 1989 when Dr Mahathir underwent a heart bypass operation. After he had made a complete recovery, a reconciliation of a kind took place with the prime minister, which led to Musa's appointment as Malaysia's special representative to the United Nations with ministerial rank and then as representative to the UN Human Rights Commission. Although his political career seemed to have come to an effective end with his elevation in title from Datuk to Tan Sri, in April 2000 he was appointed chairman of Malaysia's newly-formed Human Rights Commission.

see also: Mahathir Mohamad, Datuk Sri; May 13 Racial Riots 1969; Rahman, Tunku Abdul; Razak, Tun Abdul; Razaleigh Hamzah, Tengku; UMNO.

## Muslim Unity Front (Malaysia) see Angkatan Perpaduan Malaysia.

## Mustapha bin Datuk Harun, Tun (Malaysia/Sabah)

Tun Mustapha was chief minister of Sabah between May 1967 and April 1976, during which he governed in the style of a Suluk chieftain and entertained ideas about taking Sabah out of Malaysia. Tun Mustapha was born on 31 August 1918 in Kudat, where he succeeded his father as a native chief. He was the founding president of the **United Sabah National Organization** (USNO). He was appointed head of state on Sabah's entry into Malaysia in September 1963, holding the office for two years before becoming federal minister for Sabah affairs. In April 1967 he secured election to the

Sabah legislature and became chief minister in May. As chief minister, he encouraged mass conversion to **Islam** and also promoted Muslim insurgency in the south of the Philippines.

In the face of political challenge inspired from Kuala Lumpur which led to defections from t he ruling party, Tun Mustapha resigned as chief minister but remained head of USNO. He retained his parliamentary seat in elections in April 1976 won by dissidents from USNO grouped in *Berjaya* (Sabah People's Union) but remained in the political wilderness. In April 1985 he mounted an abortive constitutional coup which delayed the appointment as chief minister of **Datuk Joseph Pairin Kitingan**, whose **Sabah United Party** (*Parti Bersatu Sabah*) had won a clear majority of elective seats. After Datuk Kitingan's party defected from the federal *Barisan Nasional* (National Front) just before the general elections in October 1990, Tun Mustapha became reconciled with the government in Kuala Lumpur. In May 1991 he stood as a successful candidate in a by-election for the Sabah legislature on behalf of **UMNO** (United Malays National Organization) within which USNO had been subsumed. The federal constitution was then amended specifically so that he could resume the office of minister for Sabah affairs. However, in January 1994 in a shock decision, he resigned his portfolio and also his party membership in a personal reaction to the failure of **Ghafar Baba** to retain his position as deputy president of UMNO and as deputy prime minister. In late February 1994 he joined the Sabah United Party, which had just won a narrow victory in state elections but was then overturned by defections from among its ranks. He died on 2 January 1995 aged 76.

*see also: Barisan Nasional*; *Berjaya*; Ghafar Baba, Abdul; Islam; Kitingan, Datuk Joseph Pairin; Sabah United Party; UMNO; United Sabah National Organization.

# N

## Nacionalista Party (Philippines)

The Nacionalista Party was the first political organization advocating independence which was permitted after the imposition of United States colonial rule in 1898. It represented a vehicle for the prosecution of elite family interests and as such was vulnerable to fragmentation. The party was formed in March 1907. From elections in June that year, it came to dominate Philippine political life up to the advent of the Pacific War in 1941 under the leadership of Manuel Quezón and Sergio Osmena. These two political rivals split the party over the struggle for the presidency in the early 1930s. The two factions healed the breach in June 1935 shortly before the establishment of the self-governing Commonwealth in November with Quezón as president. After the war, the Nacionalista Party split again as a result of personal rivalry and its so-called 'Liberal Wing' assumed power as the **Liberal Party**. The Nacionalista Party continued as a mirror-image elite network and a vehicle for personal political ambitions and patronage. Both **Ramón Magsaysay** and **Ferdinand Marcos** became presidents under its banner in 1953 and in 1965 respectively after defecting from the rival Liberal Party. Marcos was re-elected in 1969 as the Nacionalista Party candidate but after the introduction of martial law in 1972, it became defunct. Later in the decade, Marcos established his own alternative **New Society Movement** to manipulate the electoral process until his downfall in 1986. The Nacionalista Party was revived in 1989 to serve as the electoral vehicle for Salvador Laurel who, as Mrs **Corazón Aquino**'s running mate, had been elected as vice-president in 1986. In the presidential elections in May 1992, he secured a mere 3.4 per cent of the vote, which left the party politically moribund.
*see also:* Aquino, Corazón; Liberal Party; Magsaysay, Ramón; Marcos, Ferdinand; New Society Movement.

## Nahdatul Ulama (NU) (Indonesia)

*Nahdatul Ulama* (NU), which translates as Religious Scholars, is a traditional Islamic organization which was founded in east Java in 1926 in reaction to the modernism represented by **Muhammadiyah** (Followers of the Prophet Muhammad). It commands the support of some 30 million Indonesian Muslims mainly in Java and is led by **Abdurrahman Wahid**, whose grandfather Hashim Ashiri founded the movement. Active in education and welfare, it became part of the wider *Masyumi* (Consultative Council of Indonesian Muslims) set up first under Japanese auspices in 1943 and then reconstituted as a political party after the proclamation of independence in 1945. The NU split from *Masyumi* in 1952 and contested the first national elections in 1955 in its own right, securing third place with 18.4 per cent of the vote. Religious prerogative was its priority and its leadership supported President **Sukarno**'s attack on parliamentary democracy, thus securing preferment under his political system of **Guided Democracy**. Alienation set in with the growing influence of the Communist Party of Indonesia and after an abortive coup (*see* **Gestapu**) in October 1965, NU members joined with the military in exacting a bloody retribution.

The NU held its 1955 level of support in parliamentary elections in 1971. In 1973 it was forcibly merged with three other Islamic parties into the **United Development Party**, which has been permitted only a perfunctory political role at elections every five years. In 1984 the NU withdrew from the United Development Party to devote itself to its educational and welfare roles when the government's policy obliging all organizations to accept the state philosophy of *Pancasila* as their sole principle appeared to threaten its identity. Nonetheless, in the following year, when the law making *Pancasila* the sole philosophical principle was passed, the NU endorsed it. When, in December 1990, President **Suharto** sought to counter military resistance to his continuation in office by mobilizing Islamic support through **ICMI** (Association of Indonesian Muslim Intellectuals), the NU was not a party to his initiative and has continued to command significant popular support. In mid-1991

Abdurrahman Wahid set up an alternative *Forum Demokrasi* (Democracy Forum) as a counter to the attempt to mobilize the Islamic community on confessional grounds for President Suharto's political purpose. He also visibly displeased the president by refusing to have the NU nominate him for a further five-year term of office from March 1993. Under the leadership of Abdurrahman Wahid, the NU has been guided in the direction of religious tolerance and away from an Islamic political exclusivism. In the wake of Suharto's political downfall, Abdurrahman Wahid founded the National Awakening Party (*Partai Kebangkitan Bangsa*–PKB), which drew on his NU constituency. In parliamentary elections in June 1999, the PKB secured some 17 per cent and 51 out of 462 elective seats. In the following October, Abdurrahman Wahid attracted support from a coalition of Islamic-based parties to secure presidential office. A para-military youth wing of the NU has been deployed to intimidate critics of President Wahid in the media.

*see also:* Crocodile Hole; *Forum Demokrasi*; *Gestapu*; Guided Democracy; ICMI; Islam; *Masyumi*; *Muhammadiyah*; National Awakening Party; *Pancasila*; Suharto; Sukarno; United Development Party; Wahid, Abdurrahman.

## Nair, Devan (Singapore)

Devan Nair was president of Singapore from October 1981 until he was obliged to resign in March 1985 after admitting that he was an alcoholic, following an embarrassing episode during a private visit to Sarawak. Devan Nair was born on 5 August 1923 in Malacca in Malaya (now Malaysia). He was educated in Singapore and went on to become a schoolteacher. He entered politics through leadership of the teachers' trade union and was detained by the colonial administration during 1951-3 for left-wing activities. He became a founder member of the **People's Action Party** (PAP) in 1954, serving on its central executive committee until again being detained from 1956 to 1959. Devan Nair was a close political confidant of **Lee Kuan Yew** and, when the PAP assumed office, he played a key role in purging the trade unions of Communist influence. He served as the sole

PAP Member of the Malaysian Parliament from 1964, where he remained after Singapore's independence in 1965. He returned to political life in Singapore in 1969 to resume trade union responsibilities before becoming a Member of Parliament in 1979 and then president of the republic after the death of Benjamin Sheares. After his resignation, he spent time in the United States, returning to Singapore in 1987 where his public utterances on politics attracted the wrath of the prime minister, Lee Kuan Yew, who brought a libel suit against him. Fearful of being detained, Devan Nair went into political exile in the United States.

*see also:* Lee Kuan Yew; People's Action Party.

## Najib Tun Razak, Datuk Sri Mohamad (Malaysia)

Najib Tun Razak resumed the defence portfolio after elections in November 1999 in which his personal majority was reduced to 241 votes. He had held that portfolio before becoming minister of education in May 1995, which was seen as a political promotion. His return to defence by the prime minister, Dr **Mahathir Mohamad**, was interpreted as a penalty for his poor electoral showing and an indication of declining political fortunes. Nonetheless, Najib remains one of the most senior members of **UMNO**. He was elected one of its three vice-presidents in its General Assemblies in November 1993 and in October 1996. In May 2000, he secured the highest number of votes among the contenders for vice-presidential office. Datuk Sri Mohamad Najib Razak was born on 23 July 1954 in Kuala Lipis in the state of Pahang. His father, **Tun Abdul Razak**, became prime minister of Malaysia in 1970 but died prematurely in 1976. Najib was educated at the University of Nottingham in England and on his return to Malaysia began his career with the national oil company Petronas. He entered Parliament after elections in 1978 and held a series of junior ministerial appointments, including education and finance. In 1982 he stood successfully for the Pahang state legislature and was then appointed chief minister. He returned to national politics in the elections of 1986 and held the portfolio of youth and sports and subsequently that of defence. During the intense struggle within UMNO in

1986-7, which led to an unsuccessful challenge to the position of the prime minister, Dr Mahathir Mohamad, by **Tengku Razaleigh Hamzah**, Datuk Najib's position was somewhat equivocal. He avoided committing himself irrevocably to either figure but after Dr Mahathir's victory, he was able to use his Pahang state base to revive his political career.

see also: Mahathir Mohamad, Datuk Sri; Razak, Tun Abdul; Razaleigh Hamzah, Tengku; UMNO.

## Nam Thai Party (Thailand)

The Nam Thai (Dynamic Thai) Party was established in July 1994 at the initiative of Amnuay Virawan after he had resigned from the **New Aspiration Party** and also given up the office of deputy prime minister in the coalition government led by **Chuan Leekpai**. In elections in July 1995, Nam Thai secured only 18 seats in the Parliament of 319 members but was invited at a late stage to join the seven-party ruling coalition headed by **Banharn Silpa-archa**. Amnuay returned to the office of deputy prime minister with a special responsibility for international economic affairs, while party colleague and former permanent head of the Foreign Ministry, Kasem Kasemsri, assumed the Foreign Affairs portfolio. Amnuay has a background in banking and in the early 1980s had held the office of finance minister. His intention in establishing Nam Thai was to create a political vehicle for sustaining Thailand's modernization. To that end, he put together a mix of candidates with managerial, bureaucratic, academic experience and attracted the support of the former prime minister, **Anand Panyarachun**. In the event, Nam Thai's platform failed to appeal to a growing urban electorate, especially in the capital Bangkok, but made some impact in the rural north-east of the country. The party was effectively wiped out in elections in November 1996 in which it secured only one parliamentary seat.

see also: Anand Panyarachun; Banharn Silpa-archa; Chuan Leekpai; New Aspiration Party.

## Nasakom (Indonesia)

Nasakom is an acronym and slogan conceived by President **Sukarno** to indicate the trinity of socio-political elements which were legiti-mately part of the political system of **Guided Democracy** that he inaugurated in July 1959. The acronym was drawn from the Indonesian nasionalisme, agama and kommunisme, meaning nationalism, religion and communism, represented as the three dominant strains in society. It reflected the syncretic disposition of Sukarno, who had published an essay entitled Nationalism, Islam and Marxism as early as 1926. The prime function of the slogan was to justify the political participation of the Communist Party of Indonesia, which served as a mobilizing vehicle for Sukarno against the armed forces. In the wake of an abortive coup (see **Gestapu**) in October 1965 in which the Communists were implicated and which discredited Sukarno politically and also led to the dismantling of Guided Democracy, Nasakom soon disappeared from Indonesia's political lexicon.

see also: Crocodile Hole; Gestapu; Guided Democracy; Sukarno.

## Nasution, General Abdul Haris (Indonesia)

General Nasution was a distinguished military leader during and after the period of national revolution in Indonesia who conceived of t he 'middle way' doctrine (see **Dwi Fungsi**) justifying the prerogative political role of the armed forces. Abdul Haris Nasution was born in 1918 in Sumatra and trained before the Pacific War as an officer in the colonial army. During the Japanese occupation, he was involved with militant youth organizations in Bandung and then in the period of national revolution distinguished himself as a young commander of the west Java Siliwangi Division. After independence, as head of the army, he was responsible for a display of force before the non-elected parliament but backed away from a coup. He resigned office at the end of 1952 but was reinstated in 1955. He played a critical role in crushing regional uprisings in the late 1950s and encouraged President **Sukarno** to introduce his authoritarian **Guided Democracy** in July 1959 but was then manoeuvred away from the centre of power. In October 1965 General Nasution narrowly avoided assassination during an abortive coup (see **Gestapu**), which claimed the life of his young daughter. He threw his weight behind General **Suharto**, who took the lead in restoring order, but did not play a central role in shaping the new political system based on military power. He served for a time as speaker of the **People's Consultative Assembly** but went into early retirement in the 1970s, becoming an open critic of President Suharto's **New Order**. He signed the **Petition of Fifty** to the Parliament in 1980 complaining of the perversion of the constitution, which angered the president into denying him foreign travel, among other restrictions. In mid-1993, however, in the wake of his further re-election in March, President Suharto received General Nasution, his former commander, in an act of reconciliation. He was then allowed to travel abroad for medical treatment. General Nasution leaves behind a mixed reputation as a military commander and thinker and also as someone who was always out of his depth in politics, in which he was incapable of decisive action. He died on 6 September 2000.

see also: Crocodile Hole: *Dwi Fungsi*; *Gestapu*; Guided Democracy; New Order; People's Consultative Assembly; Petition of Fifty; Suharto; Sukarno.

## National Awakening Party (Indonesia)

The National Awakening Party (in Indonesian: *Partai Kebangkitan Bangsa–PKB*) was established specifically to contest parliamentary elections in June 1999 in the wake of the political downfall of former President Suharto in May 1998. It was set up as the political arm of the *Nahdatul Ulama* (NU), a rural-based Islamic organization of 30 million adherents with a liberal pluralist agenda, which had withdrawn from active politics in 1984. Its chairman was Matori Abdul Djalil but its effective leader was **Abdurrahman Wahid**, who headed the NU. In the elections in June 1999, it secured third place behind the **Indonesian Democratic Party** and *Golkar* with 17.4 per cent of the vote and 51 out of 462 elective seats. In the event, in October 1999, as a result of coalition politics designed to block the assumption to high office of **Megawati Sukarnoputri**, Abdurrahman Wahid was elected President of Indonesia by the **People's Consultative Assembly**.

see also: *Golkar*; Indonesian Democratic Party; Megawati Sukarnoputri; *Nahdatul Ulama*; People's Consultative Assembly; Wahid, Abdurrahman.

## National Democratic Front (NDF)
(Philippines)

The National Democratic Front (NDF) was established by the Communist Party of the Philippines on 24 April 1973 in an attempt to capitalize on opposition to President **Ferdinand Marcos**'s declaration of martial law in September 1972. The object was to create a political wing under which diverse opposition groupings could be mobilized in the party's interest. A manifesto was proclaimed in April 1973 which called for the unity of all anti-imperialist and democratic forces in order to establish a coalition government that would be truly democratic. The NDF attracted interest from left-wing clergy, intellectuals, students and labour groups and became especially active after general elections in 1978. It made a major strategic blunder in early 1986 in failing to appreciate the measure of popular support which had brought Mrs **Corazón Aquino** to high office in succession to President Marcos. In negotiations with her government, unrealistic demands were made for inclusion in a national coalition as the price for a political settlement. The NDF remained outside of the national political consensus; parties attracting its support failed abysmally to make any impact in the referendum in February 1987 on a new constitution and also in elections in May for a new Congress. The main threat to Mrs Aquino came from the right and not from the left; after her succession by **Fidel Ramos**, he was confident enough to permit the legalization of the Communist Party in September 1992. That party and the NDF has suffered an evident marginalization reinforced by internal divisions. Since the late 1980s the NDF has enjoyed more of a presence in Holland than in the Philippines; it has maintained an office in Utrecht for fund raising and international public relations. The intellectual head of the party, **José María Sisón**, has lived in Holland in exile for a number of years, ever since he was released from prison by Mrs Aquino under an amnesty. Negotiations between the NDF and the government in Manila were initiated in the early 1990s through the good offices of Vietnam in an attempt to find a place for the Communist front in national political life. However, intra-party squabbles have been an important factor in preventing those negotiations from bearing political fruit. The NDF took part in peace talks with the Philippines government in Utrecht in October 1994, which broke down. They were resumed in Brussels in June 1995 but lasted only one day ostensibly because Manila refused to release Sotero Llama, a communist military commander arrested the previous May, who had been named subsequently as a member of NDF negotiating panel. Talks were resumed in the Netherlands in June 1996 after Llama was released but then broke down after the **New People's Army** (NPA), the military wing of the NDF, had seized hostages. They were resumed again in early 1998. In February, representatives of the NDF and the government in Manila met in the Hague where an agreement on human rights was signed. The following month, they signed a second agreement on social and economic reforms. Despite this progress, the NDF was unwilling to continue negotiations in the Philippines, citing reasons of security. Moreover, in May 1999, they called off further talks because the government had entered into a new visiting forces agreement with the United States. By the end of the year, there were indications of a revival of the activity and strength of the NDF's military wing, which was estimated at around 6,000 men.

see also: Aquino, Corazón; Marcos, Ferdinand; New People's Army; Ramos, Fidel; Sisón, José María.

## National Justice Party (Malaysia)

The National Justice Party (in Malay: *Parti Keadilan Nasional*) was established in April 1999 by Wan Izizah Wan Ismail, the wife of the former deputy prime minister, **Anwar Ibrahim**, shortly before he was sentenced to six years' imprisonment on charges of corruption (abuse of power). The party served as a vehicle for mobilizing support in Anwar's cause and in challenging Prime Minister **Mahathir Mohamad**, deemed responsible for the attempt to destroy him politically. In June, the National Justice Party entered into an alliance with the opposition *Parti Islam se-Malaysia* (PAS), the Demo-

cratic Action Party (DAP) and the *Parti Ra'ayat Malaysia* (Malaysian People's Party) to confront the ruling **Barisan Nasional** in forthcoming elections. In those elections in November 1999, the National Justice Party secured five federal parliamentary seats attracting support from younger educated Malays alienated by the governmental authoritarianism. In the federal parliament, it remained within the **Barisan Alternatif** (Alternative Front) opposition coalition. By mid-2000, it had begun to display signs of internal discord.

see also: Anwar Ibrahim; *Barisan Alternatif*; *Barisan Nasional*; Democratic Action Party; Mahathir Mohamad; *Parti Islam se-Malaysia*.

## National League for Democracy
(Burma/Myanmar)

The National League for Democracy was formed on 24 September 1988 as a political challenge to the **State Law and Order Restoration Council** (SLORC), which had assumed power on behalf of the military establishment six days before. That seizure of power followed a bloody confrontation on the streets of Rangoon and other major towns in which the armed forces had opened fire on unarmed demonstrators. The National League for Democracy was set up by **Aung San Suu Kyi**, the daughter of the nationalist leader and martyr, **Aung San**, and by Aung Gyi and Tin U, former senior officers who had become opponents of **Ne Win**'s regime. Aung Gyi left the party in December 1988, while Aung San Suu Kyi was arrested in July 1989. Nonetheless, the National League for Democracy participated in general elections in May 1990, winning 392 out of 485 seats for the newly created People's Assembly with some 60 per cent of the popular vote. (SLORC's **National Unity Party** won only ten seats.) However, the military establishment refused to convene the legislature until a new constitution had been drafted. SLORC also began to take repressive measures against members of the National League for Democracy, many of whom were deprived of their parliamentary status on spurious grounds, while Aung San Suu Kyi was expelled from the party. A National Convention to draft a new constitution began work in January 1993 and concluded over a year later, with the armed forces provided with a prerogative political role. Selected members of the National League for Democracy attended but as voting cannon-fodder for the military establishment, which has remained unwilling to recognize the outcome of the elections of May 1990. When Aung San Suu Kyi was released from detention in July 1995, the party had been reduced to a shadow of its former self through repression by SLORC. The NLD has been subject to recurrent harassment and enforced resignations, although it was permitted to hold a congress in May 1998 to commemorate its electoral victory in May 1990. Aung San Suu Kyi has been prevented from visiting party members outside Rangoon. NLD headquarters were sealed off by security forces in September 2000 after Aung San Sun Kyi had been forcibly returned to her residence after trying to leave the capital.

*see also:* Aung San; Aung San Suu Kyi; National Unity Party; Ne Win; State Law and Order Restoration Council.

## National Liberation Front of South Vietnam (NLF)  (Vietnam)

The National Liberation Front of South Vietnam (NLF) was set up on 20 December 1960 through the initiative of the Communist Party to mobilize popular support south of the 17th parallel of latitude against the government of President *Ngo Dinh Diem* in Saigon. In its composition and declared political aspirations, which avoided Communist associations and reference to early unification, it replicated the **Viet Minh** (standing for the League for the Independence of Vietnam), which had served as a corresponding vehicle for the party from 1941. The NLF was established in a jungle area close to the Cambodian border under the figurehead chairmanship of Nguyen Huu Tho, a French-educated lawyer of liberal persuasion. It functioned through a myriad of functional groupings headed also by prominent personalities whose nationalist credentials were not touched by Communist affiliations. In effect, the NLF's activities were soon directly controlled by the People's Revolutionary Party, which was established in 1962 as a southern branch of the national party. In June 1969 the NLF, which had attracted a membership of several million,

became a constituent part of the **Provisional Revolutionary Government of the Republic of South Vietnam**. This attempt to demonstrate a fuller international identity arose from the NLF's participation in quadrapartite peace negotiations in Paris from January 1969. After the military collapse of the Saigon government in April 1975, the NLF had served its useful political purpose and, much to the chagrin of many of its leading non-Communist members, was merged into a northern counterpart, the Fatherland Front.

*see also:* Diem, Ngo Dinh; Paris Peace Agreements 1973; Provisional Revolutionary Government of the Republic of South Vietnam; Viet Minh; Vietnam War.

## National Mandate Party  (Indonesia)

The National Mandate Party (in Indonesia: *Partai Amanat Nasional*–PAN) was set up in the wake of the political downfall of President Suharto in May 1998 in order to contest parliamentary elections in June 1999. It was established by Dr Amien Rais, a professor at Gadjah Mada University in Yogyakarta, who had been a leading figure in **ICMI** but was removed from office because of his opposition to President Suharto, which became outspoken in the weeks prior to his resignation. Amien Rais had previously been chairman of *Muhammadiyah*, a modernist Muslim organization, which drew its support from urban dwellers. The National Mandate Party made a specific appeal to Indonesia's new middle class through a manifesto with an agenda for constitutional and other liberal reforms. In the event, it came fifth in the polls with only 7.1 per cent of the vote and 36 out of 462 elective seats. In the wake of a dismal electoral performance, Amien Rais took PAN in a more conspicuously Islamic and anti-Christian direction and promoted a coalition of like-minded parties in opposition to the presidential bid of **Megawati Sukarnoputri**, whose **Indonesian Democratic Party** had come first in the polls but without an overall majority. Amien Rais's initiative paved the way for **Abdurrahman Wahid** to be elected President of Indonesia in October 1999 by the **People's Consultative Assembly** of which he had earlier become chairman.

*see also:* ICMI; Indonesian Democratic Party;

Megawati Sukarnoputri; *Muhammadiyah*; People's Consultative Assembly; Wahid, Abdurrahman.

## National Resilience (Indonesia)

*Ketahanan Nasional* (National Resilience) is a slogan and political ideal articulated by President **Suharto** of Indonesia from the late 1960s to indicate those qualities of self-sufficiency and resourcefulness which would strengthen the economic, social and political fabric of the state in the interest of development and stability. This **New Order** concept was derived from the experience of Indonesia's armed forces in seeking a social basis for national security. It was applied also in aggregate expression as a way in which like-minded partners in regional cooperation, such as **ASEAN**, could achieve a condition of regional resilience that would deny the interventionist role of external powers in South-East Asia. After the political downfall of Suharto coincident with ASEAN's decline in cohesion and international standing, the term virtually vanished from the Association's lexicon.

*see also:* ASEAN; New Order; Suharto.

## National Unity Party (Burma/Myanmar)

The National Unity Party was set up on 26 September 1988 as the successor to the **Burma Socialist Programme Party** (BSPP) through the intervention of the **State Law and Order Restoration Council** (SLORC). SLORC had seized power eight days previously in an attempt to reinforce the control of the military establishment in the wake of a bloody confrontation between security forces and unarmed civilian demonstrators. The National Unity Party was intended to serve as the electoral vehicle for SLORC in polls held in May 1990. In the event, the National Unity Party captured only 10 seats in a People's Assembly of 485 seats, although it secured some 25 per cent of the popular vote. The opposition **National League for Democracy** won 392 seats but SLORC refused to permit the legislature to convene. Instead, a constitutional convention was held from January 1993 in which the National Unity Party participated but only as

the unpopular instrument of a resented military establishment.

*see also:* Burma Socialist Programme Party; National League for Democracy; State Law and Order Restoration Council.

## Nawaphon Movement (Thailand)

The *Nawaphon* (New Force) Movement was a right-wing patriotic organization which was active during the mid-1970s in opposition to parliamentary democracy. It was set up in 1974 by Wattana Kiewvimol, the head of the Thai Students Association in the United States, on his return from studying at Seton Hall University. With covert military support, *Nawaphon* attracted a substantial following on the basis of an emotive identification with nation, religion and monarchy seemingly challenged by left-wing forces. It played an important part in the public agitation which led to the killing of students in the **Thammasat University Massacre** in October 1976, which was followed by a military coup. With the re-establishment of a military government, support for *Nawaphon* waned because of suspicion that it was primarily a vehicle for the personal ambition of senior figures within the army.

*see also:* Thammasat University Massacre 1976.

## Ne Win, General (Burma/Myanmar)

General Ne Win, as head of a military junta ruled Burma autocratically and brutally in various guises for more than a quarter of a century. He was primarily responsible for inaugurating a pseudo-socialist order that impoverished the country, provoking popular revolt put down in 1988 with great loss of life. Ne Win was born on 14 May 1911 in Paungdle in Prome District in lower Burma to a Sino-Burmese family, who gave him the name Shu Maung. He was educated at the University of Rangoon and, although a member of the nationalist movement, was not politically prominent. He left without a degree in 1932 to begin his working life as a postal clerk. He joined the *Dobama Asiayone* (Our Burma Association), a militant nationalist movement, and through it became associated with its leader **Aung San**, who recruited him as a member of a group of thirty comrades who were exfiltrated to Japan in 1940 to undergo military training.

Ne Win, who acquired his *nom de guerre* (meaning Bright Son) in this period, returned with the Japanese army when they invaded Burma in December 1941.

Ne Win became a commander in the Japanese-sponsored Burma National Army, which in March 1945 switched to the side of the Allies as Japan's defeat seemed only a matter of time. The nationalist leader, Aung San, won the respect of Admiral Lord Mountbatten, the Supreme Allied Commander, who supported Burma's independence. Despite factional and ideological conflict within the nationalist movement, independence was set for January 1948, but in July 1947 Aung San and several cabinet ministers were assassinated. At the time, Ne Win was deputy to the commander-in-chief, Lt-General Smith-Dun, who was from the **Karen** minority who soon after rose in revolt. Smith-Dun was retired in early 1949 and Lt-General Ne Win took over as supreme commander of all armed forces and in April became deputy prime minister in charge of defence and home affairs until the following year, when the insurgent challenge to the Union of Burma had been crushed. He returned to government temporarily as prime minister from 1958 to 1960 when civilian government had to be suspended for two years.

On 2 March 1962, as commander-in-chief, he led a successful coup which established a continuous period of military rule. He set up a ruling revolutionary council and also established the **Burma Socialist Programme Party** (BSPP) under whose exclusive aegis a **Burmese Way to Socialism** was promulgated. This ideology became the blueprint for a rigid system of central planning and bureaucratic control which brought the country to the point of economic collapse, so that it had to apply to the United Nations for 'least developed status'. He became president of Burma on its establishment as a socialist republic in 1974, giving up that office in 1981 but remaining as president of the BSPP; he resigned in July 1988 in a context of political decay and chaos. Although government was placed in the charge of the **State Law and Order Restoration Council** (SLORC) in September 1988, Ne Win is believed to continue to exercise a continuing influence over the military establishment and matters of political management. After not being seen in public since 1989, he was photographed in Jakarta in September 1997 looking pale and frail having travelled to Indonesia at the invitation of President Suharto for a short stay during which he visited the grave of Madame Tien, the president's late wife. He then flew on to Singapore, which he had visited for a medical check-up in 1993. In September 1998, he returned to Singapore for treatment for a clot on the brain.

see also: Aung San; Burma Socialist Programme Party; Burmese Way to Socialism; Karen; State Law and Order Restoration Council.

## Neo Lao Hak Sat  (Laos)

*Neo Lao Hak Sat* (Lao Patriotic Front) was established in January 1956 by the Lao People's Party, in effect the Communist Party, as a national front acting on behalf of the *Pathet Lao* (Lao Nation or State) movement. Headed by Prince **Souphanouvong**, the *Neo Lao Hak Sat* was constituted formally on a functional basis with representation, for example, from trade unions and women's and farmers' groups. It served also as a political party in the late 1950s enjoying significant success in supplementary national elections whose outcome had a polarizing effect between right and left in Lao politics instead of promoting national reconciliation as intended by the terms of the **Geneva Agreements on Indochina** of 1954. Throughout its existence, until superseded by a corresponding Lao Front for National Construction in 1979, the *Neo Lao Hak Sat* was controlled by the Communist Party of Laos, initially as the Lao People's Party and then from 1972 in the name of the **Lao People's Revolutionary Party** (led by **Kaysone Phomvihan** until his death in November 1992 and then by **Khamtay Siphandon**), which has ruled the country since the end of 1975.

see also: Geneva Agreements on Indochina 1954; Geneva Agreements on Laos 1962; Kaysone Phomvihan; Khamtay Siphandon; Lao People's Revolutionary Party; *Pathet Lao*; Souphanouvong.

## New Aspiration Party  (Thailand)

The New Aspiration Party (*Kwam Wang Mai*) was formed in October 1990 as the personal political vehicle of former army commander General **Chavalit Yongchaiyuth** who had been disappointed in a brief spell as deputy prime minister in the government of the prime minister, **Chatichai Choonhavan**. The New Aspiration Party secured fifty-one seats in elections conducted in September 1992. It then joined the coalition government headed by the prime minister, **Chuan Leekpai**, with General Chavalit assuming the office of minister of the interior. Although not closely identified with the military which had employed violence against civilian demonstrators in May 1992, his party lost electoral support in September 1992 compared to its performance in March that year and has also suffered factional tensions based on regional affiliations. In July 1994, its deputy leader defected to form a new party. General Chavalit was briefly deputy prime minister from October before withdrawing from the governing coalition in December 1994 in an abortive bid to topple it. In elections in July 1995, the New Aspiration Party won fifty-seven seats and was invited to join the government headed by **Banharn Silpa-archa**, with General Chavalit as deputy prime minister and defence minister. It improved that position considerably in elections in November 1996 securing 125 seats, which made it the largest parliamentary party. General Chavalit went on to form a coalition government but was obliged to step down as prime minister in November 1997 in the wake of economic crisis for which his administration was held responsible. The New Aspiration Party was excluded from the new coalition government headed by the **Democrat Party**, and has remained in opposition. In June 2000, ninety-six of its members resigned from parliament in an abortive attempt to force a snap election.

*see also:* Banharn Silpa-archa; Chatichai Choonhavan; Chavalit Yongchaiyuth; Chuan Leekpai; Democrat Party.

## New Economic Policy (Malaysia)

In the wake of an electoral reverse in May 1969 followed by intercommunal violence, the **May 13 Racial Riots**, the Malay-dominated government of Malaysia introduced a New Economic Policy in 1971. The policy, set out within the Second Malaysia Plan, comprised two related themes. These were 'to reduce and eventually eradicate poverty, by raising income levels and increasing employment opportunities for all Malaysians, irrespective of race' and also to accelerate 'the process of restructuring Malaysian society to correct economic imbalance, so as to reduce and eventually eliminate the identification of race with economic function'. To those ends, the target was set of raising holdings of corporate assets by the Malays from some 2 per cent to 30 per cent by 1990. The New Economic Policy was driven by political considerations. **UMNO** (United Malays National Organization) had experienced an electoral seepage from its natural constituency because of Malay apprehension that Chinese economic dominance might be translated into political expression. UMNO acted to protect the political birthright of the Malays and its prerogative guardian role of their interests through economic initiative. Sustained affirmative action to the advantage of the Malay community as well as ensuring that key economic portfolios in government were held by Malay ministers had the desired political effect to UMNO's advantage. It also led to the emergence of a Malay business elite associated with UMNO who enriched themselves to form a virtual new class. In June 1991 the prime minister, Dr **Mahathir Mohamad**, announced details of his government's New Development Policy to replace the New Economic Policy which had applied between 1971 and 1990. The new policy was distinguished by an intention to moderate affirmative action in favour of the Malays and to lay greater stress on improved education and training. The target of 30 per cent of corporate assets to be held by the Malays was retained but without a set date for realization, despite their having attained only 20.3 per cent by 1990. In February 1998, former finance minister **Daim Zainuddin**, then executive director of the National Economic Action Council, announced that the New Economic Policy would be relaxed to allow non-Malays to own shares in Malay-dominated companies in order to mitigate the impact of economic crisis. However, Prime Minister Mahathir Mohamad then suggested that the relaxation of policy would be a temporary measure. In August 2000, Deputy-

Prime Minister **Abdullah Ahmad Badawi** announced that the affirmative action programme for Malays would remain in place.

*see also:* Badawi, Abdullah Ahmad; Mahathir Mohamad, Datuk Sri; Daim Zainuddin; May 13 Racial Riots 1969; UMNO

## New Emerging Forces (NEFOS)
(Indonesia)

New Emerging Forces (NEFOS) is a term devised by President **Sukarno** to represent the progressive elements in a world divided into two incompatible groupings, with the reactionary grouping described as the **Old Established Forces** (OLD-EFOS). Sukarno put forward his bipolar view of the world as a radical alternative to the policy of non-alignment on 17 August 1963 in a speech commemorating the republic's proclamation of independence. The New Emerging Forces were described as being composed of 'the Asian Nations, the Latin American Nations, the Nations of the Socialist countries, the progressive groups in the capitalist countries'. Sukarno represented Indonesia as the natural leader among this constellation of progressive elements and enjoyed transitory success in giving the New Emerging Forces an institutional form when Jakarta became the venue for the first Games of the New Emerging Forces in November 1963 through Chinese financial support. An attempt to convene a conference of New Emerging Forces with the object of confirming Indonesia's role and securing endorsement of its **Confrontation** of Malaysia failed. A preliminary conference of African and Asian states arranged for June 1965 in Algeria was postponed *sine die* because of a preceding military coup. In October 1965 an abortive coup (*see* **Gestapu**) set in train events that led to Sukarno's political downfall and a fundamental change in the nature of Indonesia's politics and foreign policy. With that change, the term New Emerging Forces disappeared from the republic's political lexicon.

*see also:* Confrontation; Crocodile Hole; Gestapu; Old Established Forces; Sukarno.

## New Order  (Indonesia)

The term New Order was employed to dignify and validate the regime established in Indonesia by General **Suharto** with the support of the armed forces in the wake of an abortive coup (*see* **Gestapu**) in October 1965. The term was intended also to differentiate that regime based on the values of the 1945 constitution and the state philosophy *Pancasila* from the alleged political deviations of President **Sukarno**. In July 1966, while Sukarno still occupied presidential office, the provisional **People's Consultative Assembly** endorsed General Suharto's seizure of power in March, which was represented as an '*ordre baru*' or New Order. The unfortunate identification with the language of European fascism of the 1930s was seized on by critics of the regime. In time, the term New Order came to be superseded by that of *Pancasila* democracy as the legitimizing trope. President Suharto's so-called New Order was effectively terminated with his resignation on 21 May 1998.

*see also:* Crocodile Hole; Gestapu; Pancasila; People's Consultative Assembly; Suharto; Sukarno; Supersemar.

## New People's Army  (Philippines)

The New People's Army is the military arm of the Communist Party of the Philippines which was reconstituted on Maoist lines at a conference held between 26 December 1968 and 7 January 1969 in southern Tarlac Province on the island of Luzón. The New People's Army was established on 29 March 1969 in the same vicinity and drew support not only from a younger generation of political activists but from members of the long-standing Communist *Hukbalahap* **Movement** insurgency which had degenerated into banditry. Bernabe Buscayno (also known as Commander Dante) became the military leader in October 1970 after the capture of Faustino del Mundo (Commander Sumulong), who had switched political allegiance. The New People's Army, inspired by Maoist thought, adopted a strategy of military decentralization, exploiting the archipelagic condition of the Philippines to avoid a vulnerable concentration of forces. This strategy proved to be increasingly successful with the evident failure of the martial law regime of President **Ferdinand Marcos**, inaugurated in September 1972. The deteriorating economic condition of the country and the feckless brutality of a rapidly expanded armed forces attracted recruits to the Communist cause.

That cause was served further by the assassination of opposition leader **Benigno Aquino** in August 1983. By the mid-1980s, the New People's Army had an estimated strength of some 15,000 effectives and had established fighting presences in sixty-three of the country's seventy-three provinces where they engaged in ambush and selective assassination. Moreover, it demonstrated an organizational resilience, despite the capture of some of its senior figures, leading a Pentagon official to warn that it could seize power within ten years unless basic reforms were introduced.

The momentum of its military challenge was arrested, however, after the fall of President Marcos and the assumption to office of Mrs **Corazón Aquino** in February 1986. A miscalculation of political mood, expressed in a rejection of the constitutional process, led to a drain in popular support. Moreover, the Communist movement became subject to internal divisions as a consequence of the change in political system. Under new leadership, the security forces improved their performance and by the time that Mrs Aquino was succeeded as president by former army chief of staff, **Fidel Ramos**, in elections in May 1992, the New People's Army had declined as a fighting force. President Ramos was helped by the closure of all US military bases, such as the **Clark Air Base** and the **Subic Bay Naval Base**, which had long been a central nationalist demand by the Communist movement and in September 1992 he was sufficiently self-confident to persuade the Congress to legalize the Communist Party. The New People's Army has not been disbanded and still deploys some thousands of insurgents who have continued to engage in guerrilla activities in rural areas where poverty is still the norm. The government has been engaged in intermittent negotiations with the **National Democratic Front**, which represents its interests but without being able to bring the limited insurgency to an end. The New People's Army has shown an ability to attack police stations and to kidnap senior military personnel. In November 1999, Defence Secretary Orlando Mercado warned that the New People's Army had grown in strength. By mid-2000, ambushes of security forces had been mounted in three provinces.

*see also:* Aquino, Benigno; Aquino, Corazón; Clark Air Base; *Hukbalahap* Movement; Marcos, Ferdinand; National Democratic Front; Ramos, Fidel; Sisón, José María; Subic Bay Naval Base.

## New Society Movement (Philippines)

The *Kilusang Bagong Lipunan* (New Society Movement) was established by President **Ferdinand Marcos** on 1 February 1978 as his political vehicle for dominating the first elections to be permitted since martial law was inaugurated in 1972. Elections for an interim National Assembly were held in April with a decisive, albeit fraudulent, victory for Marcos, who then assumed the office of prime minister as well as holding that of president. The New Society Movement was an attempt to demonstrate popular organizational expression for the term employed by Marcos to dignify his seizure of power. In the event, it proved to be little more than an electoral device which was employed again in 1984, when there were also strong suspicions of polling malpractice. The New Society Movement effectively disappeared with the fall of President Marcos in February 1986. His widow **Imelda Marcos** revived the title and stood under its aegis in presidential elections in May 1992, when she secured 10 per cent of the vote in an unsuccessful bid to assume her husband's political mantle.
*see also:* Marcos, Ferdinand; Marcos, Imelda.

## Ngo Dinh Diem (Vietnam) *see* Diem, Ngo Dinh.

## Nguyen Ai Quoc (Vietnam) *see* Ho Chi Minh.

## Nguyen Co Thach (Vietnam) *see* Thach, Nguyen Co.

## Nguyen Dy Nien (Vietnam)

Nguyen Dy Nien was appointed foreign minister of Vietnam in January 2000. He was born in 1935 and trained as an academic specializing in Indian history studying at Varanasi University during the 1960s but then transferred to the foreign service. He was appointed deputy foreign minister in 1987 with responsibilities for

Cambodia and for normalizing relations with China. He was elected a member of the central committee of the Communist Party in June 1991.

## Nguyen Manh Cam  (Vietnam)

Nguyen Manh Cam was appointed Vietnam's foreign minister in August 1991 in succession to **Nguyen Co Thach**, who had become an obstacle to rapprochement with the People's Republic of China. He was a long-standing career diplomat chosen for his professional skills rather than for his political standing. Nguyen Manh Cam was born in 1929 in central Nghe Tinh Province and joined the Communist Party at the age of 17. He is believed to have received a university education and showed an early aptitude for diplomacy. He has served extensively in Europe, including two periods as ambassador in Moscow, where he was in post at the time of his appointment as foreign minister. Possibly because he had not been directly involved in difficult negotiations with Chinese counterparts, Nguyen Manh Cam was regarded as a suitable plenipotentiary for repairing Sino-Vietnamese relations. He has also been active in developing relations with **ASEAN** (Association of South-East Asian Nations), which Vietnam joined in July 1995. Nguyen Manh Cam became a member of the party's Politburo at its mid-term conference held in January 1994. In September 1997, he was appointed additionally to the office of deputy prime minister, which he retained on being succeeded as foreign minister by **Nguyen Dy Nien** in January 2000.

see also: ASEAN; Thach, Nguyen Co; Nguyen Dy Nien.

## Nguyen Tat Thanh  (Vietnam) see Ho Chi Minh.

## Nguyen Van Linh  (Vietnam) see Linh, Nguyen Van.

## Nguyen Van Thieu  (Vietnam) see Thieu, Nguyen Van.

## Nien, Nguyen Dy  (Vietnam) see Nguyen Dy Nien.

## Nixon Doctrine 1969  (Vietnam)

On 25 July 1969 at a press briefing at a United States military base on the island of Guam shortly before embarking on a tour of southern Asian countries, US President Richard Nixon set out revised criteria for his government's policy in the region. It was made explicit that the object of that revision was to avoid direct United States involvement in any future **Vietnam War**-type conflicts. In a speech in November and then in a report to Congress in February 1970, the president spelled out the terms of what had come to be known as the Nixon Doctrine. These terms were that

> The United States will keep all its treaty commitments; we shall provide a shield if a nuclear power threatens the freedom of a nation allied with us, or of a nation whose survival we consider vital to our security and the security of the region as a whole. In cases involving other types of aggression, we shall furnish military and economic assistance when requested and as appropriate. But we shall look to the nation directly threatened to assume the primary responsibility of providing the manpower for its defence.

Richard Nixon's remarks on Guam indicated the future direction of US policy in South-East Asia leading to military disengagement from Vietnam and the rest of Indochina before the end of 1973 as provided for initially in the **Paris Peace Agreements**

see also: Paris Peace Agreements 1973; Vietnam War.

## Nol, Lon  (Cambodia)

Marshal Lon Nol achieved notoriety as the leader of the coup which overthrew Prince **Norodom Sihanouk** on 18 March 1970. He ended the monarchy in Cambodia and in October 1970 established the short-lived **Khmer Republic**, which was superseded when the **Khmer Rouge** seized power in April 1975. Lon Nol was born on 13 November 1913 in Prey Veng Province. He was educated at the Lycee Sisowath from which he joined the French colonial administration, rising rapidly to become a provincial governor at the age of 32. At the end of the Pacific War, Lon Nol became chief of the Cambodian police and then transferred to military command, displaying loyalty to Norodom Sihanouk, who was then king. Lon Nol was appointed governor of the important border province of Battambang in 1954 and then chief of staff of the army in 1955. By the end of the decade, he had become both commander-in-chief and minister of defence. He was prime minister 1966–7. In September 1969 he returned to the office of prime minister as Prince Sihanouk's political grip on Cambodia began to weaken.

After the removal of Prince Sihanouk, Lon Nol, who was a practising mystic, showed himself to be an incompetent military leader in the face of a Vietnamese-led insurgent challenge. In February 1971 he suffered a stroke from which he never fully recovered, yet still held on to power with US backing. His rule was both repressive and corrupt, contributing to the ultimate victory of the Khmer Rouge. He was persuaded to go into exile on 1 April 1975 but only in return for US$1 million being deposited in his name in a United States bank. He settled in Hawaii until 1979 when he removed to California, where he died on 17 November 1985.

see also: Khmer Republic; Khmer Rouge; Sihanouk, Norodom.

**Norodom Ranariddh** (Cambodia) see Ranariddh, Norodom.

**Norodom Sihanouk** (Cambodia) see Sihanouk, Norodom.

**Nouhak Phoumsavan** (Laos)
Nouhak Phoumsavan was elected president of the Lao People's Democratic Republic on 25 November 1992 by the Supreme People's Assembly on the death of **Kaysone Phomvihan**. Nouhak and Kaysone were close colleagues and veterans of the Laotian revolutionary movement. Nouhak was born in the southern town of Savannakhet in 1916 and is known to have run a transport business between Laos and Vietnam in the early 1940s, so coming into contact with Vietnamese Communists who recruited him to their cause. He was in Hanoi at the end of the Pacific War as representative of the Laotian revolutionaries. After the outbreak

of hostilities with the French in the **Indochina Wars**, he directed guerrilla operations across the Lao-Vietnamese border. He was a *Pathet Lao* delegate to the conference that resulted in the **Geneva Agreements on Indochina** in 1954, after which he played a prominent role in the **Lao People's Revolutionary Party** following its formation in 1955. Although he engaged in negotiations with successive governments in Vientiane before 1975, his main contribution was as Kaysone's deputy as second-ranking member of the party's Politburo. After the establishment of the Communist government in 1975, Nouhak became minister of finance and then in 1982 one of four deputy prime ministers. As president, Nouhak is not believed to occupy as powerful a position as the prime minister, **Khamtay Siphandon**, who replaced Kaysone as head of the ruling party in November 1992. In March 1996, he was removed from the party's politburo and, in February 1998, he was replaced as president by Khamtay Siphandon.

see also: Geneva Agreements on Indochina 1954; Indochina Wars; Kaysone Phomvihan; Khamtay Siphandon; Lao People's Revolutionary Party; *Pathet Lao*.

**Nu, U** (Burma/Myanmar)
U Nu was the first prime minister of Burma after independence from Britain in January 1948. He came to high office in tragic circumstances following the assassination of the nationalist leader, **Aung San**, and other cabinet colleagues in July 1947. He held office until 1958 with an interruption during 1956–7 and then again from 1960 to 1962 when military intervention marked an end to civilian politics. U Nu was born on 25 May 1907 in Wakema and was educated at Rangoon University where he became president of the Students' Union in the mid-1930s. After graduation, he became a schoolteacher and was active in the nationalist organization *Dobama Asiayone* (Our Burma Association). He was interned by the colonial authorities at the outbreak of the Second World War and then released after the Japanese occupied the country. He served as foreign minister in the wartime government headed by Ba Maw and then became deputy to Aung San in the **Anti-Fascist People's Freedom League** (AFPFL) which spearheaded

the drive for independence after the defeat of the Japanese. As prime minister, he was faced with constant turbulence arising from having to cope with Communist and ethnic-minority insurrection as well as factional infighting which proved to be beyond his capacity to control. U Nu was imprisoned between 1962 and 1966. He was allowed to leave Burma in April 1969 ostensibly for Buddhist pilgrimage but sought to organize resistance from Thailand against the rule of General **Ne Win** until 1973, when he left to spend a year in the United States before passing the rest of the decade in India. He returned to Burma to retire in 1980 after an amnesty but made an ineffectual attempt to return to active politics in August 1988 in the wake of the bloody confrontation between the armed forces and civilians demonstrating for greater democracy. He set up a League for Democracy and Peace and then proclaimed a 'parallel' government in September, which proved to be empty gestures incapable of significant impact. He was placed under house arrest in December 1989 and then released in April 1992. As a politician, U Nu has always been a respected figure of integrity but regarded as unworldly and not really suited to the turbulence of public life. He died in Rangoon on 14 February 1995 aged 87.

*see also:* Anti-Fascist People's Freedom League; Aung San; Ne Win; State Law and Order Restoration Council.

# O

## Old Established Forces (OLDEFOS)
(Indonesia)

The Old Established Forces (OLDEFOS) was a category in political demonology invented by President **Sukarno**. He made clearest reference to this pejorative term in a speech on 17 August 1963, when Indonesia had launched its campaign of **Confrontation** in opposition to the formation of the Federation of Malaysia. The Old Established Forces were represented as the reactionary camp in a world divided into two alignments set in perpetual confrontation. Ranged against progressive **New Emerging Forces** (NEFOS), including the post-colonial states and the Socialist countries, were the Old Established Forces identified as the 'old forces of domination'. Their constituents were imperialism, colonialism and neo-colonialism and it was alleged that Malaysia had been conceived to serve these nefarious interests.

*see also:* Confrontation; New Emerging Forces; Sukarno.

## Ong Boon Hua (Malaya/Malaysia) *see* Chin Peng.

## *Organisasi Papua Merdeka* (OPM)
(Indonesia) *see* Free Papua Movement.

## Overseas Chinese

The term Overseas Chinese applies to a diaspora of well over 20 million people of migrant origin who are dispersed disparately within the states of South-East Asia. They comprise a majority of the population only in Singapore. Chinese migration to South-East Asia was driven by a mixture of push and pull factors and took place in the main from the southern provinces of China precipitated by adverse economic circumstances and political upheaval during the nineteenth century. It was also affected and tied up with colonialist expansion and an attendant demand for supplies of disciplined labour. The Chinese term for such migrants has been *Hua-ch'iao*, which translates as Chinese so

journers, indicating the intention of the first waves of migrants to amass sufficient wealth to return to their native villages to retire in comfort and with respect. Up to the 1930s migration was primarily a male phenomenon and there was a return traffic, but there were not many cases of peasants living in rags and returning with riches. However, with the migration of Chinese women and marriage among Chinese within South-East Asia, a pattern of permanent settlement began which has been sustained and consolidated with successor generations, so that Chinese communities are an established part of South-East Asian societies. Of the main concentrations, around 7 million reside in Indonesia, nearly 6 million in Thailand, over 4 million in Malaysia and over 2 million in Singapore.

During the colonial period, Chinese migrants distinguished themselves by their industry and acumen and established a strong position in the retail trades in particular, assisted by close-knit kin and dialect associations. Their economic success as well as continuing ties with China and engagement in Chinese politics attracted envy and suspicions. In 1914 Thailand's King Wachirawat wrote a booklet entitled *The Jews of the East*, which compared Chinese immigrants to insect pests that devour crops and leave fields dry and bare of grain. He attacked the migrant Chinese for their racial loyalty and sense of racial superiority, which stood in the way of their assimilation and transfer of allegiance to their country of residence. Ironically, although Chinese in Thailand rose to over 10 per cent of the population, their assimilation has been quite striking, with intermarriage leading to a close identification with Thai culture. Although Chinese distinctiveness has not been erased completely, assimilation has more readily occurred where the local cultures have been receptive. Thus in predominantly Buddhist Thailand and in predominantly Christian hilippines, for example, the intermarried-Chinese communities have found a social niche that has allowed them to rise to the highest offices in politics. The situation has been different in those countries where **Islam** prevails and where assimilation has required a much greater assumption of an alien identity, including a repudiation of pork-eating. Racial tension has been very high at times in Malaysia, where a violent communal confrontation (**May 13 Racial Riots**) in 1969 was a historical turning-point in shaping the political system in the interest of the indigenous Malays.

If the Chinese of South-East Asia were suspect by indigenous communities because of their attachment to their homeland, that suspicion was made acute after the acific War with the establishment of the eople's Republic of China as a revolutionary state. Earlier Chinese involvement in Communist insurrection in Malaya and Singapore had made the Chinese, like the Jews, susceptible to the charge of being both capitalist and communist at the same time. Initially, the government in Beijing carried over the *jus sanguinis* policy of its ousted Nationalist predecessor whereby any person of all or partly Chinese parentage was treated as a Chinese citizen. That policy was changed from the mid-1950s, when it began to be realized in Beijing that it was a major obstacle to promoting good state-to-state relations in the region. A landmark Dual Nationality Treaty with Indonesia, negotiated and signed by the prime minister, Zhou En-lai, in April 1955, marked a change in formal practice. However, where it has suited Chinese interests, the welfare of Overseas Chinese has been employed for political purposes, as in the case of Vietnam in the late 1970s.

The centre of Overseas Chinese achievement in South-East Asia is the Republic of Singapore, which became independent in August 1965 on its expulsion from the Federation of Malaysia. Singapore's population of just over 3 million is more than 75 per cent Chinese. Before China gave up its revolutionary mission, the government of Singapore was at great pains to play down any ethnic-Chinese identity and indeed chose Malay as the national language. Any depiction of Singapore as a third China after the eople's Republic and Taiwan (Republic of China) was strongly resisted. Since China has embarked on the road to economic modernization and with the end of the Cold

War, such inhibitions have been discarded. Indeed, with China and communism ceasing to be synonymous, a revival of pride in Chinese cultural identity has taken place, with Singapore being willing to host a World Congress of Overseas Chinese in 1991.

The term Overseas Chinese has become a misnomer and should be replaced with that of Chinese communities in South-East Asia. Nonetheless, their presence and role continues to be of political significance. Although most Chinese are by no means millionaires or the business partners of ministers and generals, they are still popularly perceived by indigenous communities with a continuing measure of envy and suspicion because of the disproportionate share of wealth and economic influence that they are seen to possess. Moreover, with a burgeoning business interest in China, investment in the mainland by Overseas Chinese firms has given rise, in Indonesia for example, to fresh charges of disloyalty. Such charges are similar to those that were levelled by the King of Thailand in 1914. The rise of China as an assertive military power with irredentist designs in the South China Sea in the wake of the Cold War has revived the predicament of South-East Asia's Chinese communities. Their vulnerability has been pointed up by recurrent kidnapping of businessmen for ransom in the Philippines, while in Indonesia their experience of violence has been pogrom-like. During the economic crisis and social unrest which preceded the political downfall of President Suharto, not only was Chinese-owned property attacked but Chinese women were raped. With the interim succession of President Habibie, the position of the local Chinese became more secure but only after a major exodus of ethnic-Chinese businessmen and their families as well as a major flight of capital. After Abdurrahman Wahid became president in October 1999, an ethnic-Chinese, Dr Kwik Kian Gie, was appointed coordinating minister for economy, finance and industry. In January 2000, the government announced a review of laws that discriminated against ethnic-Chinese citizens, while in February they were permitted to celebrate the Chinese lunar new year openly for the first time since 1967. Anti-Chinese feeling has not remained far below the surface of politics in Indonesia, however, as the country has taken longer than regional neighbours to recover from economic adversity. Elsewhere in South-East Asia where economic adversity made a significant impact at the end of the 1990s, such as in Malaysia, Thailand and the Philippines, local Chinese were not made a scapegoat for national ills. Although they remain a factor in the politics of most regional states, the Overseas Chinese of South-East Asia are better assimilated than at any time since the end of the Pacific War.

# P

## *Palang Dharma* (Thailand)

*Palang Dharma* (Moral Force party) secured twenty-three seats in the Thai elections of July 1995, twenty-four fewer than in polls in September 1992. It had been a member of the coalition government led by **Chuan Leekpai** but had precipitated its fall by defecting on a parliamentary vote of confidence. *Palang Dharma* was formed just prior to elections in July 1988 by the governor of Bangkok, retired General **Chamlong Srimuang**. General Chamlong had acquired a reputation as an ascetic and honest man, which gave him an appeal among the capital's middle class alienated by the corruption of political life. The core of the party at the outset was the *Santi Asoke* Buddhist sect, with which General Chamlong was closely identified. However, in response to criticism of the sect's narrow aims and in order to broaden his party's electoral appeal, General Chamlong distanced himself from it. He also sought to contain factional divisions by engineering the election of the former **Social Action Party** politician, Boonchu Rojanastien, as party leader. *Palang Dharma*, inspired by Chamlong, played the key role in successfully challenging the government of the non-elected prime minister, General **Suchinda Krapayoon**, on the streets of Bangkok in May 1992. His influence continued to suffuse the party, to which he was re-elected leader in September 1994. Chamlong became a deputy prime minister in December 1994 but withdrew from politics in May 1995. His place as leader of *Palang Dharma* was assumed by **Thaksin Shinawatra**, who took the party back into coalition government as deputy prime minister to **Banharn Silpa-archa**. The change of leadership reflected the changing balance of advantage between its religious and business-oriented wings. In elections in July 1995, the party's parliamentary strength was reduced from 47 to 23 seats, which also reduced its political influence. It left the government in August 1996, ostensibly because of a corruption scandal. In elections in November, it held only one seat, which precipitated Thaksin's resignation as leader. In July 1998, Thaksin set up another political party (**Thai Rak Thai**), as a vehicle for his personal political ambitions, marking the effective demise of *Palang Dharma*, which had been in decline since it lost its Buddhist orientation.

*see also:* Banharn Silpa-archa; Chamlong Srimuang; Chuan Leekpai; *Santi Asoke*; Social Action Party; Suchinda Krapayoon; Thai Rak Thai Party; Thaksin Shinawatra.

## *Pancasila* (Indonesia)

*Pancasila* is a term of Sanskrit derivation for the five principles that comprise Indonesia's state philosophy. Those principles (a belief in one supreme god, humanism, nationalism, popular sovereignty and social justice) were enunciated by nationalist leader and future president **Sukarno** on 1 June 1945 in a speech before the Investigating Committee for the Preparation of Independence set up under Japanese auspices. The most important of the five principles is the belief in one supreme deity, qualified by the right of every Indonesian to believe in his or her own particular god. The prescription was employed originally by Sukarno to counter demands by devout Muslims that Indonesia should become an Islamic state and as a way of entrenching religious pluralism and tolerance in a culturally diverse and fissiparous archipelago. Controversial as a threat to Islamic prerogative, *Pancasila* was entrenched as the state philosophy by President **Suharto**, under whose administration the five principles were made the subject of compulsory courses of instruction for civil servants. In 1978 Pancasila was incorporated into the republic's constitution, which on promulgation on 18 August 1945 had included its principles only in general terms in the preamble. In 1985 all political parties and organizations became obliged under law to adopt *Pancasila* as their sole ideological basis, described in Indonesian as *asas tunggal*. President Suharto described Indonesia's political system as *Pancasila* Democracy, which was represented as an authentic Indonesian alternative to alien western values. *Pancasila* has served as a vague but exclusive ideology which has been useful as a demobilizing device against independent political elements seeking to appeal to a national audience. The charge of acting against *Pancasila* had sufficient of a treasonable implication to intimidate political dissidents. In practice, President Suharto reserved the monopoly right to determine what constituted an acceptable expression of the state philosophy. *Pancasila* became politically controversial to the extent that it came to be seen as the instrument of President Suharto's purpose and not as a unifying neutral symbol. By May 1998, with the political downfall of President Suharto, *Pancasila* had become discredited because of the way in which it had been abused. It then lost its political centrality but remained, in principle, Indonesia's state philosophy.

see also: *Abangan*; *Forum Demokrasi*; Petition of Fifty; Santri; Suharto; Sukarno.

## Papua Freedom Movement
(Indonesia) *see* Free Papua Movement.

## Paracel Islands (Vietnam)
The Paracel Islands comprise an archipelagic cluster of some 130 barren islands, sand banks and reefs in the **South China Sea**, none of which is larger than a square mile. They are located 165 miles to the south-east of the People's Republic of China's Hainan Island and 225 miles to the east of Vietnam. The Paracel Islands comprise two main groups: the Crescent to the west and the Amphritite to the east. The islands have been fully in China's possession since January 1974 but Chinese jurisdiction is challenged by Vietnam. The position of Taiwan is synonymous with that of China; their competition has been about the government of the Chinese state, not on specific territories. The islands are known as *Xisha* by the Chinese and *Hoang Sa* by the Vietnamese.

Contention over the Paracel Islands did not arise until after the Pacific War. Chinese and Vietnamese claims based on historical associations have not been underpinned by evidence of continuous administration. France incorporated the islands within the administrative competence of its protectorate in the early 1930s but not in any effective sense. Japanese occupation followed during the Pacific War, succeeded by

that of the Nationalist Chinese until they withdrew from the mainland in 1949. France, however, did not re-establish control as it sought without success to fend off the **Viet Minh**'s military challenge. Foreign minister Zhou Enlai first asserted China's claim to the Paracels as well as that to the **Spratly Islands** in commenting on the draft Japanese Peace Treaty in August 1951. At the San Francisco Peace Conference the next month, at which that treaty was signed, the Vietnamese delegation issued corresponding claims. After the **Geneva Agreements on Indochina** in July 1954, China and the Republic of (South) Vietnam began to engage in a competitive occupation of the islands, leaving them with roughly shared control. The government of the Democratic Republic of Vietnam with its seat in Hanoi did not judge it politic then to assert a claim, given its dependence on Chinese support for its irredentist aims south of the 17th parallel of latitude. In fact, Chinese sovereignty over both the Paracel and Spratly islands was publicly acknowledged during the late 1950s. In September 1973 the government in Saigon incorporated the Spratly Islands into Phuoc Tuy Province to China's protest. This administrative act was cited by China in January 1974 when it employed superior force to dislodge the South Vietnamese from the Paracels in order to consolidate its hold over the entire archipelago before the impending victory of the northern Communist government. It was only after the unification of Vietnam that the government in Hanoi asserted claims to sovereignty over the Paracel and Spratly islands, which have been sustained ever since. In May 1996, on ratifying the 1982 United Nations Law of the Sea Convention, China employed the archipelago principle, whereby straight baselines are drawn connecting the outermost points of outermost islands, to define its maritime domain around the Paracel Islands.

see also: Geneva Agreements on Indochina 1954; South China Sea; Spratly Islands; Viet Minh.

## Paris Peace Agreements 1973
(Vietnam)
On 27 January 1973 a set of agreements to end the war in Vietnam was concluded in Paris between representatives of the United States,

the Democratic Republic of (North) Vietnam, the **Provisional Revolutionary Government of the Republic of South Vietnam** (PRG) – set up by the insurgent **National Liberation Front of South Vietnam** (NLF) in 1969 – and the Republic of (South) Vietnam. Formal talks to find a political settlement to the **Vietnam War** had begun in Paris in May 1968 between the United States and the Democratic Republic of Vietnam as a direct consequence of the impact in the United States of the dramatic **Tet Offensive** launched by the National Liberation Front in January 1968. Those talks were joined subsequently by representatives of the southern government and their revolutionary challengers who were part of a united Vietnamese Communist movement. The talks were deadlocked for some time because of the insistence of the Communist side that the United States should remove the incumbent government in Saigon as part of a political settlement. The Vietnamese Communists changed their priorities from July 1972 in the wake of their spring military offensive, which had been blunted by US aerial firepower. Their pressing concern then became to end direct US military involvement in Vietnam. That objective served as the centre-point of the agreements reached in Paris in January 1973 after an impasse from mid-December 1972 during which the intensive US '**Christmas Bombing**' of North Vietnam was authorized in order to overcome opposition from South Vietnam's President **Nguyen Van Thieu**. The agreements provided for US recognition of the territorial unity of Vietnam and a cease-fire, after which its forces would stop all military activities throughout the country as well as a total military withdrawal within sixty days of signature. In return, the Communist side agreed to return all US prisoners of war, especially air force personnel. Provision was made for a political settlement among contending Vietnamese parties through the establishment of a National Council of National Reconciliation and Concord, which was charged with organizing free and democratic elections. Provision was made also for peaceful reunification between North and South through negotiations. The last US combat soldier left Vietnam by the end of March 1973.

A political settlement did not follow, however, despite the role of an international commission of control and supervision. The Paris Agreements did not make any provision for the withdrawal of northern troops from the southern half of the country. When the contending Vietnamese parties failed to set up the National Council of National Reconciliation and Concord because of irreconcilable political differences, the matter was finally resolved through superior force. The **Ban Me Thuot Offensive** launched by Communist forces in the mountains of South Vietnam in March 1975 led to the rout of Saigon's army and the fall of the capital on 30 April 1975.

The Paris Agreements also made provision for reconciliation between the United States and the Democratic Republic of Vietnam, with the former committing itself 'to healing the wounds of war and to post-war reconstruction of the Democratic Republic of Vietnam and throughout Indochina'. Normalization of relations was long delayed, however, by American bitterness at their evident defeat and humiliation, the manner of unification and by international reaction to Vietnam's invasion of Cambodia in December 1978. In addition, the issue of Vietnam providing a full accounting for US soldiers classified as **Missing in Action** served to delay normalization of relations. It was only in February 1994 that President Bill Clinton announced an end to the long-standing US trade and investment embargo against Vietnam but without authorizing diplomatic relations with the government in Hanoi beyond liaison offices in respective capital cities in the following May. Diplomatic relations were established in August 1995, partly in response to Vietnam's active cooperation in searching for those Missing in Action.

*see also:* Ban Me Thuot Offensive 1975; Christmas Bombing 1972; Le Duc Tho; Missing in Action; National Liberation Front of South Vietnam; Provisional Revolutionary Government of the Republic of South Vietnam; Tet Offensive; Thieu, Nguyen Van; Vietnam War.

## *Partai Demokrasi Indonesia* (PDI)
### (Indonesia)

*Partai Demokrasi Indonesia* (PDI), the Indonesian Democratic Party, was established in January

1973 as part of an attempt by the government of President **Suharto** to remould the political format of the republic. The political parties of the **Sukarno** era were regarded as fractious and nationally divisive. As an alternative vehicle for mobilizing support for President Suharto's **New Order**, a so-called association of Functional Groups, known in acronym as *Golkar*, was rehabilitated for an electoral role. In order to lend legitimacy to elections as well as to control political activity, all legal parties were merged into two groupings. The PDI was formed primarily from the Indonesian National Party (*Partai Nasional Indonesia* – PNI), closely associated with Sukarno, and two Christian parties, while all Muslim parties were merged into the **United Development Party** (*Partai Persatuan Pembangunan*).

With civil servants virtually obliged to support *Golkar*, the PDI performed poorly in parliamentary elections in 1977 and in 1982. In consequence, it seemed likely to disappear and to undermine the legitimacy of the electoral process which had been devised to demonstrate the continuing legitimacy of the Suharto government. The PDI was revived to an extent in elections in 1987, in part through support from dissident elements in the armed forces and also because of growing urban discontent with the Suharto regime. Its rallies in the capital Jakarta were the most well attended and it attracted support through its identification with President Sukarno. In parliamentary elections in June 1992, the PDI made an impact by its criticism of nepotism, which was construed as an attack on the rapacious business activities of President Suharto's family, as well as calling for the tenure of office of the president to be limited to two terms only. The PDI improved further on its electoral position but still managed to secure only some 15 per cent of the total vote. In December 1993 **Megawati Sukarnoputri**, the daughter of the late President Sukarno, was elected to lead the party despite the known preference of the government for an alternative candidate. In June 1996, President Suharto contrived to remove Megawati from the party leadership at a conference in Medan. She and her supporters were excluded from the PDI list for parliamentary elections in May 1997 in which the party's

vote was reduced to 3 per cent. After the political downfall of President Suharto in May 1998, her *perjuangan* (struggle) faction of the PDI assumed the ascendency and in parliamentary elections in June 1999, it won 37.4 per cent of the vote and 154 of 462 elective seats, making it the largest party in the legislature. That electoral success gave rise to expectations that Megawati would become president but, in the event, she failed to realize that ambition and had to be content with the vice-presidency to which she was elected in October 1999. One reason for that failure was the secular-Christian image of the PDI, which alienated Islamic-based parties which formed a coalition against it. Its internal cohesion has declined since the parliamentary and presidential elections in 1999 and the participation of its leading figures in government. In August 2000, with one exception and the role of Megawati, the party was excluded from government.

*see also:* Golkar; Megawati Sukarnoputri; New Order; Suharto; Sukarno; United Development Party.

### *Partai Persatuan Pembangunan* (PPP)
(Indonesia) *see* United Development Party.

### *Partai Ra'ayat Brunei* (Brunei) *see* People's Party.

### *Parti Bangsa Dyak Sarawak*
(Malaysia/Sarawak)
Parti Bangsa Dyak Sarawak may be translated as the Dyak Race Party of Sarawak. It is a communal-based political organization which seeks to advance the interests of the Dyak peoples of the north Bornean state of Sarawak in Malaysia. The various Dyak peoples constitute the largest indigenous grouping but politics has been dominated by a Malay-Melanau Muslim leadership since the mid-1960s with support from the Malaysian federal government in Kuala Lumpur. The Dyak party was formed in 1983 as a breakaway group from the mainly Dyak **Sarawak National Party** through the initiative of Datuk Leo Moggie, who then held the federal office of minister for energy. It won seven seats in elections to the state legislature in the year of

its formation and in 1984 it became a member of the federal ruling coalition, *Barisan Nasional* (National Front). It went on to secure fifteen seats in 1987 as part of a major challenge to the leadership of the chief minister, **Abdul Taib Mahmud**, and *Parti Pesaka Bumiputera Bersatu* but then failed to hold on to its political gains in 1991, when its representation fell back to seven. Although Dyak political alienation persists in Sarawak, *Parti Bangsa Dyak Sarawak* has not been successful in mobilizing and focusing it beyond a limited constituency. In May 1994 it was admitted into the state ruling coalition. In federal elections in April 1995, all four of its candidates won their seats. In November 1999, it increased its federal parliamentary strength to six.

see also: *Barisan Nasional; Parti Pesaka Bumi-*
  *putera Bersatu;* Sarawak National Party; Taib
  Mahmud, Datuk Patinggi Abdul.

## *Parti Bersatu Sabah* (Malaysia/Sabah)
see Sabah United Party.

## *Parti Islam Se-Malaysia* (PAS)
(Malaysia)

*Parti Islam Se-Malaysia* (PAS) translates from the Malay as the Islamic Party of Malaysia. The party has long sought to entrench the religious values of **Islam** in the country's constitution and in November 1993 secured passage of a law in the Kelantan legislature which provided for an Islamic penal system. The party's origins, with support among a constituency of rural schoolteachers of leftist and pan-Malay disposition, go back to the radical Malay National Party which was founded at the end of the Pacific War. In 1951 it was reformed initially as the Pan Malayan Islamic Party which, with its fundamentalist message, posed the main Malay-Islamic challenge to **UMNO** (United Malays National Organization), which became vulnerable because of its **Alliance Party** coalition relationship with non-Malay and non-Islamic parties. The main political impact of PAS has been made in the north-east of the Malay peninsula, where it won control of the Kelantan state legislature on two occasions before becoming a member of the ruling intercommunal *Barisan Nasional* (National Front) in January 1973.

That association was short-lived, with PAS being expelled in December 1977 after a revolt within the Kelantan state legislature against a chief minister appointed from Kuala Lumpur. That upheaval led to **Datuk Mohamad Muda Asri** being removed as leader in favour of a younger generation more closely attuned to the Islamic resurgence which had become a global phenomenon. PAS has identified itself with demands for an Islamic state and to this extent has never come to terms with the political arithmetic of Malaysia, which requires non-Malay support for federal office. With the split within UMNO, which came to a head in 1987, PAS associated itself with a breakaway faction called *Semangat '46* (Spirit of 1946) and, together with a minor party, contested general elections in October 1990 as part of *Angkatan Perpaduan Ummah* (Muslim Unity Front). That coalition scored a notable success in winning all seats at the federal and state levels in Kelantan but was unable to prevent the *Barisan Nasional* from being returned to office with a two-thirds majority. In elections in April 1995, PAS held onto its seven seats in the federal Parliament and was also returned to office in the state of Kelantan. Despite this modest electoral performance, it continued to pose a threat to UMNO not only because of its Islamic credentials but also because of the probity of its leadership. PAS became the main political beneficiary of the outrage among the Malay community at the dismissal, arrest, detention, trial and imprisonment of former deputy prime minister, **Anwar Ibrahim**. In elections in November 1999, its federal parliamentary strength was increased to 27 seats, while it gained control of the state legislature and government in Terengganu, while holding on to Kelantan. Its president, Fadzil Noor, became leader of the federal parliamentary opposition, while PAS assumed the dominant position within the *Barisan Alternatif* (Alternative Front), an inter-racial coalition of opposition parties, which had begun as an electoral pact. In the wake of the elections, the editor of *Harakah* (*Struggle*), PAS's popular newspaper, was charged with sedition, while its sales were restricted to two editions a month. For its part, PAS sought to reconcile its religious priorities with a pragmatic approach to business, which drew a positive response from the non-Malay communities.

*see also:* Alliance Party; *Angkatan Perpaduan Ummah;* Anwar Ibrahim; Asri, Datuk Mohamad Muda; *Barisan Alternatif; Barisan Nasional;* Islam; *Semangat '46;* UMNO.

## Parti Pesaka Bumiputera Bersatu
(Malaysia/Sarawak)

*Parti Pesaka Bumiputera Bersatu,* which translates as the United Indigenous People's Inheritance Party, is the dominant political grouping in the north Bornean state of Sarawak in Malaysia. It was formed in 1973 as the result of a merger between the Iban-Dyak *Parti Pesaka* headed by their traditional leader, the Temenggong Jugah, and the Malay-Melanau *Parti Bumiputera* under the leadership of the chief minister, then Datuk **Abdul Rahman Yakub**, and became a member of the newly established ruling federal *Barisan Nasional* (National Front) coalition. It has been controlled continuously by its Muslim component, led by the incumbent chief minister, **Datuk Patinggi Abdul Taib Mahmud**, which was a factor in Iban alienation leading to the splinter *Parti Bangsa Dayak Sarawak* being set up in 1983. *Parti Pesaka Bumiputera Bersatu* has ruled Sarawak in a coalition known as *Barisan Tiga* (Front of Three) with the **Sarawak United People's Party** (SUPP) and the **Sarawak National Party** (SNAP). In the state elections in September 1991, it won twenty-seven seats and its coalition partners twenty-two more, to command an overwhelming majority in the fifty-six seat legislature. It retained its dominant position in state elections in September 1996. In federal elections in April 1995, all of its eleven candidates won their seats. That number was reduced to ten in federal elections in November 1999.

*see also: Barisan Nasional; Barisan Tiga; Parti Bangsa Dayak Sarawak;* Sarawak National Party; Sarawak United People's Party; Taib Mahmud, Datuk Patinggi Abdul; Yacub, Tun Abdul Rahman.

## Pathet Lao  (Laos)

*Pathet Lao,* which translates as Lao Nation or State, is the name ascribed to the Laotian revolutionary movement aligned with the Communist-led **Viet Minh** during the first phase of the **Indochina Wars**. Its origins may be traced to the association established with Vietnam's Com-

munists from October 1945 by the radical Lao nationalist Prince **Souphanouvong**. With Viet Minh military support, he organized resistance to the restoration of French colonial rule with conservative nationalists, including his half-brother Prince **Souvanna Phouma**. Driven into exile in Thailand, Prince Souphanouvong returned to Vietnam in November 1949 after an accommodation had been reached between the main body of Lao nationalists and the French. In August 1950, under Viet Minh patronage, he convened a so-called resistance congress close to the Vietnamese border. That congress set up a National Resistance government which adopted a twelve-point manifesto, at the bottom of which were the words *Pathet Lao.*

*Pathet Lao* soon became the generally accepted term for describing the Laotian revolutionary movement. The National Resistance government, however, was denied representation at the conference that led to the **Geneva Agreements on Indochina** in 1954. The cease-fire agreement for Laos concluded in July was signed between French and Vietnamese military representatives only but the latter signed on behalf of the fighting units of *Pathet Lao.* Post-Geneva, the Laotian revolutionaries set up the *Neo Lao Hak Sat* (Lao Patriotic Front) which served as a front for the guiding **Lao People's Revolutionary Party** believed to have been established in 1951. Nonetheless, the term *Pathet Lao* remained in common usage to describe the revolutionary movement which assumed total power in December 1975.

*see also:* Geneva Agreements on Indochina 1954; Geneva Agreements on Laos 1962; Indochina Wars; Lao People's Revolutionary Party; *Neo Lao Hak Sat;* Souphanouvong; Souvanna Phouma; Viet Minh.

## Pattani United Liberation Organization (PULO)  (Thailand)

The Pattani United Liberation Organization (PULO) has been the most militant Muslim separatist group in southern Thailand. Muslims constitute some 2 million of Thailand's population of around 56 million. More than half of their number live in the four southern provinces of Pattani, Narathiwat, Satun and Yala where their ancestors had been converted to **Islam** from the end of the twelfth century before coming under Thai domination from the early seventeenth century. That domination had extended to the four northern provinces of present-day peninsular Malaysia which were incorporated within the British colonial domain in a treaty of 1909. The Muslims of southern Thailand were therefore separated from their coreligionists by a political boundary not of their own making.

Muslim political alienation in Thailand dates from the late 1930s. A policy of Buddhist cultural assimilation pursued from Bangkok by the government of **Phibul Songkram** generated a flow of refugees into Malaya. Ironically, the four northern provinces of the Malay peninsula were reincorporated into Thailand by Japan for the duration of the Pacific War. Muslim separatist sentiment was stirred after the war by the success of Malay nationalism to the south. Muslim organizations to promote this end were set up both in southern Thailand and northern Malaya. A revolt of a kind was launched in southern Thailand in 1948 but it was effectively crushed, especially as coincident insurgent challenge from the Communist Party of Malaya prompted Anglo-Thai cooperation in policing a common border. Muslim cultural alienation was sustained as a result of both administrative heavy-handedness and neglect, especially in lack of provision of economic opportunity.

The Pattani United Liberation Organization was not established until 1968. Its formation represented the frustration of a younger generation of Thai Muslims, especially a small but significant number who had been educated abroad. It was founded in India by Kabir Abdul Rahman, who had studied at Aligarh Muslim University and who called himself Tengku Bira Kotanil when he went on to Mecca to establish a base for overseas recruitment. PULO became an active insurgency with the politicization of Thai students in the early 1970s and mounted a number of military actions during the decade. In the repressive climate after the restoration of military rule in October 1976, Muslim students and intellectuals were attracted to the idea of autonomy and even independence for the southern provinces of Thailand. Organized attacks on government establishments in the south of the country as well as sporadic bombings in Bangkok continued after young activists had undergone military training in Libya and Syria in camps of the Palestine Liberation Organization.

International support for PULO has taken the form of Syrian and Libyan pleas before the United Nations as well as informal representation before the Organization of the Islamic Conference. Although a measure of support has come from coreligionists in the Malaysian state of Kelantan, especially from the Malay opposition *Parti Islam Se-Malaysia* (PAS), Muslim partners of Thailand within **ASEAN** (Association of South-East Asian Nations) have never provided encouragement for its separatist goal. Popular support within Thailand for PULO and allied organizations has tended to vary with the administrative competence of local military commanders in the south but has never posed a major challenge to the authority of the government in Bangkok. Nonetheless, PULO has been responsible for sporadic bombings, for example at the railway station in the southern town of Hat Yai in August 1992, which killed three people and injured seventy-three as well as at a bridge between Hat Yai and Chana railway stations in March 1994. A revival of political violence in southern Thailand during 1993, in which arson attacks were launched against schools, was attributed to Muslim separatists but may have been an attempt to destabilize the incumbent government in Bangkok. Subsequently, only sporadic clashes have occurred with security forces. In April 1998, three alleged leaders of a new faction of PULO were extradited to Bangkok after having been arrested in Malaysia, while in the following November, the *Santiparb* (Peace) Party was formed in the south of Thailand to represent the interests of the country's Muslims. In March 2000, Indonesian sources alleged that arms for rebels in **Aceh** were being shipped across the Malacca Strait by members of PULO.

see also: Aceh; ASEAN; Emergency 1948–60; Islam; *Parti Islam Se-Malaysia*; Phibul Songkram.

**Pedra Branca** (Malaysia/Singapore) *see* Horsburgh Lighthouse.

*Pemerintah Revolusioner Republik Indonesia* **(PRRI)** (Indonesia) *see* Revolutionary Government of the Republic of Indonesia.

## Pentagon Papers (Vietnam)

The Pentagon Papers is the commonly known title of a secret *History of U.S. Decision-Making Process on Vietnam Policy* comprising forty-seven volumes which cover the period from the Pacific War until May 1968, when peace talks to end the **Vietnam War** began in Paris. (The Pentagon is the headquarters of the US Department of Defense.) The history was commissioned in June 1967 by the US secretary of defense, Robert S. McNamara, who had begun to have serious misgivings about the point of US military involvement in Vietnam. The existence of the history was revealed on 13 June 1971 when the *New York Times* began to publish articles drawing on its narrative and documents which had been leaked by an employee of the Rand Corporation. After three articles appeared, the Justice Department obtained a temporary restraining order from a federal court against further publication, which was overturned on 30 June by the Supreme Court. The Pentagon Papers served to inform debate in the United States about the merits and utility of the USA's longest war.
*see also:* Vietnam War.

## People Power (Philippines)

'People Power' is the term employed to describe the huge non-violent popular demonstration that took place from 22 February 1986 for four days in Epifanio de los Santos Avenue **(EDSA)** in Manila, close to the military camps Aguinaldo and Crame. That sustained demonstration in the wake of conspicuously fraudulent elections played a decisive part in persuading President **Ferdinand Marcos** to leave for exile in the United States and in bringing Mrs **Corazón Aquino** to office. The demonstration was precipitated by a revolt against President Marcos led by the minister of defence, **Juan Ponce Enrile**, and the deputy chief of staff of the armed forces, **Fidel Ramos**. With only some 200 supporters initially, they barricaded themselves into Camp Crame in anticipation of an armed attack. At that juncture, the Archbishop of Manila, Cardinal **Jaime Sin**, broadcast a call for people to pray and keep vigil outside the camp. The popular response was dramatic. A huge crowd established a human wall which interposed between the rebels and troops dispatched to crush them by the chief of staff of the armed forces, **Fabian Ver**. The security forces were reluctant to use force, while President Marcos prevaricated over giving an order to fire because he understood that in the event of bloodshed he would not be able to find refuge in the United States. The more he prevaricated, the more the armed forces began to side with the rebels' demand that Mrs Aquino be regarded as the rightful winner of the presidential elections. In the event, Marcos accepted the advice of US Senator Paul Laxalt, speaking for President Ronald Reagan, that he 'should cut and cut cleanly', which he did in the evening of 25 February. Without the interposing display of People Power, the revolt against Marcos might well have been expeditiously crushed and the course of Philippine history would have been different.
*see also:* Aquino, Corazón; EDSA; Enrile, Juan Ponce; Marcos, Ferdinand; Ramos, Fidel; Sin, Jaime; Ver, Fabian.

## People's Action Party (PAP)
(Singapore)

The ruling People's Action Party (PAP) has been continuously in power since the elections in May 1959 that immediately preceded Singapore's acquisition of self-governing status. The party was founded in November 1954 by English-educated professionals who sought the support of the island's Chinese-educated majority through aligning with radical trade unionists linked to the illegal Communist Party of Malaya. Their platform called for a democratic socialist non-Communist united Malaya, to include Singapore. When in 1961 a merger between peninsular Malaya and Singapore (together with British territories in northern Borneo) was sanctioned, tension arose between moderate and radical wings of the party leading to the defection of the latter, who formed the *Barisan Sosialis* (Socialist Front). The rump of the PAP governed with support in Parliament from right-wing parties. Merger into the Federation of Malaysia took place in September 1963 and in its immediate wake the PAP re-established an electoral majority in its own right.

In May 1964 the PAP made a provocative and unsuccessful electoral foray into peninsular Malaysian elections, which generated racial tensions. The outcome was Singapore's expulsion from Malaysia in August 1965, which had the effect of reinforcing popular support for the party. From elections in April 1968 until a by-election in October 1981, the PAP held every seat in the Legislative Assembly. In general elections in December 1984, two opposition candidates were successful, with the remaining seventy-seven seats going to the PAP. The opposition complement increased to four seats in the following elections in August 1991, including three won by the **Singapore Democratic Party**, in an enlarged legislature of eighty-one, with the PAP holding seventy-seven seats. In elections in January 1997, the PAP won 81 seats in a legislature enlarged to 83 seats and raised its vote from 61 per cent to 65 per cent.

Since its formation, the PAP has been dominated by the personality and intellect of its first secretary-general, **Lee Kuan Yew**. Lee Kuan Yew handed over that office to the prime minister, **Goh Chok Tong**, in August 1991. After the split within the party, Lee Kuan Yew imposed a disciplined structure through a two-tier system of cadre and ordinary members. The party is avowedly elitist, drawing parliamentary candidates from the ranks of successful bureaucrats, academics and business people. Because of the long-standing absence of credible opposition, the PAP and the government of Singapore have become virtually indistinguishable. An initial commitment to democratic socialism has given way to an authoritarian pragmatism, justified with reference to outstanding economic achievement, which has been internationally acknowledged. After the PAP's electoral victory in 1997, Prime Minister Goh Chok Tong claimed that Singapore's voters had rejected Western-style liberal democracy.

*see also: Barisan Sosialis*; Goh Chok Tong; Lee Kuan Yew; Shared Values; Singapore Democratic Party; Workers Party.

## People's Consultative Assembly (Indonesia)

The People's Consultative Assembly (*Majelis Permusyawaratan Rakyat*) is the supreme constitutional authority to which the president of Indonesia is, in principle, accountable and to whom he reports. It has responsibility for electing the president and the vice-president every five years. Provision for the Assembly was made in the original independence constitution promulgated on 18 August 1945. That constitution lapsed with the attainment of independence in December 1949 but was reinstated by President **Sukarno** in July 1959 when he inaugurated the political system of **Guided Democracy**. That constitution was retained by President **Suharto**, who restored the People's Constitutional Assembly, which enjoyed only provisional status, on a partly elected and nominated basis in March 1973. It comprises a thousand members, more than half of whom are nominated, with the rest drawn from a Parliament elected every five years. In practice, the Assembly acts as an electoral college which in a ratifying role has continuously returned. During the Suharto era, the Assembly served as a rubber-stamp electoral college returning him to highest executive office recurrently until March 1998. With his resignation in May 1998, the Assembly assumed a more active political role, especially after parliamentary elections in June 1999, which paved the way for radically new membership. In October 1999, faced with competition for highest office, it elected **Abdurrahman Wahid** as president. The chairman of the Assembly is Dr Amien Rais, the leader of the **National Mandate Party**, who has pressed for a change in the constitution, whereby the vice-president would not succeed automatically in the event of the death or incapacity of the president. In August 2000, its annual session demonstrated Indonesia's degree of political change but without posing a significant challenge to President Wahid.

*see also:* Guided Democracy; National Mandate Party; Suharto; Sukarno; Wahid, Abdurrahman.

## People's Party (Brunei)

The People's Party of Brunei (*Partai Ra'ayat Brunei*) was a radical Malay organization which mounted the abortive **Brunei Revolt** in the sultanate in December 1962. It was founded on 22 January 1956, initially as a branch of the left-wing People's Party of Malaya, but was not permitted to register until 15 August after expunging its foreign affiliation. Led by **A. M. Azahari**, the People's Party campaigned for independence within a unitary state of North Borneo under the constitutional auspices of the sultan, Sir Omar Ali Saifuddin. It opposed the agreement reached in September 1959 where-by the British protecting power granted the sultanate self-government and also the proposal in 1961 to incorporate Brunei within a Federation of Malaysia. The People's Party won all sixteen elective seats to the Legislative Council of thirty-three members in August 1962 and put down a motion opposing Malaysia for the meeting arranged for 5 December. It had planned to mount a revolt soon after, for which training had been under way for a year with Indonesian support. The sultan postponed the meeting of the Legislative Council but the revolt went ahead on 8 December, while Azahari was soliciting support in the Philippines. British troops from Singapore crushed the revolt at the request of the sultan, who banned the party on 10 December. It has remained proscribed within Brunei. In July 1973, however, a number of its leaders escaped from detention with Malaysian complicity. They reconstituted the People's Party in exile in May 1974, setting up an office in neighbouring Limbang in the Malaysian state of Sarawak (*see* **Limbang Claim**). After reconciliation between Brunei and Malaysia concurrent with the sultanate's independence and membership of **ASEAN** (Association of South-East Asian Nations) in January 1984, the external activities of the party effectively ceased.

*see also:* ASEAN; Azahari, A. M.; Brunei Revolt 1962; Confrontation; Limbang Claim.

## Permesta (Indonesia)

*Permesta* is an acronym drawn from the Indonesian term *Piagam Perjuangan Semesta Alam*, meaning Universal Struggle Charter. The term was applied to the north Sulawesi (Celebes) dimension of abortive regional rebellions, which began formally in February 1958 and had fizzled out by the end of 1961. *Permesta* was the name adopted by a regionalist army council which seized power from civilian governors in eastern Indonesia in March 1957 in order to thwart attempts by the central government to prevent smuggling of copra and rubber. Corresponding army councils had been established in Sumatra from December 1956. When a **Revolutionary Government of the Republic of Indonesia** was proclaimed in west Sumatra in February 1958, open support was proffered from *Permesta*. The rebellion in Sulawesi, as well as the more significant one in Sumatra, originated in dissatisfaction with the central government in Jakarta over the maldistribution of political power and of economic returns from regional exports of raw materials, as well as in a resentment of its tolerance of the Communist Party of Indonesia. The rebellions were not secessionist but an attempt to remould the government of the republic by reducing the rising radical influence of President **Sukarno**. The seizure of power by army councils enabled Sukarno to declare martial law; the failure of the uprisings paved the way for him to introduce his political system of **Guided Democracy** in July 1959.

*see also:* Guided Democracy; Revolutionary Government of the Republic of Indonesia; Sukarno.

## Persatuan Aliran Kesesdaran Negara (Malaysia) *see Aliran.*

## Pertamina Crisis (Indonesia)

*Pertamina* is the Indonesian acronym drawn from *Perusahan Tambang Minyak dan Gas Bumi Nasional*, which is the name of the National Oil and Gas Corporation established in 1967 as an amalgamation of three existing companies, initially under the direction of Lt-General Ibnu Sutowo. In February 1975 it was revealed that *Pertamina* had failed to repay a short-term loan of US$40 million to a group of American banks. In March, it was acknowledged that *Pertamina* owed US$1.5 billion in short and medium-term debt. By May 1976 Mohamad Sadli, the minister for mines, confirmed that *Pertamina*

owed domestic and foreign creditors more than US$10 billion, which was then about two-thirds of Indonesia's gross national product. It became apparent that *Pertamina*, at the behest of its director, had assumed huge financial obligations without either the knowledge or approval of the government, including the chartering of a large fleet of oil tankers sustained by a debt-rolling operation. The company had been run in a financially self-indulgent way virtually as the private fiefdom of Ibnu Sutowo, who was dismissed from his post in 1976. He was replaced by Major-General Piet Haryono, who introduced a new financial regime under strict government control which restricted the company's activities outside the oil sector. Indonesia was fortunate in receiving the cooperation of the aid-consortium, the Inter-Governmental Group on Indonesia (IGGI), in a debt-financing operation that enabled the country to be restored to financial good health by the late 1970s, aided by the buoyant price for oil. The *Pertamina* Crisis, which arrested the economic development of the country, indicated the extent to which President **Suharto** had based his rule on personal ties which Ibnu Sutowo had been able to exploit until he went too far in financial self-indulgence.
*see also:* Suharto.

## Peta  (Indonesia)

*Peta* is an Indonesian acronym drawn from *Pembela Tanah Air*, which translates as Defenders of the Fatherland. It was the term employed to describe the volunteer force of young Indonesians recruited by the Japanese in Java during the occupation of the Netherlands East Indies in order to supplement their military strength. Its inauguration was announced on 3 October 1943 by Lt-General Harada Kumakichi and attracted Indonesian nationalists who were provided with military training. A revolt by *Peta* forces against the Japanese in the east Javanese town of Blitar in February 1945 served as a prelude to national revolution. *Peta* was dissolved by the Japanese shortly after their surrender but it provided the nucleus of the army created after the proclamation of independence on 17 August 1945. Japanese training was limited but important in its emphasis on the role of *semangat*

(spirit), which inspired the revolutionary army and which has become an integral part of Indonesian military tradition.

## Petition of Fifty  (Indonesia)

On 5 May 1980 a group of fifty retired senior officers and former politicians signed a petition which was highly critical of the way in which President **Suharto** had appropriated the national philosophy, *Pancasila*, to his own political purposes. In March and April 1980 he had made two speeches which called on the armed forces to defend challenges to the presidential prerogative, which were represented as challenges to *Pancasila*. Prominent among the dissident group was the former army chief of staff, General Abdul Haris Nasution, who had survived an attempt at assassination during an abortive coup (*see* **Gestapu**) in October 1965. This group has maintained a continuing political identity but has served as an irritant rather than as an effective vehicle of opposition to President Suharto. Their challenge was contained from the outset through manipulation of the press and the employment of financial sanctions against individual members. In December 1997, the group made an abortive attempt to dissuade the **People's Consultative Assembly** from electing President Suharto to a seventh consecutive term of office. In May 1998, shortly before President Suharto resigned, they called on the Assembly to revoke his mandate but with his political downfall, they lost their *raison d'être*.
*see also:* Crocodile Hole; *Gestapu*; Nasution, Abdul Haris; *Pancasila*; People's Consultative Assembly; Suharto.

## Petrus  (Indonesia)

The Indonesian acronym *Petrus* is formed from *Penembakan Misterius*, which translates as Mysterious Killings. The term was applied to extensive extra-judicial killings during the early 1980s, mainly in Jakarta, of suspected criminals by hit-squads of special forces in civilian clothes. Rising urban crime linked to economic recession prompted the harsh measures, which resulted in several thousand deaths, with tacit support from the law-abiding section of urban communities. At the time, the military

authorities denied all responsibility for the killings, which attracted the attention of human rights organizations. No evidence has emerged that the killings were ever directed at the political opponents of the government but their incidence certainly generated a climate of intimidation. When President **Suharto** published a memoir in 1989, he revealed that the armed forces had been responsible for the killings, to the evident embarrassment of their former commander, General **L. B. Murdani**.
see also: Murdani, L. B.; Suharto.

## Pham Van Dong  (Vietnam)

Pham Van Dong served continuously as prime minister of the Democratic Republic of Vietnam from 1955 and then of the reunited Socialist Republic of Vietnam until he retired from office in 1987. He was born on 18 March 1906 in Quang Nai Province into a mandarin family who served the court of Emperor Duy Tan. He was educated at the National Academy in Hue and then at the law faculty in Hanoi, where he came to prominence for organizing a strike in commemoration of the death of a nationalist leader. As a member of the Revolutionary Youth League, he fled to China where he joined in a close collaboration with **Ho Chi Minh**, who placed great trust in him. He was sent back to Vietnam in 1926 to organize Communist cells and was eventually arrested and imprisoned until 1936 when after an amnesty he returned to southern China to work again in partnership with Ho Chi Minh. Pham Van Dong demonstrated great talent as an administrator and also as a negotiator. He acted as finance minister from 1946 during the course of the first phase of the **Indochina Wars**. In 1954, as foreign minister, he headed the Vietnamese Communist delegation to the conference that resulted in the **Geneva Agreements on Indochina** and became prime minister in 1955. He was reputed to be a skilled conciliator between party factions and sought also to ensure that Vietnam did not align too closely with either China or the Soviet Union. After Ho Chi Minh's death in 1969, and more so after unification in 1975, his influence waned as **Le Duan** came to dominate party councils. Pham Van Dong announced his forthcoming retirement from all governmental and party offices in December 1986 on grounds of advanced age and ill-health, giving up his posts in June 1987 to be succeeded by Pham Hung. He died in Hanoi on 29 April 2000.
see also: Geneva Agreements on Indochina 1954; Ho Chi Minh; Indochina Wars; Le Duan.

## Phibul Songkram, Field Marshal
(Thailand)

As a junior officer, Phibul Songkram was a leading military figure in the coup that overthrew Thailand's absolute monarchy in June 1932. He became virtual military dictator during the Pacific War, and again for a decade from 1948, until he was himself removed by a military coup. Phibul Songkram was born in 1897 of Sino-Thai origins and became a professional soldier after graduating from the Chulachomklao Royal Military Academy in Bangkok in 1915. He studied at the French artillery school in Fontainebleau during 1920-7; he became involved in a Thai political circle alienated by the privilege of the monarchy. After the successful coup in 1932, he held a series of command and cabinet positions. Phibul was responsible for stimulating Thai nationalism, in part at the expense of the resident Chinese community. He took Thailand close to an assertive Japan and used its support to secure territorial redress from France in Indochina. Japan invaded Thailand concurrently with its attack on the United States in December 1941. After offering a token resistance, Thailand joined Japan's side under Phibul's direction as supreme commander of the armed forces. He was eased from power in August 1944, however, when it had become apparent that Japan's defeat was only a matter of time. After the Pacific War, he was detained as a war criminal for several months but was then rehabilitated and even restored as army commander. His political fortunes revived considerably because of the Cold War and the United States' interest in an anti-Communist government. Following a military coup against the elected civilian government in November 1947, he became prime minister in April 1948, a post which he held until November 1957, when he was deposed. In 1955 Phibul returned from a tour of the United States and Britain

apparently enamoured of democracy, especially the practice of free speech which he had observed in Hyde Park in London. The political turbulence that followed provided the context for his deposition by army commander **Sarit Thanarat**. Field Marshal Phibul was then exiled to Japan, where he died in 1964.
*see also:* Sarit Thanarat.

## Phieu, Le Kha, General (Vietnam) *see* Le Kha Phieu, General.

## Philippines' Claim to Sabah (Malaysia/ Philippines)

On 22 June 1962 the government of the Philippines, in response to a diplomatic note presented to its ambassador in London on 24 May, pointed out 'there is a dispute between the Sultanate of Sulu and the Philippine Government on the one side and Her Majesty's Government on the other side regarding the ownership and sovereignty over North Borneo'. When on 16 September 1963 the British Crown transferred sovereignty over the colony of North Borneo (from then on known as Sabah) to the new Federation of Malaysia with its seat of government in Kuala Lumpur, that dispute became a matter of contention between the Philippines and Malaysia. It has remained unresolved ever since. Direct negotiations have proven fruitless, so far, in completely erasing the claim. At issue, in part, has been the question of succession to territorial domain in South-East Asia, with the Philippines reluctant to make a unilateral concession. In addition, the claim has become enmeshed in the domestic politics of the republic.

The origins of the dispute are to be found in an agreement of January 1878 between the Sultan of Sulu, the putative sovereign in the greater part of North Borneo, and representatives of a British commercial syndicate. The territory in question was either leased or ceded (depending on the translation used) in perpetuity in return for an annual payment of 5,000 Malayan dollars. In 1881 the British North Borneo Company took over the concession and began to administer the territory as well as to assume responsibility for the annual payments to the Sultan of Sulu and his heirs. These admin-

istrative arrangements were not interrupted by Britain establishing a protectorate over North Borneo in 1888. The territory was occupied by the Japanese during the Pacific War and suffered much damage. In 1946 the British North Borneo Company relinquished all of its responsibilities to the British Crown; the territory became a colony until the transfer of sovereignty to Malaysia in 1963. The prospect of a claim emerged shortly after the independence of the Philippines in 1946, especially when its government successfully negotiated the transfer of the Turtle and Mangsee islands located in the Sulu Sea, which had been subject to British administration. The primary interest at the time was private, in particular on the part of the heirs of the Sultanate of Sulu, which had been extinguished in sovereign status during the US period of colonial rule. An attempt to pursue a financial settlement in the form of a lump sum was undertaken by a son of a former president without success. However, the coincidental incumbency of President **Diasdado Macapagal** with the proposal to establish Malaysia by Malaya's prime minister, **Tunku Abdul Rahman**, brought matters to a head. Macapagal had been in charge of the Philippines Foreign Affairs Department in 1946, responsible for his country's side in the negotiations which had led to the transfer of the Turtle and Mangsee islands. An effective press campaign inspired by private interests attracted the attention of the president, who was also doubtful about the credentials of the proposed new Federation of Malaysia, which had been represented as a vehicle for serving British interests. The claim, which he was responsible for presenting, has not been formally withdrawn and has continued to cause tension between the Philippines and Malaysia.

A major rupture occurred in 1968 following a state visit to Kuala Lumpur by President **Ferdinand Marcos**, which was construed as an act of reconciliation as well as a recognition of Malaysia's sovereignty. Reports of the **Corregidor Affair**, an alleged massacre of Filipino Muslim recruits being trained for armed infiltration into Sabah, provoked a temporary suspension of diplomatic relations. Effective rapprochement did not take place during the tenure of President Marcos, while President **Corazón Aquino** proved unable to persuade her country's Congress to revoke the claim prior to the third **ASEAN** heads of government meeting at the **Manila Summit** in December 1987. Relations between the two countries improved visibly with the visit by **Fidel Ramos** to Malaysia in January 1993, which was the first by a president of the Philippines since 1968, other than for an ASEAN occasion. The prime minister, Dr **Mahathir Mohamad**, paid a reciprocal visit in February 1994. Later in the month, however, the foreign minister, **Roberto Rómulo**, felt obliged for domestic political reasons to affirm that the Philippines would continue to maintain its claim to Sabah. That position was reiterated by President Fidel Ramos in May 1994 but without its active prosecution, which has been the position under his successor President Estrada.

see also: Aquino, Corazón; Corregidor Affair 1968; Macapagal, Diasdado; Mahathir Mohamad, Datuk Sri; Manila Summit 1987; Rahman, Tunku Abdul; Ramos, Fidel; Rómulo, Roberto.

## Philippines–US Security Treaty 1951 (Philippines)

On 30 August 1951, the governments of the Philippines and the United States concluded a mutual security treaty, which was inspired by the advent of the Korean War and China's involvement and also by the need to pre-empt resistance to the Japanese Peace Treaty. Both parties agreed to act against any armed attack on the other in the Pacific with such action to be taken in accordance with each country's constitutional processes. Although the treaty has never been invoked, its terms of reference were criticized by nationalist opponents on the grounds that it did not provide the same automatic guarantee as the North Atlantic Treaty. In April 1992, after the United States had given notice of its intention to vacate all of its military bases in the Philippines, Foreign Minister **Raul Manglapus** argued that the United States was obliged to come to the defence of the Philippines under the 1951 Treaty in the event of an attack on any of its vessels or possessions in the **Spratly Islands**. The American ambassador, Frank Wisner, countered by maintaining that

his government's security obligations did not extend to the Spratly Islands, which were disputed territories. That position did not change after it was revealed in early 1995 that Chinese forces had occupied Mischief Reef claimed by the Philippines. In January 1999, US Defence Secretary William Cohen, during a visit to Manila to discuss the modernization of the Philippines' military with his counterpart Orlando Mercado, stated that his country was not taking sides in the Spratlys dispute, except to press for a peaceful solution.

see also: Manglapus, Raul; Spratly Islands.

## Pol Pot (Cambodia)

Pol Pot was the notorious leader of the Communist Party of Cambodia, who presided over a reign of terror within the country between April 1975 and December 1978, when a Vietnamese invasion drove out his government. At least 1 million Cambodians died from execution, hunger and disease under his draconian regime, which was designed to restore the glory of a national past within a Marxist model of society. Pol Pot was a *nom de guerre* made public only in April 1976 when the State of **Democratic Kampuchea** was proclaimed. Pol Pot was born Saloth Sar on 19 May 1928 in a village in northerly Kompong Thom Province, the youngest of seven children in a moderately prosperous farming family. His early education was in Phnom Penh and Kompong Cham. Possibly because of his family's royal connections through concubinage, Saloth Sar was awarded a scholarship to study electrical engineering in France from 1949. He returned to Cambodia in January 1953 after failing to complete his studies. Saloth Sar's time in France was taken up in political study within a Marxist circle heavily influenced by the Stalinist persuasion of the Communist Party of France. This period is believed to have been formative in establishing a personal bond between him and a small group of politicized fellow Khmers and in developing a sense of mission. After initial involvement in anti-monarchist politics in 1953, Saloth Sar joined a Vietnamese-led insurgency in eastern Cambodia in August. He remained in Cambodia after the 1954 **Geneva Agreements on Indochina**, which recognized the country's independence, and from 1955 to 1963 worked as a schoolteacher in Phnom Penh. When the Communist Party of Cambodia was reconstituted in secret in 1960, he became a member of its central committee. When its general secretary disappeared, probably murdered, in 1962, Saloth Sar took his place, which he is believed to hold still, despite the formal dissolution of the party.

In 1963 Saloth Sar fled the capital in fear of Prince **Norodom Sihanouk**'s police. He found refuge in a Vietnamese Communist sanctuary in the east and then moved north to spend time with tribal minorities. Their style of life with-out property, money and markets provided example and inspiration for his salvationist creed. Indeed, he and party colleagues recruited guerrilla fighters from among the deprived ranks of the tribal minorities who had a long-standing animus against urban dwellers. Armed struggle against the rule of Prince Sihanouk began in 1968 but assumed major proportions only after the coup in March 1970 which brought **Lon Nol** to power with United States support. The Vietnamese army decimated their Cambodian counterparts, so providing a shield beyond which a **Khmer Rouge** fighting force could be protected while in recruitment and training. That force seized power in April 1975 and under the leadership of the pseudonymous Pol Pot emptied the cities and then began a horrific social experiment. He was revealed as prime minister in April 1976, holding that office with an interruption for a short period later that year that was probably the result of an intra-party power struggle.

Pol Pot escaped to the Thai border after Vietnam's invasion in December 1978, holding the position of the military commander of Democratic Kampuchea until his retirement was announced in September 1985. He was then described as director of a Higher Institute for National Defence, which he gave up in June 1989. In effect, he continued to exercise leadership over the Khmer Rouge insurgents from a base close to Trat on the Thai–Cambodian border. A photograph of him with other Khmer Rouge leaders dating from 1986 was discovered in March 1994 following Cambodian government military operations in the west of the

country in March 1994. He was reported to have been present in Pattaya in June 1991 when the **Supreme National Council** convened and achieved a political breakthrough in addressing the Cambodian conflict. He is believed to have retained ultimate authority over the Khmer Rouge in its acceptance of the political settlement reached at the **International Conference on Cambodia** in Paris in October 1991. His influence is believed to have been decisive also in the subsequent boycott by the Khmer Rouge of the peace process and the elections conducted under United Nations auspices in May 1993 (*see* **UNTAC**). The failure of the Khmer Rouge to make significant military headway against the coalition government in Phnom Penh generated factional divisions within and defections from the Khmer Rouge with Pol Pot opposed to any accommodation. In June 1997, he ordered the murder of senior colleague **Son Sen**, his wife and sixteen members of his family. After fleeing with supporters into the jungle, Pol Pot was seized by **Ta Mok**, another senior figure also targeted for assassination, and put on trial in July, which was observed by Nate Thayer, an American journalist. It was the first time that he had been seen by an independent observer since December 1979. After this show trial, he was sentenced to life imprisonment in the Khmer Rouge base at Anlong Veng close to the Thai border. In an interview with Thayer in October 1997, Pol Pot was quite unrepentant about his murderous record and claimed that although several thousand may have died in Cambodia, his conscience was clear. He died on 15 April 1998, reportedly of a heart attack, although his body was cremated before conclusive evidence of the cause of death could be established. Pol Pot left a bitter legacy, which affected virtually every Cambodian family. Those who met him have testified to his personal charm and qualities of leadership but there have been few more reviled men in the history of the twentieth century.

see also: Democratic Kampuchea; Geneva Agreements on Indochina 1954; International Conference on Cambodia, Paris 1991; Khmer Rouge; Nol, Lon; Sihanouk, Norodom; Son Sen; Supreme National Council; Ta Mok; United Nations: Cambodia 1991–3; UNTAC.

## *Prachakorn Thai* (Thailand)

*Prachakorn Thai* (Thai Citizens party) has been a minor but influential factor in national politics in Thailand. It was established in 1978 by Samak Sundaravej, who had led a right-wing faction within the **Democrat Party** (*Prachathipat*). His defection to form a new party was significant because he was able to employ his personal appeal to challenge the Democrat Party in its traditional bailiwick of Bangkok. In general elections in 1979, *Prachakorn Thai* won twenty-nine out of the thirty-two seats in the capital and three seats elsewhere and gained entry to the ruling coalition led by **Prem Tinsulanond**. It improved its position marginally in elections in 1983 to remain in the government, aided by Samak's oratorical skills. The party's fortunes then became mixed, with a drop to twenty-four seats in 1986 which was raised to thirty-one in 1988. A period in opposition from 1986 was followed by a return to coalition government in 1990 at the invitation of **Chatichai Choonhavan**. That government was removed by a military coup in February 1991. Elections were held again in March 1992 when *Prachakorn Thai*, which was identified with the military establishment, had its numbers cut to seven because of the success of *Palang Dharma*, which cut into its political base. Close identification with the military led to the party being virtually eliminated in fresh elections in September in the wake of political violence and crisis in May 1992. It secured only three seats in a legislature of three hundred and sixty and had been discounted politically until it made a comeback in Bangkok in elections for the capital's assembly in March 1994, winning nineteen of the fifty-five seats. That comeback was sustained in national elections in July 1995 when *Prachakorn Thai* won eighteen seats and entered the ruling coalition under **Banharn Silpa-archa** with its leader Samak Sundharavej as a deputy prime minister. In elections in November 1996, it retained its parliamentary strength and entered the new ruling coalition headed by **Chavalit Yongchaiyut**, the leader of the **New Aspiration Party**. After Chavalit was obliged to step down from office in November 1997 because of the impact of economic crisis, twelve out of eighteen *Prachakorn Thai* members supported the new ruling coalition headed by **Chuan Leekpai**, the leader of the **Democrat Party**. It was allocated two minor posts in government. In July 2000, its leader Samak Sundaravej was elected governor of Bangkok.

*see also:* Banharn Silpa-archa; Chatichai Choonhavan; Chavalit Yongchaiyut; Chuan Leekpai; Democrat Party; New Aspiration Party; *Palang Dharma*; Prem Tinsulanond.

## *Prachathipat* (Thailand) *see* Democrat Party.

## Praphas Charusathien, Field Marshal (Thailand)

Field Marshal Praphas Charusathien was deputy prime minister of Thailand in October 1973 when student protest at the lack of constitutional progress erupted into a violent confrontation with the security forces. The civilian bloodshed prompted the intervention of King **Bhumibol Adulyadej**, which led to Praphas and the prime minister, Field Marshal **Thanom Kittikachorn**, going into exile as an act of contrition. Praphas Charusathien was born on 25 November 1912 in Udorn Province. He began his professional military training in 1933 at the Chulachomklao Royal Military Academy in Bangkok after the end of the absolute monarchy. As an infantry officer, he rose in rank as a protégé of Field Marshal **Sarit Thanarat** and served as minister of the interior under his aegis from 1957 and retained the position beyond Sarit Thanarat's death in 1963. Praphas held that post until 1973, with a brief interruption in 1971–2 when the nomenclature of his office was changed following an incumbency coup. He was also commander-in-chief of the Thai army between 1963 and 1973; his replacement by General Krit Sivara signalled a loss of political power. Praphas overshadowed Thanom and was, in effect, the strong man of Thai politics for a decade, acquiring a sinister reputation for financial manipulation and political intrigue. He was able to return to Thailand in January 1977 after a coup in October 1976 (on the same day as the **Thammasat University Massacre**) had re-established military-based rule but he ceased to play any part in public life. He died in Bangkok on 18 August 1997.

*see also:* Bhumibol Adulyadej; Sarit Thanarat; Thammasat University Massacre 1976; Thanom Kittikachorn.

## Prasong Soonsiri (Thailand)

Prasong Soonsiri was appointed foreign minister of Thailand in September 1992 as a member of the first elected civilian government, which was established following military-based rule from February 1991. He continued in office until October 1994 when, as a result of a cabinet reshuffle, he was replaced by another member of his *Palang Dharma* (Moral Force party). Prasong Soonsiri was born on 11 August 1927. He began his career in the Thai Air Force, rising to the rank of squadron leader; he received some of his training in the United States in air intelligence. In 1966 he transferred to the military division of the Secretariat of the National Security Council, rising to become its overall head in October 1980. In that role, he played a major part in influencing Thailand's hardline policy towards the Cambodian conflict, working closely with his former superior, **Siddhi Savetsila**, who had become foreign minister. From August 1986 he served for three years as secretary-general to the prime minister, **Prem Tinsulanond**, leaving office on Prem's resignation. Prasong Soonsiri then became associated with the **New Aspiration Party** led by the former army commander, General **Chavalit Yongchaiyuth**, but resigned with his supporters in January 1992 after a disagreement over allocation of constituencies in forthcoming elections. He then joined *Palang Dharma* led by the former general **Chamlong Srimaung**, winning election to Parliament in September 1992. As foreign minister, Prasong Soonsiri played a role in accelerating reconciliation with Vietnam but his views on foreign policy reflected traditional Thai geopolitical security concerns in Indochina.
*see also:* Chamlong Srimuang; Chavalit Yongchaiyuth; New Aspiration Party; Palang Dharma; Prem Tinsulanond; Siddhi Savetsila.

## Preah Vihear Temple Dispute
(Cambodia/Thailand)

A dispute over possession of the ruins of the ancient Khmer temple of Preah Vihear became a matter of tension between Cambodia and Thailand from the former's independence in November 1953, continuing even after legal resolution by the International Court of Justice in June 1962. The temple ruins are located to the north of Cambodia along the border with Thailand, on the edge of the Dang Raek escarpment which overlooks the Cambodian plain. This part of the boundary between Thailand and Cambodia (then a French protectorate) was delimited by a joint Franco-Siamese (Thai) border commission between 1905 and 1907. The commission should have based its delimitation on a boundary convention of February 1904, which stipulated that the line of demarcation follow the watershed of the Dang Raek range: this would have placed the temple in Thai territory. In the event, a French officer on the joint commission produced a map covering the area of the temple that showed its location on the Cambodian side of the boundary, which was not disputed at the time. That map was incorporated in an annexe to a subsequent boundary convention of March 1907.

Access to the ruins is exceedingly difficult from the Cambodian side, by contrast with its relative ease from the Thai side. Thailand occupied the temple site from time to time and continuously from 1949, but without objecting to the failure of the French-drawn map to reflect the terms of reference of the 1904 convention. The issue of Thailand's occupation of the temple site was raised after the end of the Pacific War, first by France and then by an independent Cambodia. A conference between the two governments in 1958 failed to resolve the issue, which was taken by Cambodia to the International Court of Justice in The Hague in the following year. The court decided in Cambodia's favour in June 1962, despite the terms of the 1904 convention, on the grounds that Thailand had never raised any objections to the authoritative map locating the temple site. The dispute over Preah Vihear reflected mutual suspicions between two states which had been historical adversaries before the advent of colonialism and which adopted different positions in the Cold War. For Cambodia under the leadership of Prince **Norodom Sihanouk**, the temple represented a symbol of a newly won independence and provided an opportunity to challenge a perceived Thai reassertion of historical hegemony. To that end, it also provided a convenient domestic focus for nation-building. From the Thai perspective, the dispute reflected a traditional condescension towards Cambodia which turned into animosity when its foreign policy of neutrality, involving diplomatic relations with the People's Republic of China, was viewed as appeasement to communism in South-East Asia. Thailand has accepted the ruling of the International Court of Justice, albeit grudgingly. Violent disorder within Cambodia for more than two decades, since the coup in March 1970 which overthrew Norodom Sihanouk, stood in the way of uncontested occupation of the temple from the Cambodian side. It has only been with the effective extinction of the **Khmer Rouge** as a fighting force that the writ of the government in Phnom Penh over the temple has been re-established.

*see also:* Khmer Rouge; Sihanouk, Norodom.

## Prem Tinsulanond, General  (Thailand)

Prem Tinsulanond served as unelected prime minister of Thailand between 1980 and 1988. He was born on 26 August 1920 and began his career as an army officer, training for the cavalry at the Chulachomklao Royal Military Academy. By 1977 he had risen to become assistant commander-in-chief of the army and served in the military government headed by General **Kriangsak Chomanan**. The **Young Turks** faction of officers, who had supported General Kriangsak, became alienated from him and engineered General Prem's succession. As prime minister, he successfully combined an activist policy towards Vietnam over Cambodia with a sober management of the economy, which flourished during his tenure. He survived two abortive coup attempts by disaffected officers and earned the respect of King **Bhumibol Adulyadej**, who sought his counsel during the street violence in May 1992 in protest at retired General **Suchinda Krapayoon** becoming unelected prime minister. One reason Prem gave for his resignation was that he believed that it was time the country had an elected prime minister; he had no inclination to participate in electoral politics. He has continued to hold advisory office as a privy councillor but refused to be drafted as head of

a governing coalition when Prime Minister **Chavalit Yongchaiyut** resigned office in November 1997 in the face of economic crisis.

*see also:* Bhumibol Adulyadej; Chavalit Yongchaiyut; Kriangsak Chomanan; Suchinda Krapayoon; Young Turks.

## *Pribumi*  (Indonesia)

*Pribumi* is the Indonesian term used to identify indigenous citizens in contradistinction to those of ethnic-Chinese origin. The term has an undoubted political significance because it is invariably applied to members of the business community and to the need to enable them to compete with Chinese entrepreneurs who have come to dominate Indonesia's economy during the rule of President **Suharto**. The more well-known and corresponding term in Malaysia is *Bumiputera*.

*see also: Bumiputera*; Suharto.

## Pridi Phanomyong  (Thailand)

Pridi Phanomyong was the most influential civilian figure in the coup group that removed the absolute monarchy in Thailand in 1932. After the Pacific War, he served briefly as prime minister. He fled into exile in November 1947 following a military coup whose instigators accused him of responsibility for the death of King **Ananda Mahidol** in 1946. Pridi Phanomyong was born in 1901 into an ethnic-Chinese family. He studied law in Bangkok and then spent seven years at university in Paris, where he was at the centre of radical thinking about Thai constitutional and economic development. On his return to Thailand, he served as an official at the Ministry of Justice before becoming a direct party to the end of the absolute monarchy. As a cabinet minister, he was a member of the constitutional drafting committee and also responsible for a controversial economic plan which led to charges of Communist inclination and his temporary banishment to France. On his return, Pridi was restored to cabinet office, including that of foreign minister. At the outbreak of the Pacific War in December 1941, he was appointed to the Regency Council in the absence of the young King Ananda, then living in Switzerland. During Thailand's alliance with Japan, he was the clandestine leader of the

Free Thai Movement and was instrumental in having the Parliament remove Field Marshal **Phibul Songkram** from the post of prime minister towards the end of hostilities. Pridi played a major part in securing Thailand's postwar international rehabilitation and took on the office of prime minister in March 1946 in difficult economic circumstances, but felt obliged to resign within two months of the violent death of King Ananda in June. He fled the country after the military coup in November 1947 and in February 1949 was implicated in an abortive attempt by the marines to restore him to power. Pridi then went to live in China, where he remained after the Communist Revolution for over twenty years. In 1970 he returned to Paris to spend the remainder of his life and died on 2 May 1983. *see also:* Ananda Mahidol; Phibul Songkram.

## Provisional Revolutionary Government of the Republic of South Vietnam (PRG) 1969–76 (Vietnam)

On 8 June 1969 the Provisional Revolutionary Government of the Republic of South Vietnam (PRG) was established in 'a liberated zone' of South Vietnam by a self-proclaimed Congress of People's Representatives. The initiative for establishing the government was taken ostensibly by the insurgent **National Liberation Front of South Vietnam** (NLF) in company with a Vietnam Alliance of National Democratic and Peace Forces. In effect, the initiative was taken by the *Lao Dong* (Workers Party), which was the name used by Vietnam's Communist Party. The object was to challenge the legitimacy of the government in Saigon by creating an alternative internationally recognized locus of authority which would be a negotiating equal in talks in Paris. A collateral purpose was to demonstrate that the insurgency in the south of Vietnam was autonomous in origin and control and that reunification between the northern and southern halves of the country would be negotiated and take place on a step-by-step basis. In the event, reunification came on northern terms in July 1976 following the military overthrow of the government in Saigon in April 1975. Moreover, members of the Provisional Revolutionary Government, which was dissolved on reunification, were not accorded any tangible role in the Socialist Republic of Vietnam by the Communist Party, whose seat was in Hanoi. *see also: Lao Dong;* National Liberation Front of South Vietnam.

## Pulau Batu Puteh (Malaysia/ Singapore) *see* Horsburgh Lighthouse.

# R

## Rahman, Tunku Abdul (Malaya/Malaysia)

Tunku Abdul Rahman was the first prime minister of Malaya and then Malaysia. In 1951, after Dato Onn bin Jafar had lost the confidence of **UMNO** (United Malays National Organization) because of his wish to permit access to members of other communities, the Tunku (as he was generally known) became its president. In this role, he forged a viable coalition, the **Alliance Party**, with Chinese and Indian communal political parties and played the leading part in negotiating the independence of the Federation of Malaya in 1957 and then in promoting the wider Federation of Malaysia which was formed in 1963. He successfully surmounted Indonesia's **Confrontation** of the new Federation but was unable to overcome intercommunal tensions aggravated by Singapore's membership. He took the fateful decision to cast Singapore out of the Federation in August 1965 but communal tensions mounted because the Malays believed that their political birthright was being compromised by the growing economic imbalance with the Chinese. The **May 13 Racial Riots** in the wake of general elections in May 1969, in which UMNO lost ground, made the Tunku's position politically untenable; he stepped down from office in 1970 in favour of his deputy, **Tun Abdul Razak**.

Tunku Abdul Rahman was born in 1903 to a Thai mother as one of forty-five children of Sultan Abdul Hamid of the state of Kedah, then part of Thailand. As a student of law in England who took many years to be called to the bar, he claimed a reputation for fast women, fast cars and not-so-fast horses. His easy-going style was carried over into his political career but it concealed a steely firmness of mind which he demonstrated in the **Baling Talks** with **Chin Peng**, the leader of the Communist Party of Malaya. After leaving high office, the Tunku served during the 1970s as head of the Islamic Secretariat in Saudi Arabia. In later life, he turned his hand to journalism, acting as the liberal conscience of a country which under the leadership of Dr **Mahathir Mohamad** became increasingly authoritarian in its politics. He died on 6 December 1990 at the age of 87.

*see also:* Alliance Party; Baling Talks 1955; Chin Peng; Confrontation; Mahathir Mohamad, Datuk Sri; May 13 Racial Riots 1969; Razak, Tun Abdul; UMNO.

## Rajaratnam, Sinnathamby (Singapore)

Sinnathamby Rajaratnam was the first foreign minister of an independent Singapore after it was separated from the Federation of Malaysia in August 1965. In that office, he participated actively in the formative stages of regional cooperation in South-East Asia and was a strident early voice in challenging Vietnam's occupation of Cambodia in the third phase of the **Indochina Wars**. He played an important part in giving Singapore a regional influence out of proportion to the island-state's geopolitical significance, employing a colourful idiom and prose to that end. Sinnathamby Rajaratnam was born in Ceylon (Sri Lanka) on 23 February 1915 and was brought to Malaya by his parents as an infant. He was educated at Raffles Institution in Singapore and then at King's College in London, where he became politically active in close company with Lee **Kuan Yew**. He worked as a journalist in Singapore during the 1950s and became a founder member of the **People's Action Party** (PAP) which, following its electoral success in 1959, has remained continuously in power. He was initially appointed minister of culture (information) and after 1965 held the office of foreign minister continuously until 1980. In June 1980 he became Second deputy prime minister with an evident elder statesman role. In January 1985 he was made senior minister within the prime minister's office until retiring from public life shortly before the general elections in September 1988.

*see also:* Indochina Wars; Lee Kuan Yew; People's Action Party.

**RAM** (Philippines) *see* Reform the Armed Forces Movement.

**Ramos, Fidel** (Philippines)

Fidel Ramos was president of the Philippines between July 1992 and June 1998. His election in May 1992 marked the first peaceful transfer of office in over a quarter of a century. Fidel Ramos has been credited with improving the governance of his country but was prohibited under the terms of the constitution from standing for a second term. He was born on 18 March 1928 in Lingayen, Pangasinan Province, and spent the greater part of his life in military service. Fidel Ramos was educated at the United States Military Academy at West Point, from which he graduated in 1950. He received further military training in the United States and saw service with Philippines forces in Vietnam. Fidel Ramos rose to become head of the paramilitary Philippine National Constabulary; when President **Ferdinand Marcos** declared martial law in 1972, Fidel Ramos served as a loyal lieutenant, rising to the position of deputy chief of staff of the armed forces. He was trusted by the president, partly because he was a cousin. He achieved fame and popular regard in February 1986 when with the defence minister, **Juan Ponce Enrile**, he led a successful military revolt against Marcos, who had tampered with the results of a snap presidential election. After **Corazón Aquino** had been confirmed as president, Fidel Ramos served her loyally, first as chief of staff and then as minister of defence. In the latter capacity, he was primarily responsible for defending constitutional government against a series of military coup attempts. President Aquino's gratitude became evident after the ruling party had rejected Fidel Ramos as their candidate for the presidential election in May 1992. He then formed his own political movement, *Lakas*-**NUCD**, and, with Mrs Aquino's support, won a closely fought contest against five other candidates with around only a quarter of the vote. Fidel Ramos became the first Protestant to occupy presidential office in the Philippines. In his first state of the nation address in July 1992, he called on the Congress to legalize the Communist Party of the Philippines in an attempt to end more than two decades of insurgency. He was a resolute chief executive but met with congressional obstacles to his programme of macro-economic reform, especially over taxation policy. He was successful, however, in overcoming military dissidence, which had posed a threat to political stability during his predecessor's tenure. Towards the end of his term, he made a controversial and abortive attempt to revise the terms of the constitution to permit him to stand for a second term. In retirement from political life, he became the chairman of the Ramos Peace and Development Foundation.

*see also:* Aquino, Corazón; Enrile, Juan Ponce; *Lakas*-NUCD; Marcos, Ferdinand.

**Ranariddh, Prince Norodom** (Cambodia)

Prince Norodom Ranariddh became chairman of Cambodia's National Assembly in November 1998 with the formation of a coalition government following general elections in the previous July. Their results, which Prince Ranariddh had initially declared to be fraudulent, confirmed the political dominance of **Hun Sen** as sole prime minister, which had been established through a violent coup in July 1997. As a result of that coup, Prince Ranariddh had been removed as First Prime Minister in favour of Foreign Minister Ung Huot and stripped of his parliamentary immunity and then tried, found guilty and sentenced to thirty-five years' imprisonment on charges of illegally importing arms and clandestine negotiations with the **Khmer Rouge**. He had been out of the country at the time of the coup and only returned to participate in national politics after his father, King **Norodom Sihanouk**, had granted him an amnesty. His diminished role stands in contrast to his prominence in Cambodian politics earlier in the 1990s. His office of chairman of the National Assembly carries with it the right to serve as acting head of state in the absence or incapacity of an ailing King Sihanouk.

Prince Ranariddh, who is the eldest son of King Norodom Sihanouk by a minor wife, was born in Phnom Penh in 1944. He showed intellectual promise as a young man and studied law at the University of Aix-en-Provence, where he obtained a doctorate in Public International Law. He joined the faculty there in 1976 but in 1983 was drawn into Cambodian exile politics when his father appointed him as his personal representative based in Bangkok. He played a prominent representative role in the protracted negotiations over a political settlement from the late 1980s until the Paris Accords at the **International Conference on Cambodia** in October 1991. When Norodom Sihanouk became chairman of the four-party **Supreme National Council** in mid-1991, Prince Ranariddh succeeded his father as head of FUNCINPEC. In that role, he demonstrated qualities of leadership and statesmanship that were not sustained after assuming office in Cambodia, however. Indeed, he gave the impression of being more interested in its pomp and circumstance than the detail of administration. He was Cambodia's First Prime Minister from October 1993 until ousted in July 1997. He assumed office in the wake of elections in May 1993 in which his party, **FUNCINPEC** (National United Front for an Independent, Neutral, Peaceful and Cooperative Cambodia), secured a plurality of votes. He shared power in a coalition with the **Cambodian People's Party** (CPP), with the former prime minister and his political adversary Hun Sen in the office of Second Prime Minister. That coalition proved to be a fragile arrangement in which power was never truly shared by the CPP, while Prince Ranariddh was outmanoeuvred politically by Hun Sen and also lost the confidence of Western governments because of his *dilettante* conduct. Prince Ranariddh's relationship with his temperamental and vain father has not been easy, while that with King Sihanouk's consort, Queen Monique, is believed to be even more difficult, primarily because of rivalry over royal succession.

*see also:* Cambodian People's Party; FUNCINPEC; Hun Sen; International Conference Cambodia, Paris, 1991; Khmer Rouge; Sihanouk, Norodom; Supreme National Council.

## Razak, Tun Abdul (Malaysia)

Tun Abdul Razak was Malaysia's second prime minister, assuming office in September 1970 in succession to **Tunku Abdul Rahman**, who had lost the confidence of the politically dominant **UMNO** (United Malays National Organization). Tun Razak was born in Pahang in 1922 and was not able to receive a higher education in Britain until after the Pacific War. He completed his legal studies in 1950 and on returning to Malaya joined the civil service but soon left to enter politics. In Britain he had played a key role in the anti-colonial Malayan Forum and also acted as a mentor to the future prime minister, Tunku Abdul Rahman, whose deputy he became, holding portfolios for defence and rural development but acting also as *de facto* foreign minister. In that latter role, he led negotiations to ward off Indonesia's **Confrontation** and to form **ASEAN** (Association of South-East Asian Nations). As prime minister, he was responsible for inaugurating the **New Economic Policy** designed to redress the balance of economic advantage from non-Malays to Malays, in part to entrench the political position of UMNO. He was responsible also for taking Malaysia into the Non-Aligned Movement in 1970 and for establishing diplomatic relations with the People's Republic of China in 1974. He died prematurely of leukemia on 14 January 1976.

*see also:* ASEAN; Confrontation; New Economic Policy; Rahman, Tunku Abdul; UMNO.

## Razaleigh Hamzah, Tengku (Malaysia)

Tengku Razaleigh narrowly lost a leadership challenge to Prime Minister Dr **Mahathir Mohamad** for the office of president of **UMNO** (United Malays National Organization) in April 1987. The following year, he established an alternative Malay party, *Semangat '46* (Spirit of 1946), which failed to make a significant impact in federal elections in October 1990. In elections in April 1995, *Semangat '46*'s parliamentary strength was reduced from eight to six seats. The party was dissolved in October 1996 when Tengku Razaleigh and his supporters resumed membership of UMNO.

Tengku Razaleigh was born in April 1937 in Kota Bharu to a former chief minister and member of the royal family of the east-coast state of Kelantan. He was educated at Queen's University, Belfast, and completed legal studies at Lincoln's Inn, London. He became active in UMNO politics in Kelantan on his return, serving for some years in the state legislature before entering the federal parliament. He achieved national prominence from 1971 as executive director of PERNAS, the organization established to promote the economic interests of the Malays. He secured the most votes in elections for the three posts of vice-president of UMNO in 1975, but was passed over for the office of deputy prime minister in favour of Dr Mahathir in 1976 on the untimely death of **Tun Abdul Razak** and the succession of **Hussein Onn**. He was appointed finance minister but in 1984 was demoted to the portfolio of trade and industry after an unsuccessful challenge to deputy Prime Minister **Musa Hitam** for the office of UMNO deputy president. He resigned from cabinet office in 1986 and in his abortive bid for the UMNO presidency ironically had Musa Hitam as his running mate. After his return to UMNO, he was not identified with the political dissidence precipitated by the dismissal, arrest, trial and imprisonment of the deputy prime minister, **Anwar Ibrahim**. He was charged with responsibility by UMNO for recovering the state legislature in Kelantan from *Parti Islam Se-Malaysia* (PAS). In elections in November 1999, Tengku Razaleigh won a federal seat in Kelantan but PAS swept the board at both federal and state levels. He was not offered a portfolio in the new cabinet and made an abortive attempt to stand for deputy president and one of the posts of vice-president of UMNO at its General Assembly in May 2000 but failed to secure sufficient nominations.

*see also:* Anwar Ibrahim; Hussein Onn; Mahathir Mohamad; Musa Hitam; *Parti Islam Se-Malaysia*; Razak, Tun Abdul; *Semangat '46*; UMNO.

# Red Gaurs Movement (Thailand)

The Red Gaurs (Wild Buffaloes) was a right-wing movement active in the 1970s, comprised primarily of lower-middle-class vocational students from Bangkok. It was organized by the Internal Security Operations Command set up to combat communism, with a key role played by ex-mercenaries who had worked for the United States' Central Intelligence Agency (CIA) in Laos. The vocational students had played a key role in challenging military rule in October 1973 but had become disillusioned when parliamentary democracy failed to meet their economic expectations. Exploiting the social distance and tension between vocational and university students, the mentors of the Red Gaurs used them as a fascist-style street army for acts of intimi-

dation and terror against political enemies. Its members were directly involved in the bloodbath in the **Thammasat University Massacre** in October 1976 which provided the pretext for overthrowing the elected government and restoring military rule.

*see also:* Thammasat University Massacre 1976.

# Reform the Armed Forces Movement (RAM) (Philippines)

The Reform the Armed Forces Movement (RAM) played a key role in the mutiny that led to the overthrow of President **Ferdinand Marcos** in 1986. During the rule of his successor, **Corazón Aquino**, it served as a focus for military discontent and was responsible for mounting abortive coups and creating a climate of political instability. Its significance declined with the election to presidential office in May 1992 of the former chief of staff of the armed forces, **Fidel Ramos**.

The movement developed out of a personal rivalry between Marcos's minister of defence, **Juan Ponce Enrile**, and the then chief of staff of the armed forces, **Fabian Ver**. Partly as a vehicle for self-protection, Enrile set out to recruit a private army within the armed forces and attracted a group of discontented young officers to his cause. The Reform the Armed Forces Movement was set up in March 1985. A plot to seize the presidential palace against the background of a snap election called for February 1986 was discovered by Marcos. Fearing arrest, Enrile retreated with his supporters to Camp Aguinaldo, the site of the Defence Ministry. He was joined there by the deputy chief of staff of the armed forces, General Fidel Ramos, and the two of them shifted their base to the more defensible Camp Crame nearby (*see* **EDSA**) which became the focus of the '**People Power**' revolt that led to Marcos giving up office and going into exile.

After Corazón Aquino became president, Enrile was reinstated as minister of defence. But they were soon alienated from one another as Enrile and his youthful military supporters resented her exercise of power, which they regarded as rightfully theirs. Enrile was replaced as defence minister in November 1986 and the first of a number of abortive coups took place in January 1987, with Fidel Ramos appointed initially as chief of staff staying loyal to the president. Perhaps the most serious of the coups took place in August 1987 and was led by Colonel Grigorio Honasan, who had been a close aide to Enrile in February 1986. Honasan evaded capture for several months and subsequently escaped from detention in 1988 to launch another abortive coup in December 1989. Honasan and other dissident officers signed an accord with the government of Fidel Ramos in December 1992, which marked the effective end of challenge by the Reform the Armed Forces Movement. A network of military dissenters has been maintained, however. In May 1995, Honasan was elected to the Senate employing the acronym RAM, revised to mean Revolutionary Alliance of the Masses. In October 1995, the government concluded an amnesty agreement with those members of the armed forces who had been party to abortive coups which restored their military ranks.

see also: Aquino, Corazón; EDSA; Enrile, Juan Ponce; People Power; Ramos, Fidel; Ver, Fabian.

## Rendel Commission (Singapore)

In 1953 Sir George Rendel, a retired British diplomat, was appointed by the colonial authorities to head a multiracial commission to review Singapore's constitution with the objective of laying the foundations for self-government in the island. In 1954 the commission recommended a significant expansion of the suffrage and a thirty-two-member Legislative Assembly, with twenty-five elected members from which a ministerial government with limited powers would be drawn. Its recommendations were accepted and its provisions were implemented with elections in April 1955, which gave rise to a coalition government headed by **David Marshall** as first chief minister.

see also: Marshall, David.

## Revolutionary Government of the Republic of Indonesia 1958–61 (Indonesia)

On 15 February 1958, a group of ill-matched dissident officers and politicians, who had met initially in Sungai Dareh in west Sumatra, proclaimed over Radio Bukit Tinggi a *Pemerintah Revolusioner Republik Indonesia* (PRRI), which translates as Revolutionary Government of the Republic of Indonesia. This reformist rather than separatist rebellion, which sought to change the structure of government in Jakarta, was rooted in regional discontent in Sumatra and Sulawesi (Celebes) in particular. It registered resentment at the distribution of power and resources between Java and the outer islands of the archipelago. It also incorporated resentment on the part of regional military commanders at the centralizing policies of the national military establishment. A revolt by the west Sumatra military command, which took over civil administration in December 1956, had precipitated corresponding actions in Sulawesi and Kalimantan (Borneo). In Sulawesi, a military movement known as *Piagam Perjuangan Semesta Alam* (in acronym **Permesta**) meaning Universal Struggle Charter, which had been declared in March 1957, allied with the Sumatran rebels on 17 February 1958. The rebellion was a reaction also to the growing assertiveness and pro-Communist radicalism of President **Sukarno**, who maintained that the source of Indonesia's political turbulence was liberal democracy imported from the west. He declared martial law in March 1957 and acted to intimidate the modernist-Muslim *Masyumi* (Consultative Council of Indonesian Muslims) and the Socialist Party. He encouraged the seizure of Dutch business enterprises at the end of November 1957 in response to a failure to secure support in the United Nations General Assembly for Indonesia's position on **Irian Jaya**. This action, by causing economic disruption including a crisis in inter-island shipping, provoked the regional rebellion into a formal declaration of an alternative government. A firm military response from the centre in March 1958, however, saw the rebellion crumble and effectively collapse by June, although final defeat was not conceded until 1961. Its failure, despite clandestine support from the United States CIA, proved to be a political turning-point. It had the effect of consolidating both the power of Sukarno and the central military establishment, who together were able to inaugurate the authoritarian political system of **Guided Democracy** in July 1959.

*see also:* Guided Democracy; Irian Jaya; *Masyumi*; *Permesta*; Sukarno.

## Rizal, José (Philippines)

José Rizal is regarded as the spiritual father of Filipino nationalism and the supreme martyr to its cause. His famous satirical novels exposing the venality of Spanish colonial rule produced an evocative response among his fellow Filipinos. He was born on 19 June 1861 in Calamba, south of Manila, to a wealthy Chinese-mestizo family. He was exceptionally gifted and went on from the Jesuit elite Ateneo High School to the University of Santo Tomas, where he qualified in medicine. Before he left the Philippines to pursue postgraduate studies in Madrid, he had suffered personal humiliation at Spanish colonial hands. He pursued a reformist political cause in metropolitan Spain and expressed his desire for equal status in two famous novels which were banned in the Philippines. He specialized in ophthalmology and spent time in England and then in Hong Kong. In June 1892 he returned to Manila, where he founded the Philippine League to advance his reformist political aims. Rizal was soon after banished to the southern island of Mindanao on a charge of sedition. In 1896 he volunteered for service in Cuba in the Spanish interest but was arrested while en route and taken back to Manila. He was charged with responsibility for the nationalist uprising which had begun in the Philippines earlier in the year and sentenced to death. Rizal was executed by firing squad on 30 December 1896 at the age of 35. His poetic last testament, *Ultimos Adios*, has served as a romantic basic text for Philippine nationalism.

## Rohingyas (Burma/Myanmar)

Rohingyas is the name of the minority Muslim community in the north of the Arakan region of Burma who are the descendants of Arab and Persian traders who settled and intermarried over a period of several hundred years from the ninth century. Under colonial rule they enjoyed the protection of the government in Rangoon; their loyalty to the British during the Japanese occupation led to friction with the majority Burman Buddhists and the first of a series of forced population movements into east Bengal.

Muslims in Arakan rose in abortive revolt with other ethnic minorities with independence in 1948 because of the central government's refusal to countenance their political autonomy.

A government campaign disguised as a search for illegal immigrants in the late 1970s produced a second major wave of refugees into newly independent Bangladesh. Recurrent harassment continued until early 1992 when a third major exodus of some 300,000 took place as a result of an evident policy of 'ethnic cleansing' by the military regime. This action attracted the hostile attention of **ASEAN** (Association of South-East Asian Nations) governments with significant Muslim communities such as Malaysia, Indonesia and Brunei, who were also exercised by the ill-treatment of Muslims in Bosnia in former Yugoslavia. The policy of the government in Rangoon has been attributed to its interest in playing on communal tensions in order to distract popular attention from its economic failings and political repression. The international repercussions of its action within South-East Asia have not helped in its attempt to solicit regional support against western attempts to condemn it for human rights violations. A process of repatriation of Rohingyas was begun in September 1992 and some 200,000 have been reported as having returned to Burma by mid-1995. In April 2000, according to the International Federation of Human Rights, tens of thousands of Rohingyas were forced to flee the country into Bangladesh as a result of a deliberate policy of ethnic-cleansing in Arakan province where some 1.5 million reside.

*see also:* ASEAN; Chin; Kachin; Karen; Shan.

## Rómulo, Carlos (Philippines)

Carlos Rómulo was a distinguished journalist and diplomat who held the office of foreign minister continuously for sixteen years. He was born on 14 January 1899 in Manila, where he studied English literature, which took him first into university teaching and then journalism. By the end of the 1930s Carlos Rómulo had become publisher-editor of a newspaper syndicate and won a Pulitzer Prize for his writing about the onset of war in Asia. In 1941 he joined the US army and became press officer to General Douglas MacArthur, with whom he was evacuated from the Philippines after the Japanese invasion. In exile, Rómulo was appointed secretary of information in the cabinet of President Manuel Quezón and then with the rank of brigadier-general took part in the liberation of the Philippines, landing on the island of Leyte with MacArthur in October 1944. He subsequently served as commissioner of the Philippines to the United States and led his country's delegation to the San Francisco Conference on whose behalf he signed the United Nations Charter. He also led the Philippines delegation to the United Nations, becoming president of the General Assembly in 1949 and in 1950 held the office of foreign minister for two years before being appointed ambassador to the United States. After a series of diplomatic and ministerial positions, as well as becoming president of the University of the Philippines, he was reappointed foreign minister in 1968 during **Ferdinand Marcos**'s administration, paying particular attention to his country's membership of **ASEAN** (Association of South-East Asian Nations) and other Asian links. He remained in post continuously until obliged to retire due to ill-health in 1984. He died on 15 December 1985 at the age of 86.

*see also:* ASEAN; Marcos, Ferdinand; Rómulo, Roberto.

## Roxas, Manuel A. (Philippines)

Manuel Roxas was the first president of the Republic of the Philippines on its independence from the United States. He was elected in April 1946 as president of the Commonwealth and then took the oath of office again in July with the full transfer of sovereignty. Manuel Roxas was born on 1 January 1892 in Capiz on the island of Panay and was educated at the University of the Philippines, where he graduated in law. He was an active politician between the two world wars, becoming speaker of the House of Representatives. He was involved in negotiating the transitional arrangement to independence set in train in 1935, after which he held the office of secretary of finance. During the Pacific War, he had remained in the Philippines as a member of the Japanese-sponsored administration headed by Jose Laurel. He was saved from the political wilderness and worse by the active intervention

of General Douglas MacArthur, who had been a close friend before hostilities. MacArthur's patronage was a decisive factor in Roxas's political rehabilitation and success. Restored as Senate president, he challenged the incumbent Sergio Osmena for high office and defected from the **Nacionalista Party** through the vehicle of its 'Liberal Wing', which was reconstituted as the **Liberal Party** under his leadership. He won a narrow victory with US support in a free-spending election. As president, he was faced with major problems of economic rehabilitation and political challenge from the peasant-based *Hukbalahap* **Movement**. He has been identified with protecting the United States' economic and military interests in the Philippines in return for payments for war damages. The military bases agreement which gave the United States a ninety-nine year tenure over twenty-three sites, including **Subic Bay Naval Base** and **Clark Air Base**, was negotiated under his aegis. Ironically he died on 15 April 1948 at Clark Air Base after making a speech to US service personnel.

*see also:* Clark Air Base; *Hukbalahap* Movement; Liberal Party; Nacionalista Party; Subic Bay Naval Base.

## *Rukunegara* 1970 (Malaysia)

Translated literally as Basic Principles of the State, *Rukunegara* was promulgated on 31 August 1970 by Malaysia's Department of National Unity. Drawing inspiration from Indonesian practice, the concept was intended to provide a set of guidelines for communal coexistence in the wake of extensive vio- lence that erupted in Kuala Lumpur in the **May 13 Racial Riots 1969**. The declaration read:

Our Nation Malaysia, being dedicated to achi eving a greater unity of all peoples; to maintaining a democratic way of life; to creating a just society in which the wealth of the nation shall be equitably shared; to ensuring a liberal approach to her rich and diverse cultural traditions; to building a progressive society which shall be oriented to modern science and technology;

We, her people, pledge our united efforts to at tain those ends guided by these principles:

Belief in God
Loyalty to King and Country
Upholding the Constitution
Rule of Law
Good Behaviour and Morality

*Runkunegara* has never assumed the standing of a national ideology and lapsed as a practical political device after Malaysia resumed parliamentary government during the 1970s. The ability of the government to proceed with its **New Economic Policy** of redistributing wealth to the particular advantage of the Malay community without unleashing communal tensions has made the stratagem underlying *Runkunegara* redundant. The concept remains available, however, for employment against political dissent with a racial connotation.

*see also:* May 13 Racial Riots 1969; New Economic Policy

# S

**Sabah United Party** (Malaysia/Sabah)
The Sabah United Party (*Parti Bersatu Sabah -* PBS) was the ruling party in the Malaysian state of Sabah in northern Borneo from April 1985 until March 1994. It was established in February 1985 as the result of defections from the ruling *Berjaya* (Sabah People's Union) because of resentment on the part of ethnic Kadazans and Chinese at the pro-Muslim policies of the chief minister, **Datuk Harris Mohamad Salleh**. In state assembly elections in April, it won twenty-five out of forty-eight seats and after overcoming an artificial constitutional impediment, its leader, **Datuk Joséph Pairin Kitingan**, was sworn in as chief minister. In time, it was accepted as a member of the ruling federal coalition, *Barisan Nasional* (National Front), and in July 1990 was returned to office despite apparent federal support for the opposition **United Sabah National Organization** (USNO). In mid-October 1990, just five days before elections to the federal legislature, PBS defected from *Barisan Nasional* to join the opposition coalition. *Barisan Nasional*, which retained office, expelled the PBS and sought to undermine its position in Sabah by establishing a branch of the politically dominant **UMNO** (United Malays National Organization) in the state as well as bringing a charge of corruption against the chief minister. This initiative appeared to backfire in April 1993, when leading members of the opposition USNO defected to join the PBS. Datuk Kitingan called state elections for February 1994, shortly before being found guilty of awarding a shop-house project to a company in which his brothers-in-law had an interest. However, he received a fine below the amount that would have disqualified him from contesting the elections. In the event, PBS was returned to power with a narrow majority. It secured twenty-five seats in the state legislature of forty-eight, with the remaining places being held by UMNO and three linked minor parties. Its parliamentary position was then undermined by a series of defections, including that of the chief minister's brother, Jeffrey Kitingan, which led to a loss of

its majority four weeks after the result of the elections. Datuk Kitingan then resigned as chief minister in favour of Sakaran Dandai, the head of the Sabah division of UMNO. The key to the failure of PBS was the refusal of the federal government to encourage the economic development of Sabah as long as it remained in office. With the resignation of Datuk Kitingan, his party began to splinter into three factions which made their own accommodations with the National Front government in the interest of sharing power and its spoils. It demonstrated its resilience in federal elections in April 1995 by holding eight seats compared to fourteen in 1990. In elections in November 1999, its federal strength was reduced to three seats, while in state elections won by the *Barisan Nasional* in the previous March, it secured seventeen out of forty-eights seat. In April 2000, however, six of its members in the state legislature defected to the ruling coalition.

see also: *Barisan Nasional*; *Berjaya*; Harris Mohamad Salleh, Datuk; Kitingan, Datuk Joséph Pairin; UMNO; United Sabah National Organization.

**Saloth Sar** (Cambodia) *see* Pol Pot.

**Samphan, Khieu** (Cambodia) *see* Khieu Samphan.

**Samrin, Heng** (Cambodia) *see* Heng Samrin.

**San Yu, General** (Burma/Myanmar)
General San Yu served as the faithful acolyte of **Ne Win** for over forty years. After Ne Win stood down as president of Burma in 1981, San Yu assumed the office until retiring from political life in 1988, when political turbulence caused the ruling military establishment to set up a new form of government. San Yu was born in Prome in 1919 and was studying medicine in Rangoon at the outbreak of the Pacific War. He became an officer in the Japanese-sponsored Burma Defence Army and continued with a

military career after the end of hostilities, with some training in the United States. He rose rapidly in the military hierarchy and was a member of the Revolutionary Council under Ne Win which seized power in 1962; San Yu became general secretary of the Central Organizing Committee of the ruling **Burma Socialist Programme Party** (BSPP) in 1964. He subsequently held the positions of deputy prime minister and also of minister of defence and was at one time seen as a likely successor to Ne Win but his political role has been that of loyal servant without great personal ambition. He died on 28 January 1996 aged 76.

*see also:* Burma Socialist Programme Party; Ne Win.

## Sangkum Reastre Niyum (Cambodia)

*Sangkum Reastre Niyum*, which translates as Popular Socialist Community, was a mass political organization established by Prince **Norodom Sihanouk** in March 1955 on his abdication from the throne. Through this organization, Prince Sihanouk commanded the heights of Cambodian politics for fifteen years until he was deposed in March 1970. The *Sangkum* served as a means through which he could encompass and also domesticate all shades of political opinion. It was employed initially to contest the general elections held in September 1955. An overwhelming victory was secured with 83 per cent of the vote, which delivered all seats in the National Assembly. The *Sangkum* functioned very much as a political stage for Prince Sihanouk, who called periodic national congresses held in the open at which he could humiliate his ministers and national assemblymen in front of an urban mass for whom the occasion provided considerable entertainment. The heyday of the *Sangkum* and its national congresses was in the late 1950s and early 1960s. However, as Prince Sihanouk's political grip became less sure, in part because of external factors, the spectacle of the national congress lost its initial attraction. By the time Prince Sihanouk was overthrown in 1970, the *Sangkum* had long ceased to serve its initial political function.

*see also:* Sihanouk, Norodom.

## Sann, Son (Cambodia) *see* Son Sann.

## Santi Asoke (Thailand)

*Santi Asoke* is the name of a Buddhist sect; it means peace and no sorrow. It was set up by a former television producer, Phra Bodhirak, ostensibly in an attempt to purge Thai **Buddhism** of superstition and impurities. Its members uphold an ascetic existence with a vegetarian diet and began by wearing brown robes instead of the traditional saffron. In the manner of Roman Catholic liberation theology, its leaders have asserted a right to be involved in politics to improve the condition of the people. In 1979 General **Chamlong Srimuang**, who went on to become governor of Bangkok, identified himself with the sect, whose members subsequently campaigned on behalf of his *Palang Dharma* (Moral Force party). In 1989 the monks of *Santi Asoke* were excommunicated by the Buddhist hierarchy, which led to General Chamlong distancing himself from the sect.

*see also:* Buddhism; Chamlong Srimuang; Palang Dharma.

## Santri (Indonesia)

*Santri* is an Indonesian term deriving from *pesantran*, which is the name for a village religious school. It has come to be employed, primarily in Java, to distinguish Indonesian Muslims of a strict orthodoxy from the *Abangan* whose **Islam** is a synthesis comprising in part animist and Hindu-Buddhist beliefs with a mystical content. Since independence, *Santri* have been identified with political parties such as *Masyumi* and the *Nahdatul Ulama* and since the merger of all Islamic parties in 1973 with the **United Development Party** (*Partai Persatuan Pembangunan*). The term is a convenient category for foreign scholars rather than a precise basis for common identity on the part of devout Muslims. It began to lose its discrete quality when former President **Suharto** sought to mobilize urban Islamic elements in his own political interest during the 1990s. With his downfall and a mushrooming of Islamic-based parties, Islamic identity has served as more of a vehicle for *Pribumi* interests than as an indication of intra-religious divisions.

*see also: Abangan;* Islam; *Masyumi; Nahdatul Ulama; Pribumi;* Suharto; United Development Party.

## Sarawak National Party (SNAP)
(Malaysia/Sarawak)
The Sarawak National Party (SNAP) is a junior member of the original *Barisan Tiga* (Front of Three); a tripartite coalition, which was formed in 1976 with *Parti Pesaka Bumiputera Bersatu* and the **Sarawak United People's Party** (SUPP) and which has continuously constituted the government in the north Bornean Malaysian state, joined additionally in coalition in 1994 by the breakaway *Parti Bangsa Dyak Sarawak*. SNAP is also part of the federal ruling coalition, the *Barisan Nasional* (National Front). The party was established in March 1961 during a period of political ferment when the proposal to incorporate the British colony of Sarawak into a Federation of Malaysia was a matter of some controversy. It drew its support primarily from the Iban–Dyak community and was led by Stephen Ningkan, a former hospital assistant with Shell in Brunei, who became the first chief minister after entry into Malaysia in September 1963. His espousal of states rights and resistance to the model of Malay-Muslim dominance established in peninsular Malaysia led to his inspired removal from office in 1966. SNAP moved into opposition but in time accommodated to the political supremacy of the minority Malay–Melanau Moslem communities. Iban–Dyak alienation at such accommodation led to defection and the breakaway *Parti Bangsa Dyak Sarawak* being established in 1983. The split within the Iban–Dyak community has ensured that SNAP remains a junior party in the coalition government, which was last returned to state office in September 1996. In federal elections in November 1999, SNAP held four seats, which was the same number secured in April 1995.
*see also: Barisan Nasional; Barisan Tiga; Parti Bangsa Dyak Sarawak; Parti Pesaka Bumiputera Bersatu; Sarawak United People's Party.*

## Sarawak United People's Party (SUPP)
(Malaysia/Sarawak)
The Sarawak United People's Party (SUPP) is a junior member of the original *Barisan Tiga* (Front of Three), a tripartite coalition formed in 1976 with *Parti Pesaka Bumiputera Bersatu* and the **Sarawak National Party** (SNAP) and

which has continuously constituted the government in the north Bornean Malaysian state, joined in 1994 by *Parti Banga Dyak Sarawak*. SUPP is also part of the federal ruling coalition, the *Barisan Nasional* (National Front). The Sarawak United People's Party was set in June 1959 in anticipation of municipal elections in Kuching and well before the proposal that the British colony be incorporated into a Federation of Malaysia had been mooted. Its founders were ethnic-Chinese businessmen who espoused a non-communal socialist agenda but support for the party was along ethnic lines. Moreover, an active Communist component within the local Chinese community used SUPP as a vehicle for an abortive opposition to Sarawak's entry into Malaysia. During the 1960s, it formed part of the state opposition. But from the early 1970s, its leadership began practical collaboration with both state and federal governments, with SUPP becoming a founding member of the *Barisan Nasional* and then a member of the state ruling coalition. It still attracts Chinese support but on the basis of economic advantage through membership of the governing state coalition, which was last returned to office in September 1996. In federal elections in November 1999, SUPP improved its parliamentary strength to eight seats from six secured in April 1995. Its founder, Ong Kui Hui, died in April 2000.
*see also: Barisan Nasional; Barisan Tiga; Parti Pesaka Bumiputera Bersatu; Sarawak National Party.*

## Sarit Thanarat, Field Marshal
(Thailand)
Sarit Thanarat was prime minister of Thailand from January 1959 until his death on 9 December 1963. He was a strong and forceful personality with an evident will to govern that commanded popular respect. During the period of political stability which he enforced as effective military dictator, the foundations were laid for Thailand's subsequent economic growth. In addition, the national standing of the monarchy was enhanced as a direct consequence of its employment by the regime to uphold its political legitimacy. Sarit Thanarat was born in the north-east of the country in 1908 and entered the Chulachomklao Royal Military Academy in

Bangkok in the late 1920s. He was a junior officer at the time of the coup against the absolute monarchy in 1932. He rose steadily as an officer and was a colonel in command of an infantry battalion in Bangkok in 1947 at the time of the first coup after the Pacific War through which the military re-established its political dominance. By 1949 he had risen to the rank of lieutenant-general with the key command of the First Army, charged with the defence of Bangkok, as part of an uneasy triumvirate with Field Marshal **Phibul Songkram** and the chief of police, General Phao Siyanond. Sarit and General Phao were direct rivals but when Sarit became commander-in-chief of the army in 1954, he was able to consolidate his power. He intervened to establish his dominance in September 1957 after a turbulent period of electoral politics fostered by the prime minister, Phibul. His deputy, General **Thanom Kittikachorn**, assumed the office of prime minister while Sarit went to the United States to receive medical treatment. Rumbling financial and political crises were not overcome until his return in October 1958 to launch a bloodless coup, after which he promulgated a new interim authoritarian constitution. Sarit assumed the office of prime minister in January 1959, drawing political inspiration from the recently established rule of Charles de Gaulle in France. In foreign policy, Thailand was sustained in its alliance relationship with the United States. After Sarit's death, a scandal arose over the number of wives he had taken as well as the considerable wealth that he had accumulated.

*see also:* Bhumibol Adulyadej; Phibul Songkram; Thanom Kittikachorn.

## Sary, Ieng (Cambodia) *see* Ieng Sary.

## Sastroamijoyo, Ali (Indonesia)

Ali Sastroamijoyo was prime minister of Indonesia from July 1953 until July 1955 and again from March 1956 until March 1957. He espoused a rhetorical left-wing nationalism and presided over unstable cabinet coalitions during a turbulent parliamentary democracy which came to an effective end with the fall of his second cabinet. He achieved a place in history for his initiative in convening the **Asian-African**

**Conference**, held in Bandung in April 1955. Ali Sastroamijoyo was born in central Java in 1903 and became active in nationalist politics as a student in Holland before the Pacific War. During the national revolution, he played a role in government as a member of the Indonesian National Party (*Parti Nasional Indonesia* – PNI) founded in 1927. He held the office of minister of education in January 1949 when the Dutch captured the republic's capital, Yogyakarta, and was sent into internal exile on the island of Bangka. After independence, he served as ambassador in Washington before returning to assume the office of prime minister as leader of the Indonesian National Party. He remained leader during the period of **Guided Democracy**, adopting a deferential political relationship with President **Sukarno** as well as echoing his ideological creed, *Nasakom*. After the armed forces led by General **Suharto** seized power in March 1966 to establish its **New Order**, Ali was removed as leader of the Indonesian National Party to spend the remainder of his life until his death in 1975 as a tolerated but suspect figure.

*see also:* Asian-African Conference, Bandung 1955; Guided Democracy; *Nasakom*; New Order; Suharto; Sukarno.

## Sawito Affair (Indonesia)

In September 1976 the Indonesian government claimed that it had discovered a plot to overthrow President **Suharto** by unconstitutional means. Its leader was alleged to be Sawito Kartwibowo, who worked as an engineer in the Department of Agriculture and who had a following as a mystic. Apparently, he had been able to persuade five distinguished national figures to sign a document entitled 'In Pursuit of Salvation' which was highly critical of the government. The signatories were the former vice-president, **Mohammad Hatta**; the chairman of the Indonesian Muslim Clergymen's Council, Professor Hamka; the chairman of the Indonesian Council of Churches and former armed forces chief of staff, General T. B. Simatupang; the chairman of the Indonesian Church's Representative Council, Cardinal Justinus Darmojuwono; and the chairman of the Joint Secretariat of the Indonesian Spiritual Association and former chief of police, General

Soekanto Tjokrodiatmodjo. All of the signatories, except Sawito, disclaimed any knowledge of the content and significance of the critical document. The short-lived episode has never been satisfactorily explained, especially the link between the six signatories, but the so-called Sawito Affair was symptomatic of an underlying discontent among members of an alienated elite at the corruption of power under the Suharto regime.

*see also:* Hatta, Mohammad; Suharto.

## SEATO (South-East Asia Treaty Organization) 1955–77 (Phillipines/ Thailand)

The South-East Asia Treaty Organization (SEATO) was the institutional expression of the South-East Asia Collective Defence Treaty concluded in the **Manila Pact** in September 1954. SEATO was established with its headquarters in Bangkok during a treaty council meeting held in the Thai capital during 23–5 February 1955. As an organization, it initially comprised representatives of all council members, made up of all ambassadors of signatory states and a corresponding member of the Thai foreign service, a military advisers group as well as three committees concerned with economics, information and security. An international secretariat and a permanent working group of junior diplomats were set up at a council meeting in Karachi in March 1956. A meeting of military planners in Singapore in June 1956 recommended the establishment of a military planning office, which was endorsed at a council meeting in Canberra in March 1957 together with the office of secretary-general. After council meetings in Manila and Wellington in 1958 and 1959, some members declared specific military units for SEATO purposes.

Although SEATO arranged series of military exercises, it never fulfilled an active military role, even during the **Vietnam War**. It found itself beset by internal tensions arising conspicuously from French dissidence but also from an underlying lack of common strategic interest. After the **Paris Peace Agreements** in January 1973, the organization began to be wound down because of its loss of any practical *raison d'être*. The military structure was abolished from 1 February

1974. At a council meeting held in New York on 24 September 1975, it was agreed to disband SEATO from 30 June 1977 but not to revoke the treaty on which it was based. Thailand, in particular, was keen to retain the vestigial security link with the United States.

*see also:* Manila Pact 1954; Paris Peace Agreements 1973.

## *Semangat '46* (Malaysia)

*Semangat '46*, which translates from Malay as the Spirit of 1946, is the name of a breakaway party from the politically dominant **UMNO** (United Malays National Organization). The schism arose from personal rivalry between the prime minister, Dr **Mahathir Mohamad**, and the former minister of trade and industry, **Tengku Razaleigh Hamzah**, and the former deputy prime minister, **Datuk Musa Hitam**. The term Spirit of 1946 refers to the year in which UMNO was established in opposition to British constitutional revisionism and was intended to register that the breakaway group was the authentic legatee of UMNO's political values and traditions. *Angkatan* (organization) *Semangat '46* was established in the wake of a decision by the federal High Court in February 1988 that UMNO was an unlawful society because thirty of its branches had not been properly registered when elections for highest party office were held at its General Assembly in April 1987. Dr Mahathir succeeded in reconstituting UMNO under the title UMNO *Bahru* (New UMNO) with the power to scrutinize the credentials of members of the deregistered party who wished to join its successor. In September 1988 Tengku Razaleigh and twelve of his supporters resigned from the *Barisan Nasional* (National Front) ruling coalition to sit as independents in the federal Parliament, to be joined in October by Datuk Musa, who then reverted to UMNO in January 1989. *Semangat '46* was officially registered as a political party in May 1989 and then entered into an electoral pact with *Parti Islam Se-Malaysia* (PAS) and a minor party in *Angkatan Perpaduan Ummah* (Muslim Unity Front) as well as a looser electoral association with the non-Malay **Democratic Action Party** (DAP). In general elections in October 1990, *Semangat '46* and its partners made a limited impact at the federal level in competition with *Barisan Nasional*, which was returned to office with a barely reduced majority. The sole significant success for *Semangat '46* was in elections in Kelantan, Tengku Razaleigh's home state, where all seats at the federal and state levels were secured by a coalition with PAS. Despite public support from the former prime ministers, **Tunku Abdul Rahman** and **Tun Hussein Onn**, seats held by *Semangat '46* at the federal level dropped from twelve to eight, while seats held by PAS increased from one to seven. The outcome of the elections revealed that the intra-UMNO revolt had effectively fizzled out and that Dr Mahathir's position was demonstrably reconfirmed. *Semangat '46*'s national position weakened further in elections in April 1995 when its parliamentary numbers were reduced to six. By 1996 its coalition with PAS had reached breaking point. In October that year, the party was formally dissolved and Tengku Razaleigh and his supporters were re-admitted to UMNO.

see also: *Angkatan Perpaduan Ummah*; *Barisan Nasional*; Democratic Action Party; Hussein Onn, Tun; Mahathir Mohamad, Datuk Sri; Musa Hitam, Datuk; *Parti Islam Se-Malaysia*; Rahman, Tunku Abdul; Razaleigh Hamzah, Tengku; UMNO.

## Sen, Hun  (Cambodia) *see* Hun Sen.

## Sen, Son  (Cambodia) *see* Son Sen.

## Seni Pramoj  (Thailand)
Seni Pramoj enjoys the unique record of having been prime minister of Thailand in 1945 and then again for two short periods in 1975 and 1976. He was born on 26 May 1905 into a junior branch of the royal family; he is the older brother of **Kukrit Pramoj** (also prime minister 1975–6). Seni Pramoj received his main education in Britain, graduating in law from Worcester College, Oxford. He practised as a lawyer and entered the judiciary before heading Thailand's legation in Washington in 1940 as minister. In that capacity, he refused to communicate Thailand's declaration of war against the Allies made at Japan's insistence. In Washington he assumed the role of leader of the overseas Free

Thai Movement; after the war he was briefly prime minister and foreign minister in interim governments before the restoration of a short-lived parliamentary democracy. He served as minister of justice in the **Democrat Party** cabinet led by Khuang Abhaiwongse during 1947–8 until it was overthrown by the military. Seni Pramoj returned to the practice of law but retained his association with the Democrat Party, becoming its leader after the death of Khuang in 1968. He re-entered Parliament in 1969 and during the democratic restoration from October 1973 until October 1976, he served for two periods as prime minister, leaving office first through electoral reverse and secondly through the military coup following the **Thammasat University Massacre**. He resigned as leader of the Democrat Party in 1979 and then retired from public life. He died on 28 July 1997 at the age of 92.

see also: Democrat Party; Kukrit Pramoj; Thammasat University Massacre 1976.

## Shan  (Burma/Myanmar)
The Shan indigenous minority inhabit a hilly plateau of about 150,000 square kilometres or a quarter of the country in the eastern part of Burma which borders the People's Republic of China, Laos and Thailand. They share a cultural and linguistic affiliation with the people of Thailand and adhere to the Theravada branch of **Buddhism**. Under British administration, the traditional political system of rule by *Sawbwas* (hereditary princes) was made part of the colonial structure. The traditional leadership agreed to membership of a Shan state within the Union of Burma at a meeting in Panglong in 1947. The Shan did not join in the separatist challenge to the Union until 1959 after an attempt was made to remove the powers of their traditional leadership. A Shan States Army fought an insurgency against the government in Rangoon until 1989, when a cease-fire agreement was reached with the ruling **State Law and Order Restoration Council** (SLORC). The Shan State Nationalities Liberation Organization formally abandoned its armed struggle against the Rangoon government in October 1994. Insurgent activity continued under the leadership of the drug baron **Khun Sa**, but in June 1995 his Mong Tai

Army split and a separate Shan State National Army resumed insurgency. In April 1997, Amnesty International reported that the Burmese army had forcibly relocated some 300,000 Shan villagers in an attempt to deny support to the Shan State National Army, torturing and killing in the process. A second Amnesty report in June 1999 maintained that military pressure was being maintained on the Shan.

see also: Buddhism; Chin; Kachin; Karen; Khun Sa; Rohingyas; State Law and Order Restoration Council.

## Shared Values (Singapore)

In January 1990 a White Paper on shared values was introduced into Singapore's Parliament. Its purpose was to promulgate an ideology for the island-state which would bond its citizens of different ethnic and cultural identities. The White Paper represented a governmental response to a disturbing religious revivalism which was a social consequence of remarkable economic development. The government had commissioned a series of studies on the need for shared values in the wake of an alleged Marxist-Leninist plot in the first half of 1987 to make Singapore into a classless society. The prime movers in that so-called conspiracy were a group of Catholic social workers. Irrespective of the validity of the charges, the government was undoubtedly concerned that the contagion of liberation theology might spread to Singapore as a reaction to its society becoming addicted to western materialist values.

The shared values in the White Paper were:

1 Nation before community and society before self;
2 Family as the basic unit of society;
3 Regard and community support for the individual;
4 Consensus instead of contention;
5 Racial and religious harmony.

The promulgation of so-called shared values has to be seen, together with legislation to promote religious harmony enacted at the end of 1990, as an instrument of social and political control. In general elections in August 1991, the ruling People's Action Party (PAP) suffered a reverse in terms of its political expectations when opposition parties won four seats in the Parliament and it failed to arrest a continuing decline in its share of the popular vote. Subsequently Singapore asserted its shared values as an East Asian phenomenon in reaction to the attempt by the US Clinton administration to promote a global doctrine of enlarging free market democracy as an alternative to the defunct one of containing international communism. With its success in elections in January 1997, the government of Singapore toned down its participation in the Asian values debate, especially as the United States had begun to take a more pragmatic attitude in dealing with authoritarian regimes in East Asia. The tenets of shared values, as articulated in 1990, have continued to be at the core of social policy in Singapore.

see also: People's Action Party.

## Shihab, Alwi (Indonesia)

Alwi Shihab was appointed foreign minister of Indonesia in October 1999. He had not had any previous diplomatic or governmental experience but had been deputy chairman of the National Awakening Party, which had been founded by President Abdurrahman Wahid. Alwi Shihab, who is of Arab ancestry, was born on 19 August 1946 in Makassar, south Sulawesi. He graduated from the Islamic Teaching Institute co-founded by his father in his birthplace and then went to higher education in Cairo where he obtained a master's degree in theology from Al Azhar University and a doctorate in Islamic philosophy from the University of Ains Shams. His main experience has been as an Islamic scholar with a special interest in comparative religion. He is a long-time associate of Abdurrahman Wahid and his role as his special adviser is as important as that of foreign minister. Alwi Shihab enjoys Western academic connections, including a visiting appointment at Harvard University. He shares the same liberal religious disposition as Abdurrahman Wahid and achieved initial prominence for his declared interest in promoting trade ties with Israel, albeit pacifying Islamic critics by stating that Indonesia would only establish diplomatic ties after the Middle East conflict was resolved peacefully.

see also: National Awakening Party; Wahid, Abdurrahman.

**Shwe, Than** (Burma/Myanmar) *see* Than Shwe.

**Siazon, Domingo L.** (Philippines)
Domingo Siazon was appointed secretary of foreign affairs of the Philippines in May 1995 in succession to **Roberto Rómulo**, who had resigned to assuage popular furore over the hanging of **Flor Contemplacion**. He is the first career diplomat to head the Philippines foreign service and prior to his appointment had been ambassador in Tokyo. Before then, from September 1985 until January 1993, he had served as the first director-general of the United Nations Development Organization (UNIDO) and as the highest placed Filipino executive in the United Nations. Domingo Siazon was born on 9 July 1939 in Appari in Cagayan Province. He received most of his higher education overseas after graduating in political science from the Ateneo de Manila. He studied physics at Tokyo University of Education and then in mid-career public administration at Harvard University. While in Tokyo, he met his Japanese wife and worked as an interpreter and translator at the Philippines Embassy before passing the Foreign Service Officer Examination and continuing in post as third secretary. He then held diplomatic appointments in Switzerland and Austria as well as representative status at UNIDO from February 1968. He was retained in office after **Joséph Estrada** was inaugurated as president in June 1998. He has brought technocratic and linguistic skills to his role as well as the absence of any political taint, which, despite the change of regime, is why he was retained as secretary of foreign affairs.
*see also:* Contemplacion, Flor; Estrada, Joséph; Rómulo, Roberto.

**Siddhi Savetsila** (Thailand)
Siddhi Savetsila served as foreign minister of Thailand from February 1980 until August 1990. During that period, he achieved prominence for his diplomatic assertiveness within **ASEAN** (Association of South-East Asian Nations) and the United Nations in challenging Vietnam's occupation of Cambodia in the third phase of the **Indochina Wars**. His removal from office came after Vietnam's withdrawal and when the

government of **Chatichai Choonhavan** wished to pursue a more conciliatory policy towards Indochina. Siddhi Savetsila was born on 7 January 1919 in Bangkok. He was educated at Chulalongkorn University and at the Massachusetts Institute of Technology. He began his career in the Royal Thai Air Force and rose to the rank of air chief marshal. At the time of Vietnam's invasion of Cambodia, he was secretary-general of the National Security Council which was advisory to the prime minister. He entered Parliament in 1983 and at the end of 1985 took over the leadership of the **Social Action Party**, which fared well in elections in July 1986; he served for a short period as a deputy prime minister. By the end of the decade the Social Action Party was in some disarray and Siddhi resigned as its leader in August 1990 after losing his cabinet portfolio and because of his disgust at political scandal. He resigned his parliamentary seat and his party membership the next month, announcing that he was tired of politics and wished to retire from public life.
*see also:* ASEAN; Chatichai Choonhavan; Indochina Wars; Social Action Party.

**Sihanouk, King Norodom** (Cambodia)
Norodom Sihanouk has been a dominating figure in the political life of Cambodia since the mid-1940s. As one of the great survivors of post-colonial politics in South-East Asia, he has drawn his staying power from a tradition of divine monarchy, a unique flamboyant personality and the failure of Cambodian regimes to transcend an endemic factionalism. He has to be regarded as a flawed personality, in part responsible for the tragedy that has befallen post-colonial Cambodia. His patriotism has always been fused with an intense personal vanity which has affected his judgement and prompted erratic behaviour.

Prince Sihanouk was born on 31 October 1922 to parents drawn from both the senior and junior wings of the royal family and received his secondary education at a French lycee in Saigon. In April 1941, after the death of King Sisowath Monivong, the colonial authorities decided to revert to the Norodom branch of the royal family because they judged that the young Sihanouk would make a malleable monarch.

Initially he proved to be an accommodating figure in dealing in turn with representatives of Vichy France, Imperial Japan and Free France. That judgement was shown to be misplaced after the Pacific War, when King Sihanouk played the nationalist card to the political disadvantage not only of the French but of contending republican and social-revolutionary groupings. In June 1952 he assumed the office of prime minister, committing himself to achieving independence within three years. In February 1953 he embarked on a world tour in a successful attempt to embarrass the French into granting his political demands. He returned in triumph from a contrived internal exile in westerly Battambang Province to the capital, Phnom Penh, on 8 November 1953 to announce national independence. That independence was confirmed in 1954 by the **Geneva Agreements on Indochina**, which also imposed obligations on Cambodia to conduct internationally observed free elections. In March 1955, in order to escape the constraints of constitutional monarchy and to out-manoeuvre his political opponents, King Sihanouk abdicated his throne in favour of his father, Norodom Suramarit. He then set up a national front called the *Sangkum Reastre Niyum* (Popular Socialist Community) which captured all the seats in the National Assembly in elections in September 1955.

Prince Sihanouk then dominated Cambodian politics in a wilful and self-indulgent manner intolerant of any dissent until his overthrow in 1970. When his father died in 1960, Prince Sihanouk had himself created head of state in a monarchy without a monarch. He was overthrown in March 1970 by a coup which was justified by a failure to remove a Vietnamese Communist presence from the eastern parts of the country. Prince Sihanouk had been a pioneer of the foreign policy of non-alignment. He attended the **Asian-African Conference** at Bandung in Indonesia in April 1955 where his meeting with the People's Republic of China's prime minister, Zhou En-lai, served to convince him that non-alignment offered the best safeguard for Cambodia's security against neighbouring historical antagonists, both of whom were allied with the United States. Prince Sihanouk went on to reject the gratuitous

protection of the **Manila Pact** of 1954 and committed his country to a foreign policy described as neutrality. Initially that policy coincided with conventional non-alignment but with the growing success of Communist insurgency in neighbouring South Vietnam, Prince Sihanouk revised the practice of neutrality to one of political accommodation to both North Vietnam and China in the hope that the government in Beijing would act as protecting patron. Toleration of Vietnamese Communist use of Cambodian territory as an active sanctuary from which to prosecute their revolutionary war against the Saigon regime provided an opportunity for his political opponents to move against him.

Prince Sihanouk was in Moscow on 18 March 1970 when he was deposed by the incumbent government in Phnom Penh headed by General **Lon Nol**. He continued a pre-arranged journey to Beijing where the prime minister, Zhou En-lai, brought him together with the Vietnamese Communist prime minister, **Pham Van Dong**, to promote an opposition united front with a group of Cambodian insurgents whom Prince Sihanouk had dubbed the **Khmer Rouge**. In May 1970 he set up a government in exile with his new-found political partners and lent his name and authority to the cause of **Pol Pot** and his minions, who between 1975 and 1978 turned Cambodia into a butcher's yard. Prince Sihanouk passed the ensuing civil war in Beijing with the exception of a clandestine visit to the battle zone in 1973, which indicated a tension between him and his coalition partners. With the victory of the Khmer Rouge in April 1975, he was reinstated as head of state but remained outside of Cambodia until the end of the year, except for a brief and disturbing visit in September. In Cambodia, Prince Sihanouk and his wife Monique lived under effective house arrest, while six of his fourteen children and a number of his grandchildren perished at Khmer Rouge hands. In April 1976, with the promulgation of the constitution for a republican **Democratic Kampuchea**, he resigned as head of state.

Coincident with Vietnam's invasion of Cambodia in December 1978, Prince Sihanouk was flown to Beijing on a Chinese aircraft and from there travelled to New York, where he denounced Vietnam's intervention before the

General Assembly of the United Nations. He then went into exile in North Korea with whose late leader Kim Il Sung he had established a close rapport. A small resistance group loyal to him was set up among refugees along the border with Thailand and were organized into **FUNCINPEC** (the French acronym for the National United Front for an Independent, Neutral, Peaceful and Cooperative Cambodia). In June 1982 Prince Sihanouk was persuaded after much external pressure to become president of a so-called **Coalition Government of Democratic Kampuchea** (CGDK) comprising his Khmer Rouge tormentors and a non-Communist resistance movement of republican disposition. During the course of the 1980s he was able to transform his initial figurehead position into one of renewed political importance as the Vietnamese were obliged to withdraw effective support from the government which they had implanted in Phnom Penh. Towards the end of the decade, he resigned his office and began bilateral but abortive negotiations with its prime minister, **Hun Sen**. The failure of an **International Conference on Cambodia** in Paris in 1989 led to a major political initiative under the aegis of the permanent members of the United Nations Security Council, who concluded a framework agreement on a peace settlement in August 1990. Prince Sihanouk was seen as central to its successful application as the head of a symbolic repository of sovereignty, the **Supreme National Council**, which would delegate administrative responsibility to the United Nations in an interim period before elections were conducted to decide the political future of the country. That settlement was endorsed by a second stage of the **International Conference on Cambodia** in Paris in October 1991 and in the following month Prince Sihanouk returned to Cambodia after an absence of almost thirteen years to be reinstalled as head of state.

The Cambodian peace settlement was based on fragile political assumptions about the contending parties' commitment to national reconciliation. Although Prince Sihanouk was greeted on his return as a national saviour, all factions sought to exploit his personal standing. The refusal of the Khmer Rouge in particular to abide by the rules of the Paris accord produced

a political impasse which proved beyond the skills of Prince Sihanouk to overcome. In failing health and lacking his former energy, he retreated to China and North Korea in periodic bouts of despair as Cambodia seemed to lapse into anarchy. UNTAC (United Nations Transitional Authority in Cambodia) persevered with its task, however, despite the refusal of the Khmer Rouge to take part in elections scheduled for May 1993. The electoral outcome was inconclusive with a near majority of votes being obtained by FUNCINPEC, once presided over by Prince Sihanouk but following his elevation to chairman of the Supreme National Council placed in the charge of his son, Prince **Norodom Ranariddh**. He entered into a provisional coalition with the **Cambodian People's Party** (CPP) led by the former prime minister Hun Sen, which excluded the Khmer Rouge. The Constituent Assembly then proceeded to restore the constitutional monarchy and on 24 September 1993, Norodom Sihanouk at the age of 70 and in poor health, was reinstated as King of Cambodia nearly forty years after he had abdicated from the throne. The powerful myth of Sihanouk contributed to the people of Cambodia and the international community turning to him as the font of national unity after Cambodia's experience of so many years of political turbulence. The record of the man, however, would suggest a greater facility for reigning than for ruling. He has been more at home with the pomp and circumstance of government than with its good practice. Indeed, his neglect of the latter when in power is part of the tragedy of modern Cambodia.

After his reinstatement as monarch, King Sihanouk returned to Beijing to receive treatment for prostate cancer. He reappeared in Phnom Penh in April 1994 and displayed some of his old political vigour in an attempt to effect an accommodation between the new coalition government and the Khmer Rouge, but to no avail. He went back to Beijing for more medical treatment in mid-May 1994 and also to demonstrate his continuing indispensability to stable government in Cambodia, pointing up the likely political vacuum that would be left with his departure from the scene. He returned to Cambodia at the beginning of 1995 without assuming an active political role. He stood above the growing rivalry between his son and Second Prime Minister Hun Sen and was publicly equivocal in response to the bloody coup in July 1997 which ousted Prince Ranariddh from senior political office. However, he did threaten to abdicate in an indication of the importance of his constitutional role to Hun Sen's consolidation of power. King Sihanouk went on to broker an agreement between Prince Ranariddh and Hun Sen initially by authorizing an amnesty for Prince Ranariddh who had been sentenced to thirty-five years' imprisonment for arms trafficking and negotiating clandestinely with the Khmer Rouge. Fresh elections were held in July 1998 in which Hun Sen's Cambodian People's Party won a plurality of seats in the National Assembly. Hun Sen became sole prime minister, while Prince Ranariddh assumed the lesser office of chairman of the National Assembly. King Sihanouk readily accommodated himself to his son's political displacement, which indicated the nature of the filial relationship and also a characteristic disposition to defer to superior power. King Sihanouk has come to the end of his days as an enfeebled constitutional monarch, a role which he has long struggled, with mixed success, to overcome.

*see also:* Asian-African Conference, Bandung 1955; Cambodian People's Party; Democratic Kampuchea; Democratic Kampuchea, Coalition Government of; FUNCINPEC; Geneva Agreements on Indochina 1954; Hun Sen; International Conference on Cambodia, Paris 1991; Khmer Rouge; Manila Pact 1954; Nol, Lon; Pham Van Dong; Pol Pot; Ranariddh, Norodom; *Sangkum Reastre Niyum*; Supreme National Council; United Nations: Cambodia 1991–3; UNTAC.

## Sim, Chea (Cambodia) *see* Chea Sim.

## Sin, Cardinal Jaime (Philippines)

Cardinal Jaime Sin, Archbishop of Manila, has been the head of the Roman Catholic Church in the Philippines since May 1976, when he was elevated to the holy consistory. He was born on 31 August 1928 in New Washington in Capiz Province on Panay Island in the central Philippines. Ordained in 1954, his early career was spent in the provincial ministry. He was surprised in January 1974 to be translated from the archdiocese of Jaro to that of Manila. He achieved political prominence as an outspoken critic of the government of President **Ferdinand Marcos** and of the self-indulgence of his wife, **Imelda Marcos**. Long before the assassination of the opposition leader **Benigno Aquino** in August 1983, which marked a turning-point in Filipino politics, Cardinal Sin had drawn public attention to growing poverty, corruption and the gross violation of human rights. After Aquino's death, he articulated the moral outrage of the Filipino people and encouraged public challenge to Marcos in the hope of promoting political reform.

Cardinal Sin has not been a radical in politics and certainly not an enthusiast for liberation theology. His self-styled stance of 'critical collaboration' towards the Marcos administration indicated an evident ambivalence. That ambivalence arose from concern that exhortation to confrontation might unleash revolutionary forces to which the Church, as well as the state, might fall victim. He was influenced by the role which Buddhist monks had played in undermining the government of **Ngo Dinh Diem** in South Vietnam, so assisting the ultimate seizure of power by the Communists. Apprehension that the Communists might secure advantage from Marcos's decaying political system moved him to persuade **Corazón Aquino**, the widow of Benigno, to stand for president against Marcos in the snap election of February 1986. When conspicuous fraud resulted in military revolt led by **Juan Ponce Enrile** and **Fidel Ramos**, Cardinal Sin encouraged the mobilization and interposition of massive popular support, '**People Power**', which prevented Marcos from employing military force in order to cling on to power. He stood by Corazón Aquino on her elevation to high office but also made known his disappointment when her new government showed itself to be less than competent in addressing the fundamental economic and social ills of the Philippines. Her failure to reverse the practice of corruption and violation of human rights did not evoke in him the same critical attitude made manifest during the Marcos era, however. His critics have put this relative political passivity down to his primary concern to protect the interests of the Roman Catholic Church in a context where the Communist threat had diminished considerably. Cardinal Sin did not appear to welcome with enthusiasm the election of Fidel Ramos as the first Protestant president of the Philippines in May 1992 and has opposed his efforts to promote birth control. He also played a prominent public role in opposing constitutional changes, which would have permitted President Ramos to stand for a second term of office. Correspondingly, he opposed constitutional changes affecting foreign ownership proposed by President **Joseph Estrada**.

see also: Aquino, Benigno; Aquino, Corazón; Diem, Ngo Dinh; Enrile, Juan Ponce; Marcos, Ferdinand; Estrada, Joseph; Marcos, Imelda; People Power; Ramos, Fidel.

## Singapore Democratic Party (SDP)
(Singapore)

The Singapore Democratic Party (SDP) became the principal parliamentary opposition when it secured three seats in elections in September 1991, the first opposition party to obtain more than a single seat since independence in 1965. It was founded in 1980 by **Chiam See Tong**, who was first elected to Parliament in 1984 and then again in 1988 as sole SDP member. The SDP has acted primarily as a moderate critic of the ruling **People's Action Party** (PAP) seeking to hold it to account for its political excesses and errors rather than posing as an alternative government. The party was very much the creation and creature of Chiam See Tong until internal differences emerged after the 1991 elections. In June 1993 Chiam See Tong resigned as secretary-general. He claimed that there were people within the party who did not share his vision. At issue ostensibly was a disagreement with the assistant secretary-general, Dr Chee Soon Juan, over his hunger strike in protest at his alleged politically motivated dismissal from a lectureship at the National University of Singapore. However, the enlargement of the parliamentary strength of the SDP had led to personal rivalry and differences over confronting the PAP on policy issues as well as revealing a cleavage between English-educated and Chinese-educated members. Chiam was replaced as leader of the

opposition in July and expelled from the SDP in August but was reinstated by the High Court in December 1993. The SDP was left a house divided and an exemplar of the continuing failure of credible political opposition in Singapore. In November 1994, a breakaway faction was registered as the Singapore People's Party. In elections in January 1997, the Singapore Democratic Party failed to win a single seat, while Chiam See Tong retained his constituency on behalf of the Singapore People's Party.

see also: Chiam See Tong; People's Action Party; Workers Party.

## Singapore Strait  (Indonesia/Malaysia/Singapore)

The Singapore Strait is a constricted and congested waterway situated south of the island of Singapore and the south-eastern tip of peninsular Malaysia and north of Indonesia's Riau Islands. Its length is approximately 70 miles. The narrowest land width is 3.2 miles; the narrowest breadth of navigable waters is 1.8 miles. At its most westerly point, the Singapore Strait merges with the **Malacca Strait**. At its corresponding easterly point, the strait merges with the **South China Sea**. Together with the linked Malacca Strait, the Singapore Strait was subject to a controversial joint statement on 16 November 1971 by Indonesia and Malaysia which challenged the customary legal regime in the context of making provision for safety of navigation. Singapore, which was a party to the provision, registered its reservations to that challenge. In the event, the three coastal states worked out a scheme for traffic separation in the linked straits on 24 February 1977 which was accepted by the maritime powers within the context of a new regime for straits used for international navigation. That regime was incorporated in the United Nations Convention on the Law of the Sea promulgated on 10 December 1982, which also recognized Indonesia's **Archipelago Declaration** of 1957.

The territorial sea boundary between Singapore and Indonesia was delimited in a treaty which was concluded on 25 May 1973. At its points of ingress and egress, the Singapore Strait is commanded by Indonesian and Malaysian territorial waters. A treaty concluded between Indonesia and Malaysia in July 1982 delimited the territorial sea boundary between the two countries recognizing as a consequence the archipelagic status of the former. A dispute obtains between Malaysia and Singapore over the island of Pedra Branca (Singapore usage) or Pulau Batu Puteh (Malaysian usage) on which is situated the **Horsburgh Lighthouse**, which has been administered from Singapore since its construction in the mid-nineteenth century. The island in dispute is bounded by Malaysian and Indonesian waters but lies close to the middle of the navigable channel at the eastern egress of the Singapore Strait.

see also: Archipelago Declaration 1957; Horsburgh Lighthouse; Malacca Strait; South China Sea; Sunda Strait.

## Singapore Summit (ASEAN) 1992
(Brunei/Indonesia/Malaysia/Philippines/Singapore/Thailand)

The fourth meeting of heads of government of **ASEAN** (Association of South-East Asian Nations) convened in Singapore on 27 and 28 January 1992. The summit took place in the wake of the **International Conference on Cambodia** in Paris in October 1991, which agreed a comprehensive political settlement of the Cambodian conflict. That conflict had engaged the corporate energies of ASEAN for more than a decade, enhancing the reputation of the Association as a diplomatic community. At issue at the summit was the ability of ASEAN to demonstrate a renewal of its terms of cooperation, especially in economic matters. To that end, the six heads of government agreed to set up **AFTA** (ASEAN Free Trade Area) using their established Common Effective Preferential Scheme as the main mechanism within a time-frame of fifteen years beginning from 1 January 1993. A Malaysian initiative to establish an **East Asian Economic Caucus** exclusive of the United States and Australia failed to attract a consensus, with Indonesia opposed in particular. Adherence to ASEAN's **Treaty of Amity and Cooperation** by regional non-members was welcomed and a declaratory commitment to a regional **ZOPFAN** (Zone of Peace, Freedom and Neutrality) was reaffirmed, but security cooperation was not advanced in any substance. It was agreed, however, that

external dialogues in political and security matters should be intensified by using the vehicle of the ASEAN post-ministerial conferences, which was undertaken from July 1992 in Manila. The heads of government agreed to meet formally every three years with informal meetings in between in a significant change from past practice. An important symbolic innovation was the decision to redesignate the secretary-general of the ASEAN Secretariat as the secretary-general of ASEAN with an enlarged mandate to initiate, advise, coordinate and implement ASEAN activities.

see also: AFTA; ASEAN; East Asian Economic Caucus; International Conference on Cambodia, Paris 1991; Treaty of Amity and Cooperation 1976; ZOPFAN.

## Sipadan-Ligitan  (Indonesia/Malaysia)

The tiny island of Sipadan, together with the nearby reef of Ligitan, is occupied by Malaysia but is also claimed by Indonesia. Sipadan is located in the Celebes Sea parallel to the eastern boundary between Malaysian Sabah and Indonesian Kalimantan. Malaysia and Indonesia base their respective claims on colonial agreements and documents, including an Anglo-Dutch boundary convention of 1891. The issue of jurisdiction arose when both states extended their territorial seas from three to twelve nautical miles. Malaysia's occupation dates from the formation of the Federation in 1963 when its troops were deployed to cope with Indonesia's **Confrontation**. The current dispute became active in the early 1980s when Indonesian patrol vessels were deployed to investigate reports of occupation by Malaysian troops, allegedly in violation of an understanding to avoid unilateral action in advance of negotiations. Malaysia has subsequently sought to develop Sipadan, which is of exceptional natural beauty, as a tourist resort. The contending claims have significance for extending jurisdiction over ocean space which could have resource implications. Indonesia has challenged Malaysia's occupation through recurrent acts of military display and in negotiations between heads of governments and officials. In September 1994, Indonesia rejected Malaysia's proposal that the dispute be referred to third-party arbitration but relented when their heads of government met again in October 1996. In May 1997, senior officials from both states concluded a draft agreement on submitting their contending claims to the International Court of Justice but Malaysia insisted on administering the islands until a judicial decision was forthcoming. At the end of April 2000, 21 people, including 10 foreign tourists, were abducted from Sipadan Island, in use as a diving resort, by armed Muslim insurgents from the Philippines.

see also: Confrontation.

## Sisón, José María  (Philippines)

José María Sisón provided the intellectual vision in the reconstitution of the Communist Party of the Philippines which took place during a so-called 'Congress of Re-establishment' in Pangasinan Province between 26 December 1968 and 7 January 1969. He was responsible for drafting the new party's constitution which acknowledged the supreme guidance of Mao Tse-tung and also assumed the post of chairman. Sisón took the name Amado Guerrero (Beloved Warrior). In 1970, under that name, he wrote *Philippine Society and Revolution*, which served as the theoretical text for the party. Sisón was born on 8 February 1939 into a middle-income family in Ilocos Sur Province. He was educated at the University of the Philippines and became a leading activist in student politics as well as a member of the Communist Party. He began his career on the staff of the Manila Lyceum School of Journalism in 1954 where he helped to form the *Kabataan Makabayan* (KM: Patriotic Youth) which was a stridently anti-American nationalist movement. Sisón was expelled from the Communist Party in April 1967 because of his personal assertiveness and rejection of discipline. He then established an alternative politburo with inspiration from China's Cultural Revolution, which led on to his initiative for an alternative party. His small group of student radicals joined up with Bernabe Buscayno, who provided the leadership for the military wing of the party which was established on 29 March 1969 as the **New People's Army**. Although Buscayno was captured soon after, the decentralized strategy adopted by the insurgents in exploiting the

geography of the archipelago posed a major challenge to the government of President **Ferdinand Marcos**, especially in its later years. Sisón was captured by security forces in November 1977. He remained in prison until after the fall of President Marcos, when he was released in March 1986 by the new government of President **Corazón Aquino**. Sisón then established the **People's Party** to exploit so-called democratic space but with his colleagues misjudged the popular mood and failed to secure congressional representation in elections in May. The inability of the revolutionary left to recapture its earlier momentum and support led to internal divisions, to which Sisón contributed. He left the Philippines at the end of 1987 to take up residence in Holland where he was granted political asylum and permitted to work for the **National Democratic Front**, which had long maintained its European office in Utrecht. Sisón continued to assert a leadership role in exile, pressing for a continuation of the initially successful strategy of peasant-based guerrilla war. In October 1988 a warrant was issued in the Philippines for Sisón's arrest after it had become known that he had resumed in exile the leadership of the Communist Party. He was involved in negotiations in Utrecht with representatives of the government in Manila in September 1992, but lost his role with a further split within the Communist Party which repudiated his leadership. He has continued to call for armed struggle in the Philippines.

see also: Aquino, Corazón; Marcos, Ferdinand; National Democratic Front; New People's Army; People's Party.

## Social Action Party  (Thailand)

The Social Action Party (*Kit Sangkhom*) is a marginal factor in Thai politics, and secured twenty-two seats in the elections in Thailand in September 1992, nine fewer than in the polls held in March 1992. It then joined the coalition government led by **Chuan Leekpai** but was dismissed in September 1993 after an abortive attempt to merge with four opposition parties in order to form the largest group in the Parliament. The Social Action Party was founded in 1974 by **Kukrit Pramoj**, a minor member of the royal family and a distinguished journalist.

It stressed rural development and secured sufficient votes in the elections in 1975 in the wake of military rule to form a short-lived coalition government under Kukrit's leadership. Elections in the following year sent the Social Action Party into the ranks of the opposition; they were suspect by the military junta which had seized power in October 1976. They secured a substantial electoral following in 1979 and during the 1980s played a regular part in coalition government but came to appear more representative of business than rural interests. Air Chief Marshal **Siddhi Savetsila** succeeded Kukrit Pramoj as leader of the party in December 1985 and managed to hold it together in the face of widespread defections. Scandal over ministerial corruption led Siddhi to resign the leadership in some disgust in August 1990, after he was removed as foreign minister, to be succeeded by Kukrit Pramoj. The party left government in December 1990 and after the military coup in February 1991 suffered notable defections. Montri Pongpanich succeeded Kukrit as leader, taking it into coalition government in 1992, but was responsible for the gamble which sent it again into opposition in 1993. In elections in July 1995, it held its twenty-two seats and joined the coalition government headed by **Banharn Silpa-archa**, with its leader as minister of agriculture. In elections in November 1996, the Social Action Party's parliamentary strength was reduced to twenty seats. It then entered the new coalition government headed by **Chavalit Yongchaiyut** with its leader in the office of deputy prime minister. In November 1997, when Chavalit was obliged to resign as prime minister in the face of economic crisis, it continued in coalition government with **Chuan Leekpai** as prime minister. In July 1999, however, the party withdrew from the government as a result of an internal feud.

*see also:* Banharn Silpa-archa; Chavalit Yongchaiyut; Chuan Leekpai; Kukrit Pramoj; Siddhi Savetsila.

## Son Ngoc Thanh  (Cambodia)

Son Ngoc Thanh was one of the earliest exponents of Cambodian nationalism but fell foul of **Norodom Sihanouk**, who treated him as a political outcast. Son Ngoc Thanh was a member of the Cambodian minority in southern Vietnam, where he was born in Travinh in 1908 into a family of prosperous landowners. He trained as a teacher as well as studying law for a year in France. He then joined the colonial administration in Indochina and in the early 1930s was working as a magistrate in Cambodia. In 1935 he became the secretary of the Buddhist Institute in Phnom Penh and in the following year jointly founded a Cambodian language newspaper *Nagaravatta* (Angkor Wat (Temple)). France's failure to resist Japanese intimidation in Indochina encouraged Thanh's anti-colonial orientation and he became involved in a demonstration in July 1942 in protest at attempts to romanize the Khmer language and to introduce the Gregorian calendar. He fled to Thailand, where the Japanese mission arranged for him to travel to Tokyo, where he spent the remainder of the war. When the Japanese overturned the French administration in Indochina in March 1945, Son Ngoc Thanh returned to Cambodia to occupy the post of foreign minister, making no secret of his republican sympathies. He assumed the office of prime minister on Japan's surrender but was arrested in September 1945 by British forces and taken to Saigon, where he was sentenced to detention in France for collaboration. He was released in October 1951 and returned to Phnom Penh to receive a rapturous public welcome which offended Sihanouk. Thanh adopted a vigorous anti-French position which he expressed in a newspaper called *Khmer Krok* (Cambodians Awake). When the newspaper was suspended in February 1952, he fled the capital and fomented a republican rebellion against French rule, which provoked Sihanouk to take the lead in the independence movement. Sihanouk then succeeded in marginalizing Son Ngoc Thanh, who remained in the jungle after Cambodia's independence had been conceded by France. Son Ngoc Thanh spent the next decade and a half leading a feckless resistance against Sihanouk's rule with Thai, South Vietnamese and US Central Intelligence Agency (CIA) support, while living in Saigon. After Prince Sihanouk was overthrown by a right-wing coup in March 1970, Thanh returned again to Cambodia in August to become an adviser to President Cheng Heng. In March

1972 he was appointed to the nominal post of First prime minister by Lon Nol, who had become executive president. When he was asked to resign by Lon Nol after fraudulent elections in September 1972, Son Ngoc Thanh left Cambodia in some despair to live again in South Vietnam in retirement, where he is believed to have died shortly after the Communists seized power in 1975.

*see also:* Nol, Lon; Sihanouk, Norodom.

## Son Sann (Cambodia)

Son Sann was the leader of the republican-inclined **Khmer People's National Liberation Front** (KPNLF) which was established in October 1979 in opposition to the **Khmer Rouge** and the incumbent **People's Republic of Kampuchea** (PRK). He was born on 5 October 1911 in Phnom Penh to a family originating from southern Vietnam. Son Sann was educated in France, where he graduated in 1933 from the School for Advanced Commercial Studies. On his return to Cambodia, he served as deputy governor of the provinces of Battambang and Prey Veng in the French administration. After the Pacific War, during which he engaged in private business, Son Sann held a series of senior government offices beginning with finance minister; in 1954, as foreign minister, he represented Cambodia at the conference leading to the **Geneva Agreements on Indochina**. He became the first governor of Cambodia's National Bank in 1955, holding that position until 1968 and serving concurrently as prime minister during 1967-8. He was never in tune politically with Prince **Norodom Sihanouk** but after Sihanouk's overthrow in 1970, Son Sann left Cambodia to take up residence in Paris, where he was living when the Khmer Rouge seized power in 1975. As leader of the KPNLF, he took his movement in June 1982 into the **Coalition Government of Democratic Kampuchea** (CGDK), in which he held the office of prime minister. Poor military performance by the KPNLF led to dissension within its ranks but Son Sann, who attracted respect for his personal probity, held on to its political leadership. He took a hard line towards the incumbent government in Phnom Penh and was a party to the negotiations which culminated in a political settlement at the **International Conference on Cambodia** in Paris in October 1991. He returned to Cambodia in December 1991 and then transformed the KPNLF into the **Buddhist Liberal Democratic Party** for the elections in May 1993 under United Nations auspices (*see* **UNTAC**). His party won only 10 out of the 120 seats in the Constituent Assembly. Son Sann was elected its chairman and supervised its role in drafting a new constitution, which was promulgated in September. After the re-establishment of the constitutional monarchy, Son Sann retired from public life, giving up his chair of the National Assembly to **Chea Sim**. He lost his position as party president to the minister of information, Ieng Mouly, in July 1995. He subsequently set up his own Son Sann Party which contested elections in July 1998 without success.

*see also:* Buddhist Liberal Democratic Party; Democratic Kampuchea, Coalition Government of; Geneva Agreements on Indochina 1954; International Conference on Cambodia, Paris 1991; Kampuchea, People's Republic of; Khmer People's National Liberation Front; Khmer Rouge; Sihanouk, Norodom; UNTAC.

## Son Sen (Cambodia)

Son Sen assumed the post of supreme commander of the insurgent national army of **Democratic Kampuchea** on the ostensible retirement of **Pol Pot** in August 1985. He was removed from that position some time after the Paris peace agreements following the **International Conference on Cambodia** in October 1991 because of contention among the **Khmer Rouge** leadership over complying with its provisions; but was reported as having been reinstated to senior command in April 1994. Son Sen was born in 1930 in southern Vietnam among the settled Cambodian minority. He was educated in Phnom Penh and then in the 1950s in Paris, where he became a member of a Marxist group of Cambodian students at whose centre was Saloth Sar (Pol Pot). On his return to Cambodia, he became director of studies at the National Teaching Institute as well as a leading member of the reconstituted Communist Party of Cambodia. He fled from the capital in 1963 to escape from Prince **Norodom Sihanouk**'s secret police and is believed to have spent time in Hanoi. By 1971 he had become chief of staff of the Cambodian People's National Liberation Armed Forces engaged in challenging the government in Phnom Penh headed by **Lon Nol**. After the Khmer Rouge seized power in April 1975, he became a deputy prime minister and minister of defence until the Vietnamese invasion at the end of 1978. He continued in that role in directing the military challenge of the ousted Khmer Rouge against the Vietnamese occupation and the government established in Phnom Penh. He was a party to the political machinery set up to implement the political settlement for Cambodia and was a Khmer Rouge member of the **Supreme National Council** in Phnom Penh until April 1993, when its delegation withdrew in protest at the forthcoming elections. At one time regarded as the fourth-ranking member of the Khmer Rouge hierarchy, he is believed to have engaged in factional rivalry with Pol Pot and to have been implicated in the murder of a British university teacher, Malcolm Caldwell, in Phnom Penh in December 1978. He was also in overall charge of the infamous **Tuol Sleng** interrogation centre. Son Sen was murdered on 10 June 1997, together with his wife and his nine children, on the instructions of Pol Pot after he had refused to attend a meeting at which the Khmer Rouge leader would have insisted on a continuation of armed struggle and on opposing a compromise deal with the government in Phnom Penh.

*see also:* Democratic Kampuchea; International Conference on Cambodia, Paris, 1991; Khmer Rouge; Nol, Lon; Pol Pot; Sihanouk, Norodom; Supreme National Council; Tuol Sleng.

## Souphanouvong, Prince (Laos)

Prince Souphanouvong was instrumental in helping to found the revolutionary movement in Laos which achieved political victory under Vietnamese patronage. He was born on 13 July 1909, the youngest of the twenty sons of Prince Boun Khong. His best-known half-brother was Prince **Souvanna Phouma**. Prince Souphanouvong was educated at a school in Hanoi and went on to study engineering in France, where he became politically active during the period of the Popular Front. He returned to Indochina in 1937 and entered the colonial public works service. Posted to southern Vietnam, he married the daughter of a hotel owner. He drew on his Vietnamese connections in September 1945 when he travelled from Laos to the headquarters of **Ho Chi Minh** to seek an alliance against the French. Ho sent him back with a military escort with which Prince Souphanouvong launched an anti-French resistance movement. This movement was driven into exile in Thailand in 1946. When its more conservative members came to terms with France in 1949, Prince Souphanouvong joined the **Viet Minh** in the jungles of Vietnam, beginning a close association with the revolutionary leaders, **Kaysone Phomvihan** and **Nouhak Phoumsavan**. In August 1950 he was a party to establishing the *Pathet Lao* (Lao Nation) revolutionary movement. Although denied representation at the **Geneva Agreements on Indochina** in 1954, a Vietnamese vice-minister of defence signed the cease-fire agreement for Laos on their specific behalf with a French counterpart.

Prince Souphanouvong was a founding member of the **Lao People's Revolutionary Party** in 1955 and subsequently played an important negotiating role on behalf of the *Pathet Lao*, participating in a short-lived coalition government after a further conference resulting in the **Geneva Agreements on Laos** in 1961–2. That conference failed to end the civil war, which was eventually concluded to *Pathet Lao* advantage in 1975 after the end of the **Vietnam War**. Possibly because of his royal origins, Prince Souphanouvong was never a truly commanding figure in the ruling Lao People's Revolutionary Party. He occupied senior positions, nonetheless, including membership of the Politburo. When the People's Democratic Republic of Laos was established in December 1975, he became its first president until obliged to give up on grounds of age and ill-health in 1986. He did not formally relinquish his office and Politburo position until the fifth national congress of the ruling party in March 1991. He died on 9 January 1995 aged 86.

*see also:* Geneva Agreements on Indochina 1954; Geneva Agreements on Laos 1962; Ho Chi Minh; Kaysone Phomvihan; Lao People's Revolutionary Party; Nouhak Phoumsavan;

*Pathet Lao*; Souvanna Phouma; Viet Minh;
Vietnam War.

## South China Sea  (Brunei/Indonesia/
Malaysia/Philippines/Vietnam)

The South China Sea has a semi-enclosed
mediterranean quality. Its area of some 648,000
square miles is bounded by China, Vietnam, the
Philippines, Indonesia, Malaysia and Brunei.
The sea provides important maritime communication routes between the Indian and Pacific
oceans, most notably for energy supply from
the Gulf of Arabia to Japan's home islands.
Within the South China Sea, there are four
main island groups, none of which is the natural geographic extension of any coastal state's
continental shelf. These groups, in different
ways, are the object of serious contention
between coastal states. The People's Republic of
China is in control of the northerly **Paracel
Islands**, which are contested by Vietnam and
Taiwan. At issue between China and Taiwan
is the question of governmental legitimacy,
not sovereignty over specific territories. Control
of the northerly Pratas Islands by Taiwan is
challenged only by China as part of its general
challenge to the government in Taipei. The Mac-
clesfield Bank is permanently submerged and
the issue of control has not yet arisen. Greatest
contention arises over the **Spratly Islands**
comprising many reefs, shoals and sandbanks
which spread out from the very centre of the
sea. Jurisdiction is contested between China,
Taiwan, Vietnam, Malaysia and the Philippines,
with Brunei concerned only with maritime
space arising from its continental shelf. The
Philippines has occupied eight of the Spratly
Islands (including reefs and shoals), while
Malaysia has occupied five with outstanding
claims respectively to nine others but not to the
entire group, which is the position with China,
Taiwan and Vietnam. China has occupied six
islands, while Vietnam has occupied twenty-
one. Taiwan has occupied Itu Aba, the largest
island in the group. The main attraction is the
prospect of discovering and exploiting extensive reserves of oil and natural gas and fishing
waters although strategic considerations may
influence governments. In July 1992 the foreign
ministers of **ASEAN** (Association of South-East

Asian Nations), at their annual meeting in
Manila, issued a **Declaration on the South China
Sea** which called on contending claimants to
resolve issues of sovereignty without resort
to force. The claim by China causes most consternation within South-East Asia because of
the transformation of strategic environment
which would follow from the projection of
its jurisdiction some 1,800 kilometres from its
mainland into the maritime heart of the region.
In May 1994 Singapore's senior minister and
former prime minister, Lee Kuan Yew, publicly
advised China to reduce anxieties over its inten-
tions in the South China Sea. Such anxieties
were reinforced in February 1995 when it
was revealed that Chinese forces had occupied
Mischief Reef, some 135 miles to the west of
the Philippines island of Palawan. Vietnam
and Indonesia have been in continuing negotiations over demarcation of the continental shelf
north of the Natuna Islands which belong to
Indonesia, while China has displayed a map
indicating a claim to maritime jurisdiction in
part of Indonesia's exclusive economic zone
arising from its jurisdiction over those islands.
ASEAN has taken the initiative to formulate a
code of conduct for states with contending
claims to jurisdiction in an attempt to build on
its declaration of July 1992 but without success,
so far. Such a code would be a confidence-
building measure and not make provision
for the settlement of conflicting claims to jurisdiction, which senior officials from ASEAN and
China, meeting in Thailand in March 2000,
agreed should be resolved on a bilateral basis.
Given the overlapping nature of most claims,
such an accord reflected the continuing impasse.
Since 1990, an informal **Workshop on Managing Potential Conflicts in the South China
Sea** has been sponsored by Indonesia with
financial support from Canada. In May 1995, the
US State Department issued a statement indicating that it would view with serious concern
any maritime claim or restriction on maritime
activity in the South China Sea not consistent
with International Law. It also stressed its interest in maintaining freedom of navigation in the
sea.

*see also:* ASEAN; Declaration on the South
China Sea; Paracel Islands; Spratly Islands;

Workshop on Managing Potential Conflicts in the South China Sea.

## South-East Asia Command 1943–6

The South-East Asia Command was the title of the military authority responsible for dispossessing Japan of territorial gains acquired during the Pacific War. After the end of hostilities in 1945 that title was adopted into conventional usage to describe the region situated to the east of the Indian sub-continent and south of China. The decision to establish the Command was taken at a conference in Quebec City in August 1943, attended by the US president, Franklin Roosevelt, and the British prime minister, Winston Churchill, which appointed Vice-Admiral Lord Louis Mountbatten as Supreme Allied Commander. Based in Kandy in Ceylon (now Sri Lanka), its initial geographic responsibilities were limited to Burma, Thailand and Malaya, including Singapore and the island of Sumatra. In July 1945 at the Potsdam Conference in Germany attended by Marshal Stalin, President Truman, Prime Minister Churchill and his successor Clement Attlee, the decision was taken to transfer extensive geographic responsibilities from the South-West Pacific Command under General Douglas MacArthur so that it could devote itself to an assault on Japan's home islands. In consequence, the South-East Asia Command was enlarged to include the whole of the Netherlands East Indies (except West Timor), northern Borneo and Indochina north of the 16th parallel of latitude. With the atomic bombing of Hiroshima and Nagasaki, its prime postwar tasks were to recover Allied prisoners of war and civilian internees and to take the surrender of Japanese forces. The Command's headquarters were transferred to Singapore in November 1945. British/Indian troops played a role in restoring French authority in southern Vietnam and came into armed conflict with Indonesian nationalists on the island of Java in the **Battle of Surabaya**. After a preliminary accord between Dutch and Indonesian representatives over the political future of the Indies in mid-November 1946, all British/Indian troops were withdrawn at the end of the month coincident with the Command being disbanded.
*see also:* Surabaya, Battle of.

## South-East Asia Nuclear Weapon-Free Zone Treaty (SEANWFZ) 1995
(Brunei/Burma(Myanmar)/Cambodia/Indonesia/Laos/Malaysia/Philippines/Singapore/Thailand/Vietnam)

On 15 December 1995, at a summit meeting in Bangkok, the heads of government of **ASEAN** together with those of Burma (Myanmar), Cambodia and Laos, signed a treaty establishing a South-East Asia Nuclear Weapon-Free Zone (SEANWFZ). The treaty was represented as contributing to the Association's declaratory commitment to a **Zone of Peace, Freedom and Neutrality (ZOPFAN)**. The terms of the treaty prohibited signatory states from manufacturing, storing or testing nuclear weapons as well as from allowing any other state to use a signatory's territory to do so. However, individual signatories were permitted to grant access to the military aircraft and naval vessels of nuclear powers. The treaty's ambit included the land area, territorial waters, 200-mile exclusive economic zones and continental shelves of the signatories. Although the treaty was of only symbolic significance, it was received with reserve by China and the United States, which the ASEAN governments had hoped would sign an attached protocol. China raised objections to the inclusion of continental shelves and exclusive economic zones of signatories on the grounds that it prejudiced its claims in the **South China Sea**. The United States indicated concern over possible impediments to the freedom of passage of its naval vessels and aircraft through regional waters and air space. By the turn of the century, none of the nuclear weapons states had signed the protocol, despite discussions to this end initiated by ASEAN. Moreover, the commission of SEANWFZ, which has been charged with drafting rules of procedure, convened only for the first time during the meeting of ASEAN's foreign ministers in Singapore in July 1999.
*see also:* ASEAN; South China Sea; ZOPFAN.

## Souvanna Phouma, Prince (Laos)

Prince Souvanna Phouma was prime minister of Laos on several occasions between 1950 and 1975 when the Communists assumed power. He was a man of liberal values who stood for a time as a symbol of national reconciliation among warring factions. His ability to fulfil that role depended in part on his personal relationship with his half-brother, Prince **Souphanouvong**, the nominal head of the pro-Communist *Pathet Lao* (Lao Nation) movement and for some years president of the People's Democratic Republic established in 1975. The obstacle which he could never overcome was that the main antagonists in Laos were never really interested in political compromise.

Souvanna Phouma was born on 7 October 1901 in Luang Prabang into the junior branch of the royal family. Trained in civil and electrical engineering in Vietnam and France, he became director of public works in French colonial Laos before the outbreak of the Pacific War. He became involved in politics at its close during the interregnum before the return of the French. With two brothers, he formed the Free Laos Movement in opposition to French rule and spent a short exile in Thailand, returning to Laos only after its independence was recognized in 1949. He first became prime minister in 1951 and negotiated the full transfer of sovereignty from France. After the **Geneva Agreements on Indochina** of 1954, which failed to resolve internal political divisons within Laos, he sought to engage the *Pathet Lao* in coalition government. Success in this enterprise prompted a right-wing military coup in July 1958 and Souvanna Phouma left office to serve as ambassador to France. He returned as prime minister after a neutralist coup in August 1960 but was forced into exile at the end of the year. He resumed high office after the **Geneva Agreements on Laos** in July 1962 as head of a government of national union. He was never able, however, to overcome deep internal divisions reinforced by external intervention. After the **Paris Peace Agreements** in January 1973, a corresponding accord for Laos, the **Vientiane Agreement on the Restoration of Peace and Reconciliation in Laos**, was concluded in the following month and Souvanna Phouma became the head of yet another coalition government. His role was little more than a caretaker one until his final resignation in December 1975. On giving up office, he was given a formal position as adviser to the new government but played no part in the political life of the People's Democratic

Republic of Laos. Souvanna Phouma died in Vientiane on 10 January 1984 aged 82.

*see also:* Geneva Agreements on Indochina 1954; Geneva Agreements on Laos 1962; Paris Peace Agreements 1973; *Pathet Lao*; Souphanouvong; Vientiane Agreement on the Restoration of Peace and Reconciliation in Laos.

## Spratly Islands  (Brunei/Malaysia/Philippines/Vietnam)

The Spratly Islands comprise a widely dispersed group of over 400 tiny islands, reefs, shoals and sandbanks in the **South China Sea** located some 500 kilometres south-east of Vietnam, 500 kilometres west of the Philippines and close to offshore Malaysian Borneo. The islands, which extend for more than 800 kilometres from north to south and which are also 1,300 kilometres from the Chinese mainland, are located along lines of maritime communications which link the Indian and Pacific oceans. They have never supported continuous human settlement or come under the effective sovereign jurisdiction of any single state. Nonetheless, the dispersed group has become the object of contending territorial claims by five coastal states.

The People's Republic of China, Taiwan and Vietnam lay claim to all of the islands; the positions of China and Taiwan are synonymous. The Philippines' claim to a concentration of islands to the west of Palawan originates from a private exploration during the mid-1950s and dates from a presidential decree in June 1978. Malaysia's claim to several islands off the coast of Borneo dates from December 1979 with the publication of an official map of the Federation's continental shelf. Brunei does not claim any territory but contests maritime space within the islands arising from its continental shelf. The most acute contention has been between China and Vietnam. The Spratly Islands are known in Chinese as Nansha and in Vietnamese as Truong Sa.

The prime attraction of the islands to the contending claimants is the prospect of discovering and exploiting large reserves of oil and natural gas as well as access to good fishing waters. The liberal extension of coastal state jurisdiction provided for under the United Nations Convention on the Law of the Sea concluded in 1982 would give governments with recognized sovereignty extensive rights beyond territorial waters.

Long-standing historical use by Chinese fishermen was never accompanied by administration; rule of a kind was not exercised until the French established colonial dominion from the late nineteenth century. Some of the Spratly Islands were occupied briefly during the Pacific War by the Japanese, who used them as submarine base facilities. After the war, the Nationalist Chinese government asserted a claim and occupied the largest island of Tai Ping Dao Dao or Itu Aba, so challenging France which sought to restore the colonial status quo. The People's Republic of China first asserted an official claim on historical grounds to both the **Paracel Islands** and the Spratly Islands in comments by the foreign minister, Zhou En-lai, in August 1951 on the draft Japanese Peace Treaty. That treaty was signed at the San Francisco Peace Conference in September at which a matching claim was registered by the Vietnamese delegation. When the Republic of Vietnam, with jurisdiction south of the 17th parallel of latitude, was established in 1955, its government reaffirmed that claim. Significantly, the government of the Democratic Republic of Vietnam, in power to its north, did not judge it politic to enter a claim to any islands in the South China Sea and even acknowledged China's sovereignty over both the Paracel and Spratly groups as early as 1956. That position changed after the unification of Vietnam, when the government in Hanoi assumed the claim of the ousted administration in Saigon to both the Paracel and Spratly islands in the context of deteriorating relations with Beijing. China had forcibly asserted control over all the Paracel Islands in January 1974. A unified Vietnam had, in turn, occupied several islands in the Spratly group held by the Saigon government in the closing stages of the **Vietnam War**. In time, a Vietnamese presence was established on some twenty-one islands within the archipelago. China began to establish a limited foothold from January 1988 and in March its forces fought a brief naval battle with Vietnam in the Spratlys, securing control of six islands in the process. In February 1992 the Standing Committee of China's National People's Congress enacted a law on territorial waters, reasserting sovereignty over islands in the East China Sea and South China Sea as well as the right to take all necessary measures to prevent and stop the so-called harmful passage of foreign vessels through its territorial waters.

Despite an initiative from 1990 by Indonesia, which does not have any claims, in convening mediatory workshops among the contending coastal states, there has not been any reconciliation of interests. The primary conflict has been between China and Vietnam with the former taking evident advantage of the latter's vulnerability, given the loss of Soviet support with the end of the Cold War and the break-up of Lenin's state. In May 1992 China signed an oil exploration agreement with the US Crestone Energy Corporation for 25,000 square kilometres at the edge of the Spratly group only some 150 kilometres south-east of Vietnamese coastal islands and in waters claimed by Hanoi as part of its continental shelf. The chairman of Crestone, Randall Thompson, revealed in June 1992 that he had received assurances from senior Chinese officials that his company would be protected with China's full naval might. The augmentation of China's naval capability for force projection in the South China Sea has caused concern in South-East Asia and beyond at possible threats to freedom of navigation through the waters of the Spratly Islands. Vietnam has responded by reasserting its sovereign jurisdiction and in October 1993 completed the construction of the first lighthouse in the archipelago on Song Tu Tay Island. A visit to China in November 1993 by Vietnam's president, **Le Duc Anh**, who met with his counterpart, Jiang Zemin, failed to record any progress over the two countries' competing claims to jurisdiction in the South China Sea. China reasserted its claim in February 1995 when its forces established a guardpost on Mischief Reef. It marked the first challenge to the claim of an ASEAN state; the reef is located some 135 miles to the west of the Philippines island of Palawan. **ASEAN** responded by reiterating its **Declaration on the South China Sea 1992** and with strong talk in a meeting with Chinese officials in April 1995. The United States registered its concern over freedom of navigation without taking a position on the legal merits of the competing claims. In July 1995, however, its navy conducted exercises with its Philippines counterpart near the contested Spratly Islands.

In the interim, ASEAN has sought to formulate a code of conduct for claimant states but without success because of intra-mural differences and because China has a separate agenda. In March 1999, Philippine reconnaissance planes revealed that China had expanded and refurbished its original structures on Mischief Reef, transforming the site into an armed forward naval station with sophisticated communications systems. In response to Philippine protests, China's foreign ministry maintained that the expanded structures were designed as shelters for fishermen. In June that year, Malaysian forces occupied Investigator Shoal on which they constructed a helipad and a two-storey building with a radar tower. In August 1999, Malaysia further occupied Erica Reef on which structures were also erected. In response to Philippine protests, the government in Kuala Lumpur maintained that the structures had been built for climatic research and marine life studies. That same month, Taiwan's defence minister, Tang Fei, confirmed that marine units stationed on Taiping (Itu Aba) would be replaced by coastguards to avoid possible conflict.

see also: ASEAN; Declaration on the South China Sea 1992; Paracel Islands; South China Sea; Vietnam War; Workshop on Managing Potential Conflict in the South China Sea.

# State Law and Order Restoration Council (SLORC) (Burma/Myanmar)

The State Law and Order Restoration Council (SLORC) was established on 18 September 1988 by the armed forces as the national instrument of government after a continuous period of public disturbance. Political disorder had been sparked off initially in September 1987 by a crude act of demonetization without government compensation, provoking student alienation which spread because of deep-seated economic discontent reaching a bloody culmination. SLORC was headed initially by the defence minister, General Saw Maung, who also assumed the post of prime minister. Martial law was introduced and all existing state organs

abolished, including the ruling **Burma Socialist Programme Party** (BSPP), which re-emerged as the **National Unity Party** a week later. Violent confrontation between student protestors and the armed forces intensified but was resolved with great loss of life through the indiscriminate use of firepower by the military.

Elections to the newly created People's Assembly were promised for May 1990 and were duly held to widespread surprise, but the overwhelming victory by the opposition **National League for Democracy** over the National Unity Party and other minor groupings did not lead to political change because SLORC refused to allow the assembly to convene. By that juncture, opposition leader **Aung San Suu Kyi** had been under detention for nearly a year, while legal powers and violence were employed after the elections to crush all dissent. SLORC pressed ahead in an attempt to give its rule constitutional legitimacy. A National Convention was convened in January 1993; it concluded its work a year later by endorsing a prerogative political role for the armed forces in any new constitutional structure. In April 1992 General Saw Maung was replaced as head of SLORC and prime minister by his deputy, General Than Shwe, after reportedly suffering from mental disturbance. The real locus of power within SLORC, however, is Brigadier-General **Khin Nyunt**, the council's First secretary and head of military intelligence. Khin Nyunt is believed to enjoy the confidence of General **Ne Win**, who gave up all formal offices in 1988, but who continues to exercise considerable political influence despite his age and poor health. In July 1995, SLORC felt able to release Aung San Suu Kyi from detention without serious fear of a challenge to its political position. On 15 November 1997, SLORC was dissolved and replaced by the **State Peace and Development Council** (SPDC). The firm grip on power by the military was not lessened in any way by this change in nomenclature.

see also: Aung San Suu Kyi; Burma Socialist Programme Party; Khin Nyunt; National League for Democracy; National Unity Party; Ne Win; State Peace and Development Council (SPDC).

## State Peace and Development Council (SPDC) (Burma/Myanmar)

On 15 November 1997, the **State Law and Order Restoration Council**, which had served as the vehicle for military rule since September 1998, was dissolved and replaced by the State Peace and Development Council (SPDC). The change of political label was purely cosmetic and was probably prompted by an attempt to improve the international image of the country following its controversial entry into **ASEAN** in the previous July. Although the change of nomenclature suggested a revision of national priorities, the authoritarian nature of government did not change. The establishment of the SPDC was accompanied by a reshuffle of senior military officers to the advantage of the Director of Defence Service Intelligence, General **Khin Nyunt**. Four generals were reportedly placed under house arrest on grounds of corruption.

see also: ASEAN; Khin Nyunt; State Law and Order Restoration Council (SLORC).

## Stephens, Donald (Malaysia/Sabah)

see Fuad, Tun Mohammad.

## Struggle of the Nationalist Filipino Masses (Philippines)

The Struggle of the Philippine Masses was established in July 1997 as an electoral vehicle for the successful bid for presidential office in May 1998 by **Joseph Estrada**, the incumbent vice-president. Estrada had stood for vice-presidential office on a ticket representing a combination of old **Nacionalista Party** and **Liberal Party** interests. His new political grouping comprised a coalition of opposition parties but was based on his personal populist appeal. The coalition is not expected to endure beyond Estrada's one-term tenure of office.

see also: Estrada, Joseph; Liberal Party; Nacionalista Party.

## Subandrio (Indonesia)

Subandrio, who like many Javanese has only one name, was foreign minister of Indonesia between April 1957 and March 1966. He was the chosen political instrument of President **Sukarno**. As such, he directed and managed the radical leftist foreign policy of **Guided Democracy**, which was marked by **Confrontation** with Malaysia and a close alignment with the People's Republic of China. Subandrio was born on 15 September 1915 and trained as a medical practitioner in Jakarta under the Dutch. After the proclamation of independence, he was posted abroad by the embryonic Ministry of Information to engage in public relations and from 1947 was the republic's representative in London, becoming ambassador to Moscow between 1954 and 1956, returning to Jakarta in 1956 to become secretary-general of the Ministry of Foreign Affairs until being appointed foreign minister in 1957. In 1963 President Sukarno appointed him first deputy prime minister. In that position, he assumed control of the Central Intelligence Bureau and openly identified with the leftwards drift in politics to the extent that speculation arose over his possible succession to President Sukarno. After the abortive coup (see **Gestapu**) in October 1965, Subandrio was subject to vociferous criticism from student and Muslim groups as well as from the armed forces. When General **Suharto** assumed executive authority in March 1966, Subandrio was arrested on charges of complicity in the alleged Communist-inspired coup attempt. After a trial before a military tribunal in October 1966, he was sentenced to death, which was commuted to life imprisonment in 1980. In August 1995, aged 81, he was pardoned and released coincident with the fiftieth anniversary of the proclamation of Indonesia's independence.

see also: Confrontation; Crocodile Hole; Gestapu; Guided Democracy; Suharto; Sukarno.

## Subic Bay Naval Base (Philippines)

Subic Bay Naval Base, situated some 50 miles west of Manila on the island of Luzon, was the most important US military installation in the Philippines. The base area comprised 62,000 acres and had been set aside for military use by US President Theodore Roosevelt in 1904. It was established as a major facility after the Philippines became independent in 1946, initially for ninety-nine years under a lease agreement concluded on 17 March 1947. It comprised a complex of facilities capable of supporting combat operations by several aircraft carrier groups throughout the Indian Ocean and the western Pacific Ocean. To serve that purpose, it became the largest US overseas supply depot. The term of the lease was reduced to twenty-five years in September 1965. The strategic significance of the base complex declined with the end of the Cold War. Nonetheless, the United States maintained an interest in retaining operational use of the facilities and engaged in protracted negotiations with the government of the Philippines from the late 1980s over the financial terms for the renewal of the lease for an additional ten years. The volcanic eruption of Mount Pinatubo close to **Clark Air Base** in June 1991 carried ash to Subic Bay in quantities that threatened the utility of the military facility. Although intergovernmental agreement on a new treaty was reached in August that year, the Philippines Senate voted against ratification the following month with members motivated in part by the potential electoral benefits of demonstrating an assertive nationalism. The Philippine government then announced that negotiations with the United States designed to sanction withdrawal of its forces over a three-year period had collapsed. The United States was subsequently served with a one-year notice of termination, which required that Subic Bay Naval Base be returned to Philippine jurisdiction before the end of 1992. The United States began to comply without protest, immediately dismantling base installations and withdrawing floating docks. After the inauguration of President **Fidel Ramos** in July 1992, negotiations were resumed with the United States government on the continued servicing and repair of American vessels at Subic Bay. However, the naval base was formally transferred to Philippine control on 30 September 1992. The Cubi Point Naval Air Station on the western edge of the base complex was relinquished on 24 November that year when the last US service personnel left the Philippines. In August 1993 the Taiwanese government signed a financial agreement whereby its affiliated China Development Corporation would undertake to convert the former base into an industrial park. President Fidel Ramos received President Lee Teng-hui of Taiwan at the site in February 1994. An international airport was inau- gurated in April 1995 from which the Ameri- can Federal

Express Company has begun operations. In July 1998, President Estrada removed Richard Gordon from his post as head of the Subic Bay Metropolitan Authority to which he had been appointed by former President Ramos. He was succeeded by Felicito Payumo.

*see also:* Clark Air Base; Estrada, Joseph; Ramos, Fidel.

## Suchinda Krapayoon, General
(Thailand)

General Suchinda Krapayoon attained political notoriety in May 1992 when responsibility was attributed to him for ordering troops to fire on demonstrators in Bangkok protesting at his appointment as prime minister without prior election to Parliament. General Suchinda had become army commander in March 1990 following the resignation of General **Chavalit Yongchaiyuth**, who had entered politics. In February 1991 General Suchinda led a bloodless coup which removed the government of the prime minister **Chatichai Choonhavan**. After a period of interim government under a former diplomat and businessman, **Anand Panyarachun**, national elections were held in March 1992. The military-backed *Samakkhi Tham* party (meaning Unity in Virtue) formed specifically for the elections, secured the largest number of seats and established a governing coalition with other pro-military parties. After their leader Narong Wongwan had been publicly discredited, General Suchinda resigned as army commander and accepted appointment as prime minister on 7 April; despite his commitment in November 1991 not to do so. Two weeks later demonstrations against his appointment were mounted in Bangkok, inspired by a fast by **Chamlong Srimuang**, the leader of the opposition *Palang Dharma* (Moral Force party). Demonstrations continued into May and after an initial use of armed force by the military, Chamlong was arrested, which inflamed political passions leading to an even bloodier confrontation with up to 200 deaths reported. On 20 May King **Bhumibol Adulyadej** summoned General Suchinda and Chamlong to his palace for a televised meeting which defused the crisis. General Suchinda resigned office three days later and departed the country.

Suchinda Krapayoon was born on 6 August 1933 in Phra Nakhon in north-east Thailand. He went straight from secondary school into the Chulachomklao Royal Military Academy in Bangkok, enrolling in its fifth class, whose cohort have dominated their military generation. He received advanced training in the United States at Fort Leavenworth Army Staff College and at Fort Seal Advanced Artillery College. His early career was spent as an artillery commander but he also spent three years in Washington in the early 1970s as deputy military attaché before transferring to army intelligence, whose head he became by 1982. On his way to the post of army commander-in-chief, he was army assistant chief of staff for operations in 1985 and army assistant commander-in-chief in 1987. General Suchinda represented a military tradition which assumed a prerogative role in public life and which had not been able to come to terms with the political consequences of economic and social change which had challenged that assumption.

see also: Anand Panyarachun; Bhumibol Adulyadej; Chamlong Srimuang; Chatichai Choonhavan; Chavalit Yongchaiyuth; *Palang Dharma*.

## Sudarsono, Professor Juwono
(Indonesia)
Juwono Sudarsono was appointed Indonesia's first civilian defence minister in some four decades in the cabinet of President **Abdurrahman Wahid**, which assumed office in October 1999. He had served briefly as environment minister in the last administration of President **Suharto** and as education minister in the interim administration of President **Habibie**. Juwono Sudarsono was born on 5 March 1942 in Ciamis, West Java. He was educated at the University of Indonesia, the University of California at Berkeley and at the London School of Economics. He taught political science at the University of Indonesia, becoming dean of the Faculty of Social and Political Sciences in 1988. In 1995, he was appointed vice-governor of the National Defence College where he commanded the respect of the military establishment even though he could be outspoken about the deficiencies of President Suharto's rule. As defence minister,

he has registered civilian supremacy and presided over the armed forces transition to greater professionalism, while demonstrating an understanding of the sensibilities of his constituency. He has been consistent in warning that Indonesia was not necessarily ready for democracy and that if the country's civilian leaders fail to create a healthy and strong political atmosphere, the military would seek to return to power. He was replaced in August 2000 and returned to the University of Indonesia.

see also: Habibie, B. J; Suharto; Wahid, Abdurrahman.

## Suharto, President (Indonesia)
President Suharto dominated political life in Indonesia from 11 March 1966, when he seized power, until 21 May 1998 when he resigned from high office. In March 1966, he had used the threat of military force to assume executive authority from the incumbent President **Sukarno**. He concentrated and exercised power ruthlessly without significant challenge until Indonesia was beset by a devastating economic crisis from late 1997, unprecedented during his rule. He ruled Indonesia much like an erstwhile Javanese monarch employing a quiet but decisive authority. In so doing, he was moved by the conviction that he had been entrusted with a divinely inspired mission to guide the country along the path of political order and economic development. With evident success in this endeavour up to the late 1990s, he became the logical chairman of the Non-Aligned Movement whose heads of government met in Jakarta in September 1992. At the end of the month, he addressed the General Assembly of the United Nations as the movement's spokesman, so demonstrating the international standing of the republic and his own personal achievement. His personal credibility and that achievement were virtually dissipated overnight as he failed to comprehend, and to take appropriate action to cope with, the enormity of Indonesia's economic ills. On relinquishing office, he was succeeded initially by his vice-president, Dr B. J. **Habibie**.

Suharto, like many Javanese, has only one name; he was born on 8 June 1921 in the village of Kemusu, near the town of Yogyakarta in central Java. He came from a peasant background and received only an elementary education but in June 1940 enlisted in the Royal Netherlands Indies Army, rising to the rank of sergeant before the Japanese occupation in 1942. In 1943 he joined the Japanese-sponsored **Peta** (*Pembela Tanah Air*, meaning Defenders of the Fatherland) within which he received officer training, rising to the rank of company commander. After the proclamation of Indonesia's independence in August 1945, Suharto joined the national army and distinguished himself as a brigade commander against the Dutch, rising to the rank of lieutenant-colonel by the transfer of sovereignty in December 1949. He subsequently commanded the central Java Diponegoro Division and the forces deployed to liberate the western half of the island of New Guinea (**Irian Jaya**) from the Dutch. In May 1963, as a major-general, he became commander of the army's Strategic Reserve (*Kostrad*) based in Jakarta, in the event a fateful posting.

In the early hours of 1 October 1965, dissident army units abducted and murdered six senior generals at the outset of an abortive coup (*see* **Gestapu**). For reasons still not satisfactorily explained, Suharto's name was not on the list of generals abducted despite Kostrad's assigned role in countering a coup attempt. Suharto seized the initiative and acted with skill and resoluteness to crush the revolt and then set about dismantling the political system of **Guided Democracy** established and dominated by President Sukarno. Responsibility for the abortive coup was attributed to the Communist Party of Indonesia, which had enjoyed the patronage of Sukarno. Suharto swept both away, leaving the armed forces under his command as the key national institution (*see* **Supersemar**).

In March 1967 as a full general, Suharto was elected acting president by the provisional **People's Consultative Assembly**. In March 1968 that assembly confirmed him in office for a full term. He was re-elected unopposed by a formally constituted People's Consultative Assembly in 1973 and then again in 1978, 1983, 1988 and 1993. From the outset, Suharto was instrumental in revising many of the republic's public priorities adopted by his predecessor. He set out to reverse the decline in Indonesia's economy by applying western orthodoxies, so

attracting the support of the governments of the United States and Japan. To demonstrate a commitment to development and in repudiation of Sukarno's flamboyant adventurism, he brought the campaign of **Confrontation** against Malaysia to a speedy end. He also embarked on an unprecedented exercise in regional cooperation with the founding in August 1967 of **ASEAN** (Association of South-East Asian Nations), which has remained at the centre of the republic's foreign policy. If seemingly attuned to western political sensibilities, Suharto has been no less a nationalist than his ill-fated predecessor. He was ruthless over the incorporation of Irian Jaya into the republic in 1969 and brutal in annexing **East Timor** from 1975.

Internally, Suharto imposed his so-called **New Order** through political demobilization. Political parties were obliged to amalgamate and subordinate their identities, while an existing organization of Functional Groups, *Golkar* (set up initially by the military to counter the Communists) became the electoral vehicle of a military establishment which he managed and manipulated. In addition, conscious of Indonesia's lack of a single cultural tradition, Suharto set out to impose nationally the syncretic formula **Pancasila**, devised originally by Sukarno at the outset of independence in 1945 as a way of containing Islamic claims on the identity of the state. By the early 1990s, Suharto's political control had begun to slip a little as senior military officers became alienated by the extent to which his rule had become quasi-monarchical. Moreover, the rapacious business activities of his children and other relatives had generated a growing popular resentment and desire for political change. Suharto retained power, despite growing dissent, through a masterly understanding of human weaknesses and for manipulating them. The death of his wife, Ibu Tien, in April 1996, is believed to have affected his political judgement and also to have placed him under the malign influence of his greedy children. In March 1998, he was elected to a seventh consecutive term of office by the People's Consultative Assembly indicating confidence that he could continue until 2003. The social and political consequences of economic crisis intervened to cut short his term. Social

unrest was precipitated by sharp rises in fuel, transport and electricity prices, while basic staples, including children's milk powder, were in short supply. A rising chorus of protest came to a head on 12 May 1998 when security forces in Jakarta opened fire on a student rally killing four young people. Urban violence assumed an anti-Chinese dimension with destruction and looting of property as well as the rape of Chinese women. In the middle of this mayhem, Suharto made a fundamental error of judgement in travelling to an international conference in Cairo in an attempt to demonstrate that his authority remained unimpaired. He was obliged to cut short his visit. He made an abortive attempt to form a so-called reform government but could not find candidates to fill its ranks. He left office as a reviled figure. In August 2000, he faced trial on a charge of siphoning off nearly US$600 million from charitable foundations but refused to appear in court on medical grounds.
*see also:* ABRI; ASEAN; Confrontation; Crocodile Hole; *Gestapu*; *Golkar*; Guided Democracy; Habibie, B.J.; Irian Jaya; New Order; *Pancasila*; People's Consultative Assembly; *Peta*; Sukarno; *Supersemar*; Timor, East.

## Sukarno, President  (Indonesia)

Sukarno, who in the Javanese tradition had only one name, was the first president of Indonesia. He was the pre-eminent nationalist leader of his generation. He enjoyed remarkable oratorical skills and an extraordinary ability to communicate with and mobilize the mass of the Indonesian people. He became a controversial international figure from the late 1950s when he led Indonesia into **Confrontation** successively with Holland and Malaysia. His political career ended in disgrace, however, in the wake of the abortive coup (*see* **Gestapu**) in October 1965 (attributed to Indonesia's Communist Party) in which he appeared to be implicated. His political successor, General (later President) **Suharto**, kept him under virtual house arrest from March 1966 until his death in June 1970.

Sukarno was born in Blitar in east Java on 6 June 1901, the son of a schoolteacher. He was brought up in a politicized environment in the home of one of the early nationalist leaders. He

graduated as a civil engineer from the Advanced School for Technical Studies in Bandung in 1925. Architecture was part of the curriculum, which Sukarno practised for a while but without much success. An active induction into nationalist politics occurred during his higher education. In 1927, he played the leading role in founding the secular Indonesian Nationalist Party, which uncompromisingly demanded independence from the Dutch. He was arrested in December 1929 and tried the following year in Bandung during which he made a spirited public defence of the nationalist cause. He was sentenced to four years' imprisonment in December 1930 but released a year later. He was detained for a second time in August 1933 and in February 1934 was sent with his family into internal exile in Flores from which he was transferred to Bengkulu in Sumatra in February 1938. He was still in internal exile when the Japanese overran the Netherlands East Indies in early 1942.

Sukarno collaborated with the Japanese but undoubtedly used his position to promote the idea of an independent Indonesian archipelago among a culturally diverse but increasingly receptive people. On 17 August 1945, two days after the Japanese had capitulated, he proclaimed Indonesia's independence together with **Mohammad Hatta**, who became vice-president. During the violent independence struggle against the Dutch, he played more of a symbolic than an active role, one that was confirmed after independence in December 1949 when he became a constitutional president. However, during the 1950s, Indonesia's experiment with western parliamentary democracy began to test the integrity of the culturally diverse archipelago state. In the face of regional rebellion and a breakdown of political order, Sukarno seized the opportunity to move to the centre of the political stage. He appealed for a return to the roots of the national revolution and for the introduction of a **Guided Democracy** in keeping with the country's traditions. After a short period of martial law from March 1957, and with the support of the armed forces, Sukarno inaugurated the political system of Guided Democracy in July 1959 by reinstating the authoritarian 1945 constitution with an executive presidency.

During Guided Democracy, Sukarno acted as the personal embodiment of the Indonesian state. He enjoyed a major triumph in employing coercive diplomacy to manipulate the Dutch into transferring **Irian Jaya**, the western half of the island of New Guinea, retained after 1949, to Indonesian jurisdiction. When Sukarno sought to use the same tactic against the Federation of Malaysia, he was not successful. In addition, his close internal alignment with the Communist Party of Indonesia and external ties with the People's Republic of China alarmed the conservative military establishment which seized power after the failed coup in 1965 and proceeded to cast Sukarno into political oblivion (*see Supersemar*). In his period of executive power, Sukarno was literally the resounding voice of Indonesia but brought his country more notoriety than prestige. In one respect, however, he demonstrated remarkable prescience. At the first meeting of the Non-Aligned Movement in Belgrade in 1961, Sukarno argued that the main problem facing the world was not that of superpower antagonism but conflict between the rich and poor countries. His management of his own country's economy was incompetent, however: on his overthrow it was in an impoverished condition as a consequence of profligate expenditure and corruption. His military usurpers have nonetheless felt it politic to resurrect his reputation posthumously and have also upheld his state philosophy of *Pancasila*, which was first enunciated in June 1945. He was undoubtedly a charismatic unifying figure at a time when the identity and integrity of the state seemed to be in jeopardy. He died on 21 June 1970 in Bogor.

see also: Confrontation; Crocodile Hole; *Gestapu*; Guided Democracy; Hatta, Mohammad; Irian Jaya; *Pancasila*; Suharto; *Supersemar*.

## Sukarnoputri, Megawati (Indonesia)
*see* Megawati Sukarnoputri.

## Sunda Strait (Indonesia)
The Sunda Strait, within which is located the famous volcanic island of Krakatau (now known as Rakata), provides the major sea link between the Indian Ocean and the Java Sea. It is approximately 50 miles in length. The narrowest land width at the point of egress into the Java Sea is

13.8 miles but the navigable channels on either side of the interposing island of Sangian are less than 3 and 4 miles in width respectively. The Sunda Strait separates the large Indonesian islands of Sumatra and Java and has long served as an important maritime passage for commercial traffic. Before the Suez Canal was opened, it was the principal corridor for direct access between Europe and East Asia and provided the point of maritime entry for the original Dutch penetration of the archipelago. Although of lesser importance than the **Malacca Strait** and **Singapore Strait**, it still carries a considerable amount of traffic from and to the western world via the Cape route, as well as from the ports of Australia. The military significance of the strait has reduced over the years. It has never been suitable for the submerged passage of US nuclear missile-carrying submarines, nor for the reactive deployment of surface naval task forces into the northern Indian Ocean. The revival of the **Five Power Defence Arrangements** and growing military cooperation within **ASEAN** (Association of South-East Asian Nations) and also between Indonesia and Australia has served to sustain military use of the strait. In September 1988 Indonesia provoked controversy and protest by temporarily suspending passage through the straits of Sunda and Lombok, ostensibly to conduct naval firing exercises.

see also: ASEAN; Five Power Defence Arrangements 1971–; Malacca Strait; Singapore Strait.

## Supersemar (Indonesia)
*Supersemar* is an acronym from the Indonesian term *Surat Perintah Sebelas Maret*, which was an order signed by President **Sukarno** on 11 March 1966 to Lt-General **Suharto**, recently appointed minister/commander-in-chief of the army, instructing him 'to take all necessary steps to guarantee security and calm and the stability of the Government and the course of the Revolution'. The effect of the order was to transfer executive authority: it marked a critical stage in the ultimate deposition of President Sukarno. The use of the acronym *Supersemar* was to provide a basis in legitimacy for the transfer through invoking the name of *Semar*, a clowngod of Hindu mythology with a reputation for invincible authority. The process of transfer

was precipitated by an abortive coup (*see Gestapu*) in October 1965, which had the effect of undermining Sukarno's authority and also encouraging the leadership of the armed forces to seize power. Matters came to a head during a cabinet meeting in the presidential palace in Jakarta on 11 March 1966 against a background of rising student protest. Troops without insignia surrounded the palace, and Sukarno and close political associates fled by helicopter to the nearby resort town of Bogor. Three senior generals then drove to Bogor, where they confronted Sukarno who agreed to transfer executive authority. Lt-General Suharto then ordered the Communist Party of Indonesia banned and reconstituted the government. The transfer order was confirmed by the provisional **People's Consultative Assembly** in March 1967, with Sukarno retaining only nominal title. General Suharto was confirmed as president in succession to Sukarno in March 1968.

*see also:* Crocodile Hole; *Gestapu*; People's Consultative Assembly; Suharto; Sukarno.

## Supreme National Council
(Cambodia)

The Supreme National Council was described in the accords on Cambodia reached at the **International Conference on Cambodia** in Paris on 23 October 1991 as 'the unique legitimate body and source of authority in which, throughout the transitional period, the sovereignty, independence and unity of Cambodia are enshrined'. Central to the contention over resolving the protracted Cambodian conflict was the problem of power-sharing between the warring Khmer factions in the transitional period before elections to determine the political future of the country. This problem was responsible for the failure of an earlier **International Conference on Cambodia, Paris 1989**. In the event, an initiative for a United Nations role in resolving the conflict gave rise to the proposal for a symbolic device comprising representatives of all factions which would be formally vested with sovereignty. Once established, it was to assume the Cambodian seat in the United Nations General Assembly and also delegate executive powers to **UNTAC** (United Nations Transitional Authority in Cambodia), which would run key ministries, oversee the

disarmament and demobilization of contending forces, and organize national elections in a neutral political environment. The Council took on a formal existence at a meeting in the Indonesian capital, Jakarta, on 10 September 1990 and assumed a practical role after Prince **Norodom Sihanouk** was elected chairman in Beijing on 17 July 1991. After the accords reached in Paris in October 1991, the Supreme National Council convened for the first time in Cambodia on 30 December 1991. That meeting had been delayed because of political disorder in the capital Phnom Penh over the participation of **Khmer Rouge** representatives. Once established, it coexisted uneasily with the incumbent administration established by Vietnamese force of arms. The Khmer Rouge justified its failure to assume the government of Cambodia as an excuse for leaving the Council and for boycotting elections held under United Nations auspices in May 1993. The Supreme National Council was replaced when a provisional coalition government was established in Phnom Penh in July 1993 without Khmer Rouge membership.

*see also:* International Conferences on Cambodia, Paris 1989, 1991; Khmer Rouge; Sihanouk, Norodom; UNTAC.

## Surabaya, Battle of, 1945 (Indonesia)

Surbaya is the principal port of east Java which serves as a base for Indonesia's navy. In November 1945 it was the site of the biggest battle of Indonesia's national revolution, which took place between Republican and British forces and not the Dutch. Japan had occupied Indonesia during the course of the Pacific War; after the Japanese surrender, British forces from the **South-East Asia Command** assumed initial responsibility for administering the Netherlands East Indies. They landed in small numbers some six weeks after the proclamation of national independence and faced the obvious suspicion that they were intent on helping to restore Dutch colonial rule. In early November 1945 Indonesian irregulars objected to a demand from the local British commander for the surrender of their arms, viewing it as a preliminary to a landing by Dutch troops. A violent confrontation ensued in which an entire brigade, comprising mainly Indian soldiers under British command, came

close to being overrun. The refusal of Indonesian irregulars to heed an ultimatum to withdraw after a British brigadier had been killed while attempting to uphold a truce provoked a military onslaught at divisional strength. From 10 November, there followed three weeks of courageous and fanatical resistance by the Indonesians, who were ultimately pacified by superior force. The Battle of Surabaya is celebrated every year in Indonesia as Heroes' Day. At the time, it marked a turning-point both for the British military authorities and Indonesia's nationalist leadership. Both parties saw the virtue of a negotiated solution to the problem of Indonesian independence. The British were conscious of the political costs of continued confrontation. The nationalist leadership judged it practical to give up a policy of armed struggle in favour of negotiations with the Dutch in part because of concern not to alienate the great power support seen to be required for achieving full independence. In addition, that leadership had been disturbed by the prospect of being displaced by a radical youth element which had been prominent at Surabaya and which would be politically advantaged through continuing violence.
see also: South-East Asia Command

## Surin Pitsuwan  (Thailand)

Surin Pitsuwan was appointed foreign minister in the administration of **Chuan Leekpai** which assumed office in November 1997. He was born on 28 October 1949 to an impoverished southern Thai family. His father was a prominent Muslim teacher. He received his higher education in the United States, acquiring a doctorate in political science from Harvard University in 1982. He then pursued an academic career, holding a post at Thammasat University in the mid-1980s. He entered politics in 1986 and was elected to parliament for the **Democrat Party** for a southern constituency in Nakhon Sri Thammarat Province, attracting strong support from the Muslim community whose faith he shares. He has served as private secretary to Chuan and also as speaker of the parliament. He was deputy foreign minister in Chuan's first administration, making a strong impression internationally for his fluency in English and for his political sophistication.

see also: Chuan Leekpai; Democrat Party.

## Sutan Syahrir  (Indonesia) see Syahrir, Sutan.

## Syahrir, Sutan  (Indonesia)

Sutan Syahrir was the first prime minister of the revolutionary Republic of Indonesia, assuming office in November 1945. He was born in west Sumatra on 5 March 1909 and after showing great promise at secondary school went to Holland to study law in Leiden. He returned to the Netherlands East Indies in 1931 at the suggestion of his more senior fellow-student **Mohammad Hatta** to help in organizing a new nationalist party, which he sought to infuse with socialist convictions. He was arrested in 1934 and sent into internal exile, first to New Guinea and then to Banda. During the Japanese occupation, he refused to collaborate and organized a small resistance movement whose members formed the core of the postwar Indonesian Socialist Party which he led. His anti-Japanese credentials were the key to his appointment as prime minister because of **Sukarno**'s taint of collaboration in the eyes of the Dutch and the western powers. Syahrir was an advocate of diplomasi (negotiation) as the way to attain independence, which became a controversial strategy as the Dutch sought to re-establish their colonial dominion by force. He was displaced in June 1947 and then pleaded Indonesia's case before the United Nations but never again held public office. After independence, he became a marginal political figure despite a following of like-minded and gifted young people who came under the spell of his intelligence and personality. He led the Socialist Party but it went into decline after securing only 2 per cent of the vote in the first national elections in 1955. Syahrir was arrested in 1962 on suspicion of involvement in regional rebellion, but when his health deteriorated in 1965, he was permitted to leave the country for medical attention in Switzerland, where he died in April 1966. His political vision was set out in a pamphlet entitled 'Our Struggle' published in October 1945.
see also: Guided Democracy; Hatta, Mohammad; Sukarno.

# T

## Ta Mok (Cambodia)

Ta Mok is the *nom de guerre* of the most notorious military commander of the **Khmer Rouge**. His true name is Chhit Choeun and he held senior military positions in the early 1970s during the successful challenge to the government of **Lon Nol**. He was seriously wounded in the fighting, losing a leg which was replaced with a wooden limb. Little is known of his personal background. His notoriety arises from his role as party secretary in the south-western region in conducting murderous purges after the Khmer Rouge came to power in April 1975, which is when he took the name Ta Mok, meaning Old Man. After their ouster by the Vietnamese, Ta Mok became vice-chairman of the supreme commission of the national army of **Democratic Kampuchea** and established a military fiefdom along Cambodia's northern border with Thailand. That position began to be challenged by the government which came to office in Cambodia in October 1993 after general elections held under United Nations aegis (*see* **UNTAC**). In a military encounter in February 1994, the government forces temporarily seized Ta Mok's base camp of Anlong Veng, but he had been able to move his headquarters some weeks before, so keeping intact his guerrilla force which then successfully counter-attacked. In June 1997, forces loyal to Ta Mok arrested **Pol Pot** who was the subject of a show trial. Ta Mok then seized control of the rump of Khmer Rouge forces but was driven from his last camp into jungle along the Thai border by government units in June 1998. He was captured along the border in March 1999 and in September was charged with genocide under a decree issued in 1979 by the **People's Republic of Kampuchea**. His trial in Cambodia has been a matter of contention with the United Nations, which has sought a credible international participation in any judicial tribunal addressing the murderous legacy of the Khmer Rouge.

see also: Democratic Kampuchea; Kampuchea, People's Republic of;Khmer Rouge; Nol, Lon; Pol Pot; UNTAC.

## Taib Mahmud, Datuk Patinggi Abdul (Malaysia/Sarawak)

Abdul Taib Mahmud has been chief minister of Malaysia's north Bornean state of Sarawak since March 1981, succeeding his uncle **Abdul Rahman Yakub**. He leads the *Parti Pesaka Bumiputera Bersatu*, which is dominated by a Muslim Malay-Melanau constituency of which he and his uncle are members. Datuk Taib was born on 21 May 1936 in Miri, Sarawak, and studied law at the University of Adelaide in South Australia. He began his career as a Crown Counsel but entered Sarawak state politics when the former British colony joined Malaysia. He assumed ministerial position from the outset, holding first the portfolio of communications and works and then at the end of the 1960s entering the federal Parliament to assume cabinet office. Among his responsibilities during the 1970s were the Ministry of Defence as well as that for Sarawak Affairs. His tenure as chief minister was marred after a time by tension with his uncle Abdul Rahman Yakub, who had become Sarawak's governor in 1981 but stood down from office in 1985. In March 1987 financially induced defections from the governing state coalition designed to unseat Datuk Taib led to early elections which returned his government to office, but with a reduced majority. In subsequent elections in September 1991, Datuk Taib restored his coalition's fortunes with a resounding victory and in April 1995 delivered twenty-six out of twenty-seven Sarawak constituencies in federal elections. Datuk Taib has cultivated good relations with the federal government and his ability to deliver Sarawak to the ruling *Barisan Nasional* (National Front) has been a key factor in his long political tenure. In September 1996, he led the ruling *Barisan Nasional* to victory in elections to the state legislature securing 57 out of 62 seats. It also secured the overwhelming majority of seats in Sarawak in federal elections in November 1999.

see also: Barisan Nasional; Parti Pesaka Bumiputera Bersatu; Yakub, Tun Abdul Rahman.

## Tan, Tony  (Singapore)

Tony Tan Keng Yam returned to the government of Singapore in August 1995 as deputy prime minister and minister of defence after an absence of nearly four years. He had previously held senior cabinet portfolios for over a decade but left the government in December 1991 to become chairman and chief executive officer of the Oversea-Chinese Banking Corporation. Tony Tan was born in Singapore on 7 February 1940. He had a distinguished academic career, with first-class honours in physics from the University of Singapore and then a masters degree in operational research from the Massachusetts Institute of Technology followed by a doctorate in applied mathematics from the University of Adelaide. He returned to the University of Singapore as a lecturer in mathematics in 1967 but within two years left to join the Oversea-Chinese Banking Corporation as a sub-manager rising to general manager of the bank in 1978. Dr Tan was elected to Parliament for the **People's Action Party** (PAP) in February 1979 and was immediately appointed senior minister of state for education and in June 1980 was elevated to minister for education and concurrently vice-chancellor of the revamped National University of Singapore and over the following decade also held the portfolios of Trade and Industry and Finance.

In speaking openly about his likely successor as prime minister, **Lee Kuan Yew** indicated his preference for Tony Tan over **Goh Chok Tong**, who eventually succeeded him in November 1990. It is not thought that Tony Tan left the government from a sense of political pique. His return, however, which involved the removal of an overseeing responsibility for defence from deputy prime minister **Lee Hsien Loong**, aroused speculation of two contrasting kinds. First, that Lee Hsien Loong might have experienced a recurrence of cancer, which was strongly denied. Second, that Tony Tan had been brought back to the cabinet in a very senior position in order to lend support to the position of prime minister Goh Chok Tong. Tony Tan is a taciturn character without populist political qualities but he commands respect for his ability and judgement. In addition to his formal defence responsibilities, he has been charged with overseeing the regeneration of Singapore's higher education system.

*see also:* Goh Chok Tong; Lee Hsien Loong; Lee Kuan Yew; People's Action Party.

## Tanjung Priok Riot 1984  (Indonesia)

A violent confrontation between Muslim protestors and security forces took place with great loss of life during the night of 12 September 1984 in the Tanjung Priok port area of Jakarta, the capital of Indonesia. The protest had been precipitated by the arrest of four members of a local prayer hall, who had attacked two army officers in the course of demanding an apology for their having allegedly violated its sanctity. The large crowd which sought the release of the detainees was met at the police station by a hail of bullets from members of an air defence regiment, resulting in up to 200 deaths. The bloody episode took place against the background of Muslim resistance to the government's attempt to require all organizations to accept *Pancasila*, the state philosophy, as their sole principle. Agitation against government policy had become vociferous in and around the Tanjung Priok prayer hall, leading to a military investigation which had in turn given rise to the incident that led on to the violence. After the fatal clash, there followed a series of fires and explosions in Jakarta; in January 1985, several small bombs went off within the historic Borobudur Buddhist monument near Yogyakarta. Acts of Muslim-inspired violence petered out by the end of the 1980s as the result of action by intelligence and security forces. Political Islam ceased to be a violent factor during the 1990s, especially as President **Suharto** went out of his way to coopt its urban elite within **ICMI**. Nearly a year after his political downfall, public interest was expressed in a full accounting of the Tanjung Priok episode with the senior officers concerned being questioned by the Human Rights Commission.

*see also:* ICMI; Islam; *Pancasila*; Suharto.

## Tet Offensive 1968  (Vietnam)

Tet is the name of the holiday celebrated on the Vietnamese lunar new year. On the night of 30 January 1968, during that holiday, forces of the **National Liberation Front of South Vietnam**

(NLF) launched a series of coordinated surprise attacks throughout South Vietnam. Apart from the capital Saigon, where the presidential palace was penetrated, thirty-four out of forty-four provincial capitals were attacked and ten were held temporarily. The citadel of the ancient capital of Hue was not retaken by United States and South Vietnamese forces until the end of February. The declared purpose of the attacks was to generate a popular uprising against the government of President **Nguyen Van Thieu**. To that end, the offensive, which involved a costly expenditure of human resources by the NLF, was a military failure. Politically, however, it proved to be a remarkable success by its visual impact on television within the United States, where the **Vietnam War** had become increasingly unpopular. The domestic impact of the Tet Offensive led to the announcement by President Lyndon Johnson on 31 March that he would not seek re-election in November 1968 and that the bombing of North Vietnam would be restricted in order to start negotiations to end the war with the Vietnamese Communists. The Tet Offensive proved to be a critical psychological turning-point in the Vietnam War, following which American resolve to fight the war was never the same.

see also: National Liberation Front of South
Vietnam; Thieu, Nguyen Van; Vietnam War.

## Thach, Nguyen Co (Vietnam)

Nguyen Co Thach was Vietnam's foreign minister between February 1980 and June 1991. He had prime responsibility for managing the adverse diplomatic consequences of the invasion of Cambodia, defending his country's interests with skill and determination in negotiations with **ASEAN** (Association of South-East Asian Nations) and the People's Republic of China. He was forced from office at the seventh national congress of the Communist party as part of the price of Vietnam's rapprochement with China. Nguyen Co Thach was born on 15 May 1923 into a peasant family in northern Vietnam. He entered the revolutionary movement as a young man and was arrested by the French. He rose to become a staff officer in the **Viet Minh** army and took part in the **Battle of Dien Bien Phu** in 1954. He then entered the

diplomatic service and spent four years in New Delhi as consul-general. On returning to Hanoi, he played an important role in a series of international negotiations beginning with the **Geneva Agreements on Laos** in 1961–2. By the end of the 1970s he had risen to become the most senior official in the Ministry of Foreign Affairs. He was made an alternate member of the party Politburo in 1982 and a full member in 1986, the first diplomat to attain such rank. In March 1987 he was appointed a deputy prime minister, holding that office until June 1991 when all of his party and state posts were relinquished simultaneously. He died on 10 April 1998 aged 77.

see also: ASEAN; Dien Bien Phu, Battle of, 1954;
Geneva Agreements on Laos 1962; Viet Minh.

## Thai Rak Thai Party (Thailand)

The *Thai Rak Thai* (Thais Love Thais) Party was established in July 1998 by the successful entrepreneur cum politician, **Thaksin Shinawatra** who was deputy prime minister in the government headed by **Banharn Silpa-archa** and briefly in that headed by **Chavalit Yongchaiyut**. He founded the party ostensibly as a vehicle for political and economic reform drawing mainly on support from Chiangmai and the rural north and also from disaffected white-collar **Democrat Party** voters. It has yet to be tested in national elections but the business prominence of its founder and other backers have given it a strong appeal to the constituency dissatisfied with the performance of Prime Minister **Chuan Leekpai**. Its candidate failed in a bid to become governor of Bangkok in July 2000 but *Thai Rak Thai* remains the principal electoral rival of the Democratic Party.

see also: Banharn Silpa-archa; Chavalit Yongchaiyut; Chuan Leekpai; Democrat Party;
Thaksin Shinawatra.

## Thaksin Shinawatra (Thailand)

Thaksin Shinawatra, who was born on 26 July 1949, is a one-time senior police officer and successful telecommunications entrepreneur *cum* politician who was leader of the *Palang Dharma* Party from May 1995 after the withdrawal from public life of **Chamlong Srimuang**. During the first administration of **Chuan Leekpai**, he was foreign minister for three months but then resigned because of controversy over his lack of a parliamentary seat. He was elected to parliament in July 1995 and took his party back into coalition government as deputy prime minister to **Banharn Silpa-archa** but gave up office in August 1996 when *Palang Dharma* left the ruling coalition. After its dismal performance in elections in November 1996, Thaksin resigned as party leader. He was briefly deputy prime minister in the coalition headed by **Chavalit Yongchaiyut** but lost office with the latter's resignation in November 1997 in the wake of economic crisis. In July 1998, he founded the *Thai Rak Thai* (Thais Love Thais) Party. On the basis of claiming to be in favour of political and economic reform, he has emerged as a strong opposition rival to the prime minister, Chuan Leekpai, but his backers have been alleged to be among the most unsavoury elements in Thai politics. Moreover, his failure, when in office, to fulfil his promise to end Bangkok's traffic chaos has cast doubt on his modernizing credentials.

see also: Banharn Silpa-archa; Chamlong Srimuang; Chavalit Yongchaiyut; Chuan Leekpai; *Palang Dharma* Party and *Thai Rak Thai* Party.

## Thammasat University Massacre 1976 (Thailand)

On 6 October 1976 armed border patrol and other police units, together with right-wing vigilante groups, stormed the campus of Thammasat University in Bangkok. Students had assembled there in protest against the return to the country in September of the former prime minister, Field Marshal **Thanom Kittikachorn**, who had gone into exile in the wake of a violent confrontation between soldiers and students in October 1973, after which parliamentary democracy had been re-established. There is reason to believe that Thanom's return was a deliberate attempt to engineer a political crisis in the military interest. Student theatre, including a mock hanging to draw attention to the extra-legal execution of two of their number in September, was seized on as an act of *lèse-majesté* because of the striking resemblance of one of the actors to Crown Prince **Maha Vajiralongkorn**. The police onslaught led to carnage, with students being burned alive and lynched from trees as well as being shot dead. The official death toll was put at forty-six but the fatalities were almost certainly much greater, while hundreds of students were wounded and many thousands arrested. The same evening, Admiral Sangad Chaloryu, minister of defence in the elected government of the prime minister, **Seni Pramoj**, announced that a National Administrative Reform Council had seized power in order to restore law and order. The coup re-established military rule in Thailand with the evident blessing of King **Bhumibol Adulyadej**, who on 9 October appointed a former Supreme Court judge, **Thanin Kraivichian**, as a nominally civilian prime minister. He was replaced in a bloodless coup in October 1977 by a pragmatic military clique led by the army commander, General **Kriangsak Chomanan**. In the wake of the bloodbath at Thammasat University, hundreds of students fled the capital to join the insurgent Communist Party of Thailand, giving that movement a new momentum and significance less than two years after the end of the **Vietnam War**.

see also: Bhumibol Adulyadej; Kriangsak Chomanan; *Nawaphon* Movement; Seni Pramoj; Thanin Kraivichian; Thanom Kittikachorn; Vajiralongkorn, Maha.

## Than Shwe (Burma/Myanmar)

General Than Shwe was appointed prime minister of Burma and chairman of the **State Law and Order Restoration Council** (SLORC) on 23 April 1992 in succession to General Saw Maung, who was relieved from office apparently suffering from a mental disorder. Than Shwe was born on 2 February 1933 in Kyaukse. He received a secondary education only and began employment as a postal clerk. In 1953, after training, he joined the Burmese army as an infantry officer and rose steadily in rank with early experience in special operations and psychological warfare. By 1970, he was a battalion commander acquiring the rank of Lt-Colonel during 1972. Staff and divisional command posts followed and in 1985 as a major general, he was made vice-chief of staff and effectively head of the army. Than Shwe was promoted to Lt-General in November 1987 before SLORC was established and after which he became deputy minister of defence with advancement to full general in March 1990. In March 1992, he was appointed minister of defence, an office which he continued to hold on becoming prime minister and chairman of SLORC just over a month later. On 25 April 1992, he also assumed the office of commander-in-chief of defence services but gave up his army command role in March 1993. Despite his many high offices, Than Shwe enjoys the reputation of a political figurehead and is believed to have less effective power than Lt-General **Khin Nyunt**, the First Secretary of SLORC since its establishment. He assumed the office of chairman of the **State Peace and Development Council** in November 1997 on its replacement of SLORC.

see also: Khin Nyunt; State Law and Order Restoration Council; State Peace and Development Council.

## Thanat Khoman  (Thailand)

Thanat Khoman served as Thailand's foreign minister between 1959 and 1971. His major contribution was in promoting regional reconciliation and cooperation. He played a key role in mediating between Indonesia and Malaysia in the mid-1960s; the choice of Bangkok as the venue for the founding meeting of **ASEAN** (Association of South-East Asian Nations) in August 1967 was a testament to his active part in institution-building. Thanat Khoman was born in 1914 in Bangkok into a Sino-Thai family. He studied law in France and entered his country's diplomatic service in 1940. He served in Tokyo during part of the Pacific War but on his return to Bangkok associated himself with the resistance to Japan's dominion. In that company, he was a member of a clandestine mission to the headquarters of the Allied **South-East Asia Command** in Ceylon (Sri Lanka) in February 1945. After the war he held several diplomatic posts, rising to the rank of ambassador to Washington in 1957. He was removed as foreign minister with the incumbency coup by the military in 1971, in part because of his declared interest in a rapprochement with the People's Republic of China. After stepping down as a technocratic foreign minister, he entered politics and became the leader of the **Democrat Party** between 1979 and 1982 and a

deputy prime minister between 1980 and 1982, after which he retired from political life.

see also: ASEAN; Democrat Party; South-East Asia Command.

## Thanh, Son Ngoc  (Cambodia) see Son Ngoc Thanh.

## Thanin Kraivichian  (Thailand)

Thanin Kraivichian became a controversial prime minister of Thailand in the wake of a military coup in October 1976 made opportune by the deaths of students in the **Thammasat University Massacre**. He was in office for only a year when he was deposed by another military coup, but without bloodshed. Thanin was born on 5 April 1927 in Bangkok. He was trained as a lawyer at Gray's Inn, London. After a period in legal practice, he embarked on a career as a jurist and by 1976 had attained the position of senior judge in the country's Supreme Court. Thanin did not enjoy a political base. The key to his appointment as prime minister was his close association with King **Bhumibol Adulyadej**, who was suspicious of military rule and wished the country to have a civilian conservative leader. Thanin fitted the bill as a compromise candidate acceptable to the so-called National Administrative Reform Council in whose name the military had seized power. In office, however, he showed himself to be ideologically so dogmatic and ill-attuned to political responsibility that his removal in October 1977 by General Kriangsak Chomanan was greeted with a sense of national relief.

see also: Bhumibol Adulyadej; Kriangsak Chomanan; Thammasat University Massacre 1976.

## Thanom Kittikachorn, Field Marshal  (Thailand)

Field Marshal Thanom Kittikachorn was prime minister of Thailand in October 1973 when brutal military reaction to student protest at the lack of constitutional progress prompted King **Bhumibol Adulyadej** to advise him to go into exile overseas. His return to Thailand in September 1976, ostensibly to enter a Buddhist monastery, provoked a recurrence of protest which culminated the following month in many student deaths in the **Thammasat University Massacre** in Bangkok, which provided the opportunity for a military coup. Thanom Kittikachorn was born on 11 August 1911 and began his professional military training at the Chulachomklao Royal Military Academy in Bangkok before the coup in 1932 that put an end to the absolute monarchy. After rising to the rank of lieutenant-general in the mid-1950s, he entered politics as a close associate of Field Marshal **Sarit Thanarat**, who was effective military dictator from 1957 until his death in 1963. Thanom, who was then deputy prime minister, became prime minister continuously (with one interruption) until his deposition in 1973. In that period, he depended conspicuously on the support of his deputy General **Praphas Charusathien**. Since his controversial return from exile, he has lived a private life in retirement.

see also: Bhumibol Adulyadej; Praphas Charusathien; Sarit Thanarat; Thammasat University Massacre 1976.

## Thieu, Nguyen Van  (Vietnam)

Nguyen Van Thieu was president and head of the government of the Republic of (South) Vietnam from September 1967 until April 1975, leaving Saigon for exile overseas shortly before the Communists seized power. He was born on 5 April 1923 into a Catholic family. He entered the army under French rule and received his professional training at the National Military Academy in Hue. He continued as an officer under the regime of **Ngo Dinh Diem**, receiving rapid promotion. As armed forces chief of staff and a lieutenant-general, he was a member of the coup group which overthrew Diem in November 1963. He was initially deputy prime minister and then constitutional president during 1965-7. In September 1967, however, he secured election as executive president and held on to power. In that office, he resisted negotiations with the Communist insurgents and sought to prevent a private deal between Washington and Hanoi being translated into the **Paris Peace Agreements** for Vietnam in January 1973. It was his decision to order the retreat of southern forces following the Communist **Ban Me Thuot Offensive** in the central highlands in

March 1975 which led to a military rout and the speedy collapse of his regime.

see also: Ban Me Thuot Offensive 1975; Christmas Bombing 1972; Diem, Ngo Dinh; Paris Peace Agreements 1973; Vietnam War.

## Tho, Le Duc  (Vietnam) see Le Duc Tho.

## Timor, East  (Indonesia/East Timor)

The island of Timor is part of the Lesser Sundas group of the Indonesian archipelago, situated some 300 miles to the north of Australia. Its eastern part, comprising some 7,500 square miles (just under half of the island's area), was settled and colonized by Portuguese friars in the sixteenth century. The western half of the island, with the exception of a small enclave of Oecusse, fell under Dutch control with the formal demarcation of colonial jurisdictions completed only in 1913. That demarcation survived Indonesia's national revolution after August 1945, with independence sought only within the domain of the Netherlands East Indies. It also escaped the romantic political lusts of President **Sukarno** during the first half of the 1960s, when **Confrontation** was directed only against Holland and Malaysia.

Indonesian interest in East Timor was generated by radical political change in Portugal in April 1974, which paved the way for accelerated decolonization in the country's overseas possessions. Within East Timor, political activity and ferment followed which aroused concern in Jakarta at the prospect of sharing a common border with a radical state at the margin of a fissiparous archipelago. That concern was reinforced with the emergence of the *Fretilin* (derived from the Portuguese for Revolutionary Front for an Independent East Timor) demanding early and complete self-rule. Indonesian attempts to sponsor a client political party in favour of integration with the neighbouring republic served to heighten political tension, which culminated in an inept and unsuccessful coup attempt in August 1975. By mid-September, *Fretilin* had established control in the administrative capital, Dili, and had crushed all opposition except along the border with Indonesian West Timor. The outbreak of civil war disrupted

Portuguese plans for orderly decolonization and prompted the retreat of its officials to the neighbouring island of Atauro.

Indonesian calculations were made in the context of revolutionary Communist success in Indochina in April 1975. Sensitive to the attitude of western aid donors, Indonesia sought to control East Timor through the vehicle of a collective police action under the aegis of formal Portuguese sovereignty. After the failure of this initiative and the evident consolidation of *Fretilin* control, more direct action was undertaken, employing Indonesian forces in an insurgent role, ostensibly as volunteers on behalf of its domestic opponents in East Timor. *Fretilin* proclaimed the independence of the Democratic Republic of East Timor on 28 November 1975. The next day, its Indonesian-backed adversaries were mobilized to declare East Timor an integral part of Indonesia. A formal declaration of support followed on 1 December from Indonesia's foreign minister, **Adam Malik**, who announced that the solution to the conflict lay on the battlefield. Decisive military intervention by so-called volunteers on behalf of East Timorese brothers began on 7 December, delayed by the presence in Jakarta of US President Gerald Ford accompanied by his secretary of state, Dr Henry Kissinger. The intervention was a less than competent military action in the face of vigorous resistance but the balance of forces and the absence of any external support for *Fretilin* put the incorporation of the eastern half of the island within Indonesia beyond any doubt. The human costs of the brutal annexation were heavy. Out of an original population of some 650,000, an estimated 100,000 inhabitants died as a direct or indirect result of the invasion and consequent pacification operations. The management of political integration was expedited within several months through a spurious process of self-determination, culminating in a formal act of incorporation of East Timor as the twenty-seventh province of the Republic of Indonesia on 17 July 1976.

Within East Timor, armed resistance to Indonesian authority continued on a limited scale, encouraged by the refusal of the international community through the United Nations

to endorse the annexation. Despite concentrating development efforts in East Timor and transplanting Indonesia's educational system to the territory, political alienation persisted. President **Suharto** declared East Timor an open province at the end of 1988 which was a preliminary to a visit to its predominantly Catholic population by Pope John Paul II in October 1989. That visit was marked by public demonstrations suppressed by security forces, an episode repeated when the US ambassador, John Monjo, travelled to Dili in January 1990. The failure of Indonesia to integrate East Timor in a national sense was displayed conspicuously on 12 November 1991, when a political protest at a memorial service for two East Timorese killed by the security forces was mercilessly crushed by force with great loss of life. The massacre aroused international outrage which was mitigated by the measures taken by the Indonesian government to inquire into the bloody episode, ostensibly to punish and reprimand those soldiers responsible.

A striking feature of continuing East Timorese resistance to Jakarta's rule was the activism of a younger generation educated in the Indonesian medium for whom the original act of annexation was probably beyond their clear recollection. *Fretilin* suffered a major blow in November 1992 when its military commander, Jose 'Xanana' **Gusmao**, was captured. He was sentenced to life imprisonment, which was subsequently commuted to twenty years. Despite international pressure, President Suharto's government refused to negotiate on the issue of its sovereign jurisdiction. That position was maintained initially following his resignation in May 1998 against a background of acute economic crisis and the succession of Vice-President **Habibie**. On 27 January 1999, partly in response to the prospect of Australia withdrawing recognition of Indonesia's jurisdiction, President Habibie made an astounding offer to the people of East Timor, apparently without consulting his foreign ministry or armed forces. They were offered a choice between extensive autonomy or complete independence. This announcement came as a great shock to the armed forces, in particular, which had not only governed East Timor as a private fiefdom but had also incurred heavy casualties in the process. In the event, an agreement was reached in May 1999 between Indonesia, Portugal (as the former colonial power) and the secretary-general of the United Nations, whereby a referendum in East Timor would be supervised by an unarmed UN mission with security the exclusive responsibility of the Indonesian authorities. By that juncture, Indonesia's forces in the territory had begun to set up armed militia in an attempt to intimidate the population into voting against independence.

The United Nations Assistance Mission in East Timor (UNAMET) organized the referendum against a background of rising violence. The referendum was held on 30 August 1999 in which 78.5 per cent of registered voters opted for independence. The result was declared in early September and was met with orchestrated violence and a scorched-earth policy on the part of the armed militia taking the territory into barbarism, which seemed beyond the competence of the armed forces leadership in Jakarta to control. The UN mission was obliged to withdraw but a visit by representatives of the Security Council recommended the deployment of an international force to restore law and order. The weight of international opinion, and importantly Indonesia's vulnerability to economic pressure, persuaded President Habibie that a United Nations-sanctioned force be permitted to enter the territory, formally a province of the republic. That force was authorized by the UN Security Council on 15 September. The International Force East Timor (INTERFET), under Australian command and with the major contribution, began its initial deployment on 20 September. A firm response to initial encounters with armed militia coming across the border with Indonesian West Timor soon led to effective pacification. On 19 October 1999, Indonesia's People's Consultative Assembly ratified the result of the referendum in East Timor, while Jose 'Xanana' Gusmao, who had been released from arrest, returned to Dili on 22 October to a rapturous welcome as the prospective state's political leader. Australia's lead role in the international force had caused tensions with Indonesia and had aroused criticism with-

in ASEAN. On 25 October 1999, the United Nations Security Council voted to replace IN-TERFET with a **United Nations Transitional Administration for East Timor** (UNTAET), including a military component under a Philippine commander with an Australian deputy. The transfer of military responsibilities from INTERFET to the United Nations Peacekeeping Force took place on 23 February 2000. On 11 December 1999, the first meeting of the National Consultative Council of East Timor convened in Dili with the responsibility to make policy recommendations to UNTAET, which is expected to exercise the equivalent of trusteeship over the territory for up to three years before independence is assumed. In mid-December 1999, an international donors' meeting in Tokyo pledged US$520 million in reconstruction aid for the devastated nascent state whose basic infrastructure has to be rebuilt from scratch. In March 2000, President **Abdurrahman Wahid** visited Dili during which he apologized for Indonesia's brutal twenty-four-year occupation. By the first anniversary of the referendum, the UN had begun to create basic institutions and had established security, except along the border with West Timor penetrated still by armed militia. In September 2000, they murdered three UN refugee workers in West Timor.

see also: Ali Alatas; Fretilin; Gusmao, Jose 'Xanana'; Habibie, B. J.; Malik, Adam; Suharto; Sukarno; United Nations: East Timor; Wahid, Abdurrahman;

## Timor Gap Cooperation Treaty 1989 (Indonesia)

The Timor Gap Cooperation Treaty concluded by the governments of Indonesia and Australia on 27 October 1979 provided for the delimitation of the continental shelf boundary between the south coast of the Indonesian island of Timor and the northern coast of Australia. The treaty came into force on 9 February 1991. Delimitation took the form of three zones, two to be subject respectively to the control of Indonesia and Australia and the third to be subject to joint control and exploitation. The prospect of rich oil and natural gas reserves in the Timor Sea was a determining factor in protracted negotiations and their outcome. Initial negotiations had centred only on the continental shelf between the western half of the island of Timor and corresponding territory in northern Australia over which agreements had been reached in 1971 and 1972. Before December 1975 the eastern half of Timor had been subject to Portuguese jurisdiction but negotiations between Lisbon and Canberra over the continental shelf had not taken place. In December 1975 Indonesia invaded **East Timor**, which was formally annexed in July 1976. That act of annexation was highly controversial and has not been recognized by the United Nations. Australia recognized the integration of East Timor into the Republic of Indonesia in 1978, however, and negotiations to delimit the eastern sector of the continental shelf began in the following year.

Contention over the terms of delimitation arose because of variations in the depth of the continental shelf overall. A shallow and vast continental shelf lies adjacent to the Australian coast whereas a narrow and deep continental shelf lies adjacent to the Timor coast. In between the two shelf features is the area known as the Timor Gap with a maximum depth of 3,000 metres. This depression lies some 300 miles north of Australia but only 60 miles south of Timor. The Australian government argued that because of the nature of that depression there were, in fact, two continental shelves between the two countries, which were themselves divided by the Timor Gap, which should itself be delimited equitably. The Indonesian government countered by maintaining that there was only one continental shelf and that the Timor Gap should not be the basis for delimitation because it was only a depression in the single shelf. They insisted on the employment of a median line between the two coasts, with obvious advantages for the Indonesian side. In the event, compromise was reached through Australian initiative in the form of a proposal for a zone of joint exploration and exploitation comprising approximately half of the delimited area. The conclusion of the treaty was important, not only because it resolved a long-standing problem of competitive access to natural resources but because it set the seal on reconciliation between Jakarta and Canberra, especially over the issue of East Timor. That issue was revived as a bone of political contention after the massacre of Timorese demonstrators by Indonesian security forces in the capital, Dili, in November 1991. That bloody episode, which provoked public protest in Australia, was not allowed to stand in the way of the practical implementation of the Timor Gap Cooperation Treaty. In December 1991 Indonesia and Australia signed agreements with a number of international oil companies, permitting them to explore for oil and natural gas in the zone of joint administration in the Timor Sea. The discovery of oil in the joint sea-bed zone was announced in February 1994. Portugal brought an action against Australia before the International Court of Justice (ICJ) on the grounds that its rights as administering power had been violated by the treaty. In July 1995, the ICJ ruled that it did not have jurisdiction in the matter; it could not rule on the annexation of East Timor by Indonesia, which had not recognized the compulsory jurisdiction of the court and was not a party to the action. After the UN-supervised referendum in August 1999 in which the vast majority of registered voters opted for independence, which was ratified by Indonesia's People's Consultative Assembly in the following October, the status of the treaty was clarified. Acting on behalf of East Timor, in February 2000, the United Nations signed a Timor Gap oil and gas exploration treaty with Australia, which had the effect of upholding the terms of the 1989 treaty in favour of East Timor (not Indonesia) and Australia.

*see also:* Timor, East.

## Tonkin Gulf Incident 1964 (Vietnam)

An alleged attack of two United States destroyers on patrol in the Gulf of Tonkin by North Vietnamese torpedo boats on 4 August 1964 prompted a US congressional resolution on 7 August. That resolution endorsed US military reprisals against naval bases and oil storage facilities and sanctioned a subsequent sustained aerial bombardment. It was revealed later that for the previous six months the United States had been sponsoring clandestine armed raids against North Vietnam and had also prepared a draft resolution for Congress which, if and when passed, would serve as a declaration of war and permit overt military action north of the 17th parallel of latitude. The retaliatory air strikes, launched some twelve hours after reports of the alleged North Vietnamese attacks had reached Washington, were possible only because of prior target planning. The Gulf of Tonkin Resolution, which authorized the president to 'take all necessary measures to repel any armed attack against the forces of the United States', was approved with only two dissenting votes. In January 1971 in an expression of congressional disillusionment with the conduct of the **Vietnam War**, the Gulf of Tonkin Resolution was repealed. *see also:* Vietnam War.

## Tran Duc Luong, President (Vietnam)
*see* Luong, President Tran Duc.

## Treaty of Amity and Cooperation (ASEAN) 1976 (Brunei/Burma (Myanmar)/Cambodia/Indonesia/Laos/ Malaysia/Philippines/Singapore/ Thailand/ Vietnam)

A Treaty of Amity and Cooperation in South-East Asia was concluded by the heads of government of **ASEAN** (Association of South-East Asian Nations) on the island of Bali on 24 February 1976. Based on respect for the sanctity of national sovereignty, the **Bali Summit** treaty set out a code of conduct for regional relations. It also made provision for the pacific settlement of disputes with a High Council to facilitate that end among signatories in the event of a failure to resolve matters through direct negotiations. The promulgation of the treaty was part of an attempt by ASEAN to display political solidarity and confidence in the wake of revolutionary Communist success in Indochina during 1975. It was also made open for accession by other regional states in an abortive effort at the time to build political bridges to Indochina. In addition to Brunei, which signed the treaty on joining ASEAN in January 1984, Papua New Guinea, which had enjoyed observer status, adhered to the document in July 1989.

It was not until after the end of the Cold War that Vietnam and Laos formally sought to adhere to the treaty. The ASEAN states approved their accession at the annual meeting of ASEAN foreign ministers in Manila in July 1992. Reference to the utility of employing the dispute settlement provisions of the treaty was incorporated into the **Declaration on the South China Sea** issued at the same meeting. A corresponding reference was included also in the statement issued after the meeting of senior officials held in Singapore in May 1993, preliminary to the inauguration of the **ASEAN Regional Forum** in July. The machinery for dispute settlement has never been invoked, however, by any of the ASEAN states to resolve intra-mural differences within the Association. Cambodia and Burma acceded to the treaty in 1995.
*see also:* ASEAN; ASEAN Regional Forum; Bali Summit 1976; Declaration on the South China Sea 1992.

## Treaty of Friendship and Cooperation 1977 (Laos/Vietnam)

A Treaty of Friendship and Cooperation between the Lao People's Democratic Republic and the Socialist Republic of Vietnam, valid for a period of twenty-five years, was concluded between the two governments in Vientiane on 15 July 1977. The treaty set out to affirm the special relationship between the two states in the context of strained ties with **ASEAN** (Association of South-East Asian Nations) governments and the deteriorating association between Vietnam and the People's Republic of China. The preamble stated that the two governments 'endeavouring to protect and develop the special Vietnam-Laos relationship to make the two countries inherently united in the national liberation cause, remain united forever in national construction and defence'. The treaty made provision for defence cooperation but the actual terms were incorporated in a secret protocol, as was the basis for the demarcation of their common border. At the time, the treaty was believed to make legal provision for the deployment in Laos of Vietnamese troops which had been in the country from the early 1950s and which were not withdrawn until the late 1980s. In February 2000, General Secretary of Vietnam's Communist Party, Le Kha Phieu, while receiving a high-level military delegation from Laos, spoke of the 'special friendship' between the two countries and peoples.

## Treaty of Friendship and Cooperation 1978 (Vietnam)

A Treaty of Friendship and Cooperation between the Soviet Union and the Socialist Republic of Vietnam, valid for a period of twenty-five years, was concluded between the two governments in Moscow on 3 November 1978. Such a treaty had been sought by the Soviet Union for some time but had been resisted by Vietnam until faced with the prospect of external threat from the People's Republic of China. On Vietnam's part, signature constituted an attempt to deter China from military retaliation in response to its planned invasion of Cambodia, which began on 25 December 1978. Article 6 of the treaty stipulated that 'In case either party is attacked or threatened with attack, the two signatories to the Treaty shall immediately consult each other with a view to eliminating that threat, and shall take appropriate and effective measures to safeguard peace and security of the two countries.' In the event, the treaty failed to deter China, which launched a punitive attack on Vietnam in February 1979. The Soviet Union provided considerable economic and military assistance to Vietnam in support of its policy in Cambodia until the late 1980s, when relations with China began to be repaired. The Soviet Union also deployed aircraft and naval vessels in Vietnam but did not at any time intervene on behalf of its treaty partner.

The treaty lapsed with the break-up of the Soviet Union in December 1991 to be succeeded by a new accord with Russia in June 1994 which covered continued use of **Cam Ranh Bay** and outstanding debts by Vietnam.
*see also:* Cam Ranh Bay.

## Treaty of Peace, Friendship and Cooperation 1979 (Cambodia/ Vietnam)

A Treaty of Peace, Friendship and Cooperation between the Socialist Republic of Vietnam and the People's Republic of Kampuchea (Cambodia), valid for a period of twenty-five years, was concluded between the two governments in Phnom Penh on 18 February 1979. The incumbent Cambodian administration had been established through force of Vietnamese arms only the previous month. The treaty was intended to give legal force to a special relationship between Vietnam and Cambodia demanded from 1976 by the government in Hanoi of the **Khmer Rouge** regime, which it had overthrown. The preamble asserted that 'the independence, freedom, peace and security of the two countries are closely interrelated'. The treaty served in particular to provide a legal basis for the presence in Cambodia of Vietnamese troops, who had been represented as volunteers when they invaded in December 1978, acting on behalf of the so-called Kampuchean National United Front for National Salvation. In the event, the treaty failed in its political and military purposes. Vietnam withdrew its main force units from Cambodia in September 1989 and, in the interest of rapprochement with the People's Republic of China, was obliged to leave the government that it had implanted in January 1979 to its own political devices to come to a settlement of the Cambodian conflict.
*see also:* Kampuchea, People's Republic of; Khmer Rouge.

## Tripoli Agreement 1976 (Philippines)

In December 1976, at a meeting in the Libyan capital, Tripoli, a provisional agreement was reached on regional autonomy between the Philippines government and the insurgent **Moro National Liberation Front** (MNLF). The MNLF had launched a separatist rebellion in the Muslim-inhabited southern provinces of the Philippines in October 1972 in the wake of a declaration of martial law by President **Ferdinand Marcos** in the previous month. Negotiations had begun from the end of 1974 but soon ran into difficulty. They were resumed two years later after a visit to Tripoli in November 1976 by Mrs **Imelda Marcos**, who enlisted the good offices of President Gaddafi who had become the most prominent international backer of Muslim nationalism in the Philippines. The Tripoli Agreement provided for a cease-fire and terms for political autonomy in thirteen provinces in the islands of Mindanao, Sulu and Palawan. The agreement was never implemented with the full consent of both parties, however, and subsequent negotiations broke down. Of the thirteen provinces identified, only four had Muslim majorities because of the internal migration of Christians from the north. President Marcos went ahead unilaterally to proclaim an autonomous region in March 1977 and to hold a referendum on the terms of autonomy within the thirteen provinces in April. The outcome was a predictable vote in favour of a very limited form of autonomy and against the kind of devolution of power favoured by the MNLF. The precarious cease-fire broke down during the remainder of 1977. Negotiations did not resume until after President Marcos was succeeded in office by **Corazón Aquino**; they have continued under the rule of President **Fidel Ramos** but so far without success. At issue has been the differing interpretations of the Tripoli Agreement in the context of the changing pattern of Muslim-Christian settlement in the southern Philippines. On the basis of a plebiscite conducted in 1989, the Aquino government established the Autonomous Region for Muslim Mindanao in four provinces in 1990. At the time, the MNLF rejected the autonomous region as a violation of the Tripoli Agreement.

*see also:* Aquino, Corazón; Marcos, Ferdinand; Marcos, Imelda; Moro National Liberation Front; Ramos, Fidel.

## Truong Chinh  (Vietnam)

Truong Chinh, who was born Dang Xuan Khu, was an influential member of the hierarchy of the Communist Party of Vietnam who served as head of state between 1981 and 1987. His ideological outlook owed much to Chinese example and his *nom de guerre* was a Vietnamese translation of the term Long March. Truong Chinh was born in 1907 in Nam Dinh Province into a well-known family of scholars. He was educated in Hanoi and after acquiring his baccalaureate worked as a schoolteacher. He was attracted to **Ho Chi Minh**'s revolutionary movement as a teenager and became a member of the Communist Party of Indochina on its foundation. He spent six years in prison from 1930 and on release worked for the Communist Party as a journalist. Truong Chinh was one of Ho Chi Minh's most trusted colleagues and was elected general secretary of the Communist Party in 1941, holding that position until 1956 when he was relieved of office because of his close identification with a harsh programme of land reform. He remained a member of the Politburo during the course of the **Vietnam War**, sustaining a reputation as a party hardliner. When **Le Duan** died in July 1986, Truong Chinh replaced him as general secretary of the Communist Party until the end of the year, when a radical change of economic course was signalled at its sixth national congress. He died on 1 October 1988 from injuries sustained in a fall.
*see also:* Ho Chi Minh; Le Duan; Vietnam War.

## Tuol Sleng  (Cambodia)

Tuol Sleng is the name of the notorious interrogation centre used by the **Khmer Rouge** regime during its rule in Cambodia between April 1975 and December 1978. The centre takes its name from the suburb in which it is located, while the actual building had served as a high school. Some 20,000 prisoners were brutally interrogated and done to death in Tuol Sleng, but only after having provided detailed confessions of their political delinquency. The bulk of the inmates were themselves Khmer Rouge, including cadres of high standing, who were charged with a range of so-called counter- revolutionary offences. Tuol Sleng represented a savage symbol of the paranoia that progressively gripped the Khmer Rouge regime under **Pol Pot**, whose acts of self-purge and destruction resembled the practice of Stalin's Soviet Union in the 1930s. After Vietnam's invasion of Cambodia in December 1978 and the establishment in January 1979 of the **People's Republic of Kampuchea**, the centre was converted into a genocide museum, in part to justify the legitimacy of the implanted regime. In May 1999, Kang Kek Ieu (better known by his revolutionary *nom de guerre* of Duch), the Khmer Rouge commandant of Tuol Sleng was discovered working with relief organizations in north-western Cambodia. His whereabouts had been known to the authorities for the previous two years but he was only arrested, ostensibly into protective custody, in the same month after his location had become public knowledge. In September 1999, he was formally indicted on a charge of genocide together with Khmer Rouge military commander, **Ta Mok**.
*see also:* Kampuchea, People's Republic of; Khmer Rouge; Pol Pot; Ta Mok.

# U

## UMNO (United Malays National Organization) (Malaya/Malaysia)

The United Malays National Organization (UMNO) is the most important political party in Malaysia. It was established in May 1946 as a Malay united front with which to challenge the British **Malayan Union Proposal**. The terms of that constitutional proposal included the deposition of the Malay rulers or sultans of the states of the peninsula as well as liberal provision for citizenship for Chinese and Indians of migrant origin. The British proposal had been influenced by the perceived mixed conduct of the different communities during the wartime Japanese occupation, with the Malays regarded as collaborators. The movement's founder and first president was Dato Onn bin Jafar, then chief minister of the State of Johor. He mobilized Malays on the basis of their acute concern that they would lose their political birthright in the country of which they were the indigenous people. He also drew on the support of a powerful lobby in Britain of former members of the Malayan civil service who were committed to the Malay cause, as well as on tha.t of the Malay rulers, who constituted living symbols of Malay identity. UMNO's campaign was successful and Britain withdrew the Malayan Union Proposal in favour of one setting up a Federation of Malaya, in which the rights of the Malay rulers were restored and access to citizenship would be made more difficult.

UMNO was then institutionalized as the main political party, claiming a prerogative right to protect the interests of the Malays which it has sustained ever since. Because the British colonial authorities, facing a Communist insurrection, believed that independence could be conceded only when the racial communities had come to political terms, Dato Onn attempted to turn UMNO into a multiracial party. This initiative proved to be premature and in the face of rank-and-file resistance, he was obliged to resign in favour of **Tunku Abdul Rahman**, who led the successful campaign for independence.

To that end, he was able to work out a viable accommodation at elite level between corresponding Chinese and Indian parties which, as the **Alliance Party**, enjoyed notable electoral success. Malaya became independent in August 1957, with UMNO as the dominan party and providing the prime minister, a situation which continued with the advent of the wider Federation of Malaysia in September 1963. In the wake of an electoral reverse and communal violence in the **May 13 Racial Riots** in 1969, UMNO expanded the ruling coalition to include its main Malay political rival within a *Barisan Nasional* (National Front) which was registered as a party in 1974. However, the separate identity and political pre-eminence of UMNO was maintained and strengthened through its extensive network of business activities.

A major split in the party occurred during the late 1980s. At the UMNO General Assembly in April 1987, the prime minister, Dr **Mahathir Mohamad**, only narrowly fended off a challenge to his leadership by the minister for trade and industry, **Tengku Razaleigh Hamzah**. In February 1988 the federal High Court ruled that UMNO was an unlawful society because thirty of its branches had not been properly registered when its General Assembly and triennial elections had been held in 1987. Dr Mahathir then secured permission to register an alternative party called UMNO *Bahru* (New UMNO) to which all members of the deregistered party would have to apply to join. In May 1989 Dr Mahathir's opponents secured permission to register a Malay party called *Semangat '46* (Spirit of 1946) which was an attempt to attach legitimacy arising from the founding of UMNO to the new entity. UMNO's political dominance was restored, however, in general elections in October 1990, when having dropped the 'new' label and still leading the *Barisan Nasional*, it succeeded in maintaining a two-thirds parliamentary majority at the expense of *Semangat '46* and its Malay and Chinese partners. At the end of that month, Dr Mahathir was returned unopposed at its General Assembly as president of a politically restored party. UMNO's pre-eminent position was reinforced through a resounding electoral victory in April 1995 in which it won 88 seats out of 101 contested. That position was diminished significantly with the outcome of the next elections in November 1999. Its strength in the federal parliament was reduced to 74 seats, while three Malay cabinet ministers failed to secure re-election. It also lost control of the state of Terengganu to *Parti Islam Se-Malaysia*, which was the main beneficiary of the swing against UMNO. That swing had been precipitated by the dismissal, arrest, trial and conviction of former deputy prime minister, **Anwar Ibrahim**. He was also dismissed as deputy president and as a member of the party. UMNO's Supreme Council appointed **Abdullah Ahmad Badawi** as its deputy president in interim succession to Anwar. In May 2000, he and Dr Mahathir were elected unopposed respectively as UMNO's deputy president and president at its General Assembly.

UMNO had confined its activities exclusively to peninsular Malaysia until 1991, when it contested by-elections in Sabah in northern Borneo in an attempt to pose a more effective challenge to the ruling **Sabah United Party** (*Parti Bersatu Sabah*) than the **United Sabah National Organization** (USNO). It succeeded in this enterprise in March 1994, when defections from the Sabah United Party which had been returned to power with a narrow majority the month before led to a loss of its parliamentary position. In state elections in March 1999, UMNO won 24 of the *Barisan Nasional*'s 31 seats to command a majority in a legislature of 48. In federal elections in November 1999, the UMNO-dominated coalition led by Chief Minister Osu Sukam won 17 of Sabah's 20 seats. In April 2000, its state parliamentary strength was augmented through defections from the opposition Sabah United Party.

see also: Alliance Party; Anwar Ubrahim; Badawi, Abdullah Ahmad; *Barisan Nasional*; Emergency 1948–60; Mahathir Mohamad, Datuk Sri; Malayan Union Proposal 1946; May 13 Racial Riots 1969; *Parti Islam Se-Malaysia*; Rahman, Tunku Abdul; Razaleigh Hamzah, Tengku; Sabah United Party; *Semangat '46*; United Sabah National Organization.

## United Development Party
(Indonesia)

The United Development Party (in Indonesian, *Partai Persatuan Pembangunan* – PPP) was established in January 1973 through an enforced merger of four Muslim parties which had participated in national elections in 1971. The object of the merger was to make all political parties subordinate to the priorities of President **Suharto's New Order** whereby they accorded it constitutional legitimacy without posing any effective electoral challenge. Over the years, the United Development Party has had its composite Islamic identity diluted as it has become obliged to give up using the *Ka'abah* (the sacred rock in Mecca) as its electoral symbol and to accept *Pancasila* as its sole ideology. It was diminished as a political organization from 1984 when the *Nahdatul Ulama* (previously the separate Religious Scholars party) withdrew from formal politics to concentrate on social and educational activities. The effect was demonstrated in parliamentary elections in 1987 in which the United Development Party won only sixty-one seats compared to ninety-four seats in 1982. A marginal improvement in its electoral performance of sixty-two in 1992 had no impact on the overall political situation whereby parties were permitted to play a limited role only every five years, with the underlying purpose of endorsing the authority of the regime tied to the person of President Suharto. After his political downfall in May 1998, the PPP found itself in electoral competition with a number of newly-formed Islamic parties. In parliamentary elections in June 1999, it secured 10.7 per cent of the vote and fifty-eight seats. Nonetheless, it was influential as a member of an Islamic-based coalition in opposing the bid for the presidency of **Megawati Sukarnoputri**, who was accused of pro-Christian bias. In the event, the PPP helped to secure the election of President **Abdurrahman Wahid** in October 1999. Its leader, Hamzah Haz, was appointed coordinating minister for people's welfare, but resigned office in November that year ostensibly to concentrate on leading his party against a background of allegations of his involvement in corruption.

*see also:* Islam; Megawati Sukarnoputri; *Nahdatul Ulama;* New Order; *Pancasila;* Suharto; Wahid, Abdurrahman.

## United Nations: Cambodia 1991–3
(Cambodia)

The United Nations became actively involved in the conflict in Cambodia from December 1978, following the Vietnamese invasion of the country. Vietnam's military occupation and the legitimacy of the government that it installed in Phnom Penh from January 1979 were challenged during the 1980s through the annual passage of resolutions in the UN General Assembly and by upholding the representation of the ousted **Khmer Rouge** regime. An **International Conference on Cambodia, New York 1981**, which convened under the auspices of the UN secretary-general, failed to resolve the conflict. A second **International Conference on Cambodia, Paris 1989** (July–August), held as the Cold War was coming to an end, also proved abortive. The four contending Cambodian factions were unable to agree on terms for power-sharing during an interim period before elections under international supervision to determine the political format and future of the country. In the wake of that failure, Stephen Solarz, a US Congressman, advocated publicly that the United Nations should assume the interim administration of Cambodia as the means to promote a political settlement. This suggestion was taken up by the Australian government, which conducted a feasibility study whose results were published early in 1990. The Australian study attracted the serious attention of the five permanent members of the United Nations Security Council. Their officials proceeded to draft a framework document, which was eventually accepted on 28 August 1990 by the four Cambodian factions as the basis for settling the conflict.

Central to the United Nations plan was a provision for bypassing the problem of power-sharing, which had stood in the way of an accord. In place of an instrument for effective power-sharing, it was proposed to have a **Supreme National Council** (SNC), on which all Cambodian factions would be represented. The SNC was described as the unique legitimate body and source of authority in which, throughout the transitional period, the sovereignty, independence and unity of Cambodia would be enshrined. This body would delegate to the United Nations all powers necessary to implement a peace agreement. The SNC was set up among the Cambodian parties at a meeting in Jakarta on 10 September 1990; the framework document was then endorsed unanimously in turn by the Security Council and the General Assembly of the United Nations. Contention among the Cambodian parties delayed the election of Prince **Norodom Sihanouk** as chairman of the SNC until July 1991. His election cleared the way for the reconvening of the **International Conference on Cambodia, Paris 1991** (October), and for a comprehensive political settlement to be concluded on 23 October.

The terms of the Paris accord called on the United Nations Security Council to establish **UNTAC** (United Nations Transitional Authority in Cambodia) with civilian and military components under the direct responsibility of the UN secretary-general. UNTAC was accorded a mandate to conduct free and fair elections for a Constituent Assembly in a neutral political environment. The Constituent Assembly would approve a new constitution and then transform itself into a legislative assembly which would have responsibility for creating a new Cambodian government. To serve this end, UNTAC assumed responsibility for supervising, monitoring and verifying a cease-fire and the withdrawal of all foreign forces, as well as the regroupment, cantonment and ultimate disposition of all Cambodian forces and their weapons during the transitional period before general elections ultimately scheduled for May 1993. In addition, in order to ensure a neutral political environment conducive to free and fair elections, five key ministries of the government in Phnom Penh, which was not to be dismantled, including that of public security, were to be placed under UNTAC's direct administrative control.

UNTAC was established formally in March 1992 after the Security Council had sanctioned the dispatch of some 22,000 civilian and military forces with an initial budget of US$1.9 million in the largest and most costly United Nations peacekeeping operation then ever mounted. Headed by Yasushi Akashi, an under-secretary-general for disarmament, UNTAC faced early difficulty in upholding the cease-fire as military clashes between Khmer Rouge and Phnom Penh government forces took place in battles for territorial and population control with the elections in mind. However, even more serious problems set in from June 1992, when the demobilization of the four factions was to have begun in a part of the plan intended to regroup about 70 per cent of all contending forces in UNTAC-controlled regroupment zones. The Khmer Rouge, deployed primarily in western Cambodia, refused to cooperate. Their representatives on the Supreme National Council complained that UNTAC had not verified the withdrawal of Vietnamese forces, large numbers of whom were alleged to be still in Cambodia in disguise. They also took exception to the limited role of the SNC and the extent to which the administration of most of the country had remained in the hands of the incumbent government in Phnom Penh, which had been installed as a direct result of Vietnam's original invasion. Indeed, they asserted that UNTAC was in active collusion with that government in its exclusive political interest. Khmer Rouge obstruction took the form of active harassment of UN personnel, including their detention and appropriation of their equipment, especially vehicles. The Khmer Rouge went further in refusing to participate in the elections arranged for May 1993. In October 1992 the UN Security Council acted unanimously in setting a deadline of the following month for Khmer Rouge compliance. When this did not materialize, trade sanctions were imposed from January 1993 on Khmer Rouge-controlled zones but without real effect. Nonetheless, the Security Council reaffirmed its intention that UNTAC proceed with elections in May. To that end, its personnel had managed to register just over 4.6 million Cambodians and had also supervised the repatriation of over 300,000 refugees from camps along the border with Thailand. By the end of January 1993, a total of twenty political parties had registered to take part in

the elections. Apart from murderous intimidation by the Khmer Rouge, directed primarily at Vietnamese residents, strong evidence emerged of political violence employed by agents of the Phnom Penh government at the expense of their non- Communist electoral rivals. Despite the absence of an ideal neutral political environment, UNTAC conducted the elections in late May 1993 as planned with considerable success, in part through the failure of the Khmer Rouge to disrupt them.

With a turnout of some 90 per cent, most of the seats for the 120-member Constituent Assembly were shared between two parties, with 58 seats for **FUNCINPEC** (National United Front for an Independent, Neutral, Peaceful and Cooperative Cambodia), led by Prince **Norodom Ranariddh**, a son of Prince Sihanouk, and 51 seats for the **Cambodian People's Party** (CPP), led by **Hun Sen**. Prince Sihanouk intervened to forge an interim coalition between the two rivals after the Cambodian People's Party sought to challenge the electoral outcome through threat of territorial secession. The Constituent Assembly convened in June 1993 and by September had agreed the terms of a new constitution, based in part on the restoration of the monarchy, resumed by Norodom Sihanouk on 24 September 1993. A new coalition government was formed at the end of October with Prince Ranariddh and Hun Sen as First and Second prime ministers respectively. The constitutional process was endorsed by the United Nations, whose mandate for Cambodia came to a substantive end on 26 September with the departure of Yasushi Akashi, the head of UNTAC, although all of its peacekeeping forces were not withdrawn until mid-November 1993. Many aspects of the UN operation were flawed, in particular its quasi-administrative role in supervising and controlling key ministries within the incumbent government in Phnom Penh. Moreover, it was constrained by a peacekeeping mandate that prevented military enforcement against violent recalcitrant factions. In the event, a calculated risk in holding elections paid off because of the courage of the Cambodian people in taking part and also because the Khmer Rouge had begun to lose their military momentum and to fragment. The political settlement left in place was a fragile one, based on the role of an ageing, ailing and capricious King Sihanouk in containing the tensions within a uneasy coalition government.

see also: Cambodian People's Party; FUNCIN-PEC; Hun Sen; International Conferences on Cambodia, New York 1981, Paris 1989, 1991; Khmer Rouge; Ranariddh, Norodom; Sihanouk, Norodom; Supreme National Council; UNTAC.

## United Nations: East Timor 1999–

The United Nations Transitional Administration in **East Timor** (UNTAET) was established on 25 October 1999 by the Security Council with overall responsibility for administration and was empowered to exercise all legislative and executive authority. The United Nations has been involved with the issue of East Timor from the time of Indonesia's invasion of the former Portuguese territory in December 1975. It had never acknowledged Indonesia's jurisdiction but failed to make any impact on the government in Jakarta during the rule of President **Suharto**. With his political downfall in May 1998, Indonesia under the interim administration of President **Habibie** appeared unwilling to concede more than a status of special autonomy for the territory. That situation changed unexpectedly in January 1999 when President Habibie offered the inhabitants of East Timor the choice between autonomy and independence. In May 1999 an agreement was reached between the secretary-general of the United Nations and the foreign ministers of Indonesia and Portugal whereby Indonesia would assume responsibility for security during the referendum in August, which would be conducted by a United Nations Assessment Mission in East Timor (UNAMET). That referendum took place on 30 August against a background of rising violence mounted by pro-integrationist armed militia inspired by the local military determined to block independence. That violence became endemic with the announcement of the referendum result on 4 September; almost four-fifths of voters had supported independence. The scorched-earth policy of the armed militia precipitated the withdrawal of the UNAMET. On 15 September, the UN Security Council adopted a unanimous resolution authorizing a multinational force to use all necessary means to restore peace in East Timor. It had been understood that Australia would provide the largest contingent in the International Force East Timor (INTERFET) whose advance units flew into Dili from Darwin on 20 September under the command of an Australian major-general. That force was effective in restoring law and order to the ravaged territory but the conspicuous role of Australia generated political tensions with Indonesia and some other members of ASEAN. It was against that background that the UN Security Council established UNTAET in October 1999 and made provision for the replacement of INTERFET by a UN force led by a Philippines' general who arrived in Dili in January 2000. INTERFET's role came to a formal end on 23 February 2000 when Australia's Major-General Peter Cosgrove handed over responsibility for security in East Timor to a United Nations peacekeeping force led by Lt-General Jaime de los Santos. The initial mandate of UNTAET was set to last until 31 January 2001 but Kofi Annan, the UN secretary-general, has estimated that it will take up to three years to shepherd the ravaged embryo-state to independence.

see also: Habibie, B. J.; Suharto; Timor, East.

## United Nations: Irian Jaya 1962–9
(Indonesia)

**Irian Jaya** is the Indonesian term for the western half of the island of New Guinea which had been an integral part of the Netherlands East Indies. Although the Dutch agreed to transfer sovereignty to an independent Indonesia in December 1949, they insisted on retaining administrative control of West New Guinea, with the future of the territory to be subject to further negotiations. Their refusal to relinquish control became a matter of great controversy during the 1950s, leading to a breach in diplomatic relations, **Confrontation**, and an international crisis engaging US-Soviet competition. A United States initiative prompted renewed negotiations in 1962 with formal mediation by a US diplomat, Ellsworth Bunker, under the auspices of U Thant, then acting secretary-general of the United Nations. An accord was concluded on 15 August 1962 whereby the territory would be transferred first to United Nations and then to Indonesian administration. In addition, it was agreed that an 'act of free choice' with United Nations advice, assistance and participation would take place before the end of 1969 in order to determine whether or not the territory's inhabitants wished to remain subject to Indonesian jurisdiction.

The initial transfer to United Nations authority took effect from 1 October 1962 with administration placed under a UN Temporary Executive Authority (UNTEA). Indonesia replaced UNTEA as agreed from 1 May 1963, despite a campaign by Jakarta to advance the date of transfer to 1 January and to suggest that a determination of opinion would not be necessary. Indonesia's assumption of administration was not popular within Irian Jaya and armed resistance was mounted by a **Free Papua Movement**. In the event, an 'act of free choice' of a kind was conducted in the territory during July and August 1969. But the overseeing UN representatives were denied full opportunity to judge the true merits of a plebiscitary exercise by village notables alone, who voted by 1,025 to nil in favour of continued union with Indonesia. The report of the visiting United Nations mission on the test of opinion confirmed the result but contained clear reservations. When the report came before the General Assembly, it was endorsed but not before attracting criticism from a number of African countries, in particular. President Suharto announced Irian Jaya's incorporation into the Republic of Indonesia as its twenty-sixth province on 17 September 1969.

*see also:* Confrontation; Free Papua Movement; Irian Jaya; Suharto; Sukarno.

## United Nations: Northern Borneo 1963 (Indonesia/Malaya/Philippines)

The controversy over the formation of the Federation of Malaysia, which was contested by Indonesia and the Philippines, led to the United Nations playing a role in assessing the political preferences of the inhabitants of the British colonies of North Borneo and Sarawak. A meeting at ministerial level in Manila in June 1963 between representatives of Indonesia, Malaya

and the Philippines resulted in the **Manila Agreements** in July to welcome the formation of Malaysia, to include the Borneo territories, provided the support of their people was ' ascertained by an independent and impartial authority, the Secretary-General of the United Nations or his representative'. U Thant agreed to dispatch such a representative with a team to northern Borneo to examine the conduct and verify the outcome of recent elections in North Borneo and Sarawak and, above all, to ascertain whether or not Malaysia had been a major, if not the main, issue. Further controversy arose over the participation of Indonesian and Philippine observers and more importantly the announcement by Malaya on 29 August 1963 that Malaysia would be established on 16 September that year, even though the findings of the United Nations mission were not due to be made public until 14 September. The United Nations team of nine assessors led by Laurence Michelmore, one of its officials, did not begin its work until 26 August. Nonetheless, the secretary-general published his report on 13 September, finding that 'there is no doubt about the wishes of a sizeable majority of the peoples of these [Borneo] territories to join in the Federation of Malaysia'. He felt obliged, however, to reprimand the government of Malaya for fixing the date for the establishment of the new Federation before his conclusions had been reached and made known. The Federation of Malaysia succeeded Malaya without difficulty in membership of the United Nations but the pointed admonition by the secretary-general became the basis of Indonesia's refusal to recognize the new Federation and to reinstate its campaign of **Confrontation**.

*see also:* Confrontation; Manila Agreements 1963.

## United Sabah National Organization (USNO) (Malaysia/Sabah)

The United Sabah National Organization (USNO) was one of the first political parties to be formed in northern Borneo in the expectation of the establishment of Malaysia. It was set up in 1961 by **Tun Mustapha Harun**, a traditional Suluk leader, whose constituency was among the Muslim community. USNO played a leading part in the coalition government of the state from 1963. Tun Mustapha began his political career in the office of constitutional head of state but stepped down in 1965 to return to USNO, leading it to electoral victory in April 1967, after which he assumed the position of chief minister. USNO, with a Chinese partner within the Sabah Alliance, then dominated state politics until defeated in elections in 1976 following a split within its ranks and federal suspicion that Tun Mustapha had secessionist ambitions. Although in opposition in Sabah, USNO entered the federal **Barisan Nasional** (National Front) but was never fully a political partner, which became evident when it opposed the transfer of the island of Labuan to the authority of the central government. USNO was expelled from the *Barisan Nasional* in 1984. It contested the state elections of 1985 under the leadership of Tun Mustapha, who failed in a constitutional coup to unseat the duly elected government of **Datuk Joseph Pairin Kitingan's Sabah United Party** (*Parti Bersatu Sabah*). USNO remained in the political wilderness until the Sabah United Party withdrew from the *Barisan Nasional* just before federal elections in October 1990. This act of political betrayal revived Tun Mustapha's utility to the government in Kuala Lumpur, which with his cooperation set up a branch of the nationally dominant **UMNO** (United Malays National Organization) in Sabah. Sabah's chief minister responded by forging a state-level coalition with dissident USNO members in April 1993. The *Barisan Nasional* acted in turn to expel USNO again from membership, while Tun Mustapha was appointed as federal minister for Sabah affairs, a post which he had first held in 1966. In August 1993 USNO was formally deregistered, ostensibly on the initiative of the Registrar of Societies. A number of its senior members joined the incumbent Sabah United Party, while Tun Mustapha resigned from the federal cabinet and from UMNO after **Ghafar Baba** had been replaced as its deputy president by **Anwar Ibrahim**. Those defections were a factor in the return to office of the Sabah United Party by a narrow majority in state elections in February 1994. That victory proved ephemeral because in the following month defections from the Sabah United Party permit-

ted the *Barisan Nasional* to assume the government of the state.

*see also:* Anwar Ibrahim; *Barisan Nasional*; Ghafar Baba, Abdul; Kitingan, Datuk Joseph Pairin; Mustapha bin Datuk Harun, Tun; Sabah United Party; UMNO.

## UNTAC (United Nations Transitional Authority in Cambodia) (Cambodia)

The United Nations Transitional Authority in Cambodia (UNTAC) was established as a direct result of the peace agreement concluded at the **International Conference on Cambodia** held in Paris in October 1991. To ensure its implementation, the UN Security Council was invited to establish a transitional authority with civilian and military powers under the direct responsibility of the UN secretary-general delegated o it by the **Supreme National Council**. Apart from peacekeeping duties, UNTAC was allocated direct responsibility for ensuring a neutral political environment conducive to free and fair elections intended to resolve political conflict. UNTAC was authorized by the Security Council on 28 February 1992 and was provided with 22,000 military and civilian personnel and a budget of around US$1.7 million. It was headed by Yasushi Akashi, an under-secretary-general.

UNTAC became operational on 15 March 1992. From the outset, UNTAC faced intractable problems in implementing its mandate. Its major difficulty arose from the refusal of the **Khmer Rouge** to cooperate in implementing the military provisions of the Paris agreement from the middle of 1992. It also failed to assume control of key ministries in Phnom Penh, which allowed the incumbent government imposed by Vietnam to intimidate political opponents. Despite serious shortcomings in its peacekeeping role, UNTAC was able to conduct relatively free and fair elections and overcome a boycott and violence by the Khmer Rouge. A remarkable success was the registration of more than 90 per cent (4.7 million) of eligible voters, while some 360,000 refugees from camps along the border with Thailand were resettled within a nine-month period. Elections held in May 1993 led on to the restoration of a constitutional monarchy, with **Norodom Sihanouk** reinstated as king, despite intervening political turbulence, and then a coalition government. When Yasushi Akashi left Cambodia on 26 September 1993 on the completion of his mission as head of UNTAC, he claimed that the United Nations had succeeded in its objective of laying a firm foundation for Cambodian democracy. That statement exaggerated the achievement of UNTAC but the outcome of its intervention far exceeded all initial expectations of its peace-keeping role.

see   also:   International   Conference   on Cambodia, Paris 1991; Khmer Rouge; Sihanouk, Norodom; Supreme National Council; United Nations: Cambodia 1991–3.

# V

## Vajiralongkorn, Prince Maha
### (Thailand)

Maha Vajiralongkorn is the only son of King **Bhumibol Adulyadej** and Queen Sirikit. He was born on 28 July 1952 in Bangkok and was invested as Crown Prince in December 1972, thus making him heir apparent. His early education was spent in England and Australia; and from January 1972, he attended the Royal Military College, Duntroon, in Canberra for four years. He went on to the Royal Thai Army Command and General Staff College during 1977–8 and then trained as a pilot. He also received advanced military training at the United States Army Institute at Fort Bragg as well as spending a year at the Royal College of Defence Studies in London. In 1988 he was promoted to the rank of Lt-General as commander of the King's Own Bodyguard Regiment. His role in Thailand has been primarily ceremonial and has not involved him in political life in the manner of his father, whom he has represented at home and abroad. He has yet to command the kind of popular regard enjoyed by King Bhumibol. As the king has advanced in years, the issue of royal succession has become a matter of deep political concern because of the stabilizing influence of the current monarch and because of the close connection of the Crown Prince with the military establishment.
*see also:* Bhumibol Adulyadej.

## Vang Pao, General  (Laos)

General Vang Pao was engaged for a quarter of a century in conducting military operations against the *Pathet Lao* (Lao Nation) revolutionary forces which seized power during 1975. As a member of the *Hmong* minority, he recruited from that ethnic group, who were trained by American Special Forces and financed by the US Central Intelligence Agency (CIA). From his headquarters at Long Cheng, south of the Plain of Jars, he mounted continuing operations for over ten years until in 1975, after the United States' military withdrawal

from Indochina at the end of the **Vietnam War**, he and thousands of his forces were airlifted to Thailand. From Thailand they were transported to the United States for resettlement as refugees. Vang Pao was born in 1931 in Xieng Khouang Province. He attended an army officer training college from the age of 20 under French auspices and saw active service in the royal capital, Luang Prabang, in 1953 against the **Viet Minh**, who acted as a vanguard for the *Pathet Lao*. He was a battalion commander after the **Geneva Agreements on Indochina 1954** when Laos became subject to incipient civil war. Aligned first with the rightist General Phoumi Nosovan, he was appointed to the rank of general in December 1964 by the prime minister, Prince **Souvanna Phouma**, after which his close connection with the CIA was formed. In exile as a naturalized US citizen, Vang Pao sought to keep alive the flame of *Hmong* resistance against the government in Vientiane through a so-called Lao National Liberation Front but without signal success. In February 1994 the Thai military authorities filed a law suit against him to deter his return to the border with Laos.
*see also:* Geneva Agreements on Indochina 1954; *Hmong*; *Pathet Lao*; Souvanna Phouma; Viet Minh; Vietnam War.

## Ver, General Fabian  (Philippines)

General Fabian Ver was chief of staff of the armed forces of the Philippines from August 1981 until February 1986, when he resigned his post in the interest of a beleaguered President **Ferdinand Marcos**. During the final stage of the martial law regime, Fabian Ver combined the role of head of the armed forces with that of principal bodyguard to Ferdinand Marcos, to whom he was closely related. General Ver was born in 1920 in Ilocos Norte, the birthplace of President Marcos. He was educated at the University of the Philippines, which provided an opportunity for entry into the Reserve Officer Training Corps and then into the paramilitary Philippine Constabulary. He took part in counter-insurgency operations against the *Hukbalahap* **Movement** guerrillas specializing in military intelligence. Fabian Ver's career took off after Marcos became president in 1966. In 1971 he had become chief of the Presidential Security Command and director-general of the National Intelligence and Security Authority. His power was based on his close personal relationship with President Marcos and also with **Imelda Marcos**, which permitted him considerable scope for patronage through control of military promotions. He acquired a reputation as a heartless advocate of punitive measures against political opponents of the president and was widely suspected of direct involvement in the assassination of **Benigno Aquino** in August 1983. He was charged with being an accessory in his murder in January 1985 and was suspended from military office, but President Marcos reinstated him as chief of staff on his acquittal in December. Fabian Ver resigned his post on 16 February 1986 as Marcos sought to shift responsibility for the fraudulent conduct of presidential elections in which he had been challenged by **Corazón Aquino**. It was allegedly fear of arrest by troops still loyal to General Ver that prompted an act of rebellion by the deputy chief of staff, **Fidel Ramos**, and the defence minister, Juan **Ponce Enrile**, on 22 February 1986 which led to Marcos's political downfall three days later. The president overruled General Ver's advice to use force against 'People Power' – civilian demonstrators blocking the path of his marines to the camp where the rebels were concentrated. After arriving in the United States, Fabian Ver is believed to have attempted to organize a revolt in the Philippines on Marcos's behalf. He is reported to have sought to recruit to Brunei Filipino workers, who would be armed and trained for assassination during a visit to the sultanate by Corazón Aquino in 1986 intended to precipitate such a revolt. In the event, the visit was postponed and arrests took place at a very senior level within the Brunei court. General Ver accumulated great wealth as a result of his close association with the Marcos family, which he has probably been able to enjoy in several places of exile, including a Latin American country. He accumulated vast wealth as a result of his close asso-

ciation with the Marcos family, which he enjoyed during twelve years of foreign exile. He died in Bangkok in November 1998 and, as a former chief of staff, was buried with full military honours in his home town of Sarrat.

*see also:* Aquino, Benigno; Aquino, Corazón; EDSA; Enrile, Juan Ponce; *Hukbalahap* Movement; Marcos, Ferdinand; Marcos, Imelda; People Power; Ramos, Fidel.

## Vientiane Agreement on the Restoration of Peace and Reconciliation in Laos 1973  (Laos)

The Paris **Peace Agreements** for Vietnam were signed on 27 January 1973. On 21 February a corresponding agreement was signed for Laos in Vientiane between the Royal government and the *Pathet Lao* (Lao Nation) represented as the Patriotic Forces which had been at odds with each other for nearly two decades. Internal conflict in Laos had been tied inextricably to that in neighbouring Vietnam ever since the Communist-led **Viet Minh** movement had challenged French rule at the end of the Pacific War in the first phase of the **Indochina Wars**. The revolutionary *Pathet Lao* had functioned as virtually a subordinate branch of the Viet Minh. After the division of Vietnam by the **Geneva Agreements on Indochina** in July 1954, the eastern uplands of Laos became of critical importance to Vietnam's Communists seeking to overturn the government in Saigon as an access route for personnel and military supplies from north to south. Effective control of the territory through which the **Ho Chi Minh Trail** passed was sufficient for Vietnam's Communists and their Laotian counterparts until the closing stages of the **Vietnam War**, when the United States' military disengagement undermined any residual political resolve of the government in Vientiane. The agreement reached in Vientiane provided for a cease-fire, the termination of all foreign military intervention, and the establishment within thirty days of a Provisional Government of National Union responsible for conducting national elections. A protocol providing for such a coalition government was not signed until 14 September with the date of formation set for 10 October

1973. That government with Prince **Souvanna Phouma** as prime minister was installed only on 5 April 1974. The coalition failed to function according to the Vientiane Agreement, however, as its demoralized Royalist members were subject to increasing intimidation. General elections did not take place and *Pathet Lao* forces assumed progressive control concurrently with the military campaign which brought the Communists to power in South Vietnam. By the end of 1975 power had passed to the **Lao People's Revolutionary Party**. On 3 December it was announced that King Savang Vatthana had abdicated and that the Lao People's Democratic Republic had been established with **Kaysone Phomvihan**, the general secretary of the Lao People's Revolutionary Party, as prime minister. A **Treaty of Friendship and Cooperation** was entered into with Vietnam on 18 July 1977. The Vientiane Agreement failed in its declared purpose, serving instead as the means through which the Laotian revolutionary movement came to power.

see also: Geneva Agreements on Indochina 1954; Ho Chi Minh Trail; Indochina Wars; Kaysone Phomvihan; Lao People's Revolutionary Party; Paris Peace Agreements 1973; *Pathet Lao*; Souvanna Phouma; Treaty of Friendship and Cooperation 1977; Viet Minh; Vietnam War.

## Viet Cong  (Vietnam)

Viet Cong is an abbreviation for *Viet-Nam Cong-San* (translated as Vietnamese Communists) which came into common usage in the years following the partition of Vietnam by the **Geneva Agreements on Indochina** in 1954. It was employed initially as a pejorative term by the southern government headed by **Ngo Dinh Diem** but was taken up by western governments and writers as a label for the Communist insurgent movement in the south of Vietnam. It was never used by the Vietnamese Communists, who founded the National Liberation Front of South Vietnam (NLF) in December 1960 as a political vehicle with which to challenge the government in Saigon.

see also: Diem, Ngo Dinh; National Liberation Front of South Vietnam; Vietnam War.

## Viet Minh  (Vietnam)

Viet Minh is an abbreviation of *Viet Nam Doc-lap Dong-ming Hoi* (which translates as League for the Independence of Vietnam) which was established in May 1941 in the Chinese border town of Chingsi. The Viet Minh was conceived of initially by the Communist leader **Ho Chi Minh** as a national united front with which to solicit Allied support, first for defeating Japan and then for liberating Vietnam from French colonial rule. It was founded as the result of a decision taken by the Communist Party of Indochina at the eighth plenum of its central committee. A guerrilla base was set up in the mountains of northern Vietnam where contact was established with agents of the US Office of Strategic Service, the forerunner of the Central Intelligence Agency (CIA). Viet Minh forces entered Hanoi in the **August Revolution** in 1945 in an attempt to foment a general insurrection. The independence of the Democratic Republic of Vietnam was declared by Ho Chi Minh on 2 September 1945 but the *coup de force* did not survive the Chinese Nationalist occupation and then the restoration of French rule. Armed conflict with France began at the end of 1946. In the previous May, the Viet Minh had sponsored the *Lien Viet* (League for the National Union of Vietnam) as an even broader front organization. When the Communist Party of Indochina, ostensibly dissolved in 1945, adopted the name *Lao Dong* (Vietnam Workers Party) in March 1951, the Viet Minh was absorbed into the *Lien Viet* and ceased to be employed by the Communists. Nonetheless, the term remained in general usage to describe the Communist-led nationalist movement which successfully challenged French rule in Indochina from the end of the Pacific War until their military success in the **Indochina Wars** at the **Battle of Dien Bien Phu** in May 1954.

see also: August Revolution 1945; Dien Bien Phu, Battle of, 1954; Ho Chi Minh; Indochina Wars; *Lao Dong*.

## Vietnam War  (Cambodia/Laos/ Vietnam)

The Vietnam War is commonly understood to refer to the armed conflict between the forces of the United States and the Communist Party of Vietnam which took place primarily from March 1965 until January 1973, when the **Paris Peace Agreements** were signed. The nature of the conflict was more complex and its course more protracted, but it was informed by the common feature of a struggle over the political identity of Vietnam. The Vietnam War passed through two clearly defined historical stages involving differing forms of American intervention. Its origins are to be found in the determined attempt by the Vietnamese-dominated Communist Party of Indochina (founded in 1930) to thwart the re-establishment of French colonial power after the end of the Pacific War and to set up a Marxist state. In the wake of Japan's surrender in August 1945, the Communist front, known as the **Viet Minh** (standing for the League for the Independence of Vietnam) seized power in Hanoi in the **August Revolution**; on 2 September **Ho Chi Minh** proclaimed the formation of the Democratic Republic of Vietnam. The Viet Minh attracted popular support because of its nationalist credentials, while the French were faced with rising opposition at home.

Direct military confrontation between the Viet Minh and the French first took place at the end of 1946 ostensibly over control of customs but, in effect, over entry of arms in the northern port of Haiphong. The first of the **Indochina Wars** began as a guerrilla struggle on the Communist side but progressively became one between conventional formations, culminating in the historic **Battle of Dien Bien Phu** in the early months of 1954. Dien Bien Phu is a valley in north-western Vietnam where the French had established a military redoubt, in the false hope of luring the Viet Minh into a pitched battle whose outcome would be determined by the superiority of their conventional forces. The French made a major miscalculation, above all, about the ability of the Viet Minh to deploy heavy artillery in the hills surrounding their military position. From 1950 the Viet Minh had the advantage of military assistance from the newly established People's Republic of China, whose provision of US-manufactured artillery captured during the Korean War was decisive in the Battle of Dien Bien Phu. The French had

attracted military assistance from the United States because of an ability to represent their colonial interest as part of a global struggle against international communism. It took the form of economic aid, military supplies and logistical support; by the time of the Battle of Dien Bien Phu, the United States was bearing almost 80 per cent of the total cost of France's prosecution of the war.

As the French military position became progressively more untenable with growing popular opposition to the war, an agreement was reached to convene an international conference in Geneva to discuss Korea and Indochina. The fortress of Dien Bien Phu fell to Viet Minh assault on 7 May 1954 in a great psychological victory only the day before the Indochina phase of the conference began. This dramatic triumph did not immediately decide the political future of Vietnam, in part because China and the Soviet Union wished to avoid a confrontation with the United States. They persuaded their Vietnamese allies to compromise on territorial control and to agree to a provisional demarcation of the country along the line of the 17th parallel of latitude prior to national elections in 1956. The Democratic Republic of Vietnam succeeded to power north of that line. To its south, an anti-Communist nationalist government was established, led by former exile **Ngo Dinh Diem**, who established a Republic of Vietnam in 1955 with the support of the United States. That government, with US backing, refused to implement the electoral provisions of the **Geneva Agreements on Indochina** and took effective military action against the southern branch of the Communist movement.

The second phase of the Vietnam War may be said to have begun with the establishment in December 1960 of the **National Liberation Front of South Vietnam** (NLF). This equivalent to the Viet Minh was set up on the instruction of the ruling *Lao Dong* (Workers Party) in Hanoi, which had changed its name from the Communist Party of Indochina in 1951. The NLF began a series of armed actions against the Saigon government with signal success in the rural areas. The insurgency was reinforced from the north through infiltration of personnel and supplies through a series of routes passing through Laos and then Cambodia known collectively as the **Ho Chi Minh Trail**. The United States became drawn progressively into the war in support of the southern government. This support took the initial form of economic and military assistance, including the provision of some 700 military advisers. US military intervention was incremental but the first major decision was made by President John F. Kennedy in 1961, which resulted in some 16,000 US ground troops being deployed in Vietnam by the end of 1963. The Vietnam conflict was perceived as a test case in defeating Communist-inspired national liberation wars. Countervailing American resolve was required to prevent countries falling to communism, one after another like dominoes, to use the imagery employed by President Dwight D. Eisenhower in April 1954 (*see* **Domino Theory**).

The year 1963 was a turning-point in the course of the war. The evident unpopularity of the government in Saigon in the face of Buddhist protest as well as its lamentable military performance led to a withdrawal of US support for President Ngo Dinh Diem. His assassination in November 1963, shortly before that of President Kennedy, was followed by the assumption of power by a series of military juntas, none of which demonstrated any grasp of the requirements for victory. In consequence, the United States took on a growing responsibility for the conduct of the war on the mistaken assumption that it would be possible to buy time for a better motivated South Vietnamese Army to resume the burden of fighting for their own country. But every addition of US military resources was matched from the north, which was driven by a nationalist zeal and supported materially and diplomatically by Communist allies.

In March 1965 the United States changed the nature of the conflict by embarking on the continuous aerial bombardment of North Vietnam. The United States had first bombed the north in August 1964 as an act of retaliation for alleged torpedo attacks on patrolling US destroyers in the **Tonkin Gulf Incident**. When this attempt to interdict the flow of supplies southwards and to impose a penal cost on Hanoi for prosecuting

the war failed, more US combat troops were introduced into the south. By the end of President Lyndon Johnson's term of office in January 1969, the number of those troops had reached more than half a million but without having been able to inflict a decisive defeat on the Communist forces. The turning-point in the second phase of the war came at the beginning of 1968 during the Tet festival for the Vietnamese new year. A series of well-coordinated offensives against urban targets was launched by the NLF from the end of January, which included the penetration of the US embassy compound in Saigon. The **Tet Offensive** was a military failure conducted at great loss of life by the NLF, which gave up control of rural strongholds as a consequence. It was, however, a great psychological victory because of its political impact within the United States, where a popular tide was rising in opposition to a war conducted at great expense in blood and treasure and which did not seem related to American interests. A political turning-point came in March in a primary election in New Hampshire, in which the setback suffered by President Johnson was such that he decided not to stand for re-election in November 1968 and to countenance negotiations with the Communist side, which began in Paris by the end of the year.

Johnson's successor, President Richard Nixon, realized that his political future depended on his ability to end the war but was concerned to do so in a way that did not seem to impair the global credibility of the United States. He began to reduce US force levels and advanced a new policy, the '**Nixon Doctrine**', in a press briefing on the island of Guam in July 1969, which placed the primary responsibility for conducting the war on the South Vietnamese. This policy of so-called **Vietnamization** was underpinned with continued bombing of North Vietnam from Guam and Thailand, as well as from offshore aircraft carriers. The declared US war aim was to maintain the separate political integrity of Vietnam south of the 17th parallel. This end was sustained in negotiations in Paris, which reached a turning-point at the end of 1972 following the failure of a conventional military offensive by the North Vietnamese across the 17th parallel in March 1972. The Vietnamese

Communists revised their long-held view that the United States should remove the government in Saigon and were prepared to settle for the priority of securing an American military withdrawal. After a renewal of US aerial warfare in the **Christmas Bombing**, a final peace agreement was concluded in Paris in January 1973 whereby, in addition to a cease-fire with Vietnamese forces in place, it was agreed that all US forces would be removed from Vietnam in return for the release of US prisoners of war, primarily air force personnel. A power-sharing National Council of National Reconciliation and Concord, a structure for organizing elections, could not be established, however, while the cease-fire broke down. Monitoring of the implementation of the accord by an international commission followd US military withdrawal and release of prisoners but without effect. American support for the Saigon government began to falter as the Watergate scandal undermined Richard Nixon's authority and his threat to resume bombing, should the Communists violate the peace accords.

In early 1975 the war began to move on to a dramatic culmination after the Communist side undertook military probes, which enabled them to seize the provincial capital of Phuoc Long. In March, the **Ban Me Thuot Offensive** in the central highlands led South Vietnam's President **Nguyen Van Thieu** to order a retreat to the plains, which turned into a spectacular rout. The progressive collapse of his army followed; on 30 April Communist forces entered Saigon to receive the surrender from President Dong Van Minh, who had succeeded to office after President Thieu's flight from the country into exile. The NLF had maintained that they sought an independent neutral southern state, but in July 1976 the two halves of the country were reunited formally into the Socialist Republic of Vietnam.

The Vietnam War was very costly in loss of life and casualties: 47,365 US personnel were killed in action and nearly 11,000 lost their lives through other causes, including accidents. The war memorial in Washington contains the names of 58,196 men and women who died in Vietnam. South Vietnamese military deaths amounted to 254,257. In May 1995, the government in Hanoi released approximate casualty figures of more than 1 million fatalities from North Vietnam and National Liberation Front of South Vietnam. Civilian casualties were very heavy both north and south, with more than 2 million deaths and injuries. The Vietnamese received engineering support from Chinese troops as well as material support from China, the Soviet Union and its bloc allies. The United States carried the main burden of prosecuting the war in support of the South Vietnamese, but was assisted by the limited military involvement of troops from Australia, New Zealand, South Korea, the Philippines and Thailand.

The Vietnam War had a wider Indochinese dimension. The Viet Minh had penetrated Laos and Cambodia in the early 1950s in order to pin down French forces and also to establish a fraternal political domain. Vietnamese troops remained in Laos after the Geneva accords in July 1954 to stiffen the counterpart *Pathet Lao* (Lao Nation) against the government in Vientiane, in part to ensure control of military access routes from north to south Vietnam. The Vietnamese Communist military presence was extended to Cambodia during the 1960s for a corresponding purpose, which provided a pretext for the overthrow of Prince **Norodom Sihanouk** and the expansion of the war westwards. The destruction of the Cambodian army by the Vietnamese Communists during 1970-1 played an important part in helping the **Khmer Rouge** to seize power in April 1975 some two weeks before the fall of Saigon. In the case of Laos, the **Vientiane Agreement on the Restoration of Peace and Reconciliation in Laos** was signed in February 1973, following the Paris accords for Vietnam, but Laos did not fall under Communist rule until after the end of the Vietnam War in April 1975.

*see also:* August Revolution 1945; Ban Me Thuot Offensive 1975; Christmas Bombing 1972; Diem, Ngo Dinh; Dien Bien Phu, Battle of, 1954; Domino Theory; Geneva Agreements on Indochina 1954; Ho Chi Minh; Ho Chi Minh Trail; Indochina Wars; Khmer Rouge; *Lao Dong*; Missing in Action; National Liberation Front of South Vietnam; Nixon Doctrine 1969; Paris Peace Agreements 1973; *Pathet Lao*; Sihanouk, Norodom; Tet

Offensive 1968; Thieu, Nguyen Van; Tonkin Gulf Incident 1964; Vientiane Agreement on the Restoration of Peace and Reconciliation in Laos 1973; Viet Minh; Vietnamization.

## Vietnamization (Vietnam)

Vietnamization was the term coined in the wake of President Nixon's historic press conference on the island of Guam in July 1969; the **Nixon Doctrine** presaged the United States' military disengagement from Vietnam. Vietnamization was meant to describe the assumption of principal responsibility for fighting the war by the army of the Republic of (South) Vietnam. Its first major test occurred in February 1971 with a military incursion (codenamed **Lam Son 719**) into Laos in an attempt to interdict the legendary **Ho Chi Minh Trail**. The action proved to be a military disaster. The failure of Vietnamization to substitute for US intervention was confirmed by the inability of the South Vietnamese Army to blunt the Communist offensive in March 1972 without the use of US air power. In the wake of the **Paris Peace Agreements** of January 1973, Vietnamization was exposed as no more than a slogan to extricate the United States from Vietnam when a rout of southern forces during the **Ban Me Thuot Offensive** in March 1975 led directly to decisive military defeat at the end of the following month.

see also: Ban Me Thuot Offensive 1975; Ho Chi Minh Trail; Lam Son 719; Nixon Doctrine 1969; Paris Peace Agreements 1973; Vietnam War.

## Vo Nguyen Giap, General (Vietnam)
see Giap, Vo Nguyen.

## Vo Van Kiet (Vietnam)

Vo Van Kiet was appointed chairman of the Council of Ministers of Vietnam in August 1991, elevated from the position of deputy to **Do Muoi**, who had become secretary-general of the ruling Communist Party. His appointment indicated Vietnam's continuing commitment to market-based economic reforms with which Vo Van Kiet had been closely identified. He was born in Can Tho in southern Vietnam in 1922 to a middle-class family and became involved in the revolutionary movement in the early 1940s. He rose in the party hierarchy working in the south of the country and held the post of secretary of the Saigon Municipal Party Committee at the end of the **Vietnam War** in 1975. He continued to hold high party office in what became Ho Chi Minh City but demonstrated a signal interest in practical economic matters with growing impatience for sterile dogma. In 1982 he was elected a full member of the Politburo and also a vice-chairman of the Council of Ministers. He became identified with the programme of economic reform after the Communist Party's sixth national congress in December 1986. He was appointed acting chairman of the Council of Ministers in March 1988 on the death of Pham Hung but failed to retain that position, which was filled in June by the more conservative Do Muoi. His succession to Do Muoi in 1991 was reconfirmed when the National Assembly elected him to the new office of prime minister in September 1992 in which he has concentrated on economic matters and in developing closer relationships with **ASEAN** (Association of South-East Asian Nations). He continued in office until September 1997 when he was succeeded as prime minister by **Phan Van Khai**. He resigned from the politburo of Vietnam's Communist Party in the following December.

see also: ASEAN; Do Muoi; Phan Van Kai.

# W

## Wahid, Abdurrahman (Indonesia)

Abdurrahman Wahid was elected as Indonesia's fourth president on 20 October 1999 by the **People's Consultative Assembly** (MPR). Although a prominent political figure, he had not been the front-runner for that office; his **National Awakening Party** (PKB) had come third in parliamentary elections in the previous June with just over 17 per cent, which was around half of the vote secured by *Partai Demokrasi Indonesia* (PDI) led by **Megawati Sukarnoputri**. Megawati's failure to try to build a majority within the electoral college, and the withdrawal of interim President **Habibie** from the contest against a background of a banking scandal placed Abdurrahman Wahid in a position to secure high office by a small majority. He had been nominated by a coalition of Muslim parties known as the Axis Force. In the event, the election of the liberal-minded Muslim cleric served to bridge contending communal constituencies whose differences have had recurrent violent expression as well as to attract a positive international response.

Abdurrahman Wahid (who is also known as Gus Dur) was born in Jombang in east Java on 4 August 1940 into a family of prominent Islamic intellectuals. His grandfather, Hashim Ashari, founded the *Nahdatul Ulamma* (NU-Muslim Scholars) and his father, Wahid Hashim, succeeded to its leadership. Abdurrahman Wahid followed in his father's footsteps in 1984 in leading the NU, after an Islamic education, first in Indonesia and then in Egypt and Iraq. He led the conservative rural-based NU, with a membership of around 30 million, in the direction of religious tolerance and against the idea of an Islamic state seen as a threat to the integrity of a culturally diverse Indonesia. He became a controversial figure after assuming the leadership of the *Forum Demokrasi* (Democracy Forum) in April 1991 as a counter to a more sectarian Islam and also to the attempt by President **Suharto** to cultivate Islam for political advantage. In 1998, he suffered a serious stroke

followed by another, while he is also clinically blind so that he has to rely heavily on family members for reading support and for information. He has a sharp mind and a prodigious memory.

Abdurrahman Wahid, as leader of the NU, had enjoyed a reputation as an impish, indiscreet, impetuous and erratic figure. He lived up to that reputation on assuming high office; for example, in seemingly inconsequential comment over the prospect of a referendum in Aceh. He stamped his mark on his coalition cabinet initially through forcing from office the former armed forces commander and coordinating minister for political and security affairs, General Wiranto, and then reshuffling the military high command in a demonstration of civilian authority. He worked well for a time with his vice-president, Megawati Sukarnoputri, despite her initial disappointment at failing to secure the presidency but provoked her ire by dismissing a key member of her party from the cabinet. He has aroused controversy by indicating a strong interest in establishing trade ties with Israel and also in repealing the law banning the Communist Party. He has also inherited weak institutions, which has been a factor in obstructing attempts to eradicate corruption and to repair the country's economic ills. Abdurrahman Wahid assumed office with a moral authority by occupying a unique national position in being able to cater for Islamic and liberal-democratic sensibilities. Within six months, however, he had alienated his supporters in other parties and dissipated international goodwill by inept leadership and a neglect of economic priorities as well as by appearing to abuse national office for party and personal advantage as well as by tolerating bully-boy tactics towards his critics by paramilitary youth members of his Muslim organization. Moreover, he had failed to exercise effective control over the armed forces.

*see also: Forum Demokrasi*; Habibie, B. J.; Megawati Sukarnoputri; *Nahdatul Ulamma*; National

Awakening Party; *Partai Demokrasi Indonesia*; People's Consultative Assembly; Suharto.

## Win Aung (Burma/Myanmar)

Win Aung was appointed foreign minister of Burma/Myanmar in November 1998. He had previously been ambassador in London. Win Aung was born on 28 February 1944. He received his higher education at the University of Rangoon/Yangon in chemistry and biology and then undertook military instruction graduating from the Army Officers Training School in 1965. Between 1965 and 1985, he worked in the Ministry of Defence and in the prime minister's office. In the following year, he transferred to the Ministry of Foreign Affairs and then began a series of overseas appointments, becoming ambassador concurrently to Germany, Austria and the Netherlands in mid-1990 but within three months was appointed ambassador to the Council of the European Communities/Union and then to the Commission before being accredited to London. He has been an articulate defender of the interests of the military government in Rangoon/Yangon.

## Workers Party (Singapore)

The Workers Party has had a chequered existence in Singapore politics for more than a quarter of a century, attaining only minimal parliamentary representation. It was founded in November 1957 by the former chief minister, **David Marshall**, and modelled on the British Labour Party. An immediate showing was made in city council elections with Communist support. Withdrawal of that support left it without any seats after general elections in 1959 brought the **People's Action Party** (PAP) to power. David Marshall then won a by-election in the Anson constituency in 1962 through a return of Communist backing after left-wing defection from the ruling PAP over the formation of Malaysia. After David Marshall resigned from the party in January 1963 in frustration at Communist control, the Workers Party became moribund for nearly a decade. In 1971 Marshall's law partner, **J. B. Jeyaretnam**, revived the party, which became very much a personal political vehicle. Ten years later in October 1981, Jeyaretnam became the first opposition member

of Parliament for over a decade when he also won a by-election also in Anson caused by Devan Nair resigning to assume the office of president. In the Parliament, he infuriated the prime minister, **Lee Kuan Yew**, by his carping criticism of government and was returned by his constituency in general elections in December 1984. Jeyaretnam lost his seat and was disqualified from Parliament for five years in November 1986 after the High Court confirmed his conviction for making a false declaration of the Workers Party accounts and being fined an amount which automatically carried that penalty. The Workers Party failed to secure any seats in elections in September 1988 but was successful in one constituency in August 1991. Although eligible, J. B. Jeyaretnam did not stand with party colleagues in December 1992 in a group constituency by-election caused by the resignation of the prime minister, **Goh Chok Tong**, and other PAP members in order to demonstrate popular confidence in his leadership. Although sustaining an identity as an opposition party, it has been overshadowed by the **Singapore Democratic Party**, founded by Chiam See Tong, which won three seats in elections in August 1991. It did not benefit from the internal conflict within the Singapore Democratic Party. In elections in January 1997, the sole Workers Party member retained his seat, while J. B. Jeyaretnam entered the parliament as the sole non-constituency member, a position allocated up to three losing opposition candidates.

*see also:* Goh Chok Tong; Jeyaretnam, J. B.; Lee Kuan Yew; Marshall, David; Nair, Devan; People's Action Party; Singapore Democratic Party.

## Workshop on Managing Potential Conflicts in the South China Sea 1990– (Indonesia)

The Workshop on Managing Potential Conflicts in the **South China Sea** is an Indonesian-inspired initiative in preventive diplomacy, which was prompted by Sino-Vietnamese clashes in the **Spratly Islands** during the late 1980s. Financed from a Canadian source, the object has been to engage representatives from claimant states in their personal capacities in a discussion of functional cooperation as a way of avoiding contentious issues of sovereignty and so ameliorating the political climate. The Workshop began with a meeting in Bali in January 1991 and was confined initially to representatives from **ASEAN** states, including non-claimants. At the second meeting in Bandung in July 1991, representatives from China, Taiwan, Vietnam and Laos began to participate. Meetings have continued on an annual basis around Indonesia with the Workshop seeking to address projects on living and non-living marine resources and on marine scientific research but with limited success. In addition, there have been meetings of technical working groups as well as experts' meetings. The course of the Workshop has pointed up the difficulty of differentiating between functional and political cooperation and the representatives of the contending states have been ultra-sensitive to any multilateral commitment that might prejudice their claims to sovereign jurisdiction. For example, it has proved impossible to promote cooperation over hydrocarbons. Moreover, Indonesia's efforts to promote specific confidence-building measures have met with frustration, especially as a result of the generally negative position of China's representatives. Indonesia's role in promoting the Workshop was based on its non-claimant status in the South China Sea beyond a continental shelf problem with Vietnam. However, differences with China over maritime space extending from the Indonesian-owned Natuna Islands have complicated its position.

see also: ASEAN; South China Sea; Spratly Islands.

# Y

## Yakub, Tun Abdul Rahman (Malaysia/Sarawak)

Tun Abdul Rahman Yakub was chief minister of Malaysia's north Bornean state of Sarawak from July 1970 until March 1981. In April 1981 he assumed the office of state governor, which he gave up in 1985 out of frustration with the political constraints of his constitutional role. Tun Yakub was born on 3 January 1928 in Bintulu, Sarawak. He was educated at the University of Southampton in England and went to qualify as a barrister at Lincoln's Inn in London in 1959. He began his career in the Sarawak government's legal service and played an instrumental role in building Muslim Malay-Melanau political organization on the former British colony's entry into Malaysia. His initial period in politics was at the federal level and he held the portfolios of land and mines and of education during the 1960s. During his tenure as chief minister, he consolidated the position in Sarawak of the ruling *Barisan Nasional* (National Front) federal coalition, which was formed during the early 1970s. His exit from active political life expressed itself in a quarrel with his nephew, **Datuk Abdul Taib Mahmud**, who had succeeded him as chief minister in 1981. After his failure to unseat his nephew in state elections in 1987, Tun Yakub retired from politics.

see also: *Barisan Nasional*; Taib Mahmud, Datuk Patinggi Abdul.

## Yang di-Pertuan Agong (Malaysia)

*Yang di-Pertuan Agong* (Supreme Ruler) is the official title of Malaysia's reigning constitutional monarch. Monarchy in Malaysia has long enjoyed a special political standing, in part because of its symbolic role in the emergence of Malay nationalism during the **Malayan Union Proposal** crisis from 1946. Its prerogatives have been jealously guarded but have come under challenge as economic development has generated change within Malay society. The distinctive feature about monarchy in Malaysia is that the office is held for five years only on a rotational rather than on a hereditary basis. The constitutional predecessor of Malaysia, the Federation of Malaya, was created from a number of states in the Malay peninsula which had been in formal treaty relations with the British Crown, making them sovereign entities in legal theory. On independence in 1957, the nine hereditary Malay rulers of Malaya agreed to occupy the office of Supreme Ruler in turn on an agreed notion of seniority. That arrangement has continued from the establishment of Malaysia in 1963. In April 1994 Tunku Ja'afar Abdul Rahman, the ruler of the state of Negri Sembilan, became the tenth incumbent of the rotating office.

In 1983 a political crisis occurred over the issue of the royal assent to Acts of Parliament which the government of Dr **Mahathir Mohamad** had sought to remove by constitutional amendment. Another **Constitutional Crisis** arose early in 1993 over the same government's attempt to remove the right of the hereditary rulers to immunity from criminal prosecution after an alleged act of assault by a former king. In May 1994 Malaysia's Parliament passed an amendment to the constitution whereby any Bill which had been endorsed by both its houses would be deemed to have become law within thirty days, whether or not assented to by the king. In April 1999, Salahuddin Abdul Aziz Shah, the Sultan of Selangor, was invested as the latest incumbent.

see also: Constitutional Crises; Malayan Union Proposal 1946.

## Young Turks (Thailand)

Young Turks is the name given to a group of regimental and battalion commanders who became influential in Thai politics from the mid-1970s and who promoted an abortive coup in April 1981. The core of the group were graduates of class seven of the Chulachomklao Royal Military Academy. They had experienced advanced professional training as well as service in Vietnam and involvement in counter-insurgency in Thailand. The group coalesced in the wake of the collapse of military rule in October 1973 during a highly volatile demo-cratic interlude brought to a close by a bloody coup in October 1976 following the **Thammasat University Massacre**. After an incumbency coup in October 1977 which made General **Kriangsak Chomanan** prime minister, the Young Turks, who took their name from the movement established at the heart of the Ottoman empire in 1908, played an arbiter role within a faction-alized military. Their withdrawal of support from General Kriangsak prompted his resigna-tion in February 1980 and the succession to office by General **Prem Tinsulanond**. Charging weakness of political leadership, the Young Turks organized a coup attempt on 1 April 1981 but General Prem escaped from Bangkok to Korat in the north-east of the country with the royal family. The failure to attract support from King **Bhumibol Adulyadej**, who endorsed General Prem's action, led to the collapse of the coup attempt within days. Most of the Young Turks were dismissed or transferred within the army but some of their number were involved in a subsequent abortive coup in September 1985. They represented a complex mixture of self-seeking and professional interests con-cerned both to protect military privilege and to prevent a perceived degeneration of the political process allegedly influenced by civil-ian- business participation.

*see also:* Kriangsak Chomanan; Prem Tinsul-anond; Thammasat University Massacre 1976.

# Z

## ZOPFAN (Zone of Peace, Freedom and Neutrality) 1971 (Indonesia/Malaysia/Philippines/Singapore/Thailand)

A joint declaration of determination 'to exert initially necessary efforts to secure the recognition of, and respect for, South-East Asia as a Zone of Peace, Freedom and Neutrality, free from any form or manner of interference by outside Powers' was signed on 27 November 1971 in Kuala Lumpur by the foreign ministers of Indonesia, Malaysia, the Philippines and Singapore and a special envoy of the National Executive Council of Thailand. The five delegates had convened to discuss a Malaysian proposal that South-East Asia as a region be neutralized through guarantees from the United States, the Soviet Union and the People's Republic of China. Indonesia's strong objection to virtual policing rights being accorded to outside powers was primarily responsible for collective endorsement of an alternative proposal allocating exclusive responsibility for managing regional order to regional states. The **Kuala Lumpur Declaration** of the ZOPFAN formula was adopted officially as corporate policy at the **Bali Summit**, the first meeting of **ASEAN**'s heads of government held in February 1976 when it was included within a **Declaration of ASEAN Concord**. That declaration called on member states, individually and collectively, to take active steps for the early establishment of the zone. Subsequently, there have been recurrent reaffirmations, by ASEAN of ZOPFAN's desirability but practical steps towards its realization have not been taken.

The concept of ZOPFAN has been supported most strongly by Indonesia, whose foreign policy it closely reflects. Malaysia has also been supportive because of its role in pressing for neutralization, which was acknowledged as a desirable objective in Kuala Lumpur in November 1971. Other regional states have been willing to provide only formal backing because of the practical difficulties of implementation. A major obstacle to implementation has been the absence of a shared strategic perspective among the ASEAN states, which is pointed up by the very concept of ZOPFAN. That concept reflects the view of those governments that wish to see regional order determined by the resident states of South-East Asia. Not all regional governments share this view because of a concern that they would be at the mercy of the strongest regional powers. For that reason, they prefer to maintain defence cooperation with states beyond the region in order to have access to external sources of countervailing power. It is noteworthy that all member governments of ASEAN have defence cooperation agreements of one kind or another with extra-regional states, while even Indonesia has permitted limited access by US naval vessels to its east Java port of Surabaya. Vietnam, which joined ASEAN in July 1995, still permits a residual Russian naval presence to remain in **Cam Ranh Bay**. In December 1995, in an attempt to lend substance to ZOPFAN, ASEAN's heads of government concluded a treaty purporting to establish a nuclear weapon free-zone in South-East Asia. However, by the end of the century at the meeting of ASEAN foreign ministers in Singapore in July 1999, only passing reference was made to ZOPFAN in noting consultations with nuclear weapon states over their accession to the protocol to the **South-East Asia Nuclear Weapon-Free Zone Treaty** (SEANWFZ). No reference was made at the end of the corresponding meeting in Bangkok in July 2000.

see also: ASEAN; Bali Summit 1976; Bangkok Summit 1995; Cam Ranh Bay; Declaration of ASEAN Concord 1976; Five Power Defence Arrangements 1971-; Kuala Lumpur Declaration 1971; South-East Asia Nuclear Weapon-Free Zone.

# Further Reading

## General

Acharya, Amitav (2000) *Constructing a Security Community. ASEAN and the Problem of Regional Order*, Routledge, London.

Alagappa, Muthiah (ed.) (1985) *Political Legitimacy in Southeast Asia*, Stanford University Press, Stanford.

Bloodworth, Dennis (1987) *The Eye of the Dragon: Southeast Asia Observed, 1954–1986*, Times Books, Singapore.

Brown, David (1994) *The State and Ethnic Politics in Southeast Asia*, Routledge, London.

Buszynski, Leszek (1983) *SEATO: The Failure of an Alliance Strategy*, Singapore University Press, Singapore.

—— (1992) *Gorbachev and Southeast Asia*, Routledge, London.

Colbert, Evelyn (1977) *Southeast Asia in International Politics, 1941–1956*, Cornell University Press, Ithaca, NY.

Fitzgerald, Stephen (1972) *China and the Overseas Chinese*, Cambridge University Press, Cambridge.

Jackson, Karl D., *et al.* (eds) (1986) *ASEAN in Regional and Global Context*, Institute of East Asian Studies, University of California, Berkeley, CA.

Jorgensen-Dahl, Arnfinn (1982) *Regional Organization and Order in Southeast Asia*, Macmillan, London.

Kershaw, Roger (2000) *Monarchy in South-East Asia. The Faces of Tradition in Transition*, Routledge, London.

Kroef, Justus M. van der (1981) *Communism in South-East Asia*, Macmillan, London.

Leifer, Michael (1990) *ASEAN and the Security of South-East Asia*, Routledge, London.

Lim Joo-jock and Vani, S. (eds) (1984) *Armed Communist Movements in Southeast Asia*, Institute of Southeast Asian Studies, Singapore.

Lo Chi-kin (1989) *China's Policy towards Territorial Disputes: The Case of the South China Sea Islands*, Routledge, London.

Mallet, Victor (1999) *The trouble with tigers: The rise and fall of South-East Asia*, Harper Collins, London.

Neher, Clark D. (1991) *Southeast Asia in the New International Era*, Westview Press, Boulder, CO.

Osborne, Milton (1971) *Region of Revolt*, Penguin, Harmondsworth.

—— (1990) *Southeast Asia: An Illustrated Introductory History*, Allen & Unwin, Sydney.

Pan, Lynn (ed.) (1998) *The Encyclopedia of the Chinese Overseas*, Archipelago Press, Singapore.

Sandhu, K. S., *et al.* (eds) (1992) *The ASEAN Reader*, Institute of Southeast Asian Studies, Singapore.

Shaplen, Robert (1979) *A Turning Wheel*, Random House, New York.

*Southeast Asian Affairs* (annually from 1974) Institute of Southeast Asian Studies, Singapore.

Steinberg, D. J., *et al.* (eds) (1987) *In Search of Southeast Asia: A Modern History*, University of Hawaii Press, Honolulu.

Suryadinata, Leo (1985) *China and the ASEAN States: The Ethnic Chinese Dimension*, Singapore University Press, Singapore.

Wang Gung-wu (1981) *Community and Nation: Essays on Southeast Asia and the Chinese*, Heinemann Educational, Singapore.

Wilson, Dick (1975) *The Neutralization of Southeast Asia*, Praeger, New York.

Yahuda, Michael (1996) *International Politics of the Asia-Pacific*, Routledge, London.

## Brunei

Bartholomew, James (1990) *The Richest Man in the World*, Penguin, Harmondsworth.

Braighlinn, G. (1992) *Ideological Innovation under Monarchy: Aspects of Legitimation Activity in Contemporary Brunei*, VU University Press, Amsterdam.

Hussainmiya, B. A. (1995) *Sultan Omar Ali Saifuddin III and Britain*, Oxford University Press, Sham Alam, Selangor.

Leake, Jr, David (1989) *Brunei: The Modern*

*Southeast Asian Islamic Sultanate*, Forum, Kuala Lumpur.

Singh, D. S. Ranjit (1984) *Brunei 1839–1983: The Problems of Political Survival*, Oxford University Press, Singapore.

## Burma/Myanmar

Lintner, Bertil (1989) *Outrage: Burma's Struggle for Democracy*, Review Publishing, Hong Kong.

Maung, Mya (1992) *Totalitarianism in Burma*, Paragon House, New York.

Silverstein, Josef (1977) *Burma: Military Rule and the Politics of Stagnation*, Cornell University Press, Ithaca, NY.

Smith, Martin (1991) *Burma: Insurgency and the Politics of Ethnicity*, Zed Press, London.

Taylor, R. H. (1988) *The State in Burma*, Hurst, London.

Tin Maung Maung Than (1999) *The Political Economy of Burma's (Myanmar's) development failure 1948–1988*, Insitute of Southeast Asian Studies, Singapore.

## Cambodia

Becker, Elizabeth (1986) *When the War was Over*, Simon & Schuster, New York.

Chanda, Nayan (1986) *Brother Enemy: The War after the War*, Harcourt Brace Jovanovich, San Diego, CA.

Chandler, David P. (1991) *The Tragedy of Cambodian History: Politics, War and Revolution since 1945*, Yale University Press, New Haven, CT.

Etcheson, Craig (1984) *The Rise and Demise of Democratic Kampuchea*, Westview Press, Boulder, CO.

Jackson, Karl D. (ed.) (1989) *Cambodia 1975–1978: Rendezvous with Death*, Princeton University Press, Princeton, NJ.

Kamm, Henry (1998) *Cambodia. Report from a Stricken Land*, Arcade Publishing, NY.

Leifer, Michael (1967) *Cambodia: The Search for Security*, Praeger, New York.

Osborne, Milton (1973) *Politics and Power in Cambodia*, Longman Australia, Camberwell.

—— (1994) *Sihanouk: Prince of Light, Prince of Darkness*, Allen & Unwin, Sydney.

Shawcross, William (1979) *Sideshow: Kissinger, Nixon and the Destruction of Cambodia*, André Deutsch, London.

—— (1984) *The Quality of Mercy: Cambodia, Holocaust and Modern Conscience*, André Deutsch, London.

Thion, Serge (1993) *Watching Cambodia*, White Lotus, Bangkok.

## Indonesia

Anderson, Benedict (1972) *Java in a Time of Revolution*, Cornell University Press, Ithaca, NY.

Bresnan, John (1993) *Managing Indonesia: The Modern Political Economy*, Columbia University Press, New York.

Crouch, Harold (1993) *The Army and Politics in Indonesia*, Cornell University Press, Ithaca, NY.

Feith, Herbert (1962) *The Decline of Constitutional Democracy in Indonesia*, Cornell University Press, Ithaca, NY.

Forrester, Geoff and May, R. J. (eds) (1998) *The Fall of Soeharto*, Crawford Publishing House, Bathurst, NSW.

Jenkins, David (1984) *Suharto and his Generals: Indonesian Military Politics 1975–1983*, Cornell Modern Indonesia Project, Ithaca, NY.

Kahin, George McT. (1952) *Nationalism and Revolution in Indonesia*, Cornell University Press, Ithaca, NY.

Legge, J. D. (1973) *Sukarno: A Political Biography*, Penguin, Harmondsworth.

Leifer, Michael (1983) *Indonesia's Foreign Policy*, Allen & Unwin, London.

Mackie, J. A. C. (1974) *Konfrontasi: The Indonesia–Malaysia Dispute 1963–1966*, Oxford University Press, Kuala Lumpur.

McDonald, Hamish (1980) *Suharto's Indonesia*, Fontana, London.

Polomka, Peter (1971) *Indonesia since Sukarno*, Penguin, Harmondsworth.

Ramage, Douglas (1995) *Politics in Indonesia: Democracy, Islam and the Ideology of Tolerance*, Routledge, London.

Reid, Anthony J. S. (1974) *Indonesian National Revolution 1945–50*, Longman Australia, Hawthorn.

Schwarz, Adam (1999) *A Nation in Waiting: Indonesia in the 1990s*, Allen and Unwin, St Leonards, NSW.

Suryadinata, Leo (1999) *Interpreting Indonesian Politics*, Times Academic Press, Singapore.

Vatikiotis, Michael (1998) *Indonesian Politics under Suharto*, Routledge, London.

## Laos

Adams, Nina S. and McCoy, Alfred W. (eds) (1970) *Laos: War and Revolution*, Harper & Row, New York.

Brown, Macalister and Zasloff, Joseph (1986) *Apprentice Revolutionaries: The Communist Movement in Laos, 1930–1985*, Hoover Institution Press, Stanford, CA.

Stevenson, Charles (1972) *The End of Nowhere: American Policy toward Laos since 1954*, Beacon Press, Boston, MA.

Stuart-Fox, Martin (1986) *Laos: Politics, Economics and Society*, F. Pinter, London.

Toye, H. C. M. (1968) *Laos: Buffer State or Battleground?* Oxford University Press, London.

Zasloff, Joseph J. and Unger, Leonard (eds) (1991) *Laos: Beyond the Revolution*, Macmillan, London.

## Malaysia

Chin Kin Wah (1983) *The Defence of Malaysia and Singapore*, Cambridge University Press, Cambridge.

Crouch, Harold (1996) *Government and Society in Malaysia*, Cornell University Press, Ithaca, NY.

Funston, John (1980) *Malay Politics in Malaysia*, Heinemann Educational Books (Asia), Kuala Lumpur.

Gomez, Edmund Terence and Jomo, K. S. (1997) *Malaysia's Political Economy: politics, patronage, and profits*, Cambridge University Press, Cambridge.

Heng Pek Koon (1988) *Chinese Politics in Malaysia*, Oxford University Press, Singapore.

Lee, H. P. (1995) *Constitutional Conflicts in Contemporary Malaysia*, Oxford University Press, Kuala Lumpur.

Means, Gordon (1991) *Malaysian Politics: The Second Generation*, Oxford University Press, Singapore.

Milne, R. S. and Mauzy, Diane K. (1999) *Malaysian Politics Under Mahathir*, Routledge, London.

Muzaffar, Chandra (1987) *Islamic Resurgence in Malaysia*, Penerbit Fajar Bakti SDN. BHD., Petaling Jaya.

Short, Anthony (1975) *The Communist Insurrection in Malaya 1948–60*, Frederick Muller, London.

Sopiee, Mohammad Noordin (1974) *From Malayan Union to Singapore Separation*, Penerbit Universiti Malaya, Kuala Lumpur.

## Philippines

Bonner, Raymond (1987) *Waltzing with a Dictator*, Times Books, New York.

Bresnan, John (ed.) (1986) *Crisis in the Philippines: The Marcos Era and Beyond*, Princeton University Press, Princeton, NJ.

Greene, Fred (ed.) (1988) *The Philippine Bases: Negotiating for the Future*, Council on Foreign Relations, New York.

Hedman, Eva-Lotta and Sidel, John (2000) *Philippine Politics in the Twentieth Century: Colonial Legacies, Post-Colonial Trajectories*, Routledge, London.

Karnow, Stanley (1989) *In Our Image: America's Empire in the Philippines*, Random House, New York.

Kerkvliet, Benedict J. (1977) *The Huk Rebellion*, University of California Press, Berkeley, CA.

Kessler, Richard J. (1989) *Rebellion and Repression in the Philippines*, Yale University Press, New Haven, CT.

Kirk, Donald (1998) *Looted: The Philippines After the Bases*, St. Martin's Press, New York.

McKenna, Thomas M. (1998) *Muslim Rulers and Rebels: Everyday Politics and Armed Separatism in the Southern Philippines*, University of California Press, Berkeley.

Steinberg, David Joel (1982) *The Philippines: A Singular and Plural Place*, Westview Press, Boulder, CO.

Wurfel, David (1988) *Filipino Politics: Development and Decay*, Cornell University Press, Ithaca, NY.

## Singapore

Bloodworth, Dennis (1986) *The Tiger and the Trojan Horse*, Times Books, Singapore.

Chan Heng Chee (1976) *The Dynamics of One Party Dominance*, Singapore University Press, Singapore.

Chua Beng Huat (1995) *Communitarian Ideology and Democracy in Singapore*, Routledge, London.

da Cunha, Derek (1997) *The Price of Victory. The 1997 Singapore General Election and Beyond*, Institute of Southeast Asian Studies, Singapore.

Hill, Michael and Lian Kwen Fee (1995) *The Politics of Nation Building and Citizenship in Singapore*, Routledge, London.

Leifer, Michael (2000) *Singapore's Foreign Policy. Coping with Vulnerability*, Routledge, London.

Milne, R. S. and Mauzy, Diane K. (1990) *Singapore: The Legacy of Lee Kuan Yew*, Westview Press, Boulder, CO.

Minchin, James (1986) *No Man is an Island*, Allen & Unwin, Sydney.

Sandhu, K. S. and Wheatly, P. (eds) (1989) *Management of Success: The Moulding of Modern Singapore*, Institute of Southeast Asian Studies, Singapore.

Vasil, Raj (1992) *Governing Singapore*, Manderin, Singapore.

## Thailand

Alagappa, Muthiah (1987) *The National Security of Developing States: Lessons from Thailand*, Auburn House, Dover, MA.

Girling, John L. S. (1981) *Thailand: Society and Politics*, Cornell University Press, Ithaca, NY.

Hewison, Kevin (ed.) (1997) *Political Change in Thailand*, Routledge, London.

Kulick, Elliot and Wilson, Dick (1992) *Thailand's Turn*, Macmillan, London.

Morell, David and Samudavanija, Chai-anan (1981) *Political Conflict in Thailand*, Oelgeschlager, Gunn and Hain, Cambridge, MA.

Stowe, Judith A. (1991) *Siam Becomes Thailand*, Hurst, London.

## Vietnam

Brown, T. Louise (1991) *War and Aftermath in Vietnam*, Routledge, London.

Duncanson, Dennis J. (1968) *Government and Revolution in Vietnam*, Oxford University Press, London.

Evans, Grant and Rowley, Kelvin (1984) *Red Brotherhood at War*, Verso, London.

Gilks, Anne (1992) *The Breakdown of the Sino-Vietnamese Alliance, 1970–1979*, Institute of East Asian Studies, University of California, Berkeley, CA.

Herring, George (1979) *America's Longest War*, Wiley, New York.

Kahin, George McT. (1986) *Intervention*, Alfred A. Knopf, New York.

Karnow, Stanley (1983) *Vietnam: A History*, Viking Press, New York.

Kattenburg, Paul (1980) *The Vietnam Trauma in American Foreign Policy, 1945–75*, Transaction Books, New Brunswick, NJ.

Kolko, Gabriel (1986) *Intervention: Anatomy of a War 1940–1975*, Allen & Unwin, London.

Lancaster, Donald (1961) *The Emancipation of French Indochina*, Oxford University Press, London.

Morley, James W. and Nishihara, Masashi (eds) (1997) *Vietnam Joins the World*, M. E. Sharpe, Armonk, NY.

Randle, Robert F. (1969) *Geneva 1954: The Settlement of the Indochina War*, Princeton University Press, Princeton, NJ.

Ross, Robert (1988) *The Indochina Tangle*, Columbia University Press, New York.

Smith, R. B. (1983–91) *An International History of the Vietnam War, Vols I–III*, Macmillan, London.

Truong Nhu Tang (1986) *Journal of a Vietcong*, Jonathan Cape, London.

Turley, William S. (1986) *The Second Indochina War*, Westview Press, Boulder, CO.

West, Richard (1995) *War and Peace in Vietnam*, Sinclair-Stevenson, London.

Williams, Michael (1992) *Vietnam at the Crossroads*, Pinter, London.

# Index by Country

## Brunei, Sultanate of

## Burma/Myanmar

## Cambodia, Kingdom of

## Indonesia, Republic of

# Laos, People's Democratic Republic of

## Philippines, Republic of

## Vietnam, Socialist Republic of